G. Bell and sons

The Propagation of the Gospel at Home and Abroad

Volume XXXIV

G. Bell and sons

The Propagation of the Gospel at Home and Abroad
Volume XXXIV

ISBN/EAN: 9783743347038

Manufactured in Europe, USA, Canada, Australia, Japa

Cover: Foto ©Thomas Meinert / pixelio.de

Manufactured and distributed by brebook publishing software (www.brebook.com)

G. Bell and sons

The Propagation of the Gospel at Home and Abroad

THE SOCIETY'S HOUSE AT WESTMINSTER.

THE MISSION FIELD.

A MONTHLY RECORD

OF THE PROCEEDINGS OF THE

Society for the Propagation of the Gospel

AT HOME AND ABROAD.

VOLUME XXXIV.

WITH 100 MAPS AND ILLUSTRATIONS.

ARMS OF THE SEE OF CANTERBURY.

1889.

LONDON:
G. BELL & SONS, 4 & 5 YORK STREET, COVENT GARDEN,
AND ALL BOOKSELLERS.

MAPS AND ILLUSTRATIONS.

THE MISSION FIELD.

THE FIELD IS THE WORLD. THE SEED IS THE WORD OF GOD.

JANUARY 1, 1889.

THE YEAR.

IT were to repeat a happily well-known tale if we were to speak at all in detail of the great ecclesiastical event of the year 1888. The *Mission Field* during the past year has recorded much that took place in connection with that wonderful gathering of the fathers of the Church—the allocution from St. Augustine's throne at Canterbury, and the Archbishop of Canterbury's sermon in Westminster Abbey (which we printed at length), the great anniversary meeting in St. James's Hall, and the memorable concluding service in St. Paul's Cathedral, when the Archbishop of York preached, and the offertory was given to the Society. The actual results of the Conference, formally embodied in resolutions, we also printed in this Magazine. In reviewing the year, therefore, we need not dwell upon its chief feature.

Death has removed many from their work in this world, including three American prelates, two of whom were in the assembly at Lambeth. Among the Bishops who have died during the year we have also to reckon the first Bishop of Mauritius, and Bishop Parker, who bravely followed his predecessor's faithfulness unto death in Eastern Equatorial Africa. From the ranks of the Society's Missionaries some have passed to their great reward, and notably two—James A. Colbeck, the hero of Mandalay, and A. H. Sheldon, of Caledonia. Such men leave gaps which are never quite filled.

The Society in England has had the advantage of the advocacy of the Bishops from abroad, and has received the warmest and strongest expressions of admiration and love from their lordships at the meetings of the Board and the Standing Committee. It was in the fortunate position of being able to vote £10,400 in new grants out of a total of £83,867 last spring; and it has also received some notable gifts. In February there were placed in the Treasurer's hands securities of the value of £25,296, as " a thank-offering to Almighty God for the extension of the Church in the Colonies and Dependencies of the British Empire, and beyond it "; from another donor, £2,268, as a trust-gift, the income only being available; and from another the endowment of a scholarship at St. Augustine's College, Canterbury. Perhaps we may reckon as among the most noteworthy things in the Society's home work the enlargement and improvement of this Magazine. We cannot but hope that its increased circulation will tend both to the extension of the interest in Foreign Missions, and (what is equally important) the rendering that interest intelligent and continuous. A parochial association where the *Mission Field* is in circulation must be stronger than it could be without it. Advantage has been taken of the half-price system in a large number of parishes; and we hope that it will be found in many more places that there are not fewer than twenty persons who can spare one penny a month to pay for an Illustrated Missionary Magazine.

We will now attempt to give some account of the work abroad, as far as has been brought before us in the course of the year. To measure the advance of the Missionary cause in periods of twelve months would be as minute a task as to measure the growth of plants by the day. Standpoints wider apart than January and December are required for such observations. When we take a period of fifty years we can see such results as are summarised by the Bishop of Durham in words from which we have quoted on a previous occasion : —

" There are now fourteen African Bishops. Not one of those Dioceses existed till Her Gracious Majesty had been on the throne fully ten years. There are nineteen Sees in British North America, and only two of them were in existence at the commencement of this reign. There are now thirteen Australian Sees, and the first of them was created just about the time Her Majesty ascended the throne. There are eight Sees in New Zealand and the Pacific Islands, and not one of them existed at the commencement of the reign. Let us ask ourselves what a See means ? It means the completion of the framework of a settled Church government; it means the establishment of an Apostolic ministry, which we believe was especially ordained by God to be the means by which the ministrations and the gifts of the Church of Christ should flow to men. It is the enrolment, as a corporate unity, of one other member of the great Anglican communion. The question which we have to ask ourselves is, by what agency, under God, had these results been achieved ?
. . . I think we may say that if there had been no Society for the

Propagation of the Gospel there could, humanly speaking, have been no Lambeth Conference."

Of a single year's work no such estimate of development can be made; nor were there in 1888 any new Sees created, nor any incidents of a character which should at once stamp them as landmarks. But we have had the happiness of recording many notes of the advance of the army of the Kingdom of God. Turn to what land we will, we hear the same welcome news. Whether it be Burmans lending willing ears at Mandalay, or Dyaks envying their kinsmen on a neighbouring river the possession of a Missionary, or Malagasy villages asking for teachers, or a Pondo chief spontaneously handing over his own sons to a Missionary for education, or heathen Basutos offering to build stone churches if teachers can be sent to use them, or Japanese students yielding to the religious influence of their English teachers, or Brahmans of Madras exhorting those who are drawn to Christianity not to fear or hesitate to change their opinion, if they have good reasons for the change,——— there is a Pentecostal complexity of listening and of utterance that should make the dullest eloquent for the cause which some would decry for smallness of success. Mere numerical growth is not an adequate gauge. For many years the large Mission of Chota Nagpore yielded not a single convert to the faithful and patient labours of the German pioneers. We can now point to nearly twelve thousand Christians there in the Society's Mission, besides an even larger number attached to the original Lutheran Mission. The absence of numerical success therefore proves nothing, except that the stage for numerical success has not yet arrived. The presence of numerical success, on the other hand, does prove something. It proves that God is faithful, and that we should not be of little faith.

While we are speaking of the numbers of the converts, it may be as well to refer briefly to a most absurd objection which has been solemnly brought forward. It is put forth as a grave proof of the failure of Foreign Missions that the natural increase of the heathen is greater than the increase among the Christians by conversion. Of course the increase is greater. We have referred to it ourselves on previous occasions as a spur to more vigorous effort. In the matter of imparting the knowledge of the true Light, the proverb *bis dat qui cito dat* much understates the case. How any one, on the other hand, can think that the fact that the natural increase of the heathen exceeds the increase of the Church by conversions is a proof of failure or even a ground for discouragement, we do not know. We can only suppose that until this recondite discovery was made there were actually some people who imagined that the few hundreds of European Missionaries in India, for instance, were able to convert a number of heathen in each year exceeding the number of annual births in a population of two hundred and fifty millions. In the days of the Apostles the natural increase of the heathen considerably exceeded the converts won to the Church, but no historian relates that such an obvious circumstance occasioned any remark.

Of course each Mission in old times in Europe became a nucleus, a centre of light and force ; and we know no reason why modern Missions should be expected to have no influence or expansive power. If each heathen in the world is only capable of being converted by the direct exertions of an European, the prospect would be indeed a sorry one, but if we are planting the living Church of the living God in Asia and in Africa, we have no doubt that while it lives it grows. If it ceases to be aggressive, it is as if it were not.

Such considerations as these make us pay much more regard to the quality than the quantity of success. Transformations of character such as take place among individuals and races under Christianity are more encouraging than would be a statistical table of larger figures relating to persons whose light was not shining before men. The boy sprung from a degraded tribe of Kohls, living formerly by rapine and pretended magic, and notorious as drunkards, who, a few years after the conversion of his family, could write in English to the Missionary, and tell of his gaining a Government allowance at the end of his school career to enable him to continue his studies, and of his formerly thriftless father possessing twenty-five cattle ; and the idle, lying Kaffirs, who have been taught handicrafts, and learnt candour, straightforwardness, and honour at such stations as Keiskamma Hoek and St. Cuthbert's, show that they have not merely substituted one set of beliefs for another, changing the false and absurd for the true, but have learnt to cast off evil, and to adorn the doctrine of God their Saviour in all things. Such as these are not mere numerical conversions.

A like evidence of quality in the work is the growth of the spirit of self-help, which is always fostered in the Society's Missions, and which we are glad to record in this Magazine, far less because money is thus saved for other work, than because it is evidence of real vitality. For the same purpose the growth of the native clergy is of the utmost importance, as showing that the Church is indeed rooting herself in foreign lands. And again, in this growth of the native ministry our satisfaction is not fastened on the numerical strength of already 116 in the Society's Missions alone, but on their character, their piety, and learning.

Regarding numerical increase as thus secondary with a view to the future of the Missions, we may at the same time point to many examples of it in the *Mission Field* for 1888, as well as to the statistical tables in the Society's Annual Report. Let us take a few instances almost at random from the former. Mahanoro is a Mission in Madagascar, which was opened only four years ago, and in one of his quarterly reports the Rev. A. Smith mentions 192 baptisms there, and several times describes

how the opportunities offered by the work exceed those which can be seized
by the workers. At Phokoane, in Basutoland, forty-three adults were
baptized on Easter Eve. At Tokyo no less than 130 Japanese were
baptized in twelve months. On the Skerang River and in other parts of
Sarawak numerous conversions have taken place. At Kalsapad, in the
diocese of Madras, the baptized Christians have in but ten years increased
from 779 to 2,514, and the communicants from 200 to 834; while all
other details of the statistics show a like character. At Ramnad, in the
same diocese, the 361 baptized Christians of fourteen years ago have
become 3,146, and instead of 91 communicants there are now 741. We
do not think we lay undue stress upon such facts as these, which it is
our privilege every month to record. Each of the many thousands of
baptized converts has caused rejoicing among the angels, and should
prompt us to utter thanksgiving and praise.

CHRISTIANITY IN RELATION TO OTHER RELIGIOUS SYSTEMS.

FROM A REPORT OF AN ADDRESS BY THE LORD BISHOP OF RIPON AT HEADINGLY ON NOVEMBER 21, 1888, AT A MEETING ON BEHALF OF THE SOCIETY.

OUR first thoughts to night run on the general subject of Missionary effort, and I want to lay down what seems to me to be one of the great principles of our faith, namely, that if our Christianity is not an expanding Christianity, it is not worthy of the name. The life which has no growth in it is not much worth living, and it is a fact that those early Churches which had no Missions were the Churches which grew stagnant. The Churches that never sought to preach the Gospel to the regions beyond seem to have died out. When the movement of Christianity took place throughout the world, flourishing Churches were planted here and there. But some how or other the places of several of them have been taken by other systems, the great cause of their disappearance lying in the fact that they did not live out Christianity as Christ intended them to live it out.

If the first theory for us to adopt concerning Christian Missions is, as I imagine it to be, that our own vitality as a Church is evidenced in proportion as we carry out the commands of Christ, we can easily understand that the seeds of decay begin at the very moment when a body becomes stagnant.

Another point which we must all have noticed is the idea which has visited some people's minds that the cause of Missions is less imperative in the present day than it was in the past. I cannot help thinking that one of the fertile causes of the lack of interest in Missions arises from the lack of appreciation of the real position of Christianity in relation to other systems of thought and religion. I am ready to grant that we have changed our modes of thought in relation to those systems, and I am thankful that that change has taken place. Christians no longer look round on the rest of the world with the feeling that it lies in the hands of what is absolutely and totally and completely evil. We are now beginning to believe in something which we may think ought to have been believed in through the long history of the Christian ages. But if I take Christianity and ask what the history of its growth and change has been, I observe that the world has not been capable of understanding the breadth of Christianity all at once, and that men have been very much what we all were in our childhood, when we were only capable of receiving one idea at a time. Hence it happens that in the history of Christianity one particular doctrine, one particular aspect of Christianity has been dominant at a particular epoch. The controversies of the past were all conflicts concerning the error and truth of a particular dogma. The history of the Arian controversy, for instance, is the history of a time when Christianity was anxious about one great truth, namely, the Divinity of our Lord. Coming later, to the period of the Reformation, we have another great conflict concerning another great dogma, in which the question of predestination, freewill, and foreknowledge was uppermost in men's minds. The Arian controversy was settled, and truth vindicated itself, and men began to leave that discussion behind, because the foundation of thought had been laid and could rest; but no sooner had one great truth been considered and settled when another came to the front.

It was through those slow debatings and controversies and conflicts of Christian thought in different times that men got hold of truths which God meant them to learn, and which it was needful they should learn at that particular epoch. This method of acquiring truth points to the providence of God. It does not necessarily mean the stupidity of man, but it means that the educating hand of God has been at work in His Church, and that He has led mankind step by step through the bitterness of controversy to the gaining and grasping of certain truths. If we were to accept all Christian truths in one moment we should not really—because we are limited—grasp the truth in its details, and comparatively, with the firmness of sincere judgment; but it is by having laboured over it, toiled over it, prayed over it, wept over it, wrestled over it, agonised over it, that we have really begun to understand the value of it, and to regard it as a precious inheritance of our own souls and of the souls of Christendom. The thought of most Christians concerning Missions at one time was this: We have light and all the rest is in the hands of the wicked. If any man now imagines that that is the true position of Christianity he has mistaken two things. He has mistaken the meaning of Providence, and he has mistaken the meaning and teaching of Christ. What our Lord came to teach was that for ever and for ever, as long as man had need and had a soul He should not be left without a witness. Our Lord's Revelation teaches us that in every country and every place all that have the fear of God and work righteousness are accepted of Him. With regard to all the systems that are non-Christian we have no right to think that they are the mere manifestations of that which is radically evil. They are rather the manifestations of the minds of those men who sought after that which represented God. What Christians say nowadays is what St. Paul said long ago—" Whom ye ignorantly worship Him declare I unto you." I frankly confess that if I did not believe that God worked before, and in anticipation of, human work, I should think that we might cease to work at all. How could we go on working if our only thought was that in our religion we had something, but that God was not working in the hearts of those who were ignorant? People tell us that Christianity is not original, and that some of its teachings could be matched by equally beautiful moral utterances of Confucius, or Zoroaster, or Buddha. Surely, however, it will be wise for us to understand what is meant by originality. When a person sets himself to be original he sets himself to try the impossible or the foolish. The only originality is that which is eternal, for that alone is original which springs from the eternal origin of things, and makes itself felt in expressions we can understand. Christ did not come to say : " I said that and nobody said it before me." He came to declare the Father, to make us understand and love Him, to make us understand the hindrances, happiness and power of our lives, and to know that the love of God was on our side and that He was helping us to the grand realisation of the external principles underlying every life. Christianity gathered all the stones that had been used in the construction of other buildings, and wherever it found they were good it used them; but it was not the resemblance of those stones or the fact that they had been used somewhere else which made the genius that displayed itself in the architecture of Christianity. The architecture is in the proportions of the building, the strength of its foundation, the nobility of its conception, and least of all in the worshippers within its walls; and Christianity has so wrought that it goes into the world with the power not of saying : " That is all wrong," but of gathering up all the strength and rays of light in other systems and saying, " These are God's; these are the gleams of that light in anticipation of the light, lighting every man."

Christianity is an expression of that which is eternal truth; therefore it came to man with the dignity of ancient ages upon it, and with that principle of eternity in it which is the noblest originality, and which provokes response in the heart of man wherever it is proclaimed. Christianity sanctions all that is true in the Platonic, the Stoical, and the Epicurean systems in that one commandment, " Thou shalt love thy neighbour as thyself." We need not then be afraid of this question of originality. The more it is investigated, the more we shall see that the glory of Christianity lies in the fact that it spreads its tent over the whole of mankind, and everything that is true to the instincts of mankind we shall find expressed, enforced, and established in Christianity. If that is the case, I say there is no reason for any hesitation about Christian Missions. The more we realise that the power of Christianity is co-existent with the needs of humanity the more we shall be persuaded that what we have in hand is not only the great principle of benefiting mankind but of manifesting our loyalty to God. We need not be afraid. We do live in days when everything is tested and examined, but the more closely Christian principles are interrogated, the more narrowly they are examined, the better they are understood, the more shall we see it to be true that among all the great doctrines of the world our Lord's has the pre-eminence, and among all those teachers to whom humanity may look for deliverence from doubt He only can become the eternal and complete Saviour of the agonising, doubting, anxious souls of the poor perishing masses of the world.

CHURCHMEN'S RESPONSIBILITY TOWARDS MISSIONS.

CHRISTIANITY is essentially aggressive. The field which it claims to occupy is the world. The last command of the Risen Christ to His disciples, and the first gift of the Ascended Christ, regarded the proclamation of the Gospel through every nation. The spiritual endowment of the Church is for the fulfilment of this office. Missions, therefore, become a test and a measure of the life both of the Society and of the individual believer.

The Gospel itself corresponds with this unlimited charge of proclaiming it. It is in its nature universal. It is not for one class, or for one race, or for one age, but for all; and it has already abundantly vindicated its claim to universality. The message of the Incarnation can indeed only be fully understood by the help of every section of humanity; and, when we look back, we can see how different races have contributed to form our own inheritance. Every progressive people has been moulded by Christian ideas, and advances by that which it has received from the Faith. This process of national evangelisation is still in the course of accomplishment. It offers opportunities for every variety of service, for zeal, for sympathy, for wisdom, for Christian statesmanship. . . . . . . In these wider labours every Christian, when once he understands their true meaning, must have some part. So far as he lives, his life must reach in prayer, or in alms, or in personal effort, to the utmost limit of the realm which his Master claims.—*Foreign Missions: a Paper on the Responsibility of Churchmen with respect to them, by the Rev. Dr. Westcott.*

THE SOUTHERN TOUNGOO MISSION.

BY THE REV. A. SALMON.

AST November we printed part of a letter from the Rev. W. E. Jones, in which he said that the division of the large Toungoo Mission (which took place last July) would, among other advantages, render possible the reinvigoration of the work among the tribes in the South. Mr. Jones had worked among them with some success a few years ago, when the illness of his senior colleague, the Rev. T. W. Windley, threw the responsibility for the whole Mission upon him, including many pressing duties at Toungoo itself, and the people of these villages were left to the care of a native clergyman, the Rev. Tarrie.

Now that the Toungoo Mission is divided into north and south districts, the Rev. A. Salmon takes charge of the latter, and has recently visited the villages with satisfactory results. This southern part of the Mission is called the Mission of SS. Peter and Paul, Toungoo, the parent Mission, being called St. Luke's. Mr. Salmon thus reports on his district:—

"The Karens of this district are for the most part of a completely different kind to those of the north, not only in language, but in habits, tastes, and characteristics altogether. Though not so varied among themselves as the Karens further north, there are a number of tribes in the south, the principal of which are the Pakus, the Monaipghahs, and the Sgaus. Further east we have the Manu-manaus, the Shokohs, the Kohpahpohs, the Pwaylohs, and the Bwai-mootors. Some of these last have lately immigrated into Paku territory, and have expressed a wish to be taught Christianity. As yet, however, we have no catechist who understands their dialect. These Bwai-mootors seem to be a very hardy, brave people, and, like the Shans, are great traders, differing considerably in this respect from the majority of Karens, who are essentially tillers of the soil. Work among the Sgaus has been practically at a standstill the last two or three years, but during the past year we have made an effort to push forward the work of evangelising them. Two new stations have been taken up, principally through the efforts of John Taw Thoo, lately a student at Bishop's College, Calcutta, and Shwe Gyno, our one deacon.

"Here we have not only the ancient superstitions of the Karens to contend with, but also a new religion started lately by one Koh Pai Sah,

an influential Karen timber merchant. He conceived the idea of com-
bining some of the more popular of the ancient religious customs of the
Karens with the teachings of Buddha and Christ as far as he knew them.
He soon became remarkably popular, and crowds of Karens flocked to

KARENS ARMED WITH WEAPONS OF OFFENCE.

the place he had built in imitation of a phongyee-kyoung (monastery) and
enrolled themselves as his disciples. The initiatory rite consists of
taking a morsel of rice from the hands of Koh Pai Sah, and paying him
Rs. 30 in the case of a man, Rs. 20 for a woman, and Rs. 15 for a child.

The new disciples undertake to eschew strong drink, and to keep the Christian Sabbath, when they have services in imitation of the Christians. These latter, however, are very peculiar, and seem to resemble more a Burmese poay (theatrical performance) than an act of worship, and are principally carried on by the younger people, the old ones looking on in great amusement. They have hymns in praise of Koh Pai Sah, but the tunes are Burmese. Although its adherents number some thousands already, it does not seem likely that this new phase of religious life will last long, as it has not the elements of stability in it.

A KAREN FAMILY.

"Work among the Paku tribes is principally in the hands of two native priests, Taruah and Tarrie. These people may be said to be wholly Christianised now, but their standard of Christianity is as yet painfully low. It must from the nature of the case take several generations to raise them as a whole to anything like the standard looked for in western countries. Still they have no great vices, and, as *far as they know*, they are perhaps as good Christians as the majority of those so called in England, their offerings in proportion to their substance are certainly as large. Taking into account every man, woman, and child connected with the Mission, the offerings amounted to 1 rupee (2 shillings) a head during the last year. In the matter of elementary education in the village schools the Pakus are rather indifferent, but that they appreciate higher education is evinced by the fact that there are 40 Paku boys in the Anglo-Vernacular School in town, most of whom will probably go through the Middle Standard (= VI & VII Standards in England) course. Besides these, there are eight young men in training with a view to becoming clergy and catechists, two being at the Kemmendine Institution under the Rev. J. Fairclough, and the other six at Toungoo under the Rev. W. E. Jones. Then there are about 30 Paku girls in the Boarding School, some of whom we hope will become village teachers, and others nurses in the future hospitals.

KAREN WOMEN WITH NECK AND LEG ORNAMENTS.

"When we compare this with the state of affairs five years ago we have reason to thank God and take courage. Then we had not a single girl at school in Toungoo, in fact we may say that throughout the whole Mission female education was a thing practically unknown. The number of boys in the Anglo-Vernacular School was then but one-fourth of the number now, and though there were spasmodic attempts at training catechists, there was no regular institution as now. Surprise has been expressed at the fact that out of a total of 1,500 or so Christians connected with this Mission only 490 are able to read. We must remember, however, that the Mission work of the Church of England here was only begun twelve years ago, and when we have deducted those who were too old to learn when they became converts, and those who are as yet too young, we shall find that 490 is a very fair percentage of the whole. Still we are far from satisfied with the educational result, nor shall we be until every man, woman, and child can read their Bible and Prayer Book at least.

"A good minor test of the advance of Church work is the number of Prayer Books sold within a given time. In the last five years just upon a thousand Prayer Books in Karen have been distributed in the whole Mission at Toungoo, of which number this Mission may claim about half. When we say *distributed*, we do not mean *given away*, but *bought* by the people, though at considerably less than cost price. A good sign, too, is the demand among the children who can read English for English Prayer Books with Hymns A. & M.

"Much remains to be done in the way of teaching the people to prepare themselves for Holy Communion and Confirmation. Our native clergy, estimable men on the whole as they are, have not been trained from their youth in Church doctrine, and consequently have very confused ideas of their duties in these matters. The European Missionary but seldom comes into contact with the mass of the Karen Christians, as they are so scattered, and for the most part at such a great distance from town. Six months of the year it is impossible to travel on the mountains on account of the incessant rainfall; the other six months have to be divided among so many villages that strictly pastoral work is almost out of the question. Thus much that we would wish to be done has to be left undone, and we can only put forth our best endeavours to raise an educated native ministry on the one hand, and, on the other hand, to keep a high standard before the people by means of our vernacular newspaper (the *Pole Star*) and other publications, such as pastorals, &c.

"With a view to assist in the more careful preparation for Holy Communion we have just issued a small book of prayers and questions for self-examination entitled '*Praeparatio*,' which we trust will be well utilised.

"As a means of establishing the disciples more firmly in the faith, and as examples of how Church doctrine and Bible truth should be definitely taught, we are now re-issuing the translation in Karen of the Rev. D. Elsdale's *Instructions on the Creed, Lord's Prayer, &c.* We have kept our printing press going with some difficulty throughout the year. For want of means we have been prevented from commencing a new edition of the Prayer Book in Karen. A new Hymn Book is needed badly.

"Of medical work we have done our utmost during the year. Wherever we travel, the sick are always in our path, and though our knowledge of the healing art is limited, we can but use what we know. Requests have come to us from several quarters to publish a small handbook of domestic medicine in Karen, and one is in course of preparation."

NEW GUINEA.

IT will be remembered that in 1887 the Society received an appeal from the Primate of Australia on behalf of New Guinea, to which the Australian Church had determined to send a Mission.

The Society at once acceeded to the Bishop's request and opened a Special Fund for New Guinea, endorsing a printed appeal issued by his Lordship. Shortly afterwards it was able to go a step farther, and appropriate a sum of £1,000 towards the initial expenses of the Mission to this new dependency of the British Empire.

We are now able to announce that the Rev. A. A. Maclaren is to be the first Missionary of the English Church to New Guinea. Mr. Maclaren, who has done excellent work in Australia, is at the present time in England, where he offered himself to the Bishop of Sydney for this work. He was accepted, and it is hoped that with at least one colleague he may shortly enter upon his new sphere of labour.

In July 1887 we published some particulars about New Guinea, and reprinted the Bishop's appeal. We may repeat a few of the details. The total area of New Guinea is reckoned to be 224,347 square miles, of which the Dutch own 147,550, the Germans 88,340, and the English, 88,457. The British possession is, therefore, almost equal in size to the whole of Great Britain. The native population of the whole island is estimated at 2,500,000. The race is considered to be a mixture of Malay and Papuan, but in the British territory the Papuan predominates. The people are tatooed, and unclothed, except with profuse barbaric ornament. Between their tribes there is constant fighting. As to religion, they appear to believe in the existence of one Supreme Being, who is, however, known under various names.

The climate affects Europeans like that of similar tropical countries. The wet summer season is unhealthy for them, but the dry season is tolerable. The coast is specially unsanitary. It is therefore proposed that the headquarters of the Mission should be placed on a healthy and accessible island, called Bentley Island, and that the coast stations should be reached by the Mission steamer. Port Moresby appears to be the only commercial port.

With regard to there being an open field for the Mission, it may be as well to quote the following words from the Bishop :—

"It is well known that noble and successful work has already been done in New Guinea under the auspices of the London Missionary Society, and substantial progress (of which, however, we have less knowledge) has also been made by a Roman Catholic Mission.   But, without the slightest interference with these good works, which touch only a few points on a coast line of more than a thousand miles, there is ample room for a new Mission ; and the Church of England is undoubtedly called to take her right place in the extension of the kingdom of our Lord to those heathen tribes, whom, though they know Him not, He claims as bought by His blood. The Australian Church has recognised this sacred duty, and has resolved to start a Mission, under the general direction of the Bishop of North Queensland, but with the support of all the dioceses represented in the General Synod."

We have been favoured with a very interesting account of a visit to New Guinea, by the Rev. Zouch H. Turton, Curate of Horton-cum-Piddington, Northampton, and formerly the Society's Missionary at Lahaina, Mani, in the diocese of Honolulu. Mr. Turton writes :—

"A letter I recently addressed to the *Standard* on the subject of New Guinea excited so much interest that I feel the present would be a most favourable time for bringing this country before the readers of the *Mission Field*, with a hope that some interest in its spiritual welfare may be aroused thereby.   It has been said the Australian Church should make herself responsible for the evangelisation of our latest colony ; perhaps so, but our sympathies and our prayers should not be withheld from our sister Church in her work, and these we shall be better able to give by knowing more of the nature of that work.

" This great island continent, fourteen hundred miles long, and nearly four hundred miles broad in its widest part, was visited by me in the early part of the year 1884 ; the difficulties that had to be overcome in reaching so little known and so little frequented a region were very great. At length, after innumerable delays, we left Thursday Island on Sunday, January 27, 1884, in a little vessel drawing only five feet of water ; for some days we were among the islands of the Torres Straits, getting on as well as we could when it was light, and dropping anchor off the lee of some island as soon as it became dark, fearing to proceed amidst the many reefs which there abound. We at last reached the open waters of the Gulf of Papua, and after sailing in a northerly direction for two days were much disappointed at not seeing land. Having no instruments

PORT MORESBY, NEW GUINEA.

on board by which to take solar observations, it was a delicate question as to where we were ; night came on, the breeze freshened, and we began to entertain fears that we might feel the land before we saw it, unless by chance the bonfires of some cannibal feast might warn us off. Sail was shortened and other precautions taken ; at nine that night it was announced that we were in shallow water, so we dropped anchor and awaited morning.

" When daylight returned, we found we had got into a bight, the land was all round us, that dark mysterious land which has never yet been crossed, with its millions of people who have not only never heard the names of Jehovah and Christ, but who live as ignorant of the civilised world beyond them as if they lived in some remote planet of our solar system. We felt, indeed, that we were on the threshold of the great Unknown, the world of every-day life was behind us, we seemed to be parted from it and to live again in that lonely sea which scarce keel has ever ploughed and in those dark though exquisitely beautiful shores, feelings of pleasure and excitement mingled with those of loneliness and solitude. What possibilities did this land not possess. My wife, who had determined to accompany me on this hazardous expedition, perhaps felt all this even more than I did; in all probability she was the first foreign woman who had ever gazed upon that scene which was new to all on board.

" We now made for the nearest land, which, when approached, turned out to be covered with a thick belt of cocoa-nut trees, stretching as far in all directions as the eye could reach, and extending, as we afterwards found out, with uninterrupted solidity along the whole of this part of the island. Soon we observed four or five canoes, they seem undecided what course to pursue, at length, one more venturesome than the rest,

NATIVES OF NEW GUINEA.

boldly struck out and made for us. Having loaded our guns and revolvers, we brought our vessel to and awaited their approach, we could see that they were paddling with all their might, and when they came within a hundred yards or so we could hear a confused noise like the chattering of monkeys. As soon as they were alongside they tried to rush the schooner, but we gave them to understand that we would each keep our own vessel, we had now an opportunity of examining them more closely, they consisted of twelve men and a boy, all naked, saving for their shell necklaces and other ornaments, their canoe was hollowed out of the trunk of a large tree and had no outrigger, it was only partially closed at one end, and the reason of bringing the boy seemed to be that his body might act as a stop gap, for he was carefully packed into the aperture, we gladly took their cocoa-nuts in exchange for some thin strips of red cloth, as the cocoa-nuts were handed up we could see that they had concealed some bows and arrows, which showed that our friends had been as suspicious of us as we had been of them. We now bid adieu, and, putting our vessel before the wind, followed the coast to the east. During the whole of that day we were sailing close to the land, a land as fair as any that could be found on this side of Paradise, the weather was charming, the breeze invigorating, and the palm trees in all their richness of green and gold, amongst which was here and there to be seen the moving form of some dusky Papuan warrior. Ever and anon, the palm trees would open out to allow some silent stream to float its waters into the ocean's brine, some of these rivers, whose banks have never looked down on anything more formidable than a canoe full of its own children, were of considerable size.

PAPUAN HOUSE, NEW GUINEA.

" Towards evening we reached a village called Orocolo, which was known to Mr. Goldie, the owner and captain of our vessel, he having been there before, we were soon surrounded by a small flotilla of canoes, Mr. Goldie receiving the most enthusiastic reception, one greasy native going so far as to insist upon rubbing noses, a brisk business was at once commenced, shell necklaces being freely exchanged for fishhooks or tiny strips of coloured cloth. The want of light soon put a stop to further bargaining, and our friends returned to their village. As day dawned we could see them making great preparations to come out in force, and no doubt they were much disappointed at seeing us weigh anchor before a single bargain was struck. We, however, had to catch the wind, or we might not reach our destination before night, which would probably have meant our having to put to sea, well enough under favourable circumstances, but not in a 14-ton vessel full of cockroaches, and having eight souls on board, five being Lascars. That day the coast presented by no means so pleasing an appearance as it had done the day before, the palm trees became more scattered, and the land more open, canoes occasionally set out from the villages that we passed to try and intercept us, but their efforts were generally unavailing.

" About two that afternoon we made for the mouth of a small river, and crossed the bar in safety with one foot of water to spare, the lead showing six feet on the bar, whilst we drew five. Having anchored at

VILLAGE NEAR PORT MORESBY.

the mouth of the river, on the right bank of which is the village Caremme, we went ashore, and were received with the greatest enthusiasm by the natives, my wife, the first white woman they had ever seen being a special object of attraction. The women and children, however, had not the courage to face us, but fled at our approach, peeping at us from behind trees and houses, but retreating still farther if they saw they were observed. The houses are built on piles raised several feet above the ground, and we saw two temples, looking like enormous boats stood upon one end, raised on piles about ten or twelve feet high like the houses, only rather more elevated ; horizontal bars are fastened across

the vertical poles to assist the climber. By the aid of a native in front
and two behind we managed to mount to one of the temples. It was
dark inside, yet light enough for us to see that it was filled with idols.
Whether they are worshipped or not I cannot say, but I imagine not, as
we found no difficulty in purchasing them. Our captain amused the
natives immensely by showing off the powers of his rifle. Their admiration was unbounded when they saw the bullet strike the water a mile
out to sea. They fully realised its deadly effect, and were sorry so much
energy should be wasted. They pointed to a village on the opposite bank
of the river, said they were their enemies, and that it would be
just as amusing, besides a good deal more useful, if Mr. Goldie
would direct his shots in that direction. Towards evening we
rejoined our vessel, around which an alligator was playing. An old
chief wished very much to sleep on board to protect us, as he said, but we
thought it better not to do so, and he was sent ashore with the rest. The
next morning when we wanted to start we found we were aground, and
had to wait five hours, much to the delight of the natives, who did a
roaring trade with some of our party. That day we kept near the land,
travelling east, and had many visits from enterprising natives, who had
set out in their canoes to try and reach us in the hope of barter; if they
came near enough we threw them a rope and thus they managed to keep
alongside. We received, as indeed all along this coast, pressing invita-
tions to go ashore and pitch our tent, every village seemed anxious to
have us. By three P.M. on the next day we had safely rounded
the hilly Island of Yule and were lying peacefully in a magnificent
harbour off the village of Delena. Here we said good-bye to Mr. Goldie
and his vessel, who went on to Port Moresby, and took up our quarters
with one of the South Sea Missionary teachers, who work in New Guinea
under the auspices of the London Missionary Society. These teachers
are delightful people.

"After a day's rest we came to Maiva in the teacher's whale boat.
Maiva is a village or group of villages about fourteen miles to the west
of Delena, and the farthest point touched by the London Missionary
Society. Here on Septuagesima Sunday, at six o'clock in the morning, I
had the privilege of offering what was almost certainly the first Eucharist
of the English Church that had ever been offered on this great Island
Continent.

"In our farther travels we had the pleasure of meeting with and
receiving the greatest kindness from Mr. and Mrs. Lawes and Mr.
Chalmers, of the London Missionary Society, whose names as missionaries
and travellers are too well known to require comment, and who must
have so often ventured into parts where neither white man nor white
woman had ever been seen before. They were, at the time of my visit, the
only Europeans permanently resident on the island with the exception of
Mr. Goldie."

ST. JOHN'S, KAFFRARIA.

REPORT OF ARCHDEACON GIBSON FOR THE MIDSUMMER QUARTER—DISCIPLINE
—MTSHAZI—LOCAL SUPPORT—EXTENSION OF THE WORK—PONDOMISI
SCHOOL—AGRICULTURAL WORK—INCREASE OF THE STAFF.

HE past quarter has been more marked by consolidation than extension (although the latter has not been neglected) ; and really it is the former of which we most stand in need at present, stricter discipline and more local subsidies being our main requirements.

Under both these heads there is a real progress to be reported. In the case of those who have fallen notoriously into open sin, such persons are now publicly cut off from communion by name, and, if they persist in their sin, are excluded entirely from all Church privileges ; nor are they readmitted until after a sufficient probation, and public acknowledgment of their fault before the congregation, an acknowledgment which is followed by public absolution. Within the last four months I have had the pleasure of thus reconciling a man who years ago had been a teacher under my predecessor, but, after marrying a wife in the Church, had afterwards taken to himself a second wife (also a Christian woman) by native customs. His real wife died some two years ago, and now both he and his partner in sin have been readmitted to the fellowship of the Church, and quietly married. There is no question that this public discipline is most salutary ; during the last year it has been the means of making two persons give up sinful courses, and has deterred a third from taking to himself a second wife, and there may probably be other cases of which I know nothing where it has also acted as a deterrent. Occasion for sin has been very often given in the past by the marriage customs, which have sprung up and been allowed to stereotype themselves in connection with Christian weddings. The most reprehensible feature in these has been the all-night singing of lads and girls, without any supervision, and in circumstances most calculated to give rise to temptation. This is now strictly forbidden by the Bishop, and his lordship's new " marriage rules " (of which this is only one) are being strenuously enforced, not without difficulty at first (thus at St. Augustine's fifteen young persons have been suspended from communion for three months, and at Roza the assistant-priest refused to marry the couple because the instructions were disregarded), but they are steadily making their way.

With reference to the second point, I can report that my Easter efforts among the white people have so far realised £20 for the local clergy fund, and there is more still to be collected. In making up recently my year's accounts, from June 1887 to June 1888, I noted that the local contributions amounted to about £240 from all sources, of which £110 came from natives and £130 from Europeans. This is not yet what it should be, but it still marks an advance on the past. In the course of next month I shall visit all the native stations in person to collect the harvest offerings. The people at St. Cuthbert's and at one or two other places give well, but at many centres the amount set apart for God is very disproportionate to the amount reaped. In order to enforce the payment of school-fees, we are now trying to carry out the suggestion of the Inspector of Schools (Canon Woodrooffe, of Grahamstown), to the effect that a promissory document should be signed by the headmen of each location, in order that, if the people fail to meet their liabilities, the Inspector may take action against them before the magistrate. This would enforce payment, and yet save individual Missionaries the odium of a resort to law.

Sunday services are now supplied regularly from St. Cuthbert's at Ntuli's location, about six miles away; and week-day ones from St. Augustine's, at the Nxasa and G. Mabandhta's kraal. Beyond the Tsitsa, the Rev. S. Adonis has purchased a hut for Church purposes at Culungea in a spot central to our people, and holds Sunday services there every month. The new station at Mkuzi's, among heathen people, of which I spoke in my last report, has been opened, and appears to be doing well. At the Roza a good stone school is now half erected.

I hope by the end of this quarter to have established the Rev. E. Jwara, now at St. Patrick's, Ggagata, at Mount Frere. The Christian natives belonging to the Church in that neighbourhood guarantee £14 a year towards his salary, which is as much as could be expected of them at present. Mr. Jwara's duties would be to itinerate from the Tina to the Umzimhtava, holding services, instructing and examining classes, instructing preachers, and baptizing. He is an able man, and this kind of work is congenial to him and such as he is likely to perform well.

Mr. Webber's itineration and the increased services among the Europeans are beginning to tell. The best proof of this is that at or near Mount Frere there are four candidates for confirmation; at or near Qumbu two; at Tsolo one; and in the Maclear district some twelve. The preparation of these is no light task, and involves long and frequent journeys. In fact, it is just at St. Cuthbert's, our nominal home, that Mr. Webber and myself are most frequently not to be found.

Two new boys have entered during the past quarter, and two more
are expected when the school meets again. I am now able to introduce
a firmer discipline than was possible at first, and the following rules are
to come into force at the beginning of next term :—(1) No boy will be
readmitted who does not bring with him a bag of grain or 3s., except
orphans, who are excused. (2) No exeats will be allowed, or leave to go
home given, except under very urgent circumstances. (3) As a general
rule, there will be an hour's manual labour on five afternoons in the
week. (4) In the evenings there will be night-school. This last rule
has been added at the request of the boys themselves, who certainly are
anxious to get on. I am fortunate in being able to leave them in the
hands of Mr. F. Rütters, who is very well fitted for the duty of looking
after them.

As regards Mtshazi, I am about to take a very important step. The
time has now arrived when, according to the custom of the tribe, he
should be circumcised, which, with a Kaffir, is tantamount to coming of
age. Considerable pressure has already been brought to bear upon him
in this matter, and he fears that, if he remains here, the tribe will compel him to be circumcised, and afterwards will not allow him to return
to school. As he is extremely anxious to continue his education for two
or three years more, he asked me to remove him to some more advanced
school far away, if possible in England. In many ways, his request falls
in with my own wishes. It is, I fancy, not generally recognised at home
that, while Christianity has made much progress among the Fingoes, it
has really touched very slightly the Amaxosa Kaffirs. The reason of this
lies, without doubt, in the Kaffir tribal system; and where a tribe sub-
sists as a tribe, the only hope of Christianising it lies through the chiefs.
After all, this is simply the principle on which the Celtic and English
Missions worked, and to which, under God, they owed their success.
Apply this to the present case. Here you have a lad brought up for three
and a half years mainly on a Mission station, and that station the only
place in his country where he feels safe ; a lad who has seen much of the
evils of heathenism as exemplified in this abominable witchcraft system,
and who is well disposed towards Christianity in itself; a lad who,
whether the Government may recognise him as a headman or not, will
always be to the people what he is indeed in their eyes already, their
chief—surely, through him, there is a grand opening for the introduction
of Christianity. The great obstacle at present which stands between
him and the catechumenate is the influence of the tribe ; if he be removed
from that, and be brought entirely under Christian influences, and be
shown the power of Christianity in civilised European countries, I believe
that there is a very strong probability that, by the grace of God, Mtshazi
would become a Christian, and that his conversion would entail the
conversion of many of his countrymen. I have accordingly resolved to

send him at the end of July to Lovedale, with the hope that, if he does well there, I may be able to make arrangements for his going on to England next year under proper supervision. His companion will be his cousin Sogotgo, whom I hope to baptize on July 22. This move is so important a one, and may be fraught with such consequences to the Pondomisi, that I most earnestly ask the Society for their prayers that God's blessing may rest upon it.

I have already shown how we are trying to obtain more help from the people for the work. This is not the only way in which we are trying to make ourselves more independent. In a month or two more, I hope that the water-furrow will be completed. Its course will be two or three miles long, and in places it has to be carried over "dongas" in troughs, while elsewhere the rock has had to be cut away for it; but, once completed, it will be a great benefit. There will soon be a large amount of glebe land under cultivation, and the growing of our own wheat and vegetables, as well as mealies and fodder for horses, will effect a very large saving in the personal expenditure. In fact, in about two years' time, if all goes well, I believe that our living ought to cost us almost nothing.

I am hoping by the end of this year to obtain the assistance of an old friend, the Rev. P. H. Case, M.A. Cantab. If the Bishop approved, my own wish is that this present parish should be formed into three: (a) the Pondomisi location, which I would keep in my own hands; (b) the Fingo work, which I should propose to hand over to the Rev. P. H. Case, assisted by the Revs. S. Adonis and E. Jwara, and an efficient staff of catechists and other workers; (c) the Europeans, to whose pastoral care the Rev. H. B. Webber has a fair claim. I believe that, in this way, we might be able to bring about a very great development of work. I should be so near to Mr. Case as to be able to place at his disposal any knowledge that I may have of the Fingo work; and should for my own part be able to give myself up to the Pondomisi, to whom I am attached by such strong personal ties, and also to the archidiaconal work, which is capable of being worked up almost indefinitely.

THE MISSIONARIES' CHILDREN EDUCATION FUND.

ALTHOUGH this Special Fund has not received so much support as was anticipated by those who started it, nor, indeed, as it well deserves, yet it has been productive of some very useful results, with which supporters of the Missionary cause may like to be made acquainted.

It has been the means of affording valuable information and advice to Missionaries regarding schools suitable for their children.

It has called forth from many persons engaged in the work of teaching, liberal offers of education, in some instances altogether gratuitous, and in others at greatly reduced terms, for children of Missionaries.

By means of its agency holiday homes have been provided for a great many children of Missionaries, as well as for some students at Missionary Colleges; and thus an increased interest in the cause of Church Missions has been engendered in many families, the full effect of which for good is such as it is impossible to estimate.

It would not be at all desirable to mention the names of those whom this Fund has benefited, but contributors to the Fund may be glad to be informed of some of the noteworthy instances of benefits conferred upon the Missionary cause by its means.

The following may be taken as examples of benefits which have arisen.

The only son of a Missionary, who died of fever caught from one of his flock, received a free education at an excellent school, then obtained admission into one of the best Colleges at Oxford, where he took his degree. He was afterwards ordained, and is now working at a curacy in England, with the full intention of returning as a Missionary to the colony in which he was born, when he has obtained experience in clerical work.

Another young man, whose father had been a Missionary in Africa, obtained free education in a large school, was received by kind friends of the Missionary cause for his holidays, and is now preparing for Holy Orders in a College in connection with S.P.G. in one of the colonies.

A Colonial clergyman with a large family, whose eldest son is now assisting him at his Mission Station, was enabled through the instrumentality of this Fund to obtain gratuitous education for his younger son at a College of good repute, where he got on so well that he obtained an exhibition, enabling him to have an Oxford education. He has taken his B.A. degree, and is hoping to obtain honours in the Theological School, and then to be ordained. The clergyman who gave him a home in the holidays has proved to be a most true friend to this young man, and has greatly helped towards his University career; but he would probably never have heard of him at all if this Fund had not existed.

In connection with this Fund education was provided for two of the daughters of a clergyman who was drowned in one of the Colonies when returning from visiting a sick person. One of these daughters had a holiday home provided for her in a country Rectory, and on her leaving school the kind friends who received her into their house as one of their own family, obtained for her a situation as governess, which she still holds, and which enables her to contribute towards the support of her mother and younger sisters, who have very scanty means.

Besides these few instances, there are many others who have been helped in various ways through the agency of this Fund.

The gentleman who contributed anonymously for several years no less than £40 a year to this Fund has been removed by death. A generous contributor of £10 annually has been prevented from continuing his support in consequence of other more urgent claims upon his charity. Other contributors have been removed by death and other causes, while the general depression of the times has had its effect upon this as well as upon almost every other charitable agency. It is therefore earnestly hoped that fresh friends may be raised up to give their aid to this good work.

It would be very undesirable to diminish the contributions made towards the general fund of S.P.G. by giving to this fund; but it is suggested that even a few additional shillings, by those who cannot well afford more, might be added for this Fund when money is paid for the general work of the Society.

If any ladies or gentlemen have useful and suitable garments to bestow upon the families of Missionaries, they may be sent (as many bundles have already at various times been sent) to the Rev. J. Frewen Moor, Ampfield Vicarage, near Romsey (Chandler's Ford Station, South-Western Railway), who will endeavour to distribute them to the best of his ability, and who acts as secretary to the Fund, and is always glad to impart information on the subject, and, as far as he is able, to assist Missionaries towards the selection of schools for their children and to find holiday homes for them. He also receives contributions, large or small, towards the Fund.

J. F. M.

THE CHILDREN'S CORNER.

THE HERO OF SÁHAWAFY.—A TALE OF THE FRANCO-MALAGASY WAR.

BY THE REV. ALFRED SMITH.

CHAPTER I.

T was a cold evening in the winter season of the year of our Lord 1881. The wind cut shrilly and fiercely from the heights of Aukáratra, and swept howling over the bare hills and valleys of Imerina. The natives were shuddering and cowering in their wretched huts, under their miserable *lambas* of so-called *heavy* sheeting, manufactured for them in Massachusetts, U.S.A. The sky was dark and gloomy and covered with clouds, and as the wind tore furiously along it seemed to blow all the brightness and beauty of the tropics for ever away. For the central provinces of tropical Madagascar can be almost (not quite) as desolate and cold as England, with the bitter wind blowing from the south-east in the months of May and June. May and June—the months looked forward to with such longing and hope by thousands of boys and girls in England, as the time when all nature awakens from the long winter sleep, and calls loudly for books to be put away in musty desks, and Heigho! for romp and play among the grass in the sweet fresh fields. But we in the great African island do not look forward with such pleasure to May and June —at least we who are old stagers in the Tropics, and know what ague-fever means. New-comers like the cold. "It is so like England!" they say. Yes, like England on one of those days Dickens describes as "combining the attributes of a scolding wife and a smoky chimney."

It was just such a cold day as that in Antananarivo at the time of which I write. The bell had sounded for Evensong in the cathedral church, and a few whose homes were near at hand, together with a good number of big boys from the High School, had already entered. The church stands high up the hill on which the capital city of Madagascar is built, and to-day it lay in the very teeth of the cutting, biting, killing wind.

Within its shelter, however, the solemn voice of prayer rose up, and the song of praise ascended to the throne of the Almighty, undisturbed by the roaring wind without. It was a fitting emblem of the struggling Mission. "Small and of no reputation," like the poor building which represents the dignity of the grand English cathedrals: beaten and buffeted by many winds of adversity, oppressed and narrowed by biting poverty. And yet withal affording a little shelter, a little haven of rest, where a few humble Christian converts might watch and pray till this life's "tyranny be overpast."

The last *Amen* had been borne away on the wings of the wind, and the little congregation was dispersing. From the vestry door issued the Bishop with two of the pupils of the High School. He walked between them, with one hand resting kindly upon a shoulder of each of the boys.

"Let us stand for a moment in the shelter here. You will think well over what I have told you, my boys," he was saying to them. "It is a great responsibility for you to undertake, that of the office of catechist. Think what your duties will be! You will have charge of a Christian church and school. You will have to try and destroy among the people of your villages all the old heathen customs, to wean them from their filthy habits, and raise them to the pure light and knowledge of the blessed Gospel of Jesus. You yourselves will have to be the examples of this pure light and knowledge, and in the midst of many and powerful temptations to show yourselves faithful servants of the Lord. This will be hard work for you, my boys, but if you only truly trust Him, God's grace will be sufficient for you."

The boys murmured assent. They had long been in training in the High School for the office of catechist in one of the district churches, and were now about to be sent forth to their difficult task. Their names were Ratefy and Ralay, and both were about eighteen years of age, and of course regular communicants.

After a few moments the Bishop resumed: "By the way, you have neither of you heard anything in town to throw light upon that robbery?" Ralay glanced quickly at the Bishop's face, and his brow seemed to darken.

"No, sir," he said, "it is hardly likely that we who belong to the church here should hear anything of it. Even supposing anything was really known in town, the knowledge would be carefully concealed from us. All the world would know indeed before us." He spoke with some heat, and as he did so the eyes of the Bishop rested curiously upon him.

"Well, if you do hear anything, it will be your bounden duty, mind, to let me know at once."

Neither of the boys looked as if they agreed to this statement of their duty. The Malagasy never voluntarily offer information against each other. A man must be caught red-handed in the commission of crime before justice is able to claim a victim. Spite* or feud will sometimes discover a criminal, and sometimes also money, but nothing else will. Sense of justice never will. Your most favourite pupil, your most promising catechist, the man in whom you have the most boundless confidence, may be the most noted rascal and notorious evil-liver ; but, unless you find it out for yourself, you may go on for years, and never get a hint of the truth from his fellows. This fact is often the source of the keenest pain and disappointment to the missionary, and one often disastrous in its results.

It was the knowledge of this fact that caused the Bishop to look so curiously at Ralay. The boy was a striking type of the ordinary Hova. A longish face, yellowish brown complexion, high cheek-bones, narrow forehead, small eyes, straight black stubborn hair cut short across the forehead, full lips, flattish nose, and, lurking underneath it all, an expression of Malay cruelty and deceit. Ratefy, though presenting in appearance the same general features, was nevertheless of quite a different character. He belonged to the higher class, to the *audriana*, or superior class of the Hova race. Bright and joyous in disposition, enthusiastic in all he did, he was a general favourite both in the Mission and amongst his own people.

"No," he said with a laugh and echoing Ralay's words, "we are not likely to hear of the thieves. The police have been told to search everywhere for traces of the stolen ornaments, which means that everybody has heard of the robbery, and "—added he after a pause—"that is all."

"You don't think we shall find them, then ? " asked the Bishop.

"Who knows ? " was the sententious response.

"Well, we need not stay in the cold any longer," said the Bishop. "I am getting old, you know, and this cruel wind makes my old bones twinge in memory of past agues. Good-night, boys."

The Bishop went on his way home. "It is curious about this Ralay," he mused as he walked on. "He answered as if he imagined I suspected him of having a hand in that robbery, and I am sure his face altered somehow. Yet his character is simply excellent so far as we know. Aye, *so far as we know*—the evil of it is that we know really nothing. Well, well ! "

Arrived at his house, he found Mr. Earnshaw, the master of the High School, waiting for him.

"Oh, here you are, Earnshaw ! " he said, shaking hands. "I am glad to find you here, for I want to talk to you. Come along ; it is tea-time, and we will talk over an inspiring cup of tea."

* A day or two after this was written it was curiously proved. The church of which the writer is in charge was robbed, and all the cassocks and surplices stolen. The town was searched from end to end the following morning by the native authorities, but no trace of the thieves discovered. A day or two ago a man and his wife fell out, and the woman was so transported with rage that, in an unlucky moment, she *publicly* taunted her husband with the theft of the cassocks and surplices. When she was examined, several witnesses at once appeared, who of course could give evidence of the fact. The husband was a soldier and policeman. "When rogues fall out, honest men come by their rights."

They went into the drawing-room, where the Bishop poured out a cup of tea for Mr. Earnshaw and one for himself.

"I have been talking to Ratefy and Ralay," the Bishop began, "about their being appointed as catechists. You know we want a couple of men to take charge of Ambóhidrapéto and Ambóatány, and they are the most trustworthy and the best we have at present. Is it not so?"

"Certainly. They have both been with us a long time; they are now fairly educated as Malagasy go; and I have absolutely nothing against their moral characters. If you appoint them I trust they will both do well."

"I trust so myself; but, alas! in a country like this one can never be sure. What a horrible condition of life it is—this never being sure that your most trusted pupil will not ultimately be shown to be the most consummate hypocrite. I never read those words in the Litany about the 'crafts and assaults of the devil,' 'deceit' and 'hypocrisy' without special reference to our converts. However, we hope that all is as we believe, though, by the way, Ralay behaved rather curiously to-night."

"Yes; how was that?"

"Of course you have heard of the cathedral church having been broken into last night and robbed. The altar-cloth, hangings, surplices, even the bit of carpet in the chancel, were all stolen. What the thieves can do with the things now they have stolen them I don't know. Surely it must have been done out of spite."

"I have heard of the robbery, naturally," replied Mr. Earnshaw; "I am surprised the thieves were not afraid of robbing a church, being so very superstitious about their heathen sanctuaries."

"After all, it is not very strange. While the Malagasy have plenty of superstition they have no reverence. Superstition is based on fear and dread, while reverence is built upon love and admiration. They nave never heard of any of their people having been crippled or struck dead in any of our sanctuaries, and so they are not much afraid of them. However, I was going to tell you that I asked Ralay and Ratefy whether they had heard anything of the thieves, and I noticed Ralay answered in a peculiar manner—as if he imagined himself suspected, *I* thought. Very likely, though, there was nothing in it, only one does grow so very suspicious out here."

"Well, I have never heard anything the least against him. His conduct with me has been most satisfactory. Both boys, indeed, have done very well, and will, I hope, do as well as teachers."

After some further conversation on the subject, it was agreed that their names should be submitted to the Diocesan Committee for appointment as catechists, and the matter then dropped, while soon after Mr. Earnshaw left.

CHAPTER II

The committee meeting had taken place, and Ratefy and Ralay were both accepted as catechists, and appointed to the charge of their respective churches.

Standing on the road beneath the great stone palace, Maujáka-miádana, as it is called, which means "reigning peacefully" (soon, indeed, to belie its name, for the clouds of war were gathering thick and fast round the Malagasy shores), and looking westward, the eye ranges over one of the most striking views of the world. Just in front is the round-topped hill of Ambóhijánaháry—the "hill of the gods"—with the long and deep trenches cut through and through it by the foolish Radama, who intended to dig it down, but was soon stopped by the appearance underneath the thin soil of the living rock. In these quiet trenches now grow gold and silver ferns, as well as many other varieties dear to the souls of fern collectors. Here, too, underneath the midnight stars, their depths have echoed back in days of old the sobbing prayers of persecuted Christians, and have been watered by martyr tears. Well indeed may they now produce gold and silver ferns!

To the south of the "hill of the gods," and almost encircled by the hill of Antananarivo, as it curves round from west to south, is the famous Máhamásina, in the centre of which is the holy stone upon which all new sovereigns of Madagascar take their stand on their coronation day. Here it is that they are "made strong" (for that is the meaning of Máhamásina) by the homage of the "thousands of Imerina."

But not only has the human sovereign of Madagascar here been "made strong." A little lower down the hill from where we stand under the shadow of their palace, is the rock of "hurling down," looking down upon Máhamásina a sheer descent of three hundred feet. It was from this rock that, wrapped in filthy mats, the mortal bodies of the patient martyrs were cast, to be crushed out of all shape of humanity in the plain below. It was then that the King of kings and Lord of lords was "made strong." It was here that the Malagasy martyrs, in the words of good old Bishop Ridley, "played the man," and "lit such a candle in Madagascar as by God's grace has never been put out," and "made strong" the Gospel of Christ.

Beyond this plain is the grand valley of Bétsimitátatra, through which the river Ikopa winds its way. The whole valley is one enormous rice-field, and it is upon the produce of this valley that the whole population of Antananarivo depends. In the early spring, when the rice plants are growing, the eye rests upon their refreshing greenness with peculiar pleasure in its contrast to the dry, dull brown hills around.

Beyond this again, ranges of hills begin to rise, dotted here and there with small villages, till one comes to the dark masses of the Ankáratra mountains, over 7,000 feet high.

Among the hills of lesser note, *one* rises far above its fellows—the hill of Ambóhidrapéto—on the top of which is the village from which it derives its name. It was to this village that Ralay had been appointed catechist.

Long before the Hova were heard of in Imérina, from this hill-top reigned Rapéto, the greatest chief of the ancient inhabitants of Madagascar, whom they call the Vazimba.

They were probably an offshoot from a still existing African tribe which had found its way across the Mozambique channel. They are said to have retired north-westward from Imérina before the inroads of the Hova, perhaps to try and regain once more the mainland.

At any rate, Rapéto was one of the last of these chiefs known to have reigned in Imérina, and it was he who led his people on their north-westward retreat, with their magnificent herds of cattle.

All that now survives of them is their name, which has become a name of terror to their successors. The Vazimba are considered to be wild and revengeful spirits that linger in certain places (no doubt their old haunts in the olden time), and trouble and vex peaceful travellers. A man is found lying dead in a lonely place on the hill-tops, with no signs of violence upon him to suggest how he came by his death,—*the Vazimba have twisted his neck!* They entice people away from their homes, especially children, to lone places, and there fiercely wreak vengeance upon them. A lonely grave, with no mark or sign placed by it by sorrowing friends, is the grave of a Vazimba, and is avoided as a pestilence. A man taken suddenly ill has inadvertently stepped over such a grave, and its inhabitant is taking vengeance for the desecration. People pray, therefore, to these fierce Vazimba spirits, and offer sacrifices to them to bespeak their assistance and to turn away their rage. Poor Rapéto and his band of conquered followers, trudging over the westward hills, left their name as a terror behind them. But the superstition is now in its turn nearly dead, for the lamp of the Gospel of Christ is shining more and more towards the perfect day, and these dark terrors are fleeing away.

The ancient town of Rapéto is, however, one of the principal places which superstition still strongly haunts. High and lifted up in the air it stands, like an eagle's nest, and frowns down upon the villages round as the place where diviners and witches of all sorts congregate. Aye, even darker things were said with bated breath about these fierce eagles of the rock. Stories of robber bands and of murders, not committed by the old Vazimba of Rapéto, but by their present successors. These are mostly slaves, descendants of captives taken in war with the Betsileo tribe. Amongst these, then, Ralay had been appointed to work.

To be continued.

NOTES OF THE MONTH.

A NTIGUA Diocese lost pecuniary assistance from the State some years ago, the life interests of the Bishop and Clergy at that time receiving State stipends alone being reserved. The venerable diocesan, Dr. Jackson, whose health forbade his continuing to reside in the West Indies, has been permitted to live in England, his duties in Antigua being performed by his coadjutor. In England, however, the Bishop has rendered invaluable service to the diocese he loves so well. He has sent out many clergymen and candidates for ordination, and among many other works, the chief has been the creation of the endowment of the See for the benefit of his successors. The Society has rendered assistance by promising money in proportion to funds raised elsewhere. Fifteen thousand pounds is the sum aimed at, and fourteen thousand are now raised. The Bishop writes :

"That my life has been spared to bring me within sight of the completion of my Fund, is matter of devout thankfulness to my God. I never can forget how much this happy prospect is due to your help and encouragement."

We trust that the Bishop may have the satisfaction of seeing the remaining thousand soon raised.

I N this letter the Bishop mentions the death of an honoured clergyman in Antigua :

"A heavy blow has fallen on my Diocese in the death of Mr. J. Drinkwater. His has been for sixteen years our model parish. He was our Registrar, the Diocesan Treasurer of our Endowment Fund, and the Chaplain and trusted Counsellor of my coadjutor and myself. He kept a curate, being the Government Inspector of the schools of the Leeward Islands, and several of our best clergy owe their efficiency under God, to his training.

"We ordained him in the spring of 1861, and I question whether St. Augustine's, during its forty-six years, has ever sent forth a more useful man."

L ORD DUFFERIN'S speech at Calcutta on St. Andrew's day, on the eve of leaving India, has deservedly attracted great attention. Although its purport was political, it is of importance to all who are interested in India from any point of view. The following considerations bear closely upon the Missionary problem :

"Well, then, what is India ? It is an Empire equal in size, if Russia be excluded, to the entire continent of Europe, with a population of 250,000,000 souls, composed of a large number of distinct nationalities, professing various religions, practising diverse rites, and speaking different languages. The census report says there are 106 different Indian tongues—not dialects—of which 18 are spoken by more than a million persons, while many races are still further separated from each other by discordant prejudices, conflicting social usages, and even antagonistic material interests.

"Perhaps the most patent peculiarity of our Indian Cosmos is its division into two mighty political communities—the Hindoos, numbering 190,000,000, and the Mahomedans, 50,000,000, whose distinctive characteristics, religious, social, and ethnological, it is unnecessary to mention. To these two great divisions must be added a host of minor nationalities (though minor is a misleading term, since most of them are numbered by millions), who, though some are included in the two broader categories, are as completely differentiated from each other as Hindoos from Mahomedans. Such are the Sikhs, with their warlike habits and traditions and theocratic enthusiasm; the Rohillas, Pathans, Assamees, Belochees, and other wild and martial tribes on the frontiers; the hillmen dwelling on the Himalayas; our subjects in Burmah, Mongol in race and Buddhist in religion; the Nairs, Bheels, and other non-Aryan peoples of the centre and south of India, and the enterprising Parsees, with their rapidly developing manufactures and commercial interests.

"Again, among the numerous communities are found, at one and the same moment, all the various stages of civilisation through which mankind has passed from prehistoric ages to the present time. At one end of the scale is the naked, savage hillmen, with stone weapons, head hunting, and polyandrous habits, and childish superstitions; at the other the Europeanised native gentlemen, with the refinement, polish, and literary culture of Western philosophy and advanced political ideas; while between the two lie layer upon layer, in close juxtaposition, of wandering communities living in tents, with flocks of goats, collections of undisciplined warriors, with blood feuds, clan organisation, and loose tribal government, feudal chiefs, or barons, with picturesque retainers, seignorial jurisdiction, and medieval modes of life, and modernised country gentlemen, enterprising merchants and manufacturers, with well-managed estates and prosperous enterprises. Besides all these under our direct administration, the Government is required to exercise a certain amount of supervision over 117 native States, with their princely rulers, autocratic executives, and independent jurisdictions, and their fifty millions of inhabitants. The mere enumeration of these diversified elements must suggest to the most unimaginative mind a picture of as complicated a social and political organisation as has ever tasked human ingenuity to govern and administer.

"But even within India itself we have not reached the limits of our accountability; for we are bound to provide for the safety and welfare, not only of Her Majesty's Hindoo, Mahomedan, and other native subjects, but also for the large East Indian community, the indigenous Christian Churches, and the important planting and manufacturing interests scattered over the face of the country, as also to secure the property and lives of all British residents in India, men, women, and children, whether employed in the service of the Government or pursuing independent avocations in the midst of alien and semi-civilised multitudes, whose peaceable and orderly behaviour cannot, under all circumstances, be implicitly relied on."

This last paragraph is especially noticeable for its reference to the indigenous Christian Churches, as now a real factor in Indian life, which cannot be overlooked in the sphere of Government responsibility.

ST. PHILIP'S MISSION, in the city of Grahamstown, is under the charge of the Rev. W. H. Turpin. Besides his colonial congregation, which he says has been diminished by the rush to the Kimberley Diamond Fields, he has work among the natives. A few

words from his report will give an idea of what is being done in connection
with St. Philip's.

"I have native unpaid lay helpers who are extremely useful in the work of
evangelisation, as they go about the native location and hold short cottage lay services
at different places, two or three evenings in the week, and go as far as ten miles into
the country to preach to their heathen brethren; but they are not sufficiently educated
to take part in teaching in the schools, or to take the service in St. Philip's. There
are two young students under Canon Mullins at the Kafir Institution, from whom I

KAFIR CHILDREN.

get assistance in the Sunday services at St. Philip's. I have also some female workers
in the Mission whose work is to visit the huts of a night, talk to the females, read to
them, and bring in as many converts as they can, and they have been very successful
in winning a good many young girls about the ages of from fourteen to eighteen years.
They also look after the female Christian members of the Mission and see that they
are keeping up to their Christian duties. I have a quarterly meeting of these workers,
the men on one evening and the women on another, and I often hold these meetings
in one of the members' huts, when we talk over the work done in the quarter, report
anything wrong in any member of the Mission, sift it, and settle some plan of putting
the person right if found to be in error. Such help is invaluable."

Mr. Turpin's Missionary work is, however, more extensive than this, for he adds :

"I have also to visit the Beaufort Mission and the Peddie Missions every quarter. The former is under the Rev. D. Malgas, who is in Priest's Orders, but the Lord Bishop requested me to still superintend the work there when he appointed Mr. Malgas, although he was in Priest's Orders; and the latter are under the Rev J. Pattison, who is in Deacon's Orders at present. His Lordship has also appointed me a kind of general Missionary Inspector, and in that capacity I have visited the Missions at De Aar, Colesberg, Sand Flats, Alice, East London, and St. Luke's during the last half-year."

Mr. Turpin has also opened new work among Kama's people, which is the first Church Mission to that tribe.

FROM Mandalay the Rev. G. H. Colbeck writes at Michaelmas to say how rejoiced he is to hear that a clergyman (the Rev. G. Whitehead) is sent out to strengthen that Mission, and that he only wishes there had been two. He says that he is seeking to obtain land at Amarapura, the old capital, where it is imperative for the Church to begin a Mission, and has already warned one of the Mandalay catechists (a former Buddhist Guie Douk, or "Archdeacon") to prepare himself for work there.

Of Madaya, a new station, he reports that it is bearing fruit, for "there are several adults ready to make their profession." He hopes soon to be able to baptize many.

"The Hpoongyis are still inquiring, but they are difficult people to know what to do with. Two Sadaws or Bishops of a monastic house close by sent word the other day that they wished for a conference with me. They had heard something of Christianity, and wished to know more. They are coming to me in a day or two. Oh, that they may be led to see 'the Light.'"

IN his quarterly report the Rev. B. Markham, the Society's Missionary at Polela, in the Diocese of Maritzburg, mentions having recently baptized six Basutos at Stofelton, the Basuto settlement beyond the Umkomazana, and adds :

"I have also been in communication with the Council of Education on the subject of a grant for the school at Stofelton, and for help to start other schools. We are informed that the Superintendent of Native Schools will sometime pay us a visit and make a report."

ZULULAND seems now to be pacified. The Rev. S. M. Samuelson writes :

"All our Christians have remained faithful to me, and, I hope and pray, to God also; but none of the heathens, except two young boys, have lately joined us, and I am sorry to say that not a few of our heathen neighbours were killed in the war. The treatment the Zulus have received from the British, and the example they have received from the soldiers, have not been calculated to induce them to embrace Christianity or civilisation, but rather to harden them against it ; consequently our work among them does not seem to be more appreciated by them now than it was when they were under their heathen chiefs. It is a sad reflection that so highly educated a people as the British are, exhibit so little fear and love of God as they do in heathen lands."

A MEETING of a very interesting character took place on Sunday, November 25, at St. Bede's, Albany Street, when the Rev. H. Rowley, of the S.P.G., addressed about sixty associates and members of the Christ Church, Albany Street, Branch of the Girls' Friendly Society.

Through the medium of a Bible Class composed of the elder girls, and at the invitation of the Vicar, the Rev. Prebendary Festing, considerable interest is evinced in the cause of Missions, and a fair sum of money collected in aid of the funds of the S.P.G.

S PEAKING at a meeting of members of the University of Cambridge in the Divinity schools in November last, the Bishop of North China described the work in his Diocese, which, he stated, contained some eighty millions of heathen, and was four or five times the size of Great Britain. At Tin-Sing, the formation of a railway, and the fact of its being the port from Pekin, had attracted a large number of people there, but there was no clergyman amongst them, and the need of one was greatly felt. At Pekin it had been felt that they should have some man of ability and learning to commence a college for educating the Chinese for the ministry, for it was to that they must look for the achievement of permanent results in China. They also wanted to establish a girls' school in addition to the one for boys which they had already. At present there were not many Christians in China, but no one knew how soon they might have a flourishing Mission in that country.

O N behalf of the Synod of Trinidad the five Bishops, to whom the choice was delegated, have chosen for that See the Rev. James Thomas Hayes, M.A., Trinity College, Cambridge, who has accepted the Bishopric. Mr. Hayes was ordained in 1871, became Rector of Swynshed in 1874, and Vicar of Holy Trinity, Hinckley, in 1876.

O N Sunday, November 25, the Bishop of North Queensland held an ordination in Holy Trinity Church, Finchley, by the permission of the Bishop of London, when Mr. C. A. Vaughan and Mr. G. E. G. Dainty, who are going to that Diocese in connection with the Society, were made deacons.

I N Westminster Abbey, on St. Andrew's Day, the Venerable Charles Frederic Douèt, Archdeacon of Surrey, Jamaica, was consecrated Coadjutor-Bishop of Jamaica, and Archdeacon Sumner was consecrated Bishop of Guildford. The Archbishop of Canterbury was assisted in the acts of consecration by the Bishops of Winchester, Rochester, Jamaica, and Dover.

SUGGESTED SUBJECTS FOR PRAYER.

For the Bishop-designate of Trinidad, and for the vacant Sees in the United States.

For New Guinea, and the English and native people there.

For the Missionaries and Missions among the Karens in Burma.

That men fitted for the great work in the Missions in the diocese of Madras may offer themselves to fill the present vacancies.

MONTHLY MEETING.

THE Monthly Meeting of the Society was held at 19 Delahay Street, on Friday, November 16, at 2 P.M., the Rev. B. Compton in the chair. There were also present the Bishop of Calcutta and the Bishop of Antigua, *Vice-Presidents*; the Rev. J. W. Ayre, Canon Betham, J. M. Clabon, Esq., Canon Elwyn, General Gillilan, Sir F. J. Goldsmid, K.C.S.I., C.B., Rev. Canon Hockin, J. R. Kindersley, Esq., Rev. G. B. Lewis, General Lowry, C.B., General Maclagan, Rev. F. H. Murray, Rev. C. J. Ridgeway, H. C. Saunders, Esq., Q.C., General Tremenheere, C.B., and S. Wreford, Esq., *Members of the Standing Committee*; The Bishop of Glasgow and Galloway, Rev. J. A. Boodle, Rev. A. Cooper, Rev. J. C. Cowd, Rev. T. Darling, Rev. H. J. Day, Rev. J. Denton, Dr. de Tatham, J. C. Eckersley, Esq., Rev. J. Elkington, Rev. F. B. Gribbell, Rev. R. S. Hassard, Rev. J. N. Heale, Rev. T. Hill, H. Laurence, Esq., T. L. Murray-Browne, Esq., Rev. G. A. Ormsby, E. Pennington, Esq., J.P., Rev. G. F. Prescott, Rev. G. C. Reynell, Rev. N. H. C. Ruddock, Rev. W. Selwyn, and Rev. A. Williamson, *Members of the Society.*

1. After prayers, the Minutes of the last Meeting were read.

2. The Treasurers presented the abstract of receipts and payments from January 1 to October 31, printed on page 480 of the *Mission Field* for December 1888.

3. Read the following letter from the Lord Bishop of Guiana :—

" October 31, 1888.

" My dear Mr. Tucker,—I cannot take leave of the dear old land without expressing to you my thankfulness for all the benefits I have received from the Society during the lengthened period of my Episcopate.

" It is no new thing to have to acknowledge the obligations under which all Colonial Churches are to the venerable Society which you so faithfully serve as Chief Secretary ; but with this acknowledgment I desire to couple the courtesy and affectionate kindness I have always received at your hands and from your admirable fellow-workers.

" No greater calamity, as I believe, could fall upon the Church of England than any diminution of interest in the Society, and my prayers will ever go forth that increasing blessings may rest upon it. For more than half a century I have been its debtor, and in my old age my obligation to it must not be forgotten.

" You shall hear from me soon after my arrival (D.V.) in my adopted home.

" Believe me to be,

" Always faithfully and gratefully yours,

" W. P. GUIANA."

4. Read letter from the Rev. B. Edwards, of Ashill, dated November 6, 1888 resigning, in his hundredth year, the secretaryship for three Rural Deaneries in the Diocese of Norwich.

5. The Lord Bishop of Calcutta addressed the members. He said that the problem of the evangelisation of India is an anxious and difficult one, and that the conditions of the problem change perpetually. There is a steady movement both among the Hindus and the Mohammedans, which sometimes awakens hope, and sometimes causes anxiety. India, it may be, is the land where the future of Hinduism as well as of

Mohammedanism will be settled. Mohammedanism has in India to consider whether it can adapt itself to the nineteenth century. Mohammedans find that the Hindus are beating them in life, and so they also are learning English. A rich Mohammedan, Sayed Ahmed, has founded a College at Aligurh, with Cambridge graduates for its professors. The Hindus on their part know that Christianity must have much to do with the future of their country, and some will hand over their children to the Missionaries without reserve.

The Bishop pointed out how the Hindu Pantheism does not admit the idea of personality, and therefore since the individual man virtually denies his own existence, moral responsibility and conscience are excluded. Those who for centuries have inherited such beliefs must take centuries to escape altogether from them. Missions have really grasped India for only half a century—*i.e.*, since the Mutiny.

Although Christianity must certainly have its influence on the future of India, the fear cannot be excluded that it may be such a Christianity as we could not recognise; and the Bishop laid the greatest stress upon the importance of taking more care for the converts, among whom traces of their Hinduism frequently reappear.

There has been considerable disappointment in recent years, which is due to the failure of the experiment of leaving native Christians too much to themselves, and concentrating the energies of the European Missionaries on Evangelisation. Besides the difficulties of caste, the joint family life weakens the individual character. More Europeans, therefore, are wanted, and more education should be provided for native Christians. At Bishop's College the Bishop rejoices that native Christian gentlemen can be educated not necessarily with a view to ordination. The Bishop urged that the work of converting the heathen might be relaxed for a time, so that the native Christians might be rendered a truer leaven for the rest of their nation. His lordship spoke warmly of the magnificent work at Bishop's College, under the Rev. H. Whitehead, where there are thirty students, some reading for their B.A. degree; he also described the impression produced by the self-denying principles of the Oxford Mission; and, in conclusion, said that while now the state of Mission work demands the exercise of patience, he is convinced that a time is coming when there will be a great breaking up of the native religions, and the Church's opportunity will come.

6. All the candidates proposed at the meeting in July were elected into the Corporation. The following were proposed for election in January 1889 : —

W. F. G. Spranger, Esq., Windsor House, Cumberland Place, Southampton ; Rev. F. James, S. Peter's, Southampton ; Rev. W. G. G. Thompson, Highbury, Bodorgan Road, Bournemouth ; G. H. Pember, Esq., Tangier Park, Basingstoke ; Rev. J. Wybrants Johnston, Termon Vicarage, Carrickmore, County Tyrone ; and Rev. C. H. Prior, Pembroke College, Oxford.

THE SOCIETY'S INCOME.

Abstract of RECEIPTS *and* PAYMENTS *from January 1 to November 30.*

						GENERAL FUND	SPECIAL FUNDS
Subscriptions, Donations, Collections, &c.	...	...	...	...	...	£30,943*	£13,526
Legacies	...	...	...	...	...	...	8,516	
Dividends, Rents, &c.	...	...	...	...	...	3,147	5,316
	TOTAL RECEIPTS	...	...	...	...	£42,606	£18,842
	PAYMENTS	...	...	...	...	£78,232	£17,258

The Receipts under the head of Subscriptions, Donations, and Collections for the General Fund from January 1 to November 30, in five consecutive years, compare as follows : 1884, £30,385 ; 1885, £30,325 ; 1886, £29,830 ; 1887, £32,020 ; 1888, £50,943.*

* In addition, the Treasurers received in February last Securities of the value of £25,296 as "A Thank-offering to Almighty God for the extension of the Church in the Colonies and Dependencies of the British Empire and beyond it ;" also other Securities of the value of £2,288 as a Trust Gift, *the income only being available.*

THE MISSION FIELD.

THE FIELD IS THE WORLD. THE SEED IS THE WORD OF GOD.

FEBRUARY 1, 1889.

LABOUR AND PATIENCE IN MISSION WORK.

A SERMON PREACHED IN THE SOCIETY'S BEHALF IN ST. PAUL'S CATHEDRAL ON SUNDAY, DECEMBER 16, 1888, BY THE REV. CANON LIDDON, D.D.

(Reprinted from the *Family Churchman*.)

"*Behold the husbandman waiteth for the precious fruit of the earth, and hath long patience for it until he receive the early and latter rain.*"—JAMES v. 7.

THE Christian duty of working for the extension of our Lord's kingdom upon earth, by supporting missions to the heathen, is a subject which has claims on our attention at all seasons of the year, because every truth of the Christian creed, and every blessing of the Christian life, which we successively commemorate, suggests high privileges of our own and the needs of those who do not share them with us. Nothing that our Lord has done or suffered for us can fail to stir a Christian heart with a strong desire to do something, if it may be, for Him, and, whether in the successive Church seasons God is sending forth his Son, "made of a woman, made under the Law, to redeem them that are under the Law that we might receive the adoption of sons," or whether the Son of God is dying on the Cross, "the just for the unjust, that He might bring us to God," or whether He is rising again for our justification, or leaving us at His ascension that He may send to us the Holy Comforter, we must be always sensible of our indebtedness to Him, and of the obligation which lies on us to do something that others too may know and love Him. But the season of Advent suggests this duty with an emphasis that is all its own. The great act of condescension whereby our Lord, "for us men and, for our salvation, came down from heaven, and was incarnate by the Holy Ghost of the Virgin Mary, and was made man," must cause every sincere Christian to ask himself the question: "What am I doing to enable more of my brother men to know that He, the True Light of the World, is here ready to give light to them that sat in darkness and in the shadow of death, and to guide the feet of wanderers into the way of peace?" And the knowledge that God has "appointed a day, in the which He will judge the world in righteousness by that Man whom He hath ordained, whereof He hath given assurance unto all men, in that He hath raised Him from the dead," must lead a Christian seriously to consider, not only whether he is himself living in expectation of that day, but also whether he is doing anything to help his brother men to prepare to meet the Universal Judge. Assuredly activity in the cause of missions is by no means the only practical answer that is to be given to these questions, but it is an answer of a very important and substantial kind; and thus Advent, by keeping our thoughts fixed more or less steadily on the Incarnation and on the Judgment, inevitably suggests the great Christian duty which we have to consider this afternoon.

Now, it is a matter of common remark that Christian missions are often looked upon somewhat coldly even by well-disposed people—much more coldly than ought to be possible for Christians with the love of our Lord Jesus Christ in their hearts. There are more reasons than one that may be given in explanation of this; such as the mistakes which missionaries—who, after all, are but men—make now and then in carrying out their difficult work, and the mistakes which societies of earnest persons at home, who undertake to promote the missionary cause—but who also are human— make, either in the conception, or in the conduct, of their great enterprise. The wonder would be if there were no such mistakes. But whatever, or however many, they may be, they are not the main reason for the coldness about missions which is under consideration—a coldness, I repeat, which all good Christians who have the kingdom and the honour of our Lord and Saviour at heart must assuredly deplore. The main reason for this coldness is, at least in a great many cases, a mistaken estimate of what missions can be reasonably expected to achieve. People point to the large sums of money that are collected annually in this country and elsewhere, to the list of devoted men who give their lives to the missionary cause, to the sanction of Church authority, to the wide popular sympathies that are equally enlisted in the favour of missions; and then they ask : " What does all this come to ? What is the measure of achieved success? Where are the numerous converts who might be expected to be forthcoming after all this expenditure of varied effort ? " Is not the disproportion, between what is said and done and the actual result, so serious as to warrant the disappointment which is thus expressed, a disappointment which is due, not merely to a sense of failure, but to an accompanying suspicion of unreality ?

Now, the first point to be observed, in this estimate of what missions can be expected to do, is that it is the natural product of one feature of the temper of our day. The human mind is largely influenced by the outward circumstances of the successive forms of civilisation in which it finds itself, and within the last half-century railroads and telegraphs have sensibly altered human habits of thought in more respects than one. We assume that the rate at which we travel and send messages must necessarily have its counterpart in all meritorious forms of human effort; and in this way we accustom ourselves to regard rapidity in producing results as a serious and necessary test of good work, a test, failure to satisfy which is not easily, if at all, atoned for by other tokens of excellence. This impatience of delay in production may have its advantages in certain limited districts of human activity. Business need not be worse done when it is got through smartly ; and there are many houses in this great city in which time is made to go much further than was possible in the days of our fathers. But is it not a mistake to assume that all forms of human effort are improved by this acceleration of pace, or, indeed, that they will adapt themselves to it ? Take Art, and consider the old and true saying : " Time is short, and Art is long." Do what we will, Art cannot be hurried. Even if a painter or a sculptor creates with great rapidity this or that masterpiece, the rapidity is limited to the moment of production ; the real preparation which has enabled him to project the idea, and has perfected the methods of expressing it, is the work of a lifetime. And rare indeed are the occasions when a great artist can produce rapidly and to order. The demand for rapidity of completion of smaller works of art means that poor works of art will be the order of the day.

The demand for the swift execution of great enterprises in art is unfavourable to the production of any works which will be much accounted of by those who come after us. Why cannot we of this generation produce public religious monuments on the scale of the cathedrals of the Middle Ages ? To say the people do not care to spend their money in that way is only very partially true. There are generous owners of wealth in our own, as well as in former, times who know how much these splendid homes of religion affect the minds of men, and lead them to think of, and to live for, higher interests than those of sense and time. It is truer to say that we, the men of to-day, are, as a rule, too much in a hurry to achieve these great triumphs of religious art. They are the work of men who knew, not only how to work, but how to wait. They are the work, in most cases, of several generations of donors and of artists. Each was content to do what he might without being able to do all he would ; but he would do his little on a splendid scale rather than try to do much on a poor one : whereas now, as a rule, we insist on completing anything of this kind which we take in hand, and therefore we have to plan it on that comparatively insignificant scale which makes it possible for us to complete it. We have the satisfaction, such as it is, of doing it all ourselves, but the result, as compared with the great creations of our forefathers, which were the fruit of the slow, unselfish travail of many generations, is poor and disappointing. Or take Literature. As a rule, the composition of a great poem, or history, or treatise, which shall live, extends over many years, not merely because the mechanical labour involved in writing out a considerable work requires a great deal of time, but especially because to produce anything that shall have on it the stamp of maturity requires time still more urgently, time for redressing, so far as may be possible, some of the defects which necessarily attach to the first effort at production, time to reconsider what is ill-judged, to supply what is deficient, to anticipate, in some degree, the sentence which an impartial posterity would pass upon a composition in its original erudity. Horace's advice to authors about keeping their works by them for many years before publication embodies the common-sense of the ancient world. But now literature, like other things, must more or less conform to the demand for something to show at once; and writers who in past generations would have made solid contributions to literature exhaust themselves in throwing off hasty contributions to the monthly magazines. They say that they wish to be read, that people will only read something short and interesting at the moment; but, with rare exceptions, the magazines disappear for ever at the end of the month, and thus the permanent interests of literature are often sacrificed to the demand for rapid production.

Now to-day we are remarking how this impatience for immediate results, which marks our time, extends itself beyond those activities which are mainly or solely human, and claims to mould and to govern undertakings in which God is the main Agent and man only God's instrument ; only here the impatient demand is apt to meet with a different kind of reception from there. Artists and men of letters adjust their work to the temper of the day, but the Eternal Workman heeds not the varying moods and fashions of the creature whom He has made, and, in spite of the demand for rapid production, is at this hour as slow and as sure in His work as at any past time in history. And so the demand for immediate results, which, at whatever cost, is anxiously gratified by human workers, is not seldom utterly balked and disappointed when God's agency is chiefly in question. And this is the case with many of those features of the progress of the human race which fall under God's general providence, but especially it is the case with Christian missions. A mission is essentially a work in which man counts for little, although his active exertion is imperatively necessary. In a mission the influences which fertilise human effort, and the date at which this fertilisation shall take place, are alike in the hands of God. When this is felt it will be felt also that an order—so to describe it—upon a given mission for so many converts at least, with such and such a time, is an indefensible thing. But St. James, in the text, supplies us with an illustration which may enable us to see this more clearly. St. James is corresponding with some Christians who demand the second coming of our Lord, or, at least, some Divine intervention in order to redress the injustice which they are suffering. Observe the difference between St. James's way of meeting this demand, put forward by suffering Christians, and St. Peter's reply to the scoff of the mockers who asked: " Where is the promise of His coming? "   St. Peter thinks it enough to say that time does not exist for God; but St. James points to the fact that God may be seen at work in nature, that God works slowly and will not be hurried, and that those men, whose business leads them to watch and to wait upon His work, are examples of a reverent patience which Christians might do well to follow: " Be patient, therefore, brethren, unto the coming of the Lord.   Behold the husbandman waiteth for the precious fruit of the earth, and hath long patience for it until he receive the early and latter rain."   What the coming of the Lord certainly means in this passage may be open to discussion.   Our Lord comes to us in blessings and in judgments, and St. James may be thinking of some political or social event which would put a stop to the oppressions of which his correspondents had complained, or he may be thinking of our Lord's second coming to judgment; but either coming, St. James implies, is, in this respect, like the natural harvest, that, while man's activity leads up to it, it depends upon agencies which are beyond man's control.   When St. James points to the presence and operation of God in nature, every countryman in Syria would have understood him.   The corn was sown in September; in October there came the early rain which made the seed sprout; the latter rain fell, as a rule, in March or at the beginning of April, in time to make the ears swell before they ripened. In a soil of a remarkable fertility, but generally of no great depth, spread as it was over the limestone rocks, everything depended on the two rainfalls.   The husbandman could only prepare the soil and sow the seed, the rest he must leave to God; and St. James dwells on the long patience with which, as a rule, the Syrian peasant waited for the precious fruit of the earth, and for the rainfall which was so necessary to its growth; and his language illustrates an old observation that, as a rule, people who live in the country are more religious—by which I mean more constantly alive to the presence and the working of Almighty God—than are people who live in towns.   In the town almost everything speaks of man, of man's energy, man's resources.   In the country man counts for much less, and we are surrounded by the works of God. Man can make a watch or a steam-engine, but he cannot make a daisy grow, he cannot give any explanation whatever of the principle of its growth; and thus people who live in towns, and who are generally engaged in manipulating, or in witnessing the manipulation of, dead matter, are less alive to the presence of God than the countrymen who know that they can do little more than arrange the scene on which the Author and Sustainer of vegetable and animal life shall work His will.   The habit of watching God in nature is of itself a lesson in the school of faith.   Our Lord gives us one part of this lesson when he bids us look at the lilies of the field, the anemones with which the soil of Palestine was covered in March and April, and consider in them the beauty which outdid the glory of Solomon's throne, yet for which they had made no preparation of toiling or spinning.   And St. Paul gives us another such when discussing the precept about the ox which treadeth out the corn.   He says that " he that ploweth shall plow in hope, and he that thresheth in hope should be partaker of his hope." Or again, when he points to the seed-crop as presenting a natural analogy to the Resurrection—" That which thou sowest is not quickened except it die; and that which thou sowest, thou sowest not that body which shall be, but bare grain, it may chance of wheat or of some other grain, but God giveth it a body as it hath pleased Him, and to every seed his own body."   If anything is clear about God's work in nature, it is that it proceeds gradually, that it cannot be precipitated.   This truth finds, perhaps, an unintentional explanation in the modern word of which we hear so much—" Evolution." " Evolution " is one of those words which have a religious or an irreligious meaning, according to the antecedent ideas with which they are associated in the speaker's mind. If by evolution I mean the work of a self-existent force in nature, originating I know not how, and tending I know not whither, but without any break of continuity whatever, even to introduce the unexplained, the unspeakable mystery of life, then the conception is quite irreconcilable, I do not say with Christianity, but with any serious belief in God. But if by evolution I mean an observed connection between some of God's earlier and later works in nature of such a sort that one leads to the other by a graduated sequence without violence, without catastrophe, this surely is so far from being irreligious that it may illuminate our conception of some of the operations of God. Whether, however, we use the word or not, there can be no doubt about the slow and patient travail of God in nature : one period in the earth's earliest condition introduces another, one phase of natural life leads on to the confines of another ; this epoch of human history is the parent of much that first emerges into view in that : the truth being that the one presiding and controlling Mind is through- out at work, never ceasing from, never hastening His task,—He, that Eternal Wisdom which reaches from one end to another, mightily and sweetly doth order all things.

And as in nature so, as St. James implies, it is in grace. Man does his part; he sows the word of life, he prepares the soil of the soul, he plants with St. Paul, he waters with Apollos, but he can do no more ; and God who sends the early and the latter rain alone gives the increase. So it is in the history of individuals when that great change takes place which is called conversion, whether from error to truth, or from ungodliness of life to the obedience of Christ. Conversion is not so sudden a process as it may seem to be. It is sudden perhaps at last. There may be a moment when a man is conscious of passing a line from darkness to light, " from the power of Satan to God," just as there is a moment when the fruit is ripened perfectly so that it falls. But that moment has been long prepared for. Long before Saul of Tarsus lay prostrate on the road to Damascus he had brooded over the meaning of the dying words and of the death of St. Stephen—what it was in itself, what it was to him. He could not do it justice at once. He could not at once dismiss as of no account the prejudices of a life-time, the respect in which he held his Pharisee teachers, the strong and subtle ties by which his heart and his understanding alike were bound to the old religion of Israel. But in time this process of spiritual fermentation had done its work ; and so, when our Lord appeared on the road to Damascus, Saul was prepared for Him. In the same way St. Augustine tells us that, long before the change which was precipitated by his reading a passage in the Epistle to the Romans, he had met with teachers, events, examples which had set him thinking. He put those thoughts aside, but they re- turned ; he again dismissed them, again they came back to him. He was in truth ill at ease ; his Manichean creed, his dissolute private life, were the husks on which this prodigal son had long fed ; but they had—those husks—they had a work of disen- chantment to do, though time was needed in which to do it ; and at last this prepara- tory process was over, the hesitations, the misgivings, the anxieties, the yearning, the relapses, the near approaches to grace, and the shrinkings back from grace—these all had come to an end, the fruit had ripened whereby the Christian Church received the greatest of her teachers since St. Paul. And so, too, in the history of societies. It took three centuries to convert the Roman Empire to Christianity, if indeed we may rightly so describe a numerical superiority—for it was not much more—on the part of the Christians at the end of the first generation of the fourth century of our era. And yet, even so described, what a wonderful work it was! Three centuries before, such a result would have seemed impossible to any man of sense and judgment. Every- thing was against Christianity—the government, the wealthy, the influential, the intelligent as much as the people. The government from time to time exchanged a contemptuous toleration of the Christians for a bitter persecution of them. The liter- ary men only deigned to notice them occasionally in terms of extreme derision or contempt. The people regarded them as food for the lions in the amphitheatre when- ever the emperor would give a public entertainment. Again and again it seemed to the servants of Christ that the struggle was too prolonged, too unequal to be main- tained ; again and again saints and martyrs pleaded " How long, O Lord, how long ? " And yet all the while the work was proceeding, the conversion of the empire was silently going forward, the faith was making its way, sometimes penetrating, in a very fragmentary form, into the thoughts of one set of men, sometimes presenting itself to another, amid a crowd of comparatively worthless rivals, only as a new idea which was worth considering. The Divine Master walked, like the Stranger on the Emmaus road, but now in conversation with Pagan hearers, long before He flashed His God-head on them in the communion of His Church. Little by little the leaven was work-ing in all quarters of the vast lump of the old diseased society; little by little the faith made or begged its way as a stranger, living on precarious sufferance, presenting itself only to be criticised, scouted, repelled again and again before at last it could take strong possession of the souls of men. There were no missionary societies in those days, no secretaries, sermons, public meetings, annual reports. The Church was the one missionary society. She set herself down among the great heathen popula-tions, and they looked at her first fiercely, then more kindly, then more fiercely than ever, as if angry that for a moment she had succeeded in fascinating them, then with a new sense of her being a power which had a future, and with which they must reckon. Every Christian in those days carried his life in his hand. He was a mission-ary by the mere fact of being a Christian. The influence that radiated from him insensibly won first toleration, then respect, then affection and reverence. Men won-dered at a type of character which was new to them—stoicism notwithstanding—and as obviously superior as it was new. Sometimes a soldier in the ranks, sometimes a professor of literature in the capital, sometimes an artist, now and then a mechanic or a merchant, rarely someone attached to the person of the emperor, not seldom a slave —these Christians lived among the heathen, confessing Jesus Christ. When one Christian in a great family was a slave he was felt to be in the enjoyment of an elevating principle of life which placed his owners at a disadvantage. He was calm and collected; indifferent to wrongs and insults; firm and consistent in his life, as seeing an invisible Master; fearless, as fearing only God; gentle, as seeing in every man a possible brother in the faith; patient, because long discipline had conquered self-will in him; disappointed at nothing in this world, because hoping nothing from it; without anxiety, because no earthly mishap could terrify him; inaccessible to cor-ruption, because having his desires perfectly in hand; inaccessible to flattery, because at heart indifferent to any judgment but one; not dazzled by the world's splendid pageant, because himself without an ambition to share it; not cynical towards sur-rounding sins and errors, because too deeply impressed with the pathos of the scene around him. When many hundreds or thousands of men in various stations were scattered throughout the society of the great empire, and were men of this character, they were inevitably missionaries, even though they never opened their mouths. They were the little leaven that was leavening the lump; little by little their example did its work. Men saw how they lived, and, on occasions, how they could die; and, at last, the desire to share the secret of their life became too strong even for the com-plex and associated strength of paganism, and, in words that were used at the time, " the cross ceased to mark the place of public execution, and it took its true place on the diadem of the Cæsars."

In view of these natural analogies and of this history, let us turn once more to the modern demand that so many missionaries shall produce in such and such a time so many converts, and to the impatience, if not the indignation, which is felt and expressed if this expectation is not realised, as though something had taken place which was akin to a commercial fraud. What is this modern way of looking at missions but an endeavour to apply to the kingdom of Divine grace those rules of investment and return which are very properly kept in view in a house of commerce? Do you not see that this demand leaves God, the great Missionary of all, out of the calculation? God has His own times for pouring out His Spirit, His own methods of silent prepara-tion, His own measures of speed and of delay, and He does not take missionaries or the promoters of missionary societies into His confidence. He has a larger outlook than they, more comprehensive plans; and whether He gives or withholds His gifts, it

is, we may be sure, in view of the truest and broadest interests of His spiritual kingdom. We cannot compel His bounty, we can but do as He bids us, and abide His
time. "Even as the eyes of servants look unto the hands of their masters, and as the
eyes of a maiden unto the hand of her mistress, even so our eyes wait upon the Lord
our God until He have mercy upon us;" or, as St. James puts it: "Like as the
husbandman waiteth for the precious fruit of the earth, and hath long patience for it
until he receive the early and latter rain."

Not that this reverent patience in waiting for God's blessing is any excuse whatever for relaxing the zealous activity with which missionary efforts should be prosecuted by the Church of God. The husbandman does not the less plough the soil, or
the less sow the seed, because he is uncertain whether his labour will be followed by
the early and the latter rain. If he does not plough and sow, he knows that the rain
will be useless, at least to him. It is quite possible for a secret indifference to the
interests of Christ and His kingdom to veil itself under the garb of reverence for the
incalculable character of the ways of God. To refuse to help the work of Christian
missions because we do not know how far God will permit a particular mission to
effect many or striking conversions is only one of the many forms of self-deceit which
we Christians too often employ in order to avoid Christian duty. Duties are for us,
results are with God. We have no doubt, if we are Christians, about our duty in this
matter. Before us lies the greater part of the human race, "sitting in darkness and
in the shadow of death," with no true knowledge of God, or of the real meaning of
life and of that which follows it; and above and among us there rises the Cross, that
Cross to which we are indebted for peace and hope, that Cross on which He hangs,
whose Name is the only Name given among men whereby men may be saved, and
in our ears there sound the commands uttered eighteen centuries ago, but always
binding, always new: "Ye shall be witnesses unto Me"; "Go into all the world and
preach the Gospel to every creature." Our part is clear, even though, after a century
of labour, we should have to say with the Prophet, "I have laboured in vain; I have
spent my strength for nought and in vain," since even then we may add with Him:
"Yet surely my judgment is with the Lord, and my work with my God."

Yes, and there is another duty, and that is to consider—not only when unfriendly
criticism forces the subject on our attention, but simply as a matter of loyalty to God
—whether our idea of missions is such as to make it likely that God will largely bless
them. Is it not the case that at least in some quarters a missionary's life, like the
work of a clergyman at home, is regarded as a profession rather than as a vocation?
And do we not see the results of this vital mistake in the idea that a missionary must
as far as possible lead the life of men who have given up nothing that they can carry
away with them to their distant task? So long as we insist on encouraging missionaries to think that the household and the family are a necessary feature of their work,
the standard of self-sacrifice will be low and poor, and the results probably meagre.
Missionaries will be what religious opinion at home expects them to be; to paraphrase
a well-known proverb, "Like people, like priest"; what the parent Church is, such
the missionaries that it sends out will be. If we at home make few efforts in our
humbler and lower sphere of work, they will make few too in their nobler sphere. If
we expect little of them in the way of self-sacrifice, they will too easily be content not
to practise it. If they see in us any token of that fire which the Son of Man came to
kindle on the earth, it will not be long before they too feel its light and its warmth.
The impulse which creates a great mission comes from the Church at home; and let
us never forget that its source, under the Holy Spirit, is in our hearts, in our sense
of duty.

And yet, whatever our feelings, and however our present missionary system fall
short of ideal effort, it will be ungrateful not to own how indulgently God has blessed
it, and in particular how He has blessed parts of the work of the old Church of England
Society for the Propagation of the Gospel. We may listen for one moment to a prelate who speaks to us from his bed of sickness, and assuredly with an authority which

will not be disputed in this Church: "There are now," says the Bishop of Durham, "fourteen African bishops; not one of those dioceses existed until Her Majesty had been on the throne fully ten years. There are now thirteen Australian sees, and the first of them was created just about the time that the Queen ascended the throne. There are eight sees in New Zealand and the Pacific Islands, and not one of them existed at the commencement of the reign. Let us ask ourselves," Bishop Lightfoot proceeds, "what a see means?" "It means," he says, "the completion of the framework of a settled Church government; it means the establishment of an apostolic ministry which we believe was especially ordained by God to be the means whereby the ministrations and the gifts of the Church of Christ should flow to men." And then, when he asks by what means, under God, these results have been achieved, he replies: "The Society for the Propagation of the Gospel." Not that the establishment of a divinely ordained ministry, although an essential feature, is the ultimate object of a Christian mission. It is a means to an end beyond—the conversion and sanctification of souls. To take one instance at haphazard out of many, "the boy who sprung from a degraded tribe, living formerly by rapine and by a false pretension to magic, and especially addicted to drunkenness, now writes a few weeks ago to the missionary to whom he owes his faith to say that he is at the end of his school career, and has gained the Government allowance which will enable him to continue his studies and to become a useful man among his own people," illustrates a work at once civilising and spiritual which our missions are carrying forward in spite of much discouragement in all quarters of the globe. The certificate of this change is the admission of adult converts to baptism; and when we read that—to take a few instances under the auspices of this society—forty-three converts were baptized in Phokoane, in Basutoland, and at Kalsapad, in Madras, the baptized Christians have increased in ten years from 779 to 2,514, or at Ramnad, in the same diocese, that 361 baptized Christians of fourteen years ago have now become 3,146, it is impossible to say that missions are followed by no considerable results. Every one of these souls is just as dear to God as were St. Peter's converts on the day of Pentecost, or as are yours or mine. Every one of them was bought on Calvary by the blood of the Immaculate Lamb. Activity and patience, these are the two conditions, whether at home or abroad, of good missionary work. We must learn to cultivate long patience for the precious fruit of the spiritual soil without in any degree relaxing our active cultivation of the soil which yields it. When a Christian takes part in these great efforts, he rises, or should rise, above the limits of his own petty individual life; he acts as, what he is, a member of the body of Christ; and the Body of Christ, it lives, not for some thirty or forty or fifty, or at most eighty years, it lives in the centuries. Already eighteen hundred years and more have passed since its birth, and it gathers in one century the harvest whose crop was sown in the century before. To belong to a great family, to a great country, may be of itself an incitement to noble effort; what should it be if we claim fellowship with the general assembly of the Church of the Firstborn in earth and in Heaven from Pentecost till now?

Let us endeavour in spirit to associate ourselves with this larger, this nobler, this more hopeful life, and to remember, not only the privileges which it confers, but the duties which it enjoins; and, in labouring according to our measure to extend its frontier, to be content and thankful, if it should please our Divine Master to show to us of this generation His work and to our children His glory.

CALCUTTA.

THE BENGAL MISSIONS—BISHOP'S COLLEGE: REPORT FROM THE PRINCIPAL.

ENGAL, Assam, Chota Nagpore, and the North-West Provinces form the four groups of the Society's Missions in the enormous Diocese of Calcutta.

In the Bengal group are some of the oldest of the Society's Indian Missions, Tollygunge being founded in 1829, and

ST. PETER'S, BARRIPORE.

Howrah and Barripore in 1833. These places are all close to Calcutta itself, where there are also the Missions of the Cathedral and St. Saviour's.

Although only about half a century has elapsed since the foundation of these Bengal Missions, we are apt, in our impatience, to complain of the smallness of their success. They certainly cannot be compared to advantage with many of the Missions in India, where rapid, vigorous growth rejoices our hearts. Each district has its peculiar difficulties, and the character of the Bengali offers formidable ones. With the wisdom that is conspicuous after the event, we may say that mistakes were made in the early working of these Missions by the pioneers, whose

c 3

experience has helped the counsels of those who began elsewhere after
them. There are between four and five thousand converts in these
Bengal Missions. Though they are not so numerous as might be wished
and expected, yet the immediate aim is not to add to them. When
addressing the Society last November, the Bishop of Calcutta sketched
the policy which should be pursued. He stated that there has been
considerable disappointment in recent years, which is due to the failure
of the experiment of leaving native Christians too much to themselves,
and concentrating the energies of the European Missionaries on
evangelisation. Besides the difficulties of caste, the joint family life
weakens the individual character. More Europeans, therefore, are
wanted, and more education should be provided for native Christians.

The joint family life is a system which must offer enormous difficulties.
Numerous married persons form part of the one household of the family
of the husbands. All the women in the household are absolutely under
the rule of the mother or grandmother. The development of the Christian
family, in any sense which would seem real to us, must be most difficult.
To both men and women the very rudiments of the idea must be strange.

The Bishop pointed out how the Hindu Pantheism does not admit the
idea of personality, and therefore, since the individual man virtually denies
his own existence, moral responsibility and conscience are excluded. Those
who for centuries have inherited such beliefs must take centuries to escape
altogether from them. Missions have really grasped India for only half a
century—i.e., since the Mutiny. Yes, after all, fifty years is but a short time
in the history of the Church; and what we look for and aim at is not mere
numerical success, but the growth of vital Christianity. And it is for this
reason that we rejoice so much at the blessing which is attending the devoted
labours of the Rev. H. Whitehead, of Bishop's College, Calcutta. That
noble foundation of Bishop Middleton had itself been disappointing. The
oundation stone of the magnificent buildings on the banks of the Hooghly,
at Howrah, shown in the accompanying illustration, was laid in the year
1820, the land being given to the Society by the Government. Bishop
Middleton intended it to be a great central college for all India, and even
for regions beyond its borders. This great aim failed. In 1880 the Government needed the Howrah site and buildings, which were sold by the Society;
and in a less pretentious structure, but in a central position in Calcutta,
the College has entered upon a new and more useful career. There are
not only theological classes, but native Christian gentlemen are educated
in the College, not necessarily with a view to ordination. When he was
in England in 1883, the Bishop was most fortunate in securing the services
of the Rev. H. Whitehead for the principalship.

The Bishop has spoken of his work in the warmest terms to the
Society on several occasions, and indeed its results speak for themselves.
From Bishop's College we may now hope that influence of the best kind

will spread to the Christians in the Missions in and around Calcutta. This is the important thing for the present. The Bishop even urged that the work of converting the heathen might be relaxed for a time so that the native Christians might be rendered a truer leaven for the rest of their nation. The Hindus themselves know that Christianity must have much to do with the future of their country, and some will hand over their children to the Missionaries without reserve.

But although Christianity must certainly have its influence on the future of India, the fear cannot be excluded that it may be such a Christianity as we could not recognise; and his lordship laid the greatest stress upon the importance of taking more care for the converts.

The following is Mr. Whitehead's report to the Society, the encouraging features in which will speak for themselves:—

THE OLD BUILDINGS, BISHOP'S COLLEGE.

" The College has not during the past year been quite without a history, and yet, I am glad to say, has been happy. An important addition has been made to the College buildings by the repurchase of the house formerly occupied by the S.P.G. Secretary, which has enabled us to give up the damp and unhealthy house that we formerly rented for the accommodation of the students. Still more important additions have been made to the College staff. In December 1887, Mr A. H. Blakesley, of Christ Church, Oxford, arrived to take Mr. Cooper's place as Vice-Principal. As Mr. Blakesley's services are given almost gratuitously, the College owes him a deep debt of gratitude for the work he has already done for us. At the beginning of this year we were further reinforced by the Rev. C. H. Walker, of the Oxford Mission, who has very kindly undertaken several courses of lectures both in theology and English. With our staff thus strengthened, we were enabled after the Summer vacation to open a B.A. class, the need of which has long been felt to enable us to retain our hold over the students during the most important part of their University course. We have not sent any students in this year for the Oxford and Cambridge Preliminary Examination; the three who are at present reading for it will, I hope, go in next October. The result of the University examination for the F.A., which comes after the first two years of the course, was eminently satisfactory. Out of six who went up from the College five passed, two in the second-class and three in the third, while one failed, chiefly owing to continued ill-health during the year preceding the examination. Of those who passed four are now reading for the B.A. and one, C. Sells, is the headmaster of the C.M.S. school at Bhapulpur. As about 50 per cent. of the students who go up for the F.A. as a rule fail, we have no reason to be dissatisfied.

"In numbers the College has been the same this year as last. Three students left us at the beginning of the year, viz., C. R. Rudra, C. Sells, and John Tawthoo, and three new ones took their rooms,—Anna Gonesh (a boy), a Canarese, from the Cowley Mission, Bombay; Anand Daji, a Mahratta, from Ahmednuggur; and Girish, a recent convert sent by the Oxford Mission. The two former are theological scholars, and the last is preparing for secular employment.

"We have recently had another loss from the death of one of the students who came to us from Chota Nagpore, named Paul Khalhhao. He was never very well in Calcutta, and I was obliged to send him back to Ranchi last June, where he got rapidly worse and died in October. Mr. Logsdail wrote that his end was a very peaceful one, and the one thing that seemed to trouble him was that he should not be able to use in God's service the knowledge he had gained at the College.

"As his departure left a room vacant, we were enabled to admit another student from Chota Nagpore, named Daud, who holds a Government Scholarship and is reading for the University Examination. He is a steady, hard-working lad, and will, I hope, do well. I give a table showing the number of the students, with their different nationalities and the work they are doing:—

	Bengalis	Tamils	Kols	Armenians	Jew	Mahratta	Canarese	N. W.	Totals
Senior Theological	—	2	—	1	—	—	—	—	3
Junior Theological	2	—	—	—	—	—	—	—	2
M.A.	1	—	—	—	—	—	—	—	1
B.A.	5	2	—	—	1	—	—	1	9
F.A.	2	2	1	—	—	—	1	—	6
Entrance	2	—	2	1	—	1	—	—	—
Totals	12	6	3	2	1	1	1	1	27

N.B.—The list does not include Paulus Khalhhao, the Kol student who died during the year, and two students who have been engaged in teaching work in our schools.

"Our Commemoration Day this year was celebrated with unusual ceremony, as it, fortunately, coincided with the Episcopal Synod, so that we were favoured with the presence of five of the Indian Bishops, viz., the Metropolitan and the Bishops of Madras, Bombay, Colombo, and Rangoon. At the early Celebration the Bishop of Bombay celebrated, and the Bishop of Calcutta gave an impressive address on the value and power of religious education. Nearly 150 guests afterwards sat down to breakfast, including my own father and mother and sister, whose presence, I need hardly say, made the day to me a true red-letter day. After breakfast speeches were made by the Bishops of Calcutta, Madras, and Bombay.

"At the beginning of February a visit was paid to the College and its schools by Lady Dufferin, which concluded the festivities of the cold season, and left us to settle down to more serious business for the rest of the year. There has been nothing calling for special mention in the routine work of the College. A request was made by some of the heathen students in the neighbourhood to be allowed to attend the secular classes, but after careful consideration we decided, for the present at any rate, not to admit non-Christians. The only reason for doing so would be the opportunity of giving them religious teaching; but that, again, would involve an entirely different method of religious instruction from that adopted at present, and the training of the Christian students would inevitably be sacrificed in the effort to reach the heathen. Moreover, the influence of any considerable influx of non-Christian students upon the general tone of the College would probably be, on the whole, injurious.

"It has been a great pleasure during the past year to hear satisfactory accounts of several of my old students. H. C. Mitter has recently taken charge of a C.M.S. boarding-school at Chupra in the Krishnaggur district, and is well spoken of by the missionary in charge. John Tawthoo, the Karen student, writes in good spirits of the school work he has begun among his native hills, and adds characteristically, 'Everything depends on me.' The Rev. R. K. Gupta is still working as a missionary at Allahabad; the Rev. S. T. Cornelius has been appointed to an independent charge in the Madras diocese; Michael Singh is working at a school in Shillong; and the Rev. A. N. Banerji has been appointed to the responsible post of Cathedral Missionary, where he is working with great zeal and ability.

"The care of the Tamil congregation in Calcutta has been undertaken by Mr. Gnanathekan, who succeeded the Rev. S. Cornelius. The school for boys and girls started some two years ago continues very successful, and is not only a great boon to the congregation, but also an important means of missionary work, as it is attended by about twenty-five Hindu children, who all receive daily religious teaching.

"Looking forward to the future, I think that what we most need is the fuller development of our Missions in Bengal and a successful sphere of work for our Bengali students. I hope that in time the Sunderbund Missions will furnish this, but at present their organisation is not advanced enough to supply work for more than a very limited number of educated workers. But there are many branches of work which I should be glad to develop in connection with the College when we have trained up some of our own students to take part of the secular teaching off our shoulders.

"In conclusion, I most sincerely thank the Committee for the welcome assistance they have given us by granting the interest in the Secretariat fund towards a repair fund. Repairs in India are a very serious item, and now that our buildings have multiplied will be in the future a heavy charge on the College funds. But the kind grant of the Committee has for the present relieved me of what had become a source of considerable anxiety.

"Looking back on the past five years, I cannot but feel deeply grateful for the manifest revival that has taken place in the work and life of the College,

CALCUTTA CATHEDRAL.

and the connection which has now been established between it and the educational work of the diocese, and, I might even add, of India generally. The experience of these years has amply proved that there is a real and important work for the College to do, which I trust will, under God's blessing, still further grow and expand as time goes on.

"The School would demand a separate report to do it justice. I will only add, therefore, that it has kept up its numbers and efficiency under the management of the Rev. E. F. Brown, to whom our warmest thanks are due for the ungrudging labour he has spent upon it."

FIJI.

AR away in the Pacific Ocean, almost at the Antipodes, is the little British Colony of Fiji. It is a group of lovely islands, no less than 225 in number, but only 80 of them are inhabited. The aboriginal natives, though forming the bulk of the population, are not very numerous—only about 110,000. Among them the Wesleyans began work long ago, and converted them from their wild state of cannibalism to Christianity. The Church began its work in Fiji later, and has no Mission to the aborigines there.

Fiji was ceded by its chiefs to the British Crown in 1874, and the islands were formally annexed by Sir Hercules Robinson on October 10 in that year. Soon afterwards, the Society began its work of which we are now to give some account. The Rev. W. Floyd was the first Missionary, and he is labouring there still.

Apart from the aborigines, there are several elements in the population; for, in addition to 2,105 Europeans, there are half-castes, East Indians, Polynesians, and a few Chinese.

Primarily among the Europeans, and then among these other races, the Society's two Missionaries are engaged.

The political capital is Suva, in the island of Viti Levu. Here the Society's Missionary is the Rev. J. Francis Jones, who went out in the year 1886, in succession to the Rev. A. Poole; while Mr. Floyd's head-quarters are at Levuka, the old capital, the striking situation of which is shown in the accompanying illustration. The scenery is bold, rugged, and abrupt. Precipice, gorge, and beach are covered with a luxuriant vegetation, from the long grass on the mountain-top to the banana plantain and cocoa-nut tree by the sea-shore.

The Church of the Redeemer at Levuka was founded by Mr. Floyd. The material structure and the living organisation, for which it exists are monuments of his patient and faithful work.

From Suva Mr. Jones wrote thus last September: "It is now a little over two years since my arrival in this Colony to take charge of Suva. Until within the last few months I confined my ministerial labours exclusively to the European residents of this town and district. As there had been no resident clergyman before I came, there was

FIJI WAR DANCE.

VIEW OF LEVUKA FROM THE ANCHORAGE.

necessarily a good deal of work to do to organise the work. A church
had to be built, the congregation had to be brought together, towards
which I was greatly assisted by zealous laymen. By now the church

GROUP OF SOLOMON ISLANDERS.

has been finished and paid for, and I have attempted to put the place
into a workable form."

The church cost £1,000, towards which the S.P.C.K. gave £200, and

it is not a little creditable to the small community that they have been
able to build it and are out of debt. For Mr. Jones says that things
are in a bad way at Suva financially, and that, although his people have
proposed that he should collect money from them for a parsonage,
"everybody in the place is really so poor that I have not the heart to
ask them." In the meantime, they have promised him £50 a year
towards house rent, which is very expensive in Suva, in addition to £150
towards his stipend. He adds: "The population of this town has very
materially decreased during the last twelve months, owing to the

A NATIVE OF THE SOLOMON ISLANDS.

Government having to reduce its staff, and the continued depression
of trade, which has told very much indeed on these islands. I lost,
during the last six months, four large families from my congregation,
in all they numbered 27 souls. And, in addition to this number, there
are several unmarried men and women leaving us by every steamer for
the Australian colonies. Levuka has suffered even more than we in
that respect."

Rewa is a place in Mr. Jones's district, and there he holds a service
every other Sunday.

His work among the Polynesian labourers is very interesting, and
serves to remind us that there is considerable scope for the Church's

work among the heathen, although the aboriginal inhabitants are now
Christians. The official returns reckon the Polynesian labourers in Fiji
as numbering 3,266, while those from India employed in the islands
number 6,146. These numbers may seem small, and in fact are so.

A NATIVE FAMILY OF THE SOLOMON ISLANDS.

Their importance lies in the fact that these people are removed from
their home surroundings, and that an opportunity is offered by that
circumstance, and by their being brought in contact with Christianity.
This opportunity should not be lost; and the result of using it in Fiji

may be such as is found to flow from similar efforts in Guiana, Mauritius, and other countries where there is imported labour. It is found that when Indian Chinese coolies return to their native lands as Christians, they exercise a wonderful evangelistic influence upon their fellow-countrymen.

It is at present the day of very small things for Mr. Jones in this direction, for he writes: "Since last February I have taken in hand a work which was inaugurated twelve months ago by the Rev. William Floyd at Levuka. It is a Polynesian school. The school is composed of young men introduced into the country by the Government, for a certain number of years, as house servants and plantation hands. I take them twice a week, on Monday and Thursday evenings, from 8 till 10 o'clock. They are principally natives of the Solomon Islands and the New Hebrides. They are more than anxious to embrace Christianity, as can be seen from the fact that they learn more readily anything from the Bible and Prayer Book than anything else. When they came to me they did not know the Alphabet, but now the majority of them can read easy passages of Scripture, and can recite by heart the Lord's Prayer, the Creed, and the Gloria. It seems very hard, when they are so anxious to learn, that every means should not be afforded them. It grieves me much to see so many of these Polynesians here without any native teacher even to look after them. Our Lord's words are most certainly applicable to them: 'The harvest is great, but the labourers are few.' The Roman Catholics are making a bold attempt to enfold them in their Church. The number of their staff has greatly increased lately by the arrival of their Bishop, who is accompanied by four priests and six sisters. They are not going evidently to leave a stone unturned to gain the Polynesian races.

"The number of boys that attend my school is about 53. Our teaching staff consists of my wife, a Mr. Coath of the New Zealand Bank, and myself. Their Sunday School is managed by Mr. Coath, and assisted by Mrs. Pattullo, my wife's sister."

It is a small beginning, but it is an extremely hopeful one. May God's blessing attend it! We are able to place before our readers illustrations which give an idea of the type of human life in these islands. Three of them represent the Solomon Islanders, who are most numerous among the Polynesian immigrants, while one shews a war dance of the native people of Fiji.

MR. BLAKESLEY'S REPLY TO CANON TAYLOR.

OGENT answer to Canon Taylor's article in the *Fortnightly Review* on Foreign Missions is given in a pamphlet by A. H. Blakesley, Esq., B.A., Tutor of Bishop's College, Calcutta. We do not know that any writer has more satisfactorily exposed the absurdity of the criticisms in the *Fortnightly Review*.

From Mr. Blakesley's pamphlet we will quote at some length on the three following points : (1) The increase of the heathen, (2) the relative cost of successful and unsuccessful Missions, and (3) the need of asceticism.

On the first subject Canon Taylor writes : "Is the natural rate of increase among the heathen greater or less than the number of conversions ? " And after certain calculations goes on to say :—

"If this estimate is approximately correct, it would take the societies 183 years to overtake the increase of the non-Christian population in a single year. For every additional Christian we have every year 183 additional heathens or Moslems.

"In spite of all the efforts that are made, there are upwards of 10 millions more heathens and Mahomedans in the world than there were a year ago. The Missionary Societies say we are advancing, and so we are. But in spite of our advance, instead of overtaking the work, the work is overtaking us. It is like the tortoise racing with a railway train ; the longer the race continues, the further the tortoise is left behind."

To this Mr. Blakesley replies : —

"It will be observed at once on perusing these extracts that Canon Taylor has fallen into the childish fallacy of calculating increases of population on the basis of a fixed annual increment instead of a proportional one. . . . It is no doubt obvious to all our readers that in dealing with a case like the spread of a proselytising religion, such a method is absolutely valueless. It rests on the supposition that a Christian population of, say, 1,000 or 10,000 will not make a numerically greater number of converts than one of ten or five. It is clear that (to take no other cause) each fresh body of Christians becomes to a greater or less degree a source of Missionary activity. But, in fact, the analogy of the tortoise and the train bristles with fallacies. A truer parallel to the case in hand would have been afforded by two sums of money put out at compound interest. Would Canon Taylor have been prepared to

argue that a sum of £10,000, put out at compound interest at the rate
of 3 per cent., would never be equalled by a sum of £100 at 5 per cent.,
because the first year's interest is £300 in the first case and only £5 in
the second? But this even would not give a true parallel to the case of
Missions unless the further condition was added that such part of the
interest on the second sum as was due to the excess in the rate per cent.
should be paid year by year out of the first sum. Only then would the
case be parallel to that of Missions, since not only do both heathen and
Christians increase cumulatively, as it were at compound interest, but
all the increment of the Christian element over and above what is due
to the natural rise of population common to the two, is caused by conversion, which implies a corresponding diminution in the numbers of
heathen.

"This extraordinary mistake into which Canon Taylor has fallen is
the more gratuitous, because he has lately had the opportunity, without
seeking further than the *Times* and the *Nineteenth Century*, of finding
the necessary statistics as regards India, and the correct method of dealing
with them, put forward by no less able a statistician than Sir W. Hunter
(whose opinions moreover, where they agree with his own, the Canon
quotes in his article). We subjoin an extract from Sir W. Hunter's
paper in the *Nineteenth Century* for July last:—

"'The official census, notwithstanding its obscurities of classification and the disturbing effects of the famine of 1877, attests the rapid increase of the Christian
population. So far as these disturbing influences allow of an inference for all British
India, the normal rate of increase among the general population was about 8 per cent.
from 1872 to 1881, while the actual rate of the Christian population was over 30 per
cent. But, taking the Lieutenant-Governorship of Bengal as the greatest province
outside the famine area of 1887, and for whose population, amounting to one-third of
the whole of British India, really comparable statistics exist, the census results are
clear. The general population increased in the nine years preceding 1881 at the rate
of 10·89 per cent., the Muhammadans at the rate of 10·96 per cent., the Hindus at
some undetermined rate below 13·64 per cent., the Christians of all races at the rate
of 40·71 per cent., and the native Christians at the rate of 64·07 per cent.'

"To Sir W. Hunter's testimony we may add that of Sir Charles
Aitchison, given in the early part of the year at the C.M.S. meeting at
Simla. After stating that the report of the census of 1881 gives the
rate of increase of population in Bengal at 10·89 per cent., he adds:—

"'The advance in the Christian population, however, is more than 40 per cent.
But what is most remarkable is the fact that, while the increase among Christians of
all other races is only 7 per cent., the increase among Native Christians is actually 64
per cent., the rate of increase being six times that of the ordinary population. . . .
Next in the North-Western Provinces the population increased 6 per cent. The
number of Native Christians rose from 7,648 to 11,823, being 54 per cent., or at the
rate of 6 per cent. per year: exactly nine times as fast as the total population. . . . In
the Punjab there is the same story to tell. The population increased 7 per cent.
The Hindu and Mahomedan religions are practically stationary, having increased only
a fraction of 1 per cent.; the Sikh religion has declined. The Christian religion has
           five times as fast as the population.'

"If only the proportionate increase of the Christian element continues even slightly greater than that of the entire population, it is clear that the Christians will eventually equal and then surpass the non-Christians, and the simile of the tortoise and the train becomes, as we pointed out above, inadmissible. If, as is the case in Bengal and many other provinces, the Christian rate of increase has a considerable superiority, this time will arrive within a comparatively short period. For instance, the total population of the Lieutenant-Governorship of Bengal in 1881 was 69,536,861, of whom 128,135 were Christians. If we combine with these figures the rates of increase quoted above, and imagine that the Christians continue to increase only at the rate at present reached of 40·71 per cent. in nine years, while the entire population of Christians and non-Christians increases at the rate of 10·89 per cent. in the same time, we shall see that, so far from it being a tortoise and train race, the Christians will have become one-half of the population in 243 years; in other words, the Christians will by that time have equalled the numbers of all other religions put together.*

"But the assumption that the present rate of increase will not be exceeded is a violent one, and that it should be so lightly made by Canon Taylor is only another instance of his disregard of the conditions of Missionary work. We should have thought that common sense, even without the least experience, would have made it clear to any one that the actual work done in new Missions cannot be gauged by the number of converts. To imagine this is to overlook all the vast amount of laborious preparation, sometimes extending over generations, which has to be expended before actual conversions begin to be made. Christianity has to be rendered familiar to the minds of those who were perfect strangers to it; often, alas! at least in India, it then has to be distinguished from the lives of those who profess it, European or other; not unfrequently some striking event occurs which gives the last needed push to thousands of hesitating minds: sometimes a wave seems to sweep over a country, no one knows whence, reminding one once afresh of the wind blowing where it listeth. Yet in all these cases the ground has been prepared by long years of silent and patient work, of the kind which critics like Canon Taylor would improve away off the face of the earth. Or again, what a disturbance would be produced among the Canon's figures by such an altogether untoward and inconvenient accident as the national reception of Christianity by the Japanese—an event which even those now alive may look forward to with considerable hopefulness. Yet undoubtedly, if this hope is realised, it will be largely due to the efforts of the despised Missionaries, in conjunction with the unconscious Missionary influence of Western Christendom. Or, to return

---

* The rate of increase here taken as a base of calculation is that of the entire Christian population—viz., 40·71 per cent. in nine years. If foreign Christians are excluded, and the rate of increase of the native Christians— viz., 64·07 per cent., be substituted, this time will again be materially shortened.

to India, who can calculate the possible effect of social changes already
looming on the horizon, by which one entire half of the population will
for the first time be made accessible to Missionary effort? Those who
criticise the advance of Christianity in India should remember that
hitherto, by the social customs of the country, well-nigh the entire
female sex has been kept beyond the reach of all influence which is not
anti-Christian. It is difficult to imagine the change which may come
over the conditions of the problem, when once the influence of home
life ceases to lie like a heavy weight in the scales on the side of heathenism. The result, both as regards adults and children, can hardly fail to
be startling.

"We have said enough, we think, to show that the statistical method
is both unsatisfactory in itself, and also, as used in Canon Taylor's
argument, based on an entire misconception of the problem."

The second point is raised by Canon Taylor in these words:—

"It is plain that the expenditure bears little or no relation to the results. The
cause seems to be twofold. In the successful Missions the native pastors are zealous
and numerous, a few Europeans being employed to guide and superintend them. In
the unsuccessful Missions the Church is exotic, and the costly European Missionary
fails to secure results which are easily attained elsewhere by native labourers of the
right sort. The second cause seems to be due to race. The aboriginal hill tribes and
the Dravidian races of Southern India seem to be far more open to Christian teaching
than the Hindus and Moslems."

In the course of his reply to this, Mr. Blakesley says:—

"By remarking that 'in the successful Missions the native pastors
are zealous and numerous . . . in the unsuccessful Missions the
Church is exotic,' Canon Taylor has taken refuge under an ambiguity of
language. He wishes us to assume that the success of the Missions is
due to the number and zeal of the native pastors employed, while the
statement is rather true in the sense that the number and efficiency of
the native pastors is due to the success of the Missions. Canon Taylor
has, we believe, confused cause and effect. For though the number of
native pastors undoubtedly reacts again on the efficiency of the Mission,
it is quite clear that they could never have come into existence without
it. But their usefulness is not a discovery of Canon Taylor's; Missionaries themselves are eager to avail themselves of 'native labourers of the
right sort'; the deficiency is not in the demand, but in the supply.

"This obviously varies enormously in different places, according to
the age and circumstances of the Missions."

On the third point Canon Taylor uses the following words:—

"The principles of the Salvation Army—absolute self-renunciation, voluntary
poverty, and conformity to the conditions of native life—have been the distinguishing
features of successful Missions. In spite of the wildest theological differences, success
has uniformly attended Missions conducted on such methods."

Mr. Blakesley has not a word to say against such self-denying
methods: quite the contrary. But he shows that it is impossible to

claim for them the merit of producing conversions, instancing the cases of Mr. Bowen in Bombay, Father O'Neill, the Salvation Army, and the Oxford Mission to Calcutta :—

"The Salvation Army, with a reckless expenditure of life, which to many seems culpable, but which, at any rate, exemplifies the principle under discussion, has achieved results altogether inadequate to the effort made, and one still further minimised by a peculiarity in their principles; for by not insisting on baptism, involving as it does a final break with heathenism, they are enabled to number among their 'converts' many who, under other circumstances, would only be called inquirers. Lastly, the Oxford Missionaries in Calcutta, starting under apparently most favourable circumstances, have succeeded in influencing, attracting, and propitiating, but not as yet, to any considerable extent, in converting. There is no cause for despair in all this; rather, for those who believe in their own principles, an incentive to greater activity. The effort is still young, the indirect effects may be incalculably great. Doubtless, no honest, still more no heroic, work is ever really thrown away; but the one thing to which the supporters of such attempts cannot at present appeal is the number of conversions."

But the more important matter is the motives and principles upon which the ascetic life should be adopted. Mr. Blakesley writes wisely :—

"What, then, is the principle which should underlie Missions conducted on this method? Not, surely, that an exhibition of asceticism for its own sake is likely to convert India; and this for two reasons. It would, in the first place, be to give a prominence and an independent value to what in the Christian scheme of life is only subordinate and useful as a means, and would, therefore, be a dangerous departure from truth. Rather the character brought chiefly into prominence must be the one which is capable of standing as the *summum bonum* of Christian ethics—the love of God and man. It would, in the second place, be to court inevitable failure. No European could for a moment hope thus to contend on his own ground with a Hindu fakir, nor would any Christian be likely to wish to do so. Asceticism, then, must find its use as a means to an end, or, rather, to two ends. First, for self-discipline, in which capacity, however, it is bound, as it values its own function, to remain buried in secrecy, and therefore valueless for aggressive purposes. Secondly, in an aspect more familiar perhaps, under the name of self-denial, it opens up opportunities of work which must otherwise remain closed. For it is obvious that while Missions receive the niggardly support at present granted to them, much work must remain untouched for want of means; hence a system of brotherhoods, where each member was content with food and raiment, might be established in double the number that Missions on the ordinary footing could be, and much new work might in this way be started. Again, a willingness to undergo discomfort and hardship would open up spheres of work in the native quarters of large towns, or in districts where, as in Africa, the climate compels every man to carry his life in his hand. And the love which does not flinch from such sacrifices would be sure, without any conscious effort, to issue in greater sympathy with those for whose sake the work is undertaken, and so be likely to lead to greater results. It is in these ways that we should expect to see an increase of fruit from an increase of the spirit of self-denial among Missionaries; for it is thus that the latter gains its ethical character, and thus, too, that it appeals to the native mind. Self-imposed austerity can only seem to them a weak imitation of the principles of their own ascetics. Hardships cheerfully endured, when through them alone lies the road to a noble and unselfish end, is as different as possible from all they have seen in ordinary Hinduism.

"If this is so, it is beginning at the wrong end for Canon Taylor or anyone else to insist on a violent increase in the asceticism of Missionaries. Let him use all means in his power to excite in men an unselfish devotion to the work of salvation, and an unconquerable determination to take whatever course leads most clearly to that result. We need not then be afraid of their failing to brush from their path whatever obstacles seem to bar the way.

"But to start from the opposite direction, and to advocate the adoption of ascetic principles as a means of gaining influence, instead of fixing attention on those positive and deeper qualities of mind and spirit which, even in ascetic Missions, are what really impress the native imagination, can only result in failure."

It may fairly be claimed that these replies are absolute and complete. Surely there is justification for Mr. Blakesley's concluding words to the effect that—

"Canon Taylor has hastily, and without any adequate appreciation of the problem, ventured to make an attack on Mission work, which should only have been undertaken with the greatest deliberation and the fullest knowledge; that by so acting he has done his best to hamper a work which he has never offered to share; and that whatever the results of his paper may be, he himself has thereby incurred a very grave responsibility."

THE CHILDREN'S CORNER.

THE HERO OF SÁHAWAFY.—A TALE OF THE FRANCO-MALAGASY WAR.

BY THE REV. ALFRED SMITH.

(Continued from page 33.)

CHAPTER III.

RALAY had been at his post now more than a week, when one day, as he was teaching the few children gathered round him, a shadow darkened the door. Looking up he saw standing in the doorway a man of immense stature and strength, with a brutal and revolting countenance. His huge body, shining with grease, was naked, excepting for the waist-cloth and a dirty piece of native flax cloth thrown over one shoulder. His black eyes were large and prominent, and shone with a peculiar light, while his free, bold carriage had in it an air of swaggering disdain. Seating himself on the doorstep, the gigantic savage fixed his eyes mockingly on Ralay.

At site of him Ralay started, and his face grew livid with fright, while the children, who knew the man well enough, looked on in some curiosity.

"Perhaps Rabe wants to learn," they tittered one to another.

Having somewhat, by an effort, regained command of himself, Ralay approached the door.

"What have you come here for?" he demanded.

Looking him steadily in the face, Rabe (for that was the name of the savage) replied :

"I have come, sir, to look at the children of our village being taught by the new teacher. I thought it would be nice to see how well the new teacher, who has been learning to be good himself so long, knows how to teach us to be good as well."

There was a tone of contempt in the words.

"How dare you come here?" said Ralay. "Don't you know that the missionary might come up at any moment?"

"Well, sir, and suppose the missionary were to come up at any moment; what harm would there be in his seeing me? I'm not afraid of his looking at me. His medicines and charms are not worth much against mine."

"What do you want, then?" gasped Ralay.

"I'll tell you what I want," answered Rabe, in a threatening manner. "You have heard of the Vagimba's cave, haven't you? Well, there is a meeting there to-night, and I want you to know it. Take care," he added, rising and hissing the words in the other's ear, "take care you don't forget the information."

So saying, and throwing his filthy cloth over his shoulders, the savage quickly disappeared.

The condition of Ralay, when left alone, was truly pitiable. Pale, and trembling in every limb, he could scarcely stand. It was of no use trying to teach any more; so, with a word, he dismissed the children.

These, delighted to get free, were soon racing across the village.

"I wish Rabe would come and look at our teacher every day," the biggest of them said. "Didn't you see how frightened he was? I'm afraid of Rabe, and so are all the people in the village. He is a great medicine man they say, and his charms are stronger than anybody's round about here. No one can conquer him. He must have bewitched Ralay."

Ralay was indeed bewitched, but the charm that held him was not one fashioned by Rabe, but by his own guilty conscience. He sat in the empty school, with his head between his hands, in utter misery and shame.

"Oh! that I could break this horrible band that binds me to this man," he groaned; "but I can't, I can't! I dare not do it."

The whole miserable past came vividly again before him. He loitered again among the busy throng in the market-place of Anta-nanarivo; he greeted again that false friend who had been his ruin. Again he heard the invitation in the silence of the schoolroom, as he had heard it that day in the past:

"Hia! Ralay, you are just the person I was looking for. Come along! I am going to see some fun."

He saw himself hesitate again, as he did on that day; and the taunt again echoed in his ears.

"Are you looking round to see if there is a missionary about, like a chicken looks after the old hen? Come along! Don't be such a baby. You don't suppose the missionaries *know* all you do?"

He saw himself yield and follow his friend. They went down a little lane near the market-place, and entered a well-enclosed courtyard, the gateway of which was guarded by a gigantic slave. There was a house in the yard, and in it sat a number of young fellows of the better class

The house was filled with the odour of rum, and the young fellows were intent upon card-playing. They looked up from their game for a moment, with flushed faces, as the new-comers entered.

"Why, here's a Mission baby come to get a little civilisation and learn the trader's prayers," laughed one of the company whose name was Ratsimba.

"Oh, if you mean card-playing," replied Ralay's friend, "he probably knows as much about that as you do."

"Let us finish this game then, and you can both come in. Have some rum, my boys, while you wait."

The rum was brought, and, ashamed and not daring to refuse, Ralay took a little.

The game came to an end.

"Now then, drain your glasses, and come on; let's begin again. Come, Ralay, tip it up, and show your civilisation like a *vazaha*,"* cried he who had spoken to them before.

To escape being laughed at, in desperation Ralay drank the fiery potion at one gulph. The liquor went to his head with lightning speed, and soon he was sitting at play, and staking sums of money which he neither possessed nor could ever pay if he lost, with drunken recklessness.

Losing always, and drinking to forget his losses, playing wilder and wilder every game, he soon lost far more than he could ever hope to pay.

It was late in the day before they stopped.

"You are all witnesses he owes me the money," said Ratsimba, as they rose to their feet. "I'll give him two days to get the money in, and if he does not pay it down, here in this house, at the end of that time, I'll sell him for a slave. I swear it!"

Again he saw himself sitting there in that hateful house, when all were gone, his head aching, and untold misery gnawing at his heart. Where could he get the money? Nowhere. And to be sold as a slave! Worse than death—oh, far worse than death itself!

"I suppose you have lost, and can't pay," said a voice in his ear. It was the voice of the gigantic slave, who had guarded the entrance to the yard. It was the voice of Rabe.

Ralay groaned.

"If you were not afraid, I could tell you how you could get out of this little scrape very easily; but you would be angry with me."

"Where can I get money? What does a fellow like you know about money?" said Ralay in a sudden rage.

"If you don't want to hear what I was going to say, I can hold my tongue, you know."

"I *do* want to hear, if you will speak."

* *Vazaha*—foreigner.

"Well, I can't let you have the money myself, you know; but what I am going to tell you will be as good, because the man you owe it to is my master. But you'll have to join our company."

"Your company! What do you mean?"

"Our company for making money. Oh, we know a thing or two about civilisation. We have learnt several things from Europeans besides prayers. Amongst them, we have learnt how to get money when we want it."

"Good heavens! What can you mean?"

"Mean! Why, isn't it plain enough? Have you never heard of *koranty maro*?"

"Making false money!"

"That is only one branch," continued Rabe quite coolly. "We have some merry nights abroad sometimes, when people are asleep."

"And so I am to join you in making bad money, and in house-breaking, am I?" cried Ralay in anguish. "Never! Never! Oh, what a fool, *fool*, I was to have ever come into this accursed place!"

"Better join us than be *sold as a slave in the public market*," answered Rabe, as he arose and went outside.

These ominous words rang in the ears of Ralay throughout the whole of the following day: "To be sold as a slave, to be sold as a slave! Either that awful lot, or pay."

Suddenly he thought he would go and see Ratsimba. Perhaps he would have mercy, and make some easy arrangement.

On arriving at the house he found Ratsimba within.

"Well," he said, as the other entered, "have you brought the *lárijána* (*l'argent*), or have you made up your mind the other way?"

"I have come to implore you not to be so hard upon me; to have some little mercy. Think what you would feel in my place. I have never gambled before. I was mad with drink, and did not know what I was doing. For God's sake, don't be hard upon me!"

"Look here, Ralay, you are a fool. Rabe has told you, I know, how you can easily escape from this affair, and make no end of money into the bargain. We want another or two fellows like ourselves, who can keep those rascally slaves we employ in perfect check. Now look here, who is to know anything about us? Did you know anything about me before Rabe told you? It's certain death to a traitor, mind. Well, you can take your pay from the Mission, and teach, and do any other nonsense you like, and nobody know the difference. Besides, you will soon have plenty of money, and not care a button for the Mission pay one way or the other. You can do as you like, but if you don't join us, I swear to you, I'll sell you publicly for a slave in the Toma market. Take your choice."

Good and evil struggled for the soul of the miserable Ralay as they have struggled for the souls of thousands before and since.   Many a young man in Madagascar, and especially in its capital, is at this present moment undergoing the same kind of struggle under many different conditions.   A time of reaction has set in amongst the young men who have been educated by the various missions.   Formerly, the Europeans at the capital were *few*, and nearly all were missionaries ; now they are *numerous*, and their influence is no longer so firm on the side of religion. Young men are taken with the free-and-easy life of the trader, and his contempt for everything in the way of religion.   They learn, therefore, to drink and swagger, and soon, alas ! to sneer at the religion of Jesus, for which their own forefathers died.   This state of things is at the present day one of the missionary's greatest trials, and one which casts a shadow over the future of the Malagasy people.   The word " civilisation " has during the last year become a Malagasy word, and is continually on the tongues of the young men of the upper classes.   According to them it means how to sit at table and use a knife and fork ; how to propose toasts at what they call " grandiné " (*grand diner*), and how to arrange the table beforehand ; how to shake hands, and lift the hat, and carry off European clothes with a swagger ; and how to have as little as possible to do with *missionaries*.   Many a ruined young Malagasy has proudly trod this road of " civilisation," and commenced it by drinking Mauritius and Bourbon rum and playing cards as poor Ralay did. Our earnest hope, however, is that these superficialities will die out as the young nation grows in experience and learns to judge things at their own proper value.

Ten minutes passed by, and Ratsimba, with a smile of contempt on his cruel Malay face, watched the struggle.

" It is of no use ; there is no escape ; God has forsaken me, and I am lost ! " wailed Ralay in anguish.

As the wretched boy lived these minutes over again alone in the schoolroom of Ambóhidrapéto drops of agony fell from his face.

Presently he lifted his head.   " I must go to the cave," he muttered!; " it is my fate."

(*To be continued.*)

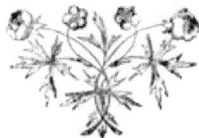

NOTES OF THE MONTH.

SAILING from England, on January 17, three Missionaries are going to reinforce the staff in the Diocese of Madras. The Rev. A. B. Vickers returns after furlough, happily restored in health; the Rev. T. H. Dodson, M.A., of Exeter College, Oxford, lately Fellow of St. Augustine's College, Canterbury, goes to be Principal of the College at Trichinopoly; and Mr. A. D. Limbrick, an Augustinian, whose location will be fixed on his arrival in Madras.

THE Rev. R. Papillon, M.A., of Exeter College, Oxford, Curate of Kirby Misperton, is to sail for India in February, to become one of the Society's Missionaries at Delhi.

IN the series entitled "Men of the Bible," issued by Nisbet & Co., the description of the life of all lives, that of "Jesus Christ, the Divine Man," has been assigned to the Rev. J. F. Vallings, M.A., Vicar of Sopley, and sometime sub-warden of St. Augustine's College, Canterbury.

Mr. Vallings' design, as stated in his preface, has been "to make some small contribution to the moral and spiritual history" of our Lord's life, and to do this "in some especial relation to Missionary work, and the contact of Christianity with non-Christian religions."

Mr. Vallings has performed his weighty task happily. The matter exhibits erudition, and the manner reverence.

WE gave an account two months ago of North Borneo, and of the arrival of the Rev. W. H. Elton, at Sandakan, on September 2. The Rev. B. Belcher, who took much interest in the opening of the Mission, has forwarded to us a later letter in which Mr. Elton says that his little flock have promised £100 a year towards his stipend, and that £500 will be required to build the Church, and £500 for the parsonage and school :—

"You will be glad to hear that we have secured an excellent site on a hill quite in the centre of the town. The church will stand on the top, and the parsonage and school on either side of the church, a little lower down the hill. It is an excellent site in every way. The temporary parsonage, made of jungle sticks and atap leaves, will be completed by the end of January, and the temporary school by the end of this year. Meanwhile, I am holding services in an old bungalow, which leaks like a sieve. I have also opened school in the same room."

RAMAINANDRO, in Madagascar, is the Mission entrusted to the Rev. E. O. McMahon, who is also the Examiner of the Mission schools of Imerina, the central province of Madagascar. In his Mission Mr. McMahon reports the baptism of 24 adults, besides 13 children, during six months; and also tells of two new stations opened recently in entirely heathen districts. Besides these he mentions the important new work among the Betsiriry, of which the Bishop spoke in a letter from which we quoted in December:—

"In May last, with two catechists, I visited the Betsiriry tribe—one of the fiercest and most self-reliant tribes of the Sakalava. These people live on the banks of the Tsiribihina and its tributaries, some 150 miles west, and are governed by a king and several chiefs. We saw some of the latter, who received us well, and the Bishop decided, on our return, to commence work amongst them, and Radaniel and Rajostina are prepared to go and live there. These people have never been visited by a European or Missionary before, and have no idea of civilisation, &c. They do not even know the value of money. We leave on Monday next, and (D.V.) shall begin work by occupying the king's town. I return here after seeing them safe and at work."

This new Mission becomes even more interesting from the fact that native Christians are maintaining it :—

"This new Mission to the Betsiriry will be commenced by subscriptions raised in Madagascar, the native Christians are giving quite nobly. At two meetings (at which no notice had been given of subscriptions) I received $20 and $4, and most of those present asked to be allowed to subscribe and pay their money later. On looking over the subscription lists I see that eight natives have already subscribed one dollar and upwards each, which sum to a native represents a good deal. We require $300 for the first year's work, the greater part of which I have in hand already, and expect the subscriptions will be over that amount."

Mr. McMahon also mentions that in a part of his Mission the native Christians had raised their endowment fund to $189.12. Such things as these are very good signs indeed.

Mr. McMahon also reports on his examination of the schools, and sends a full statistical account of them. They are 56 in number, with 2,184 scholars, of whom 1,595 were examined with satisfactory results.

CHEDDAR, in Somerset, has raised its remittance for the Society in a way that may encourage others. The Vicar writes :—

"I have special pleasure this year in sending you a remittance of over £20 from this parish for the general funds of S.P.G., because I had feared that from loss of larger subscriptions it would have fallen to £15. Thanks, however, to boxes, and an increasing interest in the cause of the Foreign Missions of the Church among the younger members of my flock, our contribution reaches the average

which I have always endeavoured to reach. The desire of the poor to help on the
work often comes out in the methods adopted to fill their boxes. One tells me she
strikes verbenas to sell for S.P.G. Another that she devotes what she can make by
the sale of her roses to her box. And I could tell you of humbler and more prosaic
ways in which the coffers of the Society are replenished."

WE inserted (on the suggestion of a lady who offered £2 if others
would do the like) a special appeal in the *Mission Field* for
December, for subscriptions to enable the Rev. A. Smith, of Mahonoro,
to place teachers at certain places in his district, where they would be
welcomed, and indeed were petitioned for. It was based on the touching
report which we had printed the month before.

It may be that our readers shared our hope that some seven or
eight people would be sure to send £2 each to provide for at least one
such teacher, and so each trusted to the generosity of others. The
hope has so far not been justified, as only four persons have written to
promise this sum. Mr. Smith's report on pages 420 and 421 of the
Mission Field for November ran thus :—

"From this point southward up to Mahela—a distance of about thirty miles—no
Missionary work has ever been attempted. The large towns of Ambináninisákaléona,
Nósivárika, Ampómánitra, Ambajáto, Mahambo, Vohitsara (where the stone elephant
is), Antanambao—all are untouched. No doubt someone will ask : Why have *you*
not taken them up ? Because I have *no money to pay a teacher* to place there.
What can I do ? Teachers must live as well as others, and I have no means whatever
of paying them. For each of these places a sum of *six dollars* per month is required
for a teacher's wages. The school-church building and the house for the teacher to
live in will be gladly provided by the people in each village. For want of this
six dollars per month the whole population for thirty miles lies in continual
spiritual darkness. The Governor of Mahela wrote to me only a few days ago : 'We
are waiting for the *teachers ;* the whole population is ready to be taught.' Yes, waiting for teachers ! 'The harvest truly is plenteous, but the labourers are few. Pray
ye the Lord of the harvest that He may send forth labourers into His harvest.' Here
surely is a way in which many people would be glad to help in the Lord's harvest, if
they only knew of the opportunity. Would not many like to pay the wages of a
teacher for some of these villages ? Only six dollars per month ! Who will of their
charity provide this sum for one of these heathen villages ? In neither place would
the school number less than seventy children."

FROM Peking the Rev. W. Brereton reports the completion of the
school buildings :—

"Our boys' school, which we began to rebuild in March, was finished in August.
We have also been able to put up a building large enough to accommodate a girls'
school, or the germ of one. It is gratifying after so much care and anxiety to have a
good solid building, such as the boys' school is, added to our premises ; and still more
gratifying to know that we are not in debt for it. The building can accommodate
twenty-four boarders, with an addition of as many more day scholars. This enlarged
accommodation is in excess of our present needs, but not of our hopes, and reasonable
expectations based on past growth and expansion.

"The girls' school has not yet been opened. The boys' school was formally opened
on September 8. We began the day with Holy Communion at 8 A.M."

A FTER the service the clergy, including the Rev. Chang Ching-Lan, with the native Christians and others, went in procession through the school compound to the large school-room :—

"A special service, consisting of benedictory prayers, lessons, psalms and hymns, partly sung and partly said, was then held. During this service the school-rooms, the industrial department, and the dormitories were each visited. The singing of the 'Te Deum' in the large school-room closed the ceremony. The whole ceremony was very bright, orderly, and encouraging.

"I ought to mention that nearly one-fifth of the whole cost of the buildings (the total cost being £500) has been contributed by friends in Peking and Tientsin, chiefly English and American, and some Chinese."

S UPERSTITION retains a strong hold over the Dyaks of Borneo, and is both an obstacle in the way of their receiving the Christian faith, and a snare to them when they have done so.

The Rev. E. H. Gomes went to Temudok, in April, to take charge of the Krian Mission ; his report exemplifies this, and yet is encouraging :—

"At Temudok there are three long Dyak houses. In the one nearest the Mission House there are several Christians. In the other two houses there are very few, not more than three. I was very much surprised at my reception on my very first visit to the longest of the houses, 'Rumah Ugai,' where there were about twenty families living. On my arrival the head man of the house told me I might come there as often as I liked to teach the people, but that it was no use speaking to *him*, as *he* would never be a Christian. I told him I thought it rather strange that he should come to any conclusion at all before he heard what I had to say for myself, but of course I could do nothing more. This head man, Ugai, would sometimes come to see me at the Mission House, but *never* came for service. If he happened to be here just when service was about to begin, he would start to return to his house rather than join us in prayer.

"Well, about two months ago, one Sunday morning, he and about ten others, together with several children, came to me. I asked them what they wanted. Ugai said they had come for service. They behaved very well during service, kneeling and standing with the others. Since then Ugai has never missed coming to service on a Sunday. I have tried to teach Ugai the principles of the Christian religion. He seems a shrewd man, and has already given up a few superstitions, such as those which assert that it is unlucky to plant certain plants. He is, however, not yet prepared to give up his belief in birds, and the power they have over the paddy crops.

"The last time I was at Buder, one Dyak doctor (*manang*), Mek by name, declared that he would cease being a *manang*, but it remains to be seen whether he will keep his word or not. The evening that he was with me, sitting in the long verandah of the Dyak house, he gave an account to the Dyaks of the many deceits practised by the *manangs*. If he will always speak out the truth as boldly as he did then, his influence for good on our side, against the native doctors, will be great."

A NOTHER Borneo Missionary, the Rev. J. Perham, who is at Banting, writes of the difficulty in raising up a native Dyak Missionary :—

"During a good part of the year I have had an intelligent and promising young Dyak with me for instruction in the doctrines of the faith, to fit him for the work of Catechist. I regret we did not get hold of him earlier in life, when he might have been taught English, and have become a worker of a higher class. And here I may add that one of the elder lads of my school here, after the examinations last month, offered himself for Mission work, and will soon proceed to Kuching, to be further trained among others who are preparing there with the same prospect in view. This branch of our work is one of special interest and one of special anxiety. To say nothing of inherited tendencies to evil, the temptations of young Dyaks are so strong and so many that we look with mingled fear and hope upon any who come forward to put their hand to the Mission plough. I do not know the capabilities of other races similar to Dyaks, nor have I had experience of other Missions, and it may be on account of our sins, that God has restrained His grace and blessing from us; but I cannot help thinking that those who have any intimate acquaintance with Dyak life and character would not be surprised that we have not yet been able to develope a native ministry out of our Dyak Christians. Leaving out other considerations, this one fact only is almost a sufficient explanation—it required years of work before the Missionaries could keep young lads for any length of time. There were several reasons for this, but I need not relate them. But we have now fairly got over this difficulty, and the prospect in this direction is brightening. There are those in training now, some of whom, I thank God, have come from Banting, who seem to be of a stronger moral character, and of greater mental power, and who have been with us some years. Some of these, I do hopefully trust, the Bishop will be able to admit to Holy Orders."

The way in which the Dyaks often show a desire for the truth is wonderful:—

"I have been encouraged this year by some Dyaks, in Banting, coming forward of their own free will to ask for Christian instruction, influenced, I believe, by the example and persuasion of some of the older Christians; and this and other things leads me to hope that the Christian mind and spirit is getting a deeper hold upon our Dyaks."

The revision of the Sea-Dyak Prayer Book is now completed by Mr. Perham :—

"I do not say that it is as perfect as future work will make it, but I can assert, thanks to the suggestions and assistance of other members of the Mission, that it is a vast improvement upon what we are using now. Much of my time during this year has been spent upon it. It is now in the hands of the Mission printer."

STAPLE is a parish in Kent with 521 inhabitants, and the remittance received from it is of more than ordinary interest. For the year 1887 it was £32. 17s., but for the year 1888, £44. 13s. 7d. More than £33 being produced by the boxes in the parish, especially those in the Rectory.

FROM Kirby Misperton the Rev. W. H. Hutchings has sent the Society's Treasurers £100 as the remittance for 1888. The amounts for the four previous years had been, 1884, £91. 12s. 4d.; 1885, £86. 14s. 11d.; 1886, £91. 17s. 0½d.; 1887, £85. 1s. 7d. The population is 972, consisting mainly of farmers and farm labourers. It will be remembered how prominent a part Missionary boxes bear in the working of this Parochial Association. A valuable article on the subject from Mr. Hutchings' pen appeared in the *Mission Field* for June last.

HOW to make a Parochial Branch a success. This is the title of a four-page leaflet which is being circulated in Oxton, near Birkenhead. It begins with a letter from the Honorary Secretary, who describes the method by which the sum raised for the Society in 1888 more than doubled that of the year before. The first step was the formation of a Committee. Then a circular was distributed in the churches, and also sent separately to the boxholders and subscribers.

"The Secretary prepared a directory, divided into six little books, and drew up some simple rules; armed with these, six ladies made a house-to-house canvass, and met with great success. The service at the Parish Church also was a great success, and demonstrated that the giving of money to Missions was an act of worship. Our next half-yearly service will be held early in January. The monthly Intercession is attended by forty persons on an average. On St. Andrew's Eve an Intercessory Service was held at ' All Saints,' and on the following Sunday at the Parish Church.

"We attribute the great increase in the interest in Missions to those two principles which can never be divorced—' Faith and Works '; in other words, our intercessions and organisation.

"We lay great importance on the placing out of boxes, as being not only the most steady source of income, but also as being a constant reminder of the cause. Many a time the cause is forgotten until a call is made for the annual subscription, which then, when given, may not come from a cheerful giver.

"The value of simultaneous and united prayer has always been a great object of the Church."

The zeal of our friends at Oxton deserves warm praise, and, still more, imitation.

AT Alnwick an exhibition of various objects from foreign countries was held in December, with the object of stirring up interest in Missions, and supplying information. There were six sections for the various parts of the world, and over each were hung maps, diagrams, and pictures. There was also a publication stall.

"This was under the care of a person who was ready to explain the contents, and to point out to people that cheap and interesting information could there be obtained concerning any part of the Mission Field."

Short lectures were delivered.

" These are essential, otherwise people simply pass through and look at the things as mere curiosities.

"We secured the assistance of two Missionaries, who, at intervals, gave short lectures, explaining the Mission work of the countries in which they had been working, using the articles, &c., as illustrations. Also the local clergy, as far as they were able, did similar work.

"Where the services of Missionaries cannot be obtained to explain things, clergy or laity can do it to a large extent themselves, if they will only read up, as they understand better what people at home want to know."

The organiser of the scheme thus concludes :

" To sum up, I should like to make the following suggestions :

" 1. Let us depend upon ourselves more, and not always think it necessary to have a Missionary to inform our people of the work which is going on abroad, when we can do so much by careful reading ourselves.

" 2. Let the clergy periodically give lectures themselves, say once a month at a week-day evening service, making it a special intercession for Missionary work, and not be satisfied with the annual sermon and meeting. A large map may usefully be hung up.

" 3. Circulate a Missionary magazine in the parish. The *Mission Field* is now issued on wonderfully cheap terms.

" 4. Have a body of Missionary visitors, who will collect monthly small subscriptions."

SUGGESTED SUBJECTS FOR PRAYER.

For the Diocese of Calcutta, and the work at Bishop's College.

For the Church at home, that it may realise more fully its Missionary responsibilities and opportunities.

For Japan, that the Church may not fail to impress the truth upon the people during the change in the national character.

For English people at the goldfields in South Africa, and for the Church's work among them.

MONTHLY MEETING.

THE Monthly Meeting of the Society was held at 19 Delahay Street, on Friday, December 21, at 2 P.M., the Rev. B. Compton in the chair. There were also present the Earl of Belmore and Canon Cadman, *Vice-Presidents*; Rev. J. W. Ayre, Rev. J. M. Burn-Murdoch, C. Churchill, Esq., C. M. Clode, Esq., C.B., Canon Elwyn, General Davies, Prebendary Festing, General Gillilan, General Maclagan, J. R. Kindersley, Esq., Rev. J. R. Kindersley, Rev. C. J. Ridgeway, H. C. Saunders, Esq., Q.C., General Sawyer, General Tremenheere, C.B., and S. Wreford, Esq., *Members of the Standing Committee*; and Rev. S. Arnott, Rev. Astley Cooper, Dr. R. N. Cust, Rev. B. C. Davidson-Houston, Rev. H. J. Day, Dr. De Tatham, Rev. J. J. Elkington, H. Laurence, Esq., Rev. J. H. C. McGill, Rev. Dr. May, Rev. H. Rowley, Rev. C. A. Solbe, and Rev. R. Wheeler, *Members of the Society.*

1. After prayers, the Minutes of the last Meeting were read.

2. The Treasurers presented the abstract of receipts and payments from January 1 to November 30, printed on page 40 of the *Mission Field* for January.

3. It was announced that the following members of the Standing Committee would retire in February under Bye-law 7 : viz., *by seniority*, General Lowry, C.B., General Sawyer, and the Rev. J. W. Ayre ; and *by paucity of attendance*, the Rev. J. St. J. Blunt, the Hon. and Rev. E. C. Glyn, and the Rev. J. M. Burn-Murdoch.

4. It was announced that the Standing Committee would propose at the meeting in January for re-election in February, General Lowry, C.B., General Sawyer, and the Hon. and Rev. E. C. Glyn ; for election, Colonel Hardy, Sir H. Cartwright, and the Rev. W. Allen Whitworth ; and to supply a vacancy caused by death, the Rev. J. M. Burn-Murdoch.

5. The Rev. F. T. Whitington, Canon of Adelaide, addressed the members. He described the wonderful growth of Australia and its Church from the time—only a hundred years ago—when there was only one clergyman. Even fifty years ago there was but one bishop, where now there are thirteen. He proceeded to speak more particularly of South Australia, a colony founded in 1836 by persons who were not members of the Church of England. It contains one-third of the area of Australia, being about eight

times as large as the United Kingdom. Bishop Short, who was consecrated the first Bishop of Adelaide in 1847, after ruling for a third of a century, left the diocese with 70 clergy, half of the cathedral built, and an important grammar school, which alone supplied higher education. Mr. Whitington described the clergy as divided into three groups : the Missionary clergy for the sparsely settled districts, the Missionary incumbents, and the parochial incumbents. He described the natives as being of almost the lowest type. They have no settled life, and no villages. There are from 200 to 300 in a tribe, and they constantly change their location. Bishop Short began work with some of the children ; Bishop Hale (then Archdeacon) gave himself up to work for the natives, and founded a sheep and cattle station for them at Poonidie, erecting a church, a school, and cottages. The children became clever at farming and at field sports, as well as in the rudiments of education and religion. Poonidie has become self-supporting as a home for the elder natives, and a training school for the young. Canon Whitington described the system of church finance in South Australia, and said that its backbone was the Lee Trust, held by the Society for the Diocese.

He said that the great hindrances in South Australia were the sectarian spirit and competition, so that in a little town with a population of 200 there would be five or six forms of Christianity ; and the secular system of public education, which even prevents the reading of the Bible in schools.

He spoke also of the now interrupted work in the Northern territory, for which the Society has voted money ; and said that Port Darwin, though small, was a most important place ; he hoped that the work would soon be resumed.

Speaking, in conclusion, of the Society's grants to Adelaide in former years, Canon Whitington said that now it was not money help which Australia desired from England so much as the development of corporate union, so that it may be seen that leading Englishmen are taking note of Australian Church life, and are interested in its well-being.

6. All the candidates proposed at the meeting in October were elected into the Corporation. The following were proposed for election at the meeting in February 1889 :—

The Rev. F. Wright Anderson, Shipton Bellinger, Andover ; Rev. J. C. Harkness, Hawkley, Lyss, Hants ; W. H. Bayley, Esq., Basingstoke ; Rev. J. H. Chadwick, Basingstoke ; Major May, Basingstoke ; Ven. J. F. Sharpin, Millbrook, Ampthill ; Rev. G. H. Hopkins, Higham Ferrers ; Rev. A. S. Valpy, Holy Trinity, Guildford ; Rev. F. R. Cocks, Holy Trinity, Guildford ; Rev. C. B. Griffith, Stoke, Chester ; Rev. J. A. Greaves, Billingborough, Folkingham, Lincs. ; Rev. J. H. Light, Lambourn, Berks, R.S.O. ; Rev. H. Wells, 4 Credon Road, Rotherhithe New Road, S.E. ; Rev. H. V. Bacon, Birstwith, Ripley, Yorks. ; Rev. J. G. B. Knight, Middleham, Bedale, Yorks. ; Oliver Codrington, Esq., M.D., 85 Upper Richmond Road, Putney, S.W. ; Rev. Marshall Tweddell, 13 Warrington Crescent, W. ; Rev. Robert Armstrong, Stradbally, Queen's Co., Ireland ; Rev. H. V. White, Killesk Rectory, Arthurstown, Co. Wexford, Ireland ; Rev. H. Pearson, Lambley, Nottingham ; Rev. W. Chambers, St. Mary's, Blandford ; William Austen Leigh, Esq., 4 Norfolk Terrace, Hyde Park, W. ; Charles Eustace Grant, Esq., King's College, Cambridge ; Rev. H. E. Ryle, King's College, Cambridge ; Rev. L. L. Cooper, St. John's, Leicester ; Rev. C. A. Dutton, Lotherdale, Keighley ; William Lyon, Esq., East Court, Finchampstead, Wokingham, and Rev. W. F. Gilbanks, Great Orton, Carlisle.

REPORTS RECEIVED.

Reports have been received from the Rev. D. J. Flynn, J. R. Hill, and F. H. T. Hoppner, of the Diocese of *Calcutta* ; W. H. Gomes, of *Singapore* ; W. Brereton, of *North China* ; W. Bramley and F. Greenwood, of *Capetown* ; P. Masiza, of *St. John's* ; T. Taylor and J. R. Ward, of *Maritzburg* ; W. H. Ball and W. H. R. Bevan, of *Bloemfontein* ; E. O. MacMahon, of *Madagascar* ; C. E. Crosse, of *Perth* ; J. Neales and T. Neales, of *Fredericton* ; W. C. Bernard, of *Quebec* ; E. Gilpin and H. Harper, of *Nova Scotia* ; W. Crompton, of *Algoma* ; S. Kerr, of *Jamaica* ; and W. Cowley, of *Antigua*.

THE MISSION FIELD.

THE FIELD IS THE WORLD. THE SEED IS THE WORD OF GOD.

MARCH 1, 1889.

CONTRAST BETWEEN HINDUISM AND CHRISTIANITY.

BY THE REV. G. U. POPE, D.D., TEACHER OF TAMIL AND TELUGU IN THE UNIVERSITY OF OXFORD, AND CHAPLAIN OF BALLIOL COLLEGE.

"There be many that say, who will shew us any good?"—PSALM vi. 4.

MEN in all times and in all lands have been heard to cry, either with eager expectant hope or in despairing sadness, amid the vicissitudes of earthly things, in the presence of the awful mysteries of life, or from under the shadow of impending death, "Who will, who can, show us any real and abiding good?" It is especially the burthen of every song, the theme of every discussion in our Eastern literatures.

It is the office of religion, and of religion alone, to make known to man that highest good he is always and everywhere seeking.

Thus from time immemorial the sages of the East have confidently assured the teeming millions of India that they have discovered the sources from which conclusive blessedness flows for man; while the nations of the West have learnt to lift their eyes to One Whom they know to be the sole Dispenser of divine and eternal blessing to mankind, and to Him they offer the prayer, "Lord, lift thou up upon us the light of Thy countenance," for from Thee alone do all good things come.

The question I propose to discuss is this: "Does that vast aggregate of faith and worship which we are accustomed to regard as one religion, and to call Hinduism, which holds sway over one hundred and eighty millions* of our fellow-subjects, in any way fulfil its promise of imparting to its votaries the good they need and yearn after?"

* Parth, p. 153.

NO. CCCXCIX.   NEW SERIES.   D

In order to answer this question, I propose to compare, or, rather, contrast, the aggregate teaching of Hinduism with that of the Christian Scriptures in regard to—

I. The Being and attributes of God;

II. The way in which men may approach Him;

III. The law of life and duty;

IV. The sources of strength to weak and struggling men; and

V. The hopes man may cherish in regard to his future after death.

This discussion, of which I merely indicate the outlines, may serve to show the reason for Missionary effort, and the main topics of our Missionary teaching.

In regard to these five all-important topics, the Christian Scriptures reveal precisely those good things that man needs in every age and in every land.

For they speak (1) of the Fatherhood of God; (2) of the mediation of Christ; (3) of a perfect law, guarded by adequate sanctions, and illustrated by a perfect example; (4) of the gift to humanity, in mystic union with Christ, of the grace of the Divine Spirit, Who is the Lord and Giver of life; and (5) of the life everlasting. In contrast with this fivefold teaching we are to consider what Hinduism teaches.

I. We are to consider what Hinduism teaches its votaries of God.

Here we are met by the difficulty, that it is utterly impossible to exhibit in any harmonious summary the Brahminical doctrines regarding the Supreme Being; for the Vedas inculcate the worship of the elements, while the later Puranas speak of an infinite multitude of gods and goddesses, of whom we find scarcely a trace in the Vedas, and none of whom can be regarded as really possessed of divine attributes. Fragments of traditional truth, poetic fancies of old Rishis, wild superstitions of prehistoric Scythic origin, philosophic notions from Greece, Arabian dogmas, and the teachings of Christianity are strangely mingled in the fermenting mass of modern Hinduism as I have encountered it in South India.

So the idea of God is in India sadly and almost hopelessly confused and obscured.

Philosophic Hinduism sometimes speaks of a Divine essence imagined as including in itself the whole universe, since all other beings whatsoever are only illusory shows, having no substantial existence. Some, however, maintain that there is indeed an eternal mind, but that matter is equally eternal. It must suffice here to say that genuine Hinduism knows nothing of a Supreme Being who is really, according to our ideas, God; —who is Creator of all things, who loves His creatures and can be the object of their love and worship. In later days, owing to the influence of Muhammadanism and of Christianity, a system of *Bhakti* or devotion to some preferential deity has arisen, and in the books of the Saiva and

Mission Field.] *HINDU IDEAS OF GOD AND OF WORSHIP.* 83
Mar. 1, 1889.]

Vaishnava sects very striking and beautiful expressions of ardent affection and profound reverence abound. But then these objects of adoration are represented as themselves subject to fate and metempsychosis as man is; and the wild legendary stories of these gods, which are full of folly, cruelty, and licentiousness, do not justify trust, love, or adoration : the devotion is not in any harmony with the record.

It is plainly of no use for a man to say "I believe in God," if he has no definite idea of One Whom he can love and trust, reverence and adore; and, in this sense, it must be said that Hinduism is practically atheistic—that the mass of the Hindus are without God in the world. To them, then, the doctrine which our Missionaries teach, that God is the "Father in heaven," possessed of all perfections, the All-holy and All-loving, is the revelation of a good of which their own systems afford but few traces.

II. The modes of worship which exist in India, the whole cultus of the Hindu or Brahminical systems, bear testimony to the fact that man needs some method of approach to God, such as the mediation of Christ supplies. The idolatries of India, bewilderingly manifold, surely bear witness to this. Our fellow-creatures there, like ourselves, desire that God should dwell among them, should take a visible form, and have something like a personal history. So they have imagined sundry manifestations of their divinities, who are supposed to dwell in blissful seats, with their wives, children, attendants, and devotees. There is nothing in all these legends (save in a few where Christian influence is evident) which suggests a point of real analogy to the history of Christ; but they bear emphatic testimony to the felt necessity of some visible manifestation of God to man. Yet, though this instinctive sense of need was, in part at least, their origin, how terribly debasing are, on the whole, the idolatries of India! Innumerable are the objects of worship, generally acknowledged not to be really gods, but really taking the place of the Supreme. The absolutely infinite hosts of Puranic divinities; the powers and energies of nature; almost every animal, in some connections, especially bulls, monkeys, birds and snakes; trees, flowers, and stones, are adored. Images of every variety, some with many heads and arms, some of them frightful, some grotesque, half-human, half-bestial, are set up, and after a ceremony of consecration, called *ārāhanam*, are supposed to be the permanent, abiding homes—nay, to have become the very and effective personalities—of supernatural beings that control the destinies of man.

The minds of the worshippers rise no higher, unless other teaching has modified their beliefs and habits. Illustrations of whatever is said in Holy Scripture of the folly and wickedness of idolatry are to be seen in every street, and almost in every house in India. "They that make them are like unto them, so is everyone that putteth his trust in them."

Among the beings supposed to be manifestations (or incarnations) of Diety, and everywhere adored, are *Krishna* and *Rāma*—the heroes of their two great Epics, the Mahābhārata and the Rāmāyana. These are mere poetical creations—very interesting ones, doubtless—with some historical basis. They are, however, rightfully no more influential or important to humanity than are Æneas or Achilles.

And what shall we say of active, popular, every-day Hinduism? You go into the streets of the black town in Madras on the night of the greatest of their local festivals, when the glare of many torches turns night into day, and the harsh discordancies of native instruments of music vex the ear. The huge car of many stories, bright with flags and flowers, drawn by hundreds of hands, rolls slowly along the streets, while sacred songs and incantations are recited. What is the weird figure enthroned on the car glittering with precious stones? It is Yĕgattāl — "the only mother" — an image worshipped here before any stranger from the West had set foot on the surf-beaten shore, where her dark and squalid temple stands—one of the forms of the Indian Cybele. As she slowly passes by, with continual halts, every door opens, and the inhabitants of each dwelling come forth to present their offerings, to join in the worship. Flowers and fruit and other gifts are brought to her feet in baskets, or on salvers of brass or silver, while the image and the car and the street around are covered with garlands. Sometimes strange rites are performed. A sheep or a goat, gaily adorned, is brought out before the idol; the priest stands by with crooked knife; one dexterous flourish and the head flies off, while the image is wet with its blood.

NEI-SINGHA AVATAR.

It is the old cry, "Wherewith shall I come before the Lord, and bow myself before the High God?" Thus are men seeking for God!

We are to compare with these sad, suggestive spectacles the Christian vision of Him Who is the image of the invisible God; Whom, not having seen, we love, and Who is made known to us in so many ways, and revealed in such a divine life history.

III.   Since it is not in man that walketh to direct his steps, it is essentially necessary for him to have some clear and authoritative exposition of his duties. It is needless for me here to dwell upon the perfection of the Christian law as taught in Holy Scripture, and illustrated by the life of Christ on earth. What, then, has Brahmanism to compare with this? In the Vedas themselves there is no moral teaching. According to the ideas of the Hindu teachers, religion has nothing to do with morals, as indeed we know that the religions of ancient Greece and Rome had no distinct ethical teaching.

There are multitudes of minor compositions in Sanscrit, and in most of the vernacular languages of India, which are filled with prudential precepts of more or less value, and often expressed with great beauty. These may compare favourably with the writings of Theognis, Seneca, and Epictetus. The first moral fables were from the East. In the Puranic writings we have here and there a noble sentiment, or a generous trait of character; but side by side with these is much that is utterly frivolous, and very much which is unspeakably wicked. The "Institutes of Menu" is the great law book of India. It contains the caste regulations of Hinduism, and forbids some of those crimes that destroy the foundations of social life; but it is utterly defective as a code of morals. It is indeed a deeply disappointing book. There is also one great moral work of peculiar excellence in the Tamil language, the Kurral, but this is not a religious composition, and its author has probably derived much of his teaching from Christian sources.* We may sum up this part of our subject by saying :—

(1) That in Hinduism there is no inculcation, and can be none, of the love of the Su-

preme as the foundation of morals.

(2) The idea of humanity, of the brotherhood of man, is unknown to every form of Hinduism. There can therefore be no inculcation of duties men owe to their fellow-men; the institution of caste is essentially opposed to this.

VARAHA AVATAR.

An illustration of this is found in the fact that Hinduism makes no provision for its own extension, and asserts no claim to be an universal religion, and would indeed shrink back with repugnance from the idea of admitting others into its circle. Christianity alone has the power and the promise of universal extension.

(3) In Hinduism the objects of worship are represented as guilty of every iniquity, and there is thus no such thing as a pattern of virtue in the Hindu mythologies. The foulest vices find sanction and examples there. In fact, all in Hinduism which would most emphasize the contrast between it and the law of the Lord, which is pure, must of necessity be passed over in silence here. We appeal to the records !

(4) The doctrine of the metempsychosis is destructive of morals, for it teaches that each individual soul enters its bodily tenement with the merit or demerit of acts done in a former state of existence clinging to it; these constitute its fate, and determine the actions of the man. Of

* See the edition published by W. H. Allen & Co.

these past deeds which he has done he has no remembrance; yet their resistless current is bearing him onward. Hence, every man, when convicted of sin, has a ready excuse, and cannot be brought to feel remorse for any evil brought home to him. No moral teacher is able to say to him, "Thou art the man." In fact (and it cannot be too much insisted upon), the Hindu has lost his own *personality*, and with it all sense of moral obligation.

(5) And lastly, it follows from the sketch here given of Hindu systems that, were the moral teaching ever so perfect, the motives to obedience and the sanctions of the law are altogether wanting.

IV. Christianity is presented to us in a great organisation which is described by the Apostle as one great body animated by the ever present Spirit of God. Here is seen "supernal grace contending with sinfulness of man."

In the Hindu system there is not the faintest recognition of man's need of Divine grace, or of the possibility of his obtaining it. Hinduism says much of the misery and degradation of human existence, but has no glimpse of any spiritual help afforded to man. Even Buddha, who was a reforming Brahmanist, knew nothing of sin as moral evil, but only of misery as the result of corporeal existence. Of Divine " grace " he knew absolutely nothing. In some of its phases, Hinduism counsels meditation and rigorous subjugation of the senses; and it prescribes a series of ascetic practices by which the soul is to free itself from corporeal bonds; but it breathes not a word of any help given to man from above. There is none to aid him, none to sympathise with him in his struggles. The Christian belief in the gift of the Holy Spirit, who is the *Lord and Giver of life*, would seem to be the one thing that the nations of the East most need, and of any analogy to which their systems are most absolutely destitute. Where help is not expected, prayer is not used. Hence the *Mantras* are charms or incantations, not prayers. The most sacred of these, the *Gâyatri*, is not understood by the millions who recite it, is hardly susceptible of any definite meaning, and was probably at first an address to the sun. If it be allowed to introduce into our comparison the thought of the joys of Christian communion with God in prayer, and of the indwelling of the Spirit in the hearts of the faithful—if we know these to be real and rapturous—how poor must any system seem which knows nothing of them! What a *good* thing is given to any man when he is taught to pray!

V. In regard to man's future after death there would seem to be in all oriental systems a substantial unity of teaching. The soul of man, as Hindus imagine it, is allied to successive organisms, human or otherwise, and is at length, as the result of meditation and rites prescribed, to obtain emancipation, *i.e.* absorbtion into the supreme essence, whatever that may be. This is called *Môksha* (deliverance), *Nirvâna* (extinction, as of

a flame by the wind), *Vidu* (utter relinquishment).   There is no belief
generally in the conscious immortality of any human soul.   Buddhism
especially denies the existence of a soul in man.   A man may pass at
death into any of the lower forms of organised life; he may become a
demon or a god sojourning in the heaven of some deity, or tormented in
one of the nine hells; he may pass through any number of human or
other births: the end of all is—the merging of his being into the Infinite and Impersonal.   This is illustrated in every variety of figure.
As a drop of water may be withdrawn from the ocean, may hang glittering on the petals of a flower, or rise in invisible vapour to the clouds,
or mingle with earth and sink into its depths, but at last finds its way
to the ocean from which it was taken, so the human soul changes its
abodes, passes through infinite vicissitudes, but is lost at last in that
unknown, impersonal existence to which some name which we errone-
ously translate "God" is attached.   It is unnecessary for me to dwell on
the contrast between this _____ ness of God, living unto
vague expectation of what Him through endless
is in itself surely annihi- ages.   O happy Christian
lation, with the Christian hope!
hope which is founded   Oriental systems are
on the resurrection of hopeless; or rather,
Christ from the dead. what they bid men hope

We believe that in our for and strive after is
flesh we shall see God, a delusion.   Thus the
and that our feet shall two systems stand con-
stand within the gates trasted.
of Jerusalem.   We shall   I will conclude with a
circle the throne of God brief reference to one or
rejoicing. There we shall two points of practical
be filled with all the ful- importance.

KALKI AVATAR.

First, it is instructive to note that in so far as any form of Brahmanism
claims authority, it is without credentials, has no evidence to adduce.

Christianity has a mass of evidence to prove it divine.   There
stands the Christ, risen from the dead, and thus proved to be the
Son of God with power.   Wherever there is the faculty to weigh evidence, the fact of the Resurrection of Christ must compel assent and
submission.

Of course, it cannot be said that Hinduism has any such fact to
announce.   Christianity has triumphed for eighteen hundred years
because she proclaims Jesus and the Resurrection.

On this we must still and for ever insist.

Much is said about methods of Missionary operation, but I am sure
that everywhere and always the Apostolic method of preaching the
whole Gospel of the risen and living Lord will alone prevail.

Secondly, anyone acquainted with the early Sanscrit philosophical treatises would have imagined that from such transcendental theories nothing could spring but a refined, if somewhat fruitless, philosophical religion. We see what its result has been, however, in India. If some of the crude theories of non-Christian writers of the present day could possibly gain a wide acceptance amongst men, we may safely predict that the result would be the development from a bewildering and unsatisfying agnosticism, of a most licentious gnosticism, and the ultimate sway of extravagant superstitions among the great masses of the people, who would translate the abstractions of the philosopher into the grossest forms of idolatrous worship. Indeed, the life of Comte shows us how easy is the descent from vague philosophy to most palpable superstition. Not the civilisation of the nineteenth century, but historic and catholic Christianity it is that keeps men from every excess of licentious practice and of degrading superstition. And this message the Missionary brings back from heathendom to the dwellers in Christian lands.

Thirdly, I think the history of Brahminism affords a warning in regard to theories of development. The word " Veda " is ever on the lips of the Hindu, yet nothing of the Vedas but the name practically survives. The objects of the worship of the last twenty centuries in India are not even named in those writings. The application is obvious. A Christianity without the central Christ, and without the Word of God, would be a sorry development of our most holy religion! Yet to this some minds seem tending.

The Word of God is incorruptible seed, and the Church of Christ, whose truth rests on it, cannot fail. But Hinduism is not the only system where dogmas have been developed into their contradictories.

There stand the old Vedas, and Upanishads, supposed to be the pillar and ground of truth—though very meagre and mixed it is. Here are the Puranas which overwhelm them with legend. Here are the mystical Tantras which turn their worship into absolute obscenity. Here are the Epics which bring in wild fantastic dreams of divine and heroic story. Then come the six philosophies which arrange and analyse and annihilate all! Compare the records. They weigh down our shelves.

Yet the Hindu clings to his Veda, of which he knows absolutely nothing! Let us learn, if we would uphold the cause of the propagation of the Gospel, to contend earnestly for the holy catholic faith, once for all delivered to God's saints, enshrined in the revealed Word, and out of IT taught by the Church of Christ to the world. Not the Christianity of Calvin, or of Dante, or of Milton, but the Christianity of the New Testament must be taught in our Missions; taught with scientific theologic accuracy, but with a most reverent, guarded and thoughtful care, lest we lay any stumbling-block in the way of men, whom we would bring to the feet of the only Master of mankind.

Fourthly. Again, it will be seen how close, in all essential respects,

HINDU DEITY.

is the resemblance between the paganism of India and old classical paganism.

Over that Christianity gained a wonderful and final and conclusive victory.

And Druidism, and Teutonic and Scandinavian paganism, are dead, smitten by the sword of the Lord.

> " The oracles are dumb,
> No voice or hideous hum
> Runs thro' the archèd roof in words deceiving.
> Apollo from his shrine
> Can no more divine
> With hollow shriek the steep of Delphos leaving.
> Nor all the gods beside
> Longer dare abide ! "

And surely it is not presumptuous for the Christian Missionary to anticipate the fall of Hindu paganism by the same means.

Already a vast and increasing body of educated Hindus is seen renouncing idolatry. Some of her best sons are in the Christian ministry. Many a Christian community is flourishing in India. These are oases in the desert—paradises half of whose charm is derived from the vast ring of barrenness, in which like gems they are set.

But may we not believe that the time will come when all the wilderness shall blossom as the rose ?

Remember in hopeful intercession that work which your Lord has given His Church to do for Him, and the accomplishment of which He is expecting on His throne of glory.

Lastly, I think I may venture, as the result of this comparison, zealously to say that I have made plain the duty of labouring more to introduce into every part of India, which is bound to us by so many ties, the religion that imparts such inestimable benefits to mankind. Let us tell the Hindus of our Father and their Father, of our God and their God. Let us tell the worshippers of idols and of imaginary deities of the one Mediator between God and man. Let us teach them the perfect law which Christ has taught us by His words and by His life. Let us proclaim to them the words of our Father in heaven who has promised to give His Holy Spirit to them that ask Him. Let us tell those who have no hope of everlasting life, of Him who hath opened the kingdom of heaven to all believers. In fine, if they are saying " Who will show us any good ? " let us be prompt to reply " *That will we ; freely have we received, freely will we give.*"

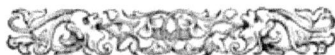

TWO YEARS IN THE MISSION OF SANDWICH BAY, LABRADOR.

BY THE REV. F. W. COLLEY.

ALL who have read the life of our good Bishop Feild, and I presume that most people who take an interest in Church work in Newfoundland have done so, may perhaps remember that early in his Episcopate he wrote to inquire whether Labrador formed part of his Diocese.

He was afterwards satisfied that it did, and exerted himself to provide for its spiritual requirements.

It was his wish to establish three Missions on the coast—at Forteau, at Battle Harbour, and Sandwich Bay.

His wish was, however, only partly gratified. Forteau and Battle Harbour were provided for, but the people to the north were left to get on as best they could.

If you know anything about Battle Harbour Mission, you are well acquainted with the names of Dysney and Hutchinson. Would that we had more men of their stamp to-day! Their words have not been forgotten, and their conduct on many a trying occasion convinced the people that their teachers were holy men, men who cared not what they endured; who had a work to do and did it; a message to deliver which they delivered. The Battle Harbour Mission extends north as far as Seal Island; but at least on one occasion Mr. Hutchinson's love of souls constrained him to go as far north as Sandwich Bay—no light undertaking. He was the first and only clergyman who visited these people during the winter until two years ago.

Bishop Feild and Bishop Kelly made a point of going as far north as Cartwright every time they visited the Labrador; but unfortunately both were prevented from visiting a very large part of my Mission (Hamilton Inlet). To this day I regret it. Where the Bishop is, we are told on good authority, there is the Catholic Church. The Church of God is a greater reality to the people of Sandwich Bay than to those further north, partly, I believe, from the effect of these visits. Bishop Feild performed at least one function peculiar to the Episcopal office. The graveyard at Cartwright, which the people delight to tell you is consecrated ground, has proved a sort of link between them and their chief pastor, and, let us hope, taught them on many a sad occasion to believe more firmly in the "Communion of Saints."

Until this summer the present Bishop of Newfoundland always made Seal Island his turning point. Before his peculiarly Episcopal work could be performed, it was deemed necessary that a priest should be sent to prepare the people. And Mr. Shears on three occasions, and Mr. Johnson on one, at his request, visited what we now term the Mission of Sandwich Bay. Their visits were very hurried, but the people were charmed to see them, and good results followed. Mr. Shears was the first clergyman to visit Esquimaux Bay (in Hamilton Inlet). An old man, an Englishman, who has been nearly half a century on the coast, told me how grateful he was when he landed at Bluff Head in the summer of 1878. "He was the first minister that I had seen, sir, since I left England, over 40 years ago; and my old woman and I had often prayed that one of the Church ministers would visit this part and administer the

Holy Communion to us before our death." "English Tom," as the people call him
(occasionally also "honest Tom "), is a splendid old fellow, and has often and often
cheered me up. Every Sunday he has service morning and afternoon, and in the
summer he puts up his flag to let the Newfoundland fishermen know that it is prayer
time; for two months of the year he usually has a good congregation; for ten he is
contented to worship with his family.

This summer (1887) the Bishop went about twenty miles out of his way for the
purpose of confirming him and two of his daughters. Most unfortunately they were
away from home, the only day for the twelve months that Tom had been absent.
Saturday, however, brought him to Rigolet, a distance of 50 miles. Mr. Curling invited him to tea, and the Bishop gave him a large Prayer-book. The next day he and

his three daughters were confirmed, and received the Holy Communion. The old
man was very happy; he informed me before I left that the service had done him good,
he had not witnessed anything like it since he left England.

The Rev. J. Curling, Rural Dean of the Strait of Belle Isle, has been in the habit
of visiting Cartwright and Rigolet every second year since his appointment. Two
years ago he took me on board his yacht at Belle Isle, and went with me to these two
places, and introduced me to the people as their priest. Since then I have been
working among them.

Bishop Feild's idea was that the Mission should extend to Cape Harrison, and he
thought that, taking the bays into consideration, the coast line would be about 200
miles. I have not been farther north than Holton, but the coast line of Esquimaux

Bay alone is about 400 miles. The Missionary in the winter season has to go around that bay and Sandwich Bay, and up Table Bay, Sandhill, Rocky, and Porcupine Bays, and has a population of 900 to visit.

My first Missionary trip commenced the day after Mr. Curling left me, August 18, and continued until October 19—two months. It was a sort of voyage of discovery, and was very hurried, my chief object being to learn the sort of work before me.

I started for Rigolet, went ten miles farther up the bay, returned, and went out of the bay on the south side. The first day I called at six places, and held five services before I put up at Mullin's Cove for the night, where I had still another service, and gave notice of a celebration, as I found that Mr. Shears had admitted two of the people to the Holy Communion. The latter part of the day was most disagreeable; it rained in torrents, and my man and I had to row. After my last service I found that I was expected to sleep next door; so scrambling over the slippery rocks, with a native for guide, we very soon found ourselves in a tilt, containing two beds; the more comfortable one I was constrained to occupy. The rain was coming down in all parts, and everything I wished to keep dry I had to put in under the bed. The greater part of the crockery was placed upon the top of a mosquito curtain, and so arranged as to keep the rain from dropping upon me. The next day was a beautiful one. After celebration, breakfast, and a row of three miles, I came to an old Englishman's house. The owner was over eighty, and had spent between sixty and seventy years in the bay. He could not read, but was most anxious for a Prayer-book; his own was out of date, he said. I soon discovered that he did not require the book for devotional purposes; but, being out of the reach of almanacks until July of every year, its calendar proved a very good substitute.

I hoped to get to Indian Island that night, but after spending two hours at four different places, we had to put up at Tinker Harbour, owing to head wind.

To Tinker Harbour I owe a debt of gratitude. On three occasions it has afforded me shelter. One morning in June 1886, having been rowing since four a.m., we were glad to land there at eight, for the wind and rain were increasing. We repaired the tilt, and stayed there till three the same evening. We had to run our boat on shore on the weather side of the island in a gale of wind. Fortunately for us it was a rowboat, so we pulled it up, and after four hours the wind moderated sufficiently for us to make another start; we arrived at our destination at ten p.m. In August we lay there for a night in the Mission boat. But in this, my first visit, the solitary tilt had quite a population—two young women, a grandmother, three men, and a lot of little children, whose mother was spending a few days next door, about four miles away. I had prayers with them, almost in the dark. My man slept on board his boat in a sleeping-bag, and I, who had no sleeping-bag, had to utilise the only available bit of floor, and rolled myself up in my oilskins. The mosquitoes, or, I should say, black flies, teased us unceasingly. Towards morning it became cold, and our tormentors were less zealous, so it seemed probable that we should get a nap, when the darling baby commenced to yell. That child had good lungs, and amused us till it was time to make a start. The morning was very foggy, and we were afraid that we should not find our way, but after landing on an island to get breakfast, it cleared up sufficiently for us to proceed.

By one o'clock we were at Indian Island, and stayed there till Monday. On Sunday I administered the Holy Communion to five natives, examined the children, gave them lessons to learn, and held three services. It is quite unnecessary for me to give a detailed account of my travels. When engaged in visiting the natives one has to be up with the sun, to have prayers, breakfast, and then to make a start. The distance to the next house is three, five, ten, or even twenty miles. The first act on landing is to get the much-needed and invariable cup of tea and bread, sometimes butter. The children then come and say their lessons, and receive a card if they deserve it. A cottage service is held, and the priest feels that he must be off if the next house is not too far away.

In the summer, there is also much work to be done among the Newfoundland fishermen. Every creek and cove is inhabited; and if the priest of Sandwich Bay deliberately sails past the entrance to visit those that he considers have a special claim upon him, he feels that he is neglecting his duty.

I made it a rule not to pass by any settlement, if I could possibly avoid doing so. The fishermen were invariably pleased to see me. Sometimes I held service in a store, sometimes in the largest house; the congregation was nearly always a good one, and was not infrequently made up of as many Dissenters as members of the Church. Since my first summer in the Labrador, I have always felt, and do feel, that for want of men and want of means, our Church people and those who have a claim upon us, though they know it not, are grievously neglected. It is a well-known fact, that the majority of the people from many of the Newfoundland Missions are on the Labrador for four months; that these people are almost entirely devoid of spiritual supervision during that time. Every one who thinks seriously will feel that this ought not to be the case. In the last ten years Newfoundlanders, who fish between Domino and Holton—only a small portion of the coast—have expected one visit from a clergyman, and, as a rule, they have not been disappointed. True, one visit is better than no visit; but it is very little. These fishing villages are so many nurseries for the "Salvation Army" and the "Ranters." Young people leave their homes in the spring, spend their summer on the Labrador, and being removed from Church influence, are taught to believe in all sorts of schismatical teaching. On every Sunday, and on most week-days, it is possible to get a good congregation in any of these numerous settlements. One great need is two or three earnest and catholic teachers to instruct the ignorant and rebuke the careless. We require the laity of the Church at home and abroad to provide the means, and priests to offer themselves for the work, that instead of only a few of the people receiving a hurried visit, systematic work might be done on the coast.

By the end of September I had been as far south as Domino, had taken the steamer and gone north to Holton, and was making my way to Rigolet, visiting the people on the north side of the bay.

The day before we arrived at Rigolet was a fearfully rough one; it rained and blew very heavily, and we—*i.e.*, a man, woman, a little boy, and myself—went nearly 50 miles in an open boat. At the time, just after dusk, we did not know what to do for the best. We wanted to get to the other side of the bay, but there was too much wind; then we thought we would land at "Tikalaluk," unfortunately the sea was too heavy; we finally decided to run for "Double Mer." We were fearfully cold and miserable, but were much cheered when about nine p.m. we suddenly discovered a light in the land-wash, and knew that there were people much nearer to us than we had anticipated. We did not occupy much time in getting on shore; the owners of the tilt jumped out of bed when they heard us, and put a fire in the stove. We divested ourselves of our oilskins, and tried to get warm. After a cup of hot tea, I had prayers, and, refusing to take possession of the bed, lay down on the stool and fell asleep; my fellow-passengers made up a bed on the floor, and the man and his wife retired again. As soon as the fire went out I commenced to get cold, and when I awoke I was shivering; they soon put in a fire, and, it being dark, I went over by the side of it, undressed, dried my things, put them on again, and slept till morning.

I then spent a fortnight in the bay, making Rigolet my head-quarters. On October 4, I administered the Holy Communion to Mr. Fortescue, of the Hudson Bay Company, and his wife, who were about to sail for England; they had been very kind to me, and have since taken a great interest in the work, and subscribed to the support of the Missionary.

On Wednesday, the 7th, I left with them in the Hudson Bay Company's steamer. It was a beautiful day, and we arrived at Cartwright about six p.m. I said good-bye that evening, and left the next morning for "Paradise." The ground was covered with snow, and it became so thick after we started that we were afraid that we should not succeed in finding our way. Fortune, however, favoured us, and by one o'clock we were anchored in the river. I was soon on deck and looking around, for the disagreeable weather had hitherto kept me below. First impressions were not prepossessing. We appeared to be in the middle of a pond, tall trees surrounded it, three log huts on one side and three on the other. I at once went on shore, and found to my disgust that the tilt I had ordered to be erected had not been commenced; and while discussing pork cakes, learnt that three weeks would elapse before I could hope to possess a room of my own. Meanwhile I had to live with the family; Edward and Mary were most kind to me, and did everything they could to make me comfortable. There were only two rooms in the house—a bedroom and a kitchen, and so they used to go next door every night.

Sunday, October 11, is a day that will long be remembered in Newfoundland and on the Labrador. The Newfoundlanders were ready for a start; some had actually started. Saturday evening there was a fresh breeze; on Sunday it blew very heavily, and proved to be the most destructive gale that had been known on the coast for about twenty years. We found the loneliness almost overwhelming; for the first time did I realise how completely I was shut off from the rest of the world; and to render the day more dreary, four of our men were absent. They left on the Friday, and we were most anxious about them. At ten I commenced prayers; there were two men and two or three children present; the day was too rough for the rest of the people to attend. "In His hands are all the corners of the Earth," were words that had a meaning for us, but it required a very great effort for us to grasp the fact that we were engaged in Catholic worship, and though separate were united in spirit with all the members of the Church.

After visiting the other side of the bay I returned to Paradise, and spent six weeks there, or rather more; for during November and the early part of December it is impossible to travel. It was somewhat trying to find occupation. For days the river would not bear, and the trees were so covered with snow that unless one required a shower bath it would not be wise to venture under their shadow.

On Wednesdays and Fridays four children used to come and say their lessons, and at seven we had service.

On December 10 I made an attempt to get to the north side of Sandwich Bay, but when we were half way across we came to open water, the wind having driven the ice out of the bay.

On the 13th I lost my way in a snow-storm, returning from Paradise, and narrowly escaped spending a night in the woods, where for four hours I walked about by myself, the darkness, drift, and uncertainty of my whereabouts making it rather terrible.

On the 14th we crossed the bay. We took the dogs with us to the edge of the ice, about five miles, and then shouldered our knapsacks, donned our rackets, and commenced one of the hardest tramps I have ever experienced. We had to climb over a hill, or neck, about two miles wide, to cross a cove, and then climb over another neck thickly wooded. The distance was not great, being about seven miles, but we took nine hours to accomplish it, and were well fagged when we arrived at Eagle River at eight p.m. I spent a fortnight in visiting Eagle River, White Bear River, and Dove Brook, and returned to Paradise for the Christmas celebration.

On January 29 I started on a three months' trip, and it may be well to state here the requirements of the Missionary of Sandwich Bay. A cometic, or slide, about six feet long, two and a half broad, and eight inches high. A cometic box to contain his kettle, tea, biscuit, &c.; a suit of sealskin for cold weather, and of moleskin for ordinary weather; a knapsack, rackets, a hatchet, eight or nine dogs, and a sleeping-bag. This last article is most useful. How one would get on without it it is impossible to imagine. In a great number of places it is impossible to get a bed, and in a great many more it is a very doubtful advantage. A good sealskin bag, lined with deerskin, keeps out the cold most effectually. I have slept out of doors in one in the spring, and have not been any the worse for it. The only occasion on which

I nearly came to grief when sleeping in mine proved that it was not so good at keeping out the heat as the cold. I was spending the night with an old woman who had a very great respect for the parson, and a strong objection to his sleeping on the floor. So she begged me to lay my bag on two stools by the side of the stove. I soon fell asleep, and she, imagining that I would be cold in the night, sent her son to cut off some wood, which she put in the stove. In about an hour I awoke, feeling fearfully hot and uncomfortable, and noticing a smell that reminded me of roast pork. I found that my sealskin bag was scorched, and I, nearly burnt by kindness, got out of it as soon as I could, and laughingly retired to the coldest corner of the room.

The first winter I did not possess a team, and had to trust to the settlers to put me about. There were, however, so many disadvantages attached to this mode of procedure that I secured the services of a man who possessed a team to take me about the second winter.

Mr. Mackenzie, of the Hudson Bay Company, lent me his dogs on two occasions for a week. Had it not been for his kindness and the kindness that I received from other gentlemen of the same company, it would have been impossible for me to have accomplished so much as I did.

The work of the Sandwich Bay Missionary during the winter months is, I suppose, different in many ways from that of other Missionaries. He has no church, no school, and in only one of the bays a schoolmaster. He has to travel every day that it is possible to travel; nor would he hesitate to go ten, twenty, or even forty miles out of his way to

FORTEAU.

visit one family. The houses are, on an average, about ten miles apart, and, as a rule, the family at whose house he is staying are the only people present at the service that he holds every evening. Occasionally he lives on the fat of the land; venison, seal, or partridge are placed before him three times a day. " My allowance sir, is two partridges three times a day," said an old man to me. " Fresh craft " has been scarce of late years, and for weeks last winter we had to be content with bread and tea, bread, fish, and tea—very rarely butter.

There were, however, some very pleasant breaks. At Rigolet, North West River, and most places in Sandwich Bay, I was always sure of a hearty welcome, an agreeable chat, and a comfortable night.

A Missionary is not worthy of the name if he is not prepared to take the rough with the smooth, and to make the best of everything. Many of the adventures we record are not half so trying at the time we endure them as they appear to be to those who read of them. And instead of making ourselves miserable when they occur, we usually crack jokes, boil our kettle (an unfailing source of comfort), make merry, and enjoy the advantages of civilisation all the better when they come to hand.

Poverty is our great bugbear. After a journey for miles over ice and snow, the thermometer something between ten and thirty degrees below zero, to arrive at a tilt, and before you have time to take off your dicky to be asked for relief; to see hunger stamped upon the face of every child, to know that this must be removed before you can hope to teach, to be aware that many are anxious to see you, not because they wish to be taught, but because they wish to be fed—these and such like circumstances are calculated to make the priest feel that he is too much of the poor commissioner, though they ought to teach him patiently to walk in the steps of Him whom he professes to follow. Strange to say, the southern people are the poorest and the most ignorant. Two families live in many of the tilts, nor do they think any partition necessary; in some instances I have seen only one bed for the family, and in one instance no bed at all. In Sandwich Bay many of the people are most industrious and very intelligent, but all along the coast there are signs of poverty.

The Government collect taxes, but give very little in return. I brought before them the destitution of the settlers, and also wrote an account of their state to one of the local papers. It is not necessary for me to repeat what I then stated. Unfortunately, no steps have been taken to remove from the coast those who would be glad to leave, and the few barrels often forwarded will not be sufficient to keep these neglected people from starvation unless they are fortunate in their hunt the coming winter.

VISITING THE COAST MISSIONS.

After three months of constant travelling, I was very glad to find myself once more at head-quarters; and very thankful that although I had had to sleep in houses in which several of the family were sick of starvation fever, and in others in which "the air was so thick that you could cut it with a knife," owing to the number of occupants, I was in good health, and not a bit the worse for the journey. I not unnaturally indulged in a wash as soon as I conveniently could. Whether such a strange experience, the luxury of feeling clean, or the dissipation of a few days' quiet, proved too much for me, I cannot tell; all I know is that I caught cold, and was decidedly unwell for three weeks. At the end of that time I was able to take a six weeks' trip, and made my last journey on the ice on May 13.

I now rested for a month; and the ice having left the bay and the rivers, I commenced going about in a boat. My work was very similar to that which I had engaged in the previous summer, the greater part of my time being taken up in visiting the natives. At Cartwright I spent about ten days, and at Spotted Island a week. Most of the people of Hamilton Inlet were visited twice, and services were held at Domino, Indian Tickle, Black Island, Grady, Cape North, Long Island, Indian Island, Indian Harbour, Bake-Apple Bight, Horse Harbour, Fox Island, and' Holton, for the benefit of the Newfoundlanders. It was late in the season before I returned to Cartwright;

and owing to some mismanagement, the captain of the mail steamer who had promised to call for me at Indian Island neglected to do so, and in consequence I and my two men were left on a lately deserted island, and I being put on the mainland had to hire a guide and walk to Sandwich. November had arrived before I gave up boating.

I now decided on making Cartwright my head-quarters. For several reasons it is the most convenient place. Here the Hudson Bay Company carry on their business, and here most of the people of the bay meet after salmon-catching. I commenced to build a parsonage, and there is to be a large room in it set aside for public worship. We are at present short of funds.

My second winter on the coast slipped away more quickly than the first. Almost too soon April arrived; and as I had decided to try to be at St. John's in time for the Synod, I had to say good-bye to my people and face south. A week after leaving Cartwright I was in the Battle Harbour Mission; and on May 2, having travelled part of the distance with dogs and cometic and part in boat, I arrived at Battle Harbour. The last place we called at was Deep Water Creek, and in leaving the stage we noticed a boat coming around the head. On board of it was the Rev. W. S. Rafter, the clergyman of the Mission. We were very pleased to meet, for I had not seen a clergyman for nearly two years. He got into my boat. Before many hours had passed he and his wife were doing all they could to make me comfortable in the parsonage.

I visited the southern part of the Mission with him, and at his request celebrated the Holy Communion at Henley, Cape Charles, and twice at Battle Harbour. We had one or two trying times together. One night we slept in a tilt half full of snow, on another in the land-wash, and when we awoke we found it snowing thickly. We were all the more disgusted on this occasion because we were on a pleasure trip.

I did not get away from Battle Harbour till June 26; the steamer we expected did not turn up, and I should have been in St. John's earlier had I stayed north till the spring opened.

After nearly three weeks in St. John's, I returned to the Labrador to prepare for the Bishop's visit. Before I left, it had been decided that I should not remain for the winter, but that the late Missionary of Channel, the Rev. T. P. Quintin, who had volunteered to help, should succeed me.

We were fortunate in having favourable winds during the ten days that the Bishop was in my Mission; consequently we were able to visit seven places, and to spend Sunday at Cartwright and Rigolet. The Sunday at Cartwright appeared to be a great success; to begin with, it was the most convenient Sunday in the year for the people; the salmon fishery had just terminated, and they had not commenced the cod fishery. Mr. Daw, of the Hudson Bay Company, had fitted up one of the stores very nicely, so there was plenty of room, the only cause for regret being that four of the candidates were unable to attend. On Saturday evening Mr. Curling preached; on Sunday morning the Bishop confirmed the candidates, and they remained to partake of the Blessed Sacrament. In the afternoon, the children were charmed by receiving a present from him of a Jubilee Medal, which he gave them after they had been catechised. At the evening service my successor was inducted, the Bishop preached again, and spoke to the people about the work of the Church and the different orders of the Ministry.

At Rigolet we were not so fortunate. It blew very hard on Saturday and Sunday, and many of the people who were most anxious to attend were unable to do so. Four people who hoped to be confirmed nearly lost their lives in trying to cross the bay, and after receiving a good drenching had to spend Sunday night about half way between their home and Rigolet. I had not so much work for the Bishop as I ought to have had. It is most difficult to prepare candidates for confirmation when you only see them three times a year. For the first year most of the people were very shy, and some were undecided; the only safety seemed to be in presenting those that had already received the Holy Communion, or were anxious to do so.

I am truly thankful that a Bishop has at last visited Esquimaux Bay, and especially am I thankful that many of those that I have learnt to respect, and who, I believe, will, by God's grace, let their light shine before men, received the gift of the Holy Ghost by the laying on of hands before my departure. It is also a cause for gratitude that our Diocesan is now in the position to ask for volunteers to work among the Newfoundlanders during the summer months. If priests will only undertake the work, and do it faithfully, they will be convinced of its importance.

I have sometimes been asked whether it is worth while to keep a clergyman in the Sandwich Bay Mission during the winter. "If all the people lived in one bay, and could receive regular visits, there would be some sense in it; but as you are only able to see these people twice during the winter, are you not wasting your time and the Church's money?" One need not say that these 900 are as precious in the sight of God as any 900 in the world. Have not the poor, uneducated, isolated, and, in many cases, depraved inhabitants of this lonely coast an especial claim upon Christ's Gospel? Remove the priest even from one of the Newfoundland Missions and the people will still hope occasionally to receive the Sacraments from the priest of an adjoining Mission. They will still have many advantages; in most settlements at least one is able to read, and in the more important there are schoolmasters. It would be hard to find

HENLEY.

a Newfoundlander who has not occasionally worshipped in a church, and there are numbers who have so many advantages that they cease to value them. The great majority of the people who live in the Sandwich Bay Mission have never entered a House of God. I myself have often thought, "How nice it will be once more to kneel down in a church." Numbers cannot read, the distance they live from one another renders it impossible for them to have frequent intercourse, and in many a house the only chance they have of hearing of " the way of salvation " is the occasional visit of a priest, and they are only just beginning to get accustomed to that. Surely if we are Christians in anything but name, we shall not be satisfied to leave our own brethren, people descended from Englishmen, Scotchmen, Newfoundlanders, and Esquimaux, in darkness, but will do all in our power by our prayers and our alms that the Gospel may be preached to every creature.

WORK IN THE REWARI DISTRICT.

BY THE REV. T. WILLIAMS, THE SOCIETY'S MISSIONARY AT REWARI,
IN THE DIOCESE OF LAHORE.

AM glad to say that the illness caused by the heat from which I was suffering when I made my last report has entirely disappeared. It kept me, however, from going out all through July, I mean going out to distant places where exposure to the heat would have been unavoidable ; but as regards Rewari and its vicinity, I was able to pursue my work as usual. In the bazaar here, my experience during this quarter has been more encouraging, and that is due to the use of the pictures of which I spoke in my last. On three or four occasions, indeed, my experience was wholly new. The recollection of one is very vivid. The Catechists who were with me had had their say with the usual result. I began my turn by unfolding the pictures. These were held together by two of the Catechists, with the Crucifixion in front, the Resurrection behind that, and next the Ascension. The crowd around my table gradually thickened, so much so, that had there been no table the heat would have been stifling. The point to dwell on in showing the Crucifixion is, that it is a *sacrifice*. To dwell on the injustice of the condemnation of our Lord is to give occasion for misleading issues. All are ready with the objection, that if Jesus were the Son of God, the Jews could not have killed him. The form of this objection is due to the Muhammadis, but it is in the mouth of all Hindoos, and my answer to the Hindoo is crushing, as it ought to be. For I have before me on the table, heaped on one another, one volume of the Ryveda, one volume of the Taittiriya Yajurveda, the whole of the White Yajurveda, and the Samaveda, as also the Sabapathu Bráhmanu, whose authority is hardly less than the White Yajurveda itself. The *raison d'être* of all but the first is sacrifice, and the first, indeed, is the volume that contains the Ryveda account of the sacrifice of Purusta. What possible answer can the Hindoo give when he finds that his much-revered Veda is full of sacrifice, and that not only of things eatable and drinkable, but also of animals, and amongst them his much belauded cow. Nay, that men—even Prajápati, the "father of the gods"—are sacrificed, and that very much so!! Every objection is met at the threshold by replies and comparisons drawn from their own sacred books.

The Muhammadi is met, not from his Koran, but from the Taurait, *i.e.* the Pentateuch, which he believes to have descended bodily from heaven. On the occasion I refer to, I had to do with Hindoos, for the Muhammadis had not objected; and as I passed, with more clearness perhaps than usual, from picture to picture the wrapt attention became more intense, until when I finished with the Ascension, and with the teaching that a time would come when all should behold Jesus, all of us there standing together, the impression made on all was such as I had rarely ever seen before. We turned away in silence and solemnity, and we thanked God very heartily indeed in the room above our preaching place, for the blessing He had that day vouchsafed upon our work.

In the month of August I visited Sirsa. Here our two agents seem to have been working very steadily. It being the chief depôt of the Rewari Ferozepore Railway, the number of Christians is fluctuating. On the occasion of my visit, our little service in the Church was attended by twenty-one, and then there were three not able to be present. Since then, however, two families have left, and the congregation consequently is much diminished. The same contrast between Muhammadis and Hindoos is kept up, as to the attitude towards our preaching displayed by them respectively, as that I mentioned in a previous report, i.e. the Hindoos listened gladly, the Muhammadis sullenly refuse to listen. Sometimes the latter's sullenness is for a moment dispelled, as at the village of Meerpoor, on the river Gaggar, a short distance from Sirsa. The inhabitants are all Pachâdâs (Westerns), and very bigoted. The pictures were new to them and so drew them, but only to cavil and snarl. However, when I came to the Ascension, and told them that the last words of Jesus were a command to Christians to go into all the world and make disciples of all nations, and that consequently our presence there was simply in obedience to that command, the effect on them was curious. From that time up to the time of our leaving, which certainly was not many minutes after, there was no more cavilling or snarling. They are crassly ignorant, as well of the Koran as of other things; but the thought that, after all, we were but obeying the prophet Isu's (Jesus') command, put our visit in quite another light for them— that we had not of our own motion come gratuitously to cast a stone at Muhammad.

Our visit to the Hindoo portion of the village of Begu was pleasantly diversified by two or three women, on their way past us, stopping to see our pictures. The picture of the Cross, and of the Virgin Mother kneeling weeping near, with the other women, touched a chord in their hearts which clearly responded. I was much struck by the mild, motherly face of one of them. They were Jats, a fact that partly explained the freer action of the women.

In the town itself of Sirsa our preaching was well received, no Muhammadi bickering. There has been manifestly a beating down of prejudice, due to the regular addresses of our agents. Jackson's

addresses seem very effective, so that I should say he has found the
sphere for which he seems specially fitted. I should like to have him
ordained deacon. From what I myself saw, and from what Jackson
and Edwards say, the Sikhs, who live in large numbers in the north and
north-east of the district, are those that listen best to, and seem to
imbibe most readily, our teaching. They are invariably Jats, and seem
in heart least distant from Christianity. Dulip Sing, the Sikh convert,
paid us here at Rewari a visit a few days ago. Let us hope that he
will remain steadfast. It is curious that the one from whom he gets
most opposition is his blind brother, who passed the Law examination
at Lahore (notwithstanding his blindness), and is now practising at
Hissar, in our district, as a Vakeel. This man says that his brother
becoming a Christian injures his prospects, as Hindoos are therefore
less likely to become his clients.

My visit to Hissar took place in September. It was during the
Muharam, and as Hissar is the most Muhammadi of all the larger
towns in my district, I expected some rather exciting preachings in the
bazaar. Never have they been so mild, however. I had never used my
pictures at Hissar before, and they were evidently so novel a feature,
that the Muhammadis for once forgot their cavils. Nay, on my last
visit to the bazaar I had occasion to leave earlier than had been my
wont, and so had not reached the point at which I unrol my pictures, and
they were Muhammadis who asked me whether I was not going to show
them!! while not far off was the chief musjid, in which, as I stood
there, I could see the Muhammadi at their prayers.

One of the most interesting features of my Hissar visit was a morning's
preaching at Dabra, about 3 kos, i.e. 4½ miles, from Hissar. It was
the native place (and the place where, when off duty, he always lives)
of Ishri Sing, one of the native officers that visited England for the
Jubilee. He was away with his regiment at Meerut, but I saw his son
and his brothers, who all live in one large house. He wrote an account
of his journey, which was promised me, but which has not yet arrived.
I was told that Ishri Sing described his visit as going to a second heaven,
so that he was evidently thoroughly pleased with all and everything.
London struck him with amazement, in fact he does not seem to have
yet recovered from it. When I asked them what it was that seemed
to have struck him most in London, the reply was wholly unexpected.
It was the great contrast between Sunday and Monday; the universal
quiet of the former, and the unceasing roar of traffic the rest of the
week. I had with me a sheet of paper on which my wife had printed in
large letters the Lord's Prayer, Creed, and Ten Commandments, and I
showed the Fourth Commandment as that in obedience to which the
week-day roar ceased for the Sunday quiet. Of course, all that they
told me only served to illustrate the tale of Christ that I had to tell;

and though they had been visited before by me, never had they understood my story as they did on this occasion. I wish every village had one inhabitant that had visited England; my work of explanation, at any rate, would be much easier.

On visiting a neighbouring village next day, and mentioning Ishri's visit to England, the only point that an old farmer could remember of what he had heard of that visit was, that the Sirkar had given to Ishri for his own use so long as he remained in England, *a cow*. This was the only item the old man could appreciate, and that therefore struck home. The difficulty the people generally must have in really comprehending our teaching may be inferred from this.

THE CHINA FAMINE.

OF the districts in China suffering from the terrible famine, which has stirred English pity so deeply, the greater part is outside the region where the Society is working. There is, however, one province, that of Shantung, which is within the Missionary diocese of North China, and is also included in the famine area. The privations and loss of life there are stated to be enormous. In consequence of its connection with the work in North China, the Society has been requested by the Mansion House Committee to send a delegate to that body. This has been done, the Rev. J. H. Snowden being the member chosen to represent the Society. The Bishop inform us that the Rev. F. H. Sprent, one of the clergy of his diocese, is now stationed at Tai-An-Foo, in the province of Shantung, and with his lordship's advice the Society is remitting to Mr. Sprent about £150, which was available for the purpose of famine relief. The Society has no wish to plead for a famine relief fund in rivalry to that which is being raised at the Mansion House. It is believed that the distribution of that fund must be mainly through the various Missionaries engaged in the famine districts.

THE CHILDREN'S CORNER.

THE HERO OF SÁHAMAFY.—A TALE OF THE FRANCO-MALAGASY WAR.

BY THE REV. ALFRED SMITH.

(Continued from page 72.)

CHAPTER IV.

IGHT came on. A drizzling mist was driving over hill and valley as Ralay, with a dirty brown *lamba*, such as slaves only use, slipped from his house and disappeared in the mist over the brow of the hill. Descending quickly into the valley, he made for the banks of the river Ikopa. Along the bank he went, and after some minutes' sharp walking he came to the point where the river, meeting a range of hills, is forced to bend its course northward. Here he descended into the shallow river-bed, and stopped before some thick bushes overhanging the bank and almost touching the water. Stooping underneath, the entrance to the cave disclosed itself. It was but a small hole, and Ralay had to creep in on his hands and knees. But once inside, the cave became a large vaulted room. The walls were formed of huge rocks which in the upheaval of the hills had fallen against each other, while the earth and *débris* between them had been washed out into the river-bed. Quite a dozen men were sitting and lying on the dry sand which formed the floor of the cave, watching and listening to the gigantic Rabe, who had traced the mystic figures of the *sikidy* in the sands, and was beginning the divination formula.

"Awake, O god, to awaken the sun!" he muttered. "Awake, O sun, to awaken the cock! Awake, O cock, to awaken mankind! Awake, O mankind, to awaken the *sikidy*—not to tell lies, not to deceive, not to play tricks, not to talk nonsense, not to agree to everything indiscriminately; but to search into the secret, to look into what is beyond the hills and on the other side of the forest, to see what no human eye can see.

"Wake up, for thou art from *Silámo be vólo* (*i.e.*, the 'long-haired Mohammedans'), from the high mountains, from Rabórobóaka, Tapélakétsikétsika, Záfitsimaíto, Andriambávitóaláhy, Rakélihoránana, Iánakára, Andrianónisolánatra, Vazimba, Anakandríananáhitra, Rakélilávavólo. Awake! for we have not got thee for nothing, for thou art dear and expensive. We have got thee in exchange for a fat cow with a large hump, and for money on which there was no dust. Awake! for thou art the trust of the sovereign and the judgment of the people.   If thou art a *sikidy* that can tell, a *sikidy* that can see, and does not only speak about the noise of the people, the hen killed by its owner, the cattle killed in the market, the dust clinging to the feet (*i.e.*, self-evident things), awake here on the mat!

"But if thou art a *sikidy* that does not see, a *sikidy* that agrees to everything indiscriminately, and makes the dead living and the living dead, then do not arise here on the mat."[*]

Having finished this incantation, his eye glanced swiftly over the figures of his divination.

"There will be opposition," he said gloomily at last, "and blood-shed."

The men looked blankly one at the other.

"Give me the cock for sacrifice."

One of the men threw across the floor to him a cock brought beforehand in case of a sacrifice being required.

Rabe placed the bird under his knee, and seizing the head by his left hand he took up a knife which lay beside him.   Slowly he severed the head from the body, and as the bright red blood spirted out he said in a solemn voice:

"Ye demand blood, ye spirits of the dead Vazimba, ye ghosts of the long-hair Mohammedans; drink then, drink, and be appeased!"

"Drink, and be appeased!" was muttered by them all.

Slowly Rabe gathered up the seeds which he had used in his divination and placed them carefully in a bag.

Ratsimba now come to the front.

"You all know," he said, "what we intend to do.   I have heard from one of the clerks that there are 2,000 dollars in Sampson & Co.'s safe.   Well, we mean to have that money.   The night will be dark, and at half-past eleven we will meet at the old place in the churchyard of the Memorial Church, and one after the other slip into Sampson's yard.   Rabe will have his charms ready for the watchman, and when he sleeps, we will enter and carry the safe and its contents bodily off.   If we are heard and there is opposition, as the divination has shown there will be, we all know how to take care of ourselves.   We will open the safe in the churchyard and bring the money here for division.   Are you all agreed?"

Everyone but Ralay enthusiastically assented.   The division of 2,000 dollars amongst them would make them rich for life.

"That is all right.   Now we will divide what I have been able to get for those church things.   I sold the gold-thread from the altar-cloth to some of my friends to ornament their uniforms with.   However, there is not much to divide."   The division was made.

"Let everyone be at the rendezvous.   You know the oath.   Let us go."

* The Rev. L. Dahle in the "Antananarivo Annual" for the year 1888.

Eleven o'clock had struck by the clock of the Memorial Church of Ambatonakanga, when the robbers one after the other arrived and concealed themselves under the churchyard walls. Each carried a long gleaming knife, and they had with them a stout pole and a coil of ropes.

The calls of the soldiers on guard round the palace were the only sounds that broke the stillness of the night.

"Are we all here?" whispered the voice of Ratsimba, hoarsely.

"All!"

"Now, Rabe, deal with the watchman first."

With the swiftness and stealthiness of a snake Rabe glided away.

"Ralay, is your pistol all right? Mind, if we are attacked fire straight at the first man who pursues, and that will stop the rest, and we shall easily slip away."

They lay crouched under the wall for a few moments longer, in silence awaiting the return of Rabe. He returned as silently and suddenly as he had gone away.

"The watchman is in a dead sleep now. My charms have taken full effect, and now is the time for us to move. The Europeans are also sound asleep with the fumes of my medicines, and everyone in the house is as dead."

"That's all right, Rabe. Now men, one after the other! Ralay, keep good watch! If you don't——"

The men slipped off one after the other perfectly noiseless. They were all naked except for the waistcloth, and all were thickly smeared with grease. It was difficult to catch one, and it would be almost impossible to hold him when caught. In a few moments they were all standing underneath the verandah of Sampson & Co.'s house. The watchman lay there before the door sleeping like the dead. Taking no notice of him, Rabe plied a strong iron lever to one of the windows with such assurance and freedom as to prove his firm reliance on the power of his charms. Not a soul was awakened by the noise he made. Soon the window stood open. He entered, and immediately afterwards the doors swung back. All went in. The iron safe was immediately secured by ropes to the pole they had brought. Four of the robbers raised it to their shoulders, and bore it swiftly away.

They went back to the churchyard, and very soon Rabe was employed in breaking it open. The burglar-proof safe soon yielded to his manipulations, and the door flew open. The dollars were within— some in bags and some loose. Ratsimba had delivered several bags to different robbers, and was occupied in collecting the loose dollars, when a yell of mingled terror and excitement rang through the churchyard. All sprang to their feet.

In a few seconds a human form appeared over the wall, and,

brandishing a spear, was in the act of springing down into the churchyard.

" Fire at him, you Mission fool you ! " cried Ratsimba in a voice of frightful rage, and lifting his knife.

Frightened, and hardly knowing what he did, Ralay raised his pistol at the word of command. There was a loud report, which echoed far and wide over the silent sleeping city.

Before the smoke had cleared away the churchyard was empty. Not a trace of the robbers remained except the broken safe. But across a grave there on the green churchyard sod lay the watchman, his face turned up to the midnight sky, with a large bullet-hole in his forehead, from which the blood slowly trickled into the grass.

In the morning there was the usual hue-and-cry. The police went hither and thither, the people stood in groups in the street and talked, while the churchyard was crowded with visitors to look upon the scene of the murder. But at Ambóhidrapéto Rabe lay calmly sleeping in the warm morning sun, and Ralay was saying prayers in the little village church.

CHAPTER V.

It will be remembered that Ratefy had been appointed to the charge of a village called Ambóatány at the same time that Ralay had been sent to Ambóhidrapéto.

Ambóatány lies some twelve or thirteen miles to the north of Antananarivo ; and, like a great number of Hova villages, is built on the top of a high hill. In olden times, when each village had its own chief, and was independent of every other village, these hill-tops were strongly fortified with deep ditches, and were rendered as impregnable against assault as possible.

From the top of Ambóatány one looks down upon the Mission Theological College to the south-west, and standing on the slope leading down to the rice-fields. A few years ago this was a barren hill-side ; but now, amidst the pleasant greenness of numerous mango and other trees, planted and cultivated by the present principal, rise the beautiful spires of the stone church and College Library and Lecture-hall.

Above them is the house of the principal, surrounded by beautiful gardens, and farther down the hill are the rows of students' houses, each enclosed in its own little garden.

In such a solitude, " blossoming like the rose," the students are trained for their sacred and responsible calling of forming the future native ministry of the Malagasy Church. From the top of the rock of Ambóatány, and looking down upon the little colony, one's heart goes out in prayer that the work done therein may be used by the Almighty for the salvation and regeneration of the Malagasy people, and that the students therefrom may walk worthy of their sacred calling.

Across the rice-fields at the bottom of the slope is another town, from amongst the native houses of which rises the wooden turret of a Roman Catholic church.

Turning to the east, one looks across the valley to the old Malagasy capital of Ambóhimánga, where the bodies of the sovereigns of Imerina lie buried in a vast tomb, with their money and valuables placed by their sides.*

No foot of European has ever trodden and desecrated the sacred streets of Ambóhimánga. By solemn treaty with the Great Powers of Europe, the Malagasy superstition with respect to its sanctity is signed and sealed. Here lie the bones of the persecuting Queen Ranavalona I., and by her side rest those of the gentle and Christian Queen Rana-valona II.

> "The old order changeth, yielding place to new,
> And God fulfils Himself in many ways."

Yea, by means of persecution sometimes.

Ambóatány has been an important place from long ago. In the centre of the village stands a native hut, enclosed by a strong stake-fence. There is no opening in the fence so that people may go in and out, and if there were, few people probably would dare to do so. Years ago this house was the dwelling of the famous idol Ramáhavály. Here his priests performed their juggling tricks, and here the sacred snake of the idol coiled his horrible folds. Ramáhavály (he that answers) was renowned throughout Imerina, and his priests reaped a rich harvest in his service.

His fame was at its height in the time of Radama I., and he was made of one of two bullock's horns, ornamented with a few beads, some dirty bits of rag containing dried leaves, bits of stick, &c.

Being carried one day in solemn procession, he went past a large wooden house which was being erected in the king's garden at Mahúzoarívo, on which several French carpenters were employed.

One of these, whose name was Legros, on asking what it was, was answered in awful tones by the trembling natives watching the procession, that it was the god Ramáhavály.

Legros laughed in derision at the silly superstition.

"We Europeans know better than to believe such nonsense," he said. "Let Ramáhavály try what he can do to us. I'm ready to fight him any day."

The bystanders shivered with terror to hear his unbelieving words, and told the priests what had been said.

They immediately accepted the challenge.

"Ramáhavály is omnipotent," they cried. "He is the god of the sovereign. If Radama only say the word, the foreigner shall soon feel his power."

* During the war, however, a great number of dollars were removed, and went to pay for rifles ,&c.

The Frenchman was eager for the combat, and, by consent of the king, a day was fixed for the trial.

The people flocked from all the neighbourhood round to see the battle, and by common consent the foreigner was doomed to destruction. The king was also present in person.

When the day arrived, Legros stood forth to brave the anger of the bullock's horns and etcetoras. But he reckoned without his host.

From among the knot of priests a huge snake glided out into the arena. As it moved slowly along with balefully shining eyes, and darting its forked tongue hither and thither, the people fled shrieking from the frightful creature.

Rearing itself high in the air, the monster cast himself upon the miserable Frenchman paralysed with fear, and in an instant had enfolded him in his fatal coils.

Legros shrieked for mercy. In the agony of terror he recalled the proud defiance, and at a word from the king the priests caused the snake to release his victim.

By means of terrorism such as this were the minds of the people enslaved, till the light of the Gospel set them free. The day came when the bullock's horns and all the dirty rags and beads which constituted Ramáhavály were publicly consigned to the flames.

His house, however, remained; probably because no one had the courage to pull it down, although its owner was burnt. They put a fence around it, and allowed it to fall to pieces of itself. And this is exactly what the light of the Divine revelation is now doing. Dark superstitions and heathen and filthy customs are being encircled more and more by the light of truth, and are slowly but surely falling away. They cannot be destroyed all at once by an edict or proclamation, though it be promulgated by a despotic queen and prime minister.

Here, then, in the ancient stronghold of superstition Ratefy taught. His genial, sunny ways soon endeared him to the people. The little church was carefully kept, and surrounded by those he taught; the daily service of prayer and praise ascended to heaven. His own little house was cleanly and decently arranged. Pictures from the English *Graphic* ornamented the walls, and among them the one representing the atheist, Mr. Bradlaugh, taking the oath in the House of Commons in Christian England. The old heathens who trusted in the bullock's horns of Ramáhavály looking upon it must have been highly satisfied with their own condition if they had only known what the picture meant.

CHAPTER VI.

But we must not linger here. The clouds of war which had gathered thicker and thicker during the last few weeks over the island were now ready to burst. An acknowledgment of the French protectorate over the north-west coast was imperiously demanded by France, and steadily refused by the Hova. The excitement of the people was daily increasing as messenger after messenger left the Hova palace for the coast. Sermons on war and patriotism began to be preached in the various Hova churches, and inflamed still more the ardour of the people. Little by little definite work of all kinds stopped, and large bodies of soldiers were brought up to the capital, and encamped on the various plains around. And when one morning the news flew through the city that, without any formal declaration of war, the port of Tamatave had been bombarded and occupied by French troops, the excitement reached its height.

At first it was expected that all foreigners, without distinction of nationality, would be at once massacred. A "committee of safety" was therefore formed amongst the British community, and if the panic had not had its serious side it would have been irresistibly droll. The Bishop was, to his own astonishment, chosen chairman of the "committee," the chief object of which ultimately became the circulation of bits of news concerning the progress of the war.

The French Jesuit priests were ordered, together with all other French subjects, to quit the capital in a couple of days' time. No bearers could be obtained to carry their palanquins (for the slave population of Madagascar was at least loyal to that extent), and the long line of black-robed priests, Christian brothers, and sisters of mercy left the city on foot to walk thence to Tamatave, a distance of perhaps 200 miles. The tears were trickling down the pale faces of the gentle sisters, and even stood in the eyes of the priests, as they descended the hill towards the east. They were leaving converts and churches gathered in and raised with such hard and prayerful toil, and were setting forth on a journey which most of them (especially the gentle sisters) could hardly hope to finish alive. As the line wound slowly and sadly up the first ascent they all turned and looked back upon the city they had left, and, turning back, they lifted up their voices and wept. With tears dropping from his eyes, the grey-headed chief lifted his hands in prayer to God for the city and flock they were leaving behind.

And here the English committee of safety stepped in. The Bishop, as chairman, wrote to the Malagasy prime minister, and put before him in the strongest possible way the inhuman cruelty it would be to expose innocent men and women to die upon the road; for even should they not die of fatigue, they would die of starvation, for no one would sell them even a grain of rice.

In reply to this letter, a body of palanquin carriers, under the charge of officers, was immediately sent after them, and so all arrived in safety in Tamatave.

(To be continued.)

NOTES OF THE MONTH.

REFERENCE to the Treasurers' statement of the income for the year 1888 cannot fail to give our friends great satisfaction. The gross total of £138,366. 17s. 6d. exceeds that of the previous year by £28,601. 12s. 3d.

Our attention is always specially fastened upon the item of the sub-scriptions, donations and collections for the General Fund. Under this head the Society received £27,884. 7s. 11d. more than in 1887. This increase, of course, is mainly made up of the two munificent donations, one of £25,296, and one of £2,268, which have been referred to each month in the Treasurers' statements. We are glad that there is an increase independently of these, of £320. May the present condition of the Society's finances stimulate and encourage us all, so that some more adequate attempt may be made to do the work which so urgently needs to be carried on. The increased income and the large gifts should move us to praise Him, from Whom all good things do come.

WE are glad to be able to announce that the large increase in the circulation of this Magazine last year is more than maintained. The sales are now between four and five times as numerous as they were a few years ago.

DURING the year 1888 the Board of Examiners recommended to the Society twenty-seven of those who had offered themselves for Missionary work abroad. Of these, eight were Augustinians, six were graduates of the University of Oxford, three associates of King's College, London, one a graduate of London University, one a graduate of Durham, and the remainder from Dorchester, St. Aidan's, St. Bees, and other colleges. Ten of them have gone to British North America, three to the West Indies, five to India, five to Australia, and the others are distributed between Borneo, South Africa, and Madagascar.

ST. HELENA Diocese is conspicuous for its small size, and for its poverty. Doubly grateful, therefore, is the offering of £17. 15s. 3d. which the Bishop sends from his diocese for the Society. His Lordship writes:—

"Such is still the poverty of the people, and their inability to contribute sufficiently for the maintenance of the clergy and other expenses of our Church work, that I must ask for a renewal of the Society's grant of £275, which has been so long and gene-rously given to this diocese. There does not seem to be any prospect of better times for this island.

"The crippled revenue of the Government limits to a small number the labourers on public works. The imperial expenditure is greatly reduced by the completion of the military works, on which, for some years, many of our people were regularly em-ployed. The ships calling in here for supplies continue to decrease in number, and there are now *very* few persons on the island whose incomes are not too small to bear any expense beyond the wages of one or two servants. We are, by the providential goodness of God, in an abundant supply of fish saved from the starvation and misery which in most other places accompany such poverty as ours.

"Great and very trying to me are our difficulties in temporal things, but I am very thankful that, so far from having fallen back in spiritual things, our people are in religious and moral condition very far better than they were in more prosperous times. The improvement has been gradual, and much greater in the country districts than in Jamestown. The labours of some good and faithful men, such as the late Archdeacon Kempthorne and, since my arrival here, Mr. Bennet in Jamestown, and Mr. Bodily, Mr. Pennell, and the late Mr. Whitehead in the country, had begun to bear fruit when the present clergy entered into their labours, which, carried on by them with zeal and activity, are bearing more fruit. Mr. Baker has been very greatly blessed in his ministry during the last four years as Vicar of St. Paul's. His district is the most extensive on the island, and his work demands much bodily exertion and patient perseverance. He has shown himself a most kind, wise, and judicious as well as zealous parish priest, and is deservedly loved by his people. I am sorry to say that over-exertion has seriously affected his throat. I have persuaded him to leave his work in my hands, whilst he takes entire rest at the seaside, and gets set up again. Mr. Ellis is working hard in Jamestown, and during the short time that he has been there has done much good. The heat of this town has told upon him. I am in hopes of giving him some

ST. HELENA.

relief by obtaining a deacon for St. John's, as it is probable that a young man may shortly come out to me from England for ordination. Mr. Hands continues to work faithfully and quietly in Longwood district, and as Acting Military Chaplain in the garrison."

I T is but recently that the dioceses of Ely and Peterborough were called upon to mourn the loss of their Organising Secretary—the Rev. H. Field Blackett—and now again his immediate successor, not, however, actually in office when he passed away, has been taken to his rest. After an academical career of such distinction that it gained him one of the highest of University prizes—a Fellowship of Trinity College Cambridge—the Rev. Joseph Albert Lobley gave himself to the Colonial Church by accepting, in 1873, the Principalship of the Theological College in Montreal, which he held until his promotion, in 1877, to a like office in Lennoxville College, Quebec. He did good work there till 1885; when he returned, after twelve years' service abroad, to bring to the Church at home the fruits of a ripe experience. The vacancy in the organising secretaryship caused by Mr. Field Blackett's death gave the opportunity, which he readily accepted, of turning to account the knowledge he had gained in Canada as a means of arousing new Missionary interest at home. His past connection with the University of Cambridge also attracted him to resume work there, as it served to keep him in touch with the scenes of his early life. The unassuming simplicity of his character, and his genuine earnestness in the work which he had undertaken, endeared him to all those with whom he came in contact, and secured for him many new personal friends in both dioceses. A consciousness that his health was not what it had been, induced him to seek the retirement of the country in 1887, and his college offered him its living of Sedbergh, where he passed away early in January, faithful to the last, and leaving behind him the bright example of a distinguished career at Cambridge being quite compatible with that of a good soldier of the Cross for a time on foreign service. Such service is too often regarded as inferior, and beneath the dignity of a man who has won high University honours, and who might, as the phrase is, "do much better for himself" at home. But Mr. Lobley did not so interpret duty.

FROM America we have received a copy of a very useful book on Missions. It is *The Great Value and Success of Foreign Missions, proved by Distinguished Witnesses;* by the Rev. John Liggins. (The Baker & Taylor Co., New York, 237 pages). It is a handy and well-arranged collection of testimony to the success of Missions from a variety of persons, many of them being of world-wide reputation. The following is one of many striking stories. A learned Brahmin, at the close of a Missionary's lecture, said in the presence of about 200 Brahmins, officials, &c.:—

"I have watched the Missionaries and seen what they are. What have they come to this country for? What tempts them to leave their parents, friends, and country, and come to this, to them, unhealthy clime? Is it for gain or profit that they come? Some of us, country clerks in Government offices, receive larger salaries than they. Is it for an easy life? See how they work, and then tell me.

"Look at the Missionary. He came here a few years ago, leaving all, and for our good! He was met with cold looks and suspicious glances. He sought to talk with us of what, he told us, was the matter of most importance in heaven and earth; but we would not hear. He was not discouraged; he opened a dispensary, and we said, 'Let the pariahs (lowest caste people) take his medicine, we wont;' but in the time of our sickness and our fear we were glad to go to him, and he welcomed us. We complained at first if he walked through our Brahmin streets; but ere long, when our wives and daughters were in sickness and anguish, we went and begged him to come —even into our inner apartments—and he came, and our wives and daughters now smile upon us in health! Has he made any money by it? Even the cost of the medicine he has given has not been returned to him.

"Now what is it that makes him do all this for us? It is the Bible! I have looked into it a good deal in different languages I chance to know. It is the same in all languages. The Bible! there is nothing to compare with it, in all our sacred books, for goodness and purity and holiness and love, and for motives of action. Where did the English people get their intelligence and energy and cleverness and power? It is the Bible that gives it to them. And they now bring it to us and say, 'That is what raised us; take it and raise yourselves.' They do not force it upon us, as did the Mohammedans with their Koran, but they bring it in love and say, 'Look at it, read it, examine it, and see if it is not good.' Of one thing I am convinced: do what we will, oppose it as we may, it is the Christian Bible that will, sooner or later, work the regeneration of our land!"

THE Diocese of Chichester has of late had to mourn the deaths in succession of several of its leading clergy; and the Society has become a partaker in that sorrow by losing the Ven. Archdeacon Hannah and the Rev. Canon Crosse, who were its Diocesan representatives on the Standing Committee. Archdeacon Hannah was not able to attend its deliberations regularly; but he doubtless felt that his colleague amply supplied the measure of counsel to be expected from the diocese. And indeed there have been few Diocesan representatives, since their institution in 1872, to whom the Society has been under greater obligations for wisdom in counsel and for an advocacy which sprung from genuine sympathy with its work, than to Dr. Crosse, whose death came as an unexpected shock on January 8. His early legal education, his shrewd common sense, and his faculty of applying them to whatever question came before him, rendered him as valuable in council as he was effective in advocating the Society's claims upon the Church at home. The Diocese and the Society, which alike mourn his departure hence, will long cherish his memory as the wisest of counsellors and truest of friends.

FROM Kolhapur, in the Diocese of Bombay, we have an account of the heathen Ganpati festival by the Rev. A. C. Laughlin:—

"This deity, which is seemingly a second-class one, and of a standing with the classical Lares and Penates, is half-man, half-elephant, anent which monstrosity I heard an excellent tale which one of my catechists employed to illustrate the childish character of the average members of the popular Hindu Pantheon. It ran somewhat thus:—Parvati, Shiva's wife, was one day washing herself in a river. In the course of her ablutions she rubbed so much dirt, &c., from her arms that it made a lump as big as her two fists. This apparently very much took her fancy, and of the lump she made a doll, to which she gave life. She took the plaything home with her, and ordered it (or I suppose we should call it a 'he') to guard her room while she dressed for the day. In the meanwhile Shiva came home, and seeing an unknown individual in close proximity to his zenana was very wrath, and drawing his sword cut off Ganpati's head. When Parvati knew this, she was very sorry, and bitterly reproached her husband for destroying, instead of admiring, the handiwork of her own ingenuity. Her tears and entreaties prevailed over her husband, who straightway went out into the forest, vowing to slay the first creature he came across and give his head to the slaughtered plaything. Unluckily, as we might think, the first animal met was an elephant, whose head cut off was affixed to the trunk of Ganpati, who thereupon became the hideous thing our æsthetic tastes are so offended at seeing. It does not require an exhaustive commentary to show how dreadfully inconsistent are the details of this story, or what a travesty on creation, &c., is presented to the ordinary un-educated Hindu hereby."

UNITED States Churchmen always preserve with affection the memory of the Society's work in the last century in their country. The following is from the Rector of Trinity Church, Oxford, Philadelphia:—

"This venerable church of which I am now Rector was founded and nourished by the Society for the Propagation of the Gospel. Among the ministers who cared for it under the Society were Messrs. Clayton, Evans, Rudman, Clubb, Humphreys, Weyman, Howie, Ross, Neill, and Smith. I have lately been engaged in collecting portraits of the earlier ministers and rectors, and other interesting memorials of the parish, to be placed in the vestry room. It has seemed to me that my collection will be incomplete without a copy of the Society's seal, and I therefore venture to ask you to send me an impression either in wax or in print, that I may frame it and hang it upon the walls of the vestry room. It is only my exceeding interest in the matter that can excuse my trespassing thus upon your kindness. It may interest you to learn that in my study are the Bible and Prayer Book (bound together) sent out in 1746, also Poole's Synopsis (in Latin), 5 vols., sent out by the Society at an earlier date. The old church, erected 1711, is the nave of the present building, and the 'Queen Anne' chalice is used at every celebration of the Holy Communion.

"The Church has never forgotten that she owes her existence to Missionary labour, and is a constant contributor to Missionary work. In the past three years it has contributed for Missionary purposes alone, at home and abroad, nearly £1,000."

GOLD is attracting large numbers of white people into Swaziland, whose presence makes large demands upon the Church's means and resources. The Rev. Joel Jackson writes:—

"When I came to this country I had but one white neighbour within a radius of fifty miles. Since then the whole of that part, which was like a wilderness, has become populated by white people. I myself have moved on forty miles, and Europeans, chiefly English, are now more than a hundred miles ahead of me, and many are settling near to the king's chief kraal. The other week the king sent for me, as he wanted to confer with me during the sitting of the white committee. When there, a public meeting of white residents was called, and I proposed that a church be built. A ready response was made, and over one hundred pounds promised on the spot towards this object. Two other such places are urgently needed in other parts of the country at once; but the great question will be, how are these different centres to be worked? I have not a single helper for either the native or white population, and the Bishop has not been able to find me even a teacher. The heat and fatigue attending journeys quite upset me, and I have been several times warned, by breaking down, that I cannot undertake more work than I have on hand at present. If the Society does not come to our Bishop's rescue and send him more help in the way of men and means, I can see no way for carrying on the work given us to do.

"I only just now begin to see the reason why I came here, and why I have been kept here so long. The native work has not been sufficiently encouraging, and it has several times been in my mind to go to more promising fields, but something always came in the way, which seemed to tell me I must stay. It now seems plain that my presence was needed to prepare for coming events and work. At first we could not gain an entrance even into the country, now I have good reason to believe that very soon Christian marriage without the payment of cattle will be a recognised law of the land for those who desire it. The minds of the king and chiefs are expanding, and preparing to accept other changes ere long."

THE Rev. W. Crompton, of Aspdin, in the Diocese of Algoma, tells a very touching story of a young girl's life :—

"About six years ago, a poor orphan 'waif,' supposed to be eleven years old, was brought to Canada by Miss Rye. I myself paid her expenses from Toronto to Aspdin (nearly 200 miles), where she was received into, and eventually adopted into the family of one of my churchwardens. Emily became a regular attendant at my daughter's class in our Sunday school at Aspdin, and also at church. Her attention was excellent and, consequently, her progress rapid. I was much pleased with her modesty of behaviour and devotion, and I have presented few with more pleasure than I did Emily for confirmation. Circumstances which are often occurring in newly settled countries, caused Mr. C—— to remove to a place over 100 miles from Aspdin, a place, alas! found out too late, where almost every form of religion was found but that of the Church of England. I managed to pay them a visit, and received a most favourable report of my 'waif.' Emily, being of a cheerful, loving disposition, soon made for herself many friends amongst the young people around, but from these came her greatest trial. Her Church was the sport and jeer of them all, and her faith was sorely tested by kindnesses, by mockeries, insults, persecutions, and by that which young people at any time find hard to bear, and which in the case of a 'waif' who had known little of the taste of the milk of human kindness, I mean the being cast off by all, Emily had indeed to · endure hardness for the cross of Christ.'

"Emily's trial was a sore and a cruel one, but her foster-parents declare that no young girl could possibly bear better testimony to the faith she professed than she did, and that, too, with smiles, meeting all unkindness with unfailing love. When Emily found that it was really a hopeless case to expect a parson to be sent into their neighbourhood, she proposed to her adopted father that he should do what she had heard me say I did when I came into the 'bush.' He listened to the voice of the poor 'waif,' he took his Prayer Book, and Sunday after Sunday the voice of prayer and praise went up in his own house. Mr. C—— told others whom he knew to be Churchmen, and soon a goodly number were gathered together, and now, I understand, a clergyman is to be sent. Thus the wild weed gathered in the 'slums' has been an instrument to God's glory, and I hope it is not wrong for me to say, the S.P.G. will be blessed through her. He, who doeth all things well, saw that Emily had done the work He had given her to do, and during this last summer she was called 'home,' after only four hours' notice, to the inexpressible grief of her adopting parents, being just 17 years old. So much had Emily become beloved, and so well had her 'light' shone before men, that upwards of 100 persons, old and young, of every degree, came to see her laid in her bed and to cast flowers on to her coffin. There was scarcely one with dry eyes, but all seemed to mourn as at the loss of a much loved sister."

BEACONSFIELD is an important parish in the Diocese of Bloemfontein, where, as far as the white population is concerned, the Church's work is independent of the Society's aid. There is a parish church which cost £2,500, schools which cost £1,000, and other things in proportion. There is, however, scope for very large work among the natives, for which the Society makes a grant of £100. This the Rector, the Rev. C. F. Tobias, asks may be increased. He says that for the native work the Mission school-buildings and the residence for the

Missionary have been built at a cost of £600, and that no debt remains,
owing to the generosity of Archdeacon Gaul and the Rev. H. Crosthwaite.

"The Mission school has an average attendance of about 180, with 250 on the
books; two European and four coloured teachers. Well reported on by Government
Inspector.

"Services at Mission Chapel on Sunday afternoons, preceded by Sunday school.

"Matins and Evensong at a small room recently built at native location every
Sunday.

"Four Morning Services held every Sunday at native compounds of various
mining companies, involving a circuit of some four or five miles.

"This native work is the result we have to show for the Society's grant of £100
per annum. But there is a native population of somewhere about 10,000 in this
parish; what can one Missionary do?"

There are about fifty native communicants. Beaconsfield is a great
diamond-mining centre, and Mr. Tobias thus describes the conditions of
the work among the natives employed:—

"Of late the mining companies have been adopting the compound system, that is
to say, the native labourers are confined during their leisure hours in barracks, and
thus are preserved from many evils, above all from the temptations of the canteens or
liquor shops. Here is an opportunity for Christian work, for we have the *entrée* of
every compound. But you will see that this system has made the need for men more
imperative than ever. Formerly a Missionary could gather his congregation to
certain central points, now he must go to the compounds, for they are unable to come
to him.

"There are two great mines in my parish—Dutoitspan and Bultfontein. Bultfontein we are able to work with something like completeness, but Dutoitspan we
cannot touch; we have virtually abandoned it to whatever influence can be brought
to bear upon it by religious bodies outside the Church.

"I do think that the Society may be content with the work done by the present
grant; a flourishing Mission school, seven or eight services every Sunday, one man's
hard and constant work is surely a fair return, but may I not plead most earnestly
for another grant of £100? Not for the purpose of increasing the income of the
Missionary, not to pay debts already incurred, but to provide another Missionary to
work in the neglected mine. I should be quite prepared to make the grant dependent
upon the employment of another clergyman in the Mission work of the parish, and I
could, I feel sure, provide for the balance of his income.

"We have natives here from every part of Southern and Equatorial Africa; the
work in the compounds cannot produce a great number of baptisms and confirmations,
for the labourers are constantly coming and going; but think what an influence for
good throughout the dark continent our work in the Diamond Fields compounds
may be."

LAST November, after the conclusion of the Diocesan Synod, the Bishop
of St. John's, Kaffraria, began a long visitation of the northern part
of his Diocese, going through the St. Cuthbert's and Matatiela districts.
We must make two extracts from the record of this journey. The first
relates to a heathen chief, and is one of innumerable evidences of the
working of the leaven among those who live in South Africa and have
not yet acknowledged Christ for their Lord:—

"We were to sleep that night at Umnyama's, a Hlubi chief, who, though still a
heathen and a polygamist, has a strong leaning to Christianity and to the Church.

On our way to this man's location, we passed the Mandileni, where we found Mr. Green preparing the candidates for to-morrow's confirmation. After confirming one very old man in his hut, we went on to Ummyama's. He received us very heartily, and soon he asked me after the bell I promised to get him in England, and for which he had given me two sovereigns; I told him it was on the way. Ummyama is really an intelligent man, and anxious that his people should embrace Christianity and be educated. It is, I believe, the fact of his having a plurality of wives alone that keeps him back himself from baptism. He is wonderfully well up in the history of the last fifty years—of South African history from a native point of view; he has lived among Basutus and the Orange River Fingoes, as well as in the colony; and he is a great talker. At the confirmation which took place at Qlthr the next morning, 40 were confirmed, and there were 80 communicants; it was in a large hut at the chief's kraal. A church is being built 50 feet long, some six miles away, which I did not see. This interesting Mission we left at about 4 o'clock in the afternoon."

The other extract is illustrative of the faithfulness of native Churchmen :—

'From here we rode for some four hours to a Basutu village, belonging to one Isaac Masin. He has kept up his Churchmanship, for which he is indebted, under God, to the Missionaries of the Diocese of Bloemfontein, in Basutaland proper, under circumstances which might easily have daunted a less sincere Churchman. We have not many Basutus in the Diocese, and very little Church work among them. They are a most interesting people, much more amenable to new impressions, more easily civilised, more industrious, and not less warlike than the best specimens of our Kaffir tribes, the Saikar and Sealikar; physically they are hardly so fine. We have a good many Fingoes who have made some progress in refinements, but I have never seen roses and everlasting flowers twined into wreaths in any of the houses where they were expecting a visit, as we saw at Isaac's; and roses grown at his own village! In the morning there were about six people confirmed, who afterwards partook of the Communion; the singing was particularly sweet, and the whole service was reverent, in spite of its being in a dwelling house. The chief of the district, Lebenya, came, and after service we had a short interview with him, and asked him to allow a school chapel to be built in the village of Masin; he told us that he could give no answer, as he had not come prepared for such a request, but would give us an answer soon."

KILLARNEY parish numbers 244 souls in connection with the Church, but it responds wonderfully to the zeal of its Rector, Archdeacon Wynne. During 1888 this little flock raised £208 for various objects external to the parish, and of this £49. 12s. 10d. was remitted to the Society.

GREAT interest has attached to the Waldenses, and their unique position. Peter Waldo lived in the twelfth century, and the Waldenses claim an even greater antiquity than this for their religious system. Their courage, their unworldliness, and their love for the Holy Scriptures have won them a good name; but sympathy with them must be restricted; for few of their fellow-Christians can fail to be repelled by some one or other of their singular tenets. Few people, for instance, would like the whole of the following list: Abolition of all oaths, of property, and of judicial sentences, mutilation and disuse of the creeds, and a distinction between bishops, priests, and deacons,

with no true succession, and with laymen permitted to act as cele-
brants of their sacraments. *The History of the Waldenses of Italy*, by
E. Comba, D.D. (London, Truslove & Shirley), is a book of 357 pages,
describing the history, literature, and religious life of one of the
strangest bodies of Christians. Their views have been subject to frequent
change, and their doctrinal standard has a tendency downwards. Those
who wish to learn more of this curious, though not very attractive, phase
of religion will no doubt find the account in Dr. Comba's book sufficiently full and detailed.

THE Society has sustained a loss in the death of W. W. Taylor, Esq.,
J.P., of Preston, who for many years acted as the Hon. Treasurer
of the Preston S.P.G. Association. The local newspapers fully expressed
the high esteem in which he was held throughout the community. Mr.
Taylor was a constant and zealous supporter of the Society, and he realised
the truth that foreign Mission work is essential to the Church's life.

SUGGESTED SUBJECTS FOR PRAYER.

For all the Missions exposed to peril by the troubles in Eastern
Africa, for the steadfastness of the native converts, the support of the
Missionaries, and a happy issue out of all their difficulties.

For India, that the spread of Western thought among its peoples may
lead to their embracing the truth of God.

For the Missions in Madagascar, that the Church may be enabled to
seize her opportunities.

For those suffering from the famine in China, and that the recipients
of Christian charity may listen to Christian truth.

MONTHLY MEETING.

THE Monthly Meeting of the Society was held at 19 Delahay Street on Friday, January
18, at 2 p.m., the Rev. B. Compton in the chair. There were also present the Bishop of
Antigua, and Rev. B. Belcher, *Vice-Presidents;* C. Churchill, Esq., Canon Elwyn, General
Gililan, Hon. and Rev. E. C. Glyn, Sir F. J. Goldsmid, K.C.S.I., C.B., J. R. Kindersley, Esq.,
General Lowry, C.B., General Maclagan, Rev. J. Frewen Moor, Rev. F. H. Murray, H. C.
Saunders, Esq., Q.C., General Sawyer, S. G. Stopford-Sackville, Esq., General Tremenheere,
C.B., and S. Wreford, Esq., *Members of the Standing Committee;* Rev. Dr. Baker, Rev.
Canon Barker, C. G. Burke, Esq., Rev. F. J. Causton, Rev. J. C. Clark, Rev. A. Cooper,
Rev. T. Darling, Rev. H. J. Day, Dr. De Tatham, Rev. R. S. Hassard, Rev. T. Hill, Rev.
S. C. Hore, Rev. J. W. Horsley, Rev. W. F. Kelly, H. Laurence, Esq., Rev. D. Long, Rev.
J. Maconechy, General Nicolls, Rev. L. E. Owen, Rev. G. C. Reynell, Rev. G. E. Tatham,
Rev. G. Thompson, Rev. W. Wallace, J. F. Ward, Esq., *Members of the Society.*

1. After prayers, the minutes of the last meeting were read.
2. On behalf of the Standing Committee there were proposed for re-election as
members of that body in February, General Lowry, C.B., General Sawyer, and the
Hon. and Rev. E. C. Glyn; for election, Colonel Hardy, Sir H. Cartwright, and the
Rev. W. Allen Whitworth; and to supply a vacancy caused by death, the Rev. J. M.
Burn-Murdoch.
3. It was announced that the Standing Committee would propose at the February
meeting the following for election as Vice-Presidents of the Society, viz., Bishop J. F.
Mackarness, Bishop Rawle, the Bishop of Bedford, the Bishop of Penrith, the Bishop
of Leicester, the Bishop of Guildford, the Bishop of Glasgow and Galloway, the
Assistant Bishop of Jamaica, the Bishop-designate of Trinidad, the Rev. Canon Liddon,
D.D., the Rev. J. W. Ayre, and C. J. Bunyon, Esq.

4. The resignation of a member was reported in accordance with the 15th bye-law.

5. The Rev. E. Sloman, from Guiana, addressed the members. He began by claiming that the climate of Demerara was not unhealthy. The temperature ranges from 80 degrees to 90 degrees; the heat is moderated by the trade winds, while the cases of yellow fever were comparatively few.

The colony contains a great variety of races—English, Portuguese, Chinese, Negroes, Coolies from India, and the Aboriginal Indians of Guiana. There are a hundred thousand Coolies working on the sugar estates drawn from all parts of India. They have broken caste by coming, and the majority of them are really without religion; there are no zenanas with their adverse influence, and few persecuting relatives. There are, therefore, great opportunities for Mission work among them. A great difficulty is the variety of language, even on one estate. Hindustani, however, is pretty generally understood. Four of the clergy and sixteen native catechists speak Hindustani. At the training school for catechists the course lasts three years, or with a student, who promises to be fitted for ordination, five years.

The number of aboriginals is variously stated at from twenty to fifty thousand.

The Chinese were of such bad habits that the Government stopped their immigration. This checked their wickedness, and they are now the best colonists and Christians. There are ten thousand of them, half of them being Christians. They produce excellent catechists, and are liberal out of their scanty means, in one case raising £200 for building a church. Mr. Sloman described one of the Chinese congregations, which had its church, school, and catechist, without any pecuniary help from anyone. Once when he visited them he celebrated the Holy Communion in English, while they sang the responses in Chinese, and although it was a week-day there were thirty-six communicants. He also described a visit to the Missions among the aborigines, stating how one congregation sent to Georgetown, distant twenty-four hours' journey from them, in order to be able to give him better food than they could provide among themselves; while he had seen at the Holy Communion, kneeling side by side, the descendants of cannibals, who had been mortal enemies of each other. Their offerings were made not only for the work in their own Mission, but for the Missions in the diocese as a whole, for they were anxious that the gospel which had reached them should be given to the other tribes.

6. The Rev. John Tsan Baw, the first Burmese clergyman of the Church of England, also addressed the members, and described briefly his work under the Rev. J. A. Colbeck, and under the Rev. Dr. Marks in the Diocese of Rangoon.

7. All the candidates proposed at the meeting in November were elected into the corporation. The following were proposed for election in March:—

Rev. A. G. Barker, Sherfield-on-Loddon, Basingstoke; Rev. C. A. Dutton, Lothersdale, Keighley; Rev. J. R. Feilden, Honingham, Norwich; Rev. W. Cowper Johnson, jun., Yaxham, East Dereham; Rev. N. C. W. Radcliffe, 62 Bromley Common, Kent; Rev. R. W. Stockdale, 12 Laurel Grove, Armley, Leeds; Sir H. B. Bacon, Bart., Thirsk; Rev. H. R. Howard, Gainsborough; Rev. H. S. Oriel, 74 Holland Road, Kensington, W.; George Griffin Griffin, Esq., Newton Court, Monmouth; Rev. C. Grant-Dalton, Wincanton; Rev. Charles Powell, East Coker, Yeovil; Rev. Alfred Thornley, South Leverton, Lincoln; Rev. Canon J. Trebeck, Southwell, Notts; Very Rev. T. Hare, Dean of Ossory, The Deanery, Kilkenny, Ireland; Rev. W. Bedford, St. Michael's, Manchester; Rev. Ifon Ll. Harry, Coldhurst, Oldham; Rev. T. B. Armitstead, Winmarleigh, Garstang; Rev. E. A. Brown, Burnage, Manchester; Rev. J. Nunn, Ardwick, Manchester; Rev. C. Fullerton Smith, Lund, Preston; Rev. G. B. Stones, St. Thomas', Garstang; and Rev. E. T. Wigg, Royton, Oldham.

THE SOCIETY'S INCOME FOR 1888.

		£	s.	d.
I. GENERAL FUND—				
Subscriptions, Donations, and Collections	...	105,910	1	1
Legacies ...	...	8,552	11	5
Rents, Dividends, &c....	...	3,222	2	6
TOTAL RECEIPTS FOR THE GENERAL FUND	...	117,684	15	0
II. SPECIAL FUNDS ...	...	20,382	2	6
TOTAL INCOME ...	...	£138,066	17	6

In addition to the above, the Society's Treasurers had received for Invested Funds, held by the Society as a Corporation for Specific Trusts by request, the sum of £1,429. 0s. 8d.

In this sum of £105,910. 1s. 1d. are included two gifts of Securities, worth £25,296 and £2,268 respectively. The former was "A Thankoffering to Almighty God for the extension of the Church in the Colonies and Dependencies of the British Empire and beyond it;" the latter was a Memorial of one who had long been a munificent supporter of the Society.

THE MISSION FIELD.

The field is the world. The seed is the word of God.

APRIL 1, 1889.

THE MISSIONARY CANDIDATE'S STUDIES.

BY THE REV. G. F. MACLEAR, D.D., WARDEN OF ST. AUGUSTINE'S COLLEGE, CANTERBURY, AND HONORARY CANON OF CANTERBURY CATHEDRAL.

" Piety does not supply the want of learning, and, more, it is not even a true piety, a solid, an enlightened piety, if it does not inspire its possessor with a decided taste for theological learning." *

IN the *Mission Field* of November 1888 I wrote an article on " Missionary Vocation." I have been requested more than once to follow it up with a paper on the Missionary's studies, or his intellectual equipment for the great work to which he proposes, by God's help, to devote himself. This I shall now try to do, and to offer a few suggestions which may, perhaps, be found useful to those for whom they are intended, and who have not had the advantage of a University training.†

I.

I assume, then, that those whom I am thinking of possess inclination and aptitude for Missionary work, and, on the strength of certain gifts and predispositions, are justified in believing themselves called to the great and arduous task of being "ambassadors for Christ" in distant lands. Now, in what does the intellectual equipment of the Missionary candidate consist? It consists in the possession of (i.) *general* and (ii.) of *special* knowledge.

(i.) *General Knowledge.*—There must, as we saw in our last Paper, be an acquaintance with the rudiments, at least, of general knowledge, such as English grammar, geography, history, and elementary mathematics.‡ An ill-informed Missionary cannot expect to be of any real service, especially in these days when so much is being done for education in all parts of the world. It is quite true that God does not *need* a man's knowledge. But He certainly needs as little his *ignorance*, and it is mocking Him to offer Him in this high and difficult service an uninformed and uninstructed mind.

---

* L'Abbé Dubois' *Zeal in the Ministry.* 4th ed., N.Y.
† At the Universities there is no lack of teachers far better able to advise those who have had the advantage of education in our public schools.
‡ For the training of the mind to habits of exact thought, and following the steps of an argument, an acquaintance with at least two books of Euclid, thoroughly mastered, is of the utmost advantage, and the importance of a fair knowledge of elementary mathematics can hardly be over-rated.

Under the head of General Knowledge comes an acquaintance with some branch of physical science. "The perfect Theologian, if we dare to imagine such a man, would require," it has been said,[*] "to be a perfect scholar, a perfect physicist, a perfect philosopher. And the sincere student of Theology will strive, according to his opportunities and powers, to gain a firm hold on the principles, at least, of scholarship, of physics,[†] of philosophy." Now, without aiming at attaining such a high standard as this, it is certain that, of all men, missionary priests and deacons ought to be so far instructed in physical science as not to betray an utter inability to discuss intelligently some of the religious difficulties which are so often supposed to be connected with some of the teachings of science.

And next comes scholarship. If the first requisite for an intelligent study of the Holy Scriptures is a fair acquaintance with the original languages, the Missionary student must spare no efforts to attain to some degree of accurate knowledge of at least the Greek of the Greek Testament, and, if he cannot manage Hebrew,[‡] the Latin of the Vulgate.[§] As regards the Greek and Latin languages, the student will find that his most real assistance will come from a diligent handling of his grammar and lexicon. If he has the advantage of being at a Theological College, he will find comments on the text supplied partly in lecture and partly in books suggested by the lecturer. But the student will find it best to *do as much as he can himself*, and not slavishly depend on the instruction he may receive from another. If he prepares the text to the best of his ability, looks out *for himself* and notes down the rarer or more difficult words, and by diligent study *makes the portion set his own*, he will do more real good than by *trusting to the brains of any teacher*.[‖] The result of his labour may be, doubtless will be, very imperfect, but at any rate it will be honestly obtained, and will have a reality which it cannot otherwise possess, and will abundantly reward persevering toil. "The mere acquisition of secondary information exhausts and enfeebles, while all independent work strengthens and inspires."

II.

(ii.) *Special Knowledge.*—So much for the general knowledge requisite for the Missionary candidate as preparatory to the more special knowledge of Theological subjects. The study of Theology as

---

[*] By Dr. Westcott, in his paper on *Theological Examinations*.

[†] For the advantages of acquaintance with some branch of physical science, see the remarks in the previous Paper.

[‡] The study of Hebrew commences at St. Augustine's with men of the first term, and is carried on throughout the course. It is recorded of the Rev. W. H. Brett, for forty years a zealous Missionary in Guiana, that "most of the knowledge he acquired was self-acquired, and was by no means confined to a narrow range. He was a fair Latin and Greek scholar, and his knowledge of his Greek Testament was very good. He set aside a portion of every day for the reading at least of one chapter of the New Testament in the original. This he continued to do as long as his health permitted him, that is to say, to within a few months of his death." Josa's *Life of the Rev. W. H. Brett*, Wells Gardner, 1887.

[§] "It seems to me that we have lost much in every way from our neglect of a Version which has influenced the Theology of the West more profoundly than we know."—Dr. Westcott's *Introduction to the Gospel of St. John*, p. xcvi.

[‖] A word may be thrown in here on the value of retranslation. It has been well said that it is one of the most efficient and instructive tests of a knowledge of the text. "A single verse retranslated and compared with the original every day will bring a power of insight into the meaning of the Greek Testament which cannot perhaps be gained in any other way."—Dr. Westcott on *Theological Study* in the *Student's Guide to the University of Cambridge*, p. 16.

a speciality is essential to securing real ministerial efficiency. "The present is an age of technical education," said the Bishop of Lincoln the other day to the students at the Theological College in that city,* "the sciences in their progress have of necessity divided. The several organs of the body, the eye, the ear, the foot are seen to involve forces of such complexity and such divinely arranged intricacies of organisation as to require the attention of separate departments of the great medical profession, and separate hospitals have been formed for their study and their treatment. And as it is with medicine and law, so it is with the queen of sciences—Theology." Those who believe in her existence have begun to treat her with more reasonable respect, and it is recognised that she demands much of those who would be "workmen who need not to be ashamed." That the first and most important requisite is personal piety is here assumed. It was dwelt upon with sufficient fulness in the previous paper. But it cannot be too much insisted on that theological study, especially with a view to work abroad, must be prosecuted in *a becoming spirit worthy of its solemn and pre-eminent importance.* To take it up lightly, to treat it as a mere means to an end, and that end the utterly ignoble one of obtaining a position abroad by passing an examination, is to degrade the greatest and most sacred of sciences, and entails a special penalty. For an unworthy study of theology brings a Nemesis peculiarly its own. But what are the signs of this becoming spirit ? A few only can be enumerated here, but amongst others there stand out pre-eminently ; (i.) a spirit of reverence, (ii.) a spirit of enthusiasm, (iii.) a spirit of self-consecration and (iv.) a spirit of thankfulness.

(i.) *A Spirit of Reverence.*—A reverent appreciation of the sacredness of Theological study will mark the man who has the true Missionary spirit. This spirit of reverence is not so common as it ought to be. The pages of the Holy Scriptures are perused much as those of Homer or Thucydides, of Horace or Juvenal. The Gospel or the Epistle to be prepared gets to be treated as a sort of book for lectures. Unless great care is taken, the student will forget that the Bible contains "the oracles of God." "The chief and top of knowledge," says George Herbert, "consists in the Book of Books, the Store-house and Magazine of life and comfort." The true Missionary student is bound to approach the sacred volume in a spirit of reverent loyalty to Him, who Himself studied its pages during His Incarnate Life, and who with the words *It is written* proved Himself "more than conqueror" over His crafty and relentless foe. And what is true of the study of the Bible is true also of the study of dogmatics. Unless we have a deep sense of the certainty and importance of the truths of the Christian revelation, unless we regard dogma as represented in the Creeds as the expression in the logical form of doctrine of what the Bible reveals in the popular form of life and action,† we may learn nothing but

* *The Father's Business.* A sermon preached at the first festival of the Theological College, Lincoln, Nov. 27 1888. Lincoln : James Williamson, 1888.
† See Schaaf's *Creeds of Christendom,* p. 3 ; Westcott's *Historic Faith,* pp. 22, 23.

negatives or controversial facts. This is not what our people want at home or abroad. They want primitive and Catholic truth. They want it dogmatically stated. They want it as a help to practical piety. " They want it as a basis for faith and morals, not an eternal negative, a sort of Christian agnosticism." * If the student would give his people hereafter what they really need, he must cultivate a spirit of reverence in handling the oracles of God and in making himself acquainted with the doctrines that they teach.

(ii.) *A Spirit of Enthusiasm.*—The queen of the sciences demands of her students earnestness and enthusiasm. It is the zeal of *the diligent inquirer* alone which discovers the hidden treasures of the Word and the depths of the doctrines of the Church. An apathetic,† listless way of just touching sacred truths with the tips of the fingers never has and never can win any true reward. " Scripture," says St. Augustine, " has its first draughts, its second draughts, and its third draughts." The superficial dealer with the Word who studies it coldly and unwillingly, as if performing an unwelcome task, who consults the oracle and expects no lively answer from its lips, cannot expect that the *Word of Christ will dwell in him richly.* ‡ The enthusiastic student alone will delight and be able to trace in non-Christian and pre-Christian systems § sparks of " the Light which lighteneth every man." He alone will trace, as he reads ecclesiastical history, forms of modern errors, the origins of modern difficulties, and in this or that controversy " old foes with new faces." ‖ A lazy, half-hearted spirit degrades all Theological study. It wins nothing and deserves to win nothing.

(iii.) *A Spirit of Self-consecration.*—Above all is needed a spirit of self-consecration. The necessity for *really consecrating* the intellectual faculties, whether great or small, to the acquisition of Theological knowledge is not half sufficiently realised. *For their sakes I consecrate Myself,*¶ said our Lord. This was the deep underlying, all-penetrating motive of the Incarnate Son of God, the true " Pastor Pastorum," the true ideal of the Christian Missionary. *For their sakes I consecrate Myself.* " I never shall forget," said the present Professor of Pastoral Theology at Oxford the other day at Eton College,** "the emphasis with which these words were left ringing through my mind by the Bishop of Durham in an address which he gave to some of us at Cuddesdon. Ever since, they have seemed to me to mark one's highest—no, one's *only*—hope of not failing utterly in such a trust as God has given to us." " Nothing," he continues, " seems much more sure

* See Webb's *Guide for Seminarians* (James Pott, New York, 1887) ; Gore's *Hints for the Study of Theology,* p. i. (Skeffington & Son, 1888).

† The true Missionary spirit is " an enthusiasm enwrapping like a flame all the faculties of the soul, and transfiguring weak and commonplace natures by the purifying and invigorating energy of a supernatural force." Canon Liddon's *Advent in S. Paul's,* i. p. 91.

‡ Col. iii. 16.

§ The excellent little manuals, published by the Society for Promoting Christian Knowledge, on Epicureanism, Stoicism, Hinduism, Buddhism, and Confucianism ought to be in the hands of all who are seeking to plant in other lands the truth which shall absorb error.

‖ " Some of our most dangerous errors, some of our most depressing doubts, would be removed if we could learn to look on earlier seasons of conflict and trial in the Church's history through the eyes of those who witnessed them." Westcott's *Religious Office of the Universities,* p. 110.

¶ St. John xii. 19. " He showed through His life how all that is human may be brought wholly into the service of God." Westcott, *in loc.*

** See *The Hallowing of Work.* Addresses given at Eton by Professor Paget, p. 16. Rivingtons, 1888.

in human life than the law that it is only in an unselfish use that the
gifts of intellect reach their full development, and go on from strength
to strength." * This is true of all intellectual study. But it is pre-
eminently true of theological study. It loses all its purity and worth
when it is pursued for selfish ends, for display, for popularity, for social
advancement, for securing a profession. The true Missionary student will
cultivate the spirit of self-consecration. "There are those," he will often
say to himself, "who will in some distant land be committed to my
charge. For them I must consecrate myself. For their sakes I must
seek to lay by all the knowledge I can. To them I must devote my
powers of mind and intellect. My *best* work—not my second best—is due
to them. For their sakes I will consecrate my studies, and strive hereafter to bring forth out of my treasure things new and old."

(iv.) *A Spirit of Thankfulness.—In everything*, says St. Paul, *give
thanks.* From this *everything* we too often exclude our Theological
studies and any progress we may make in them. And yet, "the power
of knowing," says a great teacher, "comes from God, and for every
fresh bit of knowledge acquired thanksgiving should be offered." A
spirit of thankfulness for any knowledge we may acquire, whether from
the study of a Psalm,† or a Scripture character, or a parable of our Lord,
or the life of some greater leader in ecclesiastical history, or some eminent
pioneer in the Mission field,‡ or some instance of that secret power of
revival and renewal of which the Missionary history of the Christian
Church is so full, or some meaning discovered in some Greek or Latin
word will keep the student, to a certain extent, at least, free from those
curses of theological studies, on the one hand, self-conceit, self-display,
and intellectual pride, and, on the other, a lazy acquiescence in an average
standard of attainment. *I thank Thee, O Father*, said our Incarnate Lord,
*that Thou hast hid these things from the wise and prudent, and hast revealed
them unto babes.*§ If *He* could thus thank God, who was Himself the
Truth, shall not one, who is, at the best, a very babe in the science of
theology, thank God for anything he learns, for any fresh acquisition of
knowledge he may make in language, or history, or dogma, or the Holy
Scriptures? To ask the question is to answer it. A spirit of reverence,
a spirit of enthusiasm, a spirit of self-consecration, a spirit of thankfulness will keep the Missionary student from incurring the Nemesis which,
sooner or later, awaits the pursuit of theological studies from secondary
motives and selfish purposes. He who would be a faithful and true
pastor, a real "ambassador for Christ" in distant lands, must, of all
men, try to forget himself in his work of preparation. And forgetfulness
of self, humility, and a recognition of the infinite majesty of Him, who

---

* See *The Hallowing of Work.* Addresses given at Eton by Professor Paget, p. 14. Rivingtons 1888.
† It is not the study of the text of selected portions only of the Bible which the Missionary student shall
prosecute. It is a *general knowledge* of the contents of the Bible which is so important. "Ignorance here," it
has been remarked, "is fatal when it meets the devotion to their sacred books of those who profess other faiths
in other lands."
‡ The Missionary candidate is bound to make himself acquainted, at least, to some extent, with the history
of Missions in the past, and the progress of Missions in the present age of the Church. The records of the ventures of faith made by brave pioneers in the early ages have each and all their important lessons and encourage-
ments.
§ St. Luke x. 21.

reveals Himself in His Word, are the main handmaids of real progress in Theological science, the true helpers towards the attainment of that *full knowledge of the truth which is according to godliness.*[*]

III.—HINTS TO STUDENTS.

(*a.*) *Bible Knowledge.*—(i.) Follow and attend to the lessons read at Matins and Evensong, for they will bring before you a number of Scripture facts in their historical order. (ii.) Besides what you are preparing slowly and carefully, read other portions of Scripture rapidly with regard to the main thoughts, and the broad historical events. (iii.) Make yourself acquainted with the geography and physical features of the countries mentioned in the Bible, and with Oriental manners and customs. (iv.) Learn by heart considerable portions of Holy Scripture— strive to be a good textionist.

(*b.*) *Greek Testament or Latin Author.*—(i.) Write down every word which is new to you. (ii.) Of a verb always write down the principal tenses. (iii.) Note the derivation of each word if the Lexicon gives it. (iv.) Look over your vocabularies from time to time. (v.) If a translation of a piece has been given you in Lecture, go over it again and again by yourself, and test yourself whether you can really write it out correctly.

(*c.*) *Liturgies.*—(i.) Read your Prayer Book carefully. (ii.) Learn by heart as many Collects as you can. (iii.) Take pains with your Lecture notes, getting first a clear outline, and then fill in details. (iv.) Look at the originals to which you are directed, and make great use of you *Latin Prayer Book.*

(*d.*) *Church or Missionary History.*—(i.) Never read without an atlas. (ii.) Make a Chronological Table *for yourself*, and keep adding to it. (iii.) Always be reading *at least* two Books on the period you are studying. (iv.) Group the facts round the life of one or more great men who lived in it. (v.) When you are to begin a period, (*a*) first read the whole period right through in some full sketch, without pausing on details; (*b*) then study it in detail; (*c*) then try to see it all as a great unity, and trace in it a continuous purpose.

(*e.*) *Note Books.*—Write on the right hand side only; leave the left hand side for additional notes. Make a short analysis of the important Divisions, and master this analysis. *Often look through your Note Books,* and call up to mind the thought or information which your analysis suggests. If a man simply makes his notes in his book, and does not *get them up,* "his mind will be empty, and his self-content perfect." †

(*f.*) *Examinations.*—The wise way to prepare for Examination is to take time by the forelock, *to read up and digest your notes gradually, to assimilate* what you have acquired, and to test yourself by frequent self-questioning whether you really know your Books. To leave everything to the last is bad with all studies, but it is a positive degradation of Theological studies.

<hr>

° Titus i. 1.   † Archbishop Benson, *Vigilemus et Oremus,* p. 21.

MADAGASCAR.

I HAVE just returned from a visitation tour on the coast, and will, therefore, report to you first the progress of our work in that direction.

My first point was Mahanoro, which is at present the centre of the more southern portion of our work. I hope, however, that your Committee will before long enable us to establish a fresh centre at Masindrano, commonly called Mananjara, which is four days' journey, about 100 miles south of Mahanoro.

You will remember that when I was here last year the schools were in vacation. I was unable, therefore, personally to inspect the work. This year, however, I was able so to time my visit that I found everything in full operation. In Mahanoro itself we have two very good schools—we have a boarding-school for the girls as well as a day-school—which are under the care of our admirable lady superintendent, Miss Lawrence, who is ably assisted by Miss Tessier, whom she has trained herself. On the day appointed for the inspection of this school, the Governor, Rainisolofo, attended by his officers, was present, and expressed great satisfaction at the efficiency of the school. Miss Lawrence has, however, great difficulties to contend against, and from a source the existence of which English people will hardly credit. Will it be believed that the creole traders look upon the young girls of this school as their legitimate prey, and that the utmost care and watchfulness are necessary to hinder their abduction? And this evil is increased by the horrible fact that the mothers of these children assist the designs of the profligate creoles! I can give you no better idea of the utter shamelessness of these men than the fact that one of them wrote a letter, which appeared in the *Madagascar Times*, complaining of Miss Lawrence's conduct in endeavouring to raise a sense of decency and shame in the hearts of her pupils, and this letter bore the strange signature of "Justitia." These creoles are, I grieve to say, generally British subjects from Mauritius.

The inspection of the boys' school, which was also attended by the Governor and his suite, gave very satisfactory results. It has been for some years under the charge of Philip Ravelonanosy, formerly a student at St. Paul's College, and I think the best native that we have trained; he is an excellent teacher and a good man. My last act at Mahanoro was to ordain him deacon, and he is now transferred to the very difficult post of Vatomandry.

In company with Mr. Alfred Smith, the priest in charge of this district, I proceeded to visit several other towns in the south.

At Betsizaraina we have another college man. He has a very difficult post, amid a practically heathen population, degraded by drunkenness and its attendant abominations, but we had a good muster of some 70 children in the school, and they gave evidence of having been carefully taught.

The following day we proceeded for some distance up the Mangoro River, and then for about two hours inland, where we found a considerable town rejoicing in a wonderful name. This is quite a new station and exceedingly promising. The chief of the village was most friendly. There appeared more than 100 children at the roll-call, and here we have a total freedom from the miserable opposition of the Hova—the native Independent. Our only difficulty here is that we have not at present a teacher strong enough for the place, but, on the other hand, this fact in itself is most satisfactory as indicating the extension of our work. Some years ago the pessimist cry was, "We shall never find work enough for the men whom we are turning out year by year from our college." Now, on the other hand, our difficulty is to find efficient teachers for the new stations which are constantly, and especially on the coast, opening out to us.

The next town we visited was Ambodiharina. There we have an excellent man, John Shirley, whose name you will probably remember. He has been attached to us from his childhood, having been originally handed over to Mr. Chiswell by his master at Foule Point. We had, however, by the help of friends in England, to purchase his freedom. He passed his examination for entrance into the college before we could complete his purchase, and he was, therefore, unable to reside for a year. At the end of that time we were able to set him free. He resided two years at the college, and as he was urgently required for work on the coast we made his an exceptional case, and allowed him to pass out of the college after a residence of two years. He is a native of the coast, and therefore very acceptable to the Betsimisaraka. I have never been in a place in which the work seemed to be more satisfactory. He has a native churchwarden, a most intelligent man, with a keen interest in natural history, full of anecdote, and not afraid to discourse about the traditions and superstitions of the Betsimisaraka, which makes him a most agreeable companion. In this town we seemed to be entirely free from the pernicious influence of the Hova. John Shirley is remarkable for his care and reverence in the services of the Church and for his skill in teaching music. He is intellectually inferior to Philip Ravelonanosy, but is a valuable man, and his wife is also a notable woman. There are about 150 children in the school, all in beautiful order.

We started south on the following day, and reached Andranotsara for breakfast. There we have a man named Abel, a Betsimisaraka, as teacher. Thirteen years ago this man, then a boy of ten years, accompanied me in my previous journey to the north, after which he became an inmate of my house and was a scholar at the high school for five years. We did not think it advisable to send him to college, but he is a good teacher, with a fair knowledge of his Bible, and, what is very rare in Madagascar, a high character for truth and probity. He surprised us with 47 candidates for holy baptism and 5 for confirmation.

Our next point was Ampanatoana, where we met two other churches. Of course a large number of children were assembled, and with the extra congregation the little church became an impossibility, so we held our services, and with very good effect, in the open air.

I had quite intended to have penetrated further south to Masindrano, but the distance was greater than I had supposed, and it was necessary that I should return for the Ember season to Mahanoro. I resolved, therefore, to reserve my visit to the southern stations and the Vorimo tribe for next year.

On my return to Mahanoro, I ordained Philip Ravelonanosy and John Shirley as deacons, and after that left for Vatomandry, accompanied by the former, whom I established as pastor of that district. This will, I am afraid, be for some time a very difficult post, since " the powers that be" are in strong opposition to us, but some day there will be a change of governors, which will make matters more satisfactory.

I proceeded next to Andovoranto, which is just a day's journey distant. There I found everything in excellent order—the boys' school in the hands of a very good teacher, and Miss Parker with her happy-looking girls' boarding-school. Mr. Jones has been able to open a new and promising station besides Vatomandry, which is in his district, so that we have good progress to record here also, but the heathenism and vices of Andovoranto are appalling. I spent St. Michael's day and Sunday at the Mission-house and confirmed 46 candidates.

On Monday, October 1, I started for Tamatave. There our work is at present at a very low ebb. All was shattered and dispersed by the war, and we are working in the presence of very great difficulties. The Hova Governor is an old Independent pastor, and uses his great influence secretly and very unscrupulously against us. The Jesuits also are very strong and are in active opposition against us. It is a work requiring a good deal of faith, and no little patience, to build up our church again. The havoc wrought by the hurricane was terrible. I was able to visit Mahasoa, where I found our pretty little church entirely destroyed. We have at last been able to place a teacher at the town which I visited six years ago, two days' journey west, and from which I hope we may be able to reach many of the Betsimisaraka who hide themselves from the Hova in the forest.

On Monday, October 8, I started for the north in company with
Crispin Andrew Rakotovao, the native deacon in charge of Tamatave.
We passed by Ifontsy, where, I regret to say, all our efforts have failed;
our teacher has died, and we do not see our way to placing another there.
This is due partly to the effect of the French war, partly to the degrada-
tion caused by rum, but chiefly to the adverse influence of the Hova
Governor at Tamatave.

After passing Ifontsy we entered a district under the control of the
Governor of Foule Point. This man received us most warmly, and we
found from our catechist that he does everything in his power to
forward our work. We have a good school of about 70 children, and I
think the day is not far distant when the Hova school will combine with
ours.

We passed from thence to Mahambo, which I visited some years ago,
and where we hope to open a station soon, and so to Fenoarivo. Here
we have suffered great loss in the death of our former catechist, who was
a man universally respected, and very skilful in medicine. He was
accidentally poisoned by eating a wild yam. We have replaced him by
another college man, who promises much, but of whom it is not possible
to say much at present. Here too, as at Foule Point, we had a very
friendly reception from the Governor, who will evidently place no
obstacles in our way. We spent Sunday, October 14, here, and returned
for celebration on St. Luke's day to Foule Point, and so to Tamatave for
the following Sunday. After this, I started for the capital, spending
another Sunday at Andovoranto, and arriving at Antananarivo on
November 3, having been absent exactly two months.

There is not much more to be said about our work in Imerina,
beyond what I said in my letter of last year.

We still suffer from the fact that our only priest in the capital is of
necessity master also and chief teacher in the high school, in which
he teaches regularly eighteen hours a week; besides which he has the
care of the printing, and the charge of twenty-five stations east and west
of the city. It is obvious that these stations must be very much left to
themselves, and there can be no doubt that our influence suffers
severely from this course, for we live in the midst of fierce competition
and can with difficulty hold our own. Our cathedral is approaching its completion, but unless our staff is increased we have no
power to render its services attractive. Your Committee's first desire
is "so to strengthen each existing Mission as to render it a thoroughly
efficient centre for the propagation of the Gospel around it."

The college, with its country stations now increased to eleven, continues its useful course, and the library and lecture-rooms will, we hope,
be opened in a few months.

Shortly after I sent you my report of last year, I paid a visit to

Ramainandro, and it was most refreshing to see how our work in the west had advanced. Mr. McMahon, the priest in charge, tells me that he has lately sent you full statistics of his work in that district. I am sorry to say that political complications have for the present closed the door to the western Sakalavas. Mr. McMahon has, at imminent risk of his life, paid them a second visit, but he was not allowed to place his teachers among them. Indeed we may be very thankful that his valuable life was spared; several of his men were waylaid on their return, and were either killed or taken as slaves.

SAKALAVA PEOPLE.

We have built a good parsonage at Ramainandro, but it has been done with borrowed money which must be repaid, and I again appeal to your Committee for a grant of money for this purpose.

The stone memorial church approaches completion. It will, I hope, be opened in June next year.

Looking at our work generally, I am of opinion that our Mission has *not* advanced in and around the capital, the reason for which is that for the last two years we have been undermanned, and it is not possible with our present staff to do the work which we have in hand efficiently. I beg to call your Committee's attention to the fact that Antananarivo is the heart of the country, and that weakness at the heart means general debility.

Our work on the coast, especially south of Mahanoro, increases rapidly, and has extended beyond the strength of the single Mission priest at Mahanoro. We require another English priest to be placed at Masindrano, 100 miles south of Mahanoro.

Fenoarivo, with its neighbouring town of Mahambo, is too important a centre to be left in charge of a native catechist; our work cannot extend beyond the limits of the town itself unless we have an English mission priest located there.

I have no doubt that if we could place Mr. McMahon in the far west among the Betsirary, we could open out an entirely new Mission among the western Sakalavas. But these people will not receive teachers

E 4

from the Hova, whom they justly regard with extreme suspicion. This, however, would render it necessary to have another English priest located at Ramainandro, which is a most important centre, and ought not for many years to be left in the hands of Malagasy teachers.

It is not possible to form any opinion as to the future of this interesting country. At present I should say that there is an advance in civilisation, but that religion has received a check. The system of the Independents has placed power in the hands of the natives before they were fit to receive it, and the results are deplorable.

The system pursued by the Roman Catholics is naturally very attractive to a people like the Malagasy, conspicuous for their greed. They have boarding-schools for both sexes, in which the children have everything provided for them ; and their large staff of priests with lay brothers and sisters enables them to render their schools highly effective, and they seem always to have money at their command. But so far as I can judge they do not advance in the country districts, nor have they so far taken any of our children or our people from us. I have no doubt that the French mean to advance in Madagascar ; but against this we may put their own proverb, "Les hommes s'agissent, mais Dieu les mène." Meanwhile the Malabar, or Indian, element has appeared upon the scene. These men, chiefly, I believe, from the neighbourhood of Bombay, are frugal and industrious, and have large command of capital. They have practically become masters of the commerce of Mauritius, where they are large landed proprietors ; they have now overflowed to Madagascar, and occupy largely the town of Tamatave. I believe that the trade of this country will eventually pass into their hands. These men are British subjects and unbelievers ! Meanwhile the Hovas resist all attempts at real progress by a masterly policy of inactivity. But the existence of gold in large quantities must, in my opinion, sooner or later bring about great changes. It remains only for us to work heartily while we may, and I pray your Committee to give us the means which I have indicated for making our work more efficient.

NAZARETH.

IT was the aim of the original founders of the Tinnevelly Missions to promote the formation of villages entirely Christian; where the absence of all tumult and seduction of heathenism, the simple cheerfulness of Christian life, and the daily enjoyment of Christian ordinances, should exhibit in the most advantageous and amiable light the excellence of the knowledge of Jesus Christ our Lord over that debasing system with which it is thus placed in strong and beautiful contrast. The security the converts thus enjoyed was no inconsiderable boon; but this was as nothing in comparison with the vantage-ground thus obtained for the further extension of the Gospel. It is now matter of history, and pregnant with the richest wisdom for the future, that the Christian villages planted long ago by the foresight of our elder brethren in the work have now been made, by the blessing of Almighty God, the *foci* of light and knowledge to the surrounding districts. In 1840 Bishop Spencer, of Madras, wrote: "Among many sources of comfort during my journey through Tinnevelly, one of the greatest has been a sight for which I candidly confess I was not prepared—the sight of *whole Christian villages*. He alone who has passed some time in a heathen land engaged in the work of the ministry can understand the delight I felt at finding myself met, welcomed, and surrounded by crowds of native professing Christians, whose countenances spoke a most intelligible welcome."

Nazareth Mission is in the extreme southern point of India, close to Cape Comorin. As a Christian village it soon began to exercise an influence over the surrounding districts. In 1844 the Rev. A. Caemmerer wrote to the Bishop of Madras:—"It is now my privilege to report that nearly the whole of the *Shānār* population as far as the river—which is the northern boundary of my district, and is about four miles distant—has embraced the Gospel. Since October last, 227 families, residing in seven villages, have renounced idolatry. The number of converts in them amounts to 832, and I have little doubt that many more will soon be added. In other villages, also, already in connection with Nazareth, there have been considerable accessions; their number is between 500 and 600."

At the present time the number of Christians on the roll of the Mission is no less than 6,472, with all kinds of evidence of religious vigour and spiritual life. The whole Mission under its present Missionary, the Rev. A. Margöschis, includes the Mudalur, Kadaianodai, and Christianagram Missions, and thus occupies ninety villages, with more than 13,000 Christians. The heavy responsibility which thus rests upon Mr. Margöschis he has to bear alone, as far as European helpers are concerned. Working under him are six native clergymen. From some of these we have received reports of great interest. For instance, the Rev. V. Abraham sends an account of the comparatively new work of the Kadaianodai pastorate of the Nazareth Mission, which relates several most thankworthy things.

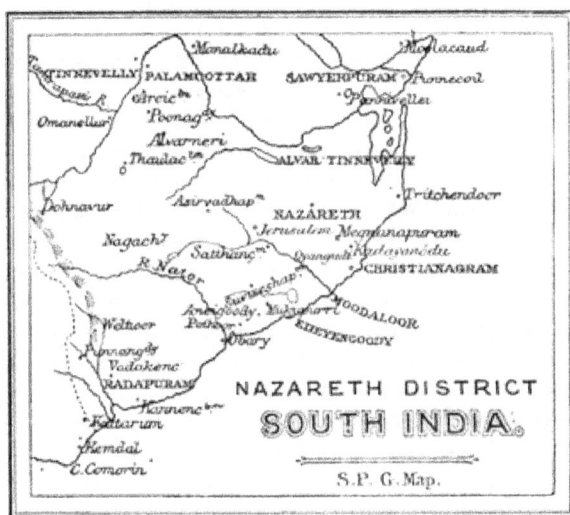

NAZARETH DISTRICT
SOUTH INDIA.
S.P.G.Map.

"In this pastorate there are 19 congregations, and the number of Mission agents is ten. The total number of Christians is 2,017, of whom 1,325 are baptised, 692 catechumens, and 461 Communicants. The number of persons who can read is 451, and there are 142 new converts.

"Nearly all are new congregations. The people can be seen only during the evening, as they are busily engaged in the daytime far from their villages. I generally go to them in the evening and stay with them, visiting many people, whom I advise and exhort in religious matters. I encourage family prayer among the people, and stir up the Mission agents to set a good example; I also advise them how to manage the congregations.

"This year there are 140 converts from heathenism, the majority of

whom are at Parkulam and Kurukatoor. Parkulam is about a mile
distant from my station; the people are landholders, who are generally
called Nadhars. They are moderately wealthy people, and were orthodox
Hindus. A few, however, were Vedantists. For many years there has
been only one single Christian soul in the place. When I visited this
place I spoke to these men about Christianity, but they would not listen
to me, and if they listened they used to argue. If any of them wished
to become Christians, the others would persecute them. They determined not to allow any church to be built in their village. My head
station being a village under their control, they tried their best to make
the Christians of that place renounce their faith by abusing them,
breaking into their houses, and carrying away their property.

"Bitter enemies of Christianity they were, but 69 of them have been
brought to the feet of Christ, and are firm in the faith. They have
given a piece of land for a church, and it is being built at their own
expense. One of them has bought a Bible and he reads it regularly.
When there was cholera in the village, this man helped the people much
by going boldly amongst them and administering medicine which he had
got from the dispensary at Nazareth.

"The Christians of Kurukatoor were converted last year and are very
firm. Sixty-one of the catechumens who had relapsed, owing to the persecution of their landlords, have since placed themselves under instruction
for Holy Baptism. There is no fear about their relapsing, because
their landlords, the Brahmins of Tenteruperi, came to the Rev. Mr.
Margöschis and promised that they would no longer molest them.
According to their promise, the Brahmins stopped their persecution, and
those who have come back are gladly learning their lessons for Baptism.
At present they hold Divine worship in a small shed which is quite
insufficient. Being very poor people, and having suffered much by
persecution, they are unable to build a church for themselves. They
have also suffered very much by cholera, which, though it carried away
ten of them and left most of them penniless, has not been able to shake
their faith.

"It gives me great pleasure to speak of the encouraging works of the
Christians of Kadaianodai. There is a small church of brick and chun-
nam here. It is called St. Thomas's Church. In my last report I said
that as the building would not hold all the people on Sundays and Festival
days, they were enlarging it at their own expense by adding a chancel and
two transepts. The work was begun in August, and finished with much
difficulty in November last. It cost Rs. 2,000 in addition to the personal
labour given without pay by the people themselves. All the labour, such
as carrying stones, sand, timber and tiles, was done by the people. The
church walls were raised and a great deal is quite new. The length
was increased by 33 ft. and the chancel is 15 ft. long. In order to make

the church cruciform, two transepts, 18 ft. by 13 ft., were added on each side of the nave. The church is now much stronger and more beautiful than it was before. The Holy Eucharist was administered for the first time in this church by the Most Rev. the Metropolitan on November 16, when the number of Communicants was 252. The dedication of this church was an event which will never be forgotten by the people, who exerted themselves to make it a joyous and festive occasion. They erected a long pandal between the church and the school which was prepared for his lordship's residence, and decorated it with leaves and plantain trees. The church was also beautifully decorated with flowers. The Metropolitan, preceded by the choir and clergy (European and Native) went in procession along the pandal into the church. The whole place resounded with music. The converts of Parkulam and Kurukatoor came and visited his lordship, who was very much pleased with them, and after giving them good advice sent them home very happy. The Rev. W. Belton, the Secretary of the M.D.C., was present, and he expressed his great pleasure at their conversion. On Sundays the harmonium is played during the service by a person who comes from Nazareth. Our heartfelt thanks are due to our Superintending Missionary, who takes so much interest in the management of all these things.

"It may be interesting to give a short account of a family at Maveedoopanni. The head of the family is ——, a widow and a good Christian. She has a daughter named Annal, who has two young sons. A time of tribulation came to the family, and the young woman lost her husband, and when her sons fell ill she became hopeless and wavering. The old mother, being a firm Christian, advised her daughter and tried to keep her steady, but without avail. At her request I often advised her myself and got other Mission agents to offer her spiritual advice. But all our endeavours were fruitless. We found that her mind was led astray by the heathen by whom she was surrounded, so we arranged to remove her two sick sons to a Mission house, where, by the grace of God, they soon got well. After this the waverer became more steady, came to church frequently, and grew regular in her religious duties. She has ever since been paying the expense of oil for lighting the church. She also sent her elder son to the Nazareth boarding-school, and he is now a good Christian example in the village. When cholera lately visited that village the mother began to be uneasy, and the heathens, who formed the bulk of the villagers, invoked their Goddess Kali to remove the disease, and hung margosa leaves in front of their houses; but the good Christian son of the widow comforted his mother, and said he was going to get a safeguard for his family. He drew two pictures of a cross, one on the right and the other on the left side of the door, and above the lintel he wrote the words, 'We are God's children.' When I went to see the family I was very much pleased with their manifestation of faith, and after advising them not to be discouraged, I offered prayer in their house.

"In my sermons, as well as when giving private advice, I exhort the Christians in my charge to pay tithes as their duty to God. As a result of my endeavours, some of them received from me a small earthenware money-box to put into it a tenth of what they earn every day. When I was wondering whether they were doing so, one day I met a man in Kadaianodai, named Gnanakanoo Vedakkan, and asked him about it. He told me that he put six pies into the box out of his daily wages before he spent anything on himself. I encouraged him to continue in this good practice. This man has always been a good and liberal person. He subscribed and paid Rs. 17 towards building the church. His sunga money, which was Rs. 1 a year, is now increased to Rs. 11–4–0. God grant that all Christians may follow his example.

"There is a visible increase in the funds for self-support in this Mission. The congregations that paid three-fourths of the salary of their Mission agents now pay the full salary, and those that paid one-third and one-fourth now give half of it. Kadaianodai, Kuluthukudy, and Pandimadal belong to the first class. Though there has been a reduction in the S.P.G. grants to the general funds of this Mission and a decrease of school grants, I trust the money required will be made up this year, as the Mission agents and the chief members of the different congregations are trying their best not to allow the funds to decrease, but rather to increase. May our gracious God bless the endeavours of our agents and our young congregations.

"Evangelisation is carried on regularly in Hindu villages, especially during Hindu festivals. The Hindus have now adopted the custom of publishing leaflets like those of our Tract Society. Their tracts speak contemptuously of Christianity and praise Hinduism to the skies. During the Kurangari Festival Hindu handbills were distributed among the heathen people in opposition to our preaching, but while persons were distributing their pamphlets, we managed to preach the Gospel to some quiet hearers in another part of the assembled crowd. I had to warn the Mission agents against preaching among drunken and quarrelsome mobs, but unfortunately some of them neglected my advice, and got into difficulties from which they could not extricate themselves till I went to their help. I understand that some Hindus have bound themselves by promises to prevent the preaching of the Gospel by all the means in their power. When such is the case, I am afraid that the Evangelistic work done by females cannot be attended to as it has been hitherto."

From Mudalur the Rev. S. Devasahayam sends an account of the terrible visitation of cholera during the year, which severely tried the Christians. It must offer peculiar difficulties in such a land of demonolatry to keep the Christians from wavering at such a time. Mr. Devasahayam writes :—

I beg to record the severe ravages made by cholera for a few months in this district, commencing from the third Sunday in Advent. Cholera made its appearance in the district first at Pohleyerpuram and next at Mudalur, and then in the other villages of Adiyal, Viravam, Kankaniarpuram, Tuckerpuram, and Thattarmudam. Of these cholera-stricken villages, Thattarmudam was affected last, and it did not leave the place till the month of April. None of the places suffered so severely as Mudalur. The total number that fell victims to it was 131. The number of deaths at Mudalur was generally larger on Sundays than on week-days. On one Sunday ten were carried off, and eight bodies were buried that day, and the remaining two bodies had to be buried on the following day, as the people were afraid to attend the burial service after sunset. That day was the most frightful Mudalur has ever witnessed within the period of ninety-one years of its existence. The people felt and confessed that such an unusual occurrence on a Sunday was designed to bring them to the sense of their neglect of Sunday duties, and their general disregard of the holy ordinances of the Church. In one family both parents died in one day, the mother at home and the father at a distance of twelve miles. In another family both parents and two boys of ten and fifteen years of age were carried off in a couple of days. A young man of very strong constitution died on the roadside three miles from his home on his way to his mother-in-law's house, whither he went by fear of cholera. There was a dead calm in the houses and streets for several weeks, when the epidemic was very fierce. People accustomed to give vent to their grief by loud cries of lamentations had to give up their dear dead ones without such expressions of regret, and without showing other tokens of affection. In a few cases the losses were so severely felt that mothers and brothers lost all soberness for weeks, as if they had become mad. In these afflictions we felt the realisation of the terrible warnings denounced by God to the Jews of old through the prophet Amos. The deaths among Christians were so many that the heathens tried to persuade our people in some places to offer sacrifices to their gods, frightening the people, who were alarmed with such terrible slaughter by the plague, that those who pay offerings to their deities can thereby escape death. Some families in Viravam, Pohleyerpuram, and Thattarmudam, by fright yielded to such advice. Some left their homes and ran away to other places. Some have given themselves to toddy and other intoxicating drinks, thinking that they can thereby be free from the terrible effects of fear. But in spite of all such false hopes and desperate attempts there were deaths also among the heathens as well as among those who adopted intoxicating drinks. The number of deaths among the Roman Catholics in this neighbourhood was also large. Among persons who ran to other places there were some who did not mee with a ready reception into the village whither they ran for protection, and had to stop in jungles for some days, till the villagers were pleased to give them entrance. Among those who remained at home there were some who murmured about such a severe slaughter. There were some who believed that Mudalur was under a curse for the repeated and unrepented sins of many of its inhabitants from time to time, and that it was time to escape the impending evils by a flight to other places. Dreamers and interpreters of dreams were on the increase. There were also sensible men who induced the people to repentance and reformed life and conduct. It was a time in which the finger of God was keenly felt and acknowledged. But notwithstanding the good resolutions that have been formed among the majority, there were also men of the worst character who took advantage of these calamities, drank to excess, robbed vacated houses and fields, and committed other mischief. Such men also were as plagues, and made the severities of the epidemic still more cruel. The darkness of the night itself was looked upon by simpletons with all prejudice and superstition. They fancied that the spirits of those who were carried away by such violent deaths were moving about in their streets in the dark, and frightening others by calling out

their names, knocking at their doors, and by doing other mischievous actions. Some
oaths were suspected to have taken place by such cases. People thought that such
spirits should be checked from wandering about from their allotted place, and one or
two men requested me, after the burial of a body, to kick against the tomb on the
headside, ordering the spirit with a stern reproof not to stir from the place of its destination. These men also said that Roman Catholic priests have done thus to check
evil spirits from doing mischief. This is a land of demonolatry, and I was not
surprised to hear the outbreak of cholera, as well as every bodily ailment, ascribed to
the influence of evil spirits. In a land which is said to be " a land where demons
stand at every span's length and demons' pagodas at every cubit's distance," "everything that had a dark appearance was a demon to the eye of him who was terror-
stricken," according to the proverbial saying in these parts. There was another false
notion among some that such sudden, painful, and violent deaths by cholera cannot
take place through the instrumentality of good angels, and they suspected that those
who fell victims were lost souls. Among those who died of cholera, there were a few
who were well known to be regular and devout Communicants, of consistent life and
conduct ; and it pleased God that in their passage from this tempestuous ocean of
troubles to the fair haven of everlasting peace they should have a violent passage.
May they rest in peace.

Notwithstanding the terrors of cholera, a woman, by name Paripooranam, a Communicant, spent whole nights in prayer in her house and in various parts of the
streets ; and in walking through the streets she used to cry out, " God Almighty, the
King of Glory, cometh. Repent of your sins, pray without ceasing, give alms and do
works of charity, attend the Church services, worship God, partake of the Lord's
Body and Blood, do not provoke God's anger, put your trust in God and be not afraid,"
and so on. She represented that she was instructed by dreams and visions what to
do and what to say. Her husband and relations tried to prevent her from exposing
herself during nights ; but she insisted that she should obey God's orders and not
yield to them. Some thought that she had become insane. But although she was
under religious excitement she was always sober. She was not easily provoked by
any remarks made by others.

Mudalur, though one of the oldest Mission stations, is not so favoured as several
other head stations in some respects. The want of a Mission Dispensary is felt
here now more than ever. The Rev. A. Margöschis, our Superintending Missionary,
supplied us with medicines from time to time, and excepting the time for Church
services I was fully engaged in distributing medicines with the help of my son and
the Cuspah catechist.

When the epidemic was violent, evening services were over before sunset, as the
people were afraid to go out at night from dread of "the pestilence that walketh in
darkness," and from fear of the destroying angel. Litanies with processional lyrics,
invoking Divine help to remove the severity of the plague, were said for several
days in each street and at church. Due notice and advice were given to all how to
behave during the epidemic, and preventive measures were also adopted. People were
so quick in seeking for help, that those who suspected the slightest symptom of disease
applied for medicine without delay, unless they were attacked late at night.

Among those who fell victims to cholera was a nephew of mine, aged twenty-two
years, who was very successful as a teacher in the Mudalur school, and who helped
me very successfully. Among the teachers of Mudalur and Adiyal all, excepting this
young man, ran to other places by fear. But he helped me to the very last. As his
last duty, he was engaged with my son in copying out a list of those who were attacked with cholera during that week, and after Evensong he was found praying on
his knees near the altar rails. At his house he had family prayers sooner than usual,
as he had the attack. At my first sight of him, a little after 7 P.M., I lost all hopes of
his recovery, as from the very first he became extremely weak. I spent the night
with him, and all possible measures were adopted for his recovery, hoping against

hope. But he knew that there was very little life left in him, and he said, "My soul is
already gone, my body only suffers in its last struggles. It is no use to give medicines,
pray for me." I prayed for him. After his death another brother and a sister of his
died one after the other. All the members in my family, excepting my wife and myself, had the attack and recovered. When my son had the attack, I had to spend some
very anxious nights with him, as I had to watch him and help him, having no other man
to help us during the night. The people got relief from their dread by the visit of tho
Rev. A. Margöschis with two Cowley Fathers, who came to us on February 9, and
cheered us by their presence, conversation, and addresses.

Our school work has suffered much by the cholera. The schools at Mudalur,
Adiyal, and Pohleyerpuram, where cholera was very violent, as well as of other places
where it was in a milder form, were either closed altogether for months or were
greatly disturbed.

Of Christianagram we have a report by the Rev. G. Eleazer, who
says that in his district there are 26 village congregations, 2,438 baptised persons, 249 catechumens, 615 Communicants, and 562 adults able
to read. In the district there are 2 native clergymen, 3 catechists, 1
medical evangelist, 7 mixed agents, 4 masters, 11 mistresses, and 3
monitors. There are 1 boys' boarding school, 9 boys' day schools, 1
boys' night school, 8 girls' day schools, and 2 mixed schools, with 510 boys
and 280 girls in them. He adds: " In reviewing our work for the past
year we have much cause for thankfulness. We are going on quietly and
steadily with our work. We have cause to be specially thankful to the
Lord for His good providence in preserving us and our congregations
from any attacks of cholera when there were so many fatal cases by that
disease in the neighbouring district of Mudalur. The returns for the
year show an increase of 48 souls in the number of baptised persons.
There is an increase of 104 boys and 94 girls in the schools over the
previous year. One girls' day school in Teriyur, 1 girls' mixed school in
Santhiadiyur, and 1 boys' night school in Christianagram have been
newly opened since July 1887."

From the head station at Nazareth the Rev. A. Pichamutthu sends a
long and interesting report, from which we take a description of the
evangelistic work, and of the organised efforts of Hindus and Mohammedans to counteract it.

" The seed of the Gospel is sown in all the heathen villages around in
obedience to the injunction of the Great Head of the Church. The
work of evangelising the heathen population is interesting indeed, and
it would be more so if it could be conducted systematically with a small
trained band of agents, able to sing Christian lyrics and selected Hindu
songs. Opposition of every kind is met with in all directions nowadays,
and reaction has set in against the slow-pervading influence of Christianity. Satan, the great adversary, set up the different sectarians
among the Jews against Jesus Christ in the days of His flesh, when He
preached the Gospel of Salvation. The same enemy is active now in
Christ's Church as well as in the heathen world, where he kindles

feelings of jealousy and hatred in the minds of all religionists against
the preachers of the good news of salvation. The contra-measures are
as follows :

" (a) Educated Hindus, in imitation of Christian prayer meetings,
have started devotional meetings named 'Pajani,' consisting of singing
penitential songs ascriptive of praise to their gods, accompanied by
musical instruments, the members of the ' Pajani' wearing garlands of
flowers during the service.

" (b) The educated community in India have recently organised
societies and associations to publish and defend the truths and rites of
their religion, which, in their opinion, have been greatly neglected by their
countrymen, owing to the influx of Western education. Various tracts
and handbills have been published by Hindu societies in defence of
their religion, and attacking our holy religion by pointing out any
apparent inconsistencies in the Holy Scriptures. Almost all the tracts
and leaflets are full of blasphemy against God, and are repulsive to
the feelings of unbiassed moralists or Vedantists, who entertain higher
views of the Great Author of Nature, the Supreme God. The Tract-
writers speak of 'The Bible-God' as distinct from the 'God of
the universe or of all nations.' It shocks Christians to read the
pamphlets issued in imitation of the handbills of the Christian Tract
Society. On thinking over the cause of such a strange movement, it
may strike a reflective mind that the educated and learned majority of
Hindus have in this way an opportunity afforded them of ' searching
the Scriptures ' (St. John v. 39), ' which are able to make wise
unto salvation' (2 Tim. iii. 15), and thereby knowing Bible truths.
Though they may not be earnest seekers after truth, yet truth will work
its way one day or other, and convert a Saul of Tarsus into a Paul of
Ephesus. There is another light in which we may view these measures
and draw a lesson of calmness and patience in this anti-Christian age.
Christian societies for a century published books, tracts, and handbills
of all descriptions, exposing the folly of idolatry and teaching the simple
truths of Christianity. One may well conclude that it is high time for
Hindus to turn the tables and criticise Christianity; for is it not the
main cause of the vast and admirable improvements India has experienced in its literary, social, moral, and religious aspects ?

" (c) Another engine of opposition employed by Hindus to counteract
the rising influence of Christ's holy religion, is to have organised bands
of preachers in important towns, who, instead of being content with
preaching the truths of their religion, condemn Christianity, attack the
Holy Scriptures, blaspheme the God-man Jesus Christ, abuse the sacred
ministry, and persecute the preachers of the Gospel. The preachers
of Hinduism mount a platform placed in a prominent position in a
town, and address the heathen crowd, attacking Christianity in highly

blasphemous language, to the provocation of Christians of all denominations and the disgust of Mahomedans who are monotheists.   Itinerant
parties have been formed among them, who go about from one village to
another preaching Hinduism and cavilling at Christianity.

   "The present agitation in India amongst Hindus reminds one of a
stanza in a Hindu poem, which is to the following purport: 'A turkey
saw a peacock in the jungle dance with its feathers spread out, so the
turkey feigned itself to be a peacock, and began to dance, spreading out
its feathers.   Thus the foolish wish to be thought wise.'

   "The Mahomedans also on their part are striving to propagate their
religion, starting societies to issue pamphlets and handbills in support
of their system and against Christianity.   A Mahomedan trader put into
my hands one day a leaflet and asked me to read it with careful attention, and at the same time obtained from me a handbill I had with me
for the purpose of distribution to the Hindus at Alvartirunagari.

   "No doubt Hinduism has some shade of truth but not the whole truth.
Fragments of truth are found in all religions, enshrined under different
forms of precepts and ceremonies, but Christianity is the only religion
of Divine authority, and contains all the revealed truths concerning God
and man, and the present and future world.   Christianity stands on its
own basis.   Let us patiently wait for the fall of the strongholds of Satan,
without attacking its walls with any violence and shouts of war-cry or
clash of arms.   Let the word of the Gospel be vigorously and hopefully
preached everywhere, commending to all nations and people the simple
truths of Christianity, and let us patiently wait for the success of our
poor and humble evangelistic work amongst the heathens of this country."

   Certainly the Tinnevelly Missions, with their steady growth, their
evidences of reality in the Christian profession of the converts, their
able and devoted native clergy and lay agents, and their numerical
success, should encourage the most faint-hearted in sharing Mr.
Pichamutthu's hope.

THE CHILDREN'S CORNER.

THE HERO OF SÁHAMAFY.—A TALE OF THE FRANCO-MALAGASY WAR.

BY THE REV. ALFRED SMITH.

(*Continued from page* 110.)

CHAPTER VI.

AND now the day came when the queen was to make her grand public appeal to the Malagasy nation to rise in defence of their fatherland. For several days previously messengers had been sent in every direction to call the whole population of Imerina together—men, women, and children—to a monster meeting in the Máhamásina plain. All day and all night bodies of men were arriving from the distant parts of Imerina, and when in the early morning of the appointed day the sullen boom of the signal cannon rang over the city and announced that the decisive day had come, it was answered by the noise of the tumult of the "thousands of Imerina," as they left the city to assemble in the plain beneath. Both sides of the roadway were lined with soldiers, from the palace doors down to the holy stone in the centre of the plain. From end to end the plain was filled, while numbers perched themselves upon places of vantage on the rocks overlooking the scene. They had, however, still a long time to wait, and while they are waiting let us glance quickly through the crowd and notice some of its peculiarities.

The soldiers lining the roadway are dressed in a longish cotton shirt, with their *lamba* rolled up and tied firmly round the waist. They carry old flint-and-steel weapons for the most part, and either stand gossiping with their friends and acquaintances, or else squat ruminatively upon their haunches. Here and there on the roadside are places marked with a red flag. These are the stations of the medical students of the Friends' Foreign Mission Association, who have been told off to succour her majesty's lieges who may meet with any mishap in the expected crowd.

As we watched the people go past we can almost tell by the dress each wears how far he is affected by European ideas. There go five or six young fellows, who have reached the "gent" period of civilisation, and represent the English 'Arry. They wear suits of ready-made clothes, which fit them more or less, solar helmets, shoes of native manufacture, with exceedingly high heels, which fit very tight indeed. Each smokes a Malagasy cigar (threepence per hundred), and they step painfully from stone to stone, the admiration of all beholders.

Then we have the compromise. This class forms the majority of the rising generation. They wear trousers with the shirt outside them, native straw hats with a black ribbon round it, and drape themselves with a Manchester print *lamba* of some gorgeous and striking pattern. When deprived of this latter article of dress they become pictures of mental and bodily distress, for they have no place left where they can hide their arms. Sometimes they make a sacrifice to civilisation and undergo " grinding torments " in a pair of native-made shoes, especially on Sundays when they go to church. They put them on the last moment before starting, and pull them off behind the churchyard wall immediately after service, and hand them to their attendant slave to be carried carefully back home. These shoes must possess at least one peculiarity to make them valuable: they must be good squeakers. Otherwise the game is not worth the candle.

Then there are the beginners. These wear the straw hat with the black ribbon, and smoke a cigar in public. There are also some who are forced to be beginners much against their will, for civilisation will have its victims. Look at that poor grey-headed old fellow hobbling along in a pair of light native-made shoes, quite new, and doing piteous penance. His trousers, of no particular cut, hardly reach below his knees. But he is a man who has several *honours*, and so *noblesse oblige*. Poor fellow! he knows nothing about *noblesse oblige*. He says: " It is my fate! Khismet! "—and with ghastly cheerfulness drees his weird.

The civilised ladies mostly wear a dress with a very long train, covered with the inevitable Manchester print *lamba*. Muffling the chin and mouth in this, they put their heads a little on one side, and trip from stone to stone barefoot.

Nothing much need be said about the uncivilised. They wear a cotton *lamba*, more or less dirty, or else one of native manufacture, and are looked upon with contempt.

Here and there also among the crowd may be seen groups of Mozambiques, gabbling away to each other in a language they call " Makoa." These African negroes, it will be remembered, were set free through English influence some twelve years ago.

The plain now presents a striking picture, and the Manchester prints of every variety of colour and pattern, specially made to suit native tastes, produce a brilliant effect.

Towards half-past ten the first gun of the royal salute is fired from the palace, giving notice that the queen is about to start. Very soon the red silk umbrellas held over the royal palanquin may be seen slowly descending the road. The good queen is elegantly attired in a European costume of silk. Before her goes a body of picked young soldiers, dressed in old French uniforms, and another such body in English red-coats follows, marching to the music of the royal band. Close around the palanquin is a number of female slaves, while on either side half-a-dozen Arabs dance, blow conches, and flourish white scarves. Preceding her likewise is a procession of palanquins, in which are seated the ladies of honour, dressed in bright yellow or bright green or bright blue silk dresses, with little cheap straw hats, trimmed with tawdry finery, stuck on the tops of their heads.

Immediately in front of the queen rides the prime minister, covered with gold lace and imitation orders, on a smart little pony, attended by his aides-de-camp.

A mountain battery of small guns is waiting in the open space called Andohalo, just below the palace. As the queen reaches this spot, in which also there is a holy stone, and rests for a moment over that object, the battery fires a royal salute. This ended, the guns take their place in the procession, and amidst an almost indescribable noise and tumult the whole moves on towards Máhamásina.

CHAPTER VII.

It is twelve o'clock before the queen reaches the platform erected over and around the holy stone. Her chair is placed upon the stone, and, surrounded by her maids of honour, the chief officers of state, and the English missionaries, their wives and children, she takes her seat upon it.

Presently silence is proclaimed, and the queen rises to read her address to the Malagasy people.

Having stated her claim to the throne in the usual formula, she told her people how she had tried to live at peace with the Great Powers of Europe, and particularly with the French; how that now the French had claimed a protectorate over the north-west coast; how, upon this having been refused, they had proceeded to bombard Mojangá and Tamatave; how that, although a woman, God helping her, she would never yield an inch of the dear fatherland to anyone soever; and how that she called upon every man, woman, and child there present, and throughout the length and breadth of the land, to rise in defence of the inheritance of their fathers.

This being ended amidst the greatest enthusiasm, it becomes the prime minister's duty to answer the appeal; and, to tell the truth, the prime minister likes nothing better than doing it on such days as these. He likes a clear space to walk up and down in during his public harangues. A signal gun is in readiness to be let off the moment he makes a point in his appeal, and the drum stands ready to keep up the enthusiasm.

He begins mildly the stereotyped formula for these occasions made and provided. Soon he enters upon his theme, and commences to walk up and down. He goes fully into the history of the French treaties with Madagascar, enlarges upon the treachery of France, and then, with a tremendous burst, he cries : " And before anyone shall succeed in taking a single inch of the fatherland from us, the rightful owners, we will die to the last man. Is it not so, soldiers ? "

Bang goes the cannon, the band gives a flourish of trumpets, the big drum hammers away with might and main, and from thousands of throats there bursts forth, as from the throats of one man, the reply : " So it is ! "

When all is ended the prime minister gives the general order for all soldiers to be brought into the neighbourhood of the palace the next day, in order that contingents may be drafted off for the defence of Tamatave and other ports.

The procession then reforms, and the sun is well down in the west before the queen enters her palace gates.

The next few days following the great Proclamation were spent in the appointment and despatch of troops to various ports both on the east and west coasts. Men were drawn for service from every clan and village throughout Imerina. It was a brilliant time for officers, chiefs, medicine-men, and men of influence of all sorts. Many made quite little fortunes by taking bribes. Those whose names were down for service on the coast, and who could afford to bribe on an extensive scale, were left to repel the French, should they ever advance as far as Imerina.

This system of bribery is *the* grand lever which moves the entire Malagasy world. It is carried on with an appearance of strict morality and ceremonious solemnity truly Pecksniffian. A bribe may (in Malagasy) be defined to be a *present* in money which a "son" or a dependent gives to a "father and mother." It looks quite innocent. The "son," however, knows quite well though that he had better give the "present," lest a worse thing happen to him. His "father and mother" would "eat him up" with an appetite if he didn't. Everything is open to a man who can judiciously bribe, from a petty clerkship in the customs to the governorship of a province.

(To be continued.)

NOTES OF THE MONTH.

"HERE, on my left hand, is a living speech. I do not know whether the patriarch of the English clergy, the Rev. Bartholomew Edwards, who is in his 97th year, intends to address you, but he has come from Norfolk to look you in the face and to express by his presence his conviction of what this Society is, and ought to be." It was in these words, at the Society's anniversary in St. James's Hall in 1885, that the present Archbishop of Canterbury presented Mr. Edwards to the meeting. On that occasion there were probably not many present who were born when Mr. Edwards first became an active friend of the Society, on his presentation in 1813 to his first and only incumbency of Ashill, in the county of Norfolk, which at his death, in February last, he had held for 76 years. In the year of his birth (1789) the income of the Society's general fund was £2,565, and he lived to see it reach last year the sum of £117,384.

For many years, of which it may with truth be said, in legal phrase, that "the memory of man runneth not to the contrary," was Mr. Edwards's voice regularly heard on behalf of the Society in many a village of West Norfolk. Always generous and hospitable, he insisted upon entertaining the Society's representative at his rectory for at least a week in the late autumn, and accompanied him to each dark evening's meeting, without regard to distance or weather, often, to the last, in an open carriage. There is many an advocate of the Society, now in foreign parts, who will hear with regret that his pleasant intercourse with the Rector of Ashill is but a memory of the past.

Mr. Edwards was elected an incorporated member in 1833, and vice-president in 1865. In addition to his annual subscription, he gave in 1873 a donation of £500 towards the purchase of the Society's house in Delahay Street, and by many other gifts he proved himself one of the Society's most generous benefactors, and the last sermon he ever preached was for the Society on the Day of Intercession, in November 1888.

In a life so far extended beyond the allotted term of man, it were but to write the contemporary history of England to recount the various reforms in Church and State which he had lived to see, and which he was apt but slowly to recognise as improvements. "Old-fashioned" was indeed an epithet which he by no means considered a term of reproach, and of which, when applied to himself, he was not a little proud. And assuredly the "old order changeth" for the worse if the "new" fail to produce men of the same sterling character as Bartholomew Edwards, who passed quietly away on February 21, within ten days of his completion of a century of life, leaving behind him a grand example of "patient continuance in well-doing" to its close.

S EVEN years have now assured the position of the *Official Year Book of the Church of England.* Its first appearance in 1883 was widely recognised as supplying what had long been needed, and each yearly issue has added to its original reputation. Persons interested in almost any kind of Church work will find in the volume information which they could not find elsewhere, and what is even more valuable, the clear tabulation and combining of what is only to be found elsewhere in fragments. The work of the Church in large towns is a very interesting feature this year, but our attention is of course mainly directed to what relates to the work of the Church abroad. This we find to be given with the fulness of previous years, and we hope the book is not without its influence in making English Churchmen realise their membership in a world-wide communion, and teaching them their more than insular responsibilities. The work of the Lambeth Conference is duly reported. We must congratulate the indefatigable Honorary Editor of the *Official Year Book,* the Rev. F. Burnside, on this year's volume, as we have done on those that have preceded it.

A RCHDEACON LIGHTFOOT, of Capetown, in sending the diocesan statistics for the year 1888, reports on the effect which the rush to the gold-fields has on the older colonies :—

Many of our clergy are just now being greatly tried by the departure to the Transvaal gold-fields of so many of their best and most enterprising parishioners. The movement has been in progress for some time now, and it naturally has a depressing influence upon much of our work. Yet it will not be right to abandon our work in these parishes—these outworks of our Church; not only on account of the large numbers of poor coloured people here residing who have become Christians and are members of my communion, but also because these villages, now more or less deserted by our English folk, will doubtless in a few years again become important centres.

W RITING on the eve of the twentieth anniversary of his consecration to the Episcopate, the Bishop of Maritzburg has sent us a summary of the condition of his diocese. His Lordship says:—

In spite of the reduction in the numbers of the clergy which we have still to deplore, the parishes of Umzinto and Umhlatuzana being still deprived of the care of a resident pastor, the Church throughout the diocese appears to be growing stronger My reports for the last few years have necessarily alluded to the commercial depression which prevailed through the whole of South Africa. We can thankfully acknowledge that this heavy cloud has passed away, and that the material condition of this Colony has considerably improved.

The Church still suffers from the absence of many who have gone to seek their fortunes at the gold-fields, but the following passage is as encouraging as anything that has reached us relating to that exodus:—

There are already instances of the recognition, on the part of those who have been successful, of the claim which the Church's work has upon their support. Our institutions in Maritzburg, the St. Cross Orphanage, the Mercy Home, and St. Albans Native College, have all received offerings in token of thankfulness to God for such success, and I hope that during the year upon which we have entered there may be increasing proofs of the prevalence of such feelings throughout the diocese.

The Bishop is anxious to be enabled to fill up the vacant cures, also to subdivide some of the larger parishes, but he pleads especially for the Missions among the natives and the immigrants from India. In both cases he urges the claim on the excellent ground that the Missions owe their origin to local zeal:—

There is one feature of considerable encouragement in the last few years to which I look with much hope in the future, the springing up of little Missions under the parish priest in different parts of the Colony, such as we have at Pinetown, Howick, and Newcastle—and I might cite the instance of Estcourt, where, since Mr. Troughton became incumbent (a period of about eighteen months), two such Missions have come into existence with scarcely any extraneous aid, one of them being rendered possible by the voluntary surrender on the part of the native catechist, Kumalo, of a part of his stipend, and the other being carried on by another native almost without pecuniary help. Such efforts as these deserve all the encouragement that we can possibly give, and I long to be able to place at the disposal of clergymen who are making these ventures in such a spirit of faith, and at the same time in so practical a shape, some regular sum, even if it be small, to develop their work.

In connection with the Indian Mission the Bishop refers to the self-sacrificing work of Dr. Booth:—

In the years 1876 and 1877, when the Indian population was flocking to these shores, and nothing at all was being done to make the Gospel known to them, the clergy out of their small incomes initiated a subscription for the commencement of Missionary effort in the parishes where the Indians were placed, and succeeded in the establishment of a few small schools. The work, however, for want of anyone who could devote himself wholly to it, made but little progress, and there was no fund out of which I could offer a stipend to a priest from India. Thus it seemed likely to languish, or even to collapse altogether, when Dr. Booth, at that time holding a large practice as a medical man in the Colony, offered his services freely for two years for this special work, for which he had other qualifications besides some knowledge of the Hindi language. You are aware that the work has steadily grown from that time.

ST. JOHN'S, Kaffraria, is showing two notable signs of growth—the increase of the native ministry and of the spirit of self-help. The Bishop is able to add what is more important, but what no mere statistics can show, namely, that the work is being consolidated, and that there is a deepening of the Christian character among the converts. His lordship says that there are now no less than six natives, well-tried and approved, looking forward to ordination ; on the second head he tells how the Diocesan Finance Board have made a reduction of one-sixth of the grants for assistant workers of whatever colour, and this is in addition to the one-third taken off a year ago, and how these reductions have been met locally :—

Thus, if a worker has £45 a year, last year £30 only of this came from headquarters, now only £25 will ; the balance of £15 or £20 is required to be made up by local sources, either by offertories, subscriptions, or donations at the harvest festivals. This was necessary, as our work has been growing, and so many openings are continually being found.

Of the character of the native Christianity his lordship writes :—

I speak of the ministry as being so all-important, and as a test, too, of the advance of the work in the past and present, and an earnest of the same in the future. I could speak at length on what is going on in the different parts of the diocese, of the extension, and especially I think of the consolidation of the work—for, indeed, our very great increase of the *number* of members of the Church has often made me tremble for the quality of their Christianity, but I feel much more confident now on this head; or, rather, without presuming to say that our people have attained any very high character of holiness, yet, as a whole, still there seems to be more life, and more appreciation of what is required of them by their profession. I think I may say this much.

MAFELLING is one of the out-stations of the St. Augustine's Mission in Zululand. The Rev. Charles Johnson thus sketches its brief but remarkable history :—

"Some six years ago I commenced going to Mafelling about once a month, when weather permitted, to hold open-air services. Sometimes we had large gatherings of three and four hundred heathen. This went on for a couple of years, when an effort was made, a small square stone building built, and a native teacher engaged. All this was done entirely by the local natives, without any outside help, so of course everything was on a very small and primitive scale, and very rough, for at that time there was not one baptised person in the district. Unfortunately, the native teacher was a failure, and this brought the work to a standstill again, and, in fact, threw it back a great deal, for it killed the energy of the people for the time being. In May 1886 the work there got a new start, and it has gone steadily ahead since.

"It was in May 1886, just after our return from England, that Mr. Wallis, who had come to our Bishop to be trained for Mission work, took Mafelling in hand. He came to it just at its worst time, just as the people were suffering from disappointment caused by the failure of the native teacher. He found no building for himself, and in fact nothing but this little bit of a square stone building for a school and service room. Dear earnest fellow, he was just the man to get on well with these simple-minded natives. I wish he could have stayed at Mafelling, but he was wanted elsewhere. He was only there a year, but in that year he managed to build a two-roomed house for the teacher, and being something of an architect, he planned the building as school-church that we have just completed, and he also gathered together a good day-school, and commenced classes of instruction for those wishing to become Christians. I have already said that when he went there in May 1886 there was not one baptised person. I will copy from Mafelling Offertory Book for last Sunday, which will give some idea how God has blessed the work there, and how it has grown :—

'EARLY CELEBRATION.

'Communicants 59
'Offertory :—Coin . . . . 4s. 9d.
      'Mealies . . . . 19 baskets
      'Fowls . . . . 1 large one
      'Pumpkins . . . . 2 very large.'

"The custom is for the people to bring whatever they have a mind to offer early before the service commences, and get bits of paper from the native catechist with their offering written on them (but not the offerer's name), and these bits of paper they put into the alms-bag at the time of the offertory. These offerings become the food of the native catechist.

"The building we have just completed is rough, but still a very nice roomy building, well adapted to the work it has to do. It is fifty feet long by twenty wide, and the walls are nice and lofty."

Mr. Johnson adds that five of the oldest and steadiest natives in his Mission have been admitted and licensed as evangelists. They go out to the kraals and preach and teach on Sunday afternoons.

THE Rev. P. Marks, Missionary at Buona Vista, in the Diocese of Colombo, sends a report from which we take the following note of the baptism of a young convert :—

"He was a most intelligent youth of between 16 and 17 years of age, a pupil of our high school at Katukurunda. He had been brought up in a Pansala, or Buddhist

THE MISSION BUILDINGS, BUONA VISTA.

school, of which a near relative of his is the priest. The lad is remarkable for his excellent knowledge of classical Singhalese and of Buddhism. I have every reason to believe that he is a sincere convert, and to hope that as he grows older he will become increasingly useful in helping to spread the Gospel."

MATALE, in the same diocese, is under the charge of the Rev. F. Mendis, who reports that the Buddhists have opened a school where English is taught in opposition to that attached to the Mission.

COFFEE PLANTATIONS AT MATALE.

"Apparently the Buddhists have been led to take this step as a reaction on their part against the lecturing in our school to Buddhist and other heathen children on Friday evenings on the evidences of Christianity. Some of our school-boys, about fifteen in number, have been drawn away by the Buddhist parents into the rival school; but happily these are, almost all of them, bad boys in our school, who were noted for irregular attendance, and so their withdrawal has not been any serious damage to our school.

" In spite of the opening of a Buddhist school, there are a good many Buddhist boys yet in our school, who are faithful to us and who gladly receive Christian instruction, and I am almost sure that many of them when they get old enough to be independent of their parents will embrace the faith."

O N his way out from England to Mauritius the Bishop stopped at the Seychelles Islands, which form part of his diocese, and spent three months there. Amidst much that was encouraging in the Creole work, he was especially pleased with that in the Island of Praslin, where he stayed nine days and confirmed forty-one persons. The Church in the Seychelles has to strive against an aggressive Roman Catholic rivalry. There are fifty European agents of that Communion in the islands. The Seychelles are 940 miles due north of Mauritius.

WATERFALL AT MATALE.

A RCHDEACON GIBSON, of St. Cuthbert's Mission, Kaffraria, has sent a valuable record of his daily work, which we regret that we have not space to print at length. The following note about the Pondo chief's son and heir, Mtshazi, about whom the Archdeacon has written several times, will be welcome to our readers. It will be remembered that Mtshazi was in the Pondomisi boarding-school :—

" Mtshazi had requested me to send him or take him to England, in order to avoid being circumcised. According to Kaffir custom, the time for his circumcision has now arrived, and the other boys of his age have to wait for him, so that great pressure is being brought to bear upon him in the matter ; on the other hand, once circumcised he will be reckoned a man, and it is not likely that the people would let him return to school. It is this which he so much dreads, as he wants to continue his education for some three years more yet. Being unable at present (through want of funds mainly) to arrange for his going to England, I promised to send him to an advanced school in the old colony. We had to act with great circumspection, and keep the matter an entire secret until a week before he was due to start, when I called all the Pondomisi chiefs together and announced my determination. The feeling was very strong against allowing their chief to leave them, but the sentiment that they could do

nothing, Mtshazi having been placed entirely in my hands by Mditshwa, was equally
strong, so that the people had to content themselves with the passive resistance of
refusing to lend horses.   At my request, Mtshazi himself said a few words, expressing
his firm intention to go, whatever the tribe might say.

On July 30, therefore, I sent him and Sogotzo off on their journey to Lovedale.
Thence they have written constantly and happily, and the reports of them from their
masters are very good.

On July 29 I had the great happiness of baptising Sogotzo, by the name of
Chelston.   He is the first of my boys to become a member of Christ.

The Archdeacon reports that the people are being taught more and
more to give of their substance, and that the harvest offerings from the
various stations in his Mission, both in cash and in kind, realised £37
clear profit.

PORT ARTHUR, in the diocese of Algoma, has recently been entrusted to the pastoral care of the Rev. C. J. Machin, who has

THUNDER BAY.

done two noteworthy things in regard to the Society.   It was a place
where the small local resources had been supplemented from the Society's
grants to the diocese.   Mr. Machin, however, determined before he went
there to be independent of this help, as he considered that the time had
come for the step.   He writes:—

When I came here, this congregation contributed towards my income 300 dols. a
year, it now gives me 1,000 dols. a year, and we receive no outside aid whatever.
The amount which I received beyond the S.P.G. grant, contributed by the organised
Canadian dioceses, now goes to my assistant, soon, I hope, to be independent.   We
have had nothing from the S.P.G. in this region (i.e. the district of Thunder Bay)
since December 31, 1885.   But you gave generous help to my predecessor in the "day
of small things" in this region; you have also pledged £50 sterling a year towards

the support of a clergyman at the silver mines, when our Bishop can procure one; therefore I have told my parishioners in Port Arthur that common honesty and elementary gratitude require of us that we should " begin to pay something back " to you. I have divided the town into districts, and appointed collectors for them.

An offertory for the Society recently produced twenty dollars, which sum Mr. Machin has remitted. He has ordered twenty copies of the *Mission Field* and forty copies of the *Gospel Missionary*, and mentions, among other incidents in connection with the establishment of the parochial association, that a prominent and influential parishioner, whom he had not expected to favour the project, agreeably surprised him by saying, " I am glad you have begun this thing, and that you have decided to send all the offerings to that Society. It is a grand Society," and describing the help which it had rendered to a place where he had previously resided.

IN Ceylon the bulk of the population are Singhalese or Tamils, but there are, in very small numbers, remains of aboriginal races, and among them the Veddas. The Rev. A. Vethecan, of Batticaloa, has congregations of Tamils and Burghers, but in connection with one of his stations—Petthale—he refers to a Vedda congregation. Although the race is a despised one, Mr. Vethecan speaks of them in very remarkable terms, saying that as they are one of the simplest so they are one of the purest tribes:—

The thought of more Gods than one true God has not once entered into a Vedda's head; the Vedda neither makes an image, nor bows down to it, nor worships it; the Vedda does not, without due regard, take the name of God into his mouth, nor does he abuse the name of the deity with rash oaths; he honours his father and mother and others like them; the Vedda does not malign with his neighbour, nor is he angry with him; he does not quarrel with him, nor seek revenge upon every light injury; adultery and fornication are unknown to him; stealing is very rare among the Veddas; as a rule, the Vedda speaks always the truth.

IN September 1887 we printed the journal of a quarter's work of the Rev. P. Masiza, a native clergyman at St. Mark's, Kaffraria. It was a most interesting document, occupying about seven pages of the Magazine, and showing in itself no slight evidence of the reality and hopefulness of the Mission work of the diocese. A native capable of doing such work as he modestly recorded, and of describing it (though in imperfect English, yet) so well, is himself a reason for taking a sanguine view of the future, as well as being, what from other sources than his own reports we know Mr. Masiza is, an excellent clergyman and Missionary.

Mr. Masiza continues to send us similar copies of the entries in his journal. Of course the space at our command does not allow us to

print them all, but our readers will, no doubt, be glad of a few extracts from his last report:—

"October 28.—Being Sunday, I conducted both Native and English services; being over, I rode on home.

"Nov. 1.—All Saints' day. I had Celebration at home.

"2.—I started for my Missionary tour round the scattered outlying Missions, and slept at Hohita; at my arrival preparation took place for Holy Communion to-morrow.

"3.—Holy Sacrament, and Mattins, being over, I rode on for Jolose. I may mention, at each station I come to I have to prepare the communicants before Celebration, and to perform all the duties waiting for me as a missionary, viz., to meet all the classes as follow—those who are to be confirmed, catechumen, and penitence, and to visit and administer the Eucharist to the sick and aged persons who can no more attend the church, and to settle every church matter which is in my power that come to me."

Day after day he visits different places :—

"Nov. 20.—Soon after sunrise Holy Communion, afterwards Mattins; being over, I rode on for Cofimvaba, and found all the people already waiting. Here I had a hill up work; however, I finished all; towards sundown I rode for Tom Sijula's location.

"21.—Celebration and Mattins, and left immediately after for Kwebulanas location, and found everything ready, and commenced at once my usual work. Here I had to speak very strongly with the congregation to use Kaffir beer moderate. Very near at sundown I left for Hanga.

"22.—After Celebration and the usual service, I rode on for Nggilis location, and found all the men at the headman's kraal, and declare my being here is that I wish to re-open the school we had here once some time back; all consent to that. From thence I rode over to Tsojana.

"23.—After Mattins, the headman Uxanti from Emhletyeni came to see me, who consult with me about several things, which I answer to his satisfaction."

On December 3 he was sent for to visit a sick woman at a distant place :—

"Dec. 4.—At sunrise I had morning prayers, and left immediately after, and reach Inbulukweza at 2 o'clock P.M. When I enter into the hut where the sick woman laying, she smile. First of all I had prayers with her, and then she asked me to administer the Eucharist, which I did at once; when I finish she said she wish to depart and be with her Redeemer; I gave her a few admonishing words, and towards sundown I went over to the Mission.

"5.—After service I went over to see her again, and had prayer with her; then I left for Kwamfula. Service took place at my arrival, and do all my duties; in the after I proceed for Caba."

RELIEF given to the sick from the Springvale Mission in the Maritzburg has not been without its effect on the heathen. The Rev. H. T. A. Thompson writes:—

"We have had a great deal of sickness amongst the natives this year; some cases we have been able to treat successfully, and this perhaps, together with the fact of our frequent visits to the sick, seems to have led some of the heathen to take more interest in our religion. Never since I came here have we had such numbers of heathen present at our services as we have had during the last two months. At St. Faith's, a district about forty miles from Springvale, but in the same parish, Napashi, chief of

SPRINGVALE MISSION BUILDINGS.

the Amacole, has asked for a teacher to be sent to teach his people. I hope to send a native schoolmaster there next winter, if I can manage it. The chief himself has promised to help in building a house and school."

FROM Mutyálápad, in the Diocese of Madras, we are glad to hear of the arrival of the Rev. H. G. Downes, who was sent out from England last autumn. He and Mrs. Downes had no little difficulty in reaching their rather remote destination. They went by train from Madras to Cuddapah, where the bullock-waggons they had ordered were not forthcoming. The wife of a L.M.S. missionary kindly gave them dinner, and sent all over the town trying to get bullocks for them, but without avail, though the attempt was only abandoned at midnight. They therefore slept at her house.

"Had it not been for her kindness, I don't know what we, ignorant of the place and language, could have done. Still the detention was very annoying, as we wanted to reach Kalsapád a day before Mr. Shepherd had to return to Mutyálápad. In the morning Mrs. C—— enlisted the sympathies of Mr. Johnson, the District Engineer, in our favour. So he sent his bullock-coach, and at 9 A.M. we started off to Mindiálampéte. It had been arranged that we should be met by a Kalsapád catechist, who would have bandies and everything necessary. Imagine our feelings on discovering that, owing to the misunderstanding caused by the suggestion that we should remain in Madras, the bandies had been recalled. Again Providence, as if to correct human mistakes, aided us. We came across two collectors, who gave us dinner, and sent us on to Mallepalle, where there was to be a tent and food awaiting us. There we arrived at 3.30 A.M., but found that here also arrangements had been upset. It was most trying, as the bullock driver naturally did not want to go on, the bullocks were tired, and no new ones to be got; we had only a loaf and a bottle of water, while there was the fear that Mrs. Downes would be knocked up. However, there was no choice, and by promising presents, and by insisting, we went on, and arrived at Kalsapád at 11 A.M., half baked, but at the time we had always meant arriving. We were neither any the worse, though all whom we have met have been astonished at the journey and how Mrs. Downes could make it. She travelled a day, a night, and the hot part of another day. It has certainly proved she possesses some of the most requisite qualities for travelling in India. And most thankful I was that it did not affect her."

Veteran missionaries would not think much of such a journey, nor does Mr. Downes; but it was certainly a rough introduction to Indian life for a young English clergyman and his wife.

M UTYÂLÂPAD, we may add, is in the Telugu country, in the northern part of the Diocese of Madras. The following account is from the *Madras Diocesan Record* for January:—

"Mutyálápad is thirty miles from Kalsapád as the crow flies; the two places are separated by a range of hills called the Nallamallais. Although the Mission was commenced in 1854, and is therefore four years older than the Kalsapád Mission, it is not so advanced in any way as the latter Mission. The Mutyálápad Mission consists of 2,320 persons who have put on Christ in holy baptism. Ten years ago the number was 1,540. In the Mutyálápad schools there are 375 scholars, of whom 129 are girls. There are 74 native agents working under the Rev. R. D. Shepherd, the Superintending Missionary of these two Missions, but not one of them is in holy orders. In addition to the 5,000 souls in the two Missions who are baptized, there are about 1,700 catechumens under instruction with a view to baptism."

SUGGESTED SUBJECTS FOR PRAYER.

For the Missions in South Africa, that the Kaffirs, Zulus and other native races may receive the truth, and that the Church may be able to use the opportunities for spreading it among them.

For all the Missions exposed to peril by the troubles in Eastern Africa, for the steadfastness of the native converts, the support of the Missionaries, and a happy end of all the difficulties.

For those suffering from the famine in China, and that the recipients of Christian charity may listen to Christian truth.

For Medical Missions, that those who receive bodily benefits may be led to seek help from the Physician of souls.

ANNUAL MEETING.

The annual meeting of the Society was held at 19 Delahay Street, on Friday, February 15, at 2 P.M., the Rev. B. Compton in the chair. There were also present the Bishop of Colchester, the Earl of Belmore, the Bishop of Columbia, and Canon Cadman, *Vice-Presidents ;* H. W. Prescott, Esq., and A. A. De Lisle Strickland, Esq., *Treasurers ;* the Rev. J. M. Barn-Murdoch, C. Churchill, Esq., J. M. Clabon, Esq., General Davies, Canon Elwyn, Rev. J. W. Festing, Sir F. J. Goldsmid, K.C.S.I., C.B., General Lowry, C.B., General Maclagan, Rev. J. F. Moor, Archdeacon Randall, General Sawyer, Rev. J. H. Snowden, General Tremenheere, C.B., and S. Wreford, Esq., *Members of the Standing Committee ;* and Rev. F. K. Aglionby, Rev. F. Ashpitel, Rev. C. Baker, Rev. Dr. Baker, Rev. J. M. Beynon, Rev. H. Brancker, Rev. W. Calvert, Rev. A. Cooper, Rev. J. C. Cowl, Dr. R. N. Cust, Rev. H. J. Day, Dr. De Tatham, Rev. R. J. Dundas, T. Dunn, Esq., Rev. J. J. Elkinton, Rev. R. Fisher, J. F. France, Esq., Rev. R. S. Hassard, Rev. J. F. Heyes, Rev. T. Hill, Rev. S. Hobson, Rev. S. C. Hore, Rev. B. Jackson, H. Laurence, Esq., W. Lovell, Esq., Rev. J. Maconochy, Rev. J. C. Moore, F. P. Morris, Esq., General Nicolls, Rev. G. A. Ormsby, Rev. G. C. Reynell, Rev. A. W. L. Rivett, Rev. H. Rowley, Rev. C. Wyatt Smith, Rev. J. S. Smith, Rev. W. Sotheby, Rev. G. S. Whitlock, and Rev. R. Wood, *Members of the Society.*

1. After prayers, the minutes of the last meeting were read.
2. The Auditors' report for the year 1888 was presented in their behalf by the Secretary.
3. The Treasurers' report for the year 1888 was presented by A. A. De Lisle Strickland, Esq., showing the Society's receipts as follows :

							£	s.	d.
I. GENERAL FUND—									
Subscriptions, Donations, and Collections	...	...	...	...	...	...	105,610	1	1
Legacies	...	...	...	...	...	...	8,552	11	5
Rents, Dividends, &c.	...	...	...	...	...	...	3,222	2	6
		TOTAL RECEIPTS FOR THE GENERAL FUND				...	117,384	15	0
II. SPECIAL FUNDS	...	...	...	...	...	...	20,982	2	6
		TOTAL INCOME	...	...	...	...	£138,366	17	6

In addition to the above, the Society's Treasurers had received for Invested Funds, held by the Society as a Corporation for Specific Trusts by request, the sum of £1,429. 0s. 8d.

In this sum of £105,610. 1s. 1d. are included two gifts of Securities, worth £25,296 and £2,268 respectively. The former was "A Thankoffering to Almighty God for the extension of the Church in the Colonies and Dependencies of the British Empire and beyond it ;" the latter was a Memorial of one who had long been a munificent supporter of the Society.

4. The surviving Vice-Presidents were re-elected, and the following were elected Vice-Presidents for the year :—

Bishop J. F. Mackarness, Bishop Rawle, the Bishop of Bedford, the Bishop of Penrith, the Bishop of Leicester, the Bishop of Guildford, the Bishop of Glasgow and Galloway, the Assistant Bishop of Jamaica, the Bishop-designate of Trinidad, the Rev. Canon Liddon, D.D., the Rev. J. W. Ayre, and C. J. Bunyon, Esq.

5. The Bishops of the Episcopal Church in the United States of America were elected Honorary Associates of the Society for the year.

6. The Rev. Prebendary Kempe, H. Barnett, Esq., A. A. De Lisle Strickland, Esq., and H. W. Prescott, Esq., were re-elected Treasurers ; W. H. Birley, Esq., Colonel A. Stewart, H. C. Kay, Esq., and General Lowndes were elected Auditors ; the Rev. H. W. Tucker was re-elected Secretary ; W. F. Kemp, Esq., and the Rev. E. P. Sketchley were re-elected Assistant Secretaries ; and J. W. Ogle, Esq., M.D., was requested to continue his valuable services as the Society's Honorary Consulting Physician.

7. The following Vice-Presidents were nominated by the Standing Committee to preside at the monthly meetings in the absence of any Bishop holding an English see :—The Lord Bishop of Colchester, the Rev. B. Compton, and J. G. Talbot, Esq., M.P.

8. The Chairman declared that General Lowry, C.B., General Sawyer, and the Hon. and Rev. E. C. Glyn were re-elected, and Colonel Hardy, Sir H. Cartwright, the Rev. W. Allen Whitworth, and (*vice* Admiral the Right Hon. Sir Astley Cooper Key, G.C.B., *deceased*) the Rev. J. M. Burn-Murdoch elected, Members of the Standing Committee.

9. The election of Representatives on the Standing Committee for the following dioceses was duly reported :—

DIOCESE OF CHICHESTER—Rev. Preb. Codrington, D.D., and Rev. Preb. C. H. Borrer ; DURHAM—R. K. A. Ellis, Esq., and Rev. J. J. Brown ; HEREFORD—Rev. C. S. Palmer and T. Martin Southwell, Esq. ; LICHFIELD—Rev. E. V. Pigot, and T. Salt, Esq., M.P. ; LINCOLN—W. Lane Claypon, Esq., and Rev. Precentor Venables ; LLANDAFF—Rev. J. C. Thompson and Rev. J. T. Harding ; LONDON—Rev. C. J. Ridgeway and Rev. J. H. Snowden ; MANCHESTER—Very Rev. Dean Oakley and Ven. Archdeacon Anson ; NEWCASTLE—Hon.

and Rev. Canon F. R. Grey and Captain F. Norman, R.N.; NORWICH—Rev. F. B. De Chair and Rev. Canon Winter; OXFORD—Ven. Archdeacon Randall and Rev. C. F. J. Bourke; ST. ALBANS—Ven. Archdeacon Lawrance and G. Alan Lowndes, Esq.; ST. ASAPH—Ven. Archdeacon Thomas and Rev. Watkin H. Williams; TRURO—Edmund Carlyon, Esq., and Rev. Canon F. Hockin; WAKEFIELD—Ven. Archdeacon J. I. Brooke and William Laycock, Esq.; WORCESTER—Alfred Baldwin, Esq., and Hon. and Rev. H. Douglas.

10. It was resolved that the cordial thanks of the Society be offered to the Treasurers, the Auditors, and the Honorary Physician for their services during the year.

11. The cordial thanks of the Society were also voted to a large number of persons for the valuable assistance which they have rendered to the Society during the year by preaching sermons, or addressing meetings in its behalf. The names of these gentlemen, both clergymen and laymen, will be printed in the annual report.

12. Power was given to affix the corporate seal to certain documents.

13. The resignation of a member was reported in accordance with the 15th by-law.

14. A copy of the regulations was placed on the table in accordance with the 32nd by-law.

15. The appointment of Canon Cadman, Dr. Robinson Thornton, Canon Curteis, Professor Fuller, and Canon Mason by the Archbishops of Canterbury and York, and the Bishop of London, to be the Board of Examiners for the year was announced.

16. The Lord Bishop of Columbia addressed the members, dwelling upon the primary importance of the colonial part of the Society's work.

17. All the candidates proposed at the meeting in December were elected into the Corporation. The following were proposed for election in April:—

C. F. Hodson, Esq., The Chantry, Bishop's Stortford; J. Flinn, Esq., Windhill, Bishop's Stortford; Rev. G. H. Westcott, The College, Marlborough; Rev. P. B. Whalley, Wretham, Norfolk; Rev. Richard Hayes, 11 Artillery Street, Londonderry, Ireland; J. T. Pilgrim, Esq., Southfields, Leicester; J. H. Williams, Esq., Knighton Park Road, Leicester; Rev F. S. Alston, Coningsby, Boston, Lincs; Rev. E. B. Birks, Trin. Coll., Cambridge; Rev. Jacob Stephenson, St. John's, Forton, Gosport; Rev. S. H. Berkeley, Heavitree, Exeter; Rev. H. Bremridge, Winkleigh, North Devon; Rev. R. E. Trefusis, Chittlehampton, South Molton; Rev. H. Vere White, Killesk, Arthurstown, Ireland; Rev. Greville T. Hales, Bradwell, Braintree; Rev. R. H. D. Acland-Troyte, 30 Rue des Cultivateurs, Pau, France; William Chamney, Esq., 15 Elgin Road, Dublin; Rev. H. W. Orford, Bradden, Towcester; Rev. James Mountain, Towcester; Rev. John Jervis, All Saints', Rotherhithe; Rev. W. P. A. Campbell, Fladbury, Pershore; Rev. R. Coachafer, King's Heath, Birmingham; Rev. C. D. Francis, Tysoe, Warwick; Rev. G. F. Hough, Holy Trinity, Worcester; Alfred C. Hooper, Esq., The College, Worcester; Rev. G. M. Isaac, St. George's, Claines, Worcester; Rev. F. Lacon, Headless Cross, Redditch; Hon. and Rev. R. C. Moncrieff, Tamworth, Birmingham; Rev. B. Potter, Wellesbourne, Warwick; Rev. J. R. Radcliffe, Snitterfield, Stratford-on-Avon; Rev. T. Rivington, St. Nicholas, Warwick; Rev. E. L. Tuson, Kingsthorpe, Northampton; Rev. T. L. Sissmore, St. Edmund's, Northampton; Rev. A. H. Snowden, St. Michael's, Northampton; Rev. C. E. Barwise, St. James's, Dallington, Northampton; Rev. T. Lea, St. Lawrence, Northampton; Rev. W. H. Deane, St. Mary's, Northampton; P. Phipps, Esq., Northampton; J. Barry, Esq., Northampton; T. Osborn, Esq., Northampton; W. Smith, Esq., Northampton; Rev. A. M. Harper, St. Paul's, Northampton; Rev. Canon G. Sowden, Hebden Bridge, Yorks; Rev. F. E. Lloyd-Jones, Holy Trinity, Halifax, Yorks; Rev. W. Davenport, Southowram, Halifax, Yorks; Henry Bert Kaye, Esq., Huddersfield; and Rev. George Herbert Tremenheere, Pusey House, Oxford.

SOCIETY'S INCOME.

Abstract of RECEIPTS *and* PAYMENTS *from January 1 to February 28.*

	GENERAL FUND	SPECIAL FUNDS
Subscriptions, Donations, Collections, &c.	£5,581	£918
Legacies	2,150	100
Dividends, Rents, &c.	886	838
TOTAL RECEIPTS	£8,617	£1,856
PAYMENTS	£10,909	£2,963

The Receipts under the head of Subscriptions, Donations, and Collections for the General Fund from January 1 to end of February, in five consecutive years, compare as follows: 1885, £5,179; 1886, £6,150; 1887, £5,803; 1888, £5,852*; 1889, £5,581.

* In addition, the Treasurers received in 1888 Securities of the value of £25,296 as "A Thankoffering to Almighty God for the extension of the Church in the Colonies and Dependencies of the British Empire and beyond it"; also other Securities of the value of £2,263 as a Trust Gift, *the income only being available.*

THE MISSION FIELD.

THE FIELD IS THE WORLD. THE SEED IS THE WORD OF GOD.

MAY 1, 1889.

THE CHURCH IN INDIA.

BY THE REV. R. R. WINTER, OF DELHI.

AT a time when men's thoughts are a good deal turned towards Christianity in India, and how so to present it to the people that it may with God's help come home to their consciences, I desire to write to the Society, so far as my observation and experience can be of any use, on the subject of the Church, and making it, as the visible expression of Christian truth, the leading means of laying that truth before the people of India; and I would base, so far as sentiment goes, on St. Peter's words, "Love the brotherhood," and on St. Paul's to Timothy, "the Church of the living God, the pillar and ground of the truth."

I have urged this subject in many Mission sermons and speeches in England on my hearers, and rejoice to see that Sir William Hunter in his lecture this year before the Society of Arts had the same opinion. I venture to think that if we would lay our plans aright for the conversion of a country or a race, we must look at them historically, and endeavour to find their characteristics, for good or evil, as shown by the facts of their history, and thus learn to utilise the good in the service of God, and see how best to counteract the evil; for, till our aim is clear, how can we tell how to deal with a people, or how to differentiate between the wants and capabilities of a Chinaman and an African, or a Japanese and an Indian? "The historical institutions of India," says Sir W. Hunter, "afford a basis for a great Christian community as firmly united by internal discipline and mutual help as was the early Church. I believe it is reserved for Christianity to develop the highest uses of Indian caste: but it will be Indian caste harmonised by a new life." If there is one thing more prominent than another in the daily life of the people of India, it is the strong hold which the idea of brotherhood, within certain strongly-marked limits, has upon them. "Each caste is in some measure a trade-guild and a mutual assurance

society, and the members are dominated by the two ideas of com-
munal life and ceremonial purity." This life of brotherhood, including
men, women and children, is to them as much all in all as the corporate side of Christianity was to St. Paul when he told the Corinthians
that all the faithful form the body of Christ, and are members one of
another. Here, then, in an embryo and distorted condition, do we not
find the idea of the Christian society? And to a people afraid to stand
alone, and looking round to the support of corporate life, we should
present Christianity not too exclusively in its individual and subjective
side, as we, as Englishmen, might be tempted to do,—nay, to far too
great an extent have already done,—but also in the common life of the
Christian Church.

Here, then, we find that truth in them which we should utilise, and
this at the same time points out to us one of the most characteristic
and fundamental errors against which we have to struggle; for the
distortion of truth is the fruitful parent of evil, and "noblest things
have vilest using," and so this beautiful idea of brotherhood, becoming
centred in self-interest, ends in disunion. The very extent to which it is
upheld within the caste, to-day seems to intensify the separation of one
caste from the other. The brotherhood is so sharply demarcated off from
the rest as to point back to the ancient life of separate tribes; to eat,
drink, smoke and intermarry with those of another brotherhood creates
ceremonial impurity, and such a man becomes outcast from the only com-
monwealth he has ever recognised. Thus the idea of common humanity is
obliterated, and man is not cared for as man but only as a caste-fellow.
Further, this intensified adhesion weakens the individual, and the very
strength of corporate life dwarfs the growth of each member of the body.
These are certain prominent facts of Indian life, and do they not teach
us that we must show them the reality of which they have only the shadow,
and that if there be unity, sympathy, and self-sacrifice in the Church of
Christ, they will there find the embodiment of that ideal human society
of which their limited brotherhoods are but broken fragments or distorted
reflections?

Now comes the question of unity. If the Catholic Church,
not only in its beliefs and the personal life of its members, but in its
corporate life as the universal society, is to be brought as part of the
essence of the faith before the Indian people, surely her unity must
be not only a leading characteristic, but would appear to be of the
essence of her being. I am writing now, not of that wide unity which,
alas! lies for the present beyond our reach, but of the unity of the
Anglo-Catholic Church within the bounds of any one country. To consider this now is a matter of no mere theory, but of present importance,
because many are inquiring whether Indian Christianity be not a thing
so wholly *sui generis* as to be in danger of losing its characteristics if

brought up in the same fold as English churchmen; that the habits of mind, thought, and life of the two races are so widely divergent as to be mutually repellant; and whether, therefore, the Indian Church should not be organised apart from the Christianity of the European and semi-European part of the population.

This, I venture to submit, seems contrary to all historic precedent. It is true that Christian people have most miserably separated from one another, but this has been because on one point or another they have differed from the main body of the Church; but do we find that the Church in any one country has deliberately divided her one body, and said, "I will cease to be one, and will now become two"?

What do we see in Italy and Gaul of the fifth and following centuries? What a babel of rival races in Italy after the fall of the Western Empire—Roman and Greek; Gaul and Goth; Lombard and Norman, all gathered within one narrow peninsula. And again, what do we find in France? The Roman of the cities, the Gaul of the country districts, the invading Visigoth, Burgundian and Frank. Where could we find more widely divergent racial characteristics? Yet did the Church say to the Southern Italian, "You are so different from these high-handed Lombards of the North, we are sure you will never develop your own line of thought or bring out your subtle characteristics, which, if left to grow, will throw so much light on Christian doctrine; we will, therefore, give you a separate organisation, that you may grow, after a friendly fashion, indeed, side by side with your neighbours, but you shall not have your characteristic thoughts, ways, and theories interfered with"? Again, could wider divergence be found than between the Latin of Southern Gaul, not yet made France, and the Teutonic Frank of the North? Yet do we find divergence in religious organisation? Abundance of confusion, it is true, everywhere, but no separation. We see Catholic unity everywhere asserted in the midst of varying races and warring nationalities; while all without was a chaos of languages, jealousies, and varying laws, in many ways akin to the present position of India, yet the one place of peace and union was the Church, which in the progress of generations lessened divergencies, smoothed jealousies, assimilated laws, till all could be brought within the bounds of one nation. Would the hard-working, plodding, down-trodden English of the soil, and the ruling, cultured, domineering Roman have ever been fused into one English nation, if their points of difference had been accentuated by the presence of two parallel Church organisations? Let me quote part of Guizot's 12th Lecture on the History of Civilisation in France. "There is one fact which dominates over all, which characterises the Christian Church in general . . . this fact is the unity of the Church, the unity of the Christian society, despite all the diversities of time, place, domination, language or origin. Singular

F 2

phenomenon! it was at the very time that the Roman empire fell to pieces and disappeared that the Christian Church rallied and definitely formed herself. Political unity perished, religious unity arose. I know not how many nations of various origins, manners, language, and destiny are thrown upon the scene; all becomes partial and local; every extended idea, every general institution, every great social combination vanishes, and at this very moment the Christian Church proclaims the unity of her doctrine, the universality of her right. This fact . . . has rendered immense services to humanity; the mere fact of the unity of the Church maintained, gave tie between countries and nations which everything else tended to separate; and from the heart of the most frightful confusion arose perhaps the most extensive and the purest idea that has ever rallied mankind—the idea of spiritual society."

Let us now look at this question of a separate Church for the Indians with reference to the other great, strictly organised, and ever active exponent of Western Christianity. There is an abundant crop of post-Reformation sects in India who do not pretend to care for unity; one phase of Protestant Christianity is much the same to them as another. These scattered fragments, good and noble work though they are doing as pioneers, will as time moves on present but little attraction to the people of India, wanting as these bodies are in antiquity, authority, and cohesion; but is this the case with the Church of Rome? She knows wisely how to adapt herself to widely differing wants of race and temperament, yet Rome will never give up her unity. At what a disadvantage then shall we of the Anglo-Catholic side of the Church be placed! Rome pointing to the antiquity and continuity of her unity, would say: "Here is no invidious distinction between race and race, no difference between a Western and an Eastern brother; with us there is one bishop, one rule, one organic whole." I believe she would win hand over hand against us, and we should be left in a corner—the best-intentioned people in the world, still lamenting over our unhappy divisions. In spite of much Indian jealousy at the present time of English interference, what they really fear is not influence or union, but *domination*: and I believe the more ignorant would be amazed, and the better educated deeply offended, if told there could not be one Church for the ruled and the ruling race.

Two evils may be said to dominate native Indian society, selfishness and clannish disunion; do we wish to *heal* these sins, or to leave them? Surely a great cure for both is the love taught of man for man, the mutual self-sacrifice, the close drawing together of opponent sympathies, aims and ambitions within the loving arms of the living and life-giving reality, the body of Christ.

It has been wisely said that we cannot transplant our dear mother the Church of England into India. For this impossibility I am not

arguing; I am simply pleading for the Catholic principle, found in
all times, places and amongst all people of the Church in her early
days, of the unity of all races within the Church of one ecclesiastical
province. At the same time, while maintaining her connection with
the rest of the Anglo-Catholic Church, the Church would be allowed,
within certain limits defined by authority, to develop her own way of
meeting the wants of her own people. Further, we must be careful not
to cast the English and Indian sections of the Church absolutely in the
same mould; difference of language used in worship must exist, probably
additional prayers and services adapted to native Indian wants will
be demanded. Many points of detail, bearing exclusively on Indian
wants or plans, would be referred to Indian sub-committees of the
Diocesan and Provincial Synods, being again brought before the whole
body for decision. Also let us by all means develop the "Panchayat"
system of Church government as much as possible by parish councils,
city councils, district councils; but let all be gathered up under the one
Bishop and his Diocesan Synod. If it be argued that the language
difficulty will be insuperable in meetings for discussion, I believe this
will be solved by patience, time, and practice. Speaking lately with
a Christian gentleman in an important Government post, on this wide
subject, he gave it as his opinion that educated natives would think
it an insult to be cut off from the Church of the English, and that all
such attempts would end in confusion and in intensifying the political
want of sympathy between the English and natives; and that when
once meeting on common ground, the Indian members would be fully
ready and able to hold their own in the presence of the English members
in matters both of understanding and of language; for we must remember how rapidly a knowledge of English is spreading, and that it bids
fair in time to become as much, or nearly so, the *lingua Franca* of
India as Urdu is now.

There is another important point urged by the advocates of leaving
India to govern her own Church; they are anxious to allow of the
growth of Indian thought and Indian expression of thought on the great
facts of our faith. No union with the English will repress the Indian
mind. Centuries of foreign rule show this, and I would ask, do they
wish to go beyond the three creeds, and to want more than satisfied the
fathers of the Greek Church?

With regard to the Thirty-nine Articles, it would not be difficult to
come to an agreement as to which should be retained and which
omitted as merely the outcome of passing controversies. The little
Church in Japan is already setting us an example of moderation and
self-restraint in this matter; I think there is great fear of our English
theologians being more Indian than the Indians, and of their being
more ready to leave optional the use of that grand treasury of worship

and belief the Anglo-Catholic Prayer Book than would be appreciated by the people themselves.

The fact is, we want the Church to do in India what she did in Italy, France and England; we want her to be able to bring into God's service the characteristic excellencies and tendencies of each race within her fold, that the one may react on the other. If the English churchman needs to be made less individual, less subjective in his ideas of religious life, so the Indian churchman needs to be made more practical; so that while his usual metaphysical thoughtfulness may add depth and breadth to our downright English ways of thought, so we may bring into the common service the hearty, breezy, wholesome way of dealing with things that is more redolent of the first than of the last.

To conclude, may I present three practical difficulties that, *inter alia*, occur to me if two Church systems are to be allowed ?

1. Who would determine the section to which each man should belong ? For we may be sure that many educated Indian churchmen would join the so-called English section, to the great loss of their poorer and more vernacular brethren, and to the still greater loss to the idea of Indian thought for the Indian Church.

2. The difficulties in the way of discipline would be almost insuperable.

3. When disestablishment comes, are we still to maintain two sets of bishops, two co-ordinate sets of priests ?

Let us then, having got the Anglican organisation and the Anglican Prayer Book in India, leave matters as they are, and make no endeavours after a theoretic division; in God's providence we *are* one. Let the Church keep to that oneness, and gradually, as generations pass on, adapt herself in language, expression of doctrine, mode of thought and ways of government to the wants of the age and her people; let her maintain the essentials of a Church in the apostolic orders, the creeds and the sacraments, and then, when the time comes, make herself as " Eastern " as she will, but let it be her own act, within the bounds of her own Unity. I have but little doubt that as India now adopts and assimilates so much of European thought and custom in matters secular, so probably her Christianity will be less distinctly different from Western forms of worship, thought and dogma than many persuade themselves she desires to be. Thus each part, supplying the wants of the other, "may grow up in all things into Him which is the Head, even Christ; from whom all the body, fitly framed and knit together through *that which every joint supplieth*, according to the working in the measure of each several part, maketh increase of the body unto the building up of itself in love."

I shall be truly thankful if I have been able to make the least contribution towards a controversy which so deeply concerns the life of the Church in India.

ZULULAND.

YOU ask for a general review of the position and prospects of the diocese. As you are aware, I was absent from the diocese from the beginning of April to the beginning of October, and naturally no important move took place while I was away. When Mr. Wallis, who had been acting as Catechist at Kwamagwaza, left to return to Capetown in February, Archdeacon Hammick went there to take charge. We always contemplated the possibility of a review of this arrangement on my return. Unfortunately an event we had not reckoned upon took place. Some members of the old Zulu royal family resisted by force the exercise of Her Majesty's authority, and for some time the whole land was in a ferment. In some places deeds of violence were done; in all there was fear and distress. The annexation, which could at one time have been so easily, and naturally, and happily carried out, had caused trouble and bloodshed at last. I am wrong. I said at one time. Say, rather, many times, for more than one or two excellent opportunities have been allowed to pass: at the end of the Zulu war; at the return of Cetshwayo; at the fall of Cetshwayo; at the partition of the land by Boer adventurers. These, at least, were grand opportunities, and had the annexation taken place when it ought, many thousands of Zulus would be alive who now have been killed by internecine strife. A vast amount of hatred and bitterness would have been prevented, much distress to both black and white would not have taken place, and Mission work, especially English Mission work, would have made good progress under the prestige of British government. But in place of this we have had a year of scares, and now political trials are going on which must have a great influence upon the land. We hope it will be for the consolidation of British power, and the introduction of a firmer and fuller system of government.

Kwamagwaza, so sadly famous in the history of the Mission, is now surrounded by farms occupied by white men—Dutch families for the most part, but with English mixed with them. At the Archdeacon's first English service seventeen attended. I myself had, with Mr. Wallis's help, held one service there in Dutch, and had baptized the child of an

Englishman named Smith, and of a Dutchman. When the disturbances took place these white people all fled, and no English public service has been held there since. The same scares put a stop to the school work

A GROUP OF ZULUS.

at Etalaneni, where, on January 4, I had opened a large school church. Between 90 and 100 was the average attendance at once, the greater part being the children of Christians who had fled from Kwamagwaza in

the previous troubles four years ago. Since they left Zululand, before the
war in which the buildings at Kwamagwaza were destroyed, they had
not had any nice place in which to assemble for worship nor for
school, and the new building was thankfully appreciated. Soon, however, came the great scares, and school work had to be suspended
again, and all hands put to work to fortify the school church in
case of an attack, which happily was not made after all. Dr. Petrie
had found it necessary to leave Kwamagwaza (the Archdeacon was
in Swaziland), and Mr. Roach was forced to bring away his wife
and children from Etalaneni to Isandhlwana and St. Augustine's, and
eventually, as there were many scares even then upon the border, to
cross over into Natal. These facts will show you into what a troublous
condition politics, with which we had nothing to do, again brought us.
While I was sitting in conference at Lambeth, and being welcomed and
entertained all over England, our Missionaries were in anxiety and
fear, and our native people, afraid to sleep in their own homes, were
lying out in grass night after night of an unusually cold winter. Yet
one or two important steps forward have been taken. Our St. Andrew's
Station, which was not well placed for Mission work, has been moved twelve
or thirteen miles higher up the Tugela, at the request of some chiefs who
were anxious to have a school right amongst their people. Such a
request from Zulus was too blessed a novelty not to be attended to, and
as the Mission funds and the Mission staff were quite inadequate to
support an additional station, the old place was pulled down and the
materials used so far as possible to put up better buildings on the new
site nearly surrounded by the little river Inembe, an affluent of the
Tugela. My first act after my return was to run up the coast of Natal
by rail, postcart, and on horseback, and formally open the new station.
Mr. and Mrs. Farmer, I am glad to find, like the place, and congregations
are large—about 80—almost entirely heathen. Much may be hoped
from this work after some years of steady, patient labour. Another
advance is now being made. The Archdeacon is giving himself entirely
to work among the white people, who are constantly increasing in number.
Vryheid, the town which was established by the Boer in-comers to be the
capital of their new Republic, has for a long time been a responsibility
thrown upon hands already over-full. The Archdeacon has visited the
place from time to time, making himself personally very acceptable to
the people. I have gone when I could, and have already held two small
confirmations there. So it has seemed best that the Archdeacon should
go there to reside permanently. And this the more as it is conveniently
situated for visits to Swaziland and the goldfields at Forbes Reef, Pigg's
Peak, and other places. He has to-day started for Vryheid to try to
make needful arrangements, and will visit on the way the Nonsweni Gold-
fields, about three hours' ride from here, where there are already between

F 3

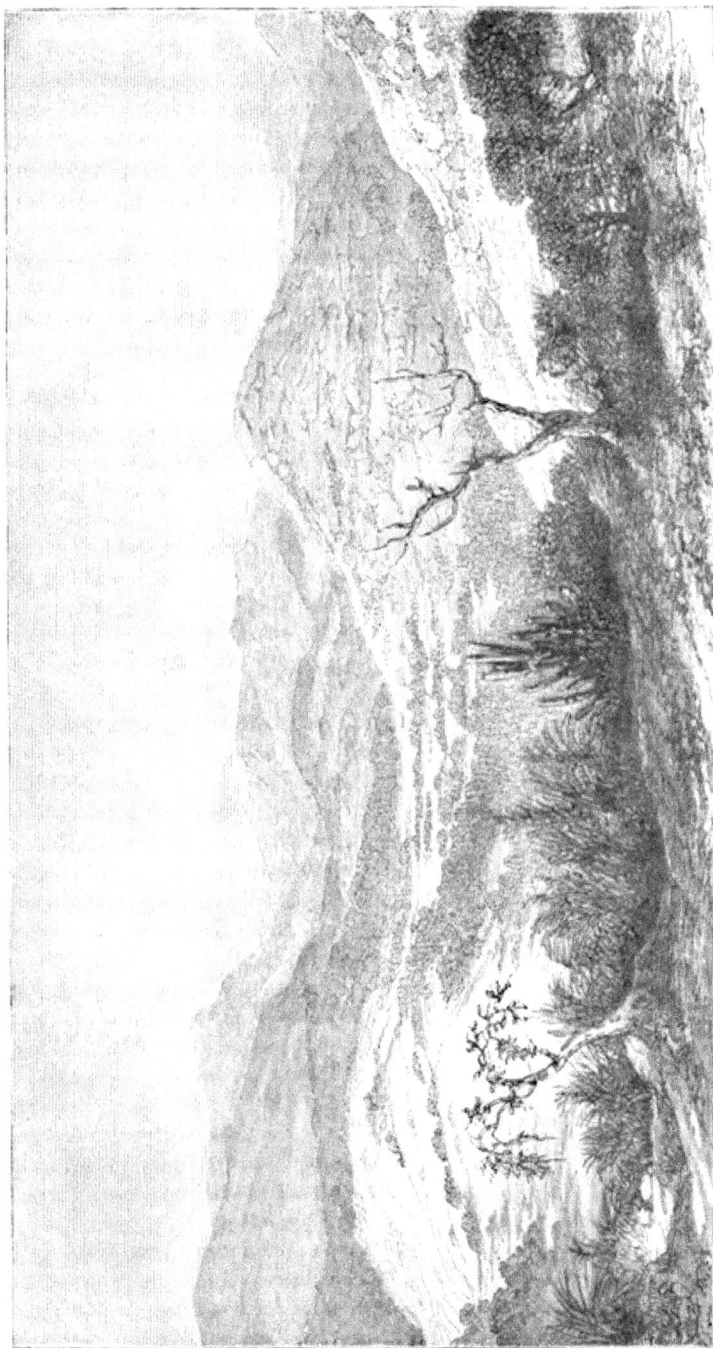

THE NGOME MOUNTAINS, LOBOMBO RANGE AND VALLEY OF THE BLACK UMVOLOSI.

thirty and forty people, three of the men having wives and children
with them. I was there last month for a Sunday afternoon service.
This is work of a very important character, and is sure to grow upon us.
Swaziland, too, is developing, and if it should be brought before long
under white man's rule, it will develop fast. A revolution has been
attempted there and failed; the Prime Minister, Sandhlana, has been put
to death, and the king's brother, who hoped to make himself king, has
fled to the Transvaal. There is already a Committee of diggers and
traders who are supposed to look after the white people in the country.

ZULULAND

S P G Map

But it does not work
smoothly at all. It
is said that the Trans-
vaal Government have
sent to the king offer-
ing to take over the
country, and to pay
the king an allowance
of £2,000 a year for
life, and that the king
has sent down to ask
the Governor of Natal
what he thinks of the
proposal. It is clear
that with gold in the
country, and white
men coming in more
and more, it will not
be possible for native
rule to be maintained
much longer; and if
E n g l a n d will not
annex Swaziland it
must consent to an-
n e x a t i o n b y t h e
Transvaal.

I asked the Society
last year to give me two more men, one for work amongst white people
in Zululand, one for corresponding work in Swaziland. Can nothing be
done this year? The want steadily increases. The Archdeacon visited
Pigg's Peak, which is across the Komati, in June last year. I hope to go
there in March or April. A considerable staff of Cornish miners is employed there who are left unshepherded. Mr. Jackson is our nearest
missionary to them. He writes to me saying that he cannot go away
to such places unless he can be enabled to support a good Catechist

F 4

who may look after the neighbourhood of the Usutu station in his absence. I received a letter by the last post from Natal, asking me to look after two young ladies who had gone as governesses to Dutch families, now in Zululand. I am told that one is a communicant and

CHURCH OF SAINT AUGUSTINE'S, ISANDHLWANA.

the other wishing for confirmation. It will be no easy matter for me to find them or do much for them when found. And as it happens, I am just now very hard pressed. Mr. Turpin, who is in Deacon's Orders, and the one of our party at Isandhlwana who speaks Zulu fluently, has broken down in health, and I am forced to give him three months' leave of absence that he may have the help of doctors in Natal, and perhaps an operation in the hospital. I had arranged for him to take the instruction classes here and at the out-station, six miles off.

I now have to take these myself, as well as the outlying services. With these classes and my two white pupils who came out with me the other day, and with whom I am reading St. Matthew's Gospel in Greek, the Acts in Latin, Sadler's Church Doctrine, Bible Truth, and Proctor and Maclear on the Prayer Book, I have nineteen hours a week of class teaching now on my time table, and two trips to Hlazakazi in addition to Sunday work.

I am hoping that the Rev. W. E. Smyth will come out in June to take on the Theological Tutor work and really learn Zulu. But I shall have to add him to the party for whom I have already to provide board and lodging from private funds. I cannot, however, lose the chance of a third class Classical Tripos, first class Theological Tripos, and a medical degree as well.

The application for Delagoa Bay is pleasant reading. It is difficult to learn the truth about that place and the prospects of the railway. I fear it is true that the climate is really deadly. I was told at the Nondweni by one who was brought away almost dead from fever after working on the line that more than 300 died while the line was being made, and that it was not through drink as we have often supposed. He is a teetotaller himself, and he says that they took fever more quickly than others. I hope to go into Tongaland in June and July, and I will then go again to Delagoa Bay. I have not been there since 1881, and I have promised Dr. Petrie to take him with me. I hope we shall be able to find out much more. I do not at present think that one man could go there alone. I have been accustomed to say that a priest, a doctor, and a catechist, at least, ought to form the mission party, and that there ought to be a station on the Lobombo mountains to which they could retire from time to time. But it is a scheme altogether beyond our means. It will be needful to find out what the railway company itself will do towards the support of a chaplain and then to see what funds S.P.G. could put at our disposal.

I ought to have said that Mr. Johnson's work at St. Augustine's makes very good progress, especially in that valuable part of the work, all too new in this Mission, the out-stations.

KEISKAMA HOEK.

GENERAL REPORT OF ST. MATTHEW'S MISSION, KEISKAMA HOEK, IN THE DIOCESE ON GRAHAMSTOWN, SOUTH AFRICA, FOR THE YEAR 1888, BY THE REV. C. TABERER, THE SOCIETY'S MISSIONARY.

HERE is necessarily much sameness in the annual reports of a Mission station. Year after year we work in the same beaten track, and this is especially the case with educational and industrial work. Old scholars and apprentices, after attaining a certain amount of proficiency, go away, and are succeeded by others who require exactly the same training as those who preceded them—and this monotony would become wearisome if we were not encouraged by the knowledge that many of our past boys and girls are really doing well in various parts of the colony, and are standing witnesses to the abiding usefulness of the work we are endeavouring to carry on.

In this report, however, what is usually called the real spiritual work must claim my first attention. For myself, I have strongly contended for many years past that educational and industrial training (especially the latter) are invaluable aids, if not absolutely necessary, to the growth of spiritual life in the native races of South Africa; invaluable and necessary because the gospel of labour, although subordinate in its degree, is part of the Gospel of Christ. For purposes of this report, however, I will speak of the work of this Mission station under three heads—Church, School, and Industrial.

Although in looking back through the past twelve months I cannot call to mind any very marked feature in the usual round of services and out-station visiting, I am glad to be able to say that there has been much more to encourage and more apparent success attendant upon our efforts during the latter half of the year. In the earlier months I was often much depressed by the apathy and indifference of many of my church members. I found it difficult to arouse any enthusiasm among them; and there was a marked falling off in the contributions to the weekly offertories, and in the annual subscriptions to the Diocesan Native Ministry Fund. To counteract all this, and to create if possible a better spirit among my people, I called special meetings at various times with the good result I have referred to above, and during the past three months especially, the services have been better attended; the offertories have increased in value; and numbers who had before refused or neglected to contribute to the Native Ministry Fund, came forward with their sub-

scriptions. Altogether, therefore, I have every reason to be thankful for
the past, and to take courage for the future. One of the first difficulties
of the work here, is the scattered condition of the congregation. The
district over which my travels extend comprises about one thousand
square miles in area with a native population—five-sixths of whom are
heathen—of from ten to twelve thousand souls ; and the members of
the church, numbering from fourteen to fifteen hundred, of all ages, are
dispersed throughout the whole of this district. It is therefore almost
impossible for me to personally visit them all in their homes, and this
probably accounts for the want of real interest in Church matters I
sometimes find so depressing, and for the occasional falling away of converts. This difficulty is partly met by the good services rendered to the
Mission by my large staff of native Catechists and Readers. These
helpers, twelve in all, attend with fair regularity the monthly meetings
of Catechists and Teachers at the Home Station, and carry out fairly
well the work allotted to them at these meetings, of visiting and holding
services at the fifteen out-stations of this Mission. It is part of our organisation that on the first Sunday of every month the out-station chapels
shall be closed in the morning, and all Catechists, Teachers and Christians
are expected to attend the 11 A.M. service at St. Matthew's. I find this
arrangement very helpful to the work generally, in bringing many of my
people to the service here, who would otherwise not visit the Home
Station for months at a time. In this way these monthly special services
are a bond of union among the members of the church, and are always
looked forward to with much pleasure. On the first Sunday in December,
there were at least 700 people present at the morning service, and it was
quite impossible to find room for all inside the church ; about 150 were
obliged to remain outside, and it will become a serious question in the
immediate future as to what is to be done to provide accommodation for
the increasing attendance. After the morning service on this occasion
150 native communicants remained to the celebration of Holy Communion.
The same thing occurred on Christmas Day, and I felt serious concern
for the numbers who were obliged to remain outside the church during
the service. On the first Sunday in October there were 132 present at
the celebration of Holy Communion, and in November 140. Our numbers appear therefore to be steadily on the increase, and I am most
thankful to be able to record this fact.

The total number of communicants on the roll is about 350.

We have had no confirmations during the year, as the Bishop has
been absent in England. About seventy-five are preparing to receive
this rite, and about twenty adult converts are being prepared for holy
baptism.

Sixty-nine children and twenty adults have been baptized during the
year.

In the school work we have scarcely been able to hold our own during the past twelve months. This partly owing to the fact that the Rev. M. A. Maggs, who had charge of the Boys' Institution last year, was taken away to fill another post in January last, and hitherto I have been unable to supply his place. His departure from here, which was a

THE MISSION AVENUE, KEISKAMA HOEK.

serious loss to St. Matthew's, will, however, prove, I trust, a great gain to the Missionary work at the Bolotwa, to which station he has been appointed.

I have also taken up a somewhat new position with reference to school work at out-stations, in insisting upon more help being rendered by the people themselves towards this object than they have hitherto given. This, to a certain extent, militates against opening new schools in my district, but it tends to create a more healthy tone in existing schools, and will eventually, I believe, have abiding good results.

We have had more than 500 names on the books of all our schools during the year, and the average attendance has been 183 boys and 219 girls—total 402.

The following letter, received by me from the Superintendent-General of Education in August last, will show how efficiently the girls' school and boarding establishment has been carried on by the lady in charge, Miss Lishman.

Department of Public Education, Cape Town,

SIR,   August 30, 1888.

I am instructed by the Superintendent-General of Education to say that he recognises your claim for special consideration, on the the ground that St. Matthew's is the only training school for native girls connected with the English Church ; and five additional allowances, at £10 each per annum, will be paid from October 1 next.

Dr. Dale thinks the Inspector's Report (of which an extra copy is sent) furnishes the most conclusive evidence of the usefulness of the institution.

I am, Sir, your obedient servant,

(Signed)   GEORGE MACONACHIE, Secretary.

The industrial departments have been somewhat crippled in their operations by the action of the Colonial Government during past years in curtailing the grants to native industrial institutions. No actual reduction in these grants has been made during the year under report, but the cutting-down process of previous years (the merits of which I fully entered into in one of my previous reports) so impaired our work in the industrial schools as to render the question a very serious one, whether we could continue this very essential and important branch of our work or not. After full consideration I determined to continue these departments, notwithstanding the great discouragements I had met with in the past, and although our numbers in the boarding schools have been necessarily smaller than they were four or five years ago, I can at the close of the year thank God and take courage for the future. I will also hope that the policy of the Colonial Government in curtailing the grants to an institution like St. Matthew's—the usefulness of which is so influentially and widely admitted—will not be continued in the future, but that the claims of the natives to a due share of the educational expenditure of the colony will be fully recognised, and I trust the day is not far distant when the eyes of colonists generally will be opened to the immense benefit indirectly conferred upon the community at large by the civilising and Christianising influences brought to bear upon the natives at these educational and industrial institutions.

We have five branches of industry regularly carried on in the boys' departments—namely, Carpentry, Waggon-making, Blacksmithing, Tinsmithing, and Gardening. The boys who come to us as scholars only are taught the latter for two hours daily. For the other trades, native lads are received as regular apprentices for a term of years, and the working hours in the shops are the same as those fixed by ordinary tradesmen in towns.

The value of the work accomplished during the year in these departments is as follows (this includes an approximate amount set down for garden work) :—Tinsmithing, £1,635 ; Carpentry, £375 ; Waggonmaking and Blacksmithing, £720 ; Gardening, £60 : Total, £2,790.

In the girls' department the usual branches of household work are taught, such as sewing, washing, ironing, &c. It would be difficult to give the exact value of the work done in this establishment, but approximately it would be about £95.

I especially draw the attention of all who have at heart the advancement and improvement of native girls, to the above letter of the Superintendent-General of Education, and I trust practical help will be forthcoming from the charitably disposed to enable me to further extend the usefulness of this department. Dr. Dale's communication is one of the brightest spots in our year's work, and is an indication, I trust, of a change of policy on the part of the Government with reference to native institutions.

The number on the books at the Home schools during the year 1888 was 217, of whom 110 were in the Boys' Institution, and 107 in the Girls'.

Boys, Native Scholars—Boarders ...	...	...	18
,, Native Apprentices—Boarders	...	...	36
,, Native Day Scholars ...	...	...	...	52
,, European Day Scholars	...	...	...	4
Girls, Native Scholars—Boarders ...	...	...	25
,, Native Apprentices— Boarders	...	...	3
,, Native Day Scholars ...	...	...	...	75
,, European Day Scholars	...	...	...	5
Total	...	...	...	...	217

The largest number of boarders in residence at any one time was, Girls, 21 ; Boys, 42 : Total 63.

The total expenditure in all departments during the year, including the industrial schools, amounted to £4,012. 16s. 8d.

There is still a debt of £1,164. 8s. on the extensive buildings I have erected at St. Matthew's during the past fifteen years at a cost of over £8,000, and for this debt I am personally responsible. I earnestly hope that substantial help will be sent to me by those who approve of my efforts, to enable me to clear off all standing liabilities and to develop and greatly extend our operations in the not very distant future.

THE TELUGU MISSIONS.

AST month we gave a brief account of Multyálápad in connection with the arrival there of the Rev. H. G. Downes.
We have now a report from the Rev. R. D. Shepherd, who
has been there for many years. It may be sufficient introduction to what he says if we remind our readers that Multyálápad is
one of the head stations in the northern part of the Diocese of Madras,
where the soft "Italian of India," Telugu, is the language of the people,
where the opportunities for missionary work have been immense and the
means for seizing them meagre, and where the number of baptized
Christians at this station alone rose in ten years from 1,540 to 2,320 in
spite of there being but one European missionary.

The Telugu people, Mr. Shepherd says, have peculiar charms for
those who are attracted by romantic and "genuine native" habits.
"The Telugus, however civilised they may once have been, however
great and powerful their empire, are now rather a rude people on the
whole than the reverse, and their manners and habits not much affected
by European influence."

We have already referred to Mr. Shepherd's having been the only
European missionary. This isolation has been aggravated by his having
the charge of another great Telugu Mission temporarily committed to
him; for in April the Rev. A. Inman took a well-earned and much-needed
furlough from the Mission of Kalasapád, which is thirty miles distant
from Multyálápad in a direct line, and much further for purposes of
inter-communication, a lofty range of hills intervening. "There are,"
writes Mr. Shepherd, "in the two Missions some eighty native agents
working." All of them, however, are laymen, and he proceeds to urge
the necessity of forming from this staff of workers a body of native
pastors. "I cannot praise too much the valuable services and efficient
work so many among them do, but, though such lay help in the absence
of clerical is so helpful, it is not the same with clerical. The Archbishop
of Canterbury once remarked that the exigencies of the case have raised
up a fresh order in India, that of Catechist. No one doubts His Grace's
meaning, but it does point to not alone a new order, but to something,

perhaps, more to be deprecated, a laico-clerical temper, to coin an appropriate word. These lay agents, village teachers, are fast acquiring the

CHURCH OF SS. PETER AND PAUL, KALASAPĀD.

position and influence of pastors; they may be looked at as lay pastors. This comes about from the missionary being unable to be anything more than chief pastor to his people; the priestly and pastoral functions, which unite in and form the *raison d'être* of the Christian ministry, are thus gradually being separated." Mr. Shepherd goes on to urge that the pressing need of these Missions is the native ministry. What is sorely wanted is a Native Pastorate, before the attainment of which no church is permanent and native of the soil.

"Give us—give these Telugu Christians of the Church of England I mean—this, and depend upon it the Church, under God's good spirit and with His divine blessing, will thrive and flourish. May I be allowed to give my opinion that to provide this at first discretion and wisdom is required? It is not wisdom to demand of natives before they be ordained that they pass tests identical with their European brethren in a language not their own. Why do we demand as much—why more—than is asked of those who have had more opportunities and much greater Christian training?"

We may hope from this that the day is not far distant when a Telugu native ministry may rapidly grow, especially as Mr. Shepherd adds that the Bishop of the Diocese remarked when he visited Multyálá-pad in 1887 that all the catechists there ought to be native pastors. "In each district there are four catechists, country ones, as we call them." There is also in each district one of the highly trained Catechists, called "M.D.C." (*i.e.* Madras Diocesan Committee) Catechists, Mr. J. F. Scott in Multyálápad, and Mr. John Appavoo in Kalasapád. "The latter, during Mr. Inman's absence, has had practical charge of the whole Mission of Kalasapád, numbering now 3,500 adherents. He has sustained the work most efficiently."

Two things seem evident from this—the high state of efficiency among the catechists, and the high standard for candidates for holy orders in the Diocese of Madras—two facts of considerable importance in view of the large numbers of the native clergy and catechists in that Diocese.

Of the rest of Mr. Shepherd's report a considerable part is occupied by his description of his visit to the Kalasapád Mission. He sends us a photograph of the Church of SS. Peter and Paul there, from which the accompanying illustration is reproduced. "I visited the whole of the villages in the Kalasapád last year—*i.e.*, every village where an agent is stationed or is working, and the work appeared very flourishing and hopeful. It is especially in the north of the Mission, in the Cunbun Telug of the Kurnool district, that the work has been spreading so much of late. It is still increasing, more villages are joining the ranks of Christianity, and the leaven of good is more and more deeply, I am convinced, working itself into the people around. If they do not well perceive the distinctive doctrines of Christianity, they cannot resist the influence of the Christians' lives; and not only so, the orderly and regular daily services at morning and evening are a feature

MISSION BUNGALOW, MULYÁLÁPAD.

which greatly strikes them, and often sets them reflecting. It sometimes is turned into a positive argument against their accepting our religion ;

they say people like themselves who have to work for their livelihood
cannot always be praying. This objection comes from the Hindus.
With the Mohammedans it is an argument in our favour, their rule
being to pray five times a day, which, however, is not very regularly
carried out, and that only by a few in the cities and larger towns.

"When preaching in the town of Cunbun, some Mohammedans
expressed themselves ready to join us, but wished first to learn a
little more about Christianity. I did not see any of them the next
day, though I invited them to my tent. One started the stock objection about God's having a Son, but he seemed to inquire in all
sincerity, and was satisfied with my answer that this doctrine is the
foundation of God's love towards us. If some regular evangelistic
work were done among them by someone knowing Hindustani (to
ingratiate them, not to make them understand, as all the Mohammedans in these parts know and speak Telugu commonly), some way
might be made among them.

"Another interesting people are the Chençus, a hill tribe inhabit-
ing the Eastern Gháts. They are like most hill tribes, very rude in
their habits, living in the meanest huts, and subsisting on the coarsest
fare. What is considered coarse food among the villagers is a luxury
to these poor people, whose common diet is a root called after them,
'chençugadda,' and other native produce of the jungles; a consequence
of this is that most of them are affected with spleen. It is not to
be wondered at that they often make grain raids upon the neighbouring villages. Those of that side of the Nallemahas are noted for this,
and, when their blood is fired with arrack, they are sometimes violent.
Their clothing is of the very scantiest, the women having only a
waistcloth, with their breasts discovered; the men have less. They
are a people to excite one's interest; and the difficulty in making
them understand is to speak Telugu pure enough, as they speak the
language simply without Sanskrit admixture, from having had so little
contact with the Aryan races. This is a proof of the antiquity of
Telugu and its entire disconnection with Sanskrit originally.

"I visited one of their encampments. They are composed of
only a few huts, not many residing together, and, with the aid of
a catechist, managed to make them understand the simple message
of salvation and deliverance from sin. It is to be hoped the seed by
being continued to be sown may bring forth fruit among them.

"It may be remarked that the deputy-collector of these parts is
said to be one of these folk; he was reared and brought up as a
Mohammedan, and is in consequence not very friendly to Christian
missions.

"Another thing to remark about these people is their utter fear-
lessness of tigers, which will not touch them; this is the more re-

markable as the Mahrattas, who reside close to them, often fall victims to these lords of the forests."

OLD MISSION COMPOUND, MULTYÁLÁPAD.

Mr. Shepherd's stay in the Kalasapád district lasted for three months. During that time he baptized 21 adults and 84 infants, and administered Holy Communion to nearly every one of the communicants.

He returned home through Nundial, which is the Society's third station in the Telugu country. Here the Rev. A. Britten is the resident missionary, and here is the training institution for native agents for the Telugu Missions. Mr. Shepherd's visit was connected with an important matter—the revision of the Telugu Prayer-book—the first meeting for the purpose being held on this occasion. He reached his own station of Multyálápad, on November 29, in time to celebrate the services of the Day of Intercession. " This," he adds, " has become a feature in our Missions from a few years back. I am desirous of awakening in the Christians' minds an interest in Missions and a slight knowledge of work being carried on in other parts of India and of the world. With this purpose we tried translating some of the *Quarterly Leaves*, which the Secretary in Madras kindly got printed. These have been distributed among the readers. Their effect has yet to be seen; but if it rouse the people to an apprehension of the greatness of Christ's Kingdom and their own share in it, this may have its fruits in increased earnestness and a spirit of self-help."

Mr. Shepherd sends some other photographs, which enable us to show two views of Multyálápad. One gives the exterior of the Mission bungalow, and the other the old compound with the school to the left, the houses of Christians to the right in the distance, and the chapel in the centre. No permanent church has as yet been erected here, but he adds : " A solid and handsome church is in course of construction at Multyálápad, the walls of which have been half completed ; the arches are in process of building. It is of blue limestone, with teak wood-work, and the whole, when completed, will hold comfortably 600 people as the natives sit. It will be an edifice worthy of the worship of God, and a monument, it is to be hoped, to the heathen of the beauty and permanence of our faith. Attached is a burial ground, a novelty in these parts, where we generally use out-of-the-way corners and the banks of streams for burying our dead. This should tend to promote reverence for the dead and greater decorum in burial both which are points to be regretted from their absence."

THE CHILDREN'S CORNER.
THE HERO OF SÁHAMAFY.—A TALE OF THE FRANCO-MALAGASY WAR.

BY THE REV. ALFRED SMITH.

(Continued from page 146.)

CHAPTER VIII.

AMONG those whose names were put down to face the French at Tamatave were those of Ralay, Ratefy, and Ratsimba. Immediately this was known, the Bishop sent for the two former. The two lads were full of excitement. They were going to fight for the Fatherland, and if need be to die for it.

"Well, well, my lads," said the Bishop, "there's an old proverb which says that it is sweet to die for the Fatherland. War is nevertheless a dreadful thing. Have you made any preparation for the road? I suppose you will have to walk down to the coast. You will find that a hard business. There is the fever!"

"We are doing what we can in the way of preparation," answered Ratefy, smiling, "but we are not rich, as you know. However, it is our fate to go, and what would you have?

"Everything is in God's hands; don't call it fate. I trust you will neither of you forget that you are Christians in this time of trial."

"God forbid we should forget that. We hope even to be able to do something in His service amongst those who go with us. We are not going as common soldiers, you know, but as attendants upon the officer in command."

"That is very good. Do try and do something to teach the soldiers, who are, I am afraid, mostly heathen. I hear many of them have been buying charms from medicine-men as a protection against the French bullets. Try, at least on Sundays, if you cannot do so daily, as you have been accustomed—try and get people to come together for prayer to God for protection. You will find, I trust, many in the camp who belong to our churches at Tamatave, and these will help you to form a little congregation."

The boys promised to do all they could.

After a few minutes' silence the Bishop resumed: "You will not leave the capital before Monday. Of course you will both come to the Holy Communion on Sunday morning, for the strengthening and refreshing of your souls before starting on this most serious and dangerous duty. You will also like to take leave of your fellow-Christians in the Church."

"O yes; we may never see any of you again," replied Ratefy, and a dark shadow passed across his face. "Somehow I feel I never shall. But I'm not afraid," he added.

"We are all of us in God's hands; let us only trust in Him. We will kneel down now and ask His Almighty protection."

They knelt down together while the Bishop, with solemn earnestness, besought Him who ruleth all things to protect the lads.

When they rose from their knees he put a sum of money into their hands. "To help you on the road," he said. "Mr. Earnshaw is getting some simple medicines for you too," he added, " in case of fever."

The lads expressed their grateful thanks; and cheered and strengthened, with lighter steps they hastened away.

A few days after, the first detachment of soldiers, 800 strong, left the capital for Tamatave, the seat of war; among them being our two friends and Ratsimba, who was attended by the slave Rabe.

The equipment of the soldiers consisted merely of their rifles (most of these being old flint and steel businesses), and a small tent made of rofia cloth. Some of them carried small sacks of rice for use on the road, and these very soon appreciated the wisdom which had prompted them so to do. The villages on the road are none of them large. The food available in any of them is very limited, and rice sufficient for 800 men could hardly be obtained in them all put together.

The road eastward winds over bare hillsides for a long day's journey till the edge of the great forest of Análamagaótra is reached. Throughout the day the men toiled along this road, where not a leaf of grateful shade afforded them a shelter from the burning heat. Many of them were still young, and hardly one of them had been far from his native village. Thus the incessant and monotonous ascending and descending these bare hillsides soon began to tell upon them. The compact body which had left Antananarivo in the morning had by midday even become a long straggling line; and when, upon arrival at the midday halting-place, many were unable to purchase even the smallest quantity of rice, symptoms of discontent rapidly began to show themselves.

CHAPTER IX.

Ratefy and Ralay were among the last to arrive. Almost the first words they heard acquainted them with the fact that there was no food obtainable. The few huts were occupied by the officers, and the men were lying in every conceivable position in and around the village. The few who had taken the precaution to bring a supply of rice with them were engaged in cooking it gipsy fashion, using the coarse grass as fuel.

The two boys threw themselves wearily on the ground, little caring where they lay.

"Well," said Ratefy at last, "if this be the beginning of sorrows, what will the end be ? I shall never reach the coast alive."

"Nor I," responded Ralay wearily, "and I don't care if I don't. We may as well die on the road with fever and starvation, as be shot by the French at Tamatave. It is our fate."

"Oh, if we are to lose heart already, we shall have no chance at all."

They were thus bewailing their fate when the slave Rabe appeared beside them.

"Have you not got any rice ? " he asked them.

"No, my friend; we did not think about it before starting, and there is none to be bought here."

" Of course not. Ratsimba has sent me to ask you to come and eat with him. I brought a good-sized bag of rice with me, knowing how it would be on the road."

" That *is* something like ! " cried Ratefy, rising to his feet with a slight groan. " Come along, Ralay. Where is Ratsimba ? "

" Just outside the village there," said Rabe, pointing in the direction his master was. " The rice is just ready."

Rabe led the way at once, and the two boys limped after him.

They found Ratsimba lying full length in the grass. A little distance from him were the remains of the fire over which Rabe had cooked the rice he had spoken of. Ratsimba was evidently in a very bad temper, and as the two came up to him he began at once to curse the hard fate which had made him a soldier and brought him this discomfort.

" However, it's of no use talking," he summed up at last. " I know what I mean to do. Come, let us eat our rice."

Rabe at once brought forward the pot of rice, and they all made a hearty meal.

" Well," said Ratefy when they had finished, " I thought I was going to die of hunger. I must have been an idiot not to have thought that 800 men would never find enough food in these villages on the road."

" Ah ! you never remembered what happened to Raitrema, I suppose," remarked Rabe.

" No ; what *did* happen to him ? "

" Raitrema one day went westward to catch wild oxen, for he was strong and used to going long distances. He was also very obstinate, and, trusting in his own strength and obstinacy, he took nothing with him but his own body. He went on and on and on, and at last came to a great desert. He had taken no food with him. After a little while he was fain to lean upon a stick, for he was weary for hunger. But he still went on. He was obstinate. At last his knees shook under him and he sat down to rest. But his obstinacy would not let him rest, and he went on again. Then his eyes grew dim and he could no longer see anything clearly, but he still went on. He sank down at the foot of a hill, and there he lay senseless and swooning. There he lay till some bee-hunters came along, and behold, a man senseless lying at the foot of the hill ! They kindled a fire with their flint and tinder and warmed some water ; then they put a little honey into it and forced it down the throat of Raitrema. So, little by little the life of Raitrema came back to him. He became able to speak, and the first words he said were : 'Of two hard things, of three hard things, hunger is the hardest of all, for it blinds the eyes and makes the knees to shake. For the future I shall lay down a law for my children, that they never leave home, even for a single morning, without taking food with them. For without food, lo ! the mighty becomes as tow.'

"Ever afterwards people always took rice with them wherever they went ; except, of course, those who are obstinate and trust in their own strength. And that is the origin of the proverb which says : 'The stomach is not rice, neither is it the shoulder.'"

"It wasn't my obstinacy, however, Rabe, that made me come without rice," said Ratefy, laughing. "I never thought of not being able to buy rice, and that's the truth."

"Rice or no rice, I don't mean to stand much more of this," said Ratsimba. "There is enough for several meals yet here with me though, so we will eat together again to-night, and we can talk over our plans. I've got a plan in my head, my friends. Come on now ; the men seem starting again for the next stopping-place, and we may as well get there as soon as we can."

CHAPTER X.

It was midday in the hottest part of a burning tropical day in the little seaport town of Tamatave. The blazing sun overhead poured its blistering rays down upon the blinding sand-dunes upon which the town stands, and the still air shimmered as fiercely as the breath of a fiery furnace. All the European "stores" were shut, and the proprietors thereof were either wrapt in heated slumber or were restless in a still more heated wakefulness. The heads of the tall cocoanut trees, which rose up here and there among the houses, seemed floating in a molten quivering liquid, like spectre trees in some Fata Morgana. At different points along the straggling street, and defying the fierce heat, stood the sentries belonging to the French marines, which at the time of which I write were in occupation of the town. The French flag hung upon the flag-staff in the circular fort at the north end of the town, and outposts had been planted at small intervals across the little peninsula upon which Tamatave stands. In the roadstead in front of the town, half a dozen men-of-war swung lazily upon the long swell of the Indian Sea.

The quarrel which had culminated in the French occupation of Tamatave on the east and Mojangá on the west coast had been simmering for several months previously, not to say years. The French have always wanted Madagascar, and have several times without success tried to take possession of it. Still, for a good number of years they have held the island of St. Marie off the east coast and that of Nósibé off the west coast of the mainland. Nósibé is one of the most charming of tropical islands that can be imagined; but it is very unhealthy. The harbour is a lovely bay, backed by hills covered with forest, whose brilliant tropical foliage can hardly be rivalled anywhere. The roads wind round and round these hills till they reach their summits, and from thence one can look over the forest top down upon the beautiful blue waters of the sea. From those same summits no doubt many an ambitious Frenchman has cast covetous eyes towards the east, where the rugged edge of the central mountain range of Madagascar cuts the horizon.

Nósibé being unhealthy in itself and of very limited extent, cannot have been ever considered as a very valuable possession for purposes of colonisation. Its value has been that it has formed a very convenient base of operation for intrigues with the wild Sakalava tribe of the north of Madagascar against the Hova race. In spite of the fact that by treaty the French had acknowledged the Hova Queen to be Queen of Madagascar, they felt themselves at liberty to make independent treaties with Sakalava chiefs. The time came when a movement among the

Sakalava towards the Hova, brought about by a mission sent by the Prime Minister, excited the jealousy of the French. A definite claim of a protectorate over the north-west coast of Madagascar was made. Upon this being refused war had broken out.

Several days before the bombardment of Tamatave the Hova governor had withdrawn from the town with the greater number of the inhabitants. Three hundred men had been left in charge of the fort, with orders that they should retire immediately hostilities began.

On Sunday morning, the 10th of June, 1883, at the time when ordinarily the Malagasy were assembling for divine service, the bombardment began. The bombarding vessels were stationed on each side of the little peninsula.

At the sound of the first cannon-shot the few natives still left in the town, together with the men in the fort, decamped with the utmost speed. Within a quarter of an hour not a single Malagasy, with the exception of a few servants who remained with their employers, was to be found within a mile of Tamatave.

The bombardment, however, went furiously on, though little seemed to come of it beyond noise and smoke. Of course there was no reply from the fort. *It was empty from the first.*

For three mortal hours the gallant Frenchmen banged away at the empty fort, and then, feeling that by that time everyone in it must surely be slain, the order to man the boats was given.

Five hundred men were put into the boats and were solemnly, with much circumspection, rowed to shore. Having landed, the serious question as to how they should find out whether there was anyone in the fort or not arose. A wretched Creole who had been watching the landing was instantly seized, questioned, and commanded to proceed instantly to the fort and find out whether there were any Malagasy in it. He soon returned with the news that it was empty.

The order was now given to " march." On the way to the fort a few servants who could not resist the temptation to go and see what the Frenchmen were doing were shot.

The fort was now " taken," and, having established themselves therein, the French turned their attention to destroying all the Malagasy huts.

It then became necessary to make domiciliary visits to the houses of the English residents of Tamatave. The gallant soldiers stuck their bayonets through mattrasses in the most fearless manner, and examined all the boxes and empty cases they could find. But they caught no Hovas.

On the outskirts of the town was a pretty little house occupied by a missionary, who was very much suspected of harbouring Hovas. This place, after being searched, was occupied by a guard of soldiers. Prowling about all over the house, they discovered at length the little wine-

cellar that contained the reverend gentleman's stock of claret. It was
of a good sort, and far superior to the vinegarish *vin ordinaire* served
out to the French marine. This was a prize indeed! With heartfelt
delight the guard, exhausted by their gallant efforts in storming the
empty fort, threw themselves upon the prize. It was not *vin ordinaire*,
I repeat; this claret had even a bouquet extraordinarily enticing to men
used to *vin ordinaire*.

"Let us drink. Vive la République!" was instantly proposed by
the sergeant.

They drank that toast, and then "Vive la France!" and then half a
dozen other "vives," and very soon the whole guard were helplessly
intoxicated.

When the officer came round to inspect the post, what was his surprise to find all the men speechless on the floor! He shook the sergeant
violently by the shoulder, and shrieked: "What's the matter *donc!*"
With a groan, the sergeant responded thickly, "Poishon!"

"Poison! Quel malheur, mes braves!" wailed the horror-stricken
officer.

"Mais oui; poishon!" repeated the sergeant thickly, and wagging
his head.

Here was a state of things! the French army poisoned by a missionary! "À bas les missionnaires!"

The poor missionary whose wine was held to be "poishon" by men
used to *vin ordinaire* was at once seized, and hurried on board one of the
men-of-war, and securely locked in one of the cabins. After being kept
there for about a fortnight, he was sent away from Madagascar, and
ultimately indemnified for the arrest.

Having thus taken complete possession of Tamatave, there was
nothing left but to await further orders before marching straight up to
Antananarivo, and taking that town also.

CHAPTER XI.

I have said that the Hova governor with his men had left Tamatave
before the French bombardment began, and had retired to the hills
several miles distant. From these hills they could look down upon
Tamatave, and watch every movement of the French, while they were
securely cut off from attack by a vast quaking bog of sweltering black
mud. The bridge which had formerly led across this bog had of course
been removed.

Here, then, the Hova settled down. Huts were soon constructed by
the soldiers, and earthworks thrown up all along the edge of the bog.

A week had already passed away before the reinforcements began to
arrive from Antananarivo, with whom were our friends Ratefy and

Ralay.   The two boys looked perhaps a little thinner than when we left them at the beginning of their journey down country, but they were both stronger and in better training.

A good many of the men had, however, deserted on the way down, and some had purchased permission to desert from their commanding officer. Among these latter was Ratsimba. The plan of which he had spoken was the old one of bribery. The officer in command was only a poor man. He had very little means of support even in Imerina, and his being able to maintain himself at the camp would depend in a great measure upon what he could get as "presents." No allowances were made by the Government to either officers or men, beyond a ration of rice, when that was to be had.   Every officer and soldier had to maintain himself as best he could, and defend his country into the bargain. What the result of this would be may be easily guessed.   One result was that Ratsimba, who was able to pay a moderate sum (say ten dollars) for permission to return to Imerina, had accordingly returned. After paying the money, all he had to do was to retire into the forest for a short time, till the last soldier had passed, and then quietly make his way back.

When the roll was called at the camp, out of the eight hundred men who had left Antananarivo, six hundred barely remained.   The rest had disappeared.

These deserters formed themselves into robber bands, and have ever since been making raids upon the villages round Antananarivo ; not infrequently, indeed, committing desperate robberies in the capital itself. Thus Ratsimba returned to his old trade.

Soon after the arrival of the reinforcements at the camp, the authorities determined to make a night attack on Tamatave.   A council of war was held, and the troops were paraded.   After telling off the men who were to make the attack, the Governor made them an energetic speech.   He described to them the awful atrocities which might be expected to be committed by the French, should they ever conquer Madagascar.   How the men would be all slain, and their wives and little ones carried away to be slaves in the sugar plantations of Bourbon. How the Malagasy race would die away, and the lands of their forefathers become the heritage of strangers.

The men were thoroughly roused by this speech, and when the band struck up the new war march, it was taken up by the whole body of soldiers.   Mingled with wild yells, the fierce chorus rolled among the hills :—

> Mandany kartirijy Frantsay,
> Tsy voarakotr' ny tratranay è,
> Raha mbola tsy maty atý,
> Arovanay 'ty tany 'ty.
>   Bómbany, bómbany re !
>   Tsy voarakotr' ny tratranay è.

NOTES OF THE MONTH.

ON Thursday, June 6, the Society's Annual Public Meeting will be held in St. James's Hall, when the President, the Archbishop of Canterbury, will take the chair.

BY the appointment of the President, the Bishop of Chester will preach the Anniversary Sermon in St. Paul's Cathedral, on Wednesday, June 19, at the 11 A.M. service.

ON the Feast of the Annunciation (March 25), at Westminster Abbey, the Rev. James Thomas Hayes, M.A., Trinity College, Cambridge, was consecrated Bishop of Trinidad. The Bishop of St. Asaph was consecrated on the same occasion. The Archbishop of Canterbury was assisted in the consecration by the Bishops of London, St. Albans, St. David's, Llandaff, Leicester, Antigua, Jamaica, and Bishop Mitchinson.

FOR the See of Tasmania, vacated by the resignation of Bishop Sandford, the Rev. Henry Hutchinson Montgomery, M.A., Trinity College, Cambridge, Vicar of St. Mark's, Kennington, has been chosen by the Archbishop of Canterbury, the Bishops of Winchester, Ely, and Manchester, and Bishop Sandford.

ON the recommendation of the Church Missionary Society, the Archbishop of Canterbury has appointed the Rev. Edward Noel Hodges, M.A., Queen's College, Oxford, to be Bishop of Travancore and Cochin.

SOME foreign Dioceses and some branches of foreign Missionary work can send home reports in which the romantic element of adventure and even of danger imparts a lively interest to the record of the work done. Without wishing for a moment to diminish that interest, we may sometimes feel that attention, sympathy, and support are withdrawn or lost from other and older spheres of hard Mission work, which have entered upon, and are now in the midst of, a crisis of great hardship and difficulty. It is well that the Church at large should know of the financial struggle with which our brethren in the Island of St. Vincent and in the unendowed Diocese of the Windward Islands, West Indies, are brought face to face. The facts will appear in the following extract from a letter written by the Bishop of Barbados, who has spiritual charge of the Windward Islands, on February 28 last, and addressed to Canon Bailey, of West Tarring, as Secretary of the Christian Faith Society.

"Men like myself have to learn the lesson every year, simply more and more to leave all things patiently and trustfully in the Hand of God. Things could hardly look worse than they do now. At the beginning of last year the whole of the Government aid was withdrawn in St. Vincent, with only six weeks' notice, and now the Legislature has brought in an Ordinance for the compulsory resignation of the three remaining State-aided Clergy there, whose rights were reserved at the time of disestablishment. And this has, I fear, received the sanction of the Colonial Office, my appeal to them notwithstanding.

"This means that the Archdeacon of St. Vincent and one of the Curates will probably retire from work altogether. They are men well advanced in years, and their retirement on pension is quite reasonable. But Canon Branch, Rector of St. Patrick's, is comparatively young and vigorous. He offers to remain if his people will make up, in addition to his pension, the sum which he has hitherto received. If this is not done he will seek work elsewhere. Taking the more favourable view, this will leave the Cathedral city, quite suddenly, without any aid from the State; and when I tell you that collections were made here in Barbados last year to aid the Clergy of St. Vincent as it is, you may suppose that the sudden removal of some £700 a year from one parish has a very grave meaning in the future for the Bishop. The S.P.G. has given me for the last three years a grant of £200 a year for Tobago, to meet the sudden collapse occasioned by the withdrawal of the State aid there. This block grant expires in June. Unless S.P.G. renew it, I shall be almost without any funds to pay the clergy. As it is, the place is so poor that I can get little beyond this and the £115 which I give them from your Grant for Catechist-Schoolmasters. You see why I say, Give my warmest thanks to the Governors for their continued thought for my poor, struggling Diocese."

MARSEILLES is one of the chaplaincies in Europe to which the Society makes grants to assist the work which is being carried on among the British sailors in the port. There is a Sailors' "Home" there, of which the sailors gladly avail themselves.

The report of the Rev. T. C. Skeggs, the Chaplain, for the last quarter, ending March 31, contains many points of interest. We append some extracts:

"As usual at this time of year, we have seen some fluctuations in the attendance of men at the Sailors' Home, owing to the closing of the Black Sea Ports during the winter months; but as soon as the ice broke up, and trade was re-established, the numbers reverted to their normal figures. One hundred and twenty-one British vessels entered this port during the quarter ending March 31, 1889, carrying 4,309 men, exclusive of yachts, which at this season of the year are numerous. These have been visited by the Scripture Reader and myself, some of them more than once, so that our total number of visits on board ship amount to 138. As opportunity has offered we have given addresses, read and expounded passages of Scripture, and conducted worship with the men on board their vessels. Including services held at the Sailors' Home, 314 addresses have been given, at which 4,743 men have been present.

"The following is copied from my diary:—February 17.—S.S. ' Rose ' left port at 10 A.M. yesterday, struck the quay on going out, but proceeded on her way. This morning she was found in distress five miles beyond Planier (the lighthouse). The crew were taken off and brought to the Home. The vessel sank with the captain on board. The men were landed in an exhausted condition from fatigue and exposure. Their wants were soon provided for by the Matron, and the men comfortably lodged for a few days until the Consul had an opportunity of sending them home.

"The s.s. ' Knight Errant ' is favoured in having for master a Captain who holds two services on board every Sunday when at sea, and one during the week, at which the hymns and canticles for the following Sunday are practised. The captain leads the tunes on his violin. At his invitation I held service in the saloon one week night, and remained for the choir practice. The discipline and high moral tone which prevails on board this ship is a striking testimony to the power of a Christianising influence. Even the Mohammedan Lascars feel it. The Captain was very pleased to receive from me a supply of tracts in Arabic, and Scripture texts in Kurdi and Hindu, for distribution among the Lascars. These native Indian crews have for some time past been much on our minds.

"The S.P.C.K. has kindly provided me with Scripture texts attractively printed on cards, and short statements of Christian doctrine in the form of tracts in the vernacular. In the absence of any special agency for Evangelistic work among this portion of our sea-going people, this is perhaps as much as we can do for them.

"The engineer of a yacht, which he had left at Nice, presented himself at the Home in a destitute condition a short time ago. He was received, provided for, and was about to be sent home by the Consul as a distressed seaman, when a gentleman called at the Home, saying he required an engineer to take a yacht to England. The kindness which this man had met with at the Home, and the good providence of God, who had delivered him out of his distress, so impressed him that he has made a public profession of religion. He found a Prayer-book on board the yacht, and now has daily prayers with his men. From what I have seen of this man I believe him to be genuine.

"I have visited the sick in hospital regularly, and communicated with their friends when they have been unable to do so themselves. The general health of the men has been exceptionally good this past quarter, so that I have only had to pay thirty-three visits in hospital.

"I have reason to hope that their moral condition has improved too. Neither the prison, nor the ' lock ' ward in the hospital have received any of our men. There have been no deaths to record, and only one case of small-pox.

"In the beginning of March our Bishop paid us a visit, inspected the Sailors' Home, and held service there one Sunday evening. He expressed himself highly gratified with all he saw."

A T St. Leonards-on-Sea the members of the S.P.G. Association received recently from the Rev. R. H. Walker an address, both simple and forcible, which is now printed by the Society. The title is "Co-operation with the Holy Spirit in the Work of the Church."

"FOREIGN Missions, and How to Aid Them," is the title of a letter from one of the Society's Organising Secretaries, which is issued by the Society in a pamphlet form. It is a very helpful paper, and though of less interest to the general reader, will be valuable to the clergy and others who have to do with the Home Organisation of the Society. It deals with such practical subjects as the distribution of the work of a deputation, evening meetings, garden meetings, and parochial associations.

THE Rev. Brymer Belcher, of Bodiam, Hawkhurst, asks us to state that he will be glad to receive volumes, or odd numbers, of the *Colonial Church Chronicle*, with a view to making up sets to present to Colonial Bishops.

FROM Berbice, in the Diocese of Guiana, Archdeacon Farrar remits to the Society half of the harvest festival offerings in that parish, a large proportion being contributed by the Chinese and Indian coolies. The Archdeacon's son is engaged in missionary work among the aborigines, and he sends us some welcome notes on this ever-interesting subject.

"You will be glad to hear that my son is doing good work on the Courentyn. The Lieut.-Governor, Mr. Bruce, and the elective members of our Court of Policy (local parliament) have just returned from a visit to the Orialla Mission. The Lieut.-Governor read the lessons in the Mission Chapel for the catechist, Mr. Farrier, and afterwards addressed some 300 Indians, belonging to this Mission and Epera, some fifty miles higher up the river, who had come down to meet the vice-regal party. On leaving, they wrote a letter to my son, offering, with his permission, to finish the catechist's residence (in their private character, of course), a very substantial and very large building, 'as a memento of their visit'; they were so pleased with all they saw. This is very gratifying for every reason, and will, I am sure, strengthen the hands of my son. He is now on a 14 days' visit to those Missions. Perhaps I ought to mention that my Chinese and coolies have given £5 (of the sum total £14)—Harvest Festival offering—very liberal for so small a band. The Bishop is up the Demerara, and talks of going to Potaro again in the autumn, when he will be 82 years old! I believe the Bishop does not think he is more than 32 years old. He is, literally, a grand old man.

METHODS of missionary work are very various. We do not pretend to be able to weigh their relative merits. The Rev. G. Ledgard, in Bombay, comes in contact with Mohammedans, and his plan is to build up, not to throw down. There can be no doubt that the principles enunciated by him commend themselves as having Scriptural warrant, as well as being naturally attractive.

"Besides the regular preaching which is now carried on in the bazaars on each morning and evening throughout the week (Sundays excepted), we have of late done a good deal by way of visiting among the Mussulmans. I place much importance upon this branch of our work, because, coming in contact with them individually, one is better able to influence them for good. I always find that men who will oppose us almost fiercely in the presence of their co-religionists will talk very freely and calmly when alone; for they have then no dread of being thought unbelievers in their own religion, whether they be so or not. A Mussulman is generally in great fear of being considered by his own people to be deviating from their received views and beliefs; and, of course, there is at all times considerable danger when teaching new truths which militate against the belief of the hearers, lest we should, at the same time, lessen or destroy the religious feeling itself. I always feel it necessary to accept and strengthen the amount of truth already held, and endeavour to build upon it a foundation for an advance to the higher truth which we have to teach. If we were once to forget this, and begin to destroy, in the first place, before giving any other resting ground, we should find it a much more difficult task afterwards to cultivate and renew the religious feeling and reverence which are necessary for any real reception of divine truth. It is for this reason that I have been endeavouring, as much as possible, to impress upon our agents the absolute necessity of abstaining from discussion in our out-door preaching, and more especially of refraining from anything like an attack upon the religious belief of those to whom we preach. This I believe to be the chief reason why the educated classes in this country are, in so many cases, sceptical in religious matters. The Government education they have received has been sufficient to destroy belief in their own religious systems, but has given them nothing in its place, so that they have come to doubt the existence of any true religion whatever."

AN American Bishop, the Bishop of Missouri, has written to thank the Society for the report of the proceedings at the memorable anniversary last year in St. James's Hall. His warm words of affection for the Church of England and for the Society form part of the abundant evidence of the daily growing love with which the Church unites those on either side of the ocean.

"I am taking a wider view of everything, and I hope it is a deeper and a better view, because of my delightful sojourn among the sacred structures and the earnest clergy and laity of the Mother Church. May God guide and bless you all.

"Even now issues among you, fraught with momentous consequences, are pending. Our hearts and love and loyalty are with you. The venerable Society, with the care of whose active interests you are charged, shall ever have my affection and grateful reverence."

IN connection with Dr. Liddon's sermon for the Society, which we printed in February, and his recent election to the position of a Vice-President, we may refer to a beautiful photograph of him—the only one, we believe, that has ever been taken. It is issued by the "Church Agency" (51 Threadneedle Street), who brought out the excellent reproduction of the photograph of the Bishops at Lambeth, which was issued with the report of the Society's Anniversary last year. The Church Agency are able to produce the photograph of Canon Liddon by reprinting the number of "Men of Mark" which contained it. The number also contains another portrait that will be valued—that of the Bishop of Lichfield.

AT St. Peter's, Belsize Park, the Bishop of Jamaica preached a most valuable sermon recently. It has been printed by the Society and added to its list of publications under the title "Christian Missions Defended."

THE Society is desirous of commending strongly the Rev. Oscar Flex, who is willing to undertake work in England as a teacher of German or Hindi. Mr. Flex is a German clergyman who was ordained by Bishop Milman of Calcutta. He speaks English perfectly. Communications for him may be addressed to him at the Society's office.

MESSRS. Cassell & Company are issuing a publication called "Conquests of the Cross." The first number has been sent to us. It contains some excellent papers on Missions, and is well illustrated. It is expected that the book will be completed in about thirty-six parts

THE death of the Rev. J. K. Best, on April 5, removes from the ranks of the Society's friends one of whom the present generation knew but little, but who nevertheless did good service in past years both to the Church abroad and to the Society at home. Ordained in 1842 by the Bishop of Madras, he served faithfully the Missions of Madura and Christianagram till 1856, when he was compelled to return to England. Then he continued to act as the Society's advocate at home until 1865, when he sought the well-earned retirement of a small incumbency in Bucks, where he maintained his interest in the Society to the last. Quiet and unobtrusive, he was faithful in every good work, and leaves behind him the record of a blameless life devoted to the service of God and of His Church.

SUGGESTED SUBJECTS FOR PRAYER.

For the Telugu Missions, that the Christians may be built up in faith and knowledge, and that fit persons may be raised up to serve in the sacred ministry of the Church.

For the Missions exposed to peril in Eastern Africa, for the steadfastness of the Missionaries, and a happy end of all the difficulties.

For the newly-consecrated Bishop of Trinidad, and for the Bishops-designate of Tasmania, and Travancore and Cochin.

For those suffering from the famine in China, and that the recipients of Christian charity may listen to Christian truth.

MONTHLY MEETING.

THE Monthly Meeting of the Society was held at 19 Delahay Street, on Friday, March 15, at 2 P.M., the Rev. B. Compton in the chair. There were also present the Bishop of Antigua and J. G. Talbot, Esq., M.P., *Vice-Presidents*; the Rev. J. M. Burn-Murdoch, Canon Betham, J. M. Clabon, Esq., Canon Elwyn, General Gillilan, Sir F. J. Goldsmid, K.C.S.I., G.C.B., Colonel Hardy, J. R. Kindersley, Esq., General Lowry, C.B., H. C. Saunders, Esq., Q.C., General Sawyer, H. D. Skrine, Esq., and General Tremenheere, C.B., *Members of the Standing Committee*; and the Rev. F. K. Aglionby, Rev. Dr. Baker, Rev. J. M. Beynon, Dr. R. N. Cust, Rev. T. Darling, Rev. H. J. Day, Dr. de Tatham, T. Dunn, Esq., Rev. J. J. Elkington, J. F. France, Esq., Rev. H. Halford-Adcock, Rev. S. Coode Hore, Rev. Dr. Jones, H. Lawrence, Esq., and Canon Trench, *Members of the Society*.

1. After prayers, the minutes of the last meeting were read.

2. The Treasurers presented the abstract of receipts and payments from January 1 to February 28, printed on page 160 of the *Mission Field*.

3. Read a telegram from the Rev. A. M. Hewlett stating that he was accidentally prevented from attending and addressing the meeting as had been announced.

4. The Rev. William John Garton, of Verden, in the Diocese of Rupertsland, addressed the members, describing the rapid settlement of Manitoba, the desire of the settlers for the ministrations of the Church, and the necessity for the assistance rendered by the Society.

5. All the candidates proposed at the meeting in January were elected into the Corporation. The following were proposed for election in May:—

Alfred Brommage, Esq., Wolverhampton; Edward Holt, Esq., Highfield, Bedford; Colonel E. R. Green, St. Mary's, Bedford; Rev. C. T. Pratt, Cawthorne, Barnsley; Rev. Thomas Anderson, Chiswick; Rev. John Hands Townsend, St. Mary's, Oatlands, Weybridge; Rev. T. G. Nicholas, West Molesey, Kingston-on-Thames; Rev. Canon G. E. Pattenden, Chertsey; W. Donald, Esq., 4 Taswell Road, Southsea; Rev. C. O. L. Riley, St. Paul's, Preston, Lancashire; Rev. P. H. Ditchfield, Barkham Wokingham.

SOCIETY'S INCOME.

Abstract of RECEIPTS *and* PAYMENTS *from January 1 to March 31.*

	GENERAL FUND	SPECIAL FUNDS
Subscriptions, Donations, Collections, &c.	£7,225	£1,370
Legacies	2,350	107
Dividends, Rents, &c.	938	838
TOTAL RECEIPTS	£10,513	£2,315
PAYMENTS	£19,754	£3,514

The Receipts under the head of Subscriptions, Donations, and Collections for the General Fund from January 1 to March 31, in five consecutive years, compare as follows: 1885, £7,478; 1886, £8,316; 1887, £8,938; 1888, £7,746*; 1889, £7,225.

° In addition, the Treasurers received in 1888 Securities of the value of £25,296 as "A Thankoffering to Almighty God for the extension of the Church in the Colonies and Dependencies of the British Empire and beyond it"; also other Securities of the value of £2,268 as a Trust Gift, *the Income only being available.*

THE MISSION FIELD.

THE FIELD IS THE WORLD. THE SEED IS THE WORD OF GOD.

JUNE 1, 1889.

ENGLISH RESPONSIBILITY FOR MISSIONS.

BY THE REV. JOHN THOMAS JEFFCOCK, M.A., RECTOR OF WOLVERHAMPTON,
PROCTOR IN CONVOCATION FOR THE DIOCESE OF LICHFIELD.

" For ask now of the days that are past, which were before thee . . . . (i.) Did ever people hear the voice of God speaking out of the midst of the fire, as thou hast heard, and live ?

*(ii.) " Or hath God assayed to go and take Him a nation from the midst of another nation . . . . according to all that the Lord your God did for you in Egypt before your eyes ! "—*DEUTERONOMY, iv. 32–34.

I.

TWO great points Moses brings out to the people of Israel, when, at the end of forty years, he reviews their history for them; first, that God had personally given to them His law of the Ten Commandments; and secondly, that He had taken them, a nation complete, from the midst of the Egyptian nation by signs and wonders and power, and made them a free people, His own people. The first makes Him the Author and the Object of each Israelite's personal religion; the second, the Author of their collective and national life. God is the Author of both; God the End of both. To an Israelite, religion, morals and politics are alike from God, and are alike to be followed with reference to God, having His sanction, and to be worked out according to His will.

* * * * *

II.

National life is not less under the ordering and control of God now than it was then. The signs and the wonders may not be miraculous to all appearance, but the mighty hand and the stretched-out arm are there still. The Book of Daniel, the Book of the Revelation of St. John, show this in prophecy. He that can understand the signs of the times may trace it in history. When the full time came that the Son of God should be manifested in the world, not only did the Jewish nation, under God's directing hand, provide Him a mother, a nurture, and a home; but the civilisation and imperial organisation of Rome and the language of the Greeks helped the spread of His Gospel ; while the Greek learning and philosophy, by their dissolving the errors of others and by their own unsatisfyingness in themselves, cleared a way for the coming in of better truths, of a life-giving religion.

Nations, too, have their terms of probation, their times of sifting and of trial, their grand opportunities, which taken at the flood lead on to fortune; which unnoticed, unemployed, abused, end in shame, disgrace or death. Spain had once this chance. Situated on the shores of the Atlantic, the mistress of the New World, with a powerful position in the Old, she might have become great, and the instrument in God's hands for great good among the heathen. But there has been for four hundred years one canker at the root of her national life—intolerance. She drove out the Moors, men skilled in science and art ; she expelled the Jews, a race thrifty, frugal, and industrious; she established the Inquisition, and crushed out by torture and death anything like freedom of thought among the more educated classes (some think that between 200,000 and 300,000 perished by its means); and so she has sunk into a third-rate power in Europe, a wreck of her former self. There is a handwriting on the wall :—Thou art weighed in the balances and art found wanting! Thy empire is divided and is passed from thee !

(i.) But it can never be the duty of the preacher to throw stones at other nations, or to cast scorn on them, only to pamper the pride of his own. We English have a national lesson to learn. As the Jews had God so nigh them by personal revelation of His name and attributes, and by the communication of His law of the two tables so we English have God very nigh to us by enjoying the blessing of an open Bible and the establishment among us of our National Church. But, my friends, are the words, "an open Bible," more to us than a platform phrase, a telling expression, calling up somewhat of our glorious history as a church and nation, and suggesting privilege which poor Spain and some other countries do not enjoy ?

Is that open Bible found open in your hands every day ? Does God commune with you in its pages, and do you commune through it with Him ? Is Thy Word, O God, indeed a lantern unto my feet and a light unto my paths, in my daily walk, my daily behaviour ? Can I say, " Lord, what delight have I in Thy Word! All the day long is my study in it " ?

If so, well. If not, cease to speak of poor Spain, poor Italy, poor

Ireland! Rather hear Christ speaking to Laodicea and to you: "Thou
sayest, I am rich, and increased with goods, and have need of nothing;
and knowest not that thou art wretched, and miserable, and poor, and
blind, and naked! I counsel thee to buy of *me!*" God dealt so with the
Jews "that they might observe His statutes and keep His laws"; and
so has He dealt with us Englishmen, that we may do likewise.

Yet we not only have an open Bible, but a pure and reformed branch
also of Christ's Church, planted in this island from ancient times. This
Church preaches the Word of God, reproves the sinful, ministers to the
sick, builds up the faithful in their most holy faith, administers the
sacraments, feeds the souls committed by Christ to her charge. Let us
each one personally use these blessings which Christ has placed within
our reach; that God may be found in the midst of His congregation here
assembled; that Christ may make Himself known of us here in the
breaking of bread.

But further, the Bible, the sacraments, the means of grace which
God gives us in His Church—were they meant for ourselves alone? Surely
not. When the Jews were brought very nigh to God, and learnt His
name and received His commandments, was it for themselves alone?
When Abraham received the promise that he should be heir of the world,
was this merely for his own glory, his own benefit? Surely not. God
fenced them off, God drove His divine knowledge into their hearts by
temptations and signs and wonders, by enslavement, by captivity, by
oppression, by persecutions, that they might learn their *lesson*—"the
Lord thy God is *one* Lord, and thou shalt love the Lord with *all* thine
heart"—well, deeply, thoroughly, with heart knowledge, with life
practice; and that that knowledge once learnt, once thoroughly ingrained
in them, should never be parted with, and should be an experience,
experienced indeed *by* them, but *for* mankind—an experience learnt by
their nation, but through them received and accepted by all nations, as
an everlasting possession, a possession for the world. This is often God's
way of dealing with mankind; one generation learns, or one people learns,
a lesson for the benefit of all generations, all peoples. For example, no
Christian seriously doubts that the Lord Jesus Christ is Son of God and
Son of man; that He is "God of God, Light of Light, Very God of Very
God; begotten, not made; being of one substance with the Father."
But this knowledge, so elementary, so necessary to be known, had to be
fought out and unravelled and definitely acquired by the Church of
Alexandria, and indeed the Church at large, through discussion and
heart-burning and trial in the fourth century. But, so acquired, so
made the Church's own, fifteen centuries ago, it has remained the Church's
possession without serious debate ever since. We are heirs now to the
fruits of the Church's pain and struggle then.

Our open Bible, then, our pure and Apostolic and Evangelical Church,

are these priceless gifts of God gifts given us for ourselves alone? God
forbid! They are meant for others also, they are meant for the world. If
ever there was a doubt about it, there can be none now. At Lambeth
there met last year 145 Bishops of the English Church from all parts
of the world, demonstrating that ours is not an island Church, an insular
establishment, but has a work to do, and, thank God! is doing it in lands
from the rising to the setting sun. God gave us the Bible that we might
spread its glorious news of God Incarnate, of a world redeemed to all
nations; He blessed us with our National Church that that Church might
be the mother of other churches in other lands.

(ii.) In knowing God, then, intimately, we English people are like the
Jews of old, we are a chosen people.

But we are very unlike the Jews in one part of God's dealing with us.
The Jews, though dwelling on a continent, between the great Hittite
nation and the civilised Egyptian, the Syrian nation and the Assyrian,
were kept by God distinct, separated, isolated, unmixed, alone. God
assayed to go and take Him a nation out of the midst of another nation,
and to keep that nation apart by itself, through all its history, to the
intent that it might be a nucleus and kernel and core in things religious
to the world.

We English, on the other hand, though dwelling on an island, God
has seen fit to drive *into the midst* of other nations, and to settle us
amidst other peoples throughout the world; so that wherever the ship
can sail, there is the English sailor to be found; wherever trade can be
had, there is the English merchant; wherever colonies are to be settled,
there is the English colonist; while in many a fair country England reigns
supreme and administers justice to a hundred peoples! Whereas God
assayed to take the nation of the Jews *out of the midst of another* nation,
to do His purposes in the world, He has put us English *into the midst* of
the nations of India, into the midst of the nations of Africa and Australia
and America—but surely to accomplish this His purpose too.

Let us look to it. The Jews were isolated in order that the germ of
true religion might be fed and developed and grow in them, and be kept
alive and consolidated till the full time came for it to come abroad, a
light to lighten the Gentiles. We English are spread abroad into all
lands; we have committed to us a genius for colonising, a talent for rule
and administration, the gift of the love of travel and adventure and
danger; but these things not by mere accident, not for nothing, still less
to use only selfishly and without reference to those we come amongst,
without reference to God. These things are talents committed to us that
we may be the vehicle of conveying the Gospel to others, of propagating
in foreign parts the knowledge of the only God, and Jesus Christ, whom
He has sent, that we may be apostles to the heathen and ministers of
grace, that we may be a power of God in making the knowledge of the

Lord to fill the earth as the waters cover the sea. The Jews were isolated to conserve the truth ; we are diffused to spread it.

Consider India. Lord Dufferin, our Viceroy in India, speaking about that country last November,* gave the statesman's view in a political speech. Yet it well brings before us as Christians, believing ourselves in the Lord Jesus Christ, and believing that He is the power of God unto salvation, the responsibility of our Church and nation to spread the Gospel in India among its 250,000,000 inhabitants. We are a Christian nation thrust in by God into the midst of a heathen nation, or rather into the midst of a congeries of heathen nations, Hindoos, Mohammedans, Buddhists and worse ; not for nothing, but to proclaim the glorious liberty of the children of God in Christ to the idolater, the pantheist, the mere cold moralist, who cannot recognise that God is Love. Here is a splendid work, lying at our doors, laid there by God, Who orders all the affairs of an individual's life, but all the affairs and circumstances of a nation's life as well. Are we to ignore this responsibility, to pretend we do not see it ? or, seeing it, are we to shirk it, saying it is too great, too hard, it involves too great self-sacrifice ? We may do so. But the nation, the church, which does not rise to its responsibility in the sight of God, soon sinks in the scale of nations, in the scale of churches. It has its opportunity ; that opportunity it neglects, lets slip, through want of courage, want of heart, want of love. The door is shut, the opportunity is at an end ; that nation, that church, allows another to take its crown, another to step in, another to do the work of God which has dropped undone from *its* hand, and that church, that nation, passes away disgraced, forgotten, undone.

I might go on to point out how we English-speaking peoples are found on every shore ; how we are spreading in numbers, in wealth, in the geographical range of our language and literature, in influence : that an enterprising nation, a colonising nation, is like a city set on a hill—it cannot be hid ; but in the counsels of Him who is " Prince of the kings of the earth," this faculty, this talent to "be fruitful and multiply and replenish the earth and subdue it," is not entrusted to us for material aggrandisement alone, but that, like a little leaven hid in three measures of meal, we Christians are put there by God to influence the world till the whole be leavened. But to him that hath an ear to hear I have said enough. Rise, my friends, to your responsibility, rise to your dignity as a Christian nation, rise to your happiness as members of the Church of God which He has purchased with His own blood. And doing so, you will never turn your back upon, or hesitate to help, with prayer and with purse, a Society which has been doing God's work and the Church of England's work for nearly 200 years—as has the Society for the Propagation of the Gospel in Foreign Parts.

* Vide The Mission Field, January 1885, pages 34, 35.

JAPAN.

NDER the title of "The Birthday of a Constitution" the Tokyo correspondent of *The Times* gave in that journal, on March 22 and April 3, a graphic description of the ceremonies and rejoicings with which the promulgation of constitutional government for Japan was accompanied.

"Twenty-one years ago the young Emperor of Japan, restored to temporal power from the seclusion, well nigh amounting to entombment, which had been endured for some eight centuries by his ancient dynasty, swore solemnly before the nobles and territorial princes of this Empire that, as one of the leading principles of his future sway, the 'government should be conducted in accordance with public opinion and popular representation.' Of the earnestness of this assurance ample proof was afforded by the measures of the succeeding decade.　*　*　*　At length in 1881 the Emperor affirmed his original assurance by a rescript proclaiming that a complete parliamentary system should be carried into effect in the year 1890. During the interval that has passed since that declaration, as in the period preceding it, the whole course of Japan's polity and method of government has been directed to the new order of things that is destined to arise next year under the terms of the Sovereign's promise. In every step, every change, and every novelty that has been adopted from time to time as occasion required, the pilots of the Japanese ark of State have kept steadily before them as their goal the sound establishment of a constitutional monarchy as understood in Europe. That the task was no easy one none can doubt. It was, indeed, surrounded with grave difficulties and perils, amid which rashness might be irreparable and error fatal. Only by vigilance and foresight of the highest order could the knotty problem of enfranchising a people that had emerged but yesterday, as it were, from the shadow of feudalism be approached with any hope of success.　*　*　*　Yesterday (February 11) was the anniversary of the birth of the Emperor Jimmu Tenno, the Sovereign from whom sprang this oldest of the world's dynasties, and who, according to the commonly received chronology, began to reign in the year 660 B.C. Yesterday, then, was chosen as an auspicious day on which the first Monarch's descendant, the Emperor Mutsuhito, might fitly ratify his Imperial vow and proclaim and

give the new Constitution to his subjects.   *   *   *   Prior to
yesterday's ceremony of promulgation the Emperor executed a solemn
oath in the Palace Sanctuary, by which he swore, in the names of
the great founder of his House and of his other Imperial ancestors,
that he would maintain and secure from decline the ancient form of
government, and would never fail to be an example to his subjects in the
observance of the new laws. Then, after a short speech, couched in
stately and kingly language and uttered with great dignity, His Majesty
publicly delivered the said laws to Count Kuroda, his Minister President
of State. These are five in number, and are entitled respectively the
Constitution of the Empire of Japan, the Imperial Ordinance concerning
the House of Peers, the Law of the Houses, the Law of Election for the
members of the House of Representatives, and the Law of Finance. In
the first, one salient and interesting feature is the care taken to affirm
with emphatic brevity the time-honoured doctrines of the sanctity of the
Emperor's title and the immutability of his dynasty. Thus, while the
first article declares that his line shall run 'for ages eternal,' the second
says simply 'The Emperor is sacred and inviolable.' Then follows a
definition of the sovereign prerogatives, from which it appears that,
while the Emperor is to remain the source of all laws, in that without
Imperial approval no parliamentary measures can become law, the
making of laws is to be the function of the Diet, and no law can be put
into force without its assent, the one exception on the latter point being
that the Emperor reserves the power of issuing ordinances in urgent
cases, on behalf of the public safety or welfare, when the Diet is not
sitting, but that such ordinances to remain law must be approved at the
next Parliamentary Session. In succeeding articles it is laid down that
the Emperor determines the organisation of every branch of the administration, appoints and dismisses all civil and military officers, and fixes
their salaries; that he has the supreme command of the army and navy,
and determines their organisations and peace standing; and that it is he
who makes war or peace, concludes treaties, confers titles of nobility, rank,
orders, and other marks of honour, and grants amnesties, pardons, and
commutation of punishment. The rights and duties of subjects are
next set forth. By these it is determined, among other things, that a
Japanese subject, while amenable to taxation and to service in the army
or navy, shall be free from all illegal arrest, detention, trial, or punishment; that, subject in every case to the provisions and limits of the
laws, he shall have liberty of abode and of change of abode; that his
house shall not be entered or searched against his will; that the secrecy
of his letters and all his rights of property shall be inviolate; and that
he shall enjoy freedom of religious belief, consistently with the duties
of the subject and the preservation of peace and order, as well as liberty
of speech, writing, publication, public meeting, and association."

The bearing of this great constitutional change upon missionary
work is obvious both in what is expressed and in what is involved. The
explicit provision that all Japanese subjects shall enjoy freedom of
religious belief, as well as liberty of speech, writing, publication, public
meeting, and association, cannot but remove many difficulties, especially
in remote districts, from the work of evangelisation. The fact that the
Emperor has made such a solemn declaration of his subjects' religious
liberty will be almost as valuable as the liberty itself, as showing that
the government no longer maintains the existing religions of Japan in
their exclusive position.

What, however, is more impressive than any of the provisions in
detail is the fact of the new Constitution's existence.

It is a land-mark of the advance of Japan in its marvellously rapid
adoption of Western ideas. European inventions, costume, and
social habits, European literature, science, and philosophy, and now
European laws and constitutions are being absorbed into Japanese life ;
and the great question remaining is the simple one relating to that
which underlies all true national greatness, as well as all individual elevation—the question of religion. The old religions are as certainly doomed
as the old political systems. Is the Japanese religion of the future to
be drawn from the same Western sources as have supplied material and
political rejuvenescence to the land of the rising sun ?

The Anglican Church is endeavouring to supply the only answer which
can be of happy augury for the nation by three organisations—the
S.P.G., the C.M.S., and the American Church. These three independent
Missions are working in perfect harmony in their endeavours to found
and to build up the Church of Christ in Japan.

What is being actually done in detail may in part be gathered from
the letters we receive from Japan. The Society's operations have, as
their two centres, Tokyo, the capital, and Kobe, an important and
rapidly growing port in the South. Here the Rev. H. J. Foss is the
missionary, and the Bishop thus briefly describes the city and the need
for more workers :—

" Kobe is a city of which the population has doubled during the last
four years. It now contains nearly two hundred thousand people. The
work of the Mission in the country round and in the island of Awaji is
on the increase. Both for the sake of town and country, the Mission
should be strong, able at the same time to superintend effectively the
organisation already established, and to undertake aggressive work
among the heathen. Mr. and Mrs. Hughes' return will bring two
trained workers to Mr. Foss' assistance. Also the first missionary of
the Ladies' Association recently accompanied my party from England,
and will shortly be able to render some assistance in such branches of
the work among the women as do not require a knowledge of the language.

THE FIRST RAILWAY IN JAPAN; A SKETCH BY A JAPANESE ARTIST.

But the Mission cannot be said to be effectively manned without a second missionary in Holy Orders. Ample work could be found for a far larger number. May I not hope that the Society will be able to send Mr. Foss, who has himself, it will be remembered, done some twelve years of faithful and fruitful labour in this country, a colleague to share with him the burden of toil and the joy of success in a great and hopeful centre of work?

"In regard to Kobe I need only further notice one or two points. Mr. Fenton, one of the young laymen who have come to Japan in connection with Mr. Lloyd's scheme for providing Christian masters in Japanese schools, has carried on the school to Mr. Foss's satisfaction since Mr. Hughes went to England last year. Mr. Foss' house has been completed, and the school and school-house, of which the ground lease had run out, are about to be re-erected on a more convenient site. This last change is being effected without any additional burden on the Society's finances, partly through the liberality of English residents in Kobe.

"I hope to ordain the worthy head-catechist of the Mission to the diaconate during next year. The congregation is already prepared to defray the required portion of his salary."

With regard to Tokyo and its manifold missionary machinery, some parts more, and some less, closely dependent on the Society, the Bishop gives this interesting summary:—

"Since last spring successful classes for youths have been carried on, on five nights in the week, by the Rev. L. B. Cholmondeley in the new St. Andrew's School-house. The Rev. A. F. King is now assisting him. During the past autumn this effort has been supplemented, through the energy of Mr. Lloyd, by a catechetical class for the training of Japanese mission-agents, in which there are at present some ten students. To this again is to be added with the new year, and under the charge of Archdeacon Shaw and Mr. Tarbet, morning classes for especially selected students, from which it is hoped we may draw in time to come a class of native Christian workers of a higher calibre than most of those who are serving the Church at present. The Rev. F. E. Freese, who left England in January, will assist in this work. In connection with these various educational efforts, and for their efficiency, a well-instructed Japanese theological teacher is urgently required. He should have a good knowledge of English and of divinity, and be fond of teaching and translation. If the Rev. J. Imai, who was admitted to the diaconate in March 1888, can be relieved of pastoral duties, he would in several respects fill very well this difficult post. The present catechist of St. Andrew's congregation would probably in this case be proposed as a candidate for Holy Orders. He has, perhaps, some qualifications for a parish priest which Mr. Imai lacks. There can be no doubt that it is to the training of the clergy of the future

that our best efforts should be devoted. * * * The Rev. A.
Chappell, whom I hope to have ordained to the priesthood before
this letter reaches you, is working in Gifu. Twenty miles from that
place is Nagoya—a place which in point of population ranks third in
the Empire. These towns will shortly be in immediate connection with
Tokyo by rail. At Nagoya a Mission has just been opened of a class on
which the Society will look with special interest. The Rev. J. Cooper
Robinson, Wiclif College, Toronto, has been sent to Japan in connection
with the Missionary Society of the Canadian Church, and will, God
willing, be joined by a colleague, a graduate of Toronto University,
during next year. * * *

"These early Missions of the Colonial Church will be of particular
interest to the Society. They cannot fail to be so, as the Society will
have a right to recognise in the converts which God gives them what
one well called 'spiritual grandchildren.'

"Mr. Lloyd's educational scheme, to which I have already referred,
has been further developed during the year, and bids fair to exercise a
wide influence on the future of Japan. He himself will be sending you
details. * * * The (Native) Japanese Missionary Society,
founded at the Synod of 1887, to which the Society, in common with the
C.M.S. and American Society, makes a small grant, has been able during
the year to open four stations, two in the neighbourhood of Tokyo, one
near Osaka, and one in the southern island of Kiushiu. The experiment
of working mission stations through the initiation of the Native Church
will be watched with interest.

"It has been a pleasure to recognise the long and faithful service
of the Rev. A. C. Shaw by appointing him Archdeacon of the Church
of England in Northern Japan.

"The Rev. A. F. King, Keble College, Oxford, accompanied me from
England. He is followed by the Rev. F. E. Freese, Trinity College,
Oxford. These two clergymen, both of whom have had considerable
experience in English parishes, will give most important assistance in
developing the work carried on from this house.

"Two members of St. Hilda's Mission have completed their first year
in Japan. Two others—one a lady nurse—have just joined them. A
boarding school was opened in the spring, and is making progress.
Next year will, I hope, see the beginning of their evangelistic and
medical work. A school, itineration in the country districts, and a
training institution for Japanese nurses are the three objects which, as
I mentioned to many English audiences last summer, this Mission has
in view. May their work be as fruitful and permanent as hers whose
name they bear. St. Hilda's Mission House, through the liberality of
the Society for Promoting Christian Knowledge, and of the members of St.
Paul's Guild, was completed in March last. It is both well situated and

KIUSIU.

serviceable. During next year we hope to add to it a chapel, with additional rooms over it. This will cost, without the fittings for the chapel, about £250. I shall be glad to receive any special donation towards this object.

"The band of English mistresses which, at the invitation of a Japanese company, undertook the teaching of a high-class institute for ladies have arrived. This letter is not the place for a record of their work. I will not say more than that it is already apparent that the expectation which was formed beforehand that they would have in their hands a unique opportunity of widest usefulness is already being justified. Several other lady workers are likely to come to Japan during next year, of whose plans and work I may have more to write hereafter. For the present they will find a home at St. Hilda's Mission House.

The native Japanese Missionary Society is more fully described by Archdeacon Shaw :—

"An interesting event in the history of the year has been the commencement of work by the Missionary Society of the Native Church. This Society was organised by the General Synod held

MOUNT FUSIYAMA.

at Osaka in the previous year. It is a missionary society directly responsible to the whole Church. According to its plan, there are four local societies in connection with, and more or less under the control of, the parent society, the latter receiving and distributing in proportion to the local contributions all moneys collected from the whole Church. In the Tokyo district two stations have been filled during the year, and one each in the districts of Osaka and Kumamoto. This work is undoubtedly one of the most hopeful signs of Church progress, and deserves in every way to be encouraged. At one of these stations the Christians have also raised the funds and have built a small church for themselves during the past few months. I was present at the opening, and it was a time of great rejoicing both for young and old. After the celebration and an address which I gave, we all adjourned to a neat little house next to the church, which has been rented for the catechist in charge, and there had a Japanese feast in honour of the occasion. Services and preaching were kept up for three days, and there seemed much earnestness among the little band. We had a similar church-opening the following month at one of the stations more directly in connection with the S.P.G.—a village called Shimo Fakuda, distant about a day's journey to the east of Tokyo. The Christians here have made good progress during the year, but it has been impossible up to the present to furnish them with a regular catechist. Certainly one of the most satisfactory aspects of the work at present is the increased activity among the village Christians, and their efforts towards self-help and independence. The Buddhists, too, have been stirred up by this, and are doing what they can to stem the tide, and now regularly send their most famous preachers to visit those parts where Christianity is especially making headway. Mr. Nanjo, who was for some years a pupil of Professor Max Müller, is now a priest stationed at the great Temple of Hougnauji, in Nagoya, and from thence he also visits the country districts in that neighbourhood. The effects, however, of his preaching a reformed Buddhism are often more disastrous than otherwise, for when he tells the people that they ought no longer to worship or reverence the idols and shrines to which they have been for ages accustomed, he is very apt to bring both the priests and people about his ears. All this, however, helps to forward the process of disintegration which is going on in the old religion, and to prepare the way for the new."

Now there can be no doubt that all this shows that an immense deal is being done with very slender resources. It is a painful fact that the Bishop's special appeal for £21,700, which was endorsed and issued by the Society last year, met with but very scant response. It is a great opportunity which Japan now offers to the Church and the Church offers to Japan. For the youngest member of the family of constitutional kingdoms our desire is that it should enter the brotherhood of Christendom, and form part of the Kingdom of the Lord of All.

LARKA COLHS.

NOTES FROM THE DIARY OF THE REV. F. KRÜGER.—THE CIVILISING OF BARBARIANS.

THE tribe of the Larka Colhs, living about 300 miles N.W. from Calcutta, in the hills of the Singbhaum district, are in every way different from the Hindus and Bengalis. They possess no written language. In every village there is a devils' priest, who has to bring sacrifices to the different devils. The Larka Colhs believe that there are water, forest, mountain, and village devils. Often, when I preached the Word of God to the Hindus or Bengalis, they used to say that they had their religion and holy books as well as the Christians. When I asked them if they thought their religion to be the right one, why had they not converted the Larka Colhs to it generally they answered: "For such unclean and stupid people as the Larka Colhs, the devil is good enough."

When, in 1867, I was sent among the Larka Colhs in Singbhaum they were all heathen. On the first Sunday our congregation consisted of three persons—viz., my wife, a Christian servant, and myself. But the Lord blessed the work, and encouraged us by giving us a good commencement. One day, a Semidar, the owner of twenty-nine villages, came to me to buy a New Testament, and I found that he knew already something of the Word of God. He told me Captain Birch, a pious man, who for several years was Deputy-Commissioner of Singbhaum, had preached to him before any missionary came to the district. After some time, I paid the Semidar a visit in his village Katbari, which lies 18 miles distant from Chaibasa. I found the man in a very poor dwelling, his house being nearly a ruin. I also found out that he was in debt of several hundred rupees, and had to pay 25 % interest to a sly Bengali. Not far from his house I saw a heap of timber, and learned from the Semidar that he intended to build of the wood a house to worship the devil in. A German proverb says: "Where God builds a church, the devil builds a chapel close by." But in the village of Katbari the contrary came to pass. In the very place where the Semidar intended to build a house for the devil, we have now a church to serve the Lord our God. After I had shown him the way to the Lord Jesus Christ, he asked for a reader, who instructed him for about six months, after which time 64 persons of his village were baptized with him. As soon as the

Hindus heard that this Colh Semidar had a mind to embrace Christianity, they did all in their power to keep him back, and even offered to accept him into the Brahmin caste. Twenty-two years have passed since that time, and our friend David the Semidar has always shown himself a true Christian. He is also much liked by the European residents, and Government made him a magistrate. One of his sons, named Dalton, who was taught in our Mission School, has now a good appointment in the Chaibasa Court. Another son is in Calcutta in a high school. For eighteen years the Katbari congregation were under my care, and I visited them about once a month. Now a native priest has been stationed at Katbari, who has the Christians of eight villages under his care. And on such Sundays when there is no priest or reader in Katbari, David the Semidar holds the service. Once I had to go to Calcutta, where the Semidar accompanied me. Arriving at the first railway station, he saw the engine moving, and he exclaimed : " Oh, wonder ! oh, wonder ! How this creature walks, and there are no bullocks pulling it ! "

Our dear Bishop Milman in Calcutta invited me and my friend to dine with him, when we found many chaplains present. Our Semidar, David, had the place of honour near the Bishop. When his Lordship saw how well our Larka Colh behaved during dinner, he said to me : " Mr. Krüger, I did not think that your savages were so civilised." Once Mr. Whitley, from Ranchi, paid us a visit ; we went to the village of Katbari, and afterwards he wrote in our record book : "After the service I went with Mr. Krüger to visit the Christians in their houses. I was very glad to see all the houses of the Christians whitewashed, and, contrary to those of the heathens, they looked all nice and clean. The village seems to make good progress. I also saw in the gardens of the Christians fruit trees which Mr. Krüger caused them to plant. A rare sight in a Colh village ! The Semidar possesses now two nice houses, has money, and is a well-to-do man. How true are the words of the Bible : 'Godliness is profitable unto all things, having promise of the life that now is, and of that which is to come.' "

ST. JOHN'S COLLEGE, RANGOON.

IN March 1864 the Rev. John E. Marks, having been relieved of the S.P.G. Mission and School in Maulmain by the Rev. H. B. Nichols, began the S.P.G. work in Rangoon by opening a Mission School in "the Cottage," the house at Ahlon wherein Mr. W. Sheriff at present resides. The Rangoon Diocesan Schools had been opened a fortnight earlier.

Mr. Marks had brought over with him ten of his old pupils from Maulmain, together with Mr. Kristnasawmy (now the Rev. John Kristna, Missionary S.P.G.) and a Burman teacher, Samuel Monng Ee. With these he made a commencement of the School, which rapidly filled with only native pupils, an agreement having been made with the Diocesan Schools to receive no European pupils. This agreement was very soon found to be embarrassing, and was annulled by mutual consent.

Mr. Marks went home very ill in December of that year, returning, against the protest of the S.P.G. Consulting Physician, after a few months' stay. The Rev. J. Fairclough and Mr. Rawlings soon joined him; and afterwards the Rev. Charles Warren and the Rev. C. H. Chard took part in the work.

In 1866 the School—then, under the advice of Sir Arthur Phayre, called St. John's College—removed into "Woodlands," the present abode of Lady Dufferin's Hospital.

In 1869 the present estate was purchased from Government at the upset price of Rs. 200 per acre, and the foundation stone of the College was laid by General Albert Fytche, and the buildings were erected from designs by Mr. J. J. Jones, of the Public Works Department. In that year Mr. Marks was called to Mandalay by King Mindoon, who built for him a grand church, together with large schools and an excellent clergy-house. Mr. Marks stayed there "in sunshine and storm" till January 1875, when he was relieved by Mr. Fairclough, and resumed his work at St. John's, assisted by the Rev. James A. Colbeck, who had been with him in Mandalay as a layman. After a short time Mr. Marks took his second furlough of a few months to England, returning early in 1876. Mr. Colbeck took over the Mission at Kemmendine as a separate charge after the visit of the present Bishop of Calcutta.

A large *tectum*, or play shed, was built on to the College in 1877, and the following year it was converted into a grand school-hall. The Bombay Burma Corporation gave the timber for two large verandahs; the school-boys, present and past, subscribed to build an annexe as bed-room for the Principal; the Bank of Bengal gave iron railings for all the windows; Mr. J. Findlay gave a staircase and landings for the English boys' rooms; Mr. H. Williams gave another staircase; Mr. Andrew Moung Zan, of Thonzai, built a verandah class-room; Government built the armoury; a Christian Chinese lady paved with Penang tiles the eastern annexe and the new dining-room; Messrs. F. C. Kennedy and R. Gordon gave two large bells for the chapel; Messrs. J. W. Darwood and W. Nicol have each given money for improvements to the buildings; and Sir Charles Bernard gave Rs. 10,000, the last education funds under his control, to build the Orphanage for Boys, and also for the fence surrounding the compound.

The land and buildings all belong to the Society for the Propagation of the Gospel in Foreign Parts, in whose name the title and all deeds are entered.

The School is conducted in accordance with the principles of that Society, and in pursuance of a scheme drawn up by Bishop Cotton approved by his successor, Bishop Milman. Bishop Titcomb, the first Bishop of Rangoon, took the liveliest interest in the Institution, visiting it almost daily, teaching classes in it, and constantly taking part in the Chapel Services.

Amongst the masters, the most distinguished have been Mr. James George Scott (Shway Yoe), of Lincoln College, Oxford, whose name is loved by all Johnians, and Mr. W. B. Tydd, who worked thoroughly well and made a great name for himself in the School. The present staff is a worthy successor to those good men and true, who, for salaries which Government servants would scorn, have maintained the reputation of St. John's. Dr. Marks says that, as the offspring of St. John's College, he reckons Little St. John's, now called St. Barnabas' S.P.G. School, at Puzoondoung; St. Michael's S.P.G. Institution at Kemmendine; the S.P.G. School at Zeloon (now closed); St. Peter's S.P.G. School at Henzada; the S.P.G. School at Moyannung (burned down in 1877); St. Andrew's S.P.G. School at Thayetmyo; and the S.P.G. Royal School at Mandalay.

No less than 8,790 boys have been admitted into St. John's College during the twenty-five years of its existence. There are about 700 pupils now in the School, of whom about 350 are boarders. This number includes the wards of the Diocesan Orphanage for Boys. The pupils are of all classes. Princes from Mandalay, the sons of English gentlemen, and the poorest of the poor. They are of fifteen or sixteen different races, but all learn and play together, though they are kept separate in their dormitories and dining-rooms. There are sixteen masters (including the Principal), of whom fifteen are resident *among* the boys.

There are two companies (H and I) of the Rangoon Volunteer Rifles, and two sanctioned bands; there is also a Volunteer Fire Brigade, 250 strong, in connection with the Municipality.

In the Chapel, which is episcopally licensed, there are daily and Sunday Services in English and Burmese, the clergy being the Principal and the Rev. John Tsan Baw, of St. Augustine's College (formerly a pupil of this School). The organist, band, and choir are all members of the College.

The educational results for this year, as far as are known, are :—

Lower Primary—fully passed, 30 ; in two or more subjects, 34.

Upper Primary—scholarships, 5 ; fully passed, 30 ; in two or more subjects, 65.

Middle School—scholarships, 3 ; fully passed, 31.

ST. JOHN'S COLLEGE, RANGOON.

It has been usual to mark the School's Birthday, but it was felt that the Twenty-fifth Anniversary ought to have a special commemoration. So at 7.30 A.M. there was a full choral celebration of the Holy Communion. The Service was "Woodward in F," and was very accurately rendered. The Celebrant was the Rev. J. Fairclough, assisted by the Rev. T. Rickard, Missionary at Puzoondoung, formerly Vice-Principal, and the Rev. John Tsan Baw. Amongst the congregation was J. M. Dunbar, Esq., the Secretary of the S.P.G. Diocesan Council.

The Rev. Dr. Marks preached a short sermon from Psalm xc. 17, "Let the beauty of the Lord our God be upon us, and establish Thou the work of our hands upon us." He alluded to the formation of the School twenty-five years ago, and spoke feelingly of those who have been at work with him, some of whom, like Charles Warren and James Colbeck, are now at rest. He exhorted masters and boys to strive to maintain the Christian character of the School, its high tone and reputation. They had received from their predecessors the heritage of a good name, an inestimable possession for a great School and all connected with it. It was for his hearers to maintain the honour of their School, so that the very fact of being a St. John's College boy might be a presumption that one was honest, true, and Christian.

In the afternoon there were sports in the spacious School grounds, amidst a whole host of spectators. The cricket field had been fenced, flagged, and marqueed off in such a way that the grounds partook of the appearance of a country fair, the bright and happy faces of 700 boys considerably adding to the general effect.

At the conclusion of the sports, Mrs. Gordon gave away the prizes, having a kind word and a smile for each successful competitor, which counted far above the more solid rewards. The following are the names of the events :—Kicking the Football ; Bamboo Race ; Half-mile Flat Race (open), prize a watch ; Non-Commissioned Officers' Race, 100 yards ; 100 yards Flat Race, Burmans only ; 100 yards Flat Race, for Europeans ; 1st Midget Race ; High Jump ; Quarter-mile Flat Race, for Europeans ; Quarter-mile Flat Race, open ; 2nd Midget Stakes ; Long Jump ; 3rd Midget Race ; Hurdle Race ; Old Boys' Race ; Three-legged Race ; Obstacle Race ; Consolation Race ; the Tug of War, eight a side ; Band Race.

We must not omit to mention a drill competition between two companies of St. John's Cadets, in which Captain Milne kindly acted as umpire.

This great College has produced, and is producing, a great effect in the whole of Burma. Scattered over the country everywhere are Dr. Marks' old pupils in important positions, and still full of veneration and respect for him and for their old School.

Dr. Marks we wish we could see in England. For his health's sake, he certainly ought to take his long delayed furlough. The great work at St. John's, Rangoon, depends so much upon his personality that he shrinks from leaving it even for a time. We can only hope that he may be induced to arrange for his absence at an early date.

MOOSE JAW.

REPORT OF A PRAIRIE PARISH FOR THE FIRST QUARTER OF THE YEAR, BY THE REV. W. NICOLLS, THE SOCIETY'S MISSIONARY AT MOOSE JAW, IN THE DIOCESE OF QU'APPELLE—SUBSTANTIAL PROGRESS.

DURING the winter I have had the assistance of two lay readers (who owing to lack of clergy have to be employed). The district according to population divides itself into three.

1. Moose Jaw and surrounding vicinity. The town consists chiefly of railway men and store-keepers. The country for ten miles round is fairly thickly settled with farmers.

2. A district north-east of Moose Jaw about twenty-five miles, with three settlements, under the charge of Mr. F. W. Outerbridge (lay reader), viz., Buffalo Lake, English Village, Cottonwood Creek—distant from each other about fourteen miles—well peopled with farmers.

3. The Canadian Pacific Railway, of which I have 150 miles to look after. This has been chiefly worked by Mr. Bernard Barton (lay reader).

In the two latter, general supervision has been exercised by myself.

1. Moose Jaw. A new church has been built and opened, resulting in the increase of the congregation and funds. The building is of concrete and was to a large extent an experiment, which has, I am glad to say, been successful. The bell, costing $120, has been paid for by the children of the parish, and is a great boon to Church people. It was intended to have seated the church with British Columbia cedar, for which the money has been raised, but owing to various circumstances it has not yet been done. The constant changing of people, for the sake of variety, from one church to another is ceasing, it being one's constant endeavour, with all charity, to draw a distinct line between the Church and the sects.

Daily services (Matins and Evensong) have been carried on since the opening of the church, with celebrations of the Holy Communion on all Sundays when I am here. It is hoped on the Bishop's return a Confirmation will be held, to include many grown-up people who have hitherto neglected the ordinance. The great point which one learns by experience is to be first on the field, and a large outlay of money at first (though often seemingly unnecessary) ensures a permanent and enlarged work in the future. All the sects are endeavouring to be first, and the consequent rivalry is immense—the field is not an open one.

Our Sunday School has reached nearly 40 in number—a good growth

from the past. Between December 25 and March 25 there were 14 Celebrations, at which 61 people communicated. The constant and regular attendance at the Communion is a very difficult point to press upon the people; many, in fact all, with one or two exceptions, being from places in which they have been brought up and trained without regard to this part of the Christian life.

2. District north-east of Moose Jaw—Buffalo Lake, English Village, Cottonwood. I visited English Village early last fall, and found a very large settlement of Church people. They expressed very earnestly their wish for services, and a man to be stationed there, promising to provide board and horse. Owing to the scarcity of men, I could find no one till January. Till that time I went up occasionally and held service on week days—generally a Celebration and sermon. They used to turn up very well indeed. There are two men and three boys who were in choirs in England, with cultivated voices. The singing, for its delightful harmony, would have put to shame many a parish choir in towns.

On January 15, I drove the lay reader (Mr. Outerbridge) up to the settlement. Since then the work has gone on wonderfully well, both at English Village and the other settlements. Services are held regularly, and at English Village the congregation has increased from 13 to 45. The Sunday School numbers over 20. The people are to build a church of lumber by the end of April.

3. The Railway line. Mr. B. Barton, lay reader. Owing to the great distances and the awkward time of trains, services have been irregular, but there are always two on a Sunday. Four places have been taken, while a fifth is waiting to be opened. There is only one place which can be called a town—Swift Current, a divisional point of the railway, where a number of men are stationed. The other places are section houses, and in two Sir John Lister Haye has the Company's farms, where there are a number of Englishmen, who have been very regular in attending, and take an interest in the work. Swift Current is 125 miles west, while Rush Lake, Gull Lake, and Chaplin are on an average forty miles apart. The clergyman is always welcomed, and they are most liberal—in one section house the contribution for one service between nine people was $4·90 = £1. The Railway has granted us a free pass.

There is a vast field open for doing good amongst the Indians, but men and means are scarce. I applied some time ago for funds, to enable me at all events to make a small beginning, in a letter to the Secretary of the Society. Near Moose Jaw there are a large band of Sioux, amongst whom no attempt has been made to Christianise them. I have been appointed agent by the Government, and by this means hope to get some hold of them. They are thoroughly deserving of help, being very moral, industrious, and at the same time independent as far as possible of charity.

THE CHILDREN'S CORNER.

THE HERO OF SÁHAMAFY.—A TALE OF THE FRANCO-MALAGASY WAR.

BY THE REV. ALFRED SMITH.

(Continued from page 193.)

CHAPTER XII.

HE war-song of the Malagasy soldiers would, in English, run thus :

> Your cartridge, ye French, fire away !
> Our bosoms are bare to the fray;
> Till the last man has died of our band,
> We will fight for our dear fatherland.
> Burst then, ye bombshells, away !
> Our bosoms are bare to the fray.

The night decided upon for the attack was moonless and dark. The men were naked, with the exception of their waist-cloths; their leaders only being armed with rifles, the men carrying only a single spear each.

Their orders were to try and get into Tamatave unobserved, and fire it in as many places as possible.

They left the camp about nine o'clock at night, and arrived at the little Mananareza stream, about a mile out of Tamatave, somewhere about eleven o'clock. Here the men divided, so as to attempt an entrance into the town on all sides at once. The party with which Ratefy and Ralay were both attached took the direct road. Nearer and nearer they crept over the smooth turf covering the plain outside of the town. At the French outpost the sentry was walking backwards and forwards, but it was impossible for him to distinguish the naked forms of the enemy creeping on hands and knees in the darkness of the *roarontaka* bushes scattered over the plain. Suddenly a bright flame shot out of the darkness, followed by a sharp report. The sentry threw up his arms, and exclaiming, " J'ai mon compte ! " fell heavily to the earth. A rifle bullet had passed through his neck.

The shot rang out clear and sharp through the silent night, and the guards at all the outposts immediately sprang to arms. A gun was fired from the battery, and soon the electric light from the war-vessels was being flashed across the plain. The quick snapping fire of a furious *mitraillade* succeeded. Firing a few shots, and uttering yells of defiance, the Malagasy were soon in full flight.

The French stood to arms the whole night through, and when morning broke the naked bodies of about forty Malagasy were found lying dead among the bushes.

Only once afterwards was the night attack repeated, and of course it led only to the same result. The Malagasy are not Zulus, and their ardour " to wash their spears " is very quickly spent. They were content to remain on the side of the quaking bog farthest from Tamatave till the French should come out to attack them. These, however, remained where they were, " waiting for orders."

Week after week went by, and the French made no sign of going up to capture Antananarivo. The patriots from the island of Bourbon, who had been pressing for war months before it actually came, and who had been airily declaring all the time that when it did come it would be only *une affaire de quelques semaines* before Madagascar lay at the feet of the conqueror—these patriots began to be very uncomfortable. Their trade was gone, and the few dollars they had made were likewise going. The outlook, too, like the score of the Dingley Dellers, was as blank as their faces. Why didn't the French march up to Antananarivo at once and take over the government of the island, so that the patriots might proceed at once to make their long-expected fortunes ?

The largest French house of business in Tamatave speedily became bankrupt. Some of the patriots now began to make out that they were really English subjects, while others tried to eke out a livelihood by supplying liquor to the French marines on the sly. This led to a stringent liquor law, and ultimately the man who had howled and written most for war was ignominiously expelled by his own countrymen for breaking that law. Thus it was that by the end of the first year's occupation of Tamatave the Bourbon patriots had repented in dust and ashes of their enthusiasm in favour of war.

The months passed by, and bad as it was for the people of Tamatave, it was equally bad for the Hova on the other side of the quaking bog. There the misery was pitiful. The men from Antananarivo suffer from coast fever even more than Europeans, and hardly one escaped it. Insufficient food and exposure to the deadly malaria product of the aforesaid quaking bog soon did their work. Men died by the dozen per day. It is the custom to bring all the members of the family to the family vault, wherever they may die ; and day by day a string of corpse-bearers might be seen wending their melancholy way to Imerina. This increased to such an extent that at last orders were issued that no more corpses were to be brought up till after the war. The effect on the general population of the sight of this terrible result of camp-life was such that to be sent to the camp was looked upon almost as a sentence of death.

To relieve the misery which now existed, the churches of Imerina made large collections for the soldiers ; but as usual under a " paternal " government, the smallest percentage only dribbled through the many avaricious native hands that handled it to the soldiers of the rank and file.

CHAPTER XIII.

In the midst of all this, however, Ratefy set himself bravely to work. Thanks to the quinine and other medicines provided for himself and Ralay by Mr. Earnshaw, he had been able to keep the fever within bounds. He found out some of the Betsimisaraka chiefs, who had belonged to the Tamatave congregation ; with their assistance a building was put up, and services held twice a day on Sundays. Those of the school-children who were in the camp were also steadily taught. Sometimes, however, they were very hurriedly dismissed from school. The French, having by this time got the range of the camp, amused themselves occasionally by firing shells into it. Sometimes they fired a dozen shells and then stopped ; at other times they would continue the whole day, firing a shell every half-hour. At the sound of the first shell whizzing over the camp the children would dart out of the school and run like rabbits for safety to the nearest hole in the earth made for protection against the shells. When all was quiet they stole out and the lessons began again.

Two years passed away in this manner, and the camp had become an ordinary native village, except that it was rather larger than they generally are, and contained many more soldiers. People had become, too, quite accustomed to the irregular bombardments, and looked upon them as ordinary incidents in the daily routine.

One day Ralay appeared at Ratefy's little cabin with a very grave face, an open letter in his hand.

" What is the matter ? " inquired Ratefy.

" I have just received this letter from Antananarivo, and it contains dreadful news."

" Dreadful news ! What do you mean ? "

" I am going to read it to you. It is about Ratsimba."

" You have heard," it says, " that there are a great number of robberies committed now in all parts of Imerina, and especially in Antananarivo and its suburbs. They are committed by the soldiers who have deserted, and are outlawed in consequence of their desertion. So numerous and bold have these now become, that in every village the men have to take turns in keeping guard throughout the night, half watching while the other half sleep. The authorities have therefore lately been trying very hard to catch one or two of these robbers to make examples of them. Some weeks ago they succeeded in catching two men, one of them being Ratsimba, a man you used to know very well, and who was sent to the camp at the same time as yourself. They were first of all sentenced to be burnt to death, in accordance with the old custom of punishing deserters, but afterwards the Prime Minister determined to deal with them as they deal with deserters in Europe, and sentenced them to be shot.

"This sentence was carried into effect yesterday, and hundreds of people went out to see the sight.

"The two miserable wretches were tied to two posts stuck in the ground. The native pastor of one of the churches said prayers, while the firing party of about forty men were stationed in front of the two men at about a *hundred yards'* distance.

"As these were now told to load their rifles, many of the women who had come out to look on fled shrieking away, covering their faces with their *lamba*. At the word of command the rifles rang out, and as the smoke cleared away the blood could be seen trickling from Ratsimba's thigh. His companion was untouched.

"'Come nearer; come close to us!' the poor wretches shouted to the soldiers. 'Kill us quickly, for God's sake!'

"'Yes,' said the officer in command, 'perhaps we had better go closer.'

"They approached to within about fifty yards and fired again. This time both of the victims were struck.

"They screamed and struggled in agony.

"'Go quite close up to them,' said the horrified officer; 'we shall never be able to put them to death like this.'

"At a few yards' distance the soldiers fired again, and so the men were put out of their misery."

After reading the above letter the two boys looked at one another in horror. They were almost afraid to speak.

"God have mercy upon them!" whispered Ratefy at length. "What an awful death to die! It would have been far, far better for Ratsimba to have done his duty, and come on here with us."

"You did not know him as I did," harshly replied Ralay. "It was his fate. As he has done to others so has it been done to him."

So saying Ralay took up his hat and left the cabin.

CHAPTER XIV.

After two years and a half's waiting the French felt now disposed to go out and take the Hova camp, and preparations were made on a grand scale for the attack.

All the marines that could possibly be spared from the vessels were landed. Five days' provisions were packed up for transport. The ambulances were inspected, and all the palanquins belonging to the Tamatave residents were requisitioned as stretchers, neatly numbered, and prepared for use. A portable bridge was likewise made for passing the quaking bog.

At break of day 1,500 men were under arms. The French ensign to be planted in the Hova camp was unfurled, and with the applause of the whole population of Tamatave the march began. A photographer hastily packed his camera (as per agreement with the French officers), and hurried after the soldiers, lest he should not be in time to take an instantaneous view of the glorious battle to be fought. Another enthusiast took out champagne wherewith the officers might quench the rage and heat of battle, together with mild lemonade for the use of the men. The English mostly went up on the roofs of their houses to watch the proceedings.

On arriving at the edge of the quaking bog, they found the Malagasy behind their earthworks ready to receive them. They had, however, very good cover.

An attempt was first of all made to make a breach by means of the field-guns in the Malagasy earthworks. A vigorous cannonade now began, the Malagasy replying to it with their rifles. The Malagasy are, however, very indifferent marksmen.

Hour after hour went by with very little change in the position of affairs. The French made no attempt to cross the quaking bog; the mere look of it, and the presence of several thousand Malagasy behind their earthworks on the opposite side, were quite sufficient.

"I am afraid," said the French admiral, who led the attack in person, to the colonel of infantry, "I am afraid we shall lose a lot of men if we attempt to cross."

"Oh, no doubt we can get across," replied the colonel, "but, as you say, we shall lose many men. Is it worth while? There may be a new Foreign Secretary to-morrow!"

Meanwhile the firing went briskly on. Here and there in the Malagasy trenches many a soldier had fallen. Towards the middle of the action it became necessary to send reinforcements into the trenches from a reserve kept behind some rising ground. But in order to reach the trenches the men must cross the bullet-swept top of the mound, and expose themselves to the full fire of the French. The chance was therefore a very desperate one, and Ratefy and Ralay were both among those who had to run it. Crawling up as near to the brow of the ascent as they possibly could, at a given signal they all started up and charged over it to the trenches.

They were met by a perfect hail of French bullets. Ralay was several yards ahead of Ratefy, when suddenly he reeled and fell.

"Oh! save me, save me!" he cried.

Instantly Ratefy stopped, seized his fallen comrade, and lifted him up. Turning again to run down to the trenches a bullet struck and shattered his right arm. It dropped heavily to his side. With a shout of agony he still struggled onward, holding on to Ralay with his teeth and left arm. Exerting himself to the utmost, he had nearly reached the shelter of the trenches when another bullet struck him full in the breast. He fell with his burden. But with a last effort he rose once more. Throwing his hands high above his head, while a smile passed across his face, he cried in ringing tones, "Veloma, ry Tánindrágako!" (Land of my Fathers, good-bye), and fell headlong—dead.

Dulce et decorum est pro patria mori. Yes. But "greater love hath no man than this, that a man lay down his life for his friend."

A cry of mingled admiration and rage burst from every Malagasy that saw the hero fall. The French could never take the camp that day. Beaten at every point they were forced to return to Tamatave carrying their dead and wounded with them.

They never again tried to take the Malagasy camp. Within a few weeks they opened negotiations for peace with the Queen of Madagascar.

After the French had retired, the Malagasy crossed the quaking bog and picked up the rifles dropped by the French wounded. These they sent up to their young Queen as trophies of their bravery; but the greatest trophy of all that was sent up from the beginning of the war to the end, and one that will last the longest, was the story of Ratefy, the Hero of Sáhamafy.

THE END.

NOTES OF THE MONTH.

AT the Annual Meeting of the Society in St. James's Hall, on Thursday, June 6, the speakers are to be :—His Grace the President, the Earl of Carnarvon, the Bishop of Ballarat, Canon Body (of Durham), the Rev. E. F. Miller (Warden of St. Thomas' College, Colombo), the Rev. G. A. Lefroy (from Delhi), and the Rev. A. A. Maclaren (Missionary to New Guinea).

IT may be as well to repeat our announcement of last month, that by the appointment of the President, the Bishop of Chester will preach the Anniversary Sermon in St. Paul's Cathedral on Wednesday, June 19, at the 11 A.M. Service, when the Holy Communion will be celebrated.

ON May 1 (the festival of SS. Philip and James), the Bishop of Tasmania (the Right Rev. Henry Hutchinson Montgomery) was consecrated in Westminster Abbey. The Archbishop of Canterbury was assisted in the act of consecration by the Bishops of Rochester, Antigua, Ballarat, and Moosonee.

AN appeal is being made for a special fund for a school at Trichinopoly. The case is this. The present buildings are two unsuitable rooms, formerly stables. The Jesuits are endeavouring to have them condemned as quite unfit, with a view to their own schools supplanting them on the Government Grant list. The Rev. T. H. Dodson, the Principal of the Society's College at Trichinopoly, accordingly feels that a determined effort should at once be made to obtain new buildings for the school, which is doing important work, and the Society has resolved to open a special fund for the purpose, and has voted £50 towards it.

NEXT month we hope to begin a series of most interesting papers, being extracts from the diary of the Bishop of Bloemfontein, during his recent remarkable journey in the regions stretching northward from his diocese.

FROM Kimberley, in the diocese of Bloemfontein, the Rev. G. Mitchell reports the completion of the new church, which is now used for services, and probably has by this time received consecration at the hands of the Bishop. After that event Mr. Mitchell promises us a further description of the church, with which he now declares he and his people are " perfectly pleased and satisfied."

ST. MARK'S Mission, in the Transkei, Kaffraria, is under the charge of the Rev. E. L. Coakes, who in a brief letter, dated April 10, mentions many details of an important and encouraging nature :—

"I am beginning to feel the benefit of the late additions to the Mission staff. Mr. Irving's visit to Cala every other month sets me free for the Fingoland portion of the district. We have a large number of people at work—84 just now; but the area is large, and the whole population is scattered, except the few who live at St. Mark's and Cala.

"I am going to-morrow to celebrate at Tshingein the opening service after the restoration of the roof, blown off in a great gale January 10. Xolobe Chapel, blown down on the same day, is not yet rebuilt. Tshingein has cost £25. Last Sunday I walked over to Mpindwein for service, where a stone hut is nearly finished. This spot—on the Mission ground—was a short time ago a favourite resting-place for a gang of cattle thieves. On March 24, the Bishop consecrated Cala Church, fifty-five miles from here. With fittings it has cost £300.

"On the 4th inst. I attended a meeting at Qutsa to settle some details about the new brick school-church they are building; and I am expecting the day to be fixed for laying the foundation-stone of a little church for Europeans and natives at Mbulu, to cost about £200. The little brick place at Mfula is nearly finished; and Masiza opened a nice sod chapel at Lufuta at the end of March.

"I am hoping soon to have the stone of the new parish church laid here. How, with all these ventures on hand, we are to raise the local £300 for the stipends I do not know. The English have—half of them—gone to the gold-fields. I wish the Society would enable us to put a man in the upper district. I have just spent nearly a month there. The people—English farmers, &c.—would pay half the salary."

IN January the Bishop of Colombo started on an Episcopal tour for the northern parts of Ceylon. He first went from Colombo to the Society's Mission of Matale; and on leaving the latter place had a narrow escape from a very serious accident :—

"When two or three miles out, the horses reared and shied at a buffalo (that with several others was very slow to move off the road), and plunged down a steep bank. Most happily and providentially none of us were injured, though the carriage partly fell upon the Bishop and one of the horsekeepers, and the Bishop incurred a few bruises. We walked back into Matale, enjoyed again the hospitality of Mr. Burrows, who was able most opportunely to supply us with another hood for the carriage, and we set out again the next morning, as the horses also came out of the accident unscathed."

BISHOP DOUET, Coadjutor of Jamaica, held his first ordination on February 17, having on the 13th presided at the meeting of the Diocesan Synod.

T HE Bishop of Wellington has been elected Primate of New Zealand, in succession to the Bishop of Christchurch, who has resigned that office.

P RESIDING over the General Synod of New Zealand in February, the Bishop of Christchurch compared the present state of the province with that of the Church in New Zealand when the first Synod was held :—

"Thirty years have passed away since the Church of this ecclesiastical province first met in her General Synod. There were present on the occasion, together with the representatives of her clergy and laity, five bishops, three of whom had been but recently consecrated, and since then there has been added to their number a bishop for this diocese of Dunedin, and a bishop as successor to Bishop Patteson in the missionary diocese of Melanesia has been associated with this Synod. The number of clergy throughout this province, including those who ministered to our Maori brethren, could not have exceeded 100; their number when we met at Auckland in 1886 had been increased to 256."

F ROM Gravenhurst, in the diocese of Algoma, the Rev. W. T. Noble writes describing his first winter, which he is told was unusually mild. The presence of a Zulu among Confirmation candidates in a Canadian diocese is a kind of type of the Church's catholicity embracing all races and localities :—

"I have found it very endurable, and in some respects pleasant. No serious mishaps have occurred, save getting a few times rolled out into the snow. Trade has been bad during the winter, and several of our church people were obliged to close, and leave town. The town has by no means recovered from the effects of the late fire; and, though some good stores have been built, it is with borrowed money, the payment of which will oppress the people for years to come. Thanks to our Ladies' Aid Society, we got a new bell in our new church on March 18. In the tower it costs $200, which is all in hand but about $25, and this was no easy task in such times as we are passing through here. But all the Christian churches have shown us practical sympathy in the matter.

"We are thus, by degrees, getting some of the many details completed in and around our new church. The Bishop held a Confirmation here on March 21, when I presented seven candidates, one of them a Zulu from Port Natal, Africa, who is living in this town. He showed very praiseworthy diligence and intelligence in the course of preparation. The congregation does not increase as I should desire, though I am told it is as good as it ever was, and I know most of the men have been away in the camps during the winter, and are only now returning. The Sunday School is making very decided and encouraging progress. We have now over 80 scholars on the book, and a band of 11 teachers, with Secretary and Librarian. My weekly Bible Class is very well attended, and my Thursday-night service has been better attended during Lent. I have a service once every two weeks at Northwood Church, seven miles out of town, and for a country place in the winter time the attendance has been very fair, though of course not all our own people. I have attended Missionary meetings at Bracebridge and Uffington. Under the Bishop's directions, I visited Port Sydney on Sunday, March 3, for the purpose of administering Holy Communion. I visited three stations, though travelling was difficult that day. I see some reasons to thank God and take courage."

FROM Upper Burma we have a brief letter, dated March 18, in which the Rev. George H. Colbeck gives many items of most encouraging news :—

"You will no doubt have heard that we have had a visit from our Bishop, which has given us much strength and encouragement.

"Mr. Stockings was admitted to Deacon's Orders on St. Matthias' Day in our beautiful Mandalay Church. A large Burmese congregation gathered together, some coming from a long distance to be present at the service.

"Before the Bishop left, Confirmations were held at Shwebo and Mandalay. We at Mandalay were able to present 36 candidates, 26 being Burmans. A larger number ought to have been presented, but from various causes we had to reduce the number.

"The new Mission Church (brick) of Madaya is going on slowly but steadily. I

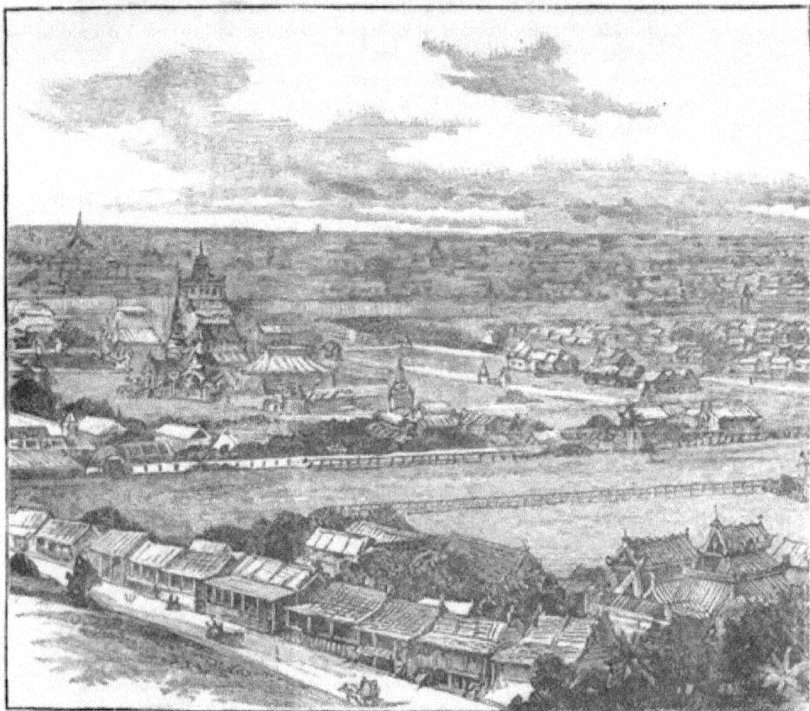

MANDALAY.

hope we shall be able to use it by Easter. Last week I had a tour in Madaya and district, visiting several new villages. People very attentive and desirous of hearing more. We hope to give them more frequent visits.

"I think I told you some time ago of the Prince of Thibaw's request that we should start a Mission in his State. He offers to build school and house, and give us his support. The Bishop had an interview with him, and gives me his permission to visit the State as soon as good opportunity arises. The eldest son of the Prince has been a pupil here for the last two years, but is now to go to England. His residence here has had this effect, that the boy professes himself a believer in Jesus; so that every care should be taken of him while he is in England. He will one day be in a position of great power and influence. I am anxious to bring the Upper Burma Missions before the Society, and also to advocate the opening of the new Shan Mission, which, I beg to state, is likely to be a most important one.

"Thibaw State is one of the most important, and is a centre of trade, not only with the Shan country, but also with China. We ought, therefore, to do our utmost to establish ourselves, especially as the offer of the Sawbwa is such a good one. You will no doubt hear from the Bishop soon.

THE ROYAL PALACE, MANDALAY.

"Whitehead is well. It is such a blessing to have him here. This last year, I must confess, has been a terribly hard one for me. I feel most thankful for God's preservation and care through it all.

"We have commenced a Tamil Mission in Mandalay. Tamil Christians have increased very rapidly lately, so we must care for them."

ON February 16, the corner-stone of a new church was laid at Thessalonica, Rio Essequibo, Guiana, by the Rev. J. Keelan, the Missionary. With the exception of some shingles for the roof, all the materials for the church have been freely given by the Indians connected with the Missions.

FROM the Diocese of the Windward Islands the Bishop sends the following description of the effects of the sudden disendowment in one of the parishes, North and South Charlotte. It is from the pen of the Rev. N. J. Clarke, who is helped by a part of the Society's grant :—

"For many years previous to 1888, South Charlotte, which contains 1,200 Anglicans, had been separately worked under the care of a perpetual curate. Early last year, however, the Government withdrew all support from the Church ; and South Charlotte was in consequence placed under my care. I may remind your Lordship that from April 1881, to January 1885, South Charlotte was in my charge, and all my time and energy were spent on, and were not enough for, the work. How much must be left undone now that that parish forms an *addition* to North Charlotte with its 6,000 Anglicans, your Lordship's experience as a parish priest will tell. It is simply impossible for one priest and a deacon to work a district which (including both parishes) extends twenty-six miles, and contains more than seven thousand Anglicans. My assistant and myself are doing our best to keep up the services. We hold one service every Sunday in each of the four chapels, and two services in the parish church. Thus we serve five places of worship, the first of which is nineteen miles distant from the fifth. In the four chapels the Holy Communion is celebrated on one Sunday in each month ; in the parish church on two Sundays every month. But our strength is spent in the long rides on the Sunday in sun or rain ; and the great danger is in the parochial work being neglected.

"Owing, no doubt, to the withdrawal of the Government grant, both the Wesleyans and Roman Catholics are without a resident minister in South Charlotte at present. Here is a district whose position should, I venture to think, awaken the sympathy of all who love Christ!

"Anglicans, Wesleyans, Roman Catholics have worked hard and long in preaching Christ. Much has been done. At the Confirmation your Lordship held a few days ago, it must have been plain that there are many in that parish who are at least anxious to hear the Word of God. A government that does not believe that it ought to provide for the spiritual wants of its subjects has suddenly withdrawn all aid. Parson, priest, and preacher have been driven away! Not only Anglicanism, but *Christianity* itself is in danger! What but a relapse into semi-paganism can be the result of the present state of things.

BISHOP BRANCH has lately had a narrow escape from death through poisoning, caused by eating unwholesome fish. We are glad to learn that his lordship is recovering.

SMALL-POX and devotion to duty have closed the useful earthly life of the Rev. A. C. Warren, the Society's Missionary at Upper Island Cove, Newfoundland. He died in March.

"This is the second clergyman who has fallen a victim to infectious disease caught in the discharge of duty at Upper Island Cove.

"More than twenty years ago Rev. W. C. Meek, in an epidemic of typhoid fever, caught the disease from his parishioners and died.

"The Rev. A. C. Warren was a Newfoundlander, and a native of St. John's. He was educated at the Church of England Academy, under the Rev. C. P. Harris, M.A., and at first thought of following the medical profession.

"In 1867 he was matriculated as a student in the Theological College, St. John's, where, under Rev. W. Pilot, B.D., he remained four years, and was ordained Deacon A.D. 1871, during the Episcopate of Bishop Feild. After serving temporarily the cures of New Harbour and Channel, he was put in charge of the Mission of St. George's Bay, from whence he was removed to Upper Island Cove in 1876.

"The Mission possesses the unenviable notoriety of being one of the poorest in the country, and the ministerial work there is sadly intensified by chronic poverty, and, we might almost add, its twin-sister, chronic disease.

"It may be remembered, too, that a few years ago Mr. Warren lost his little all by fire—the parsonage being burnt down one dreadfully stormy night in the fall of the year; his wife and family barely escaped in their night-clothes, and one of his children died a few days after from a chill then caught. Yet he laboured on, and, in spite of all his difficulties, enjoyed the goodwill and esteem of his poor people.

"He contracted the disease from visiting the man who brought the small-pox from the brig *William;* and thus Mr. Warren adds another to the roll of Anglican priests who have laid down their lives in the Great Master's service in Newfoundland."

MADAGASCAR is an example of two things so often to be seen in foreign lands. On the one hand the growth of the Church, on the other the demoralisation of natives by Europeans. The following, from the Rev. C. P. Cory, supplies material for reflection, and motive for redoubled missionary exertions, so that the net result of the contact between the Malagasy and Europeans may be a real and great gain :—

"All is well at the College. Many more people are being presented for baptism in the out-stations than formerly. I have baptized about 55 adults the last year, and Mr. Gregory as many more (or rather less perhaps). There has been less sickness on the whole, too, this term.

"The presence of the French soldiers in the capital is having a very demoralising effect upon the people, as also the European traders who flocked here as soon as the country was open again. For my first two years I never saw a drunken Malagasy, in my third year I saw one, and now I never go to the capital without meeting one or two, if not more. I am speaking of the central province, for of course on the coast drinking has been long the custom. The natives themselves say morality is getting very much lower."

HURRICANES are common in the West Indies, but that which visited Turk's Island, in the diocese of Nassau, last autumn was an exceptionally severe one :—

"It was less destructive to property than the well-remembered hurricane of 1866, but in the loss of valuable lives this last visitation has been to the full as terrible as its predecessor. A short time after sunrise on Sunday morning, the signs of approaching storm were perceived and acted upon; so that, by the time the fury of the hurricane burst upon the island, much had been done to secure life and property. Still, more than 200 houses were entirely destroyed, and the Rev. H. F. Crofton tells of the poor sufferers who came on hands and knees to seek shelter with him, and of the contrivances by which he managed to receive as many as possible.

" Three American vessels and a great number of island boats were wrecked or otherwise lost, and twenty-one lives lost. Five of these were respectable fathers of families in these islands, and their loss will be long felt in the community. At the Lower Caicos a scarcity of food, owing to the long drought up to the morning of the hurricane, must be added to the other sufferings of the poor. Over 400,000 bushels of salt, upon the export of which so much of the livelihood of the Turk's Island people depends, were destroyed, and the Acting Commissioner and committees of magistrates, who were at once appointed to inspect and record the condition of things, stated as the result of their inquiry that the distress consequent on the hurricane was too great to be adequately met by the resources of the community unaided from without. Mr. Crofton tells of several sad cases of destitution among families of the poor well known to himself."

Mr. Crofton thus describes the Bishop's visit :—

" On December 22, the Bishop of the diocese, accompanied by his brother, the Rev. H. N. Churton, arrived in the *Message of Peace*, the voyage from Nassau having taken nine days. I met them at Hawk's Nest, and we drove at once to the rectory, where they were my guests. The church bell was rung to welcome them, and evening service, with short address, was held the same evening at St. Andrew's Mission Church, at which about forty persons were present. A choral celebration was held at St. Andrew's on the following Sunday, and children's service and catechising in the afternoon. The Bishop seemed pleased with his visit on the whole, and especially with the answering of the Sunday School. His lordship addressed a crowded Temperance Meeting on the following Wednesday, after which a purse of £10, collected by some ladies of St. Thomas's congregation, was presented to him as a memorial of his first visit. His lordship kindly gave a gift of £15 to various Church objects and £5 to the Hurricane Relief Committee. His lordship and his brother, accompanied by myself, left for Salt Bay on December 27."

CAWNPORE, in the diocese of Calcutta, has a Mission with a history. The Society sent its first missionary there in 1832, when the Mutiny broke out the place was hallowed by the deaths of the missionaries who were there. They were the Rev. W. Haycock and Mr. Cockey, who with native workers and converts fell victims to the fierce fanatics in June 1857. In August 1859 work was resumed, and has been carried on ever since. A step is now to be taken which may bring to more abundant fruits the labours and patience of past years. Two brothers have been accepted for the work in Cawnpore, the Rev. G. H. Westcott, one of the masters at Marlborough College, and the Rev. Foss Westcott, curate of Sunderland. They are graduates of Peterhouse, Cambridge, sons of Professor Westcott, Canon of Westminster, and brothers of the Rev. A. Westcott, the Principal of the Society's Theological College in Madras. May they and their works be

CHRIST CHURCH, CAWNPORE.

so blessed that the few hundreds of Christians in Cawnpore may be multiplied, and let the light shine from them through the populous district of which that important city is the centre.

A N important meeting of the Society was held at Trinity College, Dublin, on May 6. The Archbishop of Armagh presided, and was supported by the Archbishop of Dublin, nearly all the Bishops of the Irish Church, and the Provost and several professors of Trinity College.

Among the speakers was the Bishop of Derry, who said :—

"We are often told that Christianity is not the only Missionary religion. I suppose it may be said that there are three other great Missionary religions. One, however, Hinduism, with its 190 millions of adherents, cannot be looked upon as Missionary. It is purely and entirely local. When it is removed from local influences and from the shrines of ancient superstition it dies out like a flower planted on some barren heath. Buddhism is very much spoken of, and beyond all question Buddhism had a most enormous success. It was said a few years ago, and I dare say that many preachers and missionaries have fallen into the error, that Buddhism numbers more heads than Christianity. It used to be said that there were 300,000,000 of Buddhists, but Professor

Williams has lately stated that there are not much more than 100,000,000, that among them everywhere disintegration is setting in, and Buddhism is giving way before the advance of that mighty wave of Christianity which is destined to sweep the whole earth. Its adherents are entirely amongst people of one type, and one constitution, and one character. Mohammedanism has been more in evidence lately. Mohammedanism, it is fair to say, is a Missionary religion by something more than the power of the sword. It helped to raise the Arab of the desert, and might also help to raise the negro. Carlyle and a succession of able men have been trying to rehabilitate it, but the claims put forward on its behalf were of a most extravagant nature. Writers have spoken of Mahomet as a great reformer, as a prophet of God, a holy prophet, much to be admired ; and one gentleman has gone so far as to write : ' Let Islamism and Christianity look upon each other as sister religions. Let them rejoice each at the success of the other ; let each supply the element wanting in the other ; and let there be a generous rivalry between them as to which can do the most for the happiness of the human family.' I advise those who can to read a book written by Dr. Coelly. It is not a pleasant subject, but I would only say that a part of Dr. Coelly's book about the domestic relations of Mahomet, drawn from contemporary documents, is absolutely fatal to the creed, and so full of abomination that it is impossible to leave the book in any house where it would lightly fall into the hands of ladies. Another book which gives immense information on the subject is published by the University Press of Cambridge. It is a volume of travels in Arabia Deserta. There Islamism has a fair field, and what did the writer of this book discover concerning it ? That hospitality and generosity are the only qualities that can be called virtues that remain amongst those people. Are we to leave the East to the religion and morality of Islamism ? Islamism has a theism frigid and sterile. It teaches its religion with impressive outward prayers ; but it has a sterile God ; it has the weight of a dead book crushing out the very life of morality, and the life of society. It has no tenderness, no humility, and, above all, it has no purity. The peace with Islam, then, that we are called on to maintain, is a peace which is both untrue to the Master and high treason against the majesty of human nature and against the purity of womanhood. In Missionary exertions, therefore, we cannot make peace with Islam. We are called upon to show our churchmanship by helping this ancient and great Society. And a great Society it is. It is a Society with a history. One glorious name of this University is associated with the Gospel Propagation Society. Berkeley, the lofty idealist, was a friend of that Society which is now girdling the earth. This work we are called upon to help by our prayers and by our alms ; and if I might venture to speak to the young men who are here assembled, I would say, that possibly in the providence of God there are other means by which you might feel called upon to help the Society for the Propagation of the Gospel. I am an old man now, and I say it to my shame, that never to me in my youth did there once come that Divine call to go elsewhere. I never knew what it was to have within my heart the superb chivalry, the divine knight-errantry of the missionaries of the Cross of Christ. Many of the young men will, no doubt, be wanted in various fields at home, and glad, indeed, would I be to see them engaged in work in their native land ; but if that Divine call does come to their hearts, God forbid that I should attempt to urge them to resist it."

SUGGESTED SUBJECTS FOR PRAYER.

For the Missions exposed to peril in Eastern Africa, for the steadfastness of the converts, and for a happy issue out of all the tribulations.

For Japan, that in their new national life the people may be renewed by the Holy Spirit.

For those engaged in the gold and diamond fields in South Africa, that Englishmen there may be strengthened against temptation, and that the natives may not be harmed by contact with Europeans, but rather may find opportunities for learning the Gospel of truth.

For those suffering from the famine in China, and that the recipients of Christian charity may be partakers of Christian faith.

MONTHLY MEETING.

THE Monthly Meeting of the Society was held at 19 Delahay Street, on Friday, April 26, at 2 P.M., the Earl of Belmore in the chair. There were also present Lord Robartes and the Rev. B. Belcher, *Vice-Presidents*; the Rev. J. M. Burn-Murdoch, C. Churchill, Esq., Prebendary Codrington, D.D., General Davies, Sir F. J. Goldsmid, K.C.S.I., C.B., Colonel Hardy, General Lowry, C.B., General Maclagan, Rev. E. V. Pigott, General Sawyer, and General Tremenheere, C.B., *Members of the Standing Committee*; the Rev. Dr. Baker, Rev. J. A. Boodle, Rev. G. F. Clarke, Rev. J. C. Cowd, Dr. Cust, Rev. H. J. Day, Rev. Dr. Deane, T. Dunn, Esq., Rev. J. J. Elkington, Rev. S. C. Hore, H. Laurence, Esq., General Mackenzie, Rev. J. H. C. McGill, Rev. J. C. Moore, Rev. Dr. Oliver, and the Rev. G. C. Reynell, *Members of the Society.*

1. After prayers, the minutes of the last meeting were read.

2. The Treasurers presented the abstract of receipts and payments from January 1 to March 31, printed on page 200 of *The Mission Field.*

3. The Secretary announced that the annual meeting of the Society in St. James's Hall would be held on Thursday, June 6, and that the annual sermon in St. Paul's Cathedral would be preached on Wednesday, June 19, by the Lord Bishop of Chester.

4. The Rev. A. M. Hewlett, who was on the eve of returning after furlough to his work in Madagascar, addressed the members. He began by stating that there were at several places in that country English, and English-speaking, people, and showing how the missionaries endeavoured to provide English services for their benefit, in addition to the work for and among the native races. He described the difficulties and the measure of success attained in the work of raising up a native ministry, and gave details of the antecedents and careers of one or two of the eight already ordained. With regard to the presence of other Missions in Madagascar, he claimed that there was ample room for the Church's work; and that in addition to the opportunities offered by the vast unoccupied districts, it was felt even by the members of other Missions that there was a place for the Church to fill in the religious life of the country. He explained how especially precious among such a people were the Church's liturgical prayers, by which babes in Christ are guided in their approach to their Heavenly Father, and the importance to them of such a thing as Church music.

5. All the candidates proposed at the meeting in February were elected into the Corporation. The following were proposed for election in June :—

The Rev. N. B. Whitby, Finningley, Bawtry; Rev. Reginald J. Hill, Salton, York; Rev. J. D. Monro Murray, Bournemouth; Rev. G. Haines Jones, Awbridge, Romsey; Rev. H. Greene, New Shildon, Darlington; Rev. Frank S. Alston, Coningsby, Boston, Lincs.; Rev. Arthur Welsh, Harewood, Leeds; Walter Rowley, Esq., Alder Hill, Meanwood, Leeds; Rev. Leonard A. Lyne, Corsham, Chippenham; Rev. H. J. Richmond, Sherburn, Durham; Rev. S. C. Lowry, Holy Trinity, Bournemouth; Rev. J. Mansfield, Rockland St. Mary, Bournemouth; Rev. Dr. Scott, Ottershaw, Bournemouth; Capt. G. Maxwell Goad, Fairlea, Bournemouth; W. W. Moore, Esq., Higham, Bournemouth.

SOCIETY'S INCOME.

Abstract of RECEIPTS *and* PAYMENTS *from January* 1 *to April* 30.

	GENERAL FUND	SPECIAL FUNDS
Subscriptions, Donations, Collections, &c.	£8,737	£3,202
Legacies ...	2,711	107
Dividends, Rents, &c....	1,579	1,189
TOTAL RECEIPTS ...	£13,027	£4,498
PAYMENTS ...	£24,218	£6,040

The Receipts under the head of Subscriptions, Donations, and Collections for the General Fund from January 1 to April 30, in five consecutive years, compare as follows : 1885, £9,159; 1886, £9,786; 1887, £10,831; 1888, £9,437*; 1889, £8,737.

* In addition, the Treasurers received in 1888 Securities of the value of £25,296 as "A Thankoffering to Almighty God for the extension of the Church in the Colonies and Dependencies of the British Empire and beyond it"; also other Securities of the value of £2,268 as a Trust Gift, *the Income only being available.*

THE MISSION FIELD.

The field is the world. The seed is the Word of God.

JULY 1, 1889.

THE SOCIETY'S ANNIVERSARY.

T the annual public meeting in St. James's Hall, on June 6, there was great warmth and heartiness. The speakers were enthusiastic and had a sympathetic audience. The proceedings opened with the singing of the grand hymn, "Jesus shall reign where'er the sun doth his successive journeys run." After prayers, and the reading of the brief report which we print at length, the Archbishop of Canterbury delivered his Presidential address, in which his Grace commented on the several points of the report, and especially spoke of the elasticity of the Society's system, praising it for thus being able to make its policy a real (because flexible and versatile) policy for the attainment of its great object, and not a misnamed policy, which consists only in adherence to a preconceived plan.

The Bishop of Ballarat spoke of the wonderfully rapid growth of Australia and its Church; explained the valuable nature of the help the Society had rendered in building it up, and the way in which the thirteen Dioceses were now practically independent of such assistance. His Lordship dwelt on the mischief consequent upon the divisions of Christendom, as exemplified by the presence in small country places in Australia of places of worship belonging to no less than five denominations.

Sir Richard Temple, Bart., G.C.S.I., combated the attacks which had been made recently on Missionary endeavours, and showed them to be groundless. He reminded his hearers how a stronger case might have been made against Missions in the early days of the Church, if there were any force in the absurd comparison between the natural growth of heathen populations and the Church's rate of increase by conversions.

Canon Body's speech fired the whole assembly. He quoted from the Society's Annual Report the words :

The painful result makes itself apparent in a multitude of Missions inadequately supported, which do not advance as might be hoped, not for lack of openings, not because of opposition, so much as from lack of the material resources necessary for legitimate and natural expansion. The moral is, that by all suitable means the conscience of the people of England must be stirred as it has never been yet stirred intelligently to grasp the position and faithfully to recognise their duty.

He proceeded to examine their accuracy, and to claim that it was the case that much greater enthusiasm and zeal should be aroused than already existed. With his fervid eloquence he pleaded for a deeper recognition of Missionary work as part of the Christian life in the great central body of the Church of England. We propose to print next month a fuller account of what he said.

During the singing of the hymn, " Thou, whose Almighty word," &c., a collection was made in the Society's behalf.

The Rev. G. A. Lefroy then made an admirable speech, describing first the work in Delhi, and, in speaking with grand confidence of the success of Missions, said he would ask those who talked of failure to say in whom they believed. If they believed in the risen and reigning Christ, they could not doubt of the triumph of His Kingdom.

The Rev. E. F. Miller, from Colombo, spoke of the many peculiar circumstances of that Diocese, its polyglot character, and its being the only one in the ecclesiastical province to which it belonged where State support was withdrawn. He showed how well under its changed conditions the Diocese had entered upon synodal action, dwelt upon the weaknesses of Buddhism, of which some people in England had formed far too high an estimate, and in conclusion paid a warm tribute to the memory of Archdeacon Matthew, whose loss the Diocese has recently had to deplore.

The Rev. A. A. Maclaren spoke of New Guinea, where he is about to become the first Missionary of the Church of England, and also of his work in Australia. He described his experience among the imported Melanesian labourers, and the lack of interest for their spiritual good displayed by those who employ them.

In conclusion, Bishop Selwyn, of Melanesia, who had just reached England, addressed a few warm words to the meeting, he having taken the Archbishop's place in the chair, and the proceedings of the day were closed by the benediction pronounced by the Venerable Bishop of Antigua.

The following is the brief Report referred to above :—

The Society and its friends throughout the world have to render thanks to Almighty God for an income during the year 1888 larger by many thousands of pounds than has ever been entrusted to its administration in any one year during its long career.

The total amount received was £138,366. 17s. 6d. as compared with £109,765, the gross income of 1887.

The bulk of this thankworthy increase comes from a noble gift of more than £25,000, "a thankoffering to Almighty God for the extension of the Church in the Colonies and Dependencies of the British Empire and beyond it"; but nevertheless every item, save those of legacies and dividends, showed a considerable increase over the corresponding receipts in 1887.

It must be the object of all the Society's friends to see to it that the income of 1888, extraordinary as it was, shall be maintained by infusing more life, more spirit, more devotion into the ordinary working of the Society's Home Machinery. Many a subscriber can double his subscription "without missing it," as the phrase runs. It is not presumptuous to express a hope that many may be moved to carry their offerings beyond this point, even to a point where self-sacrifice shall make the offering to be "missed," for until this point is reached self-sacrifice does not begin. Many a parochial association can be worked with more spirit as new members are enrolled and more information is given; then the Diocesan contributions will swell, and the Society, its members and supporters, will rejoice together in the prospect of greater facilities for spreading the Gospel of our Lord and Saviour.

The enlargement of the Society's Magazine, the *Mission Field*, and the cost incurred in illustrating it, which commenced with 1888, have proved to be very successful ventures. Not only has the magazine been well reviewed by the Press, but by its intrinsic beauty and literary merit it may safely challenge comparison with any publication of similar size and cost. Its monthly sale has increased more than fourfold, and at the same time the monthly circulation of the *Gospel Missionary*, under the editorship of Miss Frances Awdry, has increased by more than 5,000 copies.

During the year 1888 the Board of Examiners, appointed by the Archbishops of Canterbury and York and the Bishop of London, in accordance with the 26th bye-law, have recommended to the Society twenty-seven persons out of those who had offered themselves for missionary work abroad. Of these, eight were students of St. Augustine's College, Canterbury, six graduates of the University of Oxford, three associates of King's College, London, one a graduate of London University, one a graduate of Durham, and the remainder from Dorchester and other colleges. Ten of them have gone to British North America, three to the West Indies, five to India, five to Australia, and the others are distributed between Borneo, South Africa, and Madagascar.

The number of Ordained Missionaries, including ten Bishops, on the Society's list is 637; that is to say, in Asia, 199; in Africa, 148; in Australia and the Pacific, 16; in North America, 204; in the West Indies, 36; and 34 in Europe. Of these 119 are natives labouring in Asia, and 25 in Africa. There are also in the various Missions about 2,300 Lay Teachers, 2,600 Students in the Society's Colleges, and 38,000 children in the Mission Schools in Asia and Africa.

The one event of supreme interest to the whole Anglican Communion, and of no little interest to many outside that Communion, was the assemblage of the third Lambeth Conference in the month of July last. For the Society and its friends such a gathering has an interest and significance which are unique. It is permitted to see in it the fruits of the labour and prayers of all the generations of its Members since 1701. Hardly a corner of the wide Mission Field was represented in the Conference which had not at some time or other been the subject of the Society's care; and, when so calm an observer as Bishop Lightfoot declares that "if there had been no Society for the Propagation of the Gospel, there could, humanly speaking, have been no Lambeth Conference," those on whom the present conduct of its great undertaking has devolved may find in such encouraging words an inspiration and a joy.

Rarely does a year pass that does not witness a substantial extension of the Society's field of work. In the past year the territory of the North Borneo Company has been entered upon, and a clergyman of experience, gained in two of our distant colonies, has commenced his work at Sandakan as its centre. Prudence would no doubt demur to an extension of work without a reasonable expectation of enlarged means; but it is with the Society's work as with the extension of the British Empire. Ever and anon the responsibilities of enlarged dominions are deprecated by statesmen, but the dominions seem to grow as by a law which cannot be resisted; and so too the Society, as representing the Church, there come calls which cannot be denied without a sacrifice of faithfulness, even though they be listened to at the cost of prudence.

The painful result makes itself apparent in a multitude of Missions inadequately supported, which do not advance as might be hoped, not for lack of openings not because of opposition, so much as from lack of the material resources necessary for legitimate and natural expansion. The moral is, that by all suitable means the conscience of the people of England must be stirred as it has never been yet stirred intelligently to grasp the position and faithfully to recognise their duty. Three new fields are now about to be occupied. For several years the idea of sending a Mission to New Guinea has been before the Australian as well as the English Church. It was felt that the work was one incumbent on the Australian Church, and that the time had come when the thirteen Dioceses of that great continent should enter on an independent venture of missionary work. At the same time it was urged that the Mother Church should take some initial part, and the Society accordingly granted £1,000. A clergyman with Australian experience, who is among the speakers at this meeting, will shortly leave for New Guinea, and will, it is hoped, be joined by some brethren in the Colony.

It is hoped that a Mission will have been equipped for the commencement of evangelistic work in Corea before the expiration of the current year. But for circumstances over which the Society has no control a commencement would ere this have been made. The Society has been able at present to vote only £2,800, and this sum is to be spread over five years. To attempt with funds so insignificant, so great a work as a Mission to a country with a heathen population of thirteen millions, will seem to many persons to savour of indiscretion and to provoke failure. The Society cannot at present do more, but it earnestly asks for special gifts for this work to be entrusted to its administration.

Turning to another continent, the energetic Bishop of Bloemfontein has, at the wish and with the help of the Society, made a visit of exploration to the north of his Diocese, and in Mashonaland, stretching up to the Zambesi, has traversed a vast region unoccupied by missionaries, with friendly chiefs who are willing to receive teachers. Here then is the next field which ought to be entered.

These facts point to but one conclusion—the necessity of impressing on the mind of the Church the magnitude of the work which the Society has undertaken, and the need of a truer sense of proportion in the exercise of our stewardship of this world's gifts. A Society which is carrying on work in nearly fifty Dioceses scattered over the world cannot do that work on the basis of subscriptions calculated on the needs of a local hospital, or even of our home missions at large. Its resources must be more in analogy with the conditions of its work.

The Society's Missions are in touch with the many races of men, civilised and barbarian, Christian, Pagan, and Mohammedan, believers, unbelievers, misbelievers. Oh for courage to grapple with the magnitude of the work! Oh for humble faith to carry it on for the glory of God and the good of man!

THE SOCIETY'S GRANTS FOR 1890.

IT is our annual practice to set forth in some detail the Society's scheme of grants for the coming year, and we are now able to announce the votes for 1890.

The annual grants voted for the current year are, subject to some small reductions, renewed for the year 1890 to the extent of £73,218. The reductions, amounting to £629, include the lapse of £50 by the death of a pensioner in Quebec; a saving of £104, released by the growth of the Endowment Fund from the Society's guarantee of the income of the See of Qu'Appelle; the cessation of the small grant of £50 to North Queensland, and of the now unused £300 voted for the Northern Territory of South Australia; and the non-payment of £125, the rent of a Mission house in Japan, for the purchase of which the Society now votes a capital sum.

In addition to renewing the grants for £73,218, the Society has had the happiness of voting £7,100 in new grants. The additions to the annual grants amount to but £350. Of these, £50 is to enable the Bishop of Algoma to place a clergyman at the important new station of Sudbury, a place where several lines join the Canadian Pacific Railway; such grants are found to call forth at least three times their amount locally. For Port Essington and Cassiar in the Diocese of Caledonia £100 is voted. The numerous coolies in Natal offer a most valuable opportunity for Missionary work, and the grant for the Coolie Missions in the Diocese of Maritzburg is increased by £50. In Fiji financial depression has rendered the continued residence of the Society's two Missionaries there precarious, and £50 is voted in augmentation of their stipends, besides a single sum of £30 to enable one of them whose health has failed to seek a change for a time. For the ever-increasing needs of the work among the poorer settlers in various places in Europe, an additional £100 is assigned.

The remainder is voted in what are called "single sums," the chief item being the allocation of £2,500 to the Endowment Fund of the See which is being formed for Chota Nagpore, in fulfilment of long-cherished desires, and supplying a great need. It is hoped that with £5,000 from the Colonial Bishoprics Council, a like sum from the Society for Promoting Christian Knowledge, and gifts from Churchmen generally, at least £15,000 may be raised for this most necessary object. The next largest of the votes is one of £1,100 for the purchase of the Mission house at Kobé, in Japan ; this, as was said just now, will result in a saving of the high rent of £125 hitherto payable.

Two Dioceses receive small grants towards those most wise and useful of Diocesan schemes—Diocesan Clergy Endowment Funds. Such funds are provocative of local contributions, and are abundantly pro-ductive of good. The grants are, for the Diocese of British Columbia, £300, and for Grahamstown £250. To Guiana £50 is given towards the cost (estimated at £200) of a steam-launch for use in the famous Missions to the aboriginal Indians; a sum of £110 is voted towards meeting some of the pressing needs of the important Ramnad Mission in the Diocese of Madras ; and £30 to Fiji, as is stated above.

There remain eight other new grants to be mentioned. These, though all " single sums," are so far of an annual nature that their expenditure is spread over a short series of years. In this way the income of the Missions is increased without the Society's annual grants being raised above a level which would be prudent. The distress of the Church in the Windward Islands, under its sudden disendowment, has been men-tioned frequently in the *Mission Field*, and is described in the Bishop's letter in the present number. The Society votes £200 a year to the Diocese, and also set aside in 1886 £600 to be spent in three years, which are now running out. By voting £300 to be spent at the same rate, the Society virtually makes the grant to the Windward Islands £400 a year for another eighteen months, thus giving a little more " breathing time " which, it is hoped, will be useful to the Diocese for reorganising its finances. By £50 provision is made for Tristan d'Acunha for another year. The future of this lonely outpost of the Church is, of course, uncertain.

Two honoured donors have founded an endowment for Missionary Scholarships for graduates. The Society is to be the trustee and ad-ministrator of the fund ; and as the full income which it will produce is not now forthcoming, a sum of £60 given by the Society to be spread over three years enables the scheme to be set in working order at once, with two missionary scholars or exhibitioners in residence at Selwyn College, Cambridge.

When the Bishop of St. John's, Kaffraria, addressed the Society at one of its monthly meetings last year, he especially asked to be enabled to begin work in Pondoland, which occupies one quarter of the area of his Diocese, but is quite unevangelised. The Pondomese are the least civilised of the native races in the Diocese, and hitherto work among them, though attempted years ago by Bishop Callaway, has not thriven. A distinct change has now taken place, and the Bishop said that he regarded the present circumstances as offering a favourable oppor-tunity for entering on work in Pondoland. To help his Lordship to make

this beginning the Society has now voted £500 to be spent in five years.
Few Dioceses have experienced such a violent change of their conditions
as Zululand has under the recent rush to the gold and diamond fields.
In response to the Bishop's appeal, the Society votes £200 for new
Missions at the disposal of his Lordship for two years, and £100 towards
the support of a clergyman on the Lorenco-Marques Railway for the
same period. Readers of the *Mission Field* cannot but know of the
wonderful opening there is for new work in Madagascar, and will
therefore be glad to learn that for a new Mission on the coast £600 is
voted, which is to be spent in three years. Last year the Society set
aside £2,500 to be spent in five years in the Corea. Since then the
prospects of the Mission have widened, and the consecration of a
Bishop for Corea has been contemplated. The sum which might
have been sufficient for Corea as an outpost of the North China Mission
needed increase under the changed circumstances, and £300 is voted
to be spent in two years. Lastly, £300 is voted towards the support
of a Missionary chaplain at Selangor, in the Diocese of Singapore,
being £100 a year for three years. This is a grant of a kind which
encourages those for whom the chaplain will be sent to raise two or
three times as much as the Society gives, and provides the ministrations
of the Church for those whose spiritual interests are otherwise likely
to suffer terrible neglect.

Such is the list of the twenty new grants. Their character is
varied as their distribution is world-wide. Perhaps the chief thing to
notice in them is their smallness in proportion to the work it is hoped
that they may develop. How much more could be done with the
opportunities now before us, if we were able in less stinting measure to
help forward the Church's work in all parts of the world!

The following table sets forth the grants for 1890, showing the
amount of the annual grant to each Diocese :—

Montreal	£520	Jamaica (Panama)	£200
Quebec	1,450	Windward Islands	200
Toronto, Pension	32	Sierra Leone	280
Algoma	850	Capetown	1,600
Fredericton	1,250	Grahamstown, Colonial	200
Nova Scotia	865	Ditto, Heathen	2,670
Ditto, P. Edward's Island	200	Ditto, Scholarships	60
Newfoundland	2,900	St. John's	2,550
Rupertsland	1,560	Maritzburg	2,175
Qu'Appelle	988	Zululand	600
Saskatchewan and Calgary	1,300	St. Helena	275
Caledonia	300	Bloemfontein	988
New Westminster	600	Pretoria	900
Nassau	500	Mauritius	590
Antigua	850	Madagascar	3,200
Trinidad	50	Calcutta, Bp.'s Col. Pensions	375
Guiana	770	Ditto, Missions	6,625

Rangoon	...	...	...	... £3,780	Norfolk Island	...	...	...	£50
Lahore	...	...	...	... 2,300	Fiji ...	...	...	...	... 250
Ditto, Cambridge Mission			...	680	Honolulu	...	...	...	... 700
Madras, with Pensions, &c.			... 13,525		Constantinople	...	...	...	300
Bombay	...	...	...	... 4,725	Continental Chaplaincies	...		... 300
Colombo	...	...	...	... 1,500	Education of Students	...		... 170
Singapore, &c.	...	...	... 3,250						
North China	...	...	...	900	Total annual grants for 1890, £73,568				
Japan	...	...	...	... 1,835	Single sum Grants...	...		...£6,750	
Ditto, Bishop	...	...	...	500					
Perth	...	...	...	... 300	Total amount voted £80,318				
Brisbane	...	...	...	... 50					

'The grants may be summarised thus :—

	Annual Grants	Block Sums	Total
America, and the West Indies	£15,385	£650	£16,035
Africa, and the neighbouring islands	16,068	1,700	17,768
India and Ceylon	33,510	2,610	36,120
Singapore, China, Corea, and Japan	6,485	1,700	8,185
Australasia, Honolulu, &c.	1,350	30	1,380
Constantinople, Chaplaincies, and Students	770	60	830
	£73,568	£6,750	£80,318

THE LATE BISHOP RAWLE.

A FAMOUS labourer in the Mission field has been taken from us. Soon after midnight of Friday, May 10, the Right Rev. Bishop Rawle breathed his last breath in the Principal's Lodge of Codrington College, Barbados, which was for many years his happy home and the scene of his abundant labours, and whither he returned to give such help as limited powers permitted in the Theological Department of the College in September last. So great a man deserves lengthened notice in our pages, and our next number will contain an appreciative sketch of him from the pen of one who knew and loved him well, the revered Bishop of Antigua.

POVERTY OF THE CHURCH IN THE WINDWARD ISLANDS.

REPORT FROM THE BISHOP OF DISTRICTS AIDED BY
THE SOCIETY'S GRANTS.

BARBADOS was constituted a Diocese in 1824, when that of Jamaica was also established. It is thus among the very earliest of colonial sees, only three—Nova Scotia, Quebec, and Calcutta—being older than it. It included Guiana and the islands now forming the Diocese of Antigua, but was relieved in 1842 by the formation of two sees for these distant parts of the original diocese, and was further subdivided in 1872 when Trinidad became a bishopric.

In 1878 the remaining Diocese of Barbados was divided into two separately organised dioceses, called respectively Barbados and the Windward Islands, but remained under one bishop. The reason for this step was that it was found difficult to work under the same system Barbados with its State-aided establishment, and the other islands—Grenada, St. Vincent, the Grenadines, and Tobago—where the connection with the State does not now continue. Life interests were reserved in the Windward Islands at the time when the State connection was dissolved, but the time thus afforded for the Church to organise its finances on a voluntary basis has suddenly been cut short. Consequently, the Church there is in considerable difficulties.

The Society has come to its assistance with a small grant of £200 a year, and also with block sums which for four years and a half raises the grant to £400 a year. Last month we printed a letter, written by one of the clergy, which the Bishop had forwarded to us. It described vividly the crisis which has arrived. We now append some remarks from the Bishop himself as to the state of affairs in other parishes :

"Just before I came to England last year the Colonial Legislature 'suspended'—which means that they permanently withdrew—their grants in aid of the Church of England and other religious bodies. The result was an immediate reduction in the staff of clergy. The large parishes of North and South Charlotte were at once placed under the charge of one rector, the Rev. A. B. Williams, and he has now four churches to serve, with the aid of the deacon at Onia, who receives a grant from you. The churches at the extreme ends are, say, twenty miles apart. It is simply impossible for one man properly to superintend the work; but this is not a solitary case. The Rev. H. A. Melville is left alone in his parish of Calliaqua, his curate having been removed also last year.

"I have gathered such materials as I can in the brief time that I can spare from my work, and forward them as reports. 1. From Chateaubellair; 2. From Calliaqua; 3. From North Charlotte.

"1. *St. David's, Chateaubellair, St. Vincent.*—This is twelve miles distant from St. Patrick's, of which Canon Branch is the rector, and forms a district of that parish.

"It has a coast line of twelve miles, with villages dotted all along, but not extending more than half a mile from the shore. There is a newly-built stone church, which, though unfinished in some respects (the aisles are not paved, and there are no windows), is regularly used for daily and Sunday services. This district has always been a stronghold of the Wesleyans. The population is about 3,600, which may be approximately classed as—Church of England, 1,200; Wesleyans, 2,200; Roman Catholics, 125; other bodies, 75.

"They are never visited by a priest of their own. The Rev. A. B. Williams was curate here till December 31, 1887, receiving a part of your grant. The Rev. H. A. Graham, who came up from Trinidad with good testimonials from Bishop Rawle, took his place in March 1888.

"He has made a census of his parishioners, and places the households in St. David's belonging to the Church at 256, which, allowing an average of five to each house, fairly verifies the estimate of 1,200 as belonging to the Church of England.

"By the instrumentality of Canon Branch, not only the new church, but a small curate's house close to it has been built. The salary of Mr. Graham, as fixed by the Church Council, is £150, but out of this he has

WASHINGTON ROCK, ST. VINCENT, WINDWARD ISLANDS.

.to pay £20 a year for the house until a debt still remaining on it has been paid off.

"The £120 (deducting your grant) was raised in 1888 by local contributions from the whole parish. St. Patrick's raised £48 (an increase of £5 on the previous year); St. David's, £56 (an increase of £10 on 1887); so that Mr. Graham's salary (less £4) was paid in 1888. The Religious Endowment Act being repealed, the Legislature has just, with the consent of the Secretary of State, brought in an ordinance to provide for the compulsory resignation and pensions of the three remaining State-paid clergy—viz., the Archdeacon (Laborde), Canon Branch, and Rev. E. Flintof. If St. Patrick's will raise sufficient money to make up the difference between Canon Branch's pension (£180) and his former State aid (£300), he will remain at St. Patrick's; but in any case St. Patrick's will be unable for the future to give the district any aid. The coming difficulty is how to make up this, say, £50.

"There are five estates in St. David's district, but none of them contribute to Church funds. The parishioners are, with the exception of the managers and a few small shopkeepers, of the labouring class and peasant proprietors. For the first months of this year I believe Mr. Graham has received some $18 a month! But he and his brave little wife seem to have made up their minds to face straitness of means rather than surrender their post. My own very grave conviction is that eventually the district, and the parish of which it is part, must come under one priest living at St. Patrick's; but this means the surrender, I should say, of Chateaubellair to the Wesleyans. I am going to appeal to all the proprietors for aid, and ought to get £100 a year, and, if I can make the grant of £30 into £50, these poor people will get their £150.

"But then I must take from other places where the want is quite as great, where indeed the staff has been reduced already—*e.g.*, 2. *Calliaqua*, where the Rev. H. A. Melville is rector, and where the churches were destroyed by hurricane. St. Paul's is slowly but *well* rebuilding; St. Philip's is solidly rebuilt of stone, and I confirmed in it last week; St. Silvan's remains unbuilt, but services are held (as at St. Paul's) in the school-house; and St. Matthias' wooden School Chapel is rebuilt.

"Mr. Melville receives £50 a year of the S.P.G. grant. Up to February last year he had a curate, the Rev. W. G. Hutchinson, but we were compelled to give this up for lack of means.

"The parish of Calliaqua is twenty square miles in extent—Population 9,767, of whom 3,922 are Church people. The average congregation (for the most part in school-rooms) in the four places used for worship taken together was, in 1888, 448. Communicants on list, 463. Baptisms: private, 18; public, 103. Private Communions, 52. Marriages, 12. Funerals, 73. The money raised in the parish is £298. 1*s.* 7*d.*

"I have only to add that the brief record I have given of three parishes in which grants from the Society are given (Ouia being in North Charlotte) fairly represents the condition of the whole Diocese so far as I have been this year. The Rector of the Grenadines, the Rev. Canon Connell, who has done a quiet but most valuable work in these scattered islands for thirty-nine years, has retired from his work on a pension. The clergyman who succeeded him, and was removed from South Charlotte for that purpose, was sent to Begina (where the rectory is), in April, on a stipend of £150 a year; but the Church Council found they had no funds for him, and he has been obliged to maintain himself on what little assessment he can raise in the islands—Begina, Anion, and Canonan. He writes: 'My living for the last ten months has been one of extreme poverty, being compelled to subsist (with wife and children) on the meanest, coarsest fare; but,' he adds, 'we are content . . . we are exceedingly poor.'

"In town here we shall from next month be obliged to raise entirely from voluntary sources in the future the salaries of three clergymen if the present staff is maintained. Two out of the three, the Archdeacon and Mr. Flintof, have hitherto been paid entirely by the State as rector and curate.

"I don't think I can add anything now to what I have said, except that an appeal was made during my absence in England to the different parishes in Barbados for aid to pay the salaries here—and this appeal was responded to.

"*Ex pede Herculem!* From what I have said, you must judge what is the general condition of the Windward Diocese at the present time, so far as St. Vincent and Tobago are concerned. Of Grenada I must report when I go there."

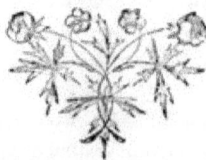

THE BISHOP OF GUIANA'S RECENT VISIT TO THE POMEROON.

BY THE REV. G. W. MATTHEWS.

S nearly as possible at the same time as the Essequibo steamer with the Bishop on board was leaving Georgetown on the morning of February 10, the large mission-boat "Kalamyhi" pushed off from Cabacaburi, our old mission station on the Upper Pomeroon with the Missionary and a fine crew of Indian paddlers, to meet his Lordship at Anna Regina. Next morning

HILL MISSION STATION, POMEROON.

about 9 A.M., the Bishop, accompanied by the Rev. W. Heard, reached Anna Regina. After availing ourselves of the kind hospitality of the Attorney, who invited us to breakfast, we were on board "Kalamyhi" and off for Cabacaburi at 10.15 A.M. Passing through a long estate trench, a narrow creek just wide enough for a boat to pass, and then a fine open lake, the "Tapacooma," we came to the artificial stop-off or watershed between the waters flowing to the coast and those joining the Pomeroon. Here we were delayed two hours until high-water; the

creek being very low on account of the dry weather. We took possession of the police-station for our picnic lunch. Having hauled over the
boat into the creek, we started off again as soon as there was sufficient
water to float us. The dull heavy " thud, thud " of the paddles gave the
people at Cabacaburi due warning of our approach long before we
arrived. All who could ran down to the waterside to greet the Bishop,
the darkness of the evening serving for the time as a covering to their
characteristic shyness. The boys and girls belonging to the school, with
their master at their head, drawn up on either side of the path leading
from the landing stage to the Mission House, greeted the Bishop, as he
stepped ashore, with a spontaneous " Good evening, my lord," and a
bow ; the effect of the latter being somewhat lost in the flickering light
of the one small lamp. Through the dimness one could see the Bishop's
face beam with pleasure as he returned the salutations of these little
Indians with natural dignity and grace, so characteristic of our venerable
prelate. Tired and hungry as he was, he lingered long to pat the cheeks
of some of the little ones, who looked up to him as if not quite sure
whether it was safe for them to be so near the " Great Parson."

It was a few minutes after 8 P.M. when we got into the Mission
House, having good appetites for dinner, as may be imagined. As
we sat and chatted afterwards, the Bishop spoke with emotion of
the history and progress of these Missions, from their earliest infancy,
in the early forties, to the present time. He spoke of his first visit to
these rivers in 1838, if I remember rightly, before Mr. Brett came and
sowed the seeds in 1840, to be followed by one who sat with us, the Rev.
W. Heard, whose devotion and powers of organisation have left such
abundant testimony behind him. Not only did he speak of the Missionaries, but he remembered minutely the work of the catechists and
schoolmasters, on whom so much responsibility rests when the Missionary is travelling from station to station. The work of the late Mr.
Kirkwood, schoolmaster, he spoke of with great praise. He was an
Englishman, who had played (in succession) the role of successful planter,
pauper, and afterwards, having reformed and given up all intoxicating
drinks, he became a distinguished schoolmaster at this station. The
history of Cabacaburi has been by no means one of continual advance,
and it seems to have suffered considerably during the long non-residence
of the Missionary before Mr. Heard came. These reminiscences we
could have listened to far into the night, but Sunday was drawing on,
and a hard day's work for the Bishop, so our little group broke up, and
we retired to our rooms, Mr. Heard preferring a hammock in the
gallery.

February 12, *Sunday.*—At five minutes to seven the church bell was
sounding its brief signal for early service, which was to consist of Confirmation service and address from the Bishop. Mr. Heard acted as

Chaplain, and the Missionary presented the candidates, 11 males and 13 females, all Indians except two. It was a very impressive sight to see these children of the forest, rescued from heathen darkness, coming forward for the holy rite, to receive the gift of the Holy Ghost through the Church's own appointed means, that they might with that help do their Christian *duty.* These are the same people who, within the memory of him who now, according to Apostolic precedent, lays his venerable hands upon them with a prayer for the gift of the Holy Ghost, knew not " whether there be any Holy Ghost."

Full Matins (Choral), at which the Bishop preached, followed by a celebration of the Holy Communion, was at 11 A.M., when there were 127 communicants, and a congregation of 265. Sunday School at 2.30 and Evensong at 4.30, at both of which the Bishop was present, completed the services for the day. There were over 300 people on the Mission, but several Carib families were absent on account of sickness.

13*th*, *Monday.*—We left Cabacaburi in " Kalamyhi " at 8.45 A.M. for Hackney, on the lower Pomeroon, where we arrived at 2.23 P.M. after a very quick passage. Hackney is a small estate, situated in the midst of a scattered population of Creoles and Portuguese, who are chiefly occupied in provision farming. The estate was bought many years ago for Missionary purposes by the late Bishop Coleridge, and has since belonged to the See of Guiana. Here there is a pretty church, capable of holding about 260 persons, built a few years ago; a school-house, Missionary's cottage, and a few labourers' cottages, forming a small Church village. Rain, unfortunately, kept the Bishop indoors for the rest of the day. Dinner over, and hammocks and nettings swung before 6 P.M. is the rule to be observed at Hackney, unless you wish to become the prey of swarms of merciless " gally-nippers." Experience had taught us this, and we were quite ready inside our fortifications when the well-known music caused by myriads of wings told us our siege had begun. We exchanged notes from under our nettings through the long evening, read, and slept. The Bishop long before it was light made an attempt to get up, but, notwithstanding his gallant effort, the mosquitoes drove him back again; a few finding their way inside the nettings continued to torture him until they were gorged. By degrees, as the day advanced, the singing outside our nettings grew fainter and fainter until we ventured to turn out, when only a few of the more desperate ones remained to take a mean advantage of us during our ablutions.

At an early hour the people began to arrive in crowded buck-shells and batteaux (the river being the only means of communication), with canisters and bundles containing their best clothes, which they put on in some friendly neighbour's cottage on the estate. Thus it is they appear in church in spotless black cloth and white drill, with polished boots without a cloud. Although this is a "week-day," the church is full, and 19 persons are confirmed, while 95 receive the Holy Communion. The afternoon the Bishop spent in visiting the schools and examining the children, and afterwards, accompanied by the Missionary, he visited all the cottages on the estate, and inspected all the church buildings and furniture. The mosquitoes were not so bad as on the previous evening, and we were able to sit up sometime after sunset by getting close round a coal-pot full of smoking grass, like the witches in Macbeth.

15th, *Ash-Wednesday.* — Matins and Commination Service at 8 A.M., and at 11.20 started for Wakapoa. This is an Indian Mission station, situated on a small creek from which it takes its name, which joins the Pomeroon on its left bank about a mile from the sea. From the wide Pomeroon we passed into the narrow creek, which we found the Indians had cleared so as to allow our boat to pass freely. At 2.40 P.M. we arrived at the Mission, which stands on a small sand island

CARIBS.

rising out of a vast savannah. The buildings embrace a very appropriate picturesque-looking church, built by the Indians (as indeed all the buildings have been), school-house, Missionary's cottage, catechist's house, and several Indian houses. We attended shortened Evensong at 4 P.M., at which a good many people were present, and others continued to arrive in their buck-shells all through the night. What a treat we found it to get to this place, where we could sleep without the necessity of hanging suffocating nettings over our hammocks! We found no mosquitoes.

16th, *Thursday.*—Confirmation at 8 A.M., when 18 Indians were

presented; 11 A.M., Matins and Holy Communion, with an address from
the Bishop. Sixty-five communicants, 145 congregation. The afternoon occupied by the Bishop in examining the school, 27 present.
4 P.M., Evensong. Indians on Mission, 178. This station, which is but
a small one compared with Waramuri and Cabacaburi, was established
by the Rev. W. Heard in 1880, and placed under the charge of an
Indian catechist, Alex. Boyan, who is still here. The Mission buildings are a model of neatness and tidiness, and have all been put up
by the Indians, the catechist being especially industrious in this way,
the Missionary's cottage, consisting of three large rooms floored
with hard wood, and a fine school-house, 35 by 25 feet, with outside

WARAU HABITATIONS.

galleries, and hard-wood floor, having been built during the last nine
months.

17th, *Friday.*—After early Matins, we started for Waramuri
Mission at 8 A.M. Our course was first into the Pomeroon, from the
mouth of which we crossed over to that of the Morucca, a distance of
about five miles. Choosing the time for crossing at low water, we found
the sea pretty calm, although the weather was rather squally. Two
hours and a half steady paddling up the Morucca brought us to Waramuri Mission. Owing to the dryness of the weather and state of the
tide, we found the trench leading from the creek to the Mission nearly
dry; so a small buck-shell was brought, into which the Bishop tran-
shipped, and was pushed over the mud by a small crowd of Indian boys

to the foot of the hill. Waramuri is the largest of the Mission stations
under the care of the "Pomeroon Missionary," there not unfrequently
being three or four hundred Indians present at one time, and on special
occasions many more. They belong to four tribes, Arawaks, Accowois,
Caribs, Waraus, the latter being the most numerous, while they are
also the most
uncivilised of
all the tribes.
The history of
this Mission
dates back to
the early days
of the Rev. W.
H. Brett, in
1843. Several
attempts have
been made, from
time to time, to
have a resident
Missionary
here, but from
one cause and
another they
have not been
successful.
The catechist,
Mr. R. Adams,
was appointed
many years ago
by Mr. Brett.
There is a
schoolmistress
and a matron
of an Orphan-
age for girls
attending the
school. It has
been found

OPENING OF THE CANNIBAL MOUND AT WARAMURI.

necessary to feed and clothe the Indian children in order to keep them at
all regular at school. This is a severe tax on our finances, and only an
average of about forty children can be kept up. The Mission buildings,
consisting of a large wooden-shingled church, school-house, orphanage
buildings, catechist's house, Missionary's cottage, boat-house, &c., have
all to be kept up by the Indians themselves, and by voluntary contri-

butions. The Indian houses, which for the most part are only occupied from Saturdays to Mondays, form quite a large village, the different tribes occupying different quarters. Waramuri was brought into notice many years ago by the visit of Governor Hincks, when a large shell-mound near the church was opened, and many fragments of stone implements and human marrow bones, split open, were discovered. The bones bore evident testimony to the dark days of the long past, when cannibalism was practised here. In July 1887 Lieut.-Governor Bruce, C.B., visited this Mission and stayed a few days, when over a thousand Indians were present.

18th, *Saturday.*—7 A.M., Matins. Afterwards baptised one adult Indian. The Bishop visited and examined the school, visited the Orphanage, in which we have at present 15 girls, while the boys, 28 in number, are under the charge of the catechist. In the afternoon we held athletic sports, in which men, women, and children joined heartily, contending in ·shooting with bows and arrows, running and jumping, for prizes of knives, combs, beads, &c., &c. We were all ready for our hammocks when the curfew tolled out its signal for retiring to rest.

19th, *Sunday.*—7 A.M., Confirmation and address by the Bishop. 27 candidates (all Indians, save one) were presented. 11 A.M., Matins and Holy Communion, with sermon by the Bishop. 167 communicants ; congregation, 287.

Having received a letter by a special messenger telling me of the dangerous illness of my little boy, I left Waramuri at 3 P.M. for Cabacaburi, which I reached after thirteen hours' almost constant paddling, at 4 A.M. next morning.

The Bishop and Mr. Heard stayed at Waramuri until Wednesday, 22nd. It had been his Lordship's intention to visit my other station, far away on the upper part of the Waini, called " Kwabanneh," but the dryness of the savannahs and small creeks through which we should have had to pass made this impossible. This journey is always a very trying one, occupying sometimes 48 hours in the passage ; there are only two or three camping places where you can get out of your boat. I was once 58 hours on this journey returning from Kwabanneh to Waramuri ; the water in the savannahs and itabos having dried up, we had to push our boat over the mud for nine hours one day, and six the next. The candidates from Kwabanneh, having had notice, walked overland to Waramuri, arriving in time to be confirmed on Sunday morning. During the Bishop's stay there were counted 537 Indians on the Mission.

22nd, *Wednesday.*—The Bishop and Mr. Heard arrived at Cabacaburi at 10.15 P.M., having been in the boat since 6.30 A.M., making only a brief stay at Hackney as they passed. That is a journey I think few men who have come to fourscore years and more would have stood better !

23rd, 24th, 25th.—These were quiet days, spent by the Bishop observing the usual routine work of the Mission. He examined the school on Thursday, and thus expressed himself in the visitors' book: "Very great improvement since my last visit—much pleased with the reading and writing of the elder children, and, indeed, of several of the younger ones. Examined the upper classes in Scripture history, chiefly asking questions out of the Acts of the Apostles, which were readily answered. The sums set by Mr. Griffith were done very well, and I confess that I hardly expected to find so much accuracy, with nicely formed figures, even with the older and more advanced pupils. School very orderly, and I had much pleasure in examining the children. Very pleased to see so much attention paid to plain sewing, which appeared to me to be neatly done by the elder girls."

WARAMURI MISSION.

Such a report reflects great credit on the schoolmaster, Mr. J. Griffith, who, when he came two years ago, found the school a wreck.

On Saturday, the Bishop, the Missionary and his wife and little family, and Mr. Heard, went up the Pomeroon as far as Maccassema, paddled by as many of the school-boys as the boat could carry.

26th, Sunday.—7 A.M., Holy Communion, the Bishop celebrant; 66 communicants. 11 A.M., Matins and sermon by the Rev. W. Heard. After Matins the Bishop confirmed six persons who had not arrived in time from their distant homes on the 12th. 2.30 P.M., Sunday School, Bishop visited. 4.30 P.M., Evensong and address by the Bishop. This was his farewell to the people, as he was to leave us early on Monday morning. The Bishop's words were full of emotion and feeling. He spoke of the recent epidemic of sickness which carried off so many from us, and left many more to mourn; and of the moral lessons sickness and death teach. He impressed upon them the duty of the strong to help the weak, and the healthy to provide for the sick and poor. The importance of sending their children to school was pointed out to them in such a way as should be remembered.

The last evening of the Bishop's visit had come all too quickly. Again reminiscences of the past history of these Missions, so full of interest, formed the ménu of our conversation. The feasibility of extending our ground and establishing stations on the Barahma and Amookooroo rivers was discussed. But we found our hands tied for the want of funds. To keep the present stations in order obliges the Missionary to draw on his own resources considerably. The Diocesan "Church Society" has just made its grants for the year, amounting in all to two hundred and fifty-seven dollars sixty cents; while the subscription from these Missions for the past year was eighty-three dollars eighty-five cents, or nearly one-third of what we get back. I have shown what the Indians have done in the way of building at Wakapoa, I might say the same of those at Cabacaburi, Waramuri and Kwabanneh; but with all this, we depend a great deal on the voluntary subscriptions of the Church.

27th, Monday.—We were all astir at 4 A.M., the Bishop as usual first, and everything was ready for a start for Anna Regina by 6.30 A.M. The Bishop and Mr. Heard travelled in the Missionary's small tent-boat " Imogodasi," the luggage following in another. They reached the coast safely soon after 2 P.M., where they were met by Mr. Heard's waggon, which conveyed them to St. John's Rectory, Suddie, where the Bishop slept the night.

28th, Tuesday.—The Bishop left Suddie by steamer for Georgetown, and arrived safely at Kingston House in the evening.

In the ordinary course of events we can hardly expect many more visits from our venerable prelate, now in his 82nd year. Since his consecration, they have been paid every other year regularly, and it will be a sad loss to the Missionary Church, above all, when his guiding hand shall be withdrawn. Our trials and privations sink into nothingness under such a sympathising " Father." In the visitation book he writes: " I am fully aware how much self-denial is required from those who devote themselves to the Ministry of souls in this remote district, and they deserve the sympathy and prayers of all the members of the Church."

FROM BLOEMFONTEIN TO THE ZAMBESI:

A GREAT MISSIONARY JOURNEY BY THE BISHOP OF BLOEMFONTEIN.

IN MATABELELAND.

THE Bishop of Bloemfontein has sent to the Secretary of the Society the diary which he kept on this journey, which was undertaken with the view of ascertaining if Mashonaland could be occupied by the Church as a Mission field.

The diary was not begun till the Bishop had arrived at Lobengula's kraal, at Enkanwini, in Matabeleland, 600 or more miles from Kimberley, the place from which the Bishop may be said to have commenced his journey. The country through which he thus passed is for the greater part of the year "a dry and thirsty ground," most difficult to travel through; and it has been adequately described in Captain Parker Gilmore's "The Great Thirst Land," and in Mr. Montague Kerr's "The Far Interior," which latter also deals with the Mashona country and the Zambesi Valley, though not with those parts which the Bishop visited.

Lobengula is the chief of the Matabele. He is the son of Umzilikatze, otherwise Mosilikatsi, one of Chaka's generals; who, being ambitious of supreme power for himself, marched away with one of his master's armies to the north-west of Zululand, and, after much fighting with the tribes he encountered, founded what is known as the Matabele kingdom. The government of Umzilikatze was, like that of Chaka, strong and cruel. His will was law; and he was merciless in his dealings with all with whom he came in conflict, and in his treatment of his own people. Lobengula, when he became chief, occupied a position not unlike that which Cetewayo held when he became supreme chief of the Zulus. He is a man of great ability and force of character. He would like to do as his father did, unfettered by any considerations of the white men; but he sees that the times are changed, and that he must govern himself accordingly, and, being afraid that the Boers of the Transvaal would molest him, he has, since the Bishop was at Enkanwini, placed his country under the protectorate of Great Britain. Nevertheless, Matabeleland is still one of the dark places of the earth that are full of the habitations of cruelty, and sooner or later the existing condition of things must be broken up by the inevitable encroachments of Christianity and civilisation.

The Bishop's servants on this journey consisted of two half-castes, Edward and William Jelly; John, a partly Mozambique and partly Bechuana man; three men from Khama, and the Christian chief of the Bamangwato; two Basuto men, Isaac and Bill; and one man of a tribe allied to the Amatonga. The need for these men, and the work they had to do, will be best shown by the Bishop's diary.

A map of the journey, from observations made by the Bishop himself, was worked out by Mr. Duncan, the Surveyor-General of Bechuanaland, but this has been unfortunately lost.

It was necessary for the Bishop to visit Lobengula, for without his consent to it the Mashonaland exploration would have been all but impossible.

The diary commences on Wednesday, May 23, 1888, as follows:—

" We arrived at the Kamalo River in the morning. The people of the village near soon knew of our arrival, and brought mealies for barter, of which basketfuls had to be bartered for separately till our sacks were full.

" The messengers from Lobengula arrived, saying that I could come on, and that the chief had said that they were each to have a present of a blanket and a bar of lead, which I gave. We arrived in the evening at Enkanwini.

" *Thursday, May 24.*—I sent John to ask the chief when I could see him, and soon after went with John to the chief's kraal. I felt that I was in a world of savage heathendom, which was far worse than I had expected. I left my horse in the outside cattle kraal, and walked into the inner one where was Lobengula, whom I saluted, and then waited for permission to speak to him. He soon said that I could speak, and I then thanked him for having told Mr. Carnegie that I could 'have the way' through his country. He replied that he had never said so. I had not expected this. Then there came some questioning and explanation as to who I was; but as John was, I think, rather frightened, and also did not put into Setabele (the Matabele language) the exact sense that I wished to convey, I proposed to visit Lobengula again with Mr. Edwards in the afternoon, which he agreed to.

" Mr. Sam. Edwards, be it said, is an Englishman who has lived for many years in the country, and has been made an 'induna' (chief) in the Tati district.

" I rode to Mr. Fry's waggon, where Mr. Edwards was, who decided to ask Mr. Tainton to interpret. Mr. Fry and Mr. Tainton, with others, were in the country trying to obtain gold concessions from Lobengula.

" In the evening after the chief had crawled into his hut, I went to him again, and Sir Sydney Shippard's letter and my 'credentials' were read to him. We then had a good deal of not very useful conversation, during which I explained that I had no intention of staying in the country now, that I had not come for gold, and that I did not wish to go anywhere against his wish. I knew that there would be gained no further end by forcing the point, so I then left.

" I learnt that nothing had been heard of Richard Foster. He was a young man who two or three years ago made a very remarkable journey along the Zambesi alone; and proposed to reach Lake Bengeolo from the Zambesi (whence he proceeded by way of Quilimaine), and then to meet me at Buluwayo. My proposal to him was that he should come with me, but he did not agree with this. I do not think that he at all anticipated the difficulties which have apparently ended in his death; for I am sure that he would be here to meet me had he been alive. A braver soul has never, I think, passed from this world to the next.

"*Friday, May 25.*—I did not feel well, and rode to Mr. Edwards to say that I would not go to Hope Fountain (the mission station), but, as I much wished to see Mr. Helm (the missionary), I nevertheless went. The sight of the mission house after my little ride of nine miles, in contrast to the chief's kraal, gave me a feeling of the blessedness of Christianity such as I had never experienced before. We talked for some time on the customs of the people, and, on my leaving, a boy was sent with me some way to show me the road.

"I was to have seen Lobengula again in the evening, but, as Mr. Tainton was away, I sent instead a present by John, consisting of three shawls, a folding chair, and four pipes.

"I am not well.

"*Saturday, May 26.*—Except for a short time I did not get up till the afternoon, when Mr. Helm came over, and I walked to the chief with him. Standing in the sun and feeling very unwell, I had to vainly explain and answer questions—the same questions repeated—such as, 'Whom do you wish to see?' 'Whose people are they?' 'Will you teach them?' 'What will you teach them?' I repeated that I would not build or stay in the country, but would come back to him; that I wished to go to the Hanyane River to see such chiefs as Shipurero and Chuzu, and to see the people by the Sabi River, along the road Mr. Selous had travelled last year. I reminded him of the Administrator's letter, and said that whatever I promised to do that I would keep to, and added, 'A kraal is built round the word of a chief.' Upon which he said that I meant to build a house there, and laughed. He was good-humoured toward the end of the interview, but gave no permission for me to go into his country.

"On leaving, I saw two halters which looked like the two that had been stolen off my horses, but I was not sure. Isaac, who had brought Mr. Helm's horse, then said he saw my knife on the young chief, but was afraid to tell me while I was at the kraal. The boy had been to the waggons asking for a present which I had refused."

On the next day, Sunday, the Bishop was ill and very weak from a severe dysenteric attack, and could not get about. He writes on Monday, May 28 :—

"Mr. Helm came over. I felt that if I could get to Hope Fountain I should get well. Rugs and a coat were put under me, but, after about a quarter of a mile, I felt that it was impossible to travel further in the waggon, so I rode the Basuto pony, and we arrived soon after dark. Mr. and Mrs. Helm were most kind. I slept in the waggon, and had a very bad night."

On the 29th the Bishop remained in the Mission House, slept on a sofa, and became better. On the 30th he writes :—

"I lay down nearly all day. Every possible kindness and attention was given me. Never shall I forget the Christian hospitality of these two people ; it showed the possibility of ' using hospitality one to another without grudging.' I trust that God will prevent a sick person ever being turned from my door.

" A boy arrived and said that Jelly was coming on from Miniani's, but that the long waggon was broken, and causing trouble.

" Mr. and Mrs. Helm sat in the room with me, and told me about the present state of the country. It is a state which can hardly be credited. An 'impi,' that is, a detachment of men sent out by the chief for raiding or other purposes, under the command of an ' induna,' has just gone out somewhere. They do not know till they have gone some distance whom they are to attack. One of the men who had been on a late raid described to Mr. Helm how they surrounded the helpless people, dragged them one by one out of the crowd, and gave them one stab with the assegai, till they had made a heap of dead bodies. Sometimes they tie up the people they go against in dry grass, and set fire to them. The wives of the late chief Umzilikatze say : ' He was a king ! He knew how to kill.' Lobengula does not kill so much, but he has lately killed, or allowed to be killed, his own brother and sister on a charge of witchcraft. The chief killing for witchcraft takes place after the ' Ingwala,' the dance of the first-fruits, which takes place in the immense kraal at Buluwayo in February, when the men come in full fighting dress. Mr. Helm found one old woman under a bush, almost reduced to a skeleton, who had been sent away by her husband, and refused admission by her son and two married daughters, between whose houses she must have wandered about 130 miles (while it was raining continually), without a single blanket. She died two days after being brought in by Mr. Helm. All that I know about the Matabele throws a light for me, such as no previous argument has done, on God's command to the Israelites to destroy a whole nation. Yet Mr. Edwards' remark that he knew the Basuto when they were worse than the Matabele is an argument for hope that allows of no refutation.

" *Thursday, May* 31.—I lay down all day except for a short walk when the buck-waggon came in. I am almost well ; the good feeding and kind care have, under God, done this.

" Jelly travelled lazily, I think, for he took eleven days to do what we did in a little over six.

" At night we had prayers, when the good missionary asked God to bless my mission to the Mashonas ; and his wife afterwards said :

What a blessing it would be if you could establish a mission amongst them ; they are so clever ! '

"*June* 1, *Friday.*—Bought mealies, and made arrangements for mending the long waggon ; then rode over with Mr. Helm to the chief. I seemed to satisfy him on all points except that I could not give the names of the little chiefs whom I wished to see. I do not know whether he cares to know or only asks to cause delay. This entails another ride of eighteen miles to-morrow, and I did not like the one to-day ; but I am much stronger.

"*June* 2, *Saturday.*—Mr. Helm and I rode to Lobengula. It was early, and he seemed cold, which made us think it best to come to him again later on. After breakfast at Mr. Fry's waggon, we went up again, but had to wait a long time while some discussion was taking place. I then gave Lobengula a list of all the chiefs whom I wished to see, and he began a long questioning. 'Who told you of the country?' said he ; and I said that Mr. Selous had first told me about it. 'Was not I the proper person to say if teachers were wanted, and to send for them?' asked he—and so on, for some time. He was reminded that I had come relying on his word that I might have the road through his country ; to which he replied that he had only said that I could come and talk about it. I then asked if I might travel through the country as an ordinary traveller to see it, and he replied, 'All countries are alike.' I assured him that I would rob his country of nothing, that what I shot for food on the road I would give him a present for when I returned. 'What?' said he. 'A horse,' said I. He then informed me that he did not wish me to go, and that he was tired, and began to tie on his monkey tail.

"The conversation lasted a considerable time, and was the more wearying from some of his people joining in it, and applauding his remarks when they saw what view he took, a proceeding which—under other circumstances, would have been ludicrous, but only added to the painfulness of my position.

"No further end would have been gained by staying, and we rode home. I can think of nothing more that I can do to get his consent. He has always refused permission for a mission to be established amongst the Mashona, probably from fear of what would happen if the subject tribes whom he raids upon should be taught ; and I think that the real reason of his dislike to my going into that country was given by one of the traders in these words : 'He knows that if you settle anywhere that it is "good-bye" to marauding there.'

"*June* 3, *Sunday.*—Isaac, Edward, and I had Holy Communion before breakfast. Afterwards I had service for John, Jelly, Isaac, William, Bill, and Mrs. Helm. In the afternoon, at Mr. Helm's request, I held a service for everyone ; five white men, Mr. and Mrs. Helm, and my own men attended. It has been a very peaceful day, and I think that the rest has done me good.

"*June* 4, *Monday.*—I had intended to ride over to Lobengula, but it was thought best for me not to ride. I have given up hope of being allowed to carry out my original plan, and mapped out another route to the N.W. This delay is very wearying, and my time is limited. Mr. Helm and I arranged and packed the medicine boxes. I gave him some.

"*June* 5, *Tuesday.*—Mr. Helm and I rode to the chief's to say that I wished to leave the country, but by the N.W. path, though I meant to try indirectly to get his consent to my original plan. He was in his mealie field. The men had just carried his corn. They were passing away like a long stream of ants, each carrying a big load on his head. We walked with the chief back to his kraal. Fortunately, it was practically empty. I waited till he had done his business and then said I thought there was no further use in my staying in the country; that he had received two letters from Sir Sydney Shippard about me, and that he had not given heed to them; that I came because I understood that he 'gave me the road' through his country, which he would not now do; that I did not wish for gold, and would have kept my promise to give him a 'salted horse' for what would be shot in his country for my men to eat.

"He asked where I wished to go. I said, Zumbo. He then said 'You may go.' I asked him if I might come round by the Sabi River, by the road that Mr. Selous came. He hesitated, but soon said, 'You will see how you can go when you get there.' He then told me that I should have to travel fast if I wished to make the journey—*i.e.*, before the bad weather set in.

"He was in a very different humour to what I had seen him before, and I attributed this, in a great degree, to his being alone. Mr. Helm thought that he had been considering the subject.

"I went out of the kraal a very much happier man than I had entered it, and rode home, and began the packing of the waggon.

"*June* 6, *Wednesday.*—After long delay we started. Bill said that he knew the road, which ended in our getting when it was dark among rocks on the top of a koppje, when I guided with a lantern. The little span (of oxen) pulled admirably, dragging the buck-waggon over a large rock. We outspanned, and waited for light until we could see Thabaginduna and make for it. This is a mountain where a large number of chiefs were killed by order of Umzilikatze.

"*June* 7, *Thursday.*—We made straight for the mountain, and under it John met us. My tracheometer measurements had been made useless by our leaving the road. The donkeys, goats, and sheep were lost in the dark. A messenger arrived from Mr. Helm asking me to send back a cow that I had bought from him, as the native who once had owned it said that he had never been paid for it by the man who sold it to Mr. Helm; he also advised me to turn back if I suffered again from dysentery.

"*June* 8, *Friday.*—We arrived at Miati after two long treks. The country between Hope Fountain and this place is very bare and uninteresting. Here two white men visited us, and one of them, a God-fearing man, said that nothing could be done with the Matabele till they had been beaten in war; and, speaking of the cruelties committed by Lobengula, said that he had seen him thrust a burning stick into a boy's eye for losing his cattle. But there are more revolting stories of the chief's cruelty than this.

"The sheep and goats, but only eight out of the ten donkeys, were brought in, and two men go back to-morrow to find the other two.

"*June* 9, *Saturday.*—I had intended to start early, and had bought three sheep and two cows (for use on the journey) when the axle-tree of my waggon was seen to be broken. It was spliced with a large bar of iron, and I remained to pass Sunday here.

"I am much relieved by John coming with me. His parents refused to allow him to go by the N.W. road. I have also engaged a man from the N.E. district who had been with Mr. Montague Kerr. He was *said* to have been to the Zambesi with him, but, as his book says that every man deserted him before he arrived at the river, this was only the common *façon de parler.* My one man who really comes from beyond the Zambesi has hurt his foot, and has been useless for some days. 'To the Zambesi' is a term used by people in South Africa, and means little. It seems to imply in many cases that the man who says it has travelled somewhere to the north of Shoshong. Again, the Zambesi at the Victoria Falls is easy to get to by a well-known road.

"Mr. Rees, the London Missionary at this the last outpost of Christianity towards the north,'-hopes that I will use his house in passing up and down; but I fear that the time has hardly come for Lobengula to allow this, and he claims the country 'as far as his father's spears went'—*i.e.*, to the Zambesi.

"*June* 10, *Sunday.*—A very happy day! Service at Mr. Martin's in the morning and evening. The afternoon I spent with Mr. Rees, who gave me valuable advice as to fever, having suffered a great deal himself. He again expressed the hope that I would always use his house in going to and fro. I do not, however, think that he quite realises the difficulties of a Mission in Mashonaland. For though I believe the Matabele power to be very inferior to what the Zulu power was, yet it seems difficult not to agree with Mr. Selous that nothing will be done with the Matabele without a war. But against this, though not one convert can be pointed to, the Mission established by Dr. Moffat *has* affected the thought of the country, yet not so far as to alter the outward rule. How far the Matabele believe in their own invincibility it would be hard to say. Lobengula once stopped an Englishman who alluded to him as the king of all the earth, not wishing his people to hear.

"*June* 11, *Monday.*—I sold 'Slug' to Mr. Martin for £20. It took me a long time to make up my mind to sell him, for he never shook me if I was not well ; but the money was worth a great deal to me, and I considered him a luxury. He is a very different pony now to what he was when I gave £4 for him.

"The bush of the buck-waggon broke soon after starting, and Edward went back to Mr. Rees for a wheel. My waggon went on to the water, and a wheel was brought back on a bough to enable the broken waggon to get there. I walked on, and went out to shoot some small birds, being afraid of eating any meat as yet, and I lost myself. I nearly always take compass bearings when leaving camp alone, but to-day I resolved to follow the course of a little dry river. After going some way I crossed it and went from it, and returned, as I thought, and followed it back ; but it broke up into little streams and gullies, and I was perfectly con- fused. I felt so sure of the general direction of the camp that twice I walked some way towards it, as I thought, but came back as I saw that the general course of the river was in a different direction. Twice I tried to find the place where I had crossed, and made up my mind to follow the river along the right bank, concluding that that must bring me back to camp. But after going some distance, I found that the stream, when it did run, ran in the opposite direction, and I then knew that I was lost. I dug a hole in the sand and found some water, and then struck into a cattle path, determined to follow it in whatever direction it led me. It was almost dark, and I had no idea where I was walking to. I felt that my head might go, and remembered how soon a man had died of thirst ; that the nights were very cold, and I was hardly well yet. I do not think any of the accidents of travelling is equal in unpleasantness to this position. But, when I began to follow the track, I felt less stupid and less dazed, and, when I saw another path join it, I made sure that I should reach a village or cattle port sooner or later. A hill in front confused me, for, when in the morning a man had climbed a tree to find some mark by which I could map the road, he reported only a forest of trees as far as he could see. But I did come to a kind of village at last, and I thanked God very sincerely. I tried to explain to a man here that I would give as much calico as would go round his waist four times if he would bring me to the waggon road, and that I wanted some water. First, he brought me snuff, then some water in a large dirty tobacco pipe, and then he and some of his friends started to show me the road. I was not very clear as to where they were taking me to till I saw rockets going up from my waggon straight in front of me. Soon I heard a shot, and then met Jelly who had ridden out towards my last shot.

"I was very much pleased with the way in which my men behaved. Isaac seems to have been in great anxiety ; Edward, as usual, had known what to do, and when he was sure that I was found began to get food ready."

(*To be continued.*)

THE CHILDREN'S CORNER.

A RECOLLECTION OF ZULULAND TWENTY YEARS AGO.

BY THE REV. C. JOHNSON.

ABOUT twenty years ago I was with a friend on the banks of the Umtamouna near the coast, amongst Umkitshwa's people. Our waggon was outspanned near the drift, and we were just preparing for our evening meal, when a young native came running up to the waggon. He was terribly out of breath, and altogether he seemed dead beat, but still he seemed to be in a state of great excitement. The poor fellow cast himself down in front of us (my friend T. F. and myself), and cried out, "Ngi fihle, Umlungu, ngi fihle!" (hide me, white man, hide me!), and in a few hurried words he showed us that his life was in danger from a party of men who were close behind him in pursuit. We quickly made a hiding-place for him under the cartel (waggon bed) in the waggon, and covered him up with empty sacks, and blankets on the top of all. Although this took us only a minute or two, we had hardly finished when a party of natives came in sight. At first I could only see one, for they were not all together, but straggling; some were following the same path the poor fugitive had appeared on; others, evidently with the idea of cutting him off, were running along a low ridge of hills ending nearly at right angles with the river. The first to reach us was a wild-looking young man, armed with assegai and shield. He had not much breath left to do much more than just roughly demand to be told which way the fugitive had taken. My friend T. F. answered in Zulu, "Watshona lapa" (he vanished there), and pointed down the banks of the river. On went the pursuing young man, and on went the other pursuers on the wrong scent. When the party had passed—and I counted fifteen men altogether—instead of eating our evening meal as we had intended, we called up the oxen, yoked them in, and started, travelling as fast as we could for about four hours. T. F. stayed behind for a short time, and then followed the waggon about half a mile in the rear, in order that, had we been pursued, he could give us sufficient warning to get the fugitive out of the waggon before the pursuers came up to us. But evidently they were either too exhausted by their running, and by their fruitless search, or they had no idea that he whom they were looking for was in the waggon, for we saw nothing more of them. When we outspanned again, our fugitive told us the following terrible story :—

"My father's name is 'Somopo, my name is Umazwi. You have helped me indeed! You have saved me! You are my fathers! But I am dead; my heart is dead! Those men, those wolves, have killed my bride, my brave bride!

"You would like to hear how it all happened?

"I had known 'Nomatopi, the daughter of Unewadi, ever since she was born, but it is only a little more than two harvests ago that she promised to be my wife. My brother Ujojo was sent as messenger from my father to Unewadi, the father of 'Nomatopi, to ask him to give her to me as my wife. My father sent a large black cow by the hands of Ujojo as a present to Unewadi to make his heart glad, so that he might more readily consent to his daughter becoming my wife. Unewadi is only an inferior man in our tribe. He received my brother very graciously and accepted the cow, but said, in answer to my father's message, that he could not say one word, good or bad, until my father, 'Somopo, sent more cattle. 'Somopo was a big man in the tribe. Let his bigness be seen in the number of cattle he sends for his son's wife. When he (Unewadi) saw a proper number of cattle coming to him, the father of 'Nomatopi, for all the trouble he had had in rearing her up to womanhood, he would then speak what was in his heart."

(This is the way the father of a girl receives the would-be bridegroom's messengers, when he feels inclined to allow his daughter to marry the suppliant.)

"My brother Ujojo returned to us with Unewadi's answer. My father said never a word for a long time, but just sat looking on the ground in great sadness of heart. I knew the cause only too well. A few years ago my father had offended the King, and the King had eaten him up;[*] and now our cattle kraal stood nearly empty, with grass growing over more than half of it.

"At last my father spoke and said:

"'My children, what can I say? Have I any cattle left? 'Newadi's words are true. The father of my son's bride ought not to have any tears in his heart, because of the small and scanty "nkulobola" (cattle paid by bridegroom to the father of bride). Are not my little children crying for milk? and I have it not to give them! How, then, can I "lobola" for my son, as 'Somopo's son ought to be lobola'd for?'

"It was agreed amongst us that my father could only give me two more cows. Ujojo said we could not dare to speak again to Unewadi unless we had at least seven head of cattle to drive to him.

---

* I have also got Umazwi's account of his father, Somopo, being eaten up by the King, and the cause, but it would take too long to insert it here, for it is a long affair.

"For more than a month my heart was heavy, and without any light. Of course I was allowed to see 'Nomatopi, but seeing her only made me more sorrowful, as I could not see how I was going to pay the 'ukulobola' cattle. I once asked her if she would run away with me to the white man's country, but she said No; but she added afterwards, 'Why do you not go to the white man and ask for cattle? He will give you some work to do, and will pay you in cattle.'

"This word of 'Nomatopi's decided me, so next day I bid good-bye to my father and relations, and started for a white man's place two days' journey away. I will not tire you with my troubles there. I worked a year and a half and got three head of cattle; with these I went home. My heart was light as I drew near my father's kraal, and I sang thanks to the 'Idhlozi lakiti' ('our guardian spirit'—the spirit of a dead ancestor), who had brought me successfully through many troubles back to my father's kraal. My father and all the family drew round me to hear how I had fared while I had been away. My old mother came and kissed me on both cheeks, and they were all joyful at welcoming me back, and yet I could see something was wrong; nor had I long to wait before learning what it was. While I had been away the old chief of the next district to ours, Matshana, a great favourite with the King, had seen 'Nomatopi as she was working in her father's maize garden. He had stopped to speak to her, and he had seemed very much struck with her, and a few days afterwards some three or four of Matshana's people came driving fifteen head of cattle to Unewadi saying: 'Matshana prays that 'Nomatopi may be given to him to wife.' Unewadi, knowing that he would get a lot more cattle, and also get the friendship of a big man who was a favourite with the King, accepted the cattle, and that the marriage feast was even now being prepared.

"My heart was very black. Was I to lose my wife now, just when I thought I was so near to her?

"The next day I sent my little sister to the garden where 'Nomatopi worked, to tell her I had come back from working for the white man, and to ask her to meet me at the old trysting-place.

"In the afternoon I saw her there, but before I could speak her father and eldest brother came up with sticks and assegais. They had heard, I suppose, that I had returned, and somehow had found out that we were to meet in the old place. They hardly waited to speak to me, but attacked me at once with their sticks. 'Nomatopi came running in between us, and I know received more than one blow that had been meant for me. At last the brother dragged her off, and, two or three more men coming up, they left off beating me, and stood simply scowling at me for some time, and then my old mother came up and dragged me away.

(To be continued.)

NOTES OF THE MONTH.

THERE was a generally expressed desire at the S.P.G. Conference, held in Dublin in January last, that the funds received by the Society from Ireland should be considerably increased, and greater exertions made on its behalf than have ever hitherto been made. To help towards this end, a member of that Conference offers to contribute £5 this year towards the Society's General Fund, if 39 other members of the Church of Ireland will do the same; a contribution of £10 will count as two of the 39.

Contributions, or promises of same, to be sent to the Rev. the Secretary S.P.G., 8 Dawson Street, Dublin.

BARBUDA is in the Diocese of Antigua, being the nearest island to the north of Antigua itself. The Rev. A. A. Humphreys, whom the Society's grant helps to maintain, reports on the work among the 900 people who form his island flock. The Church's influence to counteract poverty and weakness under temptation are shown in the following :—

"The event of a wreck tends to demoralise the people of a place to a certain extent, particularly where there are not sufficient government officers to protect life and property. The idea of having to be paid for labour rendered, while it makes some independent, makes others licentious. Then when the wages are actually paid, everyone keeps his own merry-making, a good deal of their earning is frittered away in drink, and many family wants are left unsupplied.

"Those people, however, who are full members of the Church are kept in check by the Church collectors, who are generally in and out among the crowds. This unusual and oftentimes un-Christian rejoicing among the people arises from the fact of their not being in regular employment during the year; the fact is, no employment whatever is afforded the inhabitants now whereby they can obtain money to furnish themselves with necessaries and keep up their Church subscriptions.

"The poverty among the old and infirm this year has been somewhat lamentable. A severe drought deprived us of a great deal of ground provision, so that the only hope of existence for many of the people was what their relatives would send them from Antigua in the way of money and provisions."

CHOLERA raged last year in various parts of Sarawak, Borneo. The Rev. C. W. Fowler reports that there were six cases at the Mission at Quop, and tells briefly the interesting story of one who succumbed to it :—

" One of the three fatal cases was the oldest man of the place, and the last of a generation for miles around here. He well remembered the late Raja Brook's coming, and had seen no less than from fifteen to twenty of his own great-grandchildren. He took great interest in everything up to the last, and frequently have I met him, although his eyesight was very treacherous, on his way to or from his daughter's or grand-daughter's farm, some considerable distance from his home. In former times he was the ' medicine man ' of the place, and after he had embraced Christianity was eagerly sought after, but he assured me he never again used blood, and all his prayers he addressed to ' Tapa ' (the Creator), and not to ancestors, &c. Once or twice he told me he had in his dreams seen ' the beautiful gates ajar,' and had had a peep inside, which kept him firm to his end. May he rest in peace ! I firmly believe he lived and died up to what he understood."

QUOP Church has been improved in various ways. Among other works Mr. Fowler mentions :—

" Another defect has been remedied. The floor of the nave was bilian planks on common wood ; the latter was entirely eaten away. I mentioned the matter to the people, who, being unable at that busy time to go out themselves to get material, subscribed the sum of sixteen dollars ($16) to buy it, which was just enough for the material alone, so my assistant, the Rev. Ah Luk, who is exceedingly useful in such matters, and myself took the planks up and replaced the common with bilian wood."

At this Church there is a roll of eighty-seven Communicants, in addition to those at Sentah, Batuh, Serin, and other stations.

MR. FOWLER has received some type from England, and a printing press has been made on the spot. From this there has already issued a book in the Dyak vernacular for the first standard in the schools, and one for the second is to be produced shortly.

WHEN the Bishop of Qu'Appelle recently attended a meeting of the Standing Committee of the Society, his Lordship was the bearer of the following Synodical Resolution from his Diocese :—

" That the Synod desires to express its deep gratitude to Almighty God for the help rendered to the work of laying the foundation of the Church in this Diocese through the agency of the venerable Society for the Propagation of the Gospel in Foreign Parts ; and it desires, further, to take the opportunity of the visit of the Bishop to England to convey this expression of thankfulness to the representatives of the said Society, and it would respectfully request his Lordship to place this resolution before the Society whenever he may have the opportunity of doing so personally. This Diocese, during the last four years, has received help from the Society for the Bishop, clergy, and other works to the extent of upwards of £6,000, including £1,000 for Endowment of Bishopric, £400 for Churches, and £170 Special Grants for Indian work. The security afforded by such a Society for the continuation of grants to the clergy for at least a certain number of years is of inestimable value. Work could scarcely be commenced or carried on without such security for a certain amount as a basis.

" The Synod, therefore, considers that to this venerable Society, under Almighty God, the most earnest thanks of the Diocese are due, and in the name of the Diocese it herewith renders this expression of thankfulness, trusting that the abundant blessing of the Almighty may continue to rest upon the Society, its Executive, and all its members.

" ADELBERT,
" BISHOP OF QU'APPELLE."

A REMARKABLY strong Committee has been formed at Cambridge to watch the course of events in Equatorial Africa, and to keep up the interest of English people in the sufferings of the slaves and the necessity for a free Africa. The Vice-Chancellor is Chairman, and the Committee includes ten other Heads of Colleges, and Professors Westcott, Hort, Stokes, Cayley, Sidgwick, Seeley, Clark, Macalister, Browne, Kirkpatrick, Creighton, Babington, and Sir Thomas Wade, with Dr. Routh and other influential residents. The Society's Honorary Secretary (Mr. Orpen) and the resident Organising Secretary have been added to the Committee, which had its first meeting on May 10.

DURING some heavy rains at the Lower Paarl, in the Diocese of Capetown, several houses were damaged or destroyed. The Rev. J. F. Curlewis sends some interesting accounts of the way in which persons who were exposed to danger from this cause were mercifully preserved :—

"I am glad to say that with all the falling of walls and timber no one received any serious bodily injury, although there were many narrow escapes. The wife of one of my parishioners was ill. Her husband, to secure more quiet for her of a night, took the children to sleep with him at the other end of the building, which was nothing but a longish room with a partition wall. This had been done for two nights. On the third night the woman felt very restless, but as she did not like to disturb her husband she quietly got up and went to lie near the children. This she had scarcely done when in the darkness and stillness of the night a terrible crash was heard; the whole of the end wall of the room in which she had slept had fallen flat and crushed the stretcher which was in the room which she had just left. Poor woman, it gave her a great fright, but she acknowledged the hand of God in it, and was thankful for her providential escape.

"In another house, also in this part of the parish, a nurse was about to put a dear little baby, who was sleeping in her arms, on its mother's bed, on which it usually slept in the daytime, but from some, to her unaccountable, cause she turned into another room and laid the baby down there. Within half an hour after the gable end of the house gave way and broke the bed from which the dear little one had been so mercifully and wonderfully kept. Truly may we say, 'The Lord is thy keeper.' "

LIKE most of the parishes in the Diocese of Capetown, Mossel Bay embraces work both among colonists and natives. The Rev. W. F. Taylor mentions some noticeable facts with regard to the growth of the ranks of the native Christians, who in this diocese are reached not by separate Missions, so much as by the ministry of the Colonial Church itself :—

"God is blessing our work, and especially that which is the true Missionary portion of it—the ministering to the long shamefully neglected coloured races of the land, and the bringing them within the fold of Christ's Church. Heidelberg, once an out-station of my former parish of Riversdale, in which I began the work of the Church some thirty years ago, with only a few poor English and two or three coloured people, has now been formed into a separate parish, chiefly for its Mission work, and has now 1,350 adherents, very many of whom are baptized members of the Church. In my own parish, where fourteen years ago there were not 400 baptized members of the coloured races, we have now about 1,300, and their number is steadily increasing. Last year I baptized 25 adults and 86 children of coloured blood.

"But the great difficulty is in the maintaining our work, owing to their being so widely and thinly scattered, and to their great poverty. Our little English flock here in the town, at present by no means a wealthy or prosperous one, has enough to do in providing for itself. The Dutch Boers, among whom our people dwell, and for whom they labour, give us no help, but rather oppose and hinder us. They have no wish that their *schepsels* (creatures) should be too well instructed."

S T. PETER'S-ON-INDWE is one of the Mission stations in the Diocese of Grahamstown. There are a few European traders in the neighbourhood, for whose benefit occasional services are held, but the main work is among the native races. The Rev. Alfred J. Newton's report is brief and modest, but it shows how good and patient work is telling among the Kaffirs. The "parish" of St. Peter's is reckoned to contain 400 square miles and 20,000 people. He describes a new school which he has erected, the work of the printing press done by the native converts, and after other details adds this summary :—

"The Mission which was commenced after the war of 1878 is among the Tambookie Kaffirs, and is situated on the banks of the Indwe River, in a beautiful basin surrounded by mountains, and is one of the prettiest valleys in this part of the country.

"The buildings consist of a neat chapel of red brick with iron roof, and which is of a very church-like appearance. The interior is very well furnished with church seats, handsome large font, altar with all things necessary for the reverent celebration of Holy Communion, credence table, reading desk and lectern of teak, a good harmonium, &c. It has a very comfortable little vestry at the west end, which is connected with the church by a porch. It accommodates about one hundred persons without crowding.

"Besides the work at the home or principal station, during the past year I have kept up regular services at Lady Frere for the English congregation there (20 miles from St. Peter's) ; but as a priest has now been appointed to the charge of that village, I am relieved from that duty.

"I have also regularly visited the Kaffir Mission at Queenstown, forty miles from here, which Mission was established under my care twenty-seven years ago, and is still doing a good work.

"I have also had charge of the Mission at Bolotwa, seventeen miles distant, which Mission has now been placed in charge of the Rev. M. A. Maggs.

"Another out-station has lately been commenced in connection with St. Peter's, forty-two miles in another direction ; of this I will write in another report at no distant date.

"I have another station seven miles from here where services are regularly held, as also a small day-school."

He adds that the work of Christianising and civilising the native races of South Africa, though slow and tedious, is making great progress.

"I have now been working twenty-nine years without interruption, and can thankfully testify to the great good that has been done."

J OHANNESBERG, in the Diocese of Pretoria, shares in the prosperity which has lately visited the Transvaal. It is one of the places where part of the Society's grant to the Diocese is used, but the Rev. J. J. Darragh, the Missionary, is careful to point out that this is not to help in the ordinary expenses of his or the church's maintenance:—

" In thanking the venerable Society for the assistance given during the past year, I wish it to be distinctly understood that the grant is spent entirely on native, mission, and extraneous work. The people of the town are quite able and willing to support the work among themselves, and I look forward to the time when, the great strain of providing necessary buildings being removed, *all* work in the parish will be supported by the parish itself.

" There are about 500 Indians in the town for whom hitherto no spiritual provision, specially adapted to their needs, has been made. There are a few Christians among them, coming for the most part from Dr. Booth's congregation in connection with St. Cyprian's, Durban, Natal."

Mr. Darragh mentions some interesting new features in the work:—

" The Collegiate School for girls is now completed at a cost of £3,000 for building, and about £500 for furnishing. There is every prospect of the school proving successful, though I don't anticipate a rush of pupils at the outset.

" We are now moving in the matter of establishing a Nurses' Home which, as this town develops, is very much needed. I see no reason to doubt but that before the next quarter's report comes to be written this institution will be an accomplished fact.

" The St. Mary's Benefit Society for working men is now in full swing, and has a membership of about fifty. It is confined to Cape-coloured Afrikanders, and provides maintenance, medicine, and medical attendance in sickness, and expenses of burial at death. A slight provision is also made for the widow in case there be one.

" St. Mary's Guild, which has been started during the last quarter, promises also to be a very valuable agency for good. I annex a copy of the rules. The membership, which is confined to ladies, amounts to about fifty."

IN spite of the precarious state of affairs relating to the Panama Canal, the unhealthiness, costliness, and laxity of life, we receive very encouraging reports through the Bishop of Jamaica. For instance the Rev. S. Kerr thus summarises his year's work:—

" I have been able to visit the line regularly during the year. Bas Obispo I visited ten times for preaching and Holy Communion; Monkey Hill, twenty-four times; Gorgona, fifteen times; Culebra, twenty times; Panama, twelve times, each for services, celebration of Holy Communion, and meeting committees, besides visiting and communing the sick."

There are lay workers engaged under him at the several places :—

" At Monkey Hill, Mr. A. Alexander is the catechist, and conducts regular services on Sundays and in the week. There are two held every Sunday, Sunday and day school, and I am happy to report that he is of great assistance to me in the work. A candidates' class is also held here as in Colon. I regret that the straitened condition of means raised does not allow of an increase as yet to his salary, but hope the coming year will bring about some favourable results.

" Bas Obispo is under the charge of Mr. B. Walker (the catechist). Regular services have been conducted with good results. The Committee finds it necessary to recommend Mr. Walker for Holy Orders. A letter commendatory has therefore been enclosed to his Lordship the Bishop to that effect through the Rev. E. Bassett Key, with my endorsement.

" Mr. Walker and his family have all had their share of affliction, which has had something to do with our mission work during the year, especially the last quarter. He also visits Gorgona.

" This section has the services of the assistant-layman, Mr. J. B. Johnson, who has been instrumental in keeping up almost regular services. He is desirous of being exclusively employed as catechist for this section but our limited means will not admit. He is a dispenser of medicine, and, though embarrassed under the present state of things, he still continues his help.

" I must mention that, during my recent visit to Culebra and the line, I found over 4,000 labourers unemployed, the canal contractors having stopped the work. But from recent advices some have been resumed, and there is a hope of its continuation after a few weeks. This, however, creates a panic."

ZEERUST, in the Transvaal, has received an influx of people rushing to the gold fields, followed, however, by as rapid an exodus on the failure of the fields there. The Rev. A. Temple, though thus unable to write of encouraging things with regard to his white congregation, is cheered by the Mission work among the natives:—

" I am thankful to say I have greater encouragement in my work amongst the natives, both here and amongst those at a distance. It was very cheering to see natives come a distance of fifty miles to attend the services of the Christmas Festival. And I am already endeavouring to secure a good native teacher to carry on the work of the Gospel at that outpost, whilst I have eighteen catechumens awaiting the arrival of the Bishop in our midst for the rite of confirmation."

AS long ago as 1859, the Rev. Henry Handley Brown went out as the Society's Missionary to Omata, in the Diocese of Auckland, New Zealand. Many years ago he ceased to be aided from the Society's funds, but with unabated love Mr. Brown has maintained regular correspondence with the Society, and described his work. He is now in his 76th year, and he writes:—

" During the past quarter my duties have been carried out as usual. I have had, however, to give notice to the Bishop and Archdeacon that after the expiration of the present quarter—i.e., after March 31, 1889, I shall no longer be able to undertake the care of the Inglewood-Stratford district. My spine has long suffered from my much riding. This affection of the spine has spread upward till it has affected the whole nervous system. A little enforced rest has partially restored me ; but I feel that I can never again go through the long riding needed in such an extensive district. For a time I hope to continue my duties in my own proper district—i.e., in Omata and other places south of New Plymouth ; but at the age of 75 I feel that even this cannot much longer be kept up."

IN St. Andrew's Cathedral, Sydney, Archdeacon Dawes was consecrated Assistant-Bishop for the Diocese of Brisbane, on the Festival of SS. Philip and James.

MARATHI has been enriched by two translations from the pen of the Rev. J. Taylor, one of the Society's Missionaries at Ahmednagar, in the Diocese of Bombay. The books translated by Mr. Taylor from English to Marathi are the Commentary, by the Rev. J. J. Lias, on the Epistles to the Corinthians, and Hymns Ancient and Modern.

SUGGESTED SUBJECTS FOR PRAYER.

For the Missions exposed to peril in Eastern Africa, for the steadfastness of the converts, and for a happy issue out of all the tribulations.

For India, its peoples, and its Missions, that prejudice and superstition may be dispersed by the light of Christian truth.

For the Church in the West Indies, that it may grow in spiritual graces through all temporal adversity.

For the Indian tribes of British Guiana, that they may all be brought into the Church.

MONTHLY MEETING.

THE Monthly Meeting of the Society was held at 19 Delahay Street, on Friday, May 17, at 2 P.M., the Rev. B. Compton in the chair. There were also present Prebendary Borrer, the Rev. J. M. Barn-Murdoch, C. Churchill, Esq., General Davies, Prebendary Festing, General Gillilan, Sir F. J. Goldsmid, K.C.S.I., C.B., Colonel Hardy, J. R. Kindersley, Esq., General Lowry, General Maclagan, H. D. Skrine, Esq., General Tremenheere, C.B., S. Wreford, Esq., *Members of the Standing Committee*; and W. Channcy, Esq., Rev. J. C. Cowl, Rev. T. Darling, Rev. H. J. Day, Dr. De Tatham, Baron De Teissier, Rev. R. H. Dickson, Rev. R. J. Dundas, T. Dunn, Esq., J. C. Eckersley, Esq., Rev. J. J. Elkington, Rev. Dr. Finch, Rev. T. Hill, H. Laurence, Esq., Rev. J. Maconochy, Rev. J. H. Masters, General Nicolls, Rev. G. C. Reynell, Rev. H. Rowley, Rev. W. Wallace, Rev. R. R. Watts, S. J. Wilde, Esq., Rev. Canon A. Wright, and W. Wickham, Esq., *Members of the Society.*

1. After prayers, the minutes of the last meeting were read.

2. The Treasurers presented the abstract of receipts and payments from January 1 to April 30, printed on page 240 of the *Mission Field.*

3. Power was given to affix the Corporate Seal to certain documents.

4. The Rev. A. Logsdail, who had just reached England on furlough from Chota Nagpore, in the Diocese of Calcutta, addressed the members. He said that he was sent out seven years and a half ago, and on his arrival found the first difficulty which presented itself was that of the languages used. Hindi is understood by the educated people in Chota Nagpore, but not by the villagers. Different dialects are found among the Kohls, embracing languages of the Dravidian family as well as the Kohlarian, examples of both being sometimes found in the same village.

A great difficulty in the work was the absence of railways and other means of communication, the rivers often being impassable. A more serious difficulty arose from the moral condition of the people themselves, especially in regard to the relations of the sexes. Large numbers of Kohls who are married leave Chota Nagpore to work as coolies in Assam and elsewhere, and many of them go alone. The deserted husband or wife is then in the habit of taking another partner, and such evil customs are followed by the Christians. For their correction Church discipline is enforced. Mr. Logsdail described the several stations, of which Ranchi is the chief, and showed how the area occupied by Christianity is but a small part of the whole province of Chota Nagpore. In reply to questions, he spoke of the advantages likely to follow the consecration of a Bishop for Chota Nagpore.

5. All the candidates proposed at the meeting in March were elected into the Corporation. The following were proposed for election in July:—

The Rev. H. R. Hanson, All Saints, Portsea; Rev. R. A. R. White, Titchfield, Fareham, Hants; Rev. W. R. Shepherd, Preston-on-Wye, Hereford; Rev. F. Baggallay, St. Peter's, Mancroft, Norwich; Rev. G. A. F. Quentin, Shipdham; Herbert E. Bovee, Esq., Teddington; Athelstan Riley, Esq., 2 Kensington Court, W.; Rev. J. E. Field, Benson Vicarage, Wallingford; Rev. Frank Duerdin Perrott, Ixworth, Bury St. Edmund's; Rev. G. Herbert H. Jones. Gazeley, Newmarket; Rev. Frederick Pearson, Stanstead, Sudbury; Rev. H. Power Bull, Stoke-by-Nayland, Colchester; Rev. Horatio Nelson Grimley, Norton, Bury St. Edmund's; Rev. Wm. C. Green, Hepworth, Diss; Rev. H. Aldersey Swann, Great Ashfield, Bury St. Edmund's; Rev. James Giddens, Horningsheath, Bury St. Edmunds; Rev. H. Bruce Pugh, Dalham, Newmarket; Rev. R. Sorsbie, Clare, Suffolk; Rev. T. Stantial, D.C.L., St. John's, Bury St. Edmund's; Rev. R. W. Barber, Chippenham, Soham, Cambridge; Rev. W. S. Parish, Freckenham, Soham, Cambridge; Rev. G. Moore, Denham, Bury St. Edmund's; and Rev. Prebendary Buttanshaw, St. James's Square, Bath.

SOCIETY'S INCOME.

Abstract of RECEIPTS *and* PAYMENTS *from January 1 to May 31.*

	GENERAL FUND	SPECIAL FUNDS
Subscriptions, Donations, Collections, &c.	£11,502	£3,767
Legacies	3,730	107
Dividends, Rents, &c....	1,932	2,121
TOTAL RECEIPTS	£17,164	£5,995
PAYMENTS	£33,026	£7,521

The Receipts under the head of Subscriptions, Donations, and Collections for the General Fund from January 1 to May 31, in five consecutive years, compare as follows : 1885, £12,297 ; 1886, £11,425 ; 1887, £12,909 ; 1888, £11,795* ; 1889, £11,502.

* In addition, the Treasurers received in 1888 Securities of the value of £25,296 as "A Thankoffering to Almighty God for the extension of the Church in the Colonies and Dependencies of the British Empire and beyond it"; also other Securities of the value of £2,268 as a Trust Gift, *the Income only being available.*

THE MISSION FIELD.

THE FIELD IS THE WORLD. THE SEED IS THE WORD OF GOD.

AUGUST 1, 1889.

ENTHUSIASM FOR FOREIGN MISSIONS.

CANON BODY'S ADDRESS AT THE ANNIVERSARY MEETING IN ST. JAMES'S HALL ON JUNE 6, 1889.

IN responding to the invitation to address this meeting, I have one point to which I wish to call your attention. It is a point which arises from a passage on the seventeenth page of the Society's new Annual Report. We read there of " a multitude of Missions inadequately supported, which do not advance as might be hoped, not for lack of openings, not because of opposition, so much as from lack of material resources necessary for legitimate and natural expansion. The moral is that by all suitable means the conscience of the people of England must be stirred as it has never yet been stirred, intelligently to grasp the position, and faithfully to recognise their duty." Now the point is this : I wish to ask, first, whether the latter statement is a true one ; and next, if it be true, what practical steps can we immediately take in obedience to the call that thus comes to us from the Society ?

At first sight it may seem that the statement is not a true one ; for certainly one of the arresting features of Christian life in this nine-teenth century is the wonderful revival of the Missionary spirit. It seems as though it were with us to-day almost as it was with the Christians of the first ages of the Church, and that we might say of England's sons and daughters, as it was said of the first Christians, that they are " to be found everywhere preaching the Word." In the bazaars of India, amidst the snows of Labrador, in the jungles of Africa, beneath the palm trees of the sunny Pacific, everywhere, to the glory

of this English Church and nation, are to be seen her sons and
daughters, braving hard conditions of life, facing peril, and accounting
their very lives not dear unto themselves if but they may carry the
faith of Christ to the uttermost parts of the earth. Certainly, some
will say, it is a most extraordinary charge for the oldest and most
representative Missionary Society of the Church of England to make,
that at the present time the English people have not risen to the realisation of the responsibility of their position in the Mission Field. But
my reply to that argument is this : It is quite true that there is this
wonderful awakening of the Missionary spirit at the present time ; but
that awakening is not nearly so extensive as it ought to be. It is
intense, but its intensity is within far too limited an area. It may be
said, perhaps, that I am aiming at an utopian state of things ; but
it seems to me, as a matter of fact—putting aside for a moment spiritual
considerations—that there is an immense attraction in Missions, considered even in their secondary results, and that such a work ought
to commend itself, apart from its religious aspects, to the geographer,
the archæologist, the politician, and others, so that even on these
grounds there should be a more general interest taken in them.

I fear that the great mass of Churchmen must plead guilty to this
charge of lack of Missionary enthusiasm. True, there is Missionary
enthusiasm to be found in the Church of England ; but is it not rather
to be found in the extreme sections than in the great main body that
lies between them ? Speaking of the great body which has been called
the backbone of the Church of England, is it not true, beyond possibility
of doubt, that it has not risen to the realisation of the Church's responsibility in this matter, and that it stands in saddest contrast to the other
sections of our National Church on the question of Missionary enthusiasm ?

If that is so, what is needed ? Again I appeal to the Society's
Annual Report. It insists on the necessity for an increase of life, zeal,
and devotion in parochial organisation, in all the ordinary working of
the Society's home machinery, and in each of its members. I rejoice to
notice the tone of fervour and unction in the Report for this year.
This increase of life, zeal, and devotion is just what is wanted, if the
Society is to be what a Missionary Society ought to be. If it is, in
regard to financial resources, to hold its own with the Church Missionary
Society, the first essential condition is that those who have to do with
the home work of the Society should be fired with a great deal more
zeal and devotion than as yet they have been raised to. In other
words, the first condition of this Society really rising to the present
opportunity and responding to the call made to it is this, that the
members must seek a baptism of a real enthusiasm.

An enthusiast is a God-fired man. And when God truly gives us an enthusiasm (which will be all the more real because it is disciplined, and is not impatient of restraint), in the degree in which we respond to that gift, in that same degree will the money we want come forth.

But in the next place, we not only want rousing ourselves, but we have to educate the nation as to its duty in this respect. He must be deaf indeed who cannot hear Christ plainly saying to this English nation, as He pointed to unconquered territories, "Go up and possess the land." But if this call is to be truly and really obeyed, the fact of the unique position which this English nation occupies among the nations of the earth must be brought before our people continually— the awful nature of our obligation to India must be more clearly pressed home on the English conscience—above all, the people must be taught that the spots consecrated by the blood of martyrs must not be deserted.

In the last place, the Church must recognise this great fact, that the condition for receiving blessing for home work is obedience to the Lord's command that bids her go out and occupy the fields of heathendom.

I know how hard it is to grasp that principle. For instance, I confess that I myself am conscious of a dread when I see Colonial and Missionary Bishops coming up to the Diocese of Durham, lest they should take away from us our best men. But then that feeling is utterly and absolutely wrong. We should give to them of our best.

Of this I am quite certain, that the measure of success in the work of the Church in England at home is not the measure of that work itself, but the measure of the Divine blessing that rests on that work. And if the work at home is to be blessed, the Church must stand face to face with the whole world, and look upon it as something to be won for her Lord.

Yes! If we long to see the Mission spirit in the Church's home work put forth in all its power—and that is for me the longing of my heart, and the prayer of my life—then in the measure in which the Church gives of her best to the Mission Field abroad, in that same measure will the fields at home be reaped.

BISHOP RAWLE.

THE Church in the West Indies has just sustained a severe loss in the death at Barbados, on May 10, of Bishop Richard Rawle, than whom it may be doubted whether a more distinguished scholar has ever consecrated his eminent gifts to the service of God in our colonies. A just and

eloquent tribute to his memory appeared in the *Guardian* of May 29, in which are mentioned the high double honours which he obtained in Cambridge in 1835. For twelve years he remained in England gaining experience and fresh distinction, first as Fellow and Tutor of Trinity College, and then as Rector of the important parish of Cheadle, in Staffordshire. But very early his chief interest was attracted to the Missionary and Colonial work of the Church, and in 1847 he relinquished his prospect of high preferment at home, and accepted the office of Principal of Codrington College in Barbados. Here a large number of the clergy of the West Indian Dioceses receive their training for the ministry, though the studies of the College are by no means restricted to theology; and it is at this point that the readers of the *Mission Field* will be most warmly interested in his life.

The work to which he was thus called had been auspiciously begun in 1830, and for some years carried on with singular success by the saintly John Pinder, afterwards Principal of the Theological College at Wells; and the entire self-consecration with which Mr. Rawle now threw himself into it, is not likely ever to be forgotten by any who had opportunities of knowing the high level to which he raised the reputation of the College, still less by those who in succession during seventeen years enjoyed the advantage of his masterly lectures—classical, mathematical, and theological—and the blessing of his holy and self-denying example. The hold which he gained on the admiration of the students, on their allegiance and reverence, it were not easy to exaggerate. By all he was looked up to with profound respect. To the more thoughtful among them his own spirit of earnestness and devotion was imparted, and among the senior clergy in those dioceses there are still men whose eye kindles when they speak of him, and when they recall the salutary influence which he exerted over the forming period of their lives. In several instances they have called their children after him, and in their families his name is almost a sacred one. It is not for us to measure the results to the dioceses of that memorable period in which the College was blessed with his direction and labours.

The impulse, however, which was given to the cause of education in the West Indies by Mr. Rawle's appointment to Codrington College was far from being confined to that institution and to those who were to go forth from it. Twenty-three years had now elapsed since the first two Bishops were sent out to those colonies, increased to four upon the subdivision of the Barbados Diocese, when the distinguished Bishop Coleridge retired in 1842. During that period the fetters had been struck by the Imperial Parliament from the arms of nearly a million of slaves, and schools for the instruction of these children of Africa had been established in every parish from British Guiana and Trinidad in the south, to Jamaica and the Bahamas in the north. These schools were officered with the best teachers that lay to the hands of the clergy and the ministers of other communions, and were already producing happy results among the large negro element of the population. The good and able Bishop Parry, who had now presided for five years over the Diocese of Barbados, had persuaded the Legislature to constitute a Board of Education to administer its grants, and to appoint an Inspector of Schools who should be responsible to them. But the system was still imperfect. The teachers were for the most part without efficient training, and the schools wanting in proper organisation. The managers of the schools hailed the advent of a master-hand to aid them in the work of improving them, and the new Principal gave himself with all the ardour of an enthusiast to this important department of ministerial labour. The schools on the trust-estates of the Society for the Propagation of the Gospel, in the neighbourhood of the College, at once afforded him a field on which he could prove that his gifted mind could apply itself no less to all the details of primary education than to the highest subjects of the academical lecture-room. Amid the arduous duties of principal, involving a considerable share of the classical and mathematical, as well as the theological lectures, he found time almost daily to wend his way up the steep hill which lay between the College and the Society's Chapel, and to take a personal share in the teaching of the large schools attached to it. To these he imparted an entirely new life, and very soon he gathered round him young men of mark, black and "coloured," from other parishes, and in one or two instances from other islands, whom the clergy were glad to send to benefit by his superior training. The contagion of such an example was remarkable. Time will not admit of the mention of all the measures that were now taken to raise and give efficiency to the schools, but one or two may be instanced. The Central School in Bridge Town, the capital, was placed on an entirely new footing. Established thirty years before for the education of the children of the poor whites who had formed the yeomanry of the parishes in the times of slavery, it was now thrown open to poor children of all complexions, and, under a master from England, became a normal school for the training of masters. The Board of Education appointed annually examiners, with the Principal at their head, to grant certificates of qualification to teachers. The establishment here and there, in the rural parishes, of middle schools to provide a sound commercial education for such as could afford to pay modest fees, shortly followed; and the grammar school at the Chaplain's Lodge on the S.P.G. estates, which had been in abeyance, was reopened under favourable auspices for the higher education of the well-to-do classes. In suggesting and furthering all these, the Principal bore a conspicuous share; and if his seventeen years in Barbados had left no other mark than the great stride which education had made through his efforts and example, his name could never be forgotten there.

But, after all, the great enterprise which owed to him its practical start, if not its inception (for it had occupied the mind of Bishop Parry, who was to bear his full share in its organisation), was the West Indian Church Association for the Furtherance of the Gospel in Western Africa. If Mr. Rawle was anything, he was a missionary in heart and spirit, and in the simple consecration of his life to the spreading

of Gospel light to those sitting in the darkness of ignorance and superstition. The writer regrets that he has not now before him the memorable speech in which he pressed on a crowded audience, at the annual
meeting for the S.P.G. in Bridge Town in 1850, the immediate steps
which should be taken to inaugurate such a Mission. With burning
eloquence he depicted the wrongs which, up to the beginning of the
present century, had been inflicted by the slave trade on Western Africa.
He urged the claims of that dark land upon the sympathies of Christian
hearts from its having furnished nine-tenths of the population of these
Caribbean Islands, on whom alone at that time depended the cultivation of their fruitful soils. He maintained that Codrington College
should be utilised to prepare for the work of evangelists young men
of African descent willing to offer themselves and showing an aptitude
for the high calling. "We look from our windows," he said, "straight
towards that dark land. There lies only the broad Atlantic between
our College * and Western Africa, and she seems to stretch out her
hands to us and say, Come over and help us." The idea was taken
up with ardour. At once the above-named Association was formed
to collect funds and prepare for the important undertaking. The
Principal, pleading that his own Lodge was unnecessarily large for his
accommodation, proposed to convert the western part of it into a Mission
House; and it was not long before, with some alterations and additions,
it was prepared for the reception of half a dozen students of African
blood. A fund for the maintenance of these and for the endowment of
the Mission was at once set on foot, and was aided by contributions from
England, from friends of the Principal, and from his old parishioners in
Cheadle. The College staff followed the example of their head, and took
their share in the tuition of the students; and in 1855, John Duport,
who had received his early education in one of the primary schools of
St. Kitt's, had been sufficiently prepared for Holy Orders to accompany
to Africa the Venerable Hamble Leacock, the pioneer of this Mission.
Three other students shortly followed; and as long as the Principal
remained in office, his unremitting labour was given to prepare the men
who were, under God, to carry the Gospel to the Pongas country.

One important service—vital, indeed, to the success of the Mission—
was rendered by him when, in 1861, Mr. Duport returned from Africa on
a few months' visit to Barbados and the other islands. Bringing with
him a complete Susu vocabulary and his own early translations into the
language of parts of the New Testament and of the Book of Common
Prayer, he put them into the hands of the Principal. The careful
examination of these, with his Missionary pupil at his side, was the
occupation of a long vacation; and the profound knowledge of philology
which he brought to it enabled him to supply Duport, when he returned

* The College at Barbados is on an elevated site, not half a mile from its eastern shore, on whose white sands
it looks down.

to the Pongas, with a complete grammar of that rude but not inhar-
monious language. This has been invaluable to the successive Missionaries who have, one by one, become masters of it. Not only have the
New Testament and parts of the Old, with the Liturgy of the Church of
England, in Susu, been generously printed for the Mission by the S.P.C.K.,

VIEW OF CODRINGTON COLLEGE.

but last year the Society published gratuitously two valuable Reading
Books for the schools prepared with much care by Mr. Douglin, for nearly
twenty years a devoted Missionary in the Rio Pongo, and now a parochial
clergyman in Trinidad.

But after seventeen years a constitution naturally not over strong
began to show too plainly the effect of the unceasing strain upon it

which such labours involved, and in 1864, amid the universal regret and
the profound admiration of all classes in Barbados, Mr. Rawle returned
to England. It was only for a time. He first accepted from his old
College the Vicarage of Felmersham, near Bedford, and then in 1869 the
important living of Tamworth, with its population of 10,000. Evidence
is not wanting that in both of these he was greatly valued.

His health was now completely restored. His keen interest in the
West Indies, and in the African race forming so large an element of its
population, had never languished; and when, in 1872, the unanimous vote
of the Synod in the newly-formed Diocese of Trinidad chose him for its
first Bishop, he obeyed the call. Under the license of the Archbishop, he
was consecrated in the Cathedral of Lichfield by his own diocesan, Bishop
Selwyn, then looked up to as the Father of the Colonial Episcopate,
assisted by other suffragans of Canterbury. With the fine island, hereafter to be presided over by its own Bishop, he was not unacquainted,
having on several occasions visited it; and his Missionary spirit found
now a new opportunity of displaying itself in his care for the instruction
of the many thousands of East Indian coolies, as well as Chinese, whose
introduction had in thirty years more than trebled the population. The
personal share which he here took in the pastoral and evangelistic work
of the Church may be judged from the fact that, when the large parish
of Holy Trinity became suddenly vacant by the death of its valued rector
for thirty years, the Rev. Samuel Richards, the Bishop, at his own desire,
was called to the charge of it, involving, even with the help of able and
active curates, an immense addition to his episcopal duties. These
labours, twice only relieved by a few months' visit to England, were continued with unceasing energy up to the close of 1887, when he came home
to be in readiness, after a short rest, to take his part in the Lambeth
Conference.

Here a heavy affliction awaited him. Three years after his arrival
in Barbados he had persuaded Miss Susan Blagg, the daughter of an
influential member of his flock at Cheadle, to cheer his solitary home
and to be his helpmeet in the self-sacrificing work to which he had
consecrated his life. Of the absolute devotion with which, for thirty-seven
years, she fulfilled the sacred duties of a wife it were difficult to speak in
terms of exaggeration. But all her unwearied and loving care was now
to be withdrawn from its venerated object. In midwinter they had both
suffered from bronchitis, and in February had gone to Bournemouth for
its warmer air; but late in February the Bishop was again attacked, and,
when he was recovering, his wife also more seriously, and syncope of
the heart, supervening on the bronchial affection, removed her suddenly
from his side. He bowed in all humility and trustful resignation to the
stroke. But it had entirely altered his position, and clearly indicated his
immediate course. In a letter to a friend, dated March 14, 1888, he writes:—

"In this fortnight of my mourning I have learnt much. Under the shadow of the cross I have not wanted for consolations, human and Divine. But life has now taken a different aspect for me, death still more changed, and both for the better and the truer.

"My dear wife knew well that, through decay of nature to be expected at my age, I was getting to be unfitted for, at least, the more secular and worrying part of my duties as Bishop or parish priest. But for her wise and careful management of me I should not have borne the strain of the last year or two without showing signs of impaired efficiency. Now, there is no question of being unequal to a position, whether as Bishop or Rector, which involves much anxiety and miscellaneous trouble. I must, therefore, with as little unsettlement of the Diocese as possible, resign my relation to Trinidad. I propose (D.V.) to go out on April 19, just to wind up affairs and make a becoming end. The voyage and what awaits me on the other side is a sad prospect, but in duty I have never failed for strength."

This intention was carried out. Six weeks were spent among his sorrowing flock, and in the end of June he returned to England to place his resignation in the hands of the Archbishop.

The closing months of his beautiful life are so well described by the writer of the "In Memoriam" in the *Guardian* of May 29, that there could not be a more fitting conclusion to this imperfect sketch than the following quotation:—"The theological department of his old College in Barbados was without a professor, and he was asked by the present Bishop to 'make a present of himself to Codrington College for the temporary supply of the theological element.' (His adoption of this proposal is then given in a quotation from his answer full of piety.) It was found that he had overrated his powers. Throughout the October term of last year he lectured daily on theological subjects and preached frequently, but it was evidently beyond his physical strength. Nevertheless he spent his Christmas vacation in his late Diocese, and took a series of Confirmations, his successor not having been consecrated. He returned to Barbados to find himself more unequal than ever to the discharge of the duties which he had undertaken. Then he made up his mind to return to England to die. His passage was taken by the steamer of April 29, but he was too ill to be moved. He booked to leave by the following steamer on the 13th inst., but three days before the steamer left he was taken to his rest, and in the afternoon of the 11th inst. was laid in the burial ground of the Chapel on the College Estate. Affection had suggested that he should rest in the Chapel of the College, which had been the scene for so many years of his devotions and his labours, but it was decided to lay him in that part of the common cemetery where a lofty memorial cross shall point out to after times the resting-place of a devoted servant of God."　　　W. W. ANTIGUA.

PROSPECTS OF THE CHURCH IN MANITOBA.

BY THE LORD BISHOP OF RUPERTSLAND.

THERE has not been much change in the position of the diocese during the past year. Some immigrants settled in this province, and not a few farms that had been given up were purchased, and are again being occupied. A few Missions are stronger, where two or three small towns have prospered, but on the whole our existing Missions can hardly be said to be appreciably strengthened by the accession of Church families. The general effect of immigration has rather been a further extension of occupation, and such fuller settlement of outlying and very sparsely occupied districts as to make very imperative the opening out of new Missions.

Our older Missions have not then, as a rule, advanced numerically, and the same may be said of them financially. There is no question of the wonderful fertility of much of the land here, and of the healthiness of the climate. Still there are drawbacks in the cold winter, the short seasons in spring and autumn, and other things requiring very special energy, observation, and adaptiveness on the part of farmers. It is easy to point to many industrious and energetic farmers who have achieved in a few years astonishing results. These are mainly Scotch or Canadian and but seldom Churchmen, though we have some Church farmers who have done exceedingly well. But it must be admitted that a large proportion of those who have come from England have not adapted themselves to the work here, or at any rate, from whatever cause, have not been successful. This has told seriously upon some of our Missions. Our English supporters have left, or have become less equal to helping us.

Still, though our Missions have not advanced greatly in strength, numerically or financially, yet we have been dealing with them on the supposition that where settlers have been a few years in the country they should have many things about them, and therefore be capable of doing something more for the support of the means of Grace. We therefore now have made $400 (£82) the maximum grant in aid, in the case of every new grant, and we are steadily year by year reducing the older grants to this amount. We are therefore doing all we can in this way to encourage self-reliance in our Missions.

But beyond this we can yet do little for ourselves. The settlement of this country, as I have often pointed out, is unique. In other colonies the progress of settlement has been gradual, as the opening up of the country has been gradual. But with us the vast country has been opened up in a few years by gigantic railways from means outside of us. Thus there have been all at once hundreds of settlements formed over the vast area; all weak in population and all divided in religious opinion. Speaking roughly, we may reckon on about a fourth of the population of an English-speaking settlement. The number of these settlements may be understood from the fact that there are about 600 " Protestant School Districts"; yet there are very many small settlements that have not yet been made into School Districts. The population for these schools is under 100,000. The sparse character of these settlements may be understood from the further fact that 103 School Districts in 1888 had less than 15 children each of school-age, and 104 others under 20, while 163 had between 20 and 30. Yet these schools are usually many miles apart. The rapid advance in the formation of these settlements may be thus shown. In 1871 there were 16 schools, in 1881 there were 128. This year there are nearly 600. Now, as I said, this settlement of a colony is unique. Ordinarily, after settlement has been established, as new settlements are thrown out and communication extends, the older portion becomes more densely settled. The early parishes and Missions become self-supporting, and help is required mainly for the newly-formed settlements. But actually in Manitoba, as soon as Winnipeg is left in any direction, the country becomes sparsely settled. There is the City of Winnipeg with 25,000 people. There are the two towns of Brandon and Portage-la-Prairie, each with about 3,000 people. The rest of our parishes and Missions are very much on the same footing, one being better than another as there may be a more prosperous town of a few hundred people in it, a larger proportion of Church-people for the time, or a few more liberal and earnest Churchmen. But in this Western country there is a constant movement of population, especially in the towns, so that these advantages of one Mission are often only temporary. The fact is, that in the new Missions we are forming we are expecting as much from our adherents as in the older Missions. Indeed, from the departure of people, and their places not being yet filled, some of our older Missions are our weakest. And there is still an immense extent of unsettled country. Probably only one-half, though no doubt the best half of Manitoba, is thus sparsely settled.

Now what are we doing for ourselves? It must be remembered that our little towns and hamlets have sprung up within the last seven years. Winnipeg in the the census of 1881 was under 8,000.

It must be remembered, too, that there is not one retired person with money; that our people, with few exceptions, have come to us with very

little means—often with none; and in fact that of the few who came
with some capital or have been helped from home, most have been
unable to adapt themselves to the country. They have usually belonged
to a class unaccustomed to practical farm work.

The six parishes in Winnipeg and the parishes of Portage-la-Prairie
and Brandon are self-supporting. In all we have 13 clergy supported
by endowments or their congregations, receiving no aid from Mission
funds.

Then there are 38 Missionary districts, in which we hold services
regularly. In 26 of these we have resident Missionaries. We have
resolved, in dependance on the means being furnished us by God's
Providence, to place resident Missionaries in seven of the others, as soon
as we find suitable men willing to undertake the work. We have some
five men already in view. We simply choose these districts because
the people are ready to provide from $300 to $400. The remaining five
Missions must at present be supplied from the centre. They are too
weak to raise the necessary addition to the Mission grant.

Now, what are our means for this large work? We shall require for
our Home Mission Fund:

(a) To supplement the stipends of 33 Missionaries $13,200
(b) Expenses in travelling of Central Mission to supply vacancies   1,500
(c) Working expenses, secretary, accountant, stationery, printing   1,100
(d) Outfits for new Missionaries, general diocesan purposes and in-
    cidental   1,000

                                           $16,800

Now last year, in our financial year from September 30, 1887, to
September 30, 1888, the Home Mission Fund received for Missions:

(a) From English Societies ...   . $9,126·46
(b) From ourselves—Endowment Fund and Collections ...   ...   4,245·38
(c) From Eastern Canada   ...   .   534·45

                                         $13,906·29

This will leave, if we go by last year's income, a deficiency of
$2,893·71. In other words, to meet our responsibilities this year we
require an addition of $3,000 to our income.

I have already stated that we are gradually reducing our present
grants; but the circumstances I have detailed show that this can be but
a small relief. The reduction will be very gradual.

We may hope for larger help from our self-supporting parishes and
the Diocesan Mission collections; and as our people are generous, we
may look for a good deal from this by-and-by, but we cannot expect
much advance at present.

Manitoba is still labouring under the financial blow suffered in 1882.
In 1878 there was no railway in the country. In the autumn of 1879 a
few miles were built and trains running. In the next two years

HARVEST IN NEWLY CLEARED LAND, MANITOBA.

an extraordinary opening up of the country took place. A great deal of the railway was made from the encouragement of land grants and money grants by the Dominion. This was all by means outside the country. Most extravagant expectations of immediate development and wealth were aroused in Eastern Canada, and not merely hundreds, but thousands of people, bent on speculation, crowded from the East into Winnipeg. Land in Winnipeg and in supposed townsites ran up to high values.

After some sixteen months the bubble burst. Many outside of the country suffered heavily; but in Manitoba there was ruin and embarrassment on every side. The fertile lands became unsaleable. All interests suffered. The past year has been the first year of clear advance. Land is again acquiring a value, but Winnipeg has not yet recovered. During these years all

our institutions and work have struggled with great difficulties.   But
we have kept up a good courage, knowing that the calamity was not
in the least due to the country, but was simply the outcome of undue
speculation and the consequent reaction.   Meantime, the large returns
of many of our farms in the past two years have had a great effect on
the farming population of Eastern Canada; and this year there seems
the prospect of an unexampled immigration from that quarter.   Many
thousands have already come.   We are hoping, then, for a return of
good business and adequate values of land.

We cannot, however, expect an immediate accession of any considerable amount to our Mission funds, as our self-supporting parishes have
mostly burdensome debts to be relieved from.

MARKET SQUARE, WINNIPEG.

We shall therefore have great difficulty in meeting the increased
expenditure, if the Missions are all filled.

We may hope, perhaps, for a larger amount from Eastern Canada.
The usual annual payment from this Board of Missions was not made
within our last financial year.   Since that closed, we have received $594.
The comparatively small help we receive from the Ecclesiastical Province
of Canada, has long been a matter of complaint.   We have received more
when a deputation has gone to the East and preached and held meetings
in their towns.   But our clergy, who could do this with any advantage,
are too busy to allow of this, otherwise than exceptionally.   And we
hesitate to pay out $1,200 additional for a paid secretary to raise some
$4,000, if he even did that.   The Presbyterian Body in Eastern Canada
for years have not given less than $20,000 to $30,000 for Mission and
College work in this diocese, and the Wesleyans do much.   It is said
that if we, like the Presbyterians and Wesleyans, were members of one
ecclesiastical organisation with them, then the aid would be much
greater.   But there is no real ground for this conclusion.   It is with
great difficulty that their one Diocese of Algoma is maintained.   The

main cause, I believe (beyond the social one, that I fear our people as a body spend more upon themselves and have less to give for spiritual objects, though I think they are behind none in giving for such objects as hospitals), is that every Canadian diocese has its own Home Mission Fund which monopolises its sympathy and strength. The Provincial Mission effort is consequently sickly, weak, and has little life. There is nothing of this among the Presbyterians. Their Assembly Mission Fund is their only one. I hope still that we may get larger help from Canada. I know many there recognise our difficulties and the importance of our work. I know many feel that the fact of so many of their people coming to this country and calling for our services lays upon them a strong obligation. But there are disturbing influences and causes to which I cannot allude, so that I fear we must not reckon on any appreciable increase.

I have given you a very full statement of our position. We feel deeply grateful for the large help that we have received from the Society. It has been our mainstay in our work in the new settlements. We need that help as much as ever—indeed, never more so; but the prospects of the Church, if the work can be kept up and extended with the progress of settlement, are very good.

St. John's College and Cathedral continue to be the great support of our work. One does not know what God would have raised up, but I often think that, if I had not utilised the few years after I came to the diocese before the country began to be opened up in laying the foundation of these two bodies, our Church would have been nowhere in the country. It may practically be said that there is not a parish or Mission in Winnipeg or the New Settlements, with two or three exceptions out of the thirty-eight Missionary districts, that has not been founded, nursed, and ministered to by our College and Cathedral Mission. There are never fewer than seven or eight parishes on its hands. Unfortunately, when Missions are going on satisfactorily, and grants from your Society or some other source have been enjoyed for some time, there comes a vacancy. Had not the College and Cathedral Mission been ready to step in and carry on the services, often for many months, the Mission would have gone to pieces, and the past work and expenditure have been lost.

The College has sent out a large number of very excellent clergymen, but, unfortunately, we do not keep them all; several have been drawn away to other dioceses. I am happy to say that we have this year a much larger number of students preparing for the Ministry than we have ever had before. Many are very acceptable when they take duty in the Missions.

There are some friends of the Church in England who seem, when they rejoice over the establishment of a new Bishopric, to think that when a Bishop is appointed everything necessary is effected. Such persons often resent the reappearance of a Bishop to raise funds for his work. But the Bishop finds, when he enters on his labours, that he is apparently expected to make bricks without straw. While one cannot but admire the noble devotion of means exhibited so often in England in erecting or restoring some beautiful church, yet, when viewing the number of these efforts, and the great amount of money spent on them, it cannot but seem strange to one like myself, laying the foundations of work of so vast importance in the future, that so few seem to appreciate the relative importance of different Church efforts. How seldom is a large gift, such as £25,000, given for the support of a College in a new colony? In many dioceses it may not be needed, from a College in another diocese being conveniently near, and the multiplication of colleges not absolutely required is to be deprecated. But where work is so isolated as our Church work in this country, the establishment of a strong college is a necessity. What a strength, now, such a gift to our College would add to us! Often when clergymen come to us from outside they do not satisfy our people, or our work is unsatisfactory to them. We have of course received many valuable workers from outside. But it is a great comfort when we have a man who knows our work and has been trained in its midst.

Only one thing further shall I mention. We have been asked by the Government to undertake the care of an Industrial Indian School for 80 Indian children that the Government is building. The Government allows $100 per child. We find from other institutions of the kind in Canada and the States that we cannot hope to maintain all the work, instruct, feed, and clothe the children under $150 per child. So that we must lay ourselves out to raise $4,000 per annum. This, with all our young work is, indeed, a great venture of faith.

And now, I have no space to spare for your own special work.

I think I can say that all the Missionaries receiving grants from your funds have been doing their best, several with marked success.

Several of the towns that have become most promising happen to lie in these Missions. Towns of from 500 to 800 inhabitants, as Rat Portage, Morden, Neefana, Carberry, Manitou, and Birtle. Of these, Morden, Neefana, and Carberry are of recent growth, but have specially good farming country around them. There are churches in all these places, the church in Carberry having been built this year. At Birtle there has been a great advance in the prospects of the Mission, mainly owing to the arrival a year or two ago in the district of an earnest churchman, General Wilkinson. The church at Birtle is now free of debt, and the parsonage nearly so. The young clergyman there is doing very good work. I have visited most of your Missions comparatively lately, and found good and attentive congregations. At Rat Portage, though it has no settled country about it, being a centre of a lumbering country, and only a small town, a very large portion of the adults are communicants, there being over 100 communicants attached to the congregation. By-and-by the country round will also be worked for minerals, when this may be an important point.   I 5

FROM BLOEMFONTEIN TO THE ZAMBESI: A GREAT MISSIONARY JOURNEY.

BY THE BISHOP OF BLOEMFONTEIN.

IN MASHONALAND.

MASHONALAND lies to the north-east of Matabeleland. It is a plateau elevated from 4,000 to 4,500 feet above the level of the sea. This altitude makes the climate far from very hot in summer and really cold in winter. All the year round the nights are cold. It is, therefore, generally a healthy country, a country, to use Livingstone's words of another part of the Continent, where "brisk exercise imparts elasticity to the muscles, and healthy blood circulates through the brain; the mind works well, the eye is clear, the step firm, and a day's exertion always makes repose thoroughly enjoyable."

It is a fertile land, being well watered by a network of ever running streams. When other parts of South Africa are scorched and thirsty, the Mashona plateau, says Mr. Selous, in the *Fortnightly* for May 1889, " is covered with a soft waving grass, whilst small streams or little rills run brawling down every hollow, and all live stock look fat and comfortable."

Eighty years ago this fine country was thickly populated by a well fed, industrious, and peaceable people, now the inhabitants are few and far between, for the Matabele have spread death and desolation over the land. Most of the people have been slain or captured, and the remnant that has escaped is in constant fear because of "the fierceness of the oppressor." Thus in a comparatively short time an immense extent of fertile country, that had for ages sustained in comfort a large population has been given back to nature and wild animals, and is almost deserted by man.

After getting his waggons into good order, rearranging his baggage, recovering his lost donkeys, &c., the Bishop recommenced his journey, and thus continues his diary :

"*June* 13, *Wednesday.*—The only way of mapping the road was to climb up the koppies that stood near the road. One range was fantastically beautiful, and the large boulders looked as if some baby Titans had been playing with them. In one place four single ones stood one on the top of the other. Climbing them reminded me that I had not two sound arms. (At Mafeking the Bishop broke his shoulder, and had to return to Kimberley to get it mended, so that he started on his journey later than he intended.)

"Our one Matabele man, Sekomi, asked Edward for a blanket, which he was told he could not have, when he threatened to kill Edward, and said that he had killed twenty Mashona. There is one Mashona man travelling with us. He seems very helpless and stupid. We stopped for the night some two hours and a half after passing the Sangwe River.

"*June* 14, *Thursday.*—We made but two treks to the Vungu River, where we had some difficulty in drawing the buck-waggon out; it took us one and a half hour to do so.

"As now we begin to travel only by day, we had short prayers before going to bed. We were a representative gathering—three half-castes, three Bechuana, one Matabele, one Mashona, one Matonga, two Basuto.

"*June* 15, *Friday.*—Jelly had packed the boxes badly, so that a good deal of delay was caused from their breaking. The last three sheep were allowed to stray, and were not found again. The 'bush' of my waggon has broken, and this will be a perpetual anxiety for the rest of the journey in this country. It is strange to remember on how small a thing the success of a journey may, under God, depend. If this 'bush' comes out, the waggon is useless.

"The 'impi' has passed by. Their 'spoor' was seen turning out of the road to avoid meeting us. The 'Indunas' are said to do this because they do not like the meeting with a white man. I was very much relieved at its having passed, for I thought that possibly this 'impi' might have been used by Lobengula against me if he had not wished me to go further. I remembered that he had not said any word of farewell to me (though this may have been a mistake), and there was a similarity between both myself and Captain Patterson in being allowed to go into the country after repeated requests. Captain Patterson had certainly threatened him, which I did not, and was killed with all his party, including Mr. Thomas, the Missionary's son, about two days' journey, I believe, from Iniati.

"We encamped at Gwelu River. The men refused to fetch water at night for fear of lions. When I told them to give me the cask and I would go myself, then they said they would all go, and that I was not to trouble myself; but still they complained that they 'had not come here to be thrown away.' So I took three of them, and the others followed afterwards; Edward amongst them, though it was not his work, but he came because he thought it his duty, I think, to be where I was.

"*June* 16, *Saturday.*—I stayed behind with two men to look for a harte-beest, and then rode on to get an observation from a koppie near the Ingurnia River. The grass was in some places higher than my head when on a horse. The lazier among the men wished to stay here over Sunday, but the delays had been incessant and irritating, so I went on. For about two hours there was daylight, and the trek was finished by moonlight. We met no human being all the day. The road in some parts is very beautiful, though generally flat. There are glades in places; and the latter part of the journey was through a country looking not unlike a wood in Surrey, though without the beauty of detail, which always seems wanting in South Africa. Trees had been cut down along the road by the Mashona in order to get at the large white and black caterpillars found in them, and which they dry, then roast, and eat whole, or pounded as meal.

"*June* 17, *Sunday.*—We had to make one trek to reach water, but as we did this by 7.30 A.M. little of the Sunday was broken into. After the Sunday washing and cleaning we had our Service. Camp Sundays are peaceful days, and though I am very anxious to get on, they seem in no way to retard us.

" While walking back from taking a survey from the nearest hill, we saw where a lion had killed a bastard-eland (the Dutch name for roan antelope) in the tambookie grass, which, near the waggon, is over nine feet in height. A honey-bird came to the waggon to show where honey was, but it led the men too far, and they came back without the honey. The Zaloba River, near which we are, runs constantly, though only a little brook. The days are warm, while the nights are cold, more especially towards sunrise. This rapid alternation of heat and cold is thought to be one of the causes of dysentery.

"*June* 18, *Monday.*—Sekomi led me round about in order to get meat (*i.e.* a shot at an eland or a deer), but none was obtained. I followed a honey-bird till it stood over the honey; it had been to the waggons once before in the morning.

" Isaac asked Edward how long I should be away when we left the waggons and took to walking, and on being told about three months, replied, ' Then we shall all die.'

" No human being not belonging to ourselves was seen all the day.

"*June* 19, *Tuesday.*—I went a long round and brought back a dinker, *i.e.* a small antelope. We outspanned at the Sebakwe River, a very beautiful stream. We are constantly crossing the track of the ' impi.' As far as I can understand Sekomi, they have raided on some town to the north of this, and killed the chief. He does not seem to think the killing of Mashona as anything serious. This naturally makes the Mashona treacherous and revengeful, and painful stories exist of what they have done when opportunity occurred.

" We are not able to go by the straight track (which is now lost) towards the north, as the rivers are impassable at the old fords, while above are rocks, and below the Tsetse fly. Mr. Selous and George Wood found the pass over the Machaba Hills, which we use.

"We saw for the first time one of the palm-tree family, which was between thirty and forty feet high; but we met no man, woman, or child on the road. We have passed the last Matabele town. All this country was once well peopled with Mashona, but the Matabele have killed, captured, or driven them away.

"We are now making a third fire at night in front of the oxen, on account of lions.

"My men come to prayer most willingly at night, and we have the Lord's Prayer in Sesuto.

"*June 20, Wednesday.*—I rode round and met the waggons at the pass in the Machaba Hills, which nowhere seem to attain to any great height, and are but thinly dotted with trees. We saw no one.

"*June 21, Thursday.*—We crossed the Umniati River, in which crocodiles are said to be numerous. All the rivers of sufficient size between here and Iniati seem to have the same characteristics, *i.e.* sandy and stony bottoms, steep broken banks, reeds and bushes. They are larger as we travel farther north, though it would be hard to give any correct idea of their size, owing to the stream varying in breadth according to the nature of the ground it passes through. The Umniati is perhaps twenty feet broad where it is four feet deep, and this is the dry season.

"About the time of sunset the sky is, with very small intervals, covered with clouds, which pass away, and yet there is not the remotest chance of rain. Between the rivers and brooks the ground is arid in the extreme, though the grass is still green enough in places to resist the bush-fires. The cattle prefer feeding on the ant-hills, the grass being better there on account of the moisture thrown up by the ants.

"*June 22, Friday.*—We crossed the Umgezi River this morning. Very large ant-hills, made by a small red ant, stand near it on the northern bank; one, roughly measured, was about sixteen feet high and twenty-four feet in breadth at the base.

"While going on with Sekomi a mile or more ahead of the waggons, I met the first people I have seen for some time; they were four Matabele who were hunting. Sekomi at first said they were Mashona, and would kill him, and John told me afterwards that had they been Mashona they certainly would have killed him. The town which the 'impi' destroyed is about one day on foot up the Umfuli River, from the ford where (D.V.) we shall cross it. They killed the chief, having killed his father some time ago, and all the men, and the old women who could not walk, and took the younger women, and boys, and cattle to Matabeleland. This must have happened about a fortnight ago. As we waited for the waggons, Sekomi and the four Matabele talked about it. To him it seems to be something far removed from anything serious, rather something to be laughed at.

" These men have followed us for food.

" *June* 23, *Saturday.*—While riding in front I met Count Schweinitz, who is travelling with Mr. Dunn, and, beside myself, they are the only white men in the country this year. While at the Umgezi River the ' impi ' had passed them going in, when even the Matabele men belonging to the Count's waggons hid themselves during the day, saying the ' impi ' would kill anyone. They met them also coming out, when they said that they had killed some headmen, but it was difficult to gather anything that was certain from their different accounts. They hid away the cattle, and the captives, women and children, in the bushes.

" The waggons went on to the stream, which was about four hours away, and I and Count Schweinitz, who stayed the night with me, rode on, a full moon showing us the track.

" We had quagga soup for dinner. Not a Mashona has been seen, they seem to have been frightened away by the ' impi.'

" *June* 24, *Sunday.*—Count Schweinitz stayed for our morning service, and was on the point of going away when his waggons came in. It was a pleasure to have them near, and at the evening prayers some of the Count's men attended, making fifteen in all present. There is not the slightest difficulty in getting the men to prayers, and they behave most reverently. In the evening and on week-days we stand at prayers in a circle round the fire. The Count does not hunt on Sunday.

" *June* 25, *Monday.*—I rode round with the Count and saw two ostriches, which I let alone, as there is only a small portion of them eatable, and because they represent part of the money of the country.

" Our fires have set the grass on fire, and a wind has driven the flames in the direction that we wish to go.

" The Lundaza River is now running parallel with the road. It is, perhaps, the prettiest river we have yet seen. In some places it is like a Scotch mountain stream, in others still and clear like a Wiltshire brook. A high reed grass grows on the banks, and in the small reaches a white and a lilac water-lily.

" I rode away from the road, and joined again at the Umfute Ford, just in time to see the buck-waggon upset down the opposite bank ; had I been five minutes earlier this might have been prevented.

" *June* 26, *Tuesday.*—The fog and mist that rises from the low lying damp ground in the numbing cold of the mornings before the sun has risen is a strange contrast to the dry heat of the day. Nearly the whole of the ground on which we passed to-day consisted of a black sticky soil, and must have been a morass in the rainy season, for the earth is split open in all directions from the action of the sun on the mud, and in some places there are deep holes, two or four feet wide, which apparently retained the water for some time, as there is a luxuriant growth of grass around them.

" I shot a bastard-eland to day after a quick gallop of about a mile and a half. It was a very large one, and will last the men for some time.

" Just as I had written the foregoing, a large animal that we thought must have been a hyæna came prowling near the front oxen. I shot it, but it got up and ran off, and there being only a dim moonlight we did not go after it. We sleep at the Kalangwe stream.

" (*Wednesday, June* 27, was eventless.)

" *June* 28, *Thursday.*—We reached the Hanyane River by about 8 A.M., and put the waggons higher up the hill than where Selous made his camp last year. Soon after breakfast we began to make arrangements

for continuing the journey without the waggons. We have not yet seen a single person of the country, so two men have been sent out to hunt them up, and to tell them to bring food for sale, and that I want carriers from among them to make the first stage to Magondi's.

" The making of pack-saddles has taken up nearly the whole of the day, and very little seems to have been done; there is a great deal, however, to be done before we start.

" I have arranged for Isaac to stay in charge of the waggons, and Sekomi to stay and shoot for him. It seems certain that the Mashona would kill him if we took him with us any farther.

" This is the first river we have come to that has somewhat of a tropical appearance; and it is certainly very beautiful. The reeds and the trees have a much higher degree of luxuriance, and the mass of water is greater. I heard the fish eagle for the first time.

"I am very thankful that we have had so little trouble; not a horse, ox, or donkey has been lost since leaving Mafeking about two and a half months ago. We are now some little distance in latitude to the north of the Victoria Falls.

"*June* 29, *Friday.*—From soon after sunrise till sunset, with very little intermission, we have been making pack-saddles. Fortunately I brought the necessary materials, and to-day we have made good progress.

"My two men came back with twenty-five Mashona men, who brought, however, very little food with them. They say that they cannot carry for us as their mabele is not yet threshed. Unlike the Matabele, the men alone have come, carrying their mealies chiefly in earthenware pots. They walked from soon after sunrise to sunset. There is no chief to their town now; the last one was killed some time ago by the Matabele. They are a well-mannered, inoffensive company. When they arrived they walked straight to a tree at a little distance from the waggons, and were soon at work cutting firewood for the night. Like the Matabele, they are nearly naked, and they have hair on their faces like the Amatonga. One of them will stay with the waggons, as he has nowhere to go, for last summer his town was destroyed by the Matabele, when only three persons escaped.

"*June* 30, *Saturday.*—The buying of a small sack of mealies and a few beans and nuts occupied about four hours, the small quantities that made up this amount being bought separately from each person for blue or white calico, or beads. When they were asked to make a kraal for the cattle, they wanted to be paid beforehand, but I made a compromise with each of the twelve men we employed, by letting him choose his own yard of calico, and then hanging it on a bough of a tree till the work was well done. Time, which before had seemed to be of no importance to them, now appeared of the greatest, and they ran about among the trees like ants, using axes of their own making with peculiar dexterity. One man I noticed high up in a tree, using his axe with both hands while he held on by his back and feet.

"By about sunset ten pack-saddles were finished, the idiosyncrasy of each donkey's back carefully studied, and the name of the donkey written on his saddle. I anticipate a great deal of difficulty in getting my men to put the saddles on properly; Jelly, whose power of thinking seems to be in inverse ratio to the amount of tobacco which he consumes, having arranged the halter of another donkey inside the girths of the one he ought to have been attending to. If no carriers appear, with a little more cutting down of our loads we can be independent of that painful factor in African travelling."

For several days the Bishop was engaged in arranging, weighing, sorting packs and parcels for the next stage of his journey, and writes on

"*July 4, Wednesday.*—Two oxen have been taken for the journey instead of the two horses. As I know nothing about the packing of an ox, I left it to the men. They carry a very large load.

"Count Schweinitz, who intends to hunt near Lo Magondi's, started with us. A boggy stream troubled the donkeys, two of whom had to be hauled and pushed out. Considerably after dark they arrived at the stream where we made our *skerm* and slept. *Skerm* is the name given to the enclosure of boughs made round a camp at night as a protection from wild beasts.

"*July 5, Thursday.*—We did two very long walks to-day for donkeys with heavy packs. The difficulty of packing donkeys consists in the necessity of having pack-saddles and bags which are very light and very strong. Where trees grow close together as here, several donkeys, all jostling together, or anyone trying to force his bags between two trees that refuse to allow their passage, or under a bough that is too low, requires a strong combination of leather, screws, and wood.

"The mahobiobo, with the beautiful leaf, now appears in large numbers, and whole groves of machabel in common with the mopani. The red ant has a great liking for the machabel, and it is most curious in red soil to see the trunks of a whole grove of machabels almost covered up to the beginning of the boughs with the red earth which the ants have built on them. There is a strange dearth of birds.

"*July 6, Friday.*—I should be very thankful that I have such excellent men. I have left everything at the waggons in charge of Isaac, and everything of real value is open to him; even the horses I leave with perfect confidence, knowing that at whatever moment I appear over the hill, I shall find everything as though I had never left. Scarcely anything short of an English groom could equal Edward in willingness. John is admirably good, and has recovered from the inferior example of Jelly, who has changed considerably, has become submissive, and is learning to obey; though, as his nature is to be officious, he is—*ut plerumque fit*—inefficient. His immense brute strength, however, is of great advantage whether in lifting a waggon or dragging a donkey out of a bog. He used to shout at the men, but now everyone seems on excellent terms with everyone else, even when they cannot understand each other's language, or pronounce each other's names. Antigone, the Mashona, has been left at the waggons. He sang a little song at night, ' I am a great man, and I come from a river; and it is a pity that I have not a mate '; which the men laughed at.

"The 'Matonga man was very much interested in my feet, when I took off my socks to doctor them after a walk. He said that it was

no wonder that white men required boots if they had feet like that, for
they were like little children's.

"When we arrived in the evening at the first part of Lo Magondi's
village, the people were very civil, and helped our men to cut wood,
though they have no conception of such hospitality as the Basuto would
show to a stranger.   Their clothes are very scanty.   Some of the
women wear a bead or zinc ornament through the upper lip.   There
seems to be no especial type of face, and I think that they must be a
very mixed race.   Some men wear their hair short, like the ordinary
native, others in strings.   The men are better looking than the
women, but it is very hard to know which are boys and which are
girls.

"*July* 7, *Saturday.*—I visited the few huts near our skerm, and
spoke to the headman about the life in another world, and asked him
what he thought would become of him after he was dead.   He said
that his chief, Magondi, knew, and this seemed to satisfy him.   When
I said that our God was in heaven, and that good people went there,
he admitted that it might be so, though he did not know, as he
had never seen a teacher before.   Soon after reaching Magondi's village
the son of the chief asked me not to fire off the gun then, as it would
frighten away the god, an old man who lived near, so no gun was
fired

" I made known that I wanted carriers to Sinoias, but learned that
I was out of favour because I would not give the god a present.   Lo
Magondi is away.

"*July* 8, *Sunday.*—After divine service I asked the people who
were round the skerm whether they knew what we were doing, and
deputed Sikwarri to explain through Jonas to one man.   The opening
of the Bible made the man jump up, but he was induced to sit down
again.   I do not think that the lesson was very successful."

From this place the Bishop sent back the oxen to the waggons,
as the Tsetse fly, whose bite is fatal to domestic cattle, swarmed on the
road before him, and carriers offered themselves for the next stage of
his journey.   With reference to the carriers he says :—

" On *July* 9, there was some difference of opinion as to the payment
in ' limbo ' (calico ?), during which they left in a body, and had to be
brought back.   Ultimately they were paid beforehand, on the ground
that white men, probably Portuguese half-castes trading from the North-
east, had beaten them away after their journey with them without
payment.   They carried admirably, and were no trouble whatever.

"*July* 10, *Tuesday.*—We arrived at Sinoias' town at about 10
o'clock.   The chief is Kazilamumbi.   I gave him a blanket, and
arranged about carriers to Pendoro's.   The town, which is larger than
Magondi's, is in a basin of hills, and contains a subterranean cavern

which slopes down 200 or 300 feet to a pool of water which extends into the earth, and is only visible for about fifty yards in the two directions which the cave takes. The water is of a most extraordinary blue colour from its depth and clearness, and stones at the bottom shine with a phosphorescent light. This description is given by Edward, for they would not allow a white man to go down to see it.

"The chief and people are very friendly and well mannered, the former sending me a present of some native beer immediately on my arrival. It was explained to them that I was 'a teacher,' and had not come for gold, but I do not think that they believed it.

"After the mass of people had gone away, I took John as an interpreter, and talked to about twenty men. It is, I think, usually best to speak to one only of a village, and let him repeat to his people what he has heard; for it is very hard for them not all to speak at once; but after telling these men that only one must speak at a time they were sufficiently quiet. I said that there was a man called a god at Magondi's, and asked if there was such a one here. They replied that God lived in the sky ; then, that they once had a god living with them, but the Matabele frightened him away. Furthermore, they said that they believed God made them and taught them to sow; and when I asked how they knew that God made them, replied that Magondi had taught them that. (This reference to the chief as a teacher I found nowhere else.) We talked for some time, most of them were quiet and attentive, and several said that they would like to have a teacher to live with them. Some of these people have fine faces.

" They are very poor, the great majority of them not having a blanket to sleep in, but when sleeping lie between two fires, so that in one skerm at one part there was a fire and a Mashona alternately. Yet they do not seem unhappy, for in the evening they sing and beat their drums, and dance and shout light-heartedly.

"Our road has lain for some time through uninteresting woods of dwarfed trees, without birds or animals, and with a scarcity of water."

THE CHILDREN'S CORNER.

A RECOLLECTION OF ZULULAND TWENTY YEARS AGO.

BY THE REV. C. JOHNSON.

(Concluded from page 273.)

" EXT morning the 'umtimba' (bridal party, with the bride in their midst) started for Matshana's kraal. My father, I knew, would have stopped me had I told him I was going to follow the 'umtimba,' so I bid good-bye to my people, and made as though I were going back to the white man to work again; and so got away without anyone suspecting what I was going to do. I found out that the 'umtimba' was to stay that night at a certain kraal, a short distance from Matshana's. I had formed no plan of action further than just following to see what was to become of 'Nomatopi. The name of the man at whose kraal they were going to stop at that night is 'Umzukuluka.' I thought that perhaps I might be able unseen to get a word with her while the party was at that kraal, some time during the night, but she was too well guarded. I stayed prowling round the kraal all night, but as the day broke I retired to some long grass and watched. The 'umtimba' started as the sun rose, and I followed. They halted at another kraal close to Matshana's, to put on their marriage finery. And just after the sun had turned in the heavens they started again—this time in marriage order, and singing their marriage song.

" I felt as though I were going mad as I lay down in my hiding-place and listened to their song as they passed me, and saw 'Nomatopi marching between two of her brothers, and now and again urged on by the one behind to go on quicker. But I shut my eyes and waited.

" The feasting, dancing, and singing was great that afternoon and evening at Matshana's.

" I was so well known in the district that I durst not go very near until it was dark, for fear of being recognised by some of 'Nomatopi's people, but as night set in I drew closer. Just as I got into the kraal I saw some one jump away from the midst of a group of girls and begin running away from the kraal; but evidently there were people on the watch, guarding, for the runaway was surrounded and stopped before she was really clear of the kraal. I was not near enough to see the face of the

runaway, but I felt sure it was 'Nomatopi. I saw them bring her back
and drag her roughly into a hut. The noise and feasting still went on
as though nothing had happened. I crept close behind the hut into
which I had seen them take 'Nomatopi, and listened for a long time, but
I could not hear her voice, though from time to time I could hear others
talking.

"I do not know how long I stayed there waiting and trying to think of
something I could do, when suddenly I heard a movement in the hut,
and then a struggle and a cry. I jumped up and ran for the small door
and burst it open. There was a small fire which gave a little light, just
enough to enable me to see two women struggling with something on the
ground. The old wretches took me for one of their own party, and called
on me to help them, for the 'umakoti' (bride) had got loose. I picked
up one of the lighted pieces of wood and thrust it into the thatch of the
hut, and immediately it was in a flame. I then jumped towards the
struggling women and caught hold of 'Nomatopi, shouting to the old
women to never mind the girl, but to save themselves, for the hut was on
fire, and that I would see to the ''makoti.' Directly the old women
saw the fire they thought no more of anything but saving themselves
and property. I whispered to 'Nomatopi to make for the door and turn
to the left as soon as she got out, and that I would follow. We both got
safely away in the confusion, for the cries of the old women had roused
the whole kraal, and they were running about in great confusion trying
to get water to throw on the fire. We got away safely and ran as best
we could in the darkness for a long time. And when I thought that we
were safe from pursuit, for a time at least, we turned aside and sat down
in some long grass, to think what we should do next, and form some
plan of action for the future. Of course she was quite willing now to
come away with me to the white man's country.

"I had not tasted food since I had left home the day before, and
'Nomatopi's heart had been too sore to allow of her eating, and so we
both now felt that we must get somewhere, where we could obtain food
before starting for the white man's country. Therefore we agreed to go
to my father's kraal procure food, and then go straight on as fast as we
could.

"The sun was high in the heavens as we drew near to my father's kraal.
I did not take 'Nomatopi to the kraal, but hid her in some long grass, and
went in by myself. I told my brother Ujojo all about it, and also my
mother. I could see that Ujojo was frightened when he heard about my
setting fire to Matshana's hut. He said, 'We are all dead to-day.'

"My mother gave me all the food she had cooked, and I said good-bye
to them all again, and hastened back to where I had left 'Nomatopi.
But when I reached the place she was not there, nor could I see her anywhere; but there was something I saw that startled me very much, namely,

the trampled condition of the grass. Evidently there had been a struggle. I cried out in the sorrow of my heart, and it seemed as though my cry was answered immediately, but not in the way I wished. Four men rushed on me before I could have turned to run if I had wanted to.

"It seemed that the old women who were guarding 'Nomatopi were not so flurried but that they recognised me when I spoke to them, and when they told Matshana and 'Nomatopi's brothers, they understood the whole affair at once. Matshana sent off men in different directions in pursuit, and some with orders to go straight to my father's kraal and watch close by; and so they saw where I had hidden 'Nomatopi, and laid this simple plan which secured us both.

"Makosi, ngi ya kuni tshela kanjani incino ya le'ndaba na? Inhlizeyo yami ifile! (Sirs, how shall I relate to you the end of this matter? My heart is dead!)

"I think they only intended to keep me fastened up until the forced marriage ceremony of 'Nomatopi to Matshana was finished, for they fed me and were kind to me, but kept me a close prisoner in a hut. But the spirits of our dead ancestors would not consent to this. For three days and nights was I kept tied up. About mid-day on the fourth I was untied, all but my hands, which were still fastened together behind my back with 'inkomfi' (grass string), and they led me out to a place just outside the kraal. Will my eyes ever forget what they saw there? 'Nomatopi had said she would rather die than willingly become the wife of Matshana. Two days had they kept her tied up in a hut without food, but she would not yield. Then her people and Matshana's people got into a rage, and said she should die then or yield, and they took her just outside the kraal where there was a large 'isiduli' (ant-hill). They then partially levelled it so as to thoroughly rouse the ants; and that kind, you know, has a large red head with strong nippers, strong enough to draw blood in a tender part. On the top of this prepared place they stretched my poor brave girl, laying her on her back, with her hands and feet fastened down to pegs driven into the ground. The poor, brave girl had already been there in that agony two days and a night, and now they had brought me out to try if, when I saw her suffering, I would not try and persuade her to consent to what they asked.

"When I saw her I tried to get loose, but they had tied my hands too tightly behind my back. I was led close to her as she lay stretched out with her face and body exposed to the burning sun, and the terrible little ants crawling all about her, eating her up piecemeal.

"They allowed me to kneel by her side, but my heart could hold out no longer. I cried, 'Oh! my girl—oh! my child—consent,

consent to anything.' She opened her eyes and looked at me. I could see that she was dying, but she could just manage to speak. We listened for her reply. Her words came slowly, one at a time. ' They can do nothing more to me, my body is dead ; fear not for me, I feel no more. My heart is——.' She could speak no more. I cried, ' She is dying—do not you see that she is dying ? Release her—she will consent.' Two old women undid her hands and feet, but she was quite powerless to move, having been so long stretched out. Oh ! how she must have suffered from the bites of those fierce insects, and the burning sun by day and cold by night before her body became benumbed !

" She fainted when they released her, and we all thought that she was dead. They threw water on her, but although she opened her eyes she never really revived. I jumped away from the men that were holding me, and threw myself down by her side ; but they dragged me away, and knocked me about with their sticks, but I did not feel much.

" They carried her into the shade of a tree, and when they laid her down I could see it was all over with her. In pulling me back they had stretched the ' inkomfi' fastenings of my hands, and I managed to squeeze one hand free. There was a big fellow, one of Matshana's sons, standing holding me by the arm. He had a big ' iwisa ' (knobstick) in his hand. I made a jump at him, and wrested the stick from him before he could recover from his surprise. With one blow I knocked him over. I then made for 'Nomatopi's eldest brother ; he was sitting down looking very sternly at the body. His spirit went to the spirits below with hers. I then made for the chief's hut ; he was sitting outside quietly, as though nothing were happening, with three or four of his headmen. A cry was raised by those standing round, as they saw 'Nomatopi's brother fall and saw me start for where the chief was standing. I do not know how many got in my way to stop me, or how many I knocked down, or how many I killed, but before I could reach Matshana he was surrounded by a little crowd of his people, armed with sticks, but I think no assegais. I made one last effort as I saw some men running towards me with assegais and shields. I knocked down those near me, and with one good aim I flung the ' iwisa ' at Matshana's head. I heard a cry as he fell, and they made a rush for me. Without thinking, I turned and ran. How long I had been running I do not know, when I came on to your wagon.

" There is my story !

" What shall I do now ? I do not know. I must see my father, and then try and reach the white man's country."

After he had drank a pannikin of hot coffee and eaten a bit of bread, he started on what was, I am sorry to say, his last walk. I heard afterwards that the chief, Matshana, had only been stunned by the knobkarrie thrown by Umazwi, and that when he recovered from the blow and found that his people had returned without having been able to catch the fugitive, he got into a great fury and ordered his people to muster and start off at once for 'Somopo's kraal, which they were to secretly surround and attack at daybreak. Their orders were to burn the kraal down and kill everything but the cattle, goats, &c.—*the usual thing.* Some of his headmen, I believe, got a little frightened and said, "But what will the King say?" These Matshana quieted by saying, "I will make it right with the King. Has not 'Somopo, by his son, spilt blood in my kraal? Has he not also killed me, and burnt my kraal down?" His word was carried out. 'Somopo and his family were all killed. Had Umazwi remained with us, as we wished him to do, he would have escaped; he must have got home just before the attack, or was killed as he entered the kraal.

It is the work of counteracting and altering such a dark state as shown by the above terrible account that Christ's Gospel has to do, *and, thank God, is doing.*

NOTES OF THE MONTH.

ON June 19 the Anniversary Service in St. Paul's Cathedral was held, the Archbishop of Canterbury celebrating the Holy Communion. The Bishop of Chester preached the sermon, which was a splendid vindication of the Society's position as the handmaid of the Church of England for Missionary work abroad. As his text he chose from St. Luke, xvii. 18, the words, "Returned to give glory to God." Taking that anniversary service as a thanksgiving service, the Bishop gathered up the leading facts of the past year for which the Society should glorify God. He spoke of the uses in Holy Scripture of the phrase "to give glory to God," and drew out its connection with an acknowledgment of sin and shortcoming in such cases as that of Achan. From this the preacher led his hearers to consider how the future should go far beyond the past, and to think of the way in which the present opportunities call for every possible exertion.

THE number of churches in London where the Holy Communion is celebrated on St. Peter's Day in connection with the Society's anniversary has largely increased of late years. The number this year was about 320. Besides these there were several in other dioceses, especially that of Canterbury.

FROM Colon, on the Isthmus of Panama, we have the sad news of the death of the wife of the Rev. S. Kerr. It was only last month that we printed some interesting extracts from Mr. Kerr's letters, describing the anxious and difficult, though encouraging, work in which he is engaged. Now he writes in a letter to the Bishop of Jamaica, which his lordship has kindly handed to us, as the bereaved husband desired :—

> "Of all my troubles and difficulties, combined with earthly losses, this is the keenest. For thirty-three years she helped me to endure the trials attending my work as a Missionary, and in their turn she shared in my joys. She was my counsellor, my guide, my sincere friend, as well as a devoted and faithful wife."

Mrs. Kerr's death took place on June 11, and the Colon *Telegram* describes the throng of persons at her funeral as being more numerous than had ever been seen in Colon on such an occasion :—

> "This is a mark of esteem shown by all classes towards their devoted Rector in his bereaved condition; which cannot but be gratefully appreciated."

> "She was often called upon to assist medical men in administering medicine, succour and comfort to the poor and aged; which led to the formation of a guild with other ladies devoted to Church work for the visitation of the sick and destitute in her district."

> "She was frugal in expense upon herself, so that she might have wherewithal to relieve the necessity of others when called upon."

COLON, PANAMA.

GARDEN Meetings and Sales of Work are being organised in Hampshire this season, as in previous years, in connection with the Society. The first was held on July 1, at the Training College, Winchester, when the Rev. H. and Mrs. Martin entertained a large party of guests. Sir Charles Turner, K.C.I.E., and the Bishop of Ballarat were the chief speakers. The Dean of Winchester (Dr. Kitchin) presided at a public luncheon which was previously held. Great regret was expressed at the enforced absence through illness of the Bishop of the diocese. The Organising Secretary for the county, in thanking the host and hostess, alluded to the great loss the Society in the neighbourhood had sustained through the recent bereavement of the Warden of Winchester College (the Rev. Godfrey B. Lee), and also by the death of that energetic and noble-hearted worker for the cause, the Rector of Ovington (the Rev. W. H. B. Stocker), whose parish of 110 people, with only one large house in it, had regularly contributed from £20 to £30 to the funds of the Society. He added that he was thankful to say he had every reason to hope and believe that these garden meetings and sales of work would become annual fixtures in Hampshire, and thus he was sure the funds of the Society would be much increased.

Sales of work are, we understand, arranged for during the next few months at Southsea, Bournemouth, Rowner (for Gosport), Basingstoke, Southampton, Alton, and probably at Andover. The Organising Secretary for the county (the Rev. F. C. Green, Denmead Vicarage, Cosham) will gratefully receive contributions of work, &c.

SHINTOISM—the "colourless cult"—is the aristocratic religion in Japan. The following is from a description in the *Hiogo Times* of the funeral of a Shinto gentleman :—

"In the grounds attached to the residence of the deceased in Nakanoshima were great numbers of bouquets of flowers, dwarf pines, branches of green trees and other similar offerings sent by his friends or business connections. The coffin, draped with a plain black cloth, was placed in a room looking out upon the garden, and on the right of the entrance to this apartment there was a sort of stand with twelve ducks and a number of crayfish (the latter alive) upon it. The funeral procession was headed by a person carrying a long white streamer, having on it the name of the deceased. Then came twelve priests, six of whom bore white and the other six red banners. Following these priests were about 200 coolies bearing bouquets of flowers, then a sort of kango containing offerings, the use of which was afterwards apparent, and then a band—or more properly, perhaps, a sort of choir—consisting of seven persons, playing on Japanese musical instruments. After a detachment of soldiers came the hearse, draped in white, and then more soldiers, the relatives and friends of deceased, and the general public. Not the least interesting feature in the long procession were the widow and her three children, who were all dressed in white silk crape, with their hair hanging down and bound with white paper.

"On arriving at the cemetery, our informant found that a sort of pavilion holding about sixty persons had been erected round the grave, over which was a kind of bier, kept in place above the opening by ropes. The coffin was placed in front of the bier, and the priests—arrayed, with one exception, in white robes and conical gauze hats—seated themselves to the right and left of it. Next to the priests, on the left-hand side, were the widow and female mourners, the band being stationed on the right. To the right of the hearse was placed a magnificent vase containing artificial flowers.

"The funeral ceremonies were commenced by the band playing a dirge, which continued during the remainder of the service. A young priest, bearing a vessel of white unlacquered wood containing water, stepped in front of the hearse, and dipping in two of his fingers sprinkled a little water towards the four cardinal points. Another priest then brought a tray, also of white wood, on which were two earthen bottles containing saké. This tray was decorated with sprigs of laburnum, and so were all the other vessels used in the ceremonial. The priest raised the tray slowly to the level of his head, and then presented it to another priest, who received it reverently and placed it on a stand in front of the hearse. Offerings of rice, mochi, tai, and various kinds of other fish—all on separate trays—were taken from the kango and placed on the stand before the hearse, with the same ceremony as in the case of the saké. After these came offerings consisting of a rabbit, two doves, seaweed, grapes, pears, &c., in all about twenty different articles. The priests who performed this portion of the service had their mouths covered with paper, in order that their breath should not contaminate the offerings. The band now ceased playing, and the head priest stepped in front of the coffin and thrice made obeisance, the attendant priests following him in turn. He then took a wand of white wood, and holding it almost in a perpendicular position towards the coffin between his thumbs and forefingers, he again bowed three times. Another priest now came forward and read a kind of funeral oration, eulogising the deceased, and referring to his birth, travels abroad, his important services, &c., concluding with a prayer that he might enter the rest awaiting all devout followers of the Shinto faith. When the priest ceased speaking, the widow came in front of the hearse. She carried a sprig of laburnum, and after raising it to her head, placed it among the other offerings. The relations and chief mourners then followed her example in turn, and this observance brought the funeral ceremonies to a conclusion."

A S supplementing the memoir of Bishop Rawle, the Bishop of Antigua sends to us a brief account of the impressive scene at his funeral, in the following extract from a letter dated Barbados, May 26, 1889 :—

"The funeral of Bishop Rawle was a most imposing, and at the same time picturesque one. The funeral procession moved away from the College at half-past

CHAPEL ON THE CODRINGTON ESTATE.

five in the evening, just as it was getting cool and pleasant. No hearse was used.
Black men brought the coffin from the College up the long winding hill, so that we
who were awaiting its arrival at the top of the hill could hear the College bell tolling,
and every now and then catch a glimpse of the procession winding up the steep ascent.
The procession was formed by the students of the College in surplices walking two
and two in front of the coffin, headed by one of their number bearing a tall wooden
cross; and behind the coffin followed a good many clergymen in surplices walking in
order. When the procession got to the churchyard, the surpliced clergymen took the
place of the black bearers and carried the coffin into the church. The service was
choral. The lesson was read by the Archdeacon, and the grave service by the Bishop.
At the end, the hymn was sung, 'Now the labourer's task is o'er.' This brought the
Service to a close. . . . . The spot selected for his grave was one very suitable for
him who had spent so many years as the Principal of the College. It is to the north
of the chapel, and from its elevated position commands a beautiful view of the
College; and it was also a favourite spot where Mr. Rawle and his wife used to sit
when the Sunday School was over. . . . . The College has lost a friend indeed in
Bishop Rawle!"

R EALLY the Bishop of Guiana is a marvel. The Bishop, who was
ordained in 1830, and, being consecrated as long ago as the
year 1842, is the Senior Bishop of the Anglican Communion, con-
templates, and with God's help will doubtless carry out, the following
plan :—

" On Sunday next I enter upon the task I have set myself to do, and which, with
only slight breaks here and there, will give me employment to the close of November.
During this time I shall be occupying strange beds or using my hammock in the bush,
as we term the forest, for eighty-one nights; but I am well and hearty, and I confidently
expect to get through my Visitation pleasantly, and as I hope, with some benefit to
the diocese."

S HWEBO in Upper Burma is the station of a Medical Mission
founded two years ago. The Bishop and the late Rev. J. A.
Colbeck were impressed by the importance of the place, and its suitable-
ness for a Mission centre. Accordingly in July 1887 the Rev. F. W.
Sutton, who is a qualified medical man, inaugurated the work. Shwebo
is a city with about 24,000 inhabitants, who are very poor and uncivilised, superstitious and ignorant. The medical work has won the
admiration of the people, and as Mr. and Mrs. Sutton are determined
not to let the medical character of the institution overshadow the
missionary, we may hope that a wide door will prove to have been
opened here. Our readers will be interested in the accompanying
reproduction of a photograph which Mr. Sutton has sent to us. It
represents him and his wife with some of the first natives who were
gathered to them.

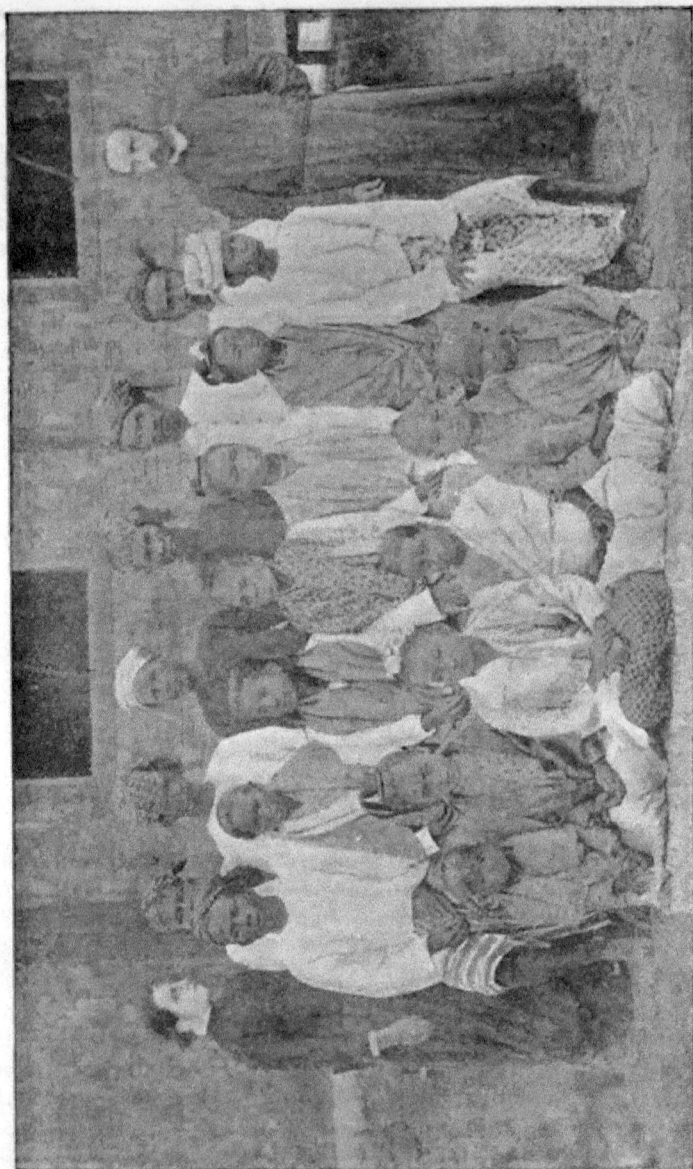

almost his last act was to send his subscription, which reached the
Society after he had passed away. Mrs. Harvey had died but eleven

hours before him, and their son-in-law, the Rev. Mowbray Trotter, writes :—

"Dear Mrs. Harvey was a true partner of his joys and sorrows, and has surely entered 'side by side' with him into our Father's Home. It will, I think, interest you to know that the accompanying cheque is the result of the offertory in my church of St. Mary de Crypt, Gloucester, at an early Communion last Tuesday (July 2), the day when we laid our dear ones to rest. Just a few friends met together with our family that morning, and it was thought that no better object could be selected than the Society for the Propagation of the Gospel to which to send the offertory, he having to the end entertained such love for the work of the S.P.G."

SUGGESTED SUBJECTS FOR PRAYER.

For the Missions exposed to peril in Eastern Africa, for the steadfastness of the converts, and for a happy issue out of all the tribulations.

For the Province of Rupertsland, that the Church may be enabled to advance in the several dioceses, and that the scattered settlers may be preserved true to the faith.

For Codrington College, and for the building up of the clergy and people of the West Indian Church in grace and knowledge, in spite of their trials and poverty.

For the Society, that blessings may result from its anniversary, that more prayers and alms may be offered in its behalf, and enlarged success attend its labours.

MONTHLY MEETING.

The Monthly Meeting of the Society was held at 19 Delahay Street, on Friday, June 21, at 2 P.M., the Lord Bishop of Chichester in the chair. There were also present the Earl of Belmore, Lord Robartes, General Sir J. Lintorn A. Simmons, G.C.B., Rev. B. Belcher, and H. W. Prescott, Esq., *Vice-Presidents* ; Canon Betham, Sir Henry E. Cartwright, Canon Churton, J. M. Clabon, Esq., Prebendary Codrington, D.D., Canon Elwyn, General Gillilan, Colonel Hardy, J. R. Kindersley, Esq., General Lowry, C.B., Prebendary Forrest, D.D., General Sawyer, General Tremenheere, C.B., and S. Wreford, Esq., *Members of the Standing Committee* ; the Rev. C. Baker, Rev. S. Blackburne, Rev. Joseph Clarke, Rev. J. C. Cowd, Dr. R. N. Cust, Rev. T. Darling, T. Dunn, Esq., J. C. Eckersley, Esq., Rev. J. J. Elkington, Rev. Dr. Finch, Rev. A. O. Hardy, Rev. R. S. Hassard, Rev. T. Hill, Rev. S. C. Hore, Rev. J. H. C. McGill, General Nicolls, Rev. H. Rowley, W. B. Simonds, Esq., Rev. W. Wallace, Rev. T. J. Williams, and the Rev. R. R. Winter, *Members of the Society.*

1. After prayers, the minutes of the last meeting were read.

2. The Treasurers presented the abstract of receipts and payments from January 1 to May 31, printed on page 280 of *The Mission Field*.

3. The following resolution relative to the decease of the late Bishop Rawle was adopted unanimously :—

"The Society for the Propagation of the Gospel, having been informed of the decease on the 11th ulto. of the Right Reverend Bishop Rawle, desires to thank Almighty God, the Giver of all good gifts, for the noble work which, by Divine grace, the late Bishop Rawle was enabled to accomplish.

"While the West Indian Province will long acknowledge itself indebted to him for the training of some generations of its Clergy at Codrington College, Barbados, for the inception of its Mission to the West Coast of Africa, and for his wise Episcopal rule in the youngest of its Dioceses, the whole Anglican Communion will cherish the noble example of one, who combined with profound learning a simple childlike faith by which he consecrated without reserve his great intellectual powers and all that he had to the glory of God."

4. The Rev. R. R. Winter, from Delhi, addressed the members. He said that the difficulty in dealing with Hindus lay less in misbelief than in want of belief. There is a moral difficulty, affecting the conception of the Divine nature, which is taken to be neither good nor evil, and therefore indifferent to evil. This excludes the sense of a personal God, the sense of responsibility, and the moral sense. Mr. Winter next discussed the question of the best agency to be employed. He urged the multiplying of native agency, and said that if the proportion of European workers to native is unduly large, the tendency is to produce a moral slackness among the native agents, who are only too ready to work in mere submission to directions. He advised the formation of sub-centres, and the fostering of the idea of the Church as the true basis and centre of Mission operations. Lastly, he strongly urged the importance of women's work in the Missions, which the native family system renders so imperatively necessary, expressing a hope that several English ladies may volunteer to join the band of workers already at Delhi.

5. The Rev. J. R. Hill, from Cawnpore, in the Diocese of Calcutta, also addressed the meeting. He began by giving a brief historical account of the Cawnpore Mission, saying that in the Mutiny all belonging to it were killed except two. At the end of 1860, Mr. Barrell had gathered some 20 souls around him; they were mostly connected with the old disbanded Sepoy regiments, and had come to Cawnpore from other stations. Now there are 400 Christians, and these are all perfectly independent of the Mission in temporal matters and self-supporting, the cotton and other mills and factories of Cawnpore having provided them with employment according to their merits, thus solving one of the gravest of the former difficulties and relieving the Mission of a trying responsibility, for most of our people are the grown-up children of the Orphanage, which was reopened in 1861 owing to famine in the surrounding districts. The boys' section of this orphanage was removed to Rurki in 1875. The girls' orphanage remains, but is much reduced in numbers, only some 20 orphans remaining in it ; but it has begun to turn itself into a boarding-school for children whose parents are living and who pay for them, and its classes are also attended by day scholars. This connects it with the work of the Ladies' Association of the S.P.G., who have three agents at Cawnpore, besides several subordinate workers.

The educational work in the town, which contains 170,000 inhabitants, has been very successful ; and in face of the powerful opposition of a Government and other secular schools, Christ Church School has held its ground and prospered, and thrown out branch schools in the town. Its pupils now number 350, and, what is of much greater importance than their success at the Government and University examinations, they have increasingly come forward for baptism. From 1860 to 1880 there were only numbered four converts from the school, and two of these fled to Allahabad and Benares to be baptized ; but since 1880 they have been more numerous, and in the last eight months Mr. Hill has had the happiness of baptizing six young men from the school, five of whom were Brahmans. The importance of the school work will be understood from the fact that the pupils often remain in the upper classes up to twenty or twenty-three years of age—the object being to pass at least the entrance examination of the university—so that the Mission has not to deal with boys only but with young men also; and it is obvious that the opportunity of converting them is in proportion to the length of their course. The Government Inspectors are urging us to build new class rooms; this is necessary, not only for the future development of the school, but for present requirements, the rooms being overcrowded.

The Cawnpore Mission has thrown out *Out-stations* also, the places where the work has crystallised in the missionaries' annual preaching-tours. The chief of these is Banda, having 36 native Christians. Here the Society has a school also, which last year yielded its first convert, a lad of the first class, seventeen years old. The native deacon, Abdul Ali, is in charge, assisted by a Bengali head-master from Bishop's College. Next in importance is Orai. The work here has grown very rapidly in the last three years—the native Christians are over 30 in number.

It is most desirable that the Society should occupy Jhansi, to which Orai is the half-way from Cawnpore. Jhansi, originally about the same size as Banda, is rapidly increasing, having been selected by Government as the great military and political centre of those regions, and by the Indian Midland Railway Company as the centre of their system.

6. An interesting discussion ensued, principally on the subject of education in India; and the statement having been made that Government educational officials had been known to speak and act in opposition to Christianity, it was agreed to bring the matter under the notice of the Standing Committee.

7. All the Candidates proposed at the meeting in April were elected into the Corporation. The following were proposed for election in October:—

Capt. J. W. F. Harvey, R.N., Stonehenge, Ashburton Road, Southsea, Hants; Rev. C. R. Bingham, Litcham, Swaffham; Rev. Langford S. R. Browne, St. Petrox, Dartmouth; Dr. Axford, Warwick House, Clarence Parade, Southsea; Rev. Norman Pares, Prescote, Southsea; Rev. F. J. Huyshe, Wimborne; Rev. F. H. Slocock, Mottisfont, Romsey; Rev. James McCall Marshall, Cathedral School, Durham; John Pares, Esq., Westfield, Southsea; Rev. W. G. C. Hodgson, Distington, Whitehaven; Rev. Archibald J. Campbell Connell, Monk's Eleigh, Bildeston S.O., Suffolk; Rev. Charles Dickens Gordon, Walsham-le-Willows, Bury St. Edmunds; Rev. S. C. Campbell, Weasenham, Brandon; Rev. E. J. Harper, Stoke Holy Cross, Norwich; Rev. A. J. Hunter, Mattishall, Dereham; Rev. H. B. Johnson, Welbourne, Dereham; Rev. G. P. Trevelyan, Wolverton St. Mary, Stony Stratford; Rev. C. O. Gordon, Goosnargh, Preston, Lancashire; Rev. J. S. L. Burn, All Saints, Middlesborough, Yorkshire; and Rev. W. C. Hawksley, North Ormesby, Middlesborough. Yorkshire.

SOCIETY'S INCOME.

Abstract of RECEIPTS *and* PAYMENTS *from January 1 to June 30.*

	GENERAL FUND	SPECIAL FUNDS
Subscriptions, Donations, Collections, &c., ...	£14,440	£5,105
Legacies	4,126	107
Dividends, Rents, &c....	2,023	2,121
TOTAL RECEIPTS	£20,589	£7,333
PAYMENTS	£42,840	£8,756

The Receipts under the head of Subscriptions, Donations, and Collections for the General Fund from January 1 to June 30, in five consecutive years, compare as follows: 1885, £14,897 * 1886, £14,410; 1887, £15,467.; 1888, £14,070* ; 1889, £14,440.

* In addition, the Treasurers received in 1888 Securities of the value of £25,296 as "A Thankoffering to Almighty God for the extension of the Church in the Colonies and Dependencies of the British Empire and beyond it"; also other Securities of the value of £2,268 as a Trust Gift, *the Income only being available.*

THE MISSION FIELD.

THE FIELD IS THE WORLD. THE SEED IS THE WORD OF GOD.

SEPTEMBER 2, 1889.

THE CONVERSION OF ENGLAND.

STUDY of contemporary Missionary enterprise can rightly exclude neither history nor forecast. It is as necessary for a due appreciation of the expansive work now being done by the Church that we should have some knowledge of the way in which she has attained her existing empire, as that we should be inspirited by the certain universality of its future. It is but an apathetic mind that can contemplate the noble river of Christian truth now before our eyes, without its flowing motion exciting any curiosity either as to its course from its Pentecostal fountain, or its onward current from our present standpoint with ever-widening volume until, like the waters covering the sea, it emerges from restricting banks and overspreads the earth with the knowledge of God.

English Christianity has its history stretching back nearly as far as any Christianity. It is claimed that the Light shone on this land during the first century. Although the traditions of St. Joseph of Arimathea, of Linus and Claudia, and of St. Paul may not rank as history, there are sufficient corroborative circumstances to make historians treat the legends with respect, and to point to the conclusion that, by whatever Missionaries the Gospel was brought, it reached our land in the earliest ages. As the epoch of traditions expands into that of history, we find the British Church covering the land. At the Council of Arles, in the year 314, there were three British Bishops present, those of York, London, and a See that was probably Caerleon, thus representing each of the three great civil divisions. Geoffrey of Monmouth says that these leading Bishops had as many as eight-and-twenty suffragans. British Bishops were probably also at the memorable Council of Nicæa in 325, and they certainly were at the Council of Ariminum in 360. The Church had strong centres of learning and Missionary force at Glastonbury, St. Albans, and many other places, and doubtless brought into her fold the whole British race. The fact that England was actually a Christian country in these early centuries is in many respects of great importance.

It is the more necessary to emphasise it from the way in which the original conversion of England has been lost sight of in the conversion, some centuries afterwards, of the heathen Teuton races—Jutes, Saxons, and Angles—who invaded the country.

Their invasions were gradual, and were spread over nearly a century and a half. They took place in the following order. In the year 449 the heathen Jutes from Northern Denmark settled in Kent on the invitation of the (Christian) British King Vortigern, who assigned that district to them in reward for their help against the Picts and Scots. In 477 Saxons who came from land to the South of Denmark, took Sussex, and, about 530, other Saxons occupied Essex.

In 547 the Angles, who came from the land between that of the Jutes and that of the Saxons, occupied Northumbria, and in 585 other Angles began to settle in East Anglia and Mercia.

Thus these Teutonic invaders possessed the whole of the Eastern and central parts of the country from North to South. Northumbria extended from the Forth to the Humber; from its borders stretched Mercia southward to the Thames; East Anglia comprised Norfolk and Suffolk, Essex being to the South of it. Across the Thames Kent was held by the Jutes; Sussex included the present county of the name with Surrey; from it Wessex stretched westwards into Hampshire, Dorset, Berks, and Wiltshire.

The Britons, and with them Christianity, were driven westwards, retaining Wales, Devon, and Cornwall, and for a long time the whole or part of Shropshire, Hereford, Monmouth, Gloucester, Somerset, and other counties. In the North-west, Lancashire, Cumberland, and Westmoreland remained in their hands, forming part of the great district of Strathclyde.

The Teutonic invasions, great as they were, by no means covered the whole country; nor were the Britons driven at first as far towards the West as they were when the Heptarchy was fully established.

We have now to sketch briefly the evangelisation of the Teutons. The earliest settlers were the first to receive Christianity. In the year 597 St. Augustine converted Ethelbert, the Jute King of Kent; and the conversion of Kent was eventually the sole direct result of his mission. Sebert, King of the East Saxons, was a nephew of Ethelbert, by whose advice he received Mellitus, one of St. Augustine's band; but his work was completely overthrown twelve years later by Sebert's sons. Paulinus, another of the Augustinian Missionaries, was consecrated Bishop for Northumbria on the marriage of Edwin, King of that country, with Ethelburga, the daughter of Ethelbert. A like disaster, however, overtook this Mission; for Penda, the heathen King of Mercia, completely destroyed it seven years afterwards; King Edwin was killed in battle, and the Bishop, Paulinus, fled. Before this happened, Paulinus had converted Eorpwald, the King of East Anglia, but his nobles were unwilling to follow his example, and killed him.

The result, therefore, of the Augustinian Mission was the conversion of Kent, and abortive Missions to Essex, Northumbria, and East Anglia. Mercia, Sussex, and Wessex were untouched. That St. Augustine's Mission thus produced the conversion of Kent alone is a fact worthy of notice both for correcting misleading exaggerations of the extent to which the conversion of England is due to that Mission, and for replying to those who think that a comparison of the success of ancient and modern Missions must be to the disadvantage of the latter.

The actual conversion of the Saxons and Angles took place by degrees, and in the following way :—

Sigbert, a brother of Eorpwald, the murdered King of East Anglia, had fled to Gaul. There he was converted from heathenism, and on becoming king in succession to his brother, invited Felix of Burgundy to East Anglia. Felix obtained the Pope's sanction, and, aided by the Celtic Missionary Fursey, succeeded in the work, founding the See of Dunwich, which was afterwards transferred to Norwich.

Oswald, who eventually succeeded Edwin as King of Northumbria (having fled to Scotland when Edwin, as yet a heathen, had robbed Oswald's father of his kingdom of Bernicia), had become a Christian at Iona. On gaining the throne he sent to that cradle of the faith for Celtic Missionaries, and in 635 St. Aidan became Bishop for Northumbria, with his seat at Lindisfarne.

Birinus, from Gaul, went to convert Wessex in 634. In the following year Oswald, the Christian King of Northumbria, sought in marriage the hand of the daughter of Cynegils, King of Wessex. By his persuasion and that of Birinus Cynegils was baptized at Dorchester in Oxford, where Birinus fixed his See.

The influence of the King of Northumbria also produced the conversion of Essex and Middlesex, the king of that district being persuaded by him to become a Christian. He asked for teachers from Lindisfarne, and St. Cedd was sent, who, in 654, revived the See of London, which had been founded twice before ; the first time by the original British Church, and the second time by Mellitus.

Mercia was converted by a Mission from Lindisfarne, Diuma being consecrated Bishop for that great central kingdom in 656.

The consecration of Theodore to the Archbishopric of Canterbury in 669 was an important epoch in the history of the English Church. He consolidated the Church, subdivided the dioceses, created the parochial system, and held the great Synods of the whole English Church at Hertford in 673, and Hatfield in 680.

It is remarkable that one important district, and that, one which lay next to Kent, was actually left without any Missionary operations until after this. It was not until the year 681 that Wilfrid, who, though a Roman partisan, was a Lindisfarne monk, began the conversion of Sussex, fixing his See at Selsey, whence it was afterwards transferred to Chichester.

We can now sum up the results of the various Missions. Wales, Devon, and Cornwall, and the counties adjoining, having Celtic or " British " Christianity, the north-western districts also retaining theirs in connection with Iona, and Kent being converted by the Mission of St. Augustine, the remainder of the whole of the country in time became Christian. Northumbria, Essex, Middlesex, and Mercia were converted entirely by Celtic Missionaries ; East Anglia by Felix of Burgundy, aided by Fursey, the Celtic Missionary ; Wessex by Birinus from Gaul, aided by Northumbrian influence ; and Sussex by Wilfrid, after the consolidation of the whole of the rest of the Church under Theodore.

Even this extremely brief summary serves to suggest some important reflections. It is not uncommon for those who have little acquaintance with the history to regard English Christianity as really owing its existence to Pope Gregory sending St. Augustine ; and in view of Roman pretensions it is useful for it to be seen how (originally) the country was wholly occupied by non-Roman Christianity, and (afterwards) how largely the conversion of the Saxons and Angles was due to non-Roman Missions. The whole of the West (from north to south) belonged to

the British Church, being entirely independent of any Roman origin ;
while the re-conversion of the rest of the country after the Teutonic
invasions was mainly effected by the Celtic Missionaries, who had, of
course, nothing to do with Rome.   Two of the smaller kingdoms were
converted by Continental Missionaries with Celtic aid, and Kent alone
was made Christian by the Augustinian band.   To this it may be added
that Theodore's organisation made the whole Church with its double
origin (British or Celtic, and Roman) one National Church, and that it
was in his days, and for long afterwards, under no bondage to the See of
Rome (though in full communion with it and the rest of Western
Christendom) any more than the Church of the United States in our
days is under bondage to the See of Canterbury.

Apart from this, more practical lessons are to be learnt.   They are
of an encouraging nature.   What could have seemed more like a death-
blow to Christianity in our land than the Teutonic invasions ?   Yet
what was their final result ?   They did not destroy British Christianity,
but moved westwards the British Christians, leaving their land to be
occupied by heathen, who in turn were to be converted.

Then the failures of the Missions of Paulinus and Mellitus surely
should teach those who fear or experience failure, that they should not
think their great cause will fail, though a particular endeavour may seem
to come to nought.   Do not many modern Missions, such, for instance, as
that of Mandalay, exemplify the same thing with an even happier sequel ?

Further, the length of time occupied by the conversion of England
supplies a cogent reply to those who complain of the rate of progress
now.   The work began in the first century, but it was not until nearly
the end of the seventh century that the Church was organised, and the
whole land won.   Even that is really too early a date, for in the following
centuries the Danes seemed almost to undo all the work.   It was as late
as A.D. 1012 that St. Alphege was martyred by them.   Modern Missions
in Equatorial and Southern Africa have suffered from wars and fightings.
We may be encouraged by reflecting how much solid work has been
accomplished by them in spite of the troubles, when we recall the more
crushing reverses endured by our spiritual forefathers with ultimate
triumph for Christian truth.

These are but instances of lessons to be deduced from the history of
the evangelisation of England.   Our object in giving a brief outline of it
will have been attained (even though no particular teaching were
suggested by it) if we have been able to help some of our readers to
realise more truly that the Missionary energy which is now spreading
the Gospel in Asia, Africa, and the isles of the sea is, with clear continuity, the same as that which, having burst forth at Pentecost in
Jerusalem, came to quicken our land centuries ago.   As it has done in
the past, so it will certainly now impart the true Life to all lands of the
earth that are as yet without the knowledge of the victory over evil which
they are to share.

MANDALAY REVISITED.

BY THE REV. DR. MARKS.

OU and very many of your readers will remember how, twenty years ago, in 1869, it pleased God to make an opening for Mission work in the capital of the then strange and but little known kingdom of Burma. In a marvellous and most unexpected manner the King, *Mindoon Min*, invited me up to Mandalay, there to exercise my vocation as a Christian priest and teacher, promising to build me a church, clergy house, and boarding and day schools, to send his sons and young nobility to me to be taught, and to support the school as a royal foundation. No one was more surprised than I at these promises, which people in India and Burma greatly doubted, and smiled incredulously when I made my report of my first interview with His Burmese Majesty. But Bishop Milman, Sir John Lawrence, General Fytche, and Captain (now Colonel Sir Edward) Sladen believed that the King would perform what he had promised. I had no doubt as to the buildings and the beginnings of things, but I felt grave uncertainty as to their continuance. What the King's motives were time alone revealed; you know the story. You remember that the King built, or rather allowed me to build, the beautiful church, the large and commodious clergy house, and the two sets of schools; and how during four years of my sojourn in his capital he let me want for nothing. You remember how he faithfully fulfilled every promise; how Bishop Milman came and consecrated the church, and how our Most Gracious Queen-Empress sent out a beautiful font to mark her sense of the kindness of the King in providing a Christian church in his capital.

You will remember too that the King, according to his promise, sent me nine of his sons, amongst whom was Thee Baw Prince, whose record from our school register I give below.[*] Of course at that time we had not the slightest idea that the dark, intelligent, quick-tempered, but

* Extracts from the Register of the S.P.G. Royal School, Mandalay :—

No. 27, THEE BAW PRINCE, Buddhist, no English school, October 12, son of H.M. the King of Burma and the Loung Shway Queen.

5 July, 1869.—Sent by H.M. the King with Prince Mine Tone and Prince Shway Koo.

28 „ „ A royal house for the Princes' accommodation, built in the compound by the King.

31 „ „ H.M. sent to ask leave of absence for the Princes every Sabbath day. Reply, " It is not our custom, but it will be granted if insisted on." It was not insisted on.

4 Aug., „ Went with royal brothers and J. E. Marks over the King's steamer.

1 Sept., „ Present with Mine Tone Prince to represent the King at the laying the foundation stone of the English Church by Major Sladen, British Resident.

otherwise amiable young Prince schoolboy, who played cricket and polo with us, and always held my hand as we walked into the palace, would be the successor of the good Mindoon Min, or the infamous blood-stained tyrant whom British power has hurled from his throne, which he so disgraced.

After about four years the old King began to tire of his last amusement. The discovery of two conspiracies amongst his elder sons made him fear to have the younger Princes go so far every day from the palace. We tried the experiment of a palace school. I soon gave that up personally, and sent an assistant instead, who, of course, could not manage a dozen self-willed young Princes. But the other school went on, all the fuller for the absence of royalties, and the King continued to pay for it, though with diminishing zeal and regularity. At last he fell greatly into arrears, and then he asked what use it was to him politically, and I had to reply *none*. He then proposed that I should go home grandly in his own sea-going steamer, with one or two of the Princes, and ask our Queen-Empress to restore to him Rangoon or Bassein, that he might have a seaport of his own. To show him the absurdity of such a proposal was not an easy or a grateful task. He was accustomed to say, *Sic volo, sic jubeo*, and it angered him to think that a scheme which he had thought over for years, and from which he had expected so much, should be thus flouted. It was a great disappointment, and he readily seized upon one or two of those little disagreements which had never been wholly absent, but which had only arisen to be talked over and adjusted, to send me word that I was no longer wanted, in fact, that it would not be safe for me to stay longer in Mandalay. This was on April 10, 1874. Of course I took no notice of the order to quit, or of the accompanying threat, but stayed on till relieved by the Rev. John Fairclough in January 1875. James A. Colbeck had joined me as a layman in March 1874, and his cheerful, manly courage was very sustaining and comforting in those anxious days. I do not believe that we were ever in any danger. Occasionally attempts were made to frighten us, but we had neither bolts to our gates nor doors to the house. Bishop Milman wrote to me urgently, "Lord Northbrook (the Viceroy) has just come into my room with an open letter from the Chief Commissioner of Burma, saying that your life is in danger, and begging me, for fear of complications between the two Governments, to recall you at once. I replied that it

---

2 Sept., 1869.—Went in a royal barge with J. E. Marks to visit the Flotilla's steamer "Colonel Fytche," Captain Bacon kindly welcomed him on board.

26 March, 1870.—Commenced to have English school in the palace, John E. Marks teaching.

April, 1871.—Moung Bah Tsee appointed palace teacher.

  ,,   1873.—Ceased to learn English and entered Buddhist Monastery

  ,,   1878.—Ascended the throne of Burma on the death of King Mindoon Min.

25 Nov., 1885.—Dethroned by General Sir Harry Prendergast and Colonel Sladen, and sent to Rangoon on board Irrawaddy Flotilla steamer "Thooreah," then deported to Ruttenaghury.

was not our custom to recall Missionaries from their posts at the first appearance of danger. That you had my full permission to retire if you thought it necessary to do so, but that while you judge it needful for your work to remain in Mandalay, I should support you in so doing. But pray let me advise caution, &c."

Mr. Fairclough relieved me in January 1875, and on the 9th I said " Good-bye to Mandalay." As my diary reminds me, " I went into the church in the early morning to return thanks for all God's mercies to me there, and to seek His pardon for all shortcomings." I must confess that I took a *stern* view of the royal city from the steamer. The annoyances and anxieties of the last year had done much to efface the kindness and liberality which I had experienced from the King in the first four years of my residence. I said, half in anger and half in jest, " I will not come here again until Mandalay is a British town." My hearers laughed, but neither they nor I thought that my words would be literally fulfilled. I reached Rangoon on the 19th, and resumed my work as Principal of St. John's. I went home to England, my second visit, in May (and returned in January 1876). Colbeck took charge of St. John's. On my return Fairclough went home, the Rev. C. H. Chard relieving him at Mandalay (1877). Then, on his accepting a Government chaplaincy, Mr. Colbeck took up the work at the Burmese capital, which he held till after the horrible palace massacres. You can well remember how nobly and bravely he bore himself during that awful time, and how he rescued many of the royal family from those who were thirsting for their blood. Acting under orders he withdrew with the British Resident, and went on with his work in Maulmein. Mandalay was left without an Anglican clergyman, and our beautiful church and buildings were left to the mercy of the Burmese. Colbeck brought away with him all the portable property that he could take from the church and used it in his mission, at Maulmein.

I need not detail the events which led to the third Burmese war in 1885. Sir Henry Prendergast led what was not inaptly called "a military picnic" up the Irrawaddy, meeting with the very slightest opposition. The King Theebaw had been kept in "a fool's paradise" with lying reports by those who were working his ruin, and are now reaping the reward of their treachery in Mandalay. The old Queen (the mother of Soopyalat, Theebaw's consort) assured me that until he heard the cannonading at Myingan the King had no idea that hostilities had really begun. Mandalay, Theebaw, and the army capitulated at once—only too quickly for our rulers. We took Mandalay long before we knew what we were going to do with it. Theebaw surrendered, and we sent him to Rangoon, and kept him on board a steamer, waiting to know what to do with him. The army, only very partially disarmed, was allowed to go off as the men chose. No effort was made to intern them, to enlist

SHRINE ERECTED OVER THE BODY OF KING MIN-DOON-MIN.

[Mission Field,
  Sept. 2, 1889.

them under the British flag, or to give them work. And so, without employment, or pay, or control, they naturally took to dacoity, and became the nucleus of bands which have kept the country in a disturbed state ever since.

On November 16, 1885, Bishop Strachan convened a meeting of Messrs. Fairclough, Chard and myself to consider about renewing the Mission at Mandalay, I thought that as I was the beginner of that Mission I had a right to take my turn there again under the altered circumstances of the capital, but the Bishop said that he had requested Mr. James Colbeck to go up again. Mr. Colbeck went up and resided in the Mission buildings, which were far less hurt by dilapidation and ill-usage than might have been expected. The Queen's Font was over-turned, and the small columns supporting it had been stolen, windows had been broken, and doors got off their hinges, but no great damage had been done. In reply to all suggestions to destroy or alienate the buildings, Theebaw (to his credit be it said) had always answered, " No, let them alone, I went to school there."

Of Mr. Colbeck's work in Mandalay amongst the Burmese and Europeans, how earnest, how zealous, how self-denying he was, how he found time for everything, it is not for me now to speak. His success amongst the Burmese was to my mind perilously great, and I was not alone in urging upon him his need for caution.

I had longed to revisit Mandalay ; especially was I anxious to do so when, in such an unexpected manner, my young friend and pupil had become king. I set out on my voyage in 1878, but when I reached Thayetmyo, our then frontier station, telegrams from the Prime Minister, the *Kin Woon Min Gyee,* forbade my further progress, and even threat-ened violence if I should persist in my plan. You gave a full account of this incident in the " Mission Field " at the time. I have since been well assured by the Queen-Mother and several ex-ministers that King Theebaw knew nothing of this incident, that he often expressed his wonder that I did not come to see him. Had I been allowed access to him then things might have gone very differently with him.

You are aware that one of the first exploits of the British Government in the newly annexed kingdom of Burma has been the narrow gauge railway which unites Mandalay to Rangoon *viâ* Toungoo, a distance of 222 miles (in all 386 miles). This work was pushed on with almost American rapidity, and in spite of cholera, dysentery, dacoits, and other difficulties the Mandalay extension was ready for its ceremonial opening on February 27. As I am at present chaplain of the Burma State Railway, in addition to my other duties, I was favoured with an invitation to attend the grand opening. A party of about forty gentlemen left Rangoon by a special train on the evening of the 25th, and travelling all night and the following day reached Mandalay, having previously been joined by Sir Chas. Crosthwaite, the Chief Commissioner, the Bishop of Rangoon, Sir Chas. Elliott, and other gentlemen.

On the platform of the Mandalay terminus I had the great pleasure to meet under their grand banner the boys of the S.P.G. Royal School, with the Revs. Geo. Colbeck, Whitehead, and Stockings, my brother Missionaries, together with the Government chaplain, who remembered me from a lecture I gave in 1875 in the Liverpool College, where he was then a pupil. After the opening ceremonies, the breakfast and the speeches, I got into a gharry and went off to find my old residence. But so utterly changed was the place from the Mandalay that I left fourteen years ago, that I actually lost my way, and it was not without difficulty and adventure that I at last got to the place. It was the same, yet greatly altered. The deep and rapid stream, the Shway T'chyoung, upon which my boys and I used to row in our double-banked twelve-oared boat in front of the school, is now a miserable little ditch, the royal fence which marked our Mission compound as a King's foundation has given way to a light railing, and the British Residency, which adjoins the S.P.G. compound, looks very seedy and dilapidated. But I was very pleased to be in the place again. I knew every post and plank and piece of carved work in the buildings, and it seemed so strange thus, after fourteen years' absence, to come back. I soon found my way into the church, and gladly remained there awhile by myself. It and the other buildings are much out of repair. These buildings and those of St. John's College were erected at the same time, and both are of teak timber. Our college was built by skilled Chinese carpenters under European surveillance. The original buildings (except the church) were roughly put together by Burmese unskilled carpenters, though I continuously improved the houses all the time I was there. Our college buildings are in perfect order, in fact their value is quadrupled, or more. But then we keep at least one carpenter regularly at work, and we are always adding and improving. We have never had such a break in occupation as occurred between James Colbeck's leaving and return to Mandalay. I believe that a considerable sum was expended to make the Mission habitable, but very much still needs to be done to preserve the buildings and to prevent their total collapse. A sum of about £350 is urgently required. Shall I be presumptuous in hoping that some of those many friends who knew me in 1875 (my last visit home), and who listened with interest to my story of Mandalay, will now come forward with help? Surely English Christians will not be less liberal than was a Buddhist King. I should feel deeply grateful if this appeal should meet with any response. I should so like to come home once again and plead for Burma. As I write, the *heim veh*, the "home longing," is very strong upon me; it is nearly fourteen years since my last visit. But I have got this great school and still greater orphanage upon my

PAGODA BUILT OVER THE THRONE ENTRANCE TO THE PALACE.

shoulders, and each year the burden grows greater, and my hopes of a
visit home grow less. But this by the way.

The bell rang for Evensong, and I was delighted again to take part
in the service in my old church. A goodly congregation of Christian
Burmans assembled. Colbeck and Whitehead sang service, and I
preached in Burmese from the words, " Lord, I have loved the habitation
of Thy house and the place where Thine honour dwelleth."

After service Colbeck and I walked to the cemetery to visit the grave
of dear James Colbeck. The road was covered with several inches of
white dust. I cannot easily forget the time when Bishop Milman, Mr.
Hardy, his chaplain, Captain Sladen, and I, with several others, went to
consecrate the little corner that the Roman Catholics gave us for our
cemetery. We had to wade part of the way, be poled in rafts the other
part, and walk the remainder, and the Consecration Service was
read from the top of the unfinished wall, which had two or three feet of
water on either side. But by the help of the Government of India I was
enabled greatly to improve the little plot, to raise it above high water
mark, to build a tight gate, and to plant it with flowering shrubs. Every
Sunday morning after service, while we were together, James Colbeck and
I used to walk to the cemetery to see that it was properly cared for.
We little thought that on my revisit after fourteen years' absence I
should stand by his grave. A simple mound of earth was all that marks
his resting-place, but I believe a suitable memorial will soon be erected.

We had very many visitors. All seemed to know me, and Burmans
know how to stay. Many of my old St. John's boys, who are in Government and other situations in Mandalay, came to see their old teacher,
and right glad was I to welcome them. Each gave his history, and
amongst them they presented me with nearly 500 rupees for the Rangoon
Orphanage. The next morning I assisted at a celebration of the Holy
Communion, and spent a pleasant hour or so in my old school. There
were no princes, but there was the usual congeries of nationalities, every
boy of a different race from his fellow. The school, though young, was
quiet and orderly. I thought the boys were showing good progress.
They did not seem to have quite the energy and go that my fellows have,
but then they are but tens to our hundreds. We drove into the city and
to Government House. All was changed. The feudal residences of the
old Burmese nobility have been cleared away. Barracks, and all the
arrangements of a large military cantonment, have taken their places. I
suppose it is improvement, but I confess to what the Burmese call *Oung
may gyin*, regretful recollections of the old houses where I have received
so much hospitality and kindness from the parents of my pupils. We
came back to the clergy house, hoping for a short rest if possible before
the return journey. But visitors crowded upon us, and rest was out of
the question. I would gladly have prolonged my stay, but I was obliged

to be in Rangoon to prepare for the celebration of the twenty-
fifth birth-day of St. John's College on March 5. But my visit
had been so hurried, and I had left so many persons and things
unnoticed, that I felt bound to make another visit as soon as
possible. That possibility you may be sure was not during Lent.
The Burmese holidays, which usually synchronise with Easter, this year,
for reasons too long to explain, did not agree, and consequently we had
great difficulty in holding on school till Easter, especially as the Government College, "our rival institution," had broken up. School rapidly
diminished, and yet we would not recognise Buddhist holidays. But we
broke up on April 12 with 489 present. This was the hottest Easter I
remember in Burma, the thermometer stood at 104 degrees in my room,
and the nights too were close and hot. So as soon as Easter Day was
over, I determined to pay my second visit to Mandalay, but this time by
one of the magnificent express steamers of the Irrawaddy Flotilla
Company. By the exceeding kindness of the Company, whose liberality
all your Burma Missionaries have so constantly experienced and acknowledged, I was enabled to travel without payment. No friends have been
kinder to us than this Company, and that from their very commencement.
They not only contribute largely to the school fund, but they give me
free passages for myself and half passages for my boys. The other day
they painted the college right throughout at their own expense. So with
three European and four Burman boys I embarked on board the SS.
"Beloo," an express boat lighted by electricity, and worked by the latest
machinery. It was one of the most luxurious boats that you can
imagine, and it was simply crowded with native passengers, though I was
the only first-class passenger the whole way.

We left on Thursday and arrived at Prome on Saturday afternoon.
I am chaplain of this station, where there is a beautiful little church
dedicated to St. Mark, the first in the Diocese consecrated by Bishop
Titcomb. It has been well cared for by the Deputy Commissioners,
especially by Colonel Geo. Alexander and Mr. F. S. Copleston, B.C.S.,
brother of the Bishop of Colombo. We stayed over Sunday, so that I
was able to have celebration of Holy Communion in the morning, and
Evensong and sermon in the evening. Next morning I had to bury a
European engineer who had died of heat apoplexy. We started at
8 A.M., and at noon on Thursday arrived in Mandalay, where we all took
up our residence at the clergy house. Colbeck had gone over to Shwebo
to visit Dr. Sutton, but Mr. Whitehead gave me a hearty welcome. The
news of my arrival soon spread, and we were besieged with visitors.
Mandalay was delightfully cool, rain falling abundantly. We planned a
succession of visits and a lot of work, but unfortunately the next morning, as I was going down the stairs of the clergy house, the stairs came
to pieces, and I had a sudden fall of about five feet. It shook and bruised

me so much that we had to send for Dr. Pedley (the brother of our kind
honorary physician here), who, of course, prescribed rest and vaseline.
The former was compulsory but very unwelcome when there was so
much that one wanted to do and see. On Sunday I was sufficiently
recovered to take part in four services. The first was at 8 A.M. Colbeck
and I took the duty of the chaplain, who was away at Myingyan. We
had parade service for the English troops (the Norfolk Regiment) and
others in the Hman Nan Daw, the grand front hall of the royal palace.
Here, in this golden apartment in which I had so often walked barefoot

EXTERIOR OF CHRIST CHURCH, MANDALAY.

and weary and anxious, waiting for hours for the appearance of one of
my prince-pupils with the joyful words, "*Caw daw moo thee*," "the King
calls you," I now stood with my back to the throne, and preached to a
large and attentive congregation from the words, "The power of His
Resurrection." In my long intervals of waiting, in days gone by, I often
used to think of the various useful purposes to which the different halls
of the palace might be put. But my wildest flights of imagination never
assigned such a purpose as that to which we were adapting the hall of audience, that of a military chapel for the British garrison. There is, of course,

a picturesqueness about making this hall, with its vermilion and gold columns and its altar-like throne, into a Christian chapel, but the place hardly lends itself to the purpose ; I trust that if Mandalay is to be retained as the capital of our newly annexed territory a suitable church will be erected by Government.   As soon as the parade service was over, Colbeck and I hurried across the enclosure to the building called Theebaw's Kyoung, one of a series of apartments, every portion of which is heavily gilded.   This also is used as a chapel for celebrations and for evening services.   It is much smaller than the palace chapel. There, for the first time in my life in the Burmese palace, I celebrated the Divine mysteries, Colbeck assisting.   There were only some half dozen communicants, but I could not help feeling what a marvellous change God has wrought.   Here, in a building erected by the last King of Burma for a Buddhist monastery within the precincts of his palace, and adjoining the chamber in which he had placed a very sacred image of Gaudama, we were celebrating the Holy Eucharist, none gainsaying or hindering us.   I cannot, however, say that this gilded chamber is well adapted for a Christian chapel.   It was exceedingly hot and close in the morning, and in the evening, when Mr. Colbeck was taking service, a dust storm drove half of his congregation to seek shelter elsewhere.

At 11 o'clock we had Burmese Mattins in our own Church.   I was glad to see a much larger congregation of Christian Burmans, but it was not so large as I expected to see, from the numerous baptisms of which I had heard.   Mr. Colbeck complains of the difficulty (not unknown elsewhere) of keeping his converts up to the mark of regularity in attendance at church.   The inevitable reaction has set in after the enthusiasm of the first ingathering on the establishment of British rule.   Colbeck held an after assembly of Christian Burmans in the clergy house, but as I know the Burman's staying powers, and it was better for the pastor and his flock to be alone, I left them to their talk, and betook myself to a long armchair on the verandah, for in truth I was tired.   In the evening (when our church becomes the parish church for Mandalay town) Mr. Whitehead sang service and I preached in English.   Compline at 9 finished this very happy Sunday, the first that I had spent in Mandalay since January 1875.

On Monday I went again into our school and gave the English headmaster, who is working very zealously but not very scientifically, a few hints as to school management, and to assimilating his plans to the system prescribed by the Educational Syndicate of Lower Burma.   I am one of the executive committee of that body, and I know that our system will be extended very shortly to Upper Burma, and it will be well for S.P.G. schools to be prepared for the change.

At 11 all my boys (for I had now 14) and I breakfasted with Mr. David, lately one of our junior masters, now the proprietor of the principal hotel in Mandalay.

On Tuesday we left, after Burmese Mattins, and embarked on board the express boat, the "Dufferin," and were soon many miles down the rapidly rising Irrawaddy. Old St. John's boys (or "Spidges," S.P.G.'s, as we call them) met us at every station, right glad to greet their old master. They are magistrates, inspectors of police, constables, clerks, traders, &c., and all proud to be called St. John's boys. One steamer clerk brought me Rs. 50, another an emerald ring, others cocoanuts and other fruits till my cabin was filled with things. We landed at Prome, whence I sent off my first detachment of eight pupils by train to Rangoon. I, with nine others, followed on Saturday, halting at Tharrawaddy, where we stayed over Sunday, holding two services in the little church there. The Chief Commissioner and his suite were sojourning with the Deputy Commissioner, Mr. Todd-Naylor, B.C.S. I dined with them, and at 2.15 A.M. we joined the night mail from Prome, which took us into Rangoon by 5.45 A.M., so that we were all ready for the re-assembling of school at 10 A.M. on Monday, May 13, after one of the longest vacations we had ever had. There were 429 boys present on the day of opening, and to-day (twenty days afterwards) we have 579 present.

NOTE.—For the illustrations which accompany this paper we are indebted to the Rev. G. H. Colbeck, who is stationed at Mandalay. They are reproduced from some photographs which he kindly sent to us.

CAWNPORE MISSION.

THE REV. J. R. HILL'S LAST REPORT OF THE WORK IN THE TOWN
AND DISTRICT.

HE last few months have been memorable here for the conversion of several young men. Last year I recorded the baptism of Ram Rattan, a youth of the third class of Christ Church High School. His younger brother, Daya Sagar, has followed him, and is now employed in the Mission at Banda. Ram Rattan has gone on to the C.M.S. Divinity School at Allahabad for the two or three years' course there. Next, also from the school, came Samuel Lakshmi Shankar Misr, a pleasing young man, and his wife has stood by him (Ram Rattan's, I am sorry to say, has not), and is a candidate for Holy Baptism, to which I have already admitted his younger brother, Daniel, a boy at school. There has also bravely stepped out a Muhammadan youth from the first class of the Banda School, Yaqub (James) Ali; his home is in the centre of the town, and his people are connected by many offices with the police. He is a fine, brave lad, and would have made his confession in Banda, but Padri Abdul Ali thought it better to bring him to Cawnpore, where I baptized him at the beginning of the year. He is tiring of reading English, which is, so far, a pity, but he is well qualified in his own language, and has already been tutor and clerk. Besides these, another Brahman, Hari Har, was accepted, but, in prudent avoidance of persecution, went to Lucknow, and was baptized at Easter by the Church Missionaries there. Besides these, there are two others. About one the only doubt has been whether this year past, during which he has been coming to me for instruction, he were old enough to defy the law forbidding minors to change their religion. The High Court of Allahabad has, however, just laid down, in a very interesting case of conversion against the American Missionaries, that sixteen is the minimum legal age for a change of faith, and eighteen of release from natural guardianship. Jawala has, however, produced his *kundali* (a document corresponding to our certificate of baptism), from which it is evident that he is nineteen. I would have baptized him, therefore, after Easter, had not the long drawn-out ceremonies and festivities of an only sister's marriage been in the way; he will, however, forthwith receive the holy rite and continue his studies.

The fact that six out of these seven young men were Brahmans, and belonged to Kursawan, the Brahman quarter of the city, and

hot-bed of bigotry and intolerance, is most significant. For how many
years have your Missionaries passed through prejudiced Kursawan on
their way to their schools, how many boys' names have they registered
whose homes were in this ward—all, it seemed, in vain ; the old Brahmans have continued to smile at us politely and sarcastically, the
youths to jeer a little at our want of success—but now it has come,
the spell at least is broken, quietly and unexpectedly the Cross of
Christ has been imprinted upon the foreheads of the youths of Kursawan.   One of the Catechists journeying in a railway carriage with
some of the old men of Kursawan was remonstrated with by them.
" We cannot tell," they said, " what has come over our boys ; we have
known for some time that they do not care for the customs of their
old religion, and prefer the Christian, and the Arya Samajis (the North
India organisation corresponding to the Brahmo Samaj of Bengal) has
not helped us, and now, if we are insistent with them, they say openly,
' We will become Christians.' "

    And it is most remarkable that this little series of conversions has
had no effect whatever upon the numbers attending school. Ten or twenty
years ago the baptism of a single Brahman boy would have half emptied it.
Instead, it is full to repletion (the Government Inspectors have twice
called our attention to the necessity for new class-rooms). Indeed, much
more fuss has been made over the death of a cow belonging to a Brahman, which had strayed into the church compound, than over these their
losses of their sons. This imaginary cow-killing case has been a most
absurd one.   The church grass-plots, &c., had suffered much from
intruding cattle, and one man, whose cow severely gored the gardener
who caught her, I prosecuted in the City Magistrate's Court.   It happened on one of my visits to Banda that a cow was caught in the evening and tied up ; in the morning when the gardener came to remove
her to the pound, she was found to be dead.   Information was at once
sent to the police station, the owner informed, and the carcase removed.
A little crowd gathered, and some ill-tempered Brahman muttered that
the Christians had killed the cow—the sacred beast. The owner, incited
by some foolish and malicious persons, brought a suit against me in the
police court, but the police refused him a summons, the whole thing
being clearly accidental and natural. But instead of this being the end
of it, the North-West Provinces Government was memorialised on the
subject, and I learnt some months afterwards the Government of India
also.   All this surely presents Hinduism in a very ridiculous light.
They have recently built some fine almshouses in old Cawnpore for
infirm and diseased cattle ; this institution has been established with
much éclat, and the agitation against the eating of beef has even
affected the English soldiers' meat market. Now the Ved, their ancient
scripture to which they are more and more turning from their Shastras

and Purans, shows plainly that their forefathers fed upon the cow; and their aversion to animal food was learnt from their great opponents, the Buddhists. Yet it is to-day the most prominent and fervent religious

CHRIST CHURCH, CAWNPORE.

tenet. And their quietly submitting to the conversion of their young men, and indignation at the death of a cow in the church compound, seems to show that they value the soul of a brute more highly than that of a Brahman.

These Brahman conversions also illustrate another curious phase in the history of our missions at present. I have been much struck by the change that has come over the character and quality of the candidates for baptism. In former days it was the low caste and no caste that came to the Missionary, seeking baptism and the social advancement that accompanied it. That taunt can no longer be made; my concern of late has been that the poor, those whom Christ especially made his own, are so hard to win, while Brahman inquirers have become numerous, and many have been at once rejected. What is the explanation of this change? I believe it to be in part due to our system, in part to the social revolution that is going on under English government. Our system and methods are mainly educational, our schools, books, lectures, and preachings act upon the most intellectually fit, that is the Brahmans. Government has been recently charged with fostering the Brahmans by its schools and colleges, in which high-caste students greatly prevail. We appeal but little to the heart, village and medical missions are few, and there is a danger of Zenanah work becoming too literary and educational. The low and less educated classes are but little reached by our efforts at present; but these are the very classes that are flourishing most in outward circumstances under English rule. The Brahman has few friends under a government that dispenses impartial justice; the wages of artisans and labourers have risen enormously, and, having plenty to eat, they feel no other care. The Brahman told them long since that they have no concern with, and are not fit for, religion, and the Sahibs evidently care for nothing more than their worldly well-being.

The growth of the out-station of Orai has been another matter of congratulation. You will remember my account of the Gajadhar family, which stood firm to Christ, though neglected and lost sight of for years. At the beginning of 1887 they and another native Christian family, eight souls in all, comprised the little Mission. Now, including Kalpi, 28 miles nearer Cawnpore, which has seven, there are 36 Christians. This is just about the same number as at Banda, but it should be understood that all the Banda Christians have been connected with it from first to last, while quite half of those at Orai have come there from other missions for their business or appointments. But it is pleasing to have so many to strengthen and assist the few faithful converts, and the work is likely to grow and develop, since Orai now has one of the best Catechists, baptized with his wife and child two years ago, at Banda, and there are several inquirers; and also because Orai is fortunate in having an excellent Deputy-Commissioner, who with his wife heartily fosters the little Mission. Orai has no church, but a good church-room is being so improved and furnished as to be fruitful in instruction and edification to the native Christians who are gathered there—the adults in the morning and the children every afternoon on Sundays.

FROM BLOEMFONTEIN TO THE ZAMBESI: A GREAT MISSIONARY JOURNEY.

BY THE BISHOP OF BLOEMFONTEIN.

(Continued from page 307.)

THROUGH MASHONALAND TO ZUMBO.

"ULY 11, *Wednesday.*—Though we began our day sometime before sunrise, it was 9 o'clock before we started. Most of the time was taken up in waiting, or arranging about payments, or seeing which men would carry the packs. Under such circumstances it is very hard to keep one's temper. When a disputed point arises there is for some considerable time a continuous roar of voices; they talk, these people, with a rapidity that is astounding, very loud, and nearly all at once. There was no trouble during the day, but we came to no water until we arrived in the evening at the Dimasamguese Brook, which springs out of Römeve mountain. A few people only live here. Gato is the name of the place, Chanetsa that of the chief.

"The carriers here said that they had been told by their chief to go no further, and when I told them that they had agreed to go to Pendoros, they replied that the place no longer existed, and that the men who had come as followers would carry to the next village. It was useless arguing with them, and they went away in the night.

"*July* 12, *Thursday.*—The relay of carriers presented themselves early in the morning, and after very little trouble, though at a high rate, were hired to go as far as the next village. I did not know where we were going, nor did I know where we were, except that we crossed the Hanyane River, and, according to the carriers, on the road to Shipuriro's. On coming near a village I saw a man run away immediately I came in sight, and the carriers explained that the people here had never seen a white man before, and might assegai or shoot me. There was, however, little cause for fear, for as we drew near to their mountain, Rurusu, we saw squatted on the top of a huge rock which crowned it nearly all the inhabitants. They were so high above us that though I examined the place very carefully I did not see them until they were pointed out to me. Even through my glass I could do little more than make out that they were human beings. They soon were induced to come down and bring us food. From them I learnt that Pendoro had gone somewhere to the East for fear of the Matabele. The carriers were given some food, which almost immediately caused a quarrel amongst them, during which the axe and the knobkerrie seemed to be their natural weapons; but the quarrel was stopped without bloodshed. These people are said to quarrel more violently over what they think is their right portion of the entrails of animals than over the flesh.

"The same carriers volunteered to go on to Shipuriro; and one of them went through an inelegant dance, at the same time singing a song, the refrain of which was—'I am going with the white man.'

"*July* 13, *Friday.*—The Moquadsi, which we crossed early in the day, is a beautiful stream running into the Hanyane, but the polished rocks made the crossing for the donkeys most difficult; both they and we shall remember it for some days.

"During the day the carriers threatened to throw down their loads if meat was not soon procured for them. Fortunately I was able to shoot an eland in the evening, and now they are happy. The carriers are very much more trouble than the donkeys, and do much shorter daily journeys. The leader of them now says that they will go no further if I do not give him a blanket. This I will not do.

"*July* 14, *Saturday.*—When we arrived at the remains of the eland this morning some of the carriers said they would go back, and one of them started off with some of the meat. I stopped him and made him give me back what he had taken. This had the effect of preventing some others from returning, but three of them went away. My own men were very good, carrying heavier weights in order to make up for the loss of the defaulting carriers. One of Khama's men said that to-day he would die, and confided in Edward that if a white man ever again asked him to go to the Zambesi, he would not do so for £200. Nevertheless he is an excellent fellow. Of our nine carriers two belong to Shipuriro, and show the way. These say that Shipuriro has changed the site of his town for fear of the Matabele, and has gone further to the East. They point out a far-distant peak which they say was Shipuriro's old station, and as such it stands in Mr. Selou's map of seven years ago.

"We are travelling much more to the East than I wish, but the men will only carry along the paths from one village to another, and indeed it is almost, if not quite necessary to do so in order to get meal.

"The same kind of trees grow here as for many miles south of the Hanyane; only where shade and water are combined is there any change. The Mahobahorbi is peculiar in its habit, growing chiefly in groves, and in one place the boundary trees were in so straight a line that it almost appeared as if they had been planted. Some of the grass that we passed through to-day must have been 11 feet high.

"We have never met a human being between any of the villages which I have mentioned. The great scarcity of water would prevent the country having anything but a scanty population. The Musiquè, a beautiful river which we crossed late this evening, is little more than a large mountain stream at this time of the year.

"To-day I saw but two water-bucks, one of which I shot. The flesh of the water-buck is not so good as that of other deer, but the Mashona are not so particular as to the quality as the quantity.

"I find it very difficult to get at the distance of any place. Two men will give different, very different distances, and the same man will give different distances on different days. I do not know whether they tell intentional falsehoods, or are very stupid; but I do know that they have a kind of weak cunning where their own interests are concerned.

"*July* 15, *Sunday.*—The men are quiet, drying and watching their meat. They dry it on platforms made of sticks. My own men have been washing themselves and their things.

"A herd of elands with a very large bull came feeding close to the camp quite unconscious of us till some sound startled them. I gave reasons why they should not be shot, among others, that it was Sunday. John said regretfully afterwards that had it not been Sunday it would have been very nice to have had some eland's fat. But to have helped some few people to understand that we should keep Sunday holy is possibly of some use.

"*July* 16, *Monday.*—While it was dark we were preparing to start, when the carriers demanded more 'limbo.' They had been paid excessively high, and I determined that this imposition must cease. I explained to them at length how well they had been paid, how kind we had been to them, how we never cheated them; but it was all useless; and though I thought with horror of our position, being left with the loads and no means of transport if they had done so, I told them to go home, but to leave the meat which had been given them on condition of their reaching Shipuriro's in two more days; and I called two of Khama's men to prevent them taking any meat away. Then they said they would go on without more payment. After this we were the best of friends for the rest of the day, and they are now sitting with my men, after helping me to map the road, and doing everything they could.

"The Mabare and Musiquè rivers are, I think, much nearer each other than is marked in Mr. Selou's map, as we walked the distance between them in four and a half hours, and for about one hour of that the donkeys were struggling and tumbling in a ravine. The Mabare is a pretty mountain stream where we crossed it, the kind of place where a water-ouzel would sit and dive.

"A snake called a seshona shato (a python) was lying almost in our path; and after I had shot a bullet through its body it made a dart at one of the men, but missed him. When it was dead we found that stretched out its length was 11 feet 3 inches.

"The natives, other than the Mashona, do not seem to have any great fear of a snake, while their dread of a lion is almost ludicrous. One of my men the other night moved his sleeping place nearer to the fire on hearing one roar far away.

"*July* 17, *Tuesday*.—I paid the men for the whole distance to Shipuriro's last night, and this morning four of them said that they wished to go back. I told them that they had been engaged for the whole distance, and that they must come on, and was pleased and surprised when they consented to do so.

"We started shortly after 6 o'clock this morning; but after walking about two hours and a half the carriers stopped, saying that they did not know where Shipuriro's was, and three of them went over a hill to a village which we had heard of to inquire. They returned about sunset, bringing with them Nyamaka, the head man of the village, and a son of Shipuriro, and also some food. The men danced in the evening, after tying the pieces of calico which had been paid to them round their bodies, and sang a song to a curious tune, the sense of which seemed to be that they would dance while they could, as the Matabele might soon come to kill them, and though they might hurry to hide themselves in holes, they would not be quick enough, their things would be taken and they would be killed.

"*July* 18, *Wednesday*.—The morning's walk brought us to Shipuriro's. I took the precaution of sending on messengers to announce our coming, and to say that we were not Matabele. He was very hospitable, and gave me some rice. He says that he has moved but a short distance from his old place, though he pointed to Mount Myambare, which is about eight miles off.

"While returning his visit he gave us a dinner; meat and boiled meal were brought to us in separate dishes, and he waited till I had had what meat I wanted, then he shared the remainder of the food with John. One of his wives, as I suppose, received the dishes, &c., from him on her knees.

"I told him that I was a teacher, and would speak to him more about this when he came to see me in the evening, but he did not come.

"*July* 19, *Thursday*.—The morning was well advanced before Shipuriro or any of his men came to me; when they did, talking began. I asked if they wished to come with me, and some seemed inclined to do so, but others objected that it was very far to Kanyembas, &c., &c. They knew that they would be paid in calico to an extent that was, to them, most extravagant; but the laziness of their lives makes exertion very hard for them, while the 'conditions of life' are very easy. I thought of the East-end London labourer waiting for hours on the chance of one day's work, as I have also thought of the East-end children when seeing the distended stomachs of children here. Then there was the usual uproar; but at length Shipuriro persuaded some of his men to go with me." (His exertions in the Bishop's behalf were not altogether disinterested, for the Bishop had promised to give him a blanket when he left, if he got a sufficient number of carriers. When the men who had agreed to go had been paid in advance, there was still a delay in starting, owing to their desire to appropriate the remains of a quagga which the Bishop had shot; but Shipuriro at last started them on the road by beating them with a stick.) Then the Bishop resumes :—

"After sending the carriers, men, and donkeys on, I stayed behind to speak to the chief about my mission; but I do not think I interested him at all. By the middle of the day the meat was nearly all gone, and the carriers said that they would go back if more was not shot for them. On crossing a small brook in the early part of the afternoon they wished to stop and sleep there, saying it was the last water; but I, not believing, made them come on, and shortly before sunset we came to a village with bad water.

"*July* 20, *Friday.*—Two hours' walking through a wood which covered small hills and valleys brought us to Chimanikeri's village. I spoke to him for a short time, telling him what I taught, and that when the teachers came he must receive them and treat them well.

"The carriers who had been engaged to go with us to Kanyemba's town here said that they would go no further, and had started for their own homes before I noticed their absence. I followed them, leaving my rifle behind, though much inclined to take it, knowing that if I frightened them with the sight of it my point in all probability would have been gained; but this I did not do, so they gained their point, and I lost my calico.

"The head man of the place did not consider the present which I gave him sufficiently good, and demanded a better. Then fresh carriers were engaged for as far as the next village, and prepaid, with a double payment to one man who was said to know the road. This occupied from 9 A.M. till about 12.30. Exclusive of a halt for breakfast, these walked for about an hour and a half, when they stopped, saying there was no water further on.

"The camp was made on the edge of the range of mountains overlooking the Zambesi plain. As far as a good glass can reach, it is in every direction an immense plain apparently covered with small trees, except that in the dim distance an indistinct hill here and there seems to spring out of the horizon. The flatness of the Zambesi valley is so extraordinary that it is hard to understand how the Geographical Society had gained the information that it was mountainous. From the great height of these mountains on which we are, the plain on a misty day might be mistaken for the sea.

"*July* 21, *Saturday.*—I had every hope this morning that as the carriers had come so short a distance there would be no difficulty in getting them to go further, but though we made the earliest preparations, the men sat sulkily round their fires and refused to move when asked to take their packs, saying that they wanted more calico. Then ensued the useless argument that leads to nothing. Each relay of carriers has been worse than the previous ones, and I thought it was time for me gently to insist; so I told John and Edward to stand near to the two smaller heaps of assegais which belonged to these men, while I stood near the other; then we took them all up at the same time, saying that if they took away our calico we must take their assegais. Unfortunately they misunderstood us and thought they would be killed, for almost together, and before a word could be spoken to reassure them, they jumped the skerm, and were starting in different directions for the wood. They were called back, however, and told why the assegais had been taken. Then a long conversation ensued, which ended in all but two of them coming on quite quietly. Then I told them that I trusted them, and gave them back their assegais. The two who would not be induced to return were heard for some time afterwards shouting in the woods. Eventually they caught us up about noon, when they were laughed at, and we became very good friends.

" There was at first little of interest in the plain below. The trees were very much larger than they appeared to be when we were on the hills, and they increased in size as we went on. Two human skulls and some bones were lying near the path, all the earthly remains of two natives who probably had not strength to face the mountains.

" The deep ravines washed out by the water from the hills were a great hindrance to the donkeys, which sometimes had to be dragged or pushed up the ascents, especially on reaching the Dande river. Long before we reached this stream the carriers stopped at a wretched pool, saying that was the last water ; fortunately we did not believe them.

" Wherever the ground is high the dryness of the soil is extreme ; but in the rainy season the plain is probably swampy; this is to be seen from the length and size of the dry grass. Edward told me that he measured one stalk, which was twenty-one feet high. Here for the first time the Baobab tree appears in numbers. To my eyes it appears a freak of nature. The trunk of one exceeded anything I had anticipated, not being very much smaller in girth than the Wellingtonian ; but it attains to no great height, and its few fat branches send out very small twigs, as though exhausted with the effort that had been made lower down. The fruit is good to eat, and is said to be most efficacious in dysentery.

" *July 22, Sunday.*—I intended to go on to Kamoti's village, but learned that it was some distance out of the road, and that there was another village on the road which we could reach about 10 A.M. I was anxious not to go any farther than was necessary, more for the donkeys' sake than our own, and the men agreed to take the loads after being paid more cloth to do so, which compact they wanted to break on further conversation with their friends from the village, but they retained the cloth. For the first time, I think, I had left the saddling up to the men, while I went to a small rise to map the country. This caused some delay which might have been fatal, but fortunately was not.

"After we had saddled up and were well on the road, delay was again caused by Jelly taking the wrong path, upon which the carriers refused to go any further till they received more cloth. Then began the usual argument, they demanding more than I had promised to give when they agreed to take on things to the next village. I learnt by degrees that the next village, instead of being close to us, could not be reached till to-morrow evening. This transpired when the question of an increased payment was discussed. We crossed the Hanyane River about midday, near to where crocodiles seemed to be numerous. We halted early, and I had a short service.

"*July* 23, *Monday.*—The carriers refused to move till they were paid for another day. I reminded them of their compact, of which they took little notice. I told the leader that I had never seen any people who told such falsehoods as they did, at which he laughed. It was the harder to submit to their extortion as I knew that by exerting the smallest amount of compulsion I should probably gain my point immediately, their power of lying being equalled only by their cowardice. However, I believe that I have done right in submitting, and should mind less were not my small stock of white calico fast disappearing, and white is demanded on almost every occasion. With a larger supply of money travelling would not be hard, though to-day Khama's man has risen in his demands. 'Not for £100 a month will I ever go to the Zambesi again,' said he.

"In coming through a small ravine where the ground had to be cut away to allow the donkeys to get out, one was by mistake left behind, and there was some difficulty in securing it. The Amatonga men not wishing to go back 'to be killed by the Mashona,' two of the carriers went, on the promise of more calico, with Sikwarri. Another donkey became so weak that to-day I ended his journey, close by where an atom of humanity had ended his. The power of the vulture to find dead things is a problem that remains to be solved. I had not seen one since we left our camp; but they soon found the poor donkey.

"After some little trouble we arrived at Namfukadza's in the evening. He is a son of Shipuriro; but here for the first time I saw the effect either of intercourse with Portuguese traders or with Central African tribes; *i.e.*, the chiefs wear long pieces of calico as a kind of 'toga'; the women wear calico round their waists; the houses are placed in a square inclosure made of Indian corn stalks, and a square is a shape unknown to South African tribes in their natural state.

"Namfukadza offered me a seat to sit on when I arrived, and came forward clapping his hands; but our conversation was cut short by his desire to go and see the donkeys. I afterwards gave him a blanket, at which he was much pleased, and brought me a small bowl of meal, apologising for its smallness by saying that there was hunger at his village. The camp was very quiet, and I talked with him for some time. He said that the Portuguese were kind to the people, though I disagreed with him on the point of giving brandy being kind. At first he said he thought that it was right for one man to have another as a slave; but when I asked him how he would like it if the Matabele were to come and take his people, he changed his mind, and said he did not think it was right. I tried to interest him by saying that we were all the children of one Father in Heaven, and that we should be kind to each other. He listened courteously; but the natives' power of attention to anything but their own subjects is very limited. He promised that when the teachers came to his town he would treat them kindly, and build them a house. He told me that a white man had been near his town before I came to it, a small man, and that he had heard that some of the people had stolen his beads. This must, I think, have been Richard Foster on his way to meet me. I did not, however, quite understand when he had gone by, nor did the chief say anything about his being dead.

"*July* 24, *Tuesday.*—True to his promise, Namfukadza appeared early this morning, so early that John and Edward were not up. I was saying my prayers when he came, and he and they remained quite quiet until I spoke to them.

"When the question of payment arose there was the usual difficulty, the men demanding twice what I understood had been agreed to last night, more indeed than I had ever paid before, and the chief also wanted another present. I paid the calico in advance on condition that they would ask for no more during the rest of the journey.

"The walking was easy, though the country through which we passed was uninteresting. For the first half of the day our course lay through Mopani trees, which always grow far apart, and seem to thrive only on the very driest and best drained soil; and where they grow there is found a kind of large agate-like stone, which evidently facilitates the drainage. About midday we struck the Oangwa River, a sand river of great breadth, where water can only be procured by digging. The prickly reed grew here in great abundance; here, too, the missing donkey arrived. We passed by a large clearing for Kaffir corn, where a few people seemed to live. Shortly before the halt for the night the mountains near Zumbo appeared in sight.

"*July* 25, *Wednesday.*—The carriers refused to move till paid again

for the day, and then on arriving at a village belonging to a son of
Kanyemba, at about eleven o'clock, refused to go any further, and with
the exception of two, who seemed somewhat ashamed of themselves, they
had to be replaced by fresh ones to Kanyemba's town.   Here we were kept
waiting some time while the messenger was informing the chief of our
arrival, but when he did appear, it was like the entrance into a new world.
A house was prepared for us, and very soon I was called to what seemed
a sumptuous meal.   It was nearly dark, and I was not particular as to
which dish provided me food, for I was hungry, and ate immensely.

"The chief was dressed in European clothes, and said that the Portuguese
brought him his civilisation.   His people are called the Mutandi.   At
the earlier part of the day we passed the village of Chipunzamongo,
whose people are called Machacunda, so that Namfukadza's town
is the last one in this direction which belongs to the Mashona.

"Kanyemba's town is surrounded by a stockade of great height,
and, but for a pigsty, is kept clean.   His people are much better
mannered than the Mashona, the custom of clapping hands for saluta-
tion and thanks being observed by them.   Some of the women wear a
modification of the lip ring (in fashion amongst the Nyassa people), and
scarcely any of the people wear skins, calico being easily obtained in
barter and service from the Portuguese.

"*July* 26, *Thursday.*—After breakfasting with Kanyemba, who made
me a present of a large sheep and a basket of meal, I started with
John for the place where the boat from Zumbo crosses the Zambesi,
thinking it was close by, and finding it fully eight miles distant.   I had
sent on earlier in the morning the letter from the Portuguese Consul
at Cape Town, and the inhabitants received me most courteously.   The
Governor was away, having gone up the river to ask Buruma, chief of
the Valenghi, why he had in May brought some 2,000 men and attacked
the settlement, which consists of about eight houses and a considerable
number of native huts.   The people of the country are Basenga,
and they call the Portuguese Basungu, which means ' white men.'

" I went to see the ruins of an ecclesiastical building, which is said
to have been a Roman Catholic Mission Station, about one mile down
the river.   The remains of what is said to be the bell of this building
is at Zumbo ; I examined it, and could find no inscription on it.

"The people on both sides of the Zambesi seem to recognise the
authority of the Portuguese, there being no chief of the Basenga on
the north side of the river, and Kanyemba and Matakenya being only
governors under them.   At Niabakobe, about four days by boat with
the stream from Zumbo, is the residence of a Portuguese ' capitani.'
The size of the river at Zumbo is imposing.   There is, however, little
that is beautiful ; reeds and sand alternately, with sometimes a reach
bordered by trees, from which a coarse but curious creeper hangs down
almost to the water, are the main features."

THE CHILDREN'S CORNER.

PERHAPS nothing makes us feel so much how we should try to turn people from darkness to light, and give the knowledge of the true God, as finding what foolish and wicked things people do for want of knowing Him. Of course this is not the whole reason why we work to spread the Church of God abroad. The chief reason is, and must be, that we desire God's glory, and want all men to know His love, and to serve Him. Many foolish and wicked things are (alas!) done in Christian countries, and among the heathen are found many people highly civilised, sensible and prudent. But such a story as the one which follows shows how the very fact that people are without the knowledge of God leads them to the most absurd kinds of false worship. Their ignorance of the Gospel is the cause of their doing things from which we might think their own common sense would keep them. But it does not, and people everywhere, who are without the knowledge of God, are constantly showing us that with Him wisdom is to be found. The Rev. H. J. Foss of Kobe sends us this story to show us that superstition is by no means rooted out of Japan. He himself witnessed the folly of the people.

"Some weeks ago," he writes, "a turtle found its way on shore in a storm, and wandering about it fell into a well. It could not get out again, and being too cramped to be able to enjoy the water, it soon died. The people to whom the well belonged pulled it out, and buried it honourably. And then the people from far and near came to worship it, and gave their alms before the spirit of the turtle, and believed that it was a sign of favour that it should have come to die there. We hear that the police stopped the collecting of alms, as they said the people were being deceived; but still divine honours are paid at the grave by the owners of the well, and their near neighbours. They used often to collect three or four shillings (1,000 to 1,500 ' cash ') daily from those who worshipped."

What strange ideas of religion such people must have! How little can a race where such a superstition is possible have had their thoughts at all turned upward, or looked upon their false gods in any way at all like that in which we can look up to our Heavenly Father!

NOTES OF THE MONTH.

HARVEST is begun early in England this year, and we trust it is good. For thankofferings we must plead on the Society's behalf. To whichever part of the world we turn we see fields fallow and fields ripening, both needing much earnest labour if spiritual fruit is to be gathered from them. The Bishop of Rupertsland's letter in our last number described the sparse character of the rapid settlement in his Diocese, and the consequent strain on the Church ; and his words apply to Qu'Appelle, Saskatchewan, and other Dioceses in Central and Western Canada. In South Africa to enumerate the opportunities for expansion would be to recite the names of the Missions, while the rush to the diamond and gold mines makes demands on the Church which are most pressing. India has its ever-growing needs with such Missions as those in Bengal, Assam, Bombay, Nazareth, Ramnad, and the Telugu country under-manned, and Secunderabad with its claims of many years' standing still unsatisfied. Burma offers successes which are almost perilous for the relatively small band of workers; and Japan presents an opportunity great, but to be seized at once, if at all. The West Indies show their poverty under disendowment. North Borneo and other new fields, should not be occupied so weakly as to court failure and loss. Such is a cursory view. The readers of the *Mission Field* know how a more detailed statement brings out the force of the appeal.

SEVERAL Missionaries will shortly be leaving England for work in various fields abroad. The Rev. L. S. R. Browne left for the diocese of Pretoria on August 2, and the Rev. A. Lloyd on August 16, for Japan, after a furlough of only a few weeks' duration, his health having necessitated his taking the voyage. The Rev. R. R. Winter returns to Delhi in October. The Rev. A. A. Maclaren is on the eve of starting for his new field of work in New Guinea. On September 12 the Rev. A. Inman is to leave for Madras, after his well-earned furlough. Mr. G. D. Iliff is sailing for North China. In the " Manora " on October 10 there will be no less than five new Missionaries sailing for India—the Rev. G. H. Westcott, the Rev. Foss Westcott, and Mr. G. H. Lusty for Calcutta ; Mr. A. J. Godden and Mr. G. F. Hart for Madras. In connection with their departure there is to be, on October 9, a celebration of the Holy Communion in the Chapel in the Society's house, to which the Society's friends are invited. On October 3, Mr. Richard Richards is to sail for Borneo.

ON June 12, the Bishop of Capetown reached his Diocese from England. The next day there was a special service, in which expression was given to the thanksgiving of the Diocese at the Bishop's restoration to his flock, and the *Te Deum* was sung.

THE following private letter from the Rev. W. H. Elton has been sent to us by the Rev. B. Belcher. It will be read with interest, as showing how important it was to send out a clergyman to North Borneo, and it is hoped that many persons will be induced to contribute towards building the church and towards the maintenance of a Chinese catechist at Kudat :—

"I hope to build the church of brick, if we can get sufficient funds. Wood in this climate decays so soon, and is always of course in danger of fire, because fire spreads so rapidly in the dry season. The pretty little church at Labuan was burnt down in ten minutes the other day—uninsured, I am sorry to say. There has been no chaplain at Labuan for some time, but the Acting Governor, Mr. Hamilton, has held service in the church for nine years. I have recommended the Bishop to put Labuan under my charge, and he has done so. Whether another church will be built, I cannot say ; there are only six Europeans on the island. I went for a Missionary tour in December, in a small steam launch, landing first at Labuan, which is about 300 miles from here. After spending some days at Government House, and visiting all the Europeans and Christians I could find, I met my wife and three children and returned with them, visiting Kudat, which lies midway between Labuan and here.

"At Kudat there are nearly 100 Christian Chinese, who are begging me to send them a schoolmaster and catechist, but I have no funds. It is a pity that a place like this cannot be provided for. I heard there were about 50 Christians five miles in the jungle, so I set off with a young Chinaman as interpreter, and, although they had only a quarter of an hour's notice of my arrival, given them by my guide, who ran on in front, they all left their work and mustered more than 40 strong in the principal house in the village. They brought me four infants to baptize, and we had a most interesting service. They also told me that a number of adults wished to be baptized, but I asked them to wait till I should send a catechist to instruct them. Thirty pounds a year would keep a catechist, who would also be schoolmaster, but I cannot raise the amount here, and the people themselves are too poor to pay it. I have already received from the different naval officers who have visited us during the eight months I have been here one hundred and thirty dollars, sufficient to build a small school at Kudat, but it is useless to build the school unless I can place a master there. My most pressing need is a young clergyman who would live with me and take charge of this place while I am travelling, and also help in the school. We took possession of the new parsonage and school the week before Easter. The parsonage is a good two-storied house, and has cost about 1,800 dollars, or £300. The school, which we use at present as church also, has cost about 600 dollars, or £100. They are both good buildings.

We are now ±100 in debt, which it will take us some time to pay off, because none of our men are well off. Unless, therefore, we get most of the money from home, I fear it will be a long time before we are able to build the church. The site of the church, parsonage, and schools is on a hill rising by itself out of the centre of the town to an elevation of 100 feet, and is clearly visible from every point. It is next to Government House, and only five minutes' walk from the Government offices and the pier. I have received, through the kindness of Lieut. Ingram, of H.M.S. 'Swift,' a number of Chinese Prayer Books, and have been able to start a Chinese service every Sunday at 11 A.M. The church is always full at these services. I hope shortly to find some means of travelling up some of the rivers to interview the inland tribes, and get them to hand me some of their sons to educate here, but I have no means for travelling, and so must wait. Besides, I should have to be away from here several months, and, in this early stage of the Mission, this would be unwise. Oh, for men and money ! There are already five Roman priests in North Borneo, and I am the only clergyman of the Church of England. You will be glad to hear that on Easter Day I had thirteen Europeans and eleven Chinese at the Holy Communion at 7.30 A.M. I have never before lived in such a trying climate. It is so intensely hot. I have had one attack of fever, and my youngest child is now down with it. I find the Governor and Mrs. Creagh a great help in every way."

WITH the hearty approval of the Bishop of Lahore, the Delhi Mission is about to open new work among the women in two towns, Rohtak and Hissar, to the north-west of Delhi. The Rev. R. R. Winter writes as to Hissar :—

" We desire to make it a centre of a village mission among the Ját peasantry of that district. Two members of the Cambridge Brotherhood are working among them, but their work is of necessity confined to the men, and it is very important to bring parallel influence to bear on the women. We therefore desire to place two English ladies in Rohtak for this work.

" Our call to Hissar is a remarkable one. A Hindu gentleman of that town has promised a subscription of twenty rupees a month for a girls' school, ' on the condition that it is superintended by a Christian lady.' This is an encouraging testimony to the estimation in which Christian ladies are held by Indian gentlemen. The call being urgent, we have already appointed one of the present Zananah missionaries of long experience to work in this place, and in the large neighbouring town of Bhiváni, but we need one other to learn the work under her, and another to supply her place in Delhi. In connection with this opening for new work therefore, four English ladies are urgently needed. The Ladies' Association of the S.P.G. has given its cordial approval to the scheme. A fifth lady is wanted for a vacancy in our Simla Zananah Mission, where the climate would enable many to work whose health would not allow them to live in the Plains. A sixth, wanted for a vacancy in the Medical Mission, has been found."

The Bishop of Lahore writes :—

".Nothing is more clearly impressed upon my mind at this time, when I am just

about to complete the primary visitation of the Diocese, than the value of the work which is being done by English ladies in the Punjab."

Mr. Winter adds :—

" All our women workers are united in a body named the Community of St. Stephen, with definite rules; this lessens isolation, and gives the support of cohesion and

HOME OF THE ZANANAH WORKERS AT DELHI.

sympathy. The community already works in three large towns besides Delhi, and, when desirable, ladies at a distance can be interchanged with those in the central house—St. Stephen's Home, in Delhi. The Mission has a House of Rest at Simla, to which all have a right of admission when their health demands it."

Letters should be addressed to Mr. Winter at 19 Delahay Street, S.W.

BISHOP HARPER, after thirty-three years of arduous labour in the See of Christchurch, has been compelled by his increasing years and infirmities, especially that of deafness, to resign his see. The primacy of New Zealand he resigned in February, and a few months afterwards he resolved to leave his diocese to a younger ruler. The Hon. H. B. Gresson, late Judge of the Supreme Court of New Zealand, was the mover of the address to his Lordship in the Synod, and in the course of his remarks said that there were some in that Synod who remembered the arrival of the Bishop thirty-three years ago. They were but few, but they would fully bear him out in his statement :—

"For the whole period during which he had presided over the Church his Lordship has been the foremost mover, and the most energetic worker, in promoting the

CHRIST CHURCH CATHEDRAL, NEW ZEALAND.

establishment of all good works in the diocese. If I were to attempt to enumerate those works in detail, my memory would fail me. I propose to refer at no great length to the prominent works which would most strike anyone who has lived in this country. It will be remembered by those who were here at the time of the

Bishop's arrival that the state of Church matters in the diocese was deplorable. If I am not mistaken, the only church in the city of Christchurch was the rickety old church of St. Michael's. It was the sole representative of the ecclesiastical institutions of Canterbury. The small house in Oxford Terrace, then occupied as a grammar school, of which the Dean was Warden, was the sole representative of our educational institutions. There were few, if any, churches in the country districts. There were a few in the most central towns, but they were of a very unsuitable and inconvenient construction and of very temporary nature. If we look at what is before us in this Synod, at the number of clergymen present, we are struck with the vast difference between the state of Church matters then and now. Most of the clergymen, if not all, have churches, and many of those churches are, notably that of the Archdeacon of Timaru, worthy of Him whose houses they are. The pastoral districts at that time were wholly without spiritual instruction. The country, of course, was a difficult one to travel. The rivers were most dangerous and treacherous, and being mostly without bridges it was necessary to ford them, and every year many persons lost their lives in attempting to do so. The only locomotion was on horseback and in drays. If we cast our eyes around now there is much to congratulate ourselves upon, and to be thankful to his Lordship for. We see a large number of churches in the city of Christchurch alone, very convenient and worthy churches, independent of the Cathedral. We also see a large number of churches in the neighbourhood of Christchurch. Throughout the whole of the pastoral districts where before there was no sort of spiritual instruction, where the inhabitants were left to themselves to live almost as heathens, religious instruction is now brought by clergymen to within easy distances of nearly all the inhabitants. Under these circumstances the organisation in such a diocese as this, because it is a large one, and includes Otago and Southland—the organisation in such a diocese and the work which has been effected must have involved immense labour, mental and physical, and not only that, but very considerable danger. His Lordship had to travel on horseback about the country, to cross those dangerous rivers, to cross immense swamps, which were numerous, and incurred many risks. I have not yet mentioned the great work of the Cathedral. It will be remembered by many how unceasingly his Lordship laboured to promote that great work, how rejoiced he was when it was brought to its present state of effectiveness, and what unceasing exertions he made to accomplish that desired end. The Bishop has been also Warden of Christ's College. As such he exerted himself with the utmost energy and unceasing efforts to put that institution upon a sound footing. And not only so, but we may fairly say that his Lordship's efforts are rewarded by success, from the position which several of the students who were educated at that institution have taken at the English Universities. If his Lordship had only confined himself to those matters which I have mentioned, I should be amply justified in moving the resolution which stands in my name. But there are a great many other works which, as those who were associated with his Lordship know, involve very great labour and constant attention and thought. I know that the Bishop does not desire that this matter should be brought forward with a shade of exaggeration. I have carefully avoided that. I know it is not his Lordship's desire to be judged by man's judgment. But of this I am convinced—there is one reward which I am sure will be satisfactory to his Lordship, and that is that there is no one within the diocese—indeed, it may truly be said in the whole of New Zealand—who does not regard his Lordship with filial affection and veneration."

O N Trinity Sunday the Bishop of Madagascar admitted to Holy Orders Samuel Ramonta and Roger Raboanar. The former has now the cure of a large district west of Ramainandro, and the latter is working in Ramainandro itself under Mr. McMahon. They are both former students of St. Paul's College, and the Bishop says that " they

have both earned a good report as catechists." His lordship tells us that
August 10th was fixed for the consecration of the Cathedral. We trust,
therefore, that this great event in the history of the Church in Madagascar has now happily taken place.

FROM the day of its consecration, more than twenty years ago,
Canon Curtis has been the Society's Chaplain at the Crimean
Memorial Church at Constantinople. He is now in England
endeavouring, with the Society's cordial approval, to raise a repair fund
for the church, which is urgently needed. Canon Curtis writes:

"The building is very lofty and exposed; the frequently sudden and violent changes
in the atmosphere have already brought it to the verge of premature ruin. Some
years ago it was struck by lightning, the shock of which threw down a person sitting
at my side at the back of the church; and the lightning-conductor being out of the
perpendicular, a portion of the stone cornice of the bell-tower fell upon the ground
below."

"The church is roofed with tiles which are continually breaking, so that the rain
falls into the nave through the wooden waggon roof, rotting the timber; rain and
snow penetrate even the stone work in the chancel, leaving deep stains, and sometimes
dripping into the organ-pipes, if these are not covered. At present there is no available method for the repair of the roof, because, the eaves overhanging the lateral
walls, there is no footing for ladders; attempts to mend it have been made from within,
but ineffectually, and now workmen have refused to go up. The long ridge-tile breaks
from time to time; heavy masses have lately tumbled from that great height upon the
path along which children daily pass to and fro. Immediately below the eaves run
narrow gutters; as these become choked up with vegetable growth, the rain-water (at
times torrential), instead of passing down the pipes, overflows and damages the parts
of the building which lie below.

"Besides, the church is peculiarly exposed to fire. The overhanging roof meets
the buttresses laid against the walls, but not the walls themselves. From buttress to
buttress, and behind, there stretches above each wall a thick oaken beam, cracked and
opened now, and above the beam an uncovered passage communicating through
spiracles with the woodwork of the waggon roof, which is laid some twenty feet below
the tile-roof. A few weeks ago a fire broke out very near the church, and the north
wind drove the smoke and burning embers against it. Had not the fire been got
under soon, our fair church might have been at this time but a blackened wreck,
burning matter being drawn and driven in through the openings beneath the eaves.
But repairs are needed, not only for the fabric of the church, but also for the walls
that enclose the church ground."

"It is a monument worth preserving, a stately structure becoming its high uses;
the only church in the city visible from the port—the only church in the world, perhaps, raised beside a mosque; meant to be not only a memento of the past, but a
sanctuary for years to come—not a cenotaph in memory of the dead, but a House of
God for the salvation of the living."

Canon Curtis will be glad to have opportunities of preaching on
behalf of the fund. Contributions are received by the Society's
Treasurers.

SUGGESTED SUBJECTS FOR PRAYER.

For the Missions exposed to peril in Eastern Africa, for the steadfastness of the converts, and for a happy issue out of all the tribulations.

For the Missionaries who are going forth to their several fields of
labour in India, China, Borneo, South Africa, New Guinea, and Japan.

For India, and especially for its women, that they may be raised
from their degradation and ignorance, and learn the truth as it is in
Christ Jesus.

For the Australasian Church, and for the guidance of those with whom
rests the choice of Bishops for its vacant Sees.

MONTHLY MEETING.

The Monthly Meeting of the Society was held at 19 Delahay Street, on Friday, July 19, at 2 P.M., J. G. Talbot, Esq., M.P., in the chair. There were also present the Rev. J. W. Ayre, the Rev. P. Belcher, and General Sir J. Lintorn A. Simmons, G.C.B., *Vice-Presidents* ; Rev. J. M. Burn-Murdoch, Rev. A. T. Brinckman, C. M. Clode, Esq., C.B., Prebendary Codrington, D.D., the Master of the Charterhouse, General Davies, Sir F. J. Goldsmid, K.C.S.I., C.B., Colonel Hardy, J. R. Kindersley, Esq., Rev. G. B. Lewis, General Lowry, C.B., General Maclagan, and the Rev. C. S. Palmer, *Members of the Standing Committee* ; and Dr. Cust, Rev. T. Darling, Rev. H. J. Day, Dr. De Tatham, Rev. Dr. Finch, Rev. F. B. Gribbell, Rev R. S. Hassard, Rev. J. R. Hill, Rev. S. Coode Hore, Rev. Blomfield Jackson, Herbert Laurence, Esq., Rev. J. H. C. McGill, W. Barrow Simonds, Esq., J. S. Smith, Esq., Rev. R. Wheeler, and S. J. Wilde, Esq., *Members of the Society.*

1. After prayers, the minutes of the last meeting were read.

2. The Treasurers presented the abstract of receipts and payments from January 1 to June 30, printed on page 320 of the *Mission Field.*

3. The Standing Committee's reply to the resolution passed at the last meeting, to the effect that they were taking steps for obtaining information on the alleged action of Government educational officials in India in opposition to Christianity, was communicated to the meeting.

4. Power was given to affix the Corporate Seal to certain documents.

5. The Venerable Archdeacon Crisp, from Bloemfontein, addressed the members. He referred to the Bishop's wonderful journey to Mashonaland, and proceeded to speak of many aspects of the Missionary work within the diocese. In particular he called attention to the opportunities afforded in the native compounds at the diamond mines. Replying to questions, he gave interesting information as to his translation work, which embraces the New Testament, the Book of Common Prayer, and 200 hymns.

6. The Rev. Dr. Batterson, of Philadelphia, gave an interesting account of the work of the American Church among the Indians and the negroes, describing the difficulties, political and moral, which beset it.

7. The Rev. W. H. Barnes, from Honolulu, also gave an address, and spoke of the work of the Church among the sailors, the 20,000 Chinese, and the half-caste natives. The King and the Court belong to the Church, which, however, has little or no work among the natives generally. The Church schools have a high reputation in the islands. Although the natives are Christians, much superstition remains, sorcery is practised, and immorality and secret vice are prevalent.

Four years ago there was only one small congregation in the Chinese Mission, which assembled in a house ; now there are two congregations, one of which has a church, and the other is ready for one. The Chinese make good Christians.

8. All the candidates proposed at the meeting in May were elected into the Corporation ; and the Rev. Thomas Palmer Abraham, of Risby Rectory, Bury St. Edmund's, was proposed for election in November.

SOCIETY'S INCOME.

Abstract of RECEIPTS *and* PAYMENTS *from January 1 to July 31.*

	GENERAL FUND	SPECIAL FUNDS
Subscriptions, Donations, Collections, &c.	£17,737	£6,407
Legacies	4,493	107
Dividends, Rents, &c.	2,694	2,491
TOTAL RECEIPTS	£24,924	£9,005
PAYMENTS	£46,647	£11,233

The Receipts under the head of Subscriptions, Donations, and Collections for the General Fund from January 1 to July 31, in five consecutive years, compare as follows : 1885, £18,205 ; 1886, £17,126 ; 1887, £17,823 ; 1888, £17,760* ; 1889, £17,737.

* In addition, the Treasurers received in 1888 Securities of the value of £25,296 as "A Thankoffering to Almighty God for the extension of the Church in the Colonies and Dependencies of the British Empire and beyond it " ; also other Securities of the value of £2,263 as a Trust Gift, *the Income only being available.*

THE MISSION FIELD.

The field is the world. The seed is the Word of God.

OCTOBER 1, 1889.

THE BIBLE IN SOUTH INDIA.

BY THE REV. G. U. POPE, D.D., TEACHER OF TAMIL AND TELUGU IN THE UNIVERSITY OF OXFORD, AND CHAPLAIN OF BALLIOL COLLEGE.

"And I saw another Angel flying in mid heaven, having an eternal Gospel to proclaim unto them that dwell on the earth, and unto every nation, and tribe, and tongue, and people."—Rev. xiv. 6.

IT is a wonderful fact that 296 versions of the Holy Scriptures into the various vernaculars of the world exist and are in active circulation; and it seems quite evident that it is the steadfast determination of Christians to carry forward this work till the Bible is put into the hands of the men of every tribe in their own dialect.

And this pledges the Christian Church to send forth her ministers to explain and expound the text-book thus prepared.

Of the versions of Holy Scripture, the Tamil is unique in its history, as it is marvellous in its excellence.

The first attempt at translation was by a Mr. Fonseca, in Jaffna, in about A.D. 1650. He rendered the Gospel of St. Matthew into Tamil from the Portuguese. Subsequently the great Dutch Missionary, Baldaeus, Dr. Kat, Dr. Ruel, and others carried on and revised the work. I think the entire Bible was not then translated, but what was done was useful at the time, and has helped subsequent translators. It was remarkable for the beauty of the type cut for it. It may be noted, by the way, that there was much zeal of a certain kind among the Dutch in Ceylon for the propagation of Christianity; though this zeal was greatly under the influence of political considerations, and often not guided by any special wisdom, or by much knowledge of oriental human nature. There is something startling in the division, seen in the history of all Dutch territory, at once into parishes, in each of which a church was erected, a

Christian pastor appointed, and schools opened. The principle acted upon was, *what is Dutch must be Christian.* Hugo Grotius wrote his celebrated work *De veritate* to aid missionaries.

On October 17, 1708, Ziegenbalg, the renowned Danish pioneer of missions in Tranquebar, began his translation, and in 1719 had advanced as far as the Book of Ruth. Portions were published as completed, and one edition of the New Testament was printed at Halle. In 1725 Schultze, a German, completed the translation, including the Apocrypha. These translations were made from the originals, with diligent comparison of the chief versions—the influence, as was natural, of Luther's grand German Bible being very marked. This was our first complete Tamil version : faithful, strong, and coarse—as uncouth, sometimes, as the marvellous type in which it was printed.

In 1754 we find Johan Philip Fabricius, a man of learning, taste, and of very considerable poetic genius, engaged in an improved version. The whole Tamil Bible seems to have been so thoroughly revised by him that it was ever afterwards called Fabricius' Version. This translation is in very colloquial language, but in its simplicity is often sublime. The Psalms and Gospels are almost perfect. He was at work at it in 1773. The next hand laid upon it was that of the venerable and learned Rottler, a Dane, Missionary of the S.P.C.K. and S.P.G. from 1776. In 1819, Dr. Rottler was still at work on it, assisted by a young Prussian, C. T. E. Rhenius, afterwards a celebrated Missionary in Tinnevelly. By this time the second version had lost much of its identity and character.

In time Rhenius undertook the work of re-translation, and executed what may be called our third version. He was a good Tamil scholar, inferior to his predecessors in knowledge of the originals, but of a singularly clear and practical mind, though unfortunately given to paraphrase where dilution of the text is inadmissible. His version was idiomatic, easy, and clear, but often unfaithful, nerveless and loose— as unlike its predecessors as it well could be.

The fourth version came from Ceylon, and now, for the first time, Englishmen, with Americans, touched the work of Tamil Biblical translation. Mr. Knight (of the C.M.S.), Messrs. Spalding and Poor (of the American Board of Missions), and Mr. Percival (at first a Wesleyan, and afterwards of the S.P.G.) were engaged for some years in the work of revision. Their work fell at last absolutely into the hands of Mr. Percival, and was beautifully printed as a tentative version by the Bible Society in 1852;—a work of undoubted erudition, it is the antithesis of that of Ziegenbalg and Schultze. Abounding in Sanskrit and High Tamil words, pedantic and polished, it is in Tamil much what Dr. Johnson's "Rambler" is in English; and is curiously ill-adapted to its purpose.

And now comes the fifth chapter of our history. Almost every
Tamil Missionary, certainly every group of Missions, had worked at revision. Almost every point had been discussed, and the proposition
was at length made by the Madras Auxiliary of the Bible Society to
the S.P.G., that the Rev. Henry Bower, one of its Anglo-Indian Missionaries, a man of pre-eminent Tamil scholarship, and of great attainments
in other ways, should be appointed permanent and sole revisor, submitting his work to certain others for advice, with a view to the issue of
an authoritative and (as far as this is possible) final version, acceptable
to all. This has been, after about four years' toil, accomplished.*

The Bible Society bore all the expenses of this undertaking, published the edition in all forms and sizes, with headings, parallel
references, &c., and without them, and liberally supplies copies to all
who need them.

This version has met with almost unanimous approval, and certainly seems to me to be equal to any version in any language that
I know of.

It is, apart from its sacred character, the longest prose work in the
language, and will be a chief standard of orthography and of prose
idiom in Tamil. Indeed, Tamil prose, Tamil typography, and the
literature generally, owe almost everything to Missionaries (from
Beschi to the present) and to Mission presses. I am only stating
what belongs to my own sphere, but others can say much the same in
regard to the Telugu, Kanarese, Malayālam, and Tuluva languages.

If we left India now, these imperishable monuments of Missionary
zeal, industry, and erudition would remain.

This very brief sketch of the history of one of the many versions
of the " sacred Books of the West," showing how a long and very varied
succession of men of many nationalities have carried on this work with
unwearied patience, enthusiastic zeal, and with no small amount of
genius and learning, from A.D. 1650 to 1880, illustrates the spirit of
modern Missions.

In such a work *how good and pleasant thing it is for brethren to
dwell* and work *in unity together.* May it not tend to gain for us that
grace which shall draw us nearer and nearer, till a United Christendom
shall advance to the work—only thus to be completely successful—of
bringing the world to accept the Revelation so presented to them.

And now I would add a few considerations affecting the use to be
made of our versions, in South India especially.

I. When I look at the Tamil literature I seem to discern great
encouragement to believe that we shall succeed in making the Bible dear to

* Mr. Bower, who received from the Archbishop of Canterbury the degree of D.D. as some acknowledgment
of his labours, and was also created a Fellow of the Madras University, is gone to his rest. A long list of useful
Tamil works attests his diligence and ability. He was a devout humble-minded, loving-hearted man.

the hearts of that people ; for it has the best literature, and is in many respects the ablest, the most progressive, and the most thorough of Indian peoples. This literature is much concerned with heroes and saints. The legends of old Sanskrit literature have been translated into excellent verse by poets not inferior to *Valmīki* and *Kalidāsa*, and also into prose Tamil, while they have been worked into dramas, romantic poems, lyrics, and hymns. Besides which, the histories of the sixty-three *Çaiva* saints and of the *Vaishnava* apostles are circulated in every form, and are full of earnestness and of genuine pathos. Epics and shorter poems of Jain origin exist, and would do honour to any literature.

What I wish to emphasize is the fact that the Tamil people are quite capable of receiving and appreciating the Bible, which gives them histories incomparably more interesting and affecting than those of their own books.

The great work of the Christian Missionary is to hold up to the love, admiration, worship, trust, and imitation of men, the Christ of the Gospels. I find vast multitudes of men to whom the name of Rāma and of Krishna, supposed incarnations of Vishnu, are inexpressibly dear. I examine these histories, and find much that is interesting, affecting, and noble, mingled inextricably with much that is puerile, revolting, and degrading. If, then, in churches, in schools, in bazaars, by word of mouth, and by our publications, the Saviour of the world is perseveringly and piously made known, who can doubt as to the result ?

When men write about the success or otherwise of our work in India, I feel inclined to urge this consideration. It cannot be denied that as the result of Missionary work the idea of the great Master in the holiness of His character, in the majesty of His works, and in the ineffable excellence of His teaching, is becoming, and must ever more and more become, familiar to the minds of all classes and all ages of men in India. This will work its way, will win affection, respect, and reverence. I look for the regeneration of India from this exhibition of Christ, who will thus draw all men unto Himself. The main question is not how many have openly renounced heathenism, but to what extent is the great body of Christian labourers able thus to introduce the idea of the great Master into the minds of men. If from every Christian institution the savour of His saving name is being spread abroad by zealous, loving Christians, no one who has faith in Him will discourage their labours, or be doubtful about the result. Organisations, just at the present, may or may not flourish, but an influence is being extended which sooner or later must surely bring all India to the Saviour's feet. There is a work over and beyond that of gathering together bodies of converts ; and it is that of creating a Christian atmosphere in which no non-Christian system can live and move and have its being. Viewed in this light the whole aggregate of Mission work in India, and especially that of Bible translation, is helpful, hopeful, and mighty.   Perhaps Christian Missionaries themselves require to be reminded of this.   Christians at home must resolutely turn their minds away from statistics, and simply take heed that the men they send forth are men whose whole mind is set on bringing the personal Saviour before the minds of those for whom He died, and whom He has graciously promised to draw unto Himself when He is thus lifted up.

II. In a previous paper I have tried to show something of the Hindu mind, of its aspirations, of its mysticism, and of the mingling in it of what is almost sublime with what is altogether nugatory; does it not seem as though it were possible that the Christian Scriptures could be presented to this people as supplying all their need ?

I think that a very thoughtful and well-weighed exposition of the essentials of our faith, connected with sympathy and respectful recognition of what is even partially good in their own systems, must be effectual with men like the Tamilians in the south.

There is need certainly, as much of what has been said will show, of a certain care, candour and sympathy in a Missionary.   A great difficulty in dealing with the mass of Hindus results from mutual misapprehension.   They are familiar with your terms, but attach to them absolutely different ideas.

(1) As to *God*.   A god is a being like man, in one stage of the Metempsychosis, destined to pass through other stages and to obtain release. The Hindu eagerly tells you that he believes in the Supreme—the One and only God—as you do.   But, stay.   He speaks of the Supreme, not as " He," but " It," as an impersonal, unconscious energy, " a characterless self."   This belief is but a form of atheism.

(2) The Hindu is of course familiar with the words *Virtue, duty, holiness*, and their opposites, *vice, sin, impurity*; but the differences in motive and in standard make it necessary to define and guard your language when talking on these subjects.   To the Hindu, " holiness " is ceremonial purity, " virtue " is the performance of certain assigned acts of charity, " duty " is a strict regard to the requirements of class or caste, " sin " is the result of any acts good or evil which tend to perpetuate embodied existence.   " Remission of sins " is immunity from Metempsychosis through the exhaustion of the effects of past action. Thus " sin " and " sinner," as we use these words, are exclusively Christian terms.*

So careful discrimination is needed.   It will appear also that many Hindu errors are half truths.   At any rate, Hindus are not, in general, to be attacked with the weapons of scorn and ridicule, or to be treated as children.

---

* Compare Bampton Lecture on Psalms by the Bishop of Derry.   Second Edition, p. 128.

There is a tangled mass of luxuriant parasitic error, but if you can clear it away you will find some venerable trunk of truth which it hides, and perhaps has well-nigh strangled. Reasonings in religion require patient, humble sympathy. Especially is this the case in India, where all appears old and is new; where all seems fixed and is changing every passing hour; where all seems profound or subtle and is really shallow and trivial; where what is loftiest and what is lowest meet in the same utterance; where pomp of words with which the sonorous, mellifluous, copious and highly organised languages of the East abound, often conceal amazing poverty and monotony of thought, and utter inconsequence in reasoning, while the men are nevertheless fervent, and mean what they say, or, at least, fancy there really is a deep significance and power in it.

The method we pursue and are pursuing in translating and laying before them, fully and without reserve, the documents of our faith, is thoroughly opposed to their own traditional methods. With them the disciple kneels at his Guru's feet, and the teacher, kneeling over the prostrate disciple, breathes into his ear the mystical and often unintelligible syllables, a knowledge of which initiates him into the sect and degree in which he has to work out his own salvation. The Christian system puts into his hands the Word of God and proceeds to guide him in its study, and if to some persons it may appear hazardous thus to introduce the study of Holy Scripture, we maintain that we are thus honouring the Holy Spirit by whose inspiration all Scripture is given, and who is able to make it powerful to the conversion and edification of men. Our belief in the Holy Ghost prepares the way for the belief in the Holy Catholic and Apostolic Church; but of course the work is but begun when the text-book is provided for teacher and learner, and we are not insensible to the difficulties presented by the form and subjects of the Divine revelation. Is it wise to introduce men at once to the Bible as a whole, with all its difficulties of criticism and interpretation? This requires judgment, but on the whole it seems the only course open to us. I have often said to an inquirer something like the following: " Study in the Gospels the life and teaching of the great Master, and when you have placed yourself at His feet all practical difficulties will disappear and you will find the whole Bible a sufficient guide." But there is an order in all things, and it is only in the New Testament that the Old Testament will by-and-by lie open to men, and in this way and with this guidance I maintain that the Bible is the proper text-book of the Missionary in every land. Meanwhile our consideration of the Missionary work of the Church emphasises the necessity for the earnest and reverent study of all that may enable us so to teach it as to present no unnecessary stumbling-blocks to the inquirer after the faith. Doubtless the Christian Missionary requires in an especial degree sobriety, candour and freedom from all that might lead him to introduce men to doubtful disputations.

It is a serious thing to add anything to or to subtract anything from the whole counsel of God.

III. The existence in Tamil of such a body of Gnomic poetry as the Kurral and other works, whatever may be the source of the enlightenment of the authors, is a help to us in propagating Christianity.*

It may be said at once that it is very desirable that Missionaries, wherever this is possible, should study thoroughly and with appreciation the native literature. Only thus can they hope to be able to purify it, to supplement it, and, where this is necessary, to supersede it. It will be found by the student more and more that Tamil literature may be made a preparation for the study of the Bible. What Tamil sages have taught inconsistently is in the New Testament taught in a complete system. The points of divergence can be seen and pointed out. It can be shown that all that they were feeling after in the darkness is clearly taught by the great Master of mankind. But this is a subject which will require much detail and many quotations, which would be out of place in this paper.

IV. The vast importance of the translations of the Bible in the native church is seen from the peculiar position of the people. There is but a scanty Christian literature. Our native clergy and superior catechists read English, but the vernacular Scriptures form their chief study. To this many add the Greek Testament.

There are, of course, great disadvantages arising from the paucity of Christian books in the literatures of South India; but such works are multiplying, and it is of the highest importance that a good English education should be given to our converts wherever this is possible. While there is a danger of too much Anglicising them, there is great gain every way in urging on sound English education. On the other hand, this want of a Christian literature makes the excellence of our vernacular versions of the Bible a matter for most heartfelt thankfulness. Our native congregations are steeped in the language of the Bible; and it is a very remarkable fact that Biblical idioms and quotations are finding their way into non-Christian mouths and writings. Under this influence even heathen literature is slowly undergoing modification. The Bible is a mighty book to introduce into the literature of a people. I hope at a future time to say a few words regarding the Book of Common Prayer and its versions, and our Christian communities in general. In this paper we have seen something of the fulfilment of what S. John beheld in visions of the future—*an angel having an eternal Gospel to proclaim to them that dwell in the earth, and unto every nation, tribe, and people.*

* In my edition of the *Kurral* of *Tiruvalluvar* (Messrs. W. H. Allen & Co.), the reader may find abundant proof of this. I am hoping to publish the *Naladiyar* at the Oxford Clarendon Press. This work is called in Tamil by a name equivalent to "The Yeoman's Bible."

REWARI.

REPORT OF THE REV. T. WILLIAMS.

AST year we took our holiday in January, and have done so this year, but only for seventeen days. We spent it in a way to benefit ourselves, both bodily and mentally. Part of our programme was to make a few days' visit to Simla, for the sake of seeing what it really is, and for the cold atmosphere that we knew we should find there. It snowed the second day of our stay. This was particularly refreshing to my wife, who is now in her eleventh year of tropical residence. (As a matter of fact, we are at Rewari a little out of the tropics, and in our temperate zone, but this fact makes no diminution of the genuinely tropical heat we have here.) This few days' visit into the Simla temperature was equal to a visit home, and that not only because of the snow to see and feel, but also because of our finding there the fir trees, the holly and ivy, the oak with its acorn, and the wild briar.

The new railway from Delhi to the foot of the Simla hills, which has just begun to be made, will make it possible to thus snatch a few days of something like home at any time of pressing need. But there was another matter that attracted me very much. It was one of ethnography. As we mounted the 6,000 feet (or thereabouts) which measures the elevation of Simla above Kálka, which lies at the base, carried along in tongas, a sort of vehicle I had used regularly in the Deccan, I noticed that the labourers on the road were unusually fair. I asked where they had come from, and was told that they belonged to the neighbouring villages, and were Paharies, i.e., mountaineers. I noticed, too, that some had the mark on the forehead such as usually Brahmans and other high castes of the plains wear. I was told these really were Brahmans—mountaineer Brahmans—and that the others without the mark were Kanéts, and were the agriculturists of the district. These were quite as fair as the Brahmans. They were, all of them, much fairer than the people of the plains. I was wholly unprepared for this, because I was steeped in the notion that the Himalayas, like the other mountain ranges of India to the south and east, were inhabited by black aborigines, such as the Bheels, who are the natives of the hills of the Deccan, where I had lived. What, then, had become of the "black-born" of the Rigveda, who, previous to the Aryan invasion, had inhabited the Punjáb plains, and the far-reaching banks of

the Sarasvati, Jamnâ, and Ganges? and resolutely, and with varying
fortunes, had withstood the advance of the invader? There is no sign
of them on the Simla hills, nor yet on those beyond, for there the
Mongolian races meet us. It is my belief that the forefathers of these
very Kanéts and Brahmans — these "Paharies" — were themselves
refugees from the plains, fleeing before, not Muhammadi enemies, but
enemies of centuries earlier, belonging to times immediately preceding
and following the Christian era—enemies then of an alien religion, but
now absorbed in Hinduism, and represented by the Goojars, Ahios, and
Jats, who now hold the very plains these mountaineers' forefathers
formerly held. Of the invasions I refer to the Brahmans have kept no
clear record, but they occupied the period when the populations of
India underwent the tremendous changes which mark the radical
differences existing between modern and Vedic times. These differences,
it has been usual to attribute to Buddhism, or the Muhammadi invasions.
But these account for but a fraction of the great social upheavals that
have really taken place—and that during the period referred to above.
The limits of this period would be about 400 B.C. and 700 A.D.

In the hope of finding some satisfactory explanation of these moun
taineers being white, and not black, as one should expect, I have searched
all the Gazetteers that refer to these hill tracts, but have found nothing to
help me. Mr. Atkinson's "Himâlayan Districts," in three portly volumes,
are very full, but do not give me the answer I ask for. Inscriptions, coins,
and archæological researches are, however, gradually lifting the thick veil
of ignorance by which this period has been hitherto enveloped.

The fifth day found us returning from Simla, and after *doing*
Amballâ and Sahârunpur, we visited Hardwâr, the very famous Hindoo
place of pilgrimage. But never was I more disappointed. I expected to
find it a large place—it is but a large village. I expected to find it
abounding in ghâts—it has but few—very few—and those small. I ex
pected to find ancient buildings—especially ancient temples—but there
is, in my opinion, not one really old building there. There are, not
far from it, actual towns and ruined sites of towns that are larger
and older than Hardwâr, as, for instance, Kanakhal and Iwâlâpur,
and amongst ruined sites there is Mayurapur. This last is mentioned in the 7th century A.D. by the Chinese pilgrim Hwen-Thsang.
The Muhammadi writers are the first to use the name "Haradwar," but
whether the name be "Haradvar" or "Haridvar," is a point contested,
and sometimes, I have heard, actually fought for, by the adherents
respectively of "Haras"-Siva and "Hari"-Vishnu. The oldest name
is Gangâdwar = door of the Gangâ—a name that has nothing polemical
in it. The change to Haradvâr or Haridvâr evidently took place when
the above two sects rose into prominence, and which took place
probably about the time of the Muhammadi invasion. The town is not

L 3

really at the point where the Gangá debouches into the plain, for this it does not at *one* point but at more than one, and Hardwár is on the more westerly branch. This indefiniteness is so genuinely characteristic of Hinduism. The " Gau Mukh " (Cow's Mouth) is usually said to be the source of the Gangá, and so it is there the pilgrims go, but the real source is that of the Jahnavi, some few hundreds of miles more in the interior, and rising in Tibet beyond the Himá-layas, in alien terri-tory. So with the Godávery (the Deccan Gangá). For the pil-grim, Trimbak is the source, but the real source is farther west and farther away, but is not so picturesque. Brahman convenience governs Hinduism. Of course shops containing articles that may be bought for souvenirs of a visit to Hardwár and specially sanctified by having been pur-chased there, abound. In some were exposed for sale necklaces of wooden beads made here in Rewari. There are, about a hundred yards from the Mission House, a few families of the carpenter caste, some of whom

AGED HINDOO VOTARY AT HARDWÁR.

do nothing else but cut out and string these beads. They are sold ridiculously cheap. It brought the matter *home* to find these things so widely bought which had been made at my very door.

On leaving the town we saw a small herd of pigs taking their bath in the river close to the most westerly ghát. It is the common belief of the

people that the mere *opus operatum* of bathing in the Ganges at
Hardwár secures Svaoga, *i.e.* Heaven. If so they must expect a good
prospect for these pigs. It is at Magnoapur, a half mile below Hardwár,
where the Ganges canal starts. At this time it carried the whole of
the Ganges water that came by Hardwár, but of course the other outlet
of the Ganges to the east of Hardwár was not interfered with. Mr.
Hoppner's (our Missionary at Rurkee) use of the fact that the canal
simply appropriates the main part of the river for so many months in
the year, and so demonstrates that the goddess has become a bond-
slave to the government, is well known.

From Hardwár we went to Rurkee, where we have the interesting
Mission worked by Mr. Hoppner. We did not remain long enough to see
the working of the Mission, but were there long enough to form a very
high estimate of the station itself as a government laboratory. There
is the best engineering college in India, well appointed in every way,
well built and in a picturesque position. There is the iron foundry,
where all sorts of things, not merely iron, but also wooden, are made.
There is the splendid canal with its over-bridge and under-bridge.
There is the water-wheel of the flour-mill and the apparatus for pump-
ing up water for the cleansing of the streets of the native town. It
struck me as a sort of oasis of European civilisation in the midst of the
desert of native stagnation. With Rurkee, our holiday of seventeen days
ended, and on reaching Rewari I proposed to spend the whole of
February in the south-eastern part of my district, where as yet I had
not gone.

MY ITINERATION IN THE SOUTH-EASTERN PART OF MY DISTRICT.

I was very agreeably disappointed with all I saw. I found myself in
the midst of a people I had had, as yet, nothing to do with. They are
the Meos. This is quite a distinct tribe, belonging undoubtedly to the
aborigines of India, but not holding the subordinate position the
aborigines have generally been reduced to, for they are the farmers
tilling nearly all the soil of the Ferosepore Jhirká and Nuh subdivisions
of the Gurgaon Zillah to which Rewari belongs. They form the main
portion of the farmer class of the state of Ulvar, which borders us on
the south. It is here that their old capital, Tijárá, is situated, a few
miles from our border, and visited by me while I stayed at Ferosepore
Jhirká. Their country, called Mewát, was small but compact, and being
hilly, it less easily succumbed to the invader, and found it less difficult
to throw off the yoke at any relaxation of the invader's grip. Being
so near Delhi it had often to bear attack from Muhammadi rulers,
but yet maintained for centuries a *quasi* independence. But while
politically it struggled hard, and not always unsuccessfully, yet
religiously its struggles were less strenuous, for, though not very many
years ago every Meo was a Hindoo by religion as well as race, now every

—absolutely every—Meo is a Muhammadi. I should say they are unique in this. As yet I have not ascertained when and how this complete change took place. I repeat that it took place not so long ago, and though universal it was not genuine, for it is only just now that the distinctly Muhammadi practices and dress are being adopted. Repeatedly have I heard both Hindoo and Muhammadi say that the Meo is neither the one nor the other. But a drifting towards what is more decidedly Muhammadi has evidently set in. In this transition state I found that they listened more attentively and intelligently to what I had to say than do the Hindoo, and, on the other hand, were not animated by the hostile animus that seems to possess the genuine Muhammadi. I often felt that this is the juncture for introducing Christianity among them, but towards this how little can a yearly visit affect, especially since that visit can only be a short one and to but a small portion of the people, for there is no tribe equal to it in number in the Gurgaon Zillah, its actual numbers, as per census 1881, being 108,678, which is 44,000 more than the Ahir tribe, the next by numbers, and who are the dominant tribe around Rewari. It is clear that the Meos ought to receive special attention.

The places belonging to the Meos that I made my centres for four or five days' preaching were Taoru, Nuh, Bhadas, and Ferosepore Jhirkà. I will tell a little about each.

1. TAORU.

This is an old, but small town, beautifully situated in a basin rimmed by ranges of low hills, at a higher elevation than Rewari, and about twenty miles from it. It was once clearly a sort of frontier post for Delhi, holding in check the neighbouring Meos, for it has many ruined tombs, said to be Baloochi, i.e. belonging to Muhammadi officers who originally hailed from Baloochistan, numbers of whom were in the pay of the Delhi kings. Our preaching place here was in a well-paved but narrow bazaar. The crowds that gathered proved a serious obstruction to the traffic of the bazaar, and therefore provoked opposition on the part of the shopkeepers. At another time we must get a room, where our audience, though smaller, will be more select. The pundit of the place, by name Umvao Singh (a rather warlike name for a Brahman) interested me much. He has tried to learn English, availing himself of all the means in his way, and it was amusing to watch him display his knowledge. He did much to secure us a good hearing, and held very liberal views for a Brahman. He himself had evidently been much impressed in favour of the English and of Christianity by what he had learnt from a Brahman of his neighbourhood who had gone as a Government emigrant to Guiana in South America. The man's friends wished

him to return, and so applied to Government. In due course he did
return. This instance of the thoroughly good faith on the part of the
English, combined with the accounts the man gave of his journey, its
distance, and the care of those in charge, as well as of the Colony of
Guiana, had most favourably impressed Umrao Singh, and all his
neighbours doubtlessly, and won from him admiration, both of the
honesty and might of the Sirkâr. I have since sent him an English
Bible, which he acknowledged by a letter beginning in English, " My
dearest Sir," all the rest being part Hindi and part Sanskrit.

2. Nuh.

This is an old, but small and decaying town, standing on an elevated
site, but surrounded by land so low, though close to a range of hills, that
for several months in the year much of it is under water, and the place
is consequently notoriously unhealthy.

Two banerjas (shopkeepers) here rather patronised our preachings,
and we certainly had audiences as crowded as our hearts could wish.
So dense was the crowd one day that it gave rise to a regular street
fight, giving one, I imagine, a very good idea as to what an Irish row
means. There must have been much treading on toes generally, but
one man thought fit to resent it by plucking off his shoe and cudgelling
the one he deemed the offender. This seemed to act like a signal, for
instantly some scores of shoes were to be seen cleaving the air, and the
crowd heaved about this way and that, swaying as if it were some
animated fluid mass. From my position I had a full view of the
struggle, and was particularly distressed to see a poor woman, an
unfortunate, in the very midst of the *mêlée*, in a very pitiable plight.
However, it did not last long. I was surprised, indeed, at the
rapidity with which the broil quieted down. There was no policeman
there. Indeed, I rather suspect that amongst the Meos this kind
of effervescence, while to me rare, is to them an ordinary thing.
One day here our preaching had point given it by a discovery we made
that morning. Outside the town is a very fine and almost new tank.
The builder, a rich shopkeeper, built also near it a temple of Krishna.
Upon visiting the temple we saw the place where the idol should be
empty, but close by was the attendant Brahman baking his bread, and
close by on the other side was the Brahman's cow, and that a well-cared-
for specimen. In reply to our inquiry as to where the idol was, the
Brahman said that he had gone to lie down in an interior room, and had
not yet risen (8 A.M.), but would in an hour's time. "What!" said I,
"does your god sleep, does he get tired, and has he need, like men, to
retire for the night?" "Oh no," said he, "it is only our way of regarding him." I need not tell what was further said, but it may well be

imagined the use we made of the incident in the evening. A grin
gradually spread over the faces of most of our audience, especially at the
racy way my catechist put the matter. It is more the bond of habit
than that of faith that now binds the Hindoo to his idol.

3. BHÂDAS.

This was my centre, but is surrounded by small towns larger than
itself. Its site is an artificial one, but is the accumulation of hundreds
of years, for it is unusually high and extensive. It must, indeed, be
very old, for the inhabitants told me that, when they dig into it, they
unearth bricks of an extraordinary length, size, and hardness, the product of a remote time, for nowhere now are bricks made either as large
or good, they say. From the highest point of this artificial mound a
very extensive view is obtained of the surrounding country in all directions, the hills to the west and south-east making the landscape the
more pleasing. At Bhâdas the Meos listened as they did not in any
other place. It was here, too, that the singing of the Meo women first
drew my attention. Their voices were unusually good—more of *timbre*
in them than I had noticed elsewhere. For some reason or other the
Meo women are physically taller and stronger than the Ahir or Jât
women. I fear the Ahir women have to work unusually hard, while the
Meos men and women live an easier life. There is, too, a real liking for
singing. The rapt attention they pay to the making a perfect unison,
and the evident pleasure that a long-drawn-out perfectly united note
gives them, shows that they have an innate fondness for song. Immediately after leaving Ferosepore Jhirkâ I met a party of six Meo women
dressed in their best, and evidently going to a marriage. I courteously
addressed them, and begged that they would give me the pleasure of
listening to one of their songs. Modestly, and yet unhesitatingly, they
complied, and standing close together in a circle, and facing inward,
they sang me one. I was much gratified, and when it was over I
thanked them very heartily, and, wishing to do something to mark my
gratification, I offered a little child a rupee. They divined my object,
and pleasantly but firmly refused it for the child, saying that they had
not sung for my money.

4. FEROSEPORE JHIRKÂ.

This small town, about 8,000 inhabitants, is prettily situated. The
hills that I mentioned as coming in the Bhâdas landscape here approach
each other very closely, and where they are closest there lies this town,
but nearer to the western range. It, in fact, stands almost in the mouth
of the gorge in which, about three miles up it, is the perennial spring
from which the town gets the name "Jhirkâ" added on to it. The
meaning is "Ferosepore of the Spring," for "Jhir" = spring; and

there is in another direction, 240 miles away, on the Sutlej, another Ferosepore, famous in the Sikh war, and one of the largest arsenals in India. To distinguish what I may call my Ferosepore from this one, the addition "Jhirkâ" is tacked on to it. The way I went, it is fifty miles away, but there is a shorter way, through the Ulwar kingdom, which is only thirty-seven miles. I paid a visit to this spring, for it is indeed a rare thing to meet with a perennial spring away from the mountains. This locality, however, is blessed with another one, and that a medicinal one, at Sohra, which I also visited on this tour. The gorge is really a most romantic one, and exhibits the geology of the district in the stratified precipices bordering in a way nowhere else to be seen. Through the gorge is the way to Tijârâ in the Ulwar territory, and by which the nearer road runs to Rewari. It is a very old place, and, as I said above, is the old Meo capital. Half of the gorge, perhaps more than half, is British territory. What a contrast between the state of the road in the British part, which is far and away the more difficult, and that in the native state! The natives of India never went in for roads. A camel track, or bullock one, was well-nigh all they cared for, and that where now are magnificent trunk roads, and even railroads, under British *régime*.

At Ferosepore I spent a very pleasant time. Our preachings were unusually well attended, though throughout the district they had been very good. Here I met for the first time with a tahsildar—*i.e.*, executive native officer—in charge of a subdivision of a jillah, who was a professed Árya Samáji, and named Jugal Kishore, a Meithil Brahman. He was really the best specimen of that sect that I had as yet met. He is certainly an honest follower of Dayânand Sarasvate, for he every Sunday holds a meeting for worship and instruction according to the Árya Samáj principles and has evidently made an impression in the place, for I attribute the *respectability* of my audience in the streets to the more influential people having been really roused up by the Arya Samáj party in their midst.

Twice the tahsildar and his followers visited me for formal discussion. I had heard of the tahsildar before leaving Rewari, for Winter had written telling me of him, consequently I had many Sanskrit books with me, as being most important for such a discussion. Our argument elicited, first, that the tahsildar knew only what Dayânand had written; second, that what he had written was not in accordance with the Vedas and Shástra; and third, that Dayânand and his followers did not scruple to misrepresent and even to falsify the Hindoo sacred books. As an illustration of their unscrupulousness, the tahsildar said that the Dayânandis (*i.e.* Árya Samajies) intended bringing out an edition of the Manu Svarti (the greatest Indian law book), in which everything said about eating flesh was to be omitted! I did exclaim at this. It shows well how these would-be reformers are actuated. No word is oftener on their lips than "truth," and yet they deliberately and systematically go in for falsehood. I cannot think they will ever dare to mutilate the Manu Svarti to that extent, but judging from what I know has been done by the Dayánandis, the only thing that will deter them is the discredit an inevitable exposure will bring.

The tahsildar and I have begun a correspondence.

5. SOHNA.

This place I visited after Taoru. It is not really in my district but in Lefroy's. I was, however, within easy visiting distance and had heard much of it, so took advantage of this opportunity of seeing it. There cannot but be many Meos in it and around, for it has often been looted by them, and kept in possession for years at different times, and is really on the very border of what is called Mewat. It nestles close under the same hill that is continued in a range to Nuh, and beyond it to Bháda and Ferosepore. It is chiefly famous for its spring, alluded to above, which is a hot sulphurous one, welling up strongly at the foot of the hill. It is said to be particularly useful in healing a virulent sore that goes by the name of the Delhi boil. In fact those suffering from any skin disease find benefit from its waters.

The Rájpoots seem to predominate in and around Sohna, but the population is very heterogeneous.

6. DHARUHERA.

With this place what I may call my Meo tour terminated. I have already said something of this large village in a report two years ago.

I do hope that next cold weather a longer and more extended visit to Mewat may be made. All but the journeys to and from Dharuhera, eleven miles from Rewari, was done on foot, and though sometimes stinted for victuals and very tired, I am convinced that the more this sort of itineration be done the better for our work.

In March I visited the south-western corner of my district just as in the previous month I went to the south-eastern. I took as my centre the town of *Shahjahanpur* (usually pronounced Shájápoor), eighteen miles from Rewari on the Jeypore road. This again is the locality of quite an independent tribe called the Minas, whose habitat originally occupied the whole of the territory now embraced by the Rajpoot kingdom of Jeypore. These and the Meos were evidently neighbouring people and aborigines, but while the latter maintained until recent times a *quasi* independence, the Minas, as being probably less hardy, soon succumbed. They are now reckoned a " criminal " class, and in British territory they have been collected and form a colony at Shahjahanpur under police supervision. This means that twice every twenty-four hours, at twelve

o'clock noon and at twelve o'clock midnight, a policeman calls over all
their names, and every absentee is punished. They are consummate and
professional thieves, sometimes not stopping short of bloodshed. I saw
a little of them, but my time was taken up with the people of the town
and in visiting neighbouring villages. I was never treated by the
banerjas (shopkeepers) so well as here. A venerable old man, when I
first took my place in the bazaar, came, and beckoning me away, led me
to an excellent preaching place in front of a building half temple and half
sarai. It was indeed a good site. There was an elevated platform
on which the holders up of my picture stood, so that while within
easy reach of my pointer-stick, they were at the same time in the full
sight of the audience. I had some unusually thank-inspiring preachings
here. The schoolboys and I struck up a mutually good acquaintance.
They seemed to me to be near—some one or other—all day long.
Never did schoolboys pass a better examination in geography than did
the highest class here. I was much pleased. As to my tracts—I took
a goodly number there, but when I left scarcely a leaflet remained.

Not far from Shahjahanpur is a small but very old town called
Nimrânâ. Oh what a wretched, dead-alive little place it is ! It is to a
certain extent an independent place, its Râjâ being the senior representative of the Chauhan clan of Râjpoots, the clan to which belonged Prthoi
Râj, the last Hindoo king of Delhi. The little town is under the shadow
of a dilapidated palace, large enough to contain all the townspeople.
The present Râjâ is a minor, and is at school at Ajmere. A very good
congregation gathered in the Government Offices to hear my story, and the
Prime Minister (!) and Head of the Police (!) were oppressively courteous.

At a place called Jaunâchâ the inhabitants are almost wholly
Brahmans, and the only Brahman that has the reputation of a pundit
for miles around lives here. He was to have met me at Shahjahanpur
for discussion, but did not turn up, so I visited him instead. Evidently
that part of the country must be badly off if he be their best pundit.
But what the old man wanted in knowledge of Sanskrit was made up by
an excess of Brahmanic pride. In the midst of repeating a verse of the
" Rigveda " he suddenly stopped short, and showed by his manner that
it was not right to proceed because there were Shûdras present, in
whose ears the sacred words must not fall, and yet it is from them the
old man gets his bread and butter ! My best listener was a Brahman
who had visited Abyssinia in the commissariat of Lord Napier's army.
He was a pensioner, and to him the English Râj was a wonderful thing.
He had evidently impressed his fellow-villagers with something of the
same regard.

I retain pleasing recollections of my visit to this locality. I was
quite alone, and during my stay went everywhere on foot. Some of the
Shahjahanpur boys have since visited me.

FROM BLOEMFONTEIN TO THE ZAMBESI: A GREAT MISSIONARY JOURNEY.

BY THE BISHOP OF BLOEMFONTEIN.

(*Continued from page* 350.)

THE RETURN FROM ZUMBO.

AVING reached Zumbo, the Bishop would gladly have commenced his return journey without delay, but the donkeys needed rest, and he was not very well, so he resolved to postpone his departure for a few days. In the meantime he went to Kanyemba's and brought back provisions, clothes, medicines, &c., and endeavoured to map the surrounding country.

On Sunday, July 29, he writes :—" We had one service as soon as the verandah where we lived was free from people. They were more or less troublesome through the day; and they stole, among other things, my only towel, which I do not care much about, and my pocket Holy Communion set, which I do very much care for.

" I have arranged to go right down the river, and not return to Zumbo, but send the donkeys to Shipuriro's, and walk from somewhere near the Umsengaisi River to Mount Myambere, and there meet them, or return to our camp by separate roads. So I sent for Jelly, and explained that he was to go back on our track as far as Shipuriro's.

"*July* 30, *Monday.*—With very little difficulty, at about nine o'clock this morning we started down the river in one of the large boats made for the Portuguese, paddled by eight men, with one to steer and one to direct. My companions were Edward and John, Wilhelm and Kleinberg.

" Before I left I had given Kanyemba a blanket and a rug, and told Jelly to give him three knives and some powder, for he had been very hospitable and courteous. I gave the Portuguese five tins of quinine, and they gave me some white calico, and beads, and a goat.

" The boat was heavy, the paddles small, the men lazy; fortunately the stream is strong. It is perhaps more to be wondered at that natives will carry a paddle at all, rather than that they seem unable morally to continue doing it long. This form of paddling is more suited to the hollowed-out trees, brought from the Ruangua River, which are chiefly used here, some of which are more than thirty feet in length. To make these canoes with the tools at their disposal argues both patience, ingenuity, and perseverance on the part of the natives. As they paddle they frequently sing; their tunes are simple and very monotonous. The director usually starts them, and repeats the words, while the others sing a chorus. One wishes that they would sing less and row more, yet it seems to help them to work, and a great deal may be tolerated to gain that. Not that I feel my own intellectual standard to be a high one just now. The only book I have beside my Bible and Prayer Book is one of Kingsley's, and that I have not read for some time.

"Though there is little of beauty in this part of the Zambesi, it is strange and interesting: the immense reaches where the river widens out with sandbanks and shallows; the great volume of water, and the great strength of the stream in the narrower parts. The Zambesi is comparatively narrow opposite Zumbo, but lower down it widens into what looks like great estuaries. As it was getting dark to-day the boat ran on a sandbank, but after a great deal of talk and disunited action it was pushed off; while a huge hippopotamus close by watched us. These sandbanks must be constantly changing; even at this time of the year the dry banks on the riversides seem to be continually crumbling away. The amount of sand carried down when in the rainy season the river rises as much, at times, as eight or nine feet in the broad parts must be immense. The sand is finer than our river sand. There are a large number of crocodiles about. The people here have a superstition against killing them, as in Matabeleland.

"On reaching Matakenya's town we found his younger brother, who lent us a large hut. The chief himself was away, having gone up the river with the Portuguese Governor to find out why Buruma had attacked Zumbo and Kanyemba's town. As far as I can gather Buruma is chief of the Valenghi people, to the west of the Ruangua River. He came in great force with his under-chiefs, but was repulsed from both places.

"Matakenya's town is palisaded round; in the centre is the house of the chief, and those of his attendants, forming a kind of inner fortress, which would resist a strong force having no guns.

"Perhaps it is needless to say that the boatmen, though working for their own masters, found means of causing us annoyance, though fear of my sending back a messenger to their masters kept them, I think, somewhat in order.

"I slept very well in the cleanest part of a rather dirty yard—it

however, being cleaner than the hut ; the odd-looking pigs betaking themselves to a corner in another part of the same yard.

" *July* 31, *Tuesday.*—I talked for some time with Kanyemba's son,
and learnt much from him. The people over whom Matakenya and his
father are governors, under the Portuguese, are called Mutandi, and extend to the Umsengaisi River. He had been educated in a Portuguese
school at Quilimaine, and the people owe their higher form of civilisation
to the Portuguese. No missionaries, however, have been here since those
who were killed near Zumbo. He seemed very ready to learn, but then
neither his nor Matakenya's family are Mutandi ; they call themselves

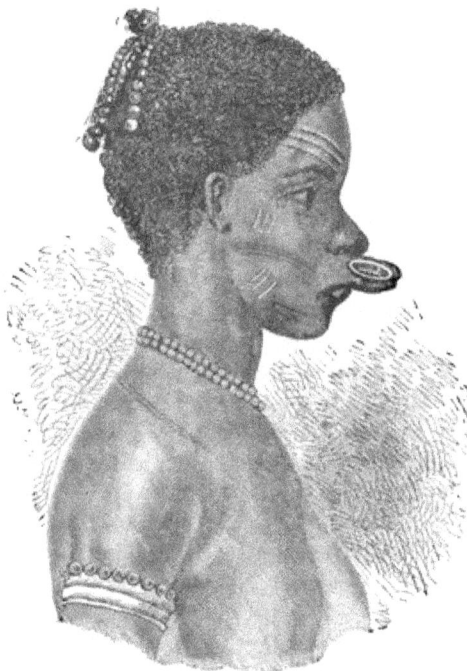

A ZAMBESI WOMAN WITH UPPER LIP RING.

Ba-Nyungwé, *i.e.*, they originally come from Tette, Nyungwé being another
name for Tette, and they are of a much higher type than the Mutandi.

" Here I saw the lip ring as worn by the Basenga women. No
description could give any idea of the disgusting appearance of this
monstrosity. I fancy that the pictures of the lip ring, as worn by the
women of the Shire River, represent only the upper lip as thrust forward,
but here both lips have the ring, and both therefore stand out. The
rings vary in size with the age of the wearers, larger ones being worn
as the women grow older. The smaller rings seem to be shaped like a

small hour-glass, while those for the older women are like huge coins. This custom gives to the women the appearance of having pigs' faces.

"These people make tiles and wooden doors, &c., for their houses. They grow the sugar-cane, and crush sugar out by an ingenious contrivance made of wooden rollers, then boil and dry it.

"The chief seems to carry on a large trade in ivory, for which he gives beads in exchange. Some very curious flint-lock guns were kept in his house; four or five of them were very heavy, they carried ten bullets, and it took two men to fire them off.

"It was very interesting to see an English Bible which had been given to Matakenya when he went to Iniati to see Lobengula, by Mr. Thomas, the London missionary.

"I gave each of the young chiefs a good knife; they gave me some food, and came down to the boat with me.

"We went on paddling and floating along till nearly sunset,. when the men stopped and insisted on sleeping on a sand-belt, for fear of lions. We tried for some time to persuade them to go on to where there was wood, but they would not; and after all, nearly any place does to eat and sleep on. The mosquitoes are numerous and have a more painful bite than any others that I have met with, but their bite is not poisonous. The water of the Zambesi is peculiarly soft, and very warm, its temperature at sunrise being 60°."

At Matakenya's the Bishop obtained the last information about his young friend Richard Foster; from which it would seem that he was at Zumbo in December 1887, having arrived there with one boy in a boat from Tette, that he went up the Ruangua River for five days, when he was obliged to return for want of food; that he came to Matakenya's, where he obtained the service of four men; that he passed through Kanyemba's country, and went on his way to Shipuriro's, at which place he never arrived. It is probable that he was killed for the sake of his beads, but where and by whom could not be ascertained.

"*August* 1, *Wednesday.*—We started soon after sunrise. The river was well bordered with trees; mountains were on the left bank, and a small hill now and again rose on the right bank, till the afternoon, when we reached Mount Manyambere, which is of great length but little height; from this place the hills on the left recede to some distance from the river. We halted near some very hot springs on the north bank, which had a strong taste of what seemed to be iron. The water was so hot that I could not keep my fingers in it for longer than a couple of seconds. Here we saw some beads lying on the bank, which the men would not take, for a man had been killed there by a lion, and these were supposed to be his beads. On leaving here we went on again till shortly before sunset, when the men stopped to get wood, but would not stay for the night on account of their childish fear of lions. They rowed to the middle of the river, and made preparations to land on a sandbank that rose about a foot out of the water, where they intended to sleep. After vainly remonstrating with them against this, I became angry, for the first time since I left the camp. It had an immediate effect, and though they had harder work than they had done throughout the day to reach the opposite bank, owing to the strength of the stream, they did it without a complaint. It was very dark, and I thought it quite possible that we should be carried anyhow down the river on to some sandbank, of which there are many hereabouts. The men are very irritating, and I was very uncertain where we should go to; yet it was hard not to laugh at their shouting and quarrelling, and the yells to go on from the director. Sometimes they would stop to talk or do nothing, when it was of great importance to keep the boat's head to the stream, and when we ran on a bank they pushed and pulled in a most helpless sort of way. I have seen a man, when helping to push the boat off a bank in the middle of the river when it was getting dark, stop to ask for a light for his tobacco. Their power of making a quarrel is also extraordinary. One man had been deputed by the Portuguese to point out the mountains, &c., to me. I, foolishly, after the experience that I had gained, said that I would give him a knife if he told me everything well. This knife he soon demanded on the ground that I intended to cheat him. The knife was given. Then he wanted to know if that was all I was going to give him for telling me the names of the mountains. He wanted calico, and he must have calico—three very long yards, when the bag was opened—or he would tell me no more names, and for a time he would not. But on being told that he should have no calico except he gave me the information I wanted, he relented. In the evening the calico was given; then he complained that it was short measure, and his friend was made to show that it was not. But the friend wanted calico also, for he had told me the names of one or two places, and so required half the quantity the other had received. Ultimately they were induced to go to their camp under the bank, wrangling and squabbling and talking as only the natives of this country seem able to do. I become more and more convinced that the power of stringing words together arises more from emptiness than fulness of brain; certainly their power of going on saying something is extraordinary. A few days ago I was attracted by the length of time that a man had been speaking to another man, who said 'Eh' after each sentence, and then I began to count the sentences, when he added 217 more. This talk was about some corn and an ox, or oxen, which he had been to see about, and which had been sent by Kanyemba."

August 2, Thursday.—After a topographical description of that part of the Zambesi plain which was within his view, the Bishop proceeds :—

"We reached Perizemgi's town, at the mouth of the Umsengaisi, quite early. Our path goes to the south from here, so far as I can learn ; but as I think the people do not know anything for certain beyond the next village, I propose starting for the next village to-morrow morning. They would not start to-day, though we could have gone more than half-way. The way in which the men pass the day, except something extraordinary occurs, is almost incredible, and one wonders that a creature with the form of a man and having an immortal soul can so exist.

"The people of this town are composed of Banyai and Chicunda. Their headman, who is now at Zumbo, is named Perizemgi ; and he is a 'Capitão' appointed by the Portuguese. The people immediately on the other side of the Zambesi are called Vapendi ; those farther away, Basenga, who are also round Zumbo. Those along the south bank from the mouth of the Umsengaisi to Kanyemba's town are Mutandi. The Shidima country is to the east of this as far as Tette. The people there are called Atavara. Some Mutandi live on the Umsengaisi ; but Banyai villages soon begin, and continue till we arrive at those of the Mashona. Some

A LION IN THE CENTRAL AFRICAN DESERT.

Banyai live among the Mutandi on the south of the Zambesi, between here and Kanyemba's.

"The trees here are much the same as those along the rivers running from Mashonaland, and on the higher ground much the same as on the higher ground there. There is a very large tree in the inclosure here, called museke ; it is more symmetrical than any that I have seen, and apparently it is growing in an old ant-heap, for its roots extend several feet above the level of the ground.

"Placed on a heap of stones in the sun, the thermometer registered 120°.

"No one who has not had dealings with heathen natives would credit what a repulsive degradation of humanity they are; seeming to combine the high development of rascality and cunning as found in professional London thieves, with a shamelessness which few of them have; while their miserable stupidity, in nearly every case where their own interests are not concerned, is only to be appreciated by those who have been subjected to it. Living somewhat intimately among them is a refutation such as nothing else could be of the belief that heathen natives are better than Christian natives, and an argument for the necessity of raising them, if only to the level of those inferior representatives of Christianity as are found in every colonial town. It is idle to speak of natives such as the Basuto, who have been raised by many years of contact with Christianity and civilisation, as specimens of heathenism, though thousands may believe in no God, and grease their bodies with pig's fat and yellow ochre.

"The boatmen who had been engaged for me by the Portuguese, and for whom I paid very highly, demanded payment from me also, and were more violent in their protestations than any I have yet had to deal with. After careful explanation I said that they would get nothing more, and they went to sleep, apparently very angry.

"*August* 3, *Friday.*—The boatmen were perfectly happy and friendly, which they certainly would not have been had they really considered themselves unpaid, as they asserted. I gave them a small present, and they wished us a prosperous journey most courteously.

"Having paid the carriers very highly, there was very little difficulty in starting them; but some, after going about 100 yards only, put down their loads to go to their houses to have food.

"We crossed the Umsengaisi River four times to-day. The road, being by the side of the river for a large part of the day, was pretty, but the walking on the high ground among the mopani trees is much the easiest. The heat has exceeded anything we have yet had. Edward has a slight touch of fever this evening, but Warburg's tincture will probably drive it away. We arrived at Makombe's before sunset. It is the first Banyai village on our route. There are no huts here, and the people are living under boughs, having been driven from their original village by the Chicunda. They seem to be living on the fruit of the baobab tree, though it is very possible that their own laziness is the cause of their having nothing else.

"*August* 4, *Saturday.*—After a good deal of trouble I hired and paid nine men to carry, and hoped that they would soon start; but then the grinding of their food began, then the cooking and eating, then the taking of snuff; all being done with a leisurely insolence which must be seen to be believed, and accompanied by the remark that it was getting late and they would not be able to reach the next village."

(Note by the Bishop some time after: " Possibly, in the wish to start quickly, sufficient allowance is not made for the inability of the native to understand the value of time; and possibly what we may consider his insolence is nothing more than good-natured contempt for one in haste.")

"We crossed the Umsengaisi three times in all to-day, and for nearly a mile walked along the bed of the large Macumburra, a sand river, on leaving which our carriers missed the track, and further delay was caused. When they rejoined us they refused to go any further, on the ground of there being no more water in front; but after a further delay they were induced to go on, having been lent a water-bottle. Edward, John, and I had filled our water-bottles for the night, but before arriving at the sleeping-place Edward had quite, and John almost, finished their water. Edward said that he could not help it. I daresay the fever made him very thirsty, and the heat was very great, as it always has been over this horrible plain. However, we managed somehow; but the carriers said they would go back to-morrow; then that they would be paid again before starting; then they complained that we had brought them where there was no water, and they had an ill-look on their faces as they eyed us over the fires. It was not a pleasant ending of a day passed chiefly in walking over a dreary flat, the object of most interest being a human skull and some few bones, the remains of a poor creature whom the men said had been killed for the sake of the poor valuables that he was carrying.

"If the people killed this man for his property, it is probable that they may have killed Richard Foster also. After a deal of questioning, I was unable to find out exactly who the man was, or who killed him. The carriers seemed to know all about it, but I could not make them explain the details sufficiently clearly for me to understand them.

"Perizemgi had a village on the Umsengaisi in our path, but is said to have left it owing to the number of lions. This seems like an immense land under an immense curse: if it be the curse of Ham, the curse of Ham was a very terrible one.

"*August 5, Sunday.*—We wished to reach water before the sun was hot, so Edward called us at 3.30, and soon afterwards we were packed and waiting for light. The men were paid again and walked very fairly. I was not sorry for a little delay, for I thought that my knee would give me trouble. John and I missed the first water, and waited half a mile ahead of the men while they were at their breakfast. Nyantequi's town, a place belonging to the Banyai, was reached early. The chief was away, but his two wives came to see me, to whom I gave a present. They gave me in return some meal and corn, and sold me more, for which I paid rather highly. I spoke to them for a short time on my Mission, and told them how they should receive a missionary when he

came among them. One of the last relay of carriers, a superior sort of man, said that they would like to have a white man to live with them; but for this reason, as it turned out, because he would teach them to grow corn, and would give them biscuits such as I had given him. As the two great ladies went away, they derided the other women of the village, saying that they were not afraid to come and sit near me.

"We had to wait a long time for some meal which I had promised

HIPPOPOTAMI.

the men, and then were delayed nearly another hour while the lazier ones smoked and ate; and after we had started, we had not gone more than two miles before the carriers wished to stop for the night, but on receiving their calico they walked on till nearly dark, covering about twenty miles.

"The Bechuana man has bad symptoms; Edward, however, is well. He says that he had a very bad headache, and was very deaf yesterday;

but then I had put a good deal of quinine into his mug without measuring, which seems effectual.

"If it should be considered wrong to travel on Sunday, I can only say that, under the circumstances, we were the best judges of that. We slept at Mamatseo's, a Banyai village.

"*August* 6, *Monday.*—The great heat of the nights has ceased, and we slept in comfort, getting up as soon as there was an appearance of dawn in the sky. The country through which we passed to-day was the most pleasing that we have gone through in all the plain; the mopani trees were numerous and grew to a great size, and clumps of fan-palm broke the monotony of the mopani; but the tsetse fly was very bad. All went well till John, who was in front, shot an eland, when the usual scene took place, and the men wished to go no further, saying, no more water was to be had. Not till they were made to understand that they would have no meat unless they came on, did they resume their journey. But they soon stopped again, declaring that there was no more water, and that they would go no further. The Kadzi here is a sand river having water under the surface. Though the meat causes trouble, it is a great help to us in walking, especially as we have but two meals a day.

"*August* 7, *Tuesday.*—Khama's man has fever. The carriers gave us trouble before they would start. Then we walked beside a good deal of water, showing how these men had lied; but one of the traits which distinguishes the heathen natives from the partially civilised, or most degraded class of Europeans, is an entire absence of shame.

"We stopped at Umsusa's, the last Banyai village. The Banyai must be a branch of the same family as the Mashona; the language is closely allied, and their appearance is much the same—very unlike the Bantu races, *i.e.*, the Zulu, Basuto, Bechuana, &c.

"To have seen these people, and to have had dealings with them—to have seen fallen humanity untouched by the regenerating influences of Christianity—is an argument for the necessity of Missions such as nothing else could provide, should the command to Christianise all nations not carry sufficient force.

During the walk to-day the mountains could be seen clearly in front, a sight for sore eyes; not that mine are sore, except where a piece of the reed, that by courtesy passes in this country for grass, had cut the white. It is a strange formation, the vast plain, with the long line of mountains rising abruptly from it; the difference of climate as seen by the growth of sub-tropical plants, such as the fan-palm, which are not found in the higher ground; and the tsetse fly, which is left immediately that the mountains are reached. Where the mopani grows—that is, on the very well drained ground—the walking is very good, and the surroundings pleasant and healthy, though generally devoid of

any interest; while in other parts, especially on our path to the
Zambesi, the country was very repulsive : the coarse yellow grass,
thicker than straw, the thorns, the masses of a kind of weed which
makes the place smell like the Zoological Gardens, the annoyance and
pain which are continually being caused in small ways when one is
brought into contact with nature. Some time ago, for instance, I took
up a large seed to examine it, and my hands were immediately rubbing
each other in order to get out the prickles from it, which were really
painful. Those of the prickly pear could not be compared to these.
Fortunately I could find my carbolic oil immediately. Edward had
some of these prickles in his chin, and he has sores there still.

" I hired another carrier to carry the sick man's things, and, after
great delay and high payments, we started for the mountains, which
were reached in the afternoon, but which the men would not go up,
though two of them went off to find the remains of some animal that
had been killed by lions.

" *August* 8, *Wednesday.*—Wilhelm is also ill with fever. We reached
Umsusa's village in the evening. The two sick men could barely get
there. Edward and John behaved admirably. The carriers went away,
after behaving during the day, like all the rest of their kind, abominably.

" *August* 9, *Thursday.*—Last night and this morning the men were
properly dosed with quinine, not small quantities by weight, but a
little meal of it. They had Warburg's mixture also. They say that
they are deaf, but they can both walk.

" With no trouble at all a new relay of carriers started. Only once
was there a difference of opinion, when some wished to go back to tell
someone else that they had heard that a Matabele man had been killed
close by. I did not believe that any Matabele would come alone into the
country, and so they went on. We soon struck into the old path and
reached Shipuriro's early, about three hours before the time I had told
Jelly to expect me. I was a good deal astonished at his being there
by the day on which I appointed ; but learnt from Edward that it was
fear that I would keep my word and not wait for him that had brought
him along. On arriving at their skerm I found Khama's other man
huddled up by the fire suffering from fever ; Jelly had it also, though
not badly. He had hired three men and two women, with the promise
of my cloth, to carry for him. It appears that his heart failed him
after he had been two days on the road. He was either afraid of the
plain or the hills, or of having some trouble with the donkeys, and
so hired these people, and drove the donkeys with scarcely anything
on them, which saved him a very great deal of trouble ; and as I had
allowed him one and a half days' margin, he was able to come up to
time. But the man brought a boy with him, whom he said Kanyemba
had given him, intending of course that he should be given to me

FALLS OF THE ZAMBESI 400 MILES ABOVE ZUMBO.

in return for my presents to him. I could only call the boy and tell him that he was free to go where he liked, and try to induce him to go back, which he, having had enough of the plain, refused to do. So I told him that if he worked for me he would be fed and paid ; not that I want him, but in order to show that the English do not have slaves. He will stay with us; but he has a bad cough, which the climate of this colder country will probably make worse.

" We rearranged the packs for to-morrow's journey. One donkey and both the dogs have died from the tsetse fly.

"*August* 10, *Friday.*—We hired three carriers, who were excellent ; and we walked to-day the distance it had taken two days to do on the journey up. We sleep at the Mabare River.

" *August* 11, *Saturday.*—A day of almost perfect rest. For twenty miles the carriers walked without a word of complaint; but then they said they ' were dead.' Some other of the donkeys are beginning to feel the effects of the tsetse fly bites, and go but slowly. We breakfasted on the south side of the Musiqué River, and sleep at the Brook Morere.

" *August* 12, *Sunday.*—We walked to Kurusu by shortly after 10 o'clock, and there made arrangements for carriers to the waggons. The chief lives on Gato Mountain, a curious formation corresponding to Kurusu. On the summit of the topmost block of stone the grain hut was built, for use in case the people were driven there. The chief's son was made a slave of by the Matabele when a boy, and is now staying here. His education among the Matabele has made him superior in dealing with white men to the Mashona. He has a rough good-natured courtesy, and a civil independence that would be hard to find among the Mashona; and he is as superior to the ordinary Matabele as he is to the ordinary Mashona.

" I told the chief to come to our skerm, when I gave him a present. The son said that he knew I was a teacher ; but I could say very little to him, as there was a great crowd of people that had been collected apparently by a beer-drinking.

" Another donkey died to-day from the tsetse fly."

On August 13, the Bishop made a long day's journey in the direction of the waggons, which were then said to be two more days off. On the 14th, before starting, he had to shoot a donkey dying from the effects of the tsetse fly, and made a painful journey to the Mozuatadzi brook with tired men and exhausted or sick animals. Indeed, two more of the donkeys died on the road. On Wednesday, August 15, he thus writes :—

" The guide said that we could reach the hill where the waggons were if but a little weight were carried. So leaving the last of my meal for the carriers, and part of my oatcakes for John, Edward, and Wilhelm, I and the Matonga started with four carriers very early.

"For the first two hours we went through wet grass; but the carriers had not stated facts accurately, for at about one o'clock we reached the waggons, after some fifteen or sixteen miles' walk only.

"Before doing anything else we thanked God for His preservation of us, and indeed we had good cause to be thankful.

"Everything was in the same order as though Isaac had expected us to-day. Without going into the question as to the value of Christianity, or the profitableness of Missions, it certainly is the greatest comfort to have Christian servants on such a journey as this. There is little in common between Isaac and the ordinary heathen here, except that they both have black skins. Everything has been done as I told him. The horses and dogs were fat and well, except that one of the latter had been caught by a crocodile, but escaped with a bad bite in the thigh.

"Mr. Dunn was just starting with Count Schweinitz's waggons for the south; but he now stays here for this evening, and rides on to-morrow. There seems to be some idea of the Indunas making difficulties on the Sabi road by saying that no road exists that way. The Count is going by the shorter road, so as to be home by Christmas. How I should like to be home by Christmas!—but I think that far the larger number of Mashonas live to the south-east, and I wish to do the work and keep faith with the Society."

(To be continued.)

LORD ADDINGTON.—IN MEMORIAM.

IN Lord Addington, the Church of England loses almost the last of a generation, now rapidly passing away, of eminent Laymen who brought to bear upon Church finance, in connection with its work in foreign parts, the same powers of practical wisdom and enterprise as distinguished the conduct of their own commercial pursuits.

What the late Mr. Philip Cazenove did for the S.P.G., that did Mr. Hubbard for the Colonial Bishoprics Fund. As one of its Treasurers from its foundation in 1841, he applied all his vast experience and knowledge of finance to the creation and extension of the Fund, which has been the chief instrument in building up the Episcopate abroad by securing for it the advantages of whole or partial endowment from the bounty of the Church at home. Whatever of stability in temporal matters is now possessed by the several dioceses which owe their origin to that Fund is almost exclusively due to the watchful care and vigilance of its Treasurer, who, first as Mr. Hubbard and afterwards as Lord Addington, maintained to the end of an honoured life that interest in its operations with which its original designs had from the first inspired him.

He dedicated his high position in the world of practical business to the advancement of the Church's interests both abroad and at home. And though the Colonial Bishoprics Fund was the first object of his regard, he always showed a warm interest in the kindred work of the S.P.G., of which he was elected a Vice-President in 1868. Indeed, his labours of love for the Church of England in every department of its work will ever be held in grateful remembrance by all who duly appreciate their value; and its best hope for the future depends on whether others among the laity will arise to emulate his example, though worthily to fill his place may involve more sacrifice of self than perhaps is given to the generation of Churchmen which succeeds him.

THE CHILDREN'S CORNER.

THE COAST OF LABRADOR.

ACCOUNT OF A WINTER'S "CRUISE," BY THE REV. J. BALL.

ON October 24, 1888, I left Mutton Bay for Old Post, remaining there until January 1889. Only two families were in the bay at the time of my leaving, their neighbours having gone to their winter houses, where there is more shelter, and wood within easy distance. Old Post is about a mile from Tabatiere, and both places are situated about four miles due north from Meccatina or Grosse Isle, Gulf of St. Lawrence, Canadian Labrador. Tabatiere is the best seal fishery on the coast.

Perhaps a brief description of the mode of catching seals might not be uninteresting. I will therefore commence by stating that seals are caught by means of nets, one end of which is fastened to iron rings attached to bolts let into the rocks; the other end is secured to a buoy-rope, attached to a heavy anchor, which is sunk in about ten fathoms of water. The foot rope of the net must be kept tight at the bottom, for when the seals find their progress checked they dive, and if any space is available will make their escape underneath the nets. The nets are loose and baggy at the ends. This plan frightens the seals, and in their bewilderment they endeavour to force themselves through, when they become entangled in the meshes of the nets. Men in boats overhaul the nets, and bring the captured seals ashore; they are then put away in store-houses until spring, when they are scalped, and the fat rendered into oil. Seals weigh from one to three hundred pounds each. Between the carcase and the pelt is a solid mass of fat, in the large ones about two inches thick. This fat is first cut from the carcase with long sharp knives, slightly curved, and afterwards skinned from the pelt. The *fonnderie* is made about the end of April, and consists of a rude furnace, with an iron boiler, into which the fat is thrown and melted. The oil is put into barrels, and is worth from 25 to 30 cents per gallon. Previous to the discovery of petroleum, it fetched 50 cents per gallon. The skins are valued at about $1·30 each. The average value is about $3·00 (three dollars) per seal, so that a good seal fishery is a valuable possession. Last year the Tabatiere fishermen secured not quite 550 seals, and Old Post 197. This was considered about half a "voyage." As many as two thousand have been captured in one season at Tabatiere, and as few as five. It is very cold work, as the seals pass along the coast during the month of December. The ice and rough weather frequently wreck the fishing craft. The fishermen also suffer great annoyance from sharks, enormous creatures, sixteen feet long. When these become entangled in the nets, they do great damage. Several seal fisheries on this coast which were once flourishing are now abandoned, the proprietors, being reduced to poverty, not being enabled to replenish their nets, owing to bad voyages. The carcases are of little value, being mostly used to feed dogs. Many people, however, eat them, fresh meat being a very scarce article during winter on the Labrador.

My time was occupied at Old Post teaching school five days a week, four of the Mutton Bay families having their winter-houses at Bay Rouge, about a mile distant. There were thirteen scholars. This, in connection with regular Sunday duties, kept me fully employed, so that when the middle of January arrived I found the winter was half gone, and had been scarcely noticed.

On January 16 I started upon my visitations along the coast. It was a bitter cold day, with a biting east wind. The bays not being frozen, we had to take the lakes in the interior. We left Old Post about 8 A.M., but did not reach Grande Coupe until near 4 P.M. The first part of the journey the wind was dead ahead, and, as it was my first day out, by the time our destination was reached my blood was almost chilled. Evensong and baptism at Grande Coupe. Next day (Harrington), evensong and two baptisms. 19th.—Started for Wolf Bay, which was reached after much difficulty. The bays being still unsafe, we had to take the inside "leads," and at Cross River the rocks were polished like glass bottles. At one place we had to unhitch the dogs and let the cometique down end foremost. There was just about ten feet to land upon, after making a very slippery descent of twenty or thirty yards down an almost perpendicular rock, and the wind seemed always ready to drive you over the cliff, at the bottom of which was open water, fathoms deep. The utmost caution was necessary in making this passage.

We reached Romaine on Monday, and put up there for the night, not being enabled to reach Musquarro that day, owing to the inside run being so much longer than outside on the bays. Here my teamster had to take a pilot, there being some dangerous rapids to pass at the Washa-cootie River. Musquarro was reached in good time, where we put up for the night. I was unable to proceed to Kegashka, owing to my teamster not being acquainted with the interior. We also learned that there was no dog food there, and, as thick weather threatened, it was deemed advisable to return. Romaine was reached next day, but such a storm of wind and snow that night. We were thankful to be in a country of which my teamster had some knowledge, and with the

prospect of getting his dogs fed when they arrived back at Wolf Bay.
There we passed a second Sunday with two services. Monday.—Very
stormy. 29th.—Left Wolf Bay at 9 A.M., arrived at J. Gallibois', Roman
Catholic, 4 P.M., distance about 18 miles; but the travelling was very
heavy, with snow falling. At this place, some years ago, Gallibois'
father was caught in a blizzard, and lost his way within a mile of his

TRAVELLING IN LABRADOR

house. He was found next morning frozen stiff. The surrounding
country thereabouts is very level, and there are few landmarks to guide
you in thick weather. We were hospitably entertained for the night, and
our host, though a Roman Catholic, harnessed his dogs next morning
and took me to Harrington, leaving my own teamster to bring the

luggage. It was an exciting run of five hours' duration. The way those dogs, seven splendid fellows, thoroughly under command, raced down the rocky hill-sides, those only can judge who have tried it. The bays were still unfrozen, and the recent snowfalls had covered the icy rocks, thereby making the return passage at Cross River more difficult and dangerous than it was two weeks previously. But Harrington was safely reached, though only just in time to escape a furious storm of wind, sleet, and rain, with piercing cold temperature, which lasted three days. We could only hold one week-night service. People could not venture out.

After visiting other places, we started on February 13 from St. Augustine River for Shecatico. We had the misfortune, however, to be caught in a blizzard, and my teamster was unwilling to proceed. So we made for an unoccupied house at L'Anse au Portage, which was reached. We were thankful to find a stove, but the pipes were choked full of snow, and when the fire was started we were almost smothered with smoke for about an hour. There was scarcely any wood, and we had no provisions. In this predicament we were thankful to discover a young harbour seal in one corner of the house, so when the stove pipes were thawed out, and a pile of fuel had been gathered somewhere, the harbour seal was placed near the stove, thawed out, scalped, and cooked. It was either that or no supper, and we had had nothing to eat since breakfast, some twelve hours having since elapsed. We found it not bad eating, our appetites being keen enough to eat anything digestible. But it was very fresh, and we had neither pepper, salt, nor bread to eat with it. The night was passed in an old chair, and for some hours we were oblivious to everything, except when the fire got low, when we were forcibly reminded that there is a great difference between lying on a feather-bed covered with blankets and sitting upon the soft side of a plank wrapped in an overcoat. My voice was rather husky for some days after, the little room in which the night was passed being about six feet by twelve, was embedded in snow, and very damp. When day broke it was somewhat clearer, but no sooner had we started than the wind began to blow and the snow to drift, which increased our difficulty in finding Mystinock Island. We were at length successful, and, having burst in the door of R. Shittler's summer-house, hoped to find some eatables ; but disappointment awaited us, only some small "rounders" (cod-fish) could be found. There being a good stove and plenty of wood at hand, a fire was kindled, and two of the fishes roasted. They were found to be very salt, but this helped to take off some of the freshness of our last night's meal. Shecatico winter-house was reached before noon, when we had the pleasure of partaking of a "good square meal." Through March I went on from one place to another until I arrived back at Old Post, on April 4, about 6 P.M., thus finishing a winter's "cruise" of exactly eleven weeks and one day.

NOTES OF THE MONTH.

FOR the loss of those, who having fought a good fight for many years, we are ever sorry; but not less deeply do we feel bereaved when a young life of great promise is cut short. Less than two years ago Arthur Holmes Blakesley went out from England to take part in the great work going on at Bishop's College, Calcutta. He was a son of the late Dean of Lincoln, and a graduate of Christ Church, Oxford. As tutor of Bishop's College under the Rev. H. Whitehead, he had already won a good report by the value of his lectures and his influence on the students. Last February we printed at some length, in the *Mission Field*, extracts from a pamphlet written by him. It is not too much to say that this pamphlet is as cogent a reply as has been made to the attacks on Missions which had been put forth in the *Fortnightly Review* and elsewhere. It is sad to think that he is no longer working in India for the cause he so ably defended; but, as he himself said, no honest work is ever thrown away, and his short career we trust has not closed without his doing much of which the future will show the result. He passed to his rest on August 20 at Calcutta.

DR. MACLEAR has added to his numerous works a valuable volume, under the title of *An Introduction to the Creeds* (Macmillan & Co., 319 pages). Although the book is of comparatively small bulk, it is by no means to be considered a mere handbook. It brings together much that cannot easily be found elsewhere. The first part is mainly historical, showing the origin of the creeds, and the various forms which they assumed in the course of their formation. These are given with fulness, and the work of the great councils is sufficiently described for the purpose of the book. The second part is an exposition of the twelve articles of the creeds. It will be found very useful in colonial and missionary work, where it is of supreme importance to keep well in view the objective teaching of the Incarnation, Passion, Resurrection, and Ascension of our Lord. The pith of the *Filioque* controversy is very well given in five pages. Appendices give the exact words of the creeds at different dates, and the book is well indexed.

WORK in the Corea is to be undertaken with the direct action of the episcopal order. The Archbishop of Canterbury has chosen the Rev. Charles John Corfe, M.A., All Souls College, Oxford,

FUSANKAI PORT, COREA.

who has accepted the position of Bishop for Corea. Mr. Corfe has been a chaplain in the Royal Navy since 1867. He has served often in Eastern seas, and knows China well, while he has taken great interest in his future Diocese for a long time. The Mission of which he is to be the head is small in its beginning, but we trust that he may be spared to see the fruit of his labours on no small scale in the land for which he is giving himself.

H AMPSHIRE has had some more of its successful garden meetings. One was held by the invitation of Sir William and Lady Parker, of Blackbrook House, which was marred somewhat by bad weather. Another was held at Malshanger on the invitation of Mrs. Wyndham Portal, which was addressed by Sir Charles

Turner, K.C.I.E., late Chief Justice of Madras, who begged his hearers
to recollect how big India was.

"It was as large as Europe, excepting Russia, and the population was 200,000,000
under British rule, and 50,000 under native rule. Down near Bengal and the Ganges
the population was 750 per square mile, being the densest rural population of any
country in the world. Sir Charles proceeded to give a sketch of the origin of
the Aryan race, and an account of their principal religious notions, from which it
appeared that they had a system of natural religion, which was afterwards corrupted
by their priests. A conspicuous feature of Hindoo society was the strong family ties
which bound them together, and these ties constituted a difficulty which the Missionary
had to deal with."

The Hon. Egerton Hubbard, M.P., who has since succeeded to the
peerage on the lamented death of his father, as Lord Addington, said :—

"I think everybody will allow that the object of all philosophy and all religion
is happiness, and that every person of sense and feeling ought to try and share his
happiness with other people. If we care for a thing, we are willing to pay in purse
or person for it. We boast of our Christianity; but do we pay in purse or person for it? In 1887 the income of this Society was £109,000. Last year it was
£138,000, but the increase was due to the fact that one person gave £25,000 and
another £2,500. We are face to face with the sad conclusion that among a population of 38,000,000 we do not raise for this purpose a shilling per family all the year
round. One man won £60,000 last year in stakes in horse-racing alone, and the
exports of beer and spirits alone amounted to £2,800,000, which was sent to Africa and
India and other parts of the world, where the use of spirits was known to drive the
people nearly mad, while only £130,000 was sent to the Society for the Propagation of
the Gospel for the purpose of teaching these poor creatures to be sober and temperate.
There are other societies doing the same work. This Society is in want of £25,000 a
year more."

ON August 19 another meeting was held at the Wakes, Selborne, on
the invitation of General and Mrs. W. Chase Parr. The Earl of
Selborne presided. His lordship spoke of the duty incumbent upon all
to take their share in the conversion of the heathen.

"Everyone should be a Missionary, at least in will, and should do all that is
possible to promote the cause of Missions by prayer and almsgiving if in no other way.
It was a Divine command to preach the Gospel to every creature. The only power
that can make good men, good women, and good children too, was the power of
Christianity." His lordship then reviewed the progress of the Missions of the Church,
showing that by them the United States of America, Canada, Australia, and New Zealand
were, at any rate in profession, Christian. He spoke of the mission work in the Islands
of the Pacific, and of the late Bishop Selwyn's wise method of preaching the Gospel.

"Japan and even China are breaking through the old traditions of hostility to
Europeans, and thus openings exist in those countries for teaching the Faith, and
opportunities are afforded us now which we ought not to be slow to seize. By helping
with our prayers and our alms the Society for the Propagation of the Gospel we shall
be doing much to carry on the work of the Church and to bring the nations of the
world to the knowledge of our Lord and Saviour Jesus Christ."

A GARDEN PARTY in aid of the Society was held at Ashford, Kent,
on the invitation of Dr. George Wilks, M.A., M.B., on August 21.

Extensive preparations had been made by the host, and several hundred guests were expected, but a downpour of rain just before the hour of commencement rendered the beautiful garden quite unfit for an outdoor meeting, and kept a large number of the invited guests at home. However, an adjoining empty house, containing capacious reception rooms, fortunately furnished a refuge to those who had braved the weather, and thither the company repaired to listen to earnest and interesting speeches from the Rev. Samuel Bickersteth, brother and commissary of the Bishop of Japan, and the Rev. H. M. Joseph, a native of Antigua. By the conclusion of the meeting the weather had sufficiently changed to allow a move to be made to the garden, where instrumental music was performed by the band of the local Rifle Volunteer Corps. Considering "the great rain," the friends of the Society have no need for discouragement at this effort to awaken interest in the vast undertakings of the S.P.G. But the Society's Ashford supporters invite prayers that God will bless this new Association, and make it a fruitful spring, from which may flow liberal alms and fervent intercessions on the Society's behalf, as well as benefitting the cause throughout the whole district of which Ashford is the centre.

SUGGESTED SUBJECTS FOR PRAYER.

For the Missions exposed to peril in Eastern Africa, for the steadfastness of the converts, and for a happy issue out of the tribulations.

For the Missionaries who are going forth to their several fields of labour in India, China, Borneo, and New Guinea.

For the Bishop-designate of Sydney, and for the Australian Church.

For the new work to be undertaken in New Guinea and Corea, and for the Bishop-designate of Corea.

SOCIETY'S INCOME.

Abstract of RECEIPTS *and* PAYMENTS *from January* 1 *to August* 31.

					GENERAL FUND	SPECIAL FUNDS
Subscriptions, Donations, Collections, &c.	...	...	...	...	£19,052	£10,394
Legacies ...	...	...	...	...	7,801	107
Dividends, Rents, &c....	...	...	...	...	2,988	2,775
	TOTAL RECEIPTS	...	...	...	£29,841	£13,276
	PAYMENTS	...	...	...	£60,561	£12,511

The Receipts under the head of Subscriptions, Donations, and Collections for the General Fund from January 1 to August 31, in five consecutive years, compare as follows : 1885, £19,797 ; 1886, £18,435 ; 1887, £20,008 ; 1888, £19,247* ; 1889, £19,052.

* In addition, the Treasurers received in 1888 Securities of the value of £25,296 as "A Thankoffering to Almighty God for the extension of the Church in the Colonies and Dependencies of the British Empire and beyond it"; also other Securities of the value of £2,268 as a Trust Gift, *the Income only being available.*

THE MISSION FIELD.

THE FIELD IS THE WORLD. THE SEED IS THE WORD OF GOD.

NOVEMBER 1, 1889.

INTERCESSION FOR FOREIGN MISSIONS.

PRAYER is a force to be employed in all religious efforts. Missionary efforts are peculiarly dependent upon its employment. In this paper we propose to put together some thoughts as to the reason of this, and to try to arrive at it by inquiring what it is that we have to pray for in our Intercession for Foreign Missions. The nature of our needs should show us something of the means by which we should endeavour to supply them, and why prayers have such a prominent part in our efforts.

What, then, do we want? What are we to pray for? It is too narrow a conception of the intention of intercession to restrict it to the privilege we have of praying, in literal obedience to the Divine bidding, that the Lord of the harvest will send forth labourers into His harvest. Yet in some minds this prayer itself becomes more limited than its words denote. The prayer is not only that God may put it into the hearts of Englishmen to offer themselves for work abroad, but that He may send forth workers in the power of His spirit, not necessarily from one land to another, but from His altar, whence the live coal has touched their lips, to those who know Him not. The sending is not geographical but spiritual, and the prayer should include with at least equal prominence the desire for the raising up and strengthening of the native ministry in heathen lands.

Further, while the need which we desire to see supplied is that of more labourers, yet it is not simply numerical. Especially with regard to those sent out from England, quality takes precedence of quantity. Numerically there are more men willing to go as workers abroad than there are means to support. The demand is for "able ministers" of

God's Word and Sacraments; "able," that is, in the possession of spiritual grace, and also in other ways. It is a mistake to speak of other than distinctly religious qualifications as if they were carnal or secular. When a Missionary is sent abroad, a human being is sent abroad, and not a spirit with a mere appendage, called a body, as it were accidentally belonging to it. The Missionary priest is a man, and should be a man able to do God's work. Physically he should be able to bear what fatigues, hardships, or extremes of climate he is to meet. If he is to preach to the heathen, he should not be deficient in powers of utterance; if he is to be in charge of the varied institutions of a large Mission, with its many native agents, he should have powers of organisation, aptitude for leading and for administration; for building up in the true faith those who have known none of it he needs, not less, but more than an ordinary acquaintance with theology.

But, as we have said, this is not the whole object of our Missionary Intercession. Our Lord has given us other petitions than this to put up. The Lord's Prayer is a Missionary prayer. Its first part is primarily this; and it is strange how the clause "Thy kingdom come" can be uttered by Christians without their realising that it is a prayer for the complete subjection to Him of that world-wide kingdom which He purchased with His precious Blood. No less direct is the next petition that on the earth—on the whole of it, not on a part—men may do the will of God as angels do it above. And with this meaning of the first clauses the remainder of the prayer harmonises. Not in the singular number, but in the plural, do we say it, even when we are alone. Not in selfishness, but in expansive charity, do we pray that redemptive mercy may forgive trespasses, and the only atonement be applied to the souls of men, "the propitiation for our sins, and not for ours only, but also for the sins of the whole world." Surely not least do the worshippers of false gods need to be delivered from evil; while those heathen in whom are the beginnings of faith have an awful claim for a share in the prayer for deliverance from the temptation of persecution, which keeps them back from acknowledging Him Whose Spirit is working in their hearts; and the converts need to be sustained by the Bread of Heaven.

Our prayers, therefore, are for Missionary work in all its departments and in all its aspects. We must ask for all sorts of blessings: for wisdom and zeal and power in the workers, for willing ears and hearts in those to whom they go, for the avoidance of strife, self-will, weakness, vice, or apostacy in the infant churches. How can we expect such blessings, unless the desire for them is felt by the Church which sends out the Missions? How can we have the desire, and expect it to be satisfied, unless it is expressed in prayer?

Further, praying for the Missionary cause is more than springs from a desire for the salvation of the heathen. Christian pity for those who know not God is a lofty and beautiful motive. Christian love that refuses limits and seeks objects in all parts of the world is a glorious fruit of the Holy Spirit. But there is a higher motive and a more sublime object than even the desire for our fellow-men's salvation. The love of our neighbour, realising an universal brotherhood, fulfils a great law of God. But it is, after all, the second Commandment. The first Commandment bids us love God, and desire His glory. What, therefore, is first of all, and above all, to be desired, is that Christians should be inflamed with the desire for the completion of the kingdom of Christ; that Churchmen should aim at the Church's winning the whole world for her Lord; and that believers should work for the consummation of that victory over death and sin in which they trust.

From our prayers, therefore, should not be excluded the cause of Foreign Missions in the heart of the Church at home. It is deplorable that the desire in England for the success of Foreign Missions should be limited and faint. That it is so is only too notorious. Whole parishes have no part nor lot in the matter, and in many more it does not really enter into the religious life of the people.

In extending the Church of Christ, God and man work together. It is His power that works, it is man that is the agent, and not the mere natural man, but men in the Spirit-bearing Body of Christ. The Church must desire the success of her Lord's cause. Her desires when expressed are prayers; for to God she pours out her longings. She is to grow and cover the earth, by having the Divine impulse within her to do so. It is to her the glorious destiny is given of completing the victory, and making its effect universal. She is to do it, not as an inanimate machine, but with ardent will. She cannot do it simply by external and visible Missionary operations. Each pure impulse to forward the cause in the world must be joined with a heavenward-directed desire. The pleading with Christ the merits of His sacrifice before the throne must accompany the efforts to tell all nations of His saving health.

ARTHUR HOLMES BLAKESLEY.

IN MEMORIAM.—BY THE REV. H. WHITEHEAD. REPRINTED FROM
THE "INDIAN CHURCHMAN."

T is with the deepest sorrow that we record the death of Mr. A.H. Blakesley, late tutor of Bishop's College and sub-editor of the *Indian Churchman.* On the night of Sunday, the 11th of August, he was seized with an acute attack of dysentery; he seemed to be getting better on the next Saturday and Sunday, but on Monday he began to sink fast, and died on Tuesday evening, at 8 P.M. He was buried the next morning at the Lower Circular Road Cemetery. The first part of the service was said in the College Chapel; the service at the grave was read by the Rev. A. G. Luckman and the Rev. H. Whitehead. Hymn 289 (A. & M.) was sung in the chapel, 225 as a processional from the cemetery gate, and 221 after the body was committed to the earth. Owing to the short notice that was given many were unable to attend the funeral who would otherwise have done so; most of the clergy of Calcutta, however, were present, and all the members of Bishop's College and the Schools attached to it.

Arthur Blakesley was the son of the late Dean Blakesley of Lincoln, well known to old Cambridge men as an accomplished scholar, and better known to the general public of thirty years ago as the "Hertfordshire Incumbent," who published during the Crimean War a series of extremely able letters in the *Times,* criticising the conduct of the campaign. Arthur Blakesley inherited his father's talents, especially his practical gifts in the management of affairs and power of dealing with statistics and business details, which, combined with accurate scholarship, the power of clear and vigorous philosophic thought, and a refined artistic taste, endowed him with a capacity for intellectual work of no mean order. He was educated at Charterhouse and thence went to Christ Church, Oxford, as a junior student in 1883. In spite of ill health he gained high honours in the Class lists, obtaining a first class in Classical Moderations, a second class in the final school of *Literæ Humaniores,* and a first class in Theology. In December 1887 he came out as tutor to Bishop's College, Calcutta. His original intention was to stay for two years and then return, as it was very uncertain whether his weak health would be able to stand against an Indian climate; with characteristic generosity, however, he soon offered to stay out a third year to enable the Principal to take a holiday in England. And as, in spite of a severe attack of fever last December, his general health seemed good, he made up his mind, at the end of June last, definitely to devote his life to the work of the Church in India.

His death is a heavy loss to Bishop's College, where he was much respected and beloved by both the students and his fellow-workers; and the influence of his teaching and example will be very greatly missed. To his personal friends it is a deep sorrow to part with him. He had a peculiarly lovable and attractive nature, and his genial humour, ready sympathy, and willingness to sacrifice himself for the sake of others, won him the affection of all who were privileged to know him well. And it is no exaggeration to say that his death has been felt by men of all parties as a public calamity to the diocese. During the short time that he was in India, his powers matured with wonderful rapidity, and, whatever sphere of work he entered upon, he soon made himself felt to be a power. Besides his ordinary college work, he had undertaken, since January 1888, most of the editorial work of the *Indian Churchman*, and many of the articles on various subjects which came from his pen showed a singular ripeness of thought and judgment. Those which he wrote in answer to Canon Taylor's criticisms on Mission work were afterwards reprinted in pamphlet form, and were very highly thought of by persons most competent to form an opinion as to their merits. He was warmly thanked for them by the Secretary of the S.P.G., and the articles were printed for distribution in England by the C.M.S. Committee; and the Archbishop of Canterbury, at a public meeting, recommended them as the best answer to Canon Taylor which he had seen. The wisdom with which he dealt with such subjects as asceticism in these articles is a striking example of the grasp of principles and the power of discerning fundamental truths which he showed in all relations of life. Those who knew him intimately could not fail to be struck by the way in which he invariably set aside mere passing sentiment as a basis of action, and sought to find solid and enduring principles of belief and conduct.

Some perhaps who only knew him slightly would have thought him lacking in enthusiasm, and to comparative strangers he seemed at first somewhat reserved, but in reality his whole character was pervaded by a deep moral earnestness and a sincere religious feeling. He spoke and wrote strongly and even vehemently on social and moral questions, and felt keenly the general indifference of society as to matters of morality and religion, and the degrading effect of the prevalent selfishness in the use of wealth. He took a great interest in all efforts for the promotion of temperance and purity, and had he lived would certainly have taken an active part in these great movements. His recent labours for the relief of the distress among the famine-stricken Christians in the Sunderbunds were only one instance out of many of his sympathy with suffering, and of the sound practical common sense which he brought to bear on its relief.

In his religious life, one striking feature was his love of sincerity. He instinctively shrank from anything that savoured of unreality, and studied to make both his words and acts strictly correspond to the inner life. His religion was of an essentially unostentatious and undemonstrative type. A regular and devout communicant, an earnest seeker after religious truth, impressed with a deep sense of his own personal responsibility to God, striving ever upward towards a high standard of duty, upheld by a humble reliance on Christ his Saviour, he yet made but little show or display of religious feeling, and was studiously simple in all his outward religious acts. He personally preferred simple services and a simple ritual, not from any doctrinal bias, but because it was natural to him to give a simple and quiet expression to his deepest feelings, and because he disliked above all things any approach to exaggeration, and dreaded the substitution of outward display for true spirituality. Yet at the same time he could join heartily in more ornate services ; and even those who differed from him in his estimate of the value of outward forms felt the highest admiration for the sterling reality and manly simplicity to which his opinions on these matters were due.

If we had to sum up in one word that which made his character so peculiarly attractive to his friends, and indeed, to all who came into close contact with him, we should say that he was "true-hearted." There was a thoroughness and sincerity about him which made people feel that they had to do not only with a man of exceptional intellectual gifts, but also with a strong and genuine character. As a friend, he could always be depended upon to speak his mind and criticise where he thought criticism was due. He was one of those who could "smite friendly," and "speak the truth in love," and few things stirred his indignation more than an unreal affectation, especially with regard to religion. His peculiar aversion was "priggishness," which was to him what metaphysics was to Carlyle, and he often caused his friends much amusement by his humorous analyses of the elements which went to make up this objectionable characteristic. Similarly in his work he was thorough and conscientious. Whatever he took up, even if it lay outside his proper sphere of work, he did it with all his might. When he was asked by the Chaplain of S. Thomas's to take a class of lads on Sunday afternoons, he threw himself as heartily into the work as though it had been one of the main reasons for which he came out to India ; and we know that it was his regular habit very carefully to prepare each lesson and afterwards to write down in his diary what the effect of the lesson had been, what faults he thought he had made, and hints for future improvement. It seems at first sight a life of great promise prematurely cut short ; but "God knoweth those that are his," and his friends, however greatly they may miss him, cannot for his sake regret that he has been called to his rest and so early won his crown.

> The morning shall awaken,
> The shadows shall decay,
> And each true-hearted servant
> Shall shine as doth the day.

SHWEBO, UPPER BURMA.

LAST August the *Mission Field* contained a portrait group of the Mission workers and converts at the new Mission of Shwebo, in Upper Burma. The Rev. F. Sutton writes about this group :—

"Some infants grow more rapidly than others, and the infant church of Shwebo has grown, I think I must confess, rather more rapidly than our faith permitted us to expect. It is the result, no doubt, of the many prayers that have continually been made at home in England and elsewhere, that God's blessing may rest upon the work of the Mission, for every mail that comes in assures us of hearty sympathy and fervent prayer from some kind friend or another. To illustrate the growth of this infant church, I may mention that in the photograph alluded to, only eleven of the figures are those of converts of the Mission ; the rest comprise mission helpers—such as schoolmaster, catechist and his wife, and moonshi—and two girls already baptized Christians, placed in the school by the late Mr. Colbeck of Mandalay. Now if we could get a photograph of all baptized in connection with this Mission, up to date, the eleven would become eighty-three, and the boarders in our school for Burman girls would number twenty-one instead of four. This boarding establishment for girls is, I consider, the most important and the most promising part of the Mission. The ignorance and superstition of the Upper Burmans far exceed that of the lower province, and both are more marked among the women than among the men. The minds of some of these girls that we have admitted seem to be a perfect blank, and their faces were equally wanting in any expression of intelligence ; but with kindness, care and education, they improve wonderfully, and assure us that their lives will be rendered not only more happy but much more useful and honourable than they ever could be without the advantages of a Christian home and education. I only wish we could extend these advantages to many more than we have ; but our funds do not suffice, or we might admit a great many more. They are given over to the Mission by written agreement for a stated number of years—varying according to the age of the child—and with full consent to baptize them into the Christian Faith whenever they are considered fit to receive the rite. A week ago I baptized the last four admitted, and all our twenty-one girls are now brought into Christ's fold. Amongst the number, we have two given to us for life. The first so admitted was a poor starved baby, ten days of age, with no parents, the father having left his wife some time before the birth of the child, and the mother dying when the child was

THE MISSION HOUSE, SHWEBO.

only four days old. I thought the child would die within forty-eight hours of admission, but I was mistaken, for she is as bright a child of fourteen months now as I have ever seen.

"The work of the Mission is becoming very interesting in another direction, namely, by its extension into the surrounding villages. Neither is this entirely the result of our itinerating into the district and visiting these villages, but it results in a great measure from our young Christians calling in their friends, and if we can only keep all our converts up to the mark in this way, there is no reason why the number of Christians should not increase steadily in different parts of the district. Of course those who live out in the villages away from the Mission head-quarters have not the privileges that those have who are living in Shwebo itself, and living in some cases alone, surrounded by heathenism and old relatives and friends still staunch in the Buddhist faith, they demand our pity and constant prayer. The largest number of Christians at present in any one village is five. The villages are from three to thirty miles from Shwebo, and as there are only two roads (and these would hardly be recognised as such at home), and the country is low and under paddy cultivation, they are very difficult to get at except in the dry season.

"With much to encourage us and to make us thankful, we have, on the other hand, our trials and disappointments. Our Christians are not always what we should wish them to be; some fall into grievous sin; in others, love seems to grow cold, and we cannot help feeling in some cases that there is a danger of them falling away. They need much patience and gentleness on our part, and we ourselves need more and more of the Holy Spirit, for the thought comes to us again and again that our Christians will be what we make them. They are, too, without many of the advantages that almost every one may have in England, and our greatest need at Shwebo is a suitable church for Divine worship."

The accompanying illustration is taken from a photograph of the Mission House at Shwebo. We are grieved to hear from the Bishop that almost immediately after writing this letter Mr. Sutton had to return to England at once in consequence of Mrs. Sutton's illness. From the first she has been an ardent and efficient worker in the Mission. In the letter announcing their leaving for England, the Bishop says, "Their departure is, so far as our limited senses extend, a terrible blow to our promising Mission at Shwebo;" and adds, "They are both most earnest and devoted Missionaries."

THE BISHOP OF ZULULAND'S JOURNEY TO DELAGOA BAY.

LEFT home on June 26, and rode to Etalaneni, my wagon having started the day before to take Mr. Morris, of the St. Augustine's Mission, the man who joined me last year, to Kwamagwaza, that he might stay some time under Dr. Petrie's care to be cured of the obstinate sores from which for some months he had been suffering. His lungs, too, have not yet made the progress we hoped for. The wagon was to meet me at the military camp at Emtonjaneni.

At Etalaneni I gave my cordial approval to a plan Mr. Robertson had made for himself. After a trip to Eshowe in his wagon he was proposing to start for a preaching and (to use a goldfields word) a prospecting tour in Sibepu's country—the north-east of Zululand—where we have never yet been able to begin work. I was forced to say that no pledge must be given that permanent work would be undertaken there, however promising the opening might seem to be. Until our hands can be strengthened by larger funds it will be quite impossible to do more. Mr. Robertson proposed to return to Etalaneni at ploughing time—probably in September.

I then rode on to Emtonjaneni, and remained over Sunday that I might preach to the soldiers. I grieve to say I found none to join with me in Holy Communion. Old Martyn the native deacon arrived with the wagon ready to accompany me on the long journey through Zululand, and Swaziland, and Tongaland to Delagoa Bay.

We made our start together on Monday, and spent Sunday, July 7, at the Pongola River. We had had a very rough road, and as regards Mission work a very useless week, for not only are the valleys of White Umfolosi, Black Umfolosi, Umkuzi, and Pongola, which had to be successively crossed, stony and full of thick bush not suitable for cattle and gardens, but a large part has been swept again and again by civil war between the Usutu or royal party and Sibepu.

From the lower drift on the Pongola our route lay along the western border of the great flat which extends from the Swazi hills to the Bombo. Here we found many more people, in spite of the scarcity of water. But it was, of course, mid-winter, the driest time, and with the exception of one short rush of rain about February the season has been unusually dry.

Sunday, July 14, we spent a little to the east of one of the great
Swazi kraals, Emafuteni (usually given on maps as Mofutani), and
there, besides finding two white men for English prayers, Martyn and I
had a nice little congregation of the rawest possible heathen from two
neighbouring kraals. We had visited them on Saturday afternoon and
invited them to come to my wagon.

We had now come into the great transport road from the western
upper country past the Swazi King's to the Bombo and the Tembe River,
and having made a sharp turn to the east were at last heading straight
for our destination. You will see that we crossed the Usutu River
much lower down than Mr. Jackson's station. It is a sandy, shifting
drift, and we did not go into the river at the right place. The wagon
was very nearly upset, the leader was frightened, the oxen were swim-
ming, the water came into the wagon a foot deep, wetting mealie meal,
blankets, and various other things, but thank God, we got over all right
at last, and, as it was only about one o'clock and the sun was bright and
hot, we were able to dry everything pretty well, before sundown, and
trek on with a splendid moon. We had been advised not to sleep in the
Bombo flat because of lions; but there are not many now, and the
amount of transport in the winter months drives them away from the
main road, while the Boers who come down from the highlands of the
Transvaal for winter pasture spend a large part of their time in hunting.
We neither saw nor heard a lion. However, we did make a forced
march across the flat, giving the oxen only about one hour, and two and
a half hours' rest between 4 A.M. and sundown. The Bombo is very
broad at that part, much broader and more stony, with less bush and
less water, than at the place above the Umfolosi River, where our
Catechist, Titus Zwani, died in 1881. On Monday night we slept on
the western edge of the plateau; on Tuesday on the eastern edge overlooking the enormous tract of flat bushy land spread out beneath us
like the sea. Here we had to rest the oxen, and we did not reach the
Tembe River until Friday morning. From this point I sent the wagon
back to the top of the Bombo to await Martyn's return, and to give the
oxen a long rest in a more healthy climate, and better grass. He and I
procured two boys (i.e. men) to carry our blankets and food, and
started to walk along the narrow paths, and through the sand and bush
of Tongaland. We were eight days in the country altogether, sleeping
in the native huts and having a good many opportunities of preaching
truth in the smaller kraals, for, as usual, the common people received us
gladly, and on four occasions food was given either for us or for the
boys, though food is very scarce this year. It was not so pleasant at
the three great royal kraals—one twelve miles west of the Usutu, one
near the east bank of the Usutu (marked Nozingele on the maps), and
one a good ten miles further east, the usual residence of the young king

M 4

Ngwanasi, and of the queen-mother, who is regent. There we had to tell our business to the stiff, hard-hearted old indunas or headmen, the worst to attempt to make an impression upon in this heathen and drunken land. And finally, we were not allowed to tell our tale to either king or queen, but had to accept a message sent out to us that they did not want any of such talk, we had better turn back at once. Unfortunately for us, Mr. Shepstone had lately been down from Swaziland, and it was said that he meant to come again with an impi or armed force. And there was actually encamped close by an exploring party, sent by a company which is supposed to have obtained some concession or right in the land, and a difficulty about comers between them and the king was actually stopping the way. To add to this, the queen had quarrelled with her son, because the boy (he is about 16) would feed his pigs on mealies in a time of scarcity. This, at least, is what we heard. So the time was not very favourable. The indunas were probably quite sure, although we declared we had not, that we really had some connection with one or other of these two parties; and the idea of a white man taking the trouble to come to them seeking nothing for himself but only wishing to do them good was too impossible to be received. I am not surprised or disappointed seriously. I thought it might be like this on the first visit, and I believe we were the first Missionaries who had ever been seen at the great place. But we have talked to not a few on our way, and we have knocked even at the royal gate. The old indunas in spite of themselves have heard a good deal, for, when I received the message of refusal from the king and queen, I began at once to tell them the chief things we believe and teach; and, to my surprise, they sat still and listened with patience for some time before they rose up and laughed and walked away.

Please God another year we shall be able to do more. They will know me and will, I trust, have come to the conclusion that I am harmless if I am an idiot. As to the land itself, I am rather agreeably surprised. It is true my visit was at the most favourable time of year, and the dry season has caused less fever anywhere than usual. But I have tried to find out all I can from residents (white) in and near. And so far as I can learn the Bombo at the part where I crossed is healthy enough. The chief danger seems to lie in going down to the flat below in summer, and then returning. People are then very liable to a chill, and a chill means fever. All agree that one who gets fever down below ought not to run away by sea to Durban, or by land to the higher levels. The change of climate seems to be too sudden. The fever patient ought to go into hospital in Delagoa Bay, or be otherwise well taken care of, and, when he is fairly well again, go away for a change. And all seem to agree that Tongaland itself is not so bad as Delagoa Bay. The whole

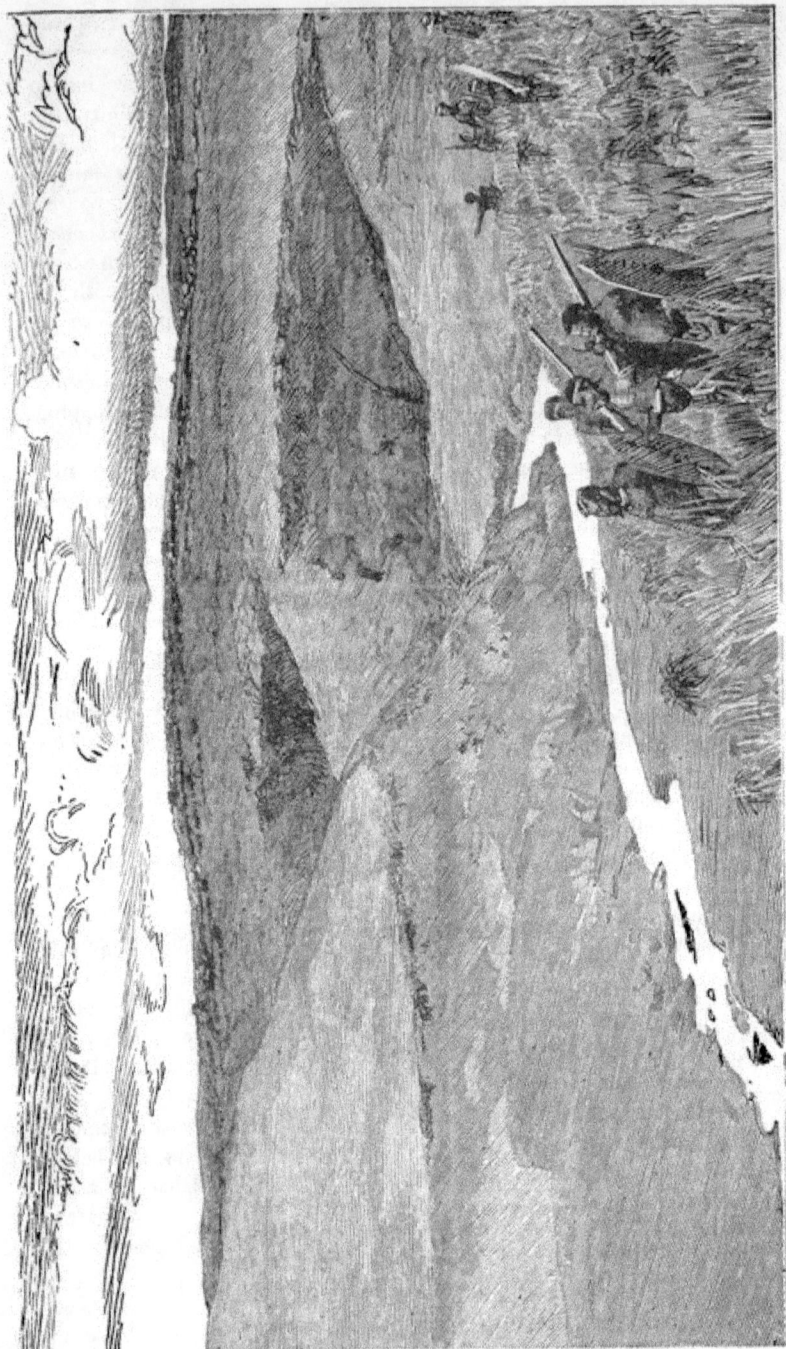

UMFOLOSI RIVER

country is sandy and flat, none much above, and some, I verily believe, below the level of the sea. The people get their drinking water either from swamps or from shallow holes, from six to ten feet deep, which they dig almost anywhere. No wonder that the water is often bad, and gives fever and dysentery to people not used to it. We were very careful only to drink tea and cocoa after the water had boiled. But my belief is that an Abyssinian tube pump could be set up almost anywhere, and would find water at a very moderate depth, and that water so obtained might be very fairly good. A filter, however, would be a necessary precaution. If, then, one of the higher spots were selected for a station, and the Missionaries took reasonable care of themselves, there does not seem to be more danger than in other hot and rather unhealthy places. Swiss Missionaries are at work north and north-west of Delagoa Bay, and we found a native teacher near the mouth of the Usutu. They do not seem to have suffered much during the two or three years they have been there. They have had slight attacks of fever and recovered. A third pastor has just come out. My conclusion, therefore, is that if we could find the funds and the men we ought to open a station on the Bombo and another below in Tongaland itself. And in several places people are very close together. They have not the same number of cattle as our Zulus, nor has there been the same devastation of the land by wars, with the evil of a subsequent portioning out the country in large lots to small families or tribes. And they do not shift their kraals so much. It would therefore be easier than in Zululand for a stationary missionary to influence a considerable number within easy reach. This seemed to be especially the case in the neighbourhood of the great Ematutwini kraal, a day's walk from the Tembe and about twelve miles from the Usutu; also about a day and a half from this place, so that supplies could be pretty easily obtained and postal communication kept up. The Portuguese *have* the land down to 26° 30′ from the sea to the Bombo, and *claim* that the boundary is the 26° 30′ line only from the sea to the Usutu and that thence it follows the river up to the Bombo. If there be anything in that claim, and Portuguese protection is worth anything, and they would move on behalf of anything English (all of them considerable *ifs*), then a Missionary placed where I propose would have some civilised protection. The Governor here, who is a thorough gentleman and speaks English well, having once been in the English navy as midshipman, says that the Tonga queen always sends to consult him about any white men in the country. Now, what are the prospects of our being enabled to take this great step forward? Next time I visit Tongaland I think I shall come by sea to this place and start off walking from here with two donkeys to carry for us. The worst part of that scheme is that the fare by steamer to Durban is £4. But the saving of time is considerable. And

I shall come if possible earlier, about the middle of June, and stay longer. We saw a good deal of one nice boy, a relation and close associate of the young king. He has been to Maritzburg for school, and is nearly a Christian now. I hope one good result of our visit will be that he will go for another two years or so to Grahamstown and be baptized while he is there. He will be a very influential man some day. It was very cheering to know that one young heart was grieved at the uncivil reception of us at court.

And now as to Delagoa Bay itself, and the application made to the Society by the English Directors. The Natal papers had told us just before I left Isandhlwana that there had been a blow up, and that the Portuguese Government had seized the line for non-fulfilment of contract. When on the Bombo I heard that the General Manager, Mr. Knee, with whom I had been in correspondence, had already left, and that many of the English *employés* had left also. On arrival here I found that this was true, but all blame the old Company far more than the Government. The position now is that the Portuguese are finishing the line to their border, and it will be complete so far within six months, when the Netherlands Company will be prepared to carry it on in the Transvaal. When complete this portion is to be sold, and I have it on pretty good authority that the Portuguese Government are sure to buy it. In that case the few English now employed will gradually leave or be got rid of, and Portuguese substituted for them. The number of English in this place has already decreased, and business has suffered, because the Englishman is well paid and will live well, which means that he scatters his money freely. The Portuguese are badly paid and hold more tightly the little they have. The prospect, therefore, of support for a clergyman from the place itself is much less hopeful than it was. On the whole it is clear that so far as the railway is concerned we must await the completion and the sale. There are not many Englishmen now employed on the line—only about 25, in addition to Mr. E. E. Sawyer, the civil engineer, and his assistant Mr. Montanaro. I went out to the Komati River, where they are now at work, on Tuesday, and in the evening we got nearly twenty together for a short service outside Mr. Sawyer's little house. It was a poor offering of prayer and praise, and I could only speak shortly and *uncomfortably* about the Good Shepherd; but it was the best we could do, and the rocks there heard for the first time, and probably many of the men almost for the first time, " Praise God from Whom all blessings flow."

Martyn and I arrived here by dint of pretty hard walking at midday on Saturday. Time was short to make arrangements for Sunday, so I accepted at once Mr. Macintosh's kind offer of his room for Sunday evening, and promised to go on board the gunboat, H.M.S. Bramble, in the morning at 10. I could not find any one ashore anxious for Communion, so again

I celebrated in Zulu in my own room at the hotel. But I was very glad to be able to start Martyn off on Monday "strengthened and refreshed" for his walk back to the Bombo to rejoin the wagon. I am not at the hotel now. Mr. Macintosh was sailing for Durban on Monday in the mail steamer, and he kindly invited me to take possession of his room and his place at table during his absence. He is the principal of the chief English place of business, and lives very comfortably with five assistants. This has saved me much expense, and given me quieter and better quarters.

The Corisland has just arrived from Mozambique, and I go on board her to-morrow. She ought to land us at Durban on Sunday afternoon or Monday morning.

There is no doubt that this town and neighbourhood badly needs the counter influence of some clergy, for it is a very drunken and corrupt place. The natives are terribly demoralised by drink and high wages, and contact with bad white men. In one kraal in the midst of a torrent of Tonga, which is so unlike Zulu we cannot understand it at all, I heard the name of God in English, but it was the common English curse !! Father, forgive them, for they know not what they do.

As to the Tonga language, while it is very unlike Zulu in many ways besides words, and sounds more like the vile stuff which we commonly call kitchen Kafir, talked by most white people in Durban and Maritzburg, it yet has affinities, so that a knowledge of Zulu is of great assistance in reading it, and the people have had so much intercourse with Zulus and Swazis that most of the men and boys can understand and talk Zulu, and a Zulu speaker could always find an interpreter. He must be prepared, however, to have his grammatical soul sorely vexed by the apparent barbarities of the dialect.

I did not know till I came here this time that any books had been printed in this language, but I find one put forth by the Swiss, Buku ya Tsikwembo, printed at Lausanne, Imprimerie Georges Bridel, 1883.

Tsikwembo is the creator, whom we call Nkulunkulu. I have not yet discovered the etymology of the name.

It is evident that the town here could be visited by Missionaries from the Bombo and from Tongaland, who would probably have to come in from time to time in any case to look after their supplies.

FROM BLOEMFONTEIN TO THE ZAMBESI: A GREAT MISSIONARY JOURNEY.

BY THE BISHOP OF BLOEMFONTEIN.

(Continued from page 391.)

WITH THE BAROTZE AND OTHERS.

THE Bishop made but a very short stay at the camp, for, all things being ready for continuing the journey, and his party being all collected together, he crossed the pass to the south-east on Thursday, August 16, and slept on the plain. On the next day he says :—

" I was riding a short distance in front of the waggons, when Edward galloped up, and asked if I had seen the troop of lions which crossed the road between me and the waggons. He pointed out the direction they had taken, towards a wood on the right, and I galloped after them for some distance, and then saw them going in single file through the trees. As I drew close to them, two or three of the hinder ones stopped and looked at me, and Sir Garnet began to go a little shifty, like a horse wishing to refuse a fence. Then I lost sight of them for a few moments, and was galloping to catch them up, when, as I was passing an ant-heap covered with grass, I heard a loud growl, and saw on the heap a lion who was sitting up looking at me. I stopped as quickly as I could, got my horse a bit round, and shot the lion. He gave a growl, and moved a few yards, but the bullet had disabled him, and two more bullets killed him. Sir Garnet behaved admirably. I shouted towards the waggons, and Sekomi came up first, and began skinning the dead lion. Then Isaac rode up, and I sent him back for more cartridges, as I had killed the beast with my last. I tied Sir Garnet to a tree about twenty yards from the edge of the long grass on the ant-hill, and was trying to find the spoor of the other lions, when I heard a very nasty growl from the hill, and saw Sekomi running past me as fast as a man can run. Another lion had been lying in the grass on the ant-hill all the time. My first impulse was to climb a tree, but almost immediately I thought of the horse. It was the one I had to give to Lobengula, and there was no money to buy another.

At any moment the lion might be on him; so I went and untied him, when he immediately ran back, and dragged the bridle out of my hand. I caught him, however, mounted, and went on to Sekomi. Isaac soon came up with more cartridges; but while we were setting fire to the grass, the brute with cat-like stealth must have crawled away on the opposite side, for we saw nothing of him. This would not have happened had not the wretched dogs all skulked back to the waggon on first seeing the lions, and refused to move for some time. I rode about in several directions, but saw no more of them. When first sighted they were standing over a dead tsessebe which they had killed.

"In the afternoon, I went with John to find the road and water near the mountains, and came right upon a herd of eland, but most of them seemed to have little calves, and so I did not like to shoot one. I shot, however, a tsessebe and a sable antelope, but the vultures got the latter.

"*August* 18, *Saturday.*—We are halting in order to get the oxen stronger before moving on, and I hope also that the runners may come from Count Schweinitz's waggon with letters, and take mine back. I wounded an eland early in the morning, which John rode round and drove nearer to the waggons, and then killed him. I went through the survey of the road which I had made since leaving Iniati. I feel that this is rather a lazy way of spending a day, but I cannot well go on, and I am not sorry for the rest.

"*August* 19, *Sunday.*—Edward, Isaac, Siquarri, and I received the Holy Communion early. Later on we had the general service, after which Isaac and Edward went on with the Morning Service. I read the Second Lesson to the men in the evening.

"*August* 20, *Monday.*—Very early this morning John and I started for Unyamwenda's. I took no present, but gave the chief a reed buck which I shot on the way. He was ill, but sent me a large pot of beer. John told the people that he and I did not drink it as it would make us tipsy, which they seemed to think very laughable, and proceeded to drink it themselves. I sent Unyamwenda some polite messages, and spoke to the people about their having teachers. They said that if a teacher came they would build him a house, and take care of him.

"The place is of very curious formation. Out of the plain four gigantic piles of boulders seem to have been thrown up, and they are in form so fantastic and quaint that it is hard to think that they had not been put there one by one by human hands. They are in strange contrast to the sugar-loaf hills close to them, which look as though they had been made with a pair of compasses, smoothed down by a plane, and had their trees planted with a yard-measure.

"The people live in these uncomfortable places for fear of the Matabele, and they seem on some occasions to defend themselves well for a time. I hear that the Impi, whose path we crossed on the way up, suffered so severely from the resistance of the Mashona that Lobengula was very angry, and sent out another in a different direction. Upon asking the people of Unyamwenda's village why they lived among rocks which were not sufficiently high to act as fortresses, they told me that they knew of holes into which they could escape when necessary. They have a few small cows and some goats. They grow rice, and are just now making the deep holes in which it is planted.

"We rode through a pass in the hills, and visited one of Unyamwenda's smaller villages, where I told the people my message; and I had a short talk with the inhabitants of another village as we came back through the hills by another pass.

"*August 21, Tuesday.*—We made one long track over the pass to good grass for the oxen. By travelling slowly I think they will gain condition for the journey.

"*August 22, Wednesday.*—John and I started very early to shoot something, for I had been told that there was no more meat for the men. Some Mashona followed us. I shot a very large eland bull, and told the Mashona that if they would carry a small part of it back for us they might have the rest. At first they refused, but afterwards agreed.

"It is a horrible sight to see these people over a dead animal, cutting away with assegais, knives, and hatchets in nearly every direction. Here one, in a kind of frenzy of haste, is clutching at the head of another's axe; there two elderly men, who look like fathers of the tribe, are dragging at the two ends of a heap of entrails, utterly unconscious that such an arrangement as sharing it is possible. It is easy to see how these wretched creatures—wretched only in character, not in physique, for they are as a rule immensely strong—fall a prey to the Matabele, though they might meet a Matabele Impi with ten to one. They have not the slightest idea of uniting; no one seems to have any authority; for no one seems to inspire respect among a people who have too little self-respect themselves to reverence others.

"In speaking of the Mashona, however, it must not be forgotten that they are a nation of slaves, taken when they are wanted apparently, and that they have inherited, possibly, the usual characteristic of slaves. Yet with all their faults they are a pleasanter people to deal with than the Matabele. In general character they are, I think, superior.

"*August 23, Thursday.*—I offered any two of the Mashona nearly anything that they wished if they would take my letters to Mr. Dunn. I believe that I can do all that I wish to do, and be back by Christmas, and am very anxious for the clergy to know it. If I do not send from here, there is no other opportunity till I get to Miati. But not one of

these people will go ; they have meat, and what more can a man want ?
I spoke civilly to them, and reminded them that we had been kind to
them, and asked them again to do this for me, but no, 'We are afraid of
the Matabele' was their answer.   I felt sure that no one would go, yet I
talked to them for some time on the foolishness of their conduct, in the way
they treated the Matabele and us.   When I had finished they shouldered
their immense loads of meat, and went off.   Meat is all-valuable to them.
A small piece held in the hollow of the cheek will serve for a whole meal
of porridge ; and it is that they may be able to dig mice, which they eat,
out of the ground more easily that every year nearly the whole country is
set on fire.

"Their treatment of stray Matabele seems to be imbecile.   I hear
that the Umbezweni Regiment is out somewhere to the south in order
to avenge some wandering Matabele who were killed last year by the
Mashona.

"We trekked to the head of a small stream running into the Hanyane.
The whole country through which we have passed has evidently been
well populated once.   Old gardens are often situated among rocks, apparently for the sake of the moisture in the ground ; the rice holes are
in the more swampy parts, of which there are a far larger number than
I have seen in most other places.

"There was a slight shower of rain as we were coming back to the
camp.

"*August* 24, *Friday.*—I wait here, probably till Monday, as the last
chance of the runners bringing the letters, and of my having an opportunity of sending mine.

"John and I rode and saw where the last of the three streams runs
into the Hanyane.   In trying to recross the Hanyane, we each had a fall
in a quicksand, and had to find another crossing place.   I do not know
whether in any place the sands are deep enough to pull a horse down.

"John's power of finding his way about is most extraordinary.   I
go out with him as confident that we shall not lose ourselves as, if I were
alone, I should be that I would.   He sees everything apparently.   In
a very fast gallop he saw that we had crossed waggon-tracks twice.   I do
not know what I should have done without him ; never in the way,
never out of the way, doing exactly what he is told, afraid of nothing,
very gentle, and speaking very little.   He is the son of a good mother,
and was educated and trained by Christian Missionaries."

From August 24 to 27 the Bishop waited at the camp for letters,
and to give his waggon oxen more rest.   They had been over-tired by
the journey from Iniati, which was rapidly made because the Bishop
had then no idea that he could do the Zambesi journey so quickly,
and gave himself more days to do it in than were actually needed.   He
did 535 or more miles in less than 40 days, notwithstanding he had

continually to hire new relays of carriers. To all who know what
African travel is in such a difficult part of the country this is a remarkable feat.

On the 27th, the Bishop resumed his journey, and records :—

" A long trek which only brought us to some bad water, and John
and I rode on to find better, and found it in holes at what had once
been a large settlement of the Mashona.

" *August* 28, *Tuesday.*—As we were making our morning trek, the only
one, a gnu in the long grass deceived us into believing him to be a lion,
till he was seen, not so far away, looking at John and me. I am not
very well.

" *August* 29, *Wednesday.*—One trek was made to good water. I could
get no meat to-day ; there seems to be little on this road, though there
are, I believe, large numbers of antelopes more to the east.

" *August* 30, *Thursday.*—Another deserted village was passed on the
right of us shortly before we reached the Nyatzimi river. Some Mashona
who came to the camp in the evening gave us some information concerning
the country, though it is very hard to gain anything from them, owing to
their seldom giving a direct answer to a question, and my having to ask
them to repeat the names again and again before I am sure that I have
them accurately. I took a long round with some of our men, and passed
through Rutope (the name of the village), a mass of granite rocks, which
was once inhabited by Chuota's people, who left it, and crossed the river,
probably to be further away from the Matebele. In coming home John,
for a wonder, mistook the Nyatzimi for the Mutedzerewe, and, had we
not happily crossed our own waggon track, we might have had a cold
time, as the sun had already set, and I was in my shirt-sleeves.

" *August* 31, *Friday.*—We made two treks to-day. I know that the
oxen will have rest at Goto's, or near it. The Mashona are still following us ; they know what my business is, but they follow for meat. In
the evening we passed a herd of sable antelopes on the other side of a
bog, and, having been a good deal in bog already, I intended to leave
them alone, but on being petitioned, and as we had no meat, I got into
this bog also, and had to dismount before my horse could get out. The
antelopes ran through a thick wood, and during our pursuit of them
John was knocked off his horse and hurt his shoulder. The Mashona
behaved very well, and carried home the deer we had shot to the camp.

" Jelly's boy is very ill. Nothing can be done for him except feed him,
and let him keep himself warm in his own way.

" *September* 1, *Saturday.*—We made one long trek, and one short and
very unsatisfactory one. Having lost the track we first turned to the
left on being told of a beacon that was known to some of the men ; but,
riding on, I found that rocks and bogs made the way to it impossible.
Then we went to the right, and the buck waggon sank beyond the naves

in bog that John and I thought was sound; and all had to be unloaded. So we slept on the apex of the watershed of the Hanyane, Umfull, and Sabi rivers, and a very nasty place it was. There was a wind and no shelter, and firewood was a long way off.

"I had been arranging for some time to ride to Sadza's Town from some point on the road; but even if I could have left the waggons, in to-day's wanderings we passed the only path to it without knowing, and it was so far back that I gave up the idea of going to it.

"*September* 2, *Sunday.*—I thought it better to move on to another place. It is windy, cloudy, and cold. As the waggons were about to move, Jelly called to me that the sick boy was dying; and in a few minutes afterwards he died. It was a most happy release for him.

"We made for Mount Wedza, and, happily, were able to take an almost direct road to a point from which I hoped to see it, by crossing a 'bottom,' and laying trees over the boggy place. Then it began to rain; but the place was sheltered.

"A good deal of time was taken in making a grave for the dead boy, and we had a little service and buried him. I read part of 1 Corinthians xv. to the men, and was very glad that there were some Mashona present.

"The boy was said to be a slave of Kanyemba's people. I saw no signs of slavery there; but at Matakenya's six Basenga women were working in chains, fastened together; yet this was said to be for stealing."

For several days nothing of importance occurred. There was rain, and some difficulty in keeping the faint track; but Mount Wedza loomed into view, and, though the country was so hilly that no straight road could be kept, the second trek, on Wednesday, September 5, brought the waggons to Goto's Town, which is situate on the top of a rocky hill, under which the Bishop made his camp, and where he resolved to give his oxen a long rest.

On September 6, Thursday, he thus writes:—

"Goto and Choto, two brothers, the chiefs whom I had sent for, came early, and I gained from them such information as I could about the people to the south and east. The chiefs promised carriers, and I gave them each a blanket, calico, and caps. The largest number of people came to the waggons that I have seen together in the country—about 300. We bought from them mealies, rice, and Kaffir meal, and I also bought a good many of their ornaments, and some axes, knives, and assegais, made by themselves. They are very clever at working in brass and iron, and the iron is said to be well tempered. The leg-bangles of the women are, some of them, of great thickness, and fifteen are sometimes worn on one leg. The little skins which they wear round their waists are very scanty. Many of them make a kind of cap by twisting beads into their hair. In disposition they seemed to be very quiet, gentle, and modest.

" The people here say that they are not Mashona, but Iriwambiri; but they speak Seshuna.

" In the middle of the buying there was a stampede of the people, and the chiefs said that news had been brought of a raiding party that was marching upon them; but I heard nothing more of it.

"*September 7, Friday.*—About 200 men and women collected early round the waggons. I heard that Kwarimba, the paramount chief, had come, and I went to him and tried to be civil. But after I had given him a blanket he said it was too small, so I gave him another and some caps; then he wished for calico before he would allow the carriers to start; then I talked to him, telling him how differently a chief of a fighting nation, such as the Basuto, would behave to a stranger, and said I would leave his town if he did not behave differently. After this there was no more trouble with him.

" I put the waggons under his care, and left Jelly, who is ill, and two of Khama's men in charge, and started for Sipiros.

" The path soon began to enter a kind of sea of mountains, and the collections of huts here and there, especially on Goto's hill, are very picturesque. They, however, give the idea of being very uncomfortably placed, more like birds' nests than houses; but everything is sacrificed to personal safety. Bofa's town, which we passed about sunset, is the most remarkable specimen of this. This hill is one immense rock, with a partly smooth face to the north, and where it is broken up, though still nearly perpendicular, there the town is placed. One of the men tells me that Sccomi said that the place would soon be destroyed; that he did not know the people had so much cattle; and that the Matabele did not know of the place. These people have great strength and activity, and more guns than the Matabele; the country has many natural fortresses; and yet their foolishness, and want of power of sufficient combination, make them more or less an easy prey. The first Missionaries here will have to be men of almost limitless patience; and the first establishing of Missions will possibly be expensive, as it may be some time before these people learn that their use consists in anything else but to be drained of their possessions. I wished to know the name of the brook at which we stopped, but ' We are hungry, we will not say,' was the reply. I bought food for them, then it was—' We want beer.' I would not buy it, upon which came the threat—' We will go home to-morrow.' Nevertheless on

" *September 8, Saturday.*—The carriers gave no trouble, and, with the exception of Magondi's men, were the only ones that did not refuse to start without more payment. A very short walk brought us to Inyampara, Sipiro's Mountain. Here we had to stop till he knew of our coming. We had heard of Gaza men being here, but I did not know that this country was tributary to the Gaza people, *i.e.* Umzila's tribe. The people of Kwarimba are also, and both give a tribute of cattle every year. Gaza men are now here collecting the tribute; so we were not allowed to be seen, and were taken round to behind a hill to wait till they should go away. I am told that the Gaza people to the south allow no white man to come among them in their own country, and that those that are now here would ask for such of our things as they wanted, and, if they were refused, would take them and kill us.

"The heat is very great, and the only water is under a rock in a hole; so I hope that these Gaza men will go away to-morrow. I was in hopes that, as the Gaza people are Zulus, Sekomi would be on good terms with them; but he says that as his Matabele have fought with them they would kill him. The son of Sipiro says that there are no people between here and the Gaza country. I can hardly believe that, for their ignorance of the surrounding country is great. They do not know in what direction the Sabi river runs, or whether the Rosarwe runs into it, nor do they care. Probably the greatest difficulty which Missionaries will have to contend with when they are allowed in the country will be an entire want of interest in anything beyond meat and calico, beads and caps. Their tongues, which, as a rule, seem to have an almost incredible power of going on saying something, lose it when they are asked for any definite or useful information; and though they crowd round one, bringing habits which one would sooner they left behind, in a perfectly unnecessary way, it is interesting to see the change when one wishes to know the names of some of the mountains round about. Then they are cold, or tired, or want to go away.

"The people here say that they are Barotze, but that they have forgotten Serotse and now speak Schona. If this be so these Barotze are an interesting study of the retrogression of the native races. They are presumably of the great Bantu race, the same race as the Basutos, originally speaking practically the same language as they, and yet in nearly every particular entirely unlike them. Is it probable that people who still call themselves Barotze can have been so lowered by contact with the Mashona? Not to go beyond the one point in which savages may be supposed to excel—fighting—here is a numerous people subject in apparent contentment to a race who live at a great distance; while in the Basuto we see a people, subject indeed to English protection, but who, when the Cape Government tried to take away their guns, fought till the Colonial forces retreated out of their country. Again, hospitality is generally supposed to be a quality possessed by savages. The Basuto chiefs as a rule are very hospitable: among the people here hospitality worthy of the name does not exist. So far as I have seen it does not exist between here and the Zambesi, except where the people are sufficiently to the north to be influenced by the Portuguese. It is an utter fallacy to say that the 'raw' native is better than the Christian native. The people who say so have no premises to argue from, for a 'raw' native has never existed in the Orange Free State, or in Kimberley, where about 10,000 natives are employed. About the Colony I cannot speak from experience, but I presume that similar conditions there produce similar results. By the time they have arrived they cease to be 'raw.' They must have come through some country, Bechuanaland, the Transvaal, the Free State, or the North of the Old Colony, and they could not have been a week at most in any of these without having the sense to conform to the customs of the country which they have come into, or being taught by .lessons which are not easily forgotten, that so long at least as they are there, they had better learn to do so. They may be almost naked till this is stopped by law, or may not understand a word of Dutch or English, but they are no more 'raw' than is meat which has gone through two or three partial cookings because it is from an animal that has only lately been killed. They have outwardly lost the very characteristics which are most distinctive of the savage in his natural state. I do not suppose that there are a dozen men in Kimberley or the Free State who have ever seen a 'raw' native, *i.e.* one in his own country, unrestricted by such force as Kimberley, or the Free State, or the Transvaal, or the Natal Government can produce. Although it is an offshoot of the question, I should not allow the title 'raw' to any nation which has had any contact with civilisation and Christianity, such as the Zulus, though few of them may have been converted to Christianity.

"Upon the question of native servants who are not Christians being better than those who are, I can only speak from my own experience. If I had a difficult journey to do again I would try to take no other than Christians."

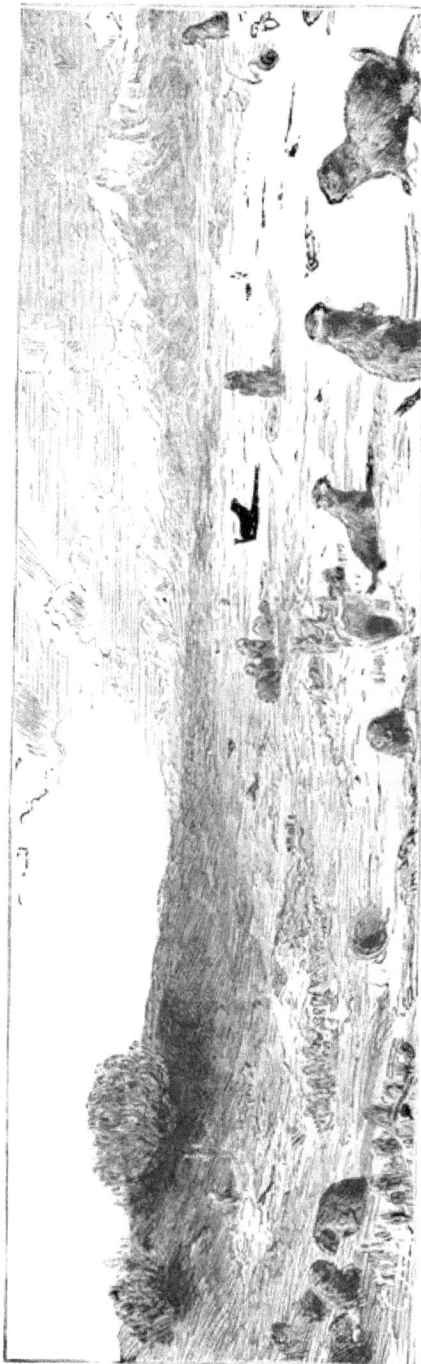

A VOICE FROM THE PRAIRIE :— MIANAMI'S OWN STORY.

WRITTEN BY MISS WINIFRED
E. WILSON, OF THE SHING-
WAUK HOME, SAULT STE.
MARIE, IN THE DIOCESE OF
ALGOMA.

A FEW days ago Mr. Smith came to me and said, " John, I want you to write a story about yourself, how you were once a wild Indian boy, and then how you were civilised and educated; I will read it over and make any alterations that may be needed, and then it shall be printed." At first I laughed much at the idea of a poor Indian Missionary writing a story, but when I saw that my good friend Mr. Smith wished me to do it, I consented. So to begin.

The first thing I can at all remember is a great prairie, miles and miles of long grass ; you could not see the beginning or the end of it. The Indian camp was right on the prairie. We lived in tee-pees ; they are something like what white people call tents, but they are of a different shape, and have skins of animals stretched over them. My father's

PRAIRIE DOGS.

name was Surgescin and my mother Anistapitaki; my own name is
Mianami; I had also one sister. We all lived in one teepee. The chief
of our tribe (the Blackfoot) lived amongst us; he was an old man, but he
had much power among the Indians, and I was often afraid of him,
and never went very close to his teepee. There were many other children
in the camp, for there were about 100 teepees altogether. We used to
run races and play games, or pick up stones and try to kill the little
gophers, or prairie dogs, which now and then peeped out of their holes,
where they lived with a rattlesnake and an owl. The men did no work,
they just smoked and talked, walking about the camp; sometimes a
party of them went off hunting, but not very often, for the white men
had not left much for the Indian to hunt. Twice a week all the Indian
people went to the agent (a white man), and he gave them out the food
which Government allows them—1 lb. of meat and 1 lb. of flour a day to
each person. When night came the drums were brought out, and the
people danced, but the children were generally asleep in the teepees.

Sometimes we had
a "sun-dance."
Then many other
Blackfoot Indians
came to our camp,
bringing their tee-
pees and ponies
and children with
them; for as Chief
Natus-ape lived in
our camp, it be-
came the head-

INDIAN SAND-HILL GRAVES.

quarters for all the other camps. I did not mind the "sun-dance" in
those days, but now it seems to me they are bad. The young men used
to fast, and they would torture themselves, stick knives and skewers into
their flesh, cut off their fingers, and do many other things that it makes
me sad to think of. But they thought it pleased the great spirit, for
we knew not of the true God, we worshipped the sun. When people
died, we thought their souls went to the sand-hills. The bodies were
wrapped in blankets, and the friends of the dead person brought moccasins,
blankets, weapons, &c., and put with the body, so that when the soul
left the body it might have plenty of things to take to the sand-hills
with it. The Blackfoot Indians do not bury the dead in the ground, but
they place the body on a sort of platform up in a tree, or sometimes on
a hill-top, but then it is put in a box. The Blackfoot Indians liked
their old ways and habits best, they did not want to give them up.
About ten miles from our camp there lived a few white men; they had
built a little school-house, and they wanted the Indians to send their

children to school. One of the white men was a clergyman; he was a good man, he wanted to teach the poor Indian the true religion, but the old men would not listen to him. I used to hear them talk something about it. There was one named Hee-pan; he was 125 years old, and the other men listened to him with great respect, for they thought him wise. Hee-pan hated the white men, for once, many years ago, they had killed his son in a fight. " Why should we listen to the white men ? " Hee-pan would say; " they have brought us nothing but sorrow; they have killed our buffalo ; they have built their cities on our land, and driven us back, and even now they are ploughing up our prairie land ; with their far-shooting guns have they killed our bravest chiefs ; they laugh at the Indian, they say he were better dead. Once there were many tribes, now they are few; it is the white man's doing; and now he wants to take

CHIEF OF THE BLACKFOOT INDIANS.

your children from you to teach them to be like white men ! We do not want them like white men, for they are not good. The agent is bad; he cheats the Indian, he hates him ; no one loves the Indian but his own people. Therefore, my sons, keep your children ; let not the white man have them." So would Hee-pan speak, and the men would say " Agsiu " (it is good). And when the white man, Mr. Grey, came to talk to them, they would not listen, and the children laughed and ran away. Once I went to his school for one morning, but it seemed very hard to me ; I cared nothing for the little marks in a book which he called alphabet, and I soon ran away. But sometimes in the evening as I stood looking over the prairie, I wondered what lay beyond ; so far as I had ever been it was prairie, but I knew it could not go on so for ever, and when the train went rushing past I stood and watched it till it was far away, and

I wondered where it came from and where it went. But I said nothing of my thoughts to anyone, lest they should think I wanted to become a white man. But one day there came a change. I was sitting in our teepee, busy skinning a gopher, when my sister came running, crying, " N'appi-akon " (white man). I took no notice, for I liked to be like the men, and not show excitement like girls and children. But by-and-by, when the skin was off the gopher, I rose and went to the door and looked out. There was Mr. Grey, and with him was a strange white man, dressed like the Missionary; he was talking and making signs to some of the women and children, and showing them pictures and beads and many other things. Soon quite a crowd came round him, but the men stood a little way off. By-and-by Mr. Grey and the stranger rose and went to the chief's teepee; many of the men followed them. I went and peeped in at the door; the stranger was talking and showing pictures to the chief, Natus-ape. Soon Natus-ape began to ask questions. " Where does the white man come from ? " he said. " From far away across the prairie, across much water," answered the white man. " What does the white man want with the Blackfoot Indians ? " continued Natus-ape. " I want to be their friend," said the white man. " For many years have I worked among my Indian brothers, the Ojibway and the Sioux ; I know them and we love each other ; now it is in my heart to help the Blackfoot Indians, and to be their friend." Much more he said in this way. I looked at the face of Natus-ape, and I saw he liked the white stranger ; they talked long together, and at the end the chief said, " Come again." Then the white man seemed glad, and he shook hands with all in the teepee before he went away. In two days he came again alone ; he brought more pictures, he talked to many of the people and bought their beadwork, and did not try to pay too little for it, and the Indians were glad and they liked him. He had a little block of paper, and with a pencil he made pictures of some of the men ; we all thought it wonderful, and many of us had our pictures drawn. He showed us some that he had made of his home. It was a big house and there were many Indian boys and girls standing round. " Who are these? " asked an old woman. " They are my boys and girls," was the answer; " they live with me and learn to do many useful things, so by-and-by they may earn money and live like good white men, or go back to their own people and teach them all that it is good to know." The people said nothing, but in my heart there arose a wish to be like the white man's boys.

One day the white man talked long with Natus-ape, and at the end Natus-ape said, " You are a good white man; I believe you are true; you shall be my son and I will be your father, and the old woman (his wife) your mother, and your name shall be Natusiasamiu (the sun looks upon him). Then Natus-ape kissed the white man, and the old woman, laughing much, kissed him also, and the white man gave his new father and mother some tobacco and went away. That night a young man ran round the camp beating a drum and calling to the people to come to a meeting in the chief's teepee. The men obeyed, but the women

BUFFALOS ON THE PRAIRIE.

did not go, for Indians take not women into their council. It was late when my father came home, but I was wide awake under my blanket, and I heard my father and mother talking. Soon I heard my name, and I listened. "The chief knows best," said my father. "Natus-ape is wise; he spoke wise words in the council. The day of the great Indian tribes is over, their sun is setting; no longer can they ride over the prairie and hunt the buffalo, the white man is too strong. . . . We old people cannot change our ways, we cling to our beliefs; we will die Blackfoot Indians and our spirits will go to the sand-hills. But for our children it must not be so; if they would be strong, they must be as the white men. Therefore will we give up our son Mianami and our daughter Anistapitaki, and they shall go with the white man and learn with him and be as white man and woman. I have spoken." Then my mother broke out into loud wailing, for she wanted not to send away her children, and she wept long. Then she rose up and took a sharp knife and cut off one of her fingers at the first joint, for so it is the Blackfoot Indians show their grief. My father said nothing and soon fell asleep, but for a long time I lay and heard the moaning of my mother; but at last I too slept.

Mr. Smith says my story is getting too long, therefore I will not say much of the days that followed. I found that another boy was also

SAULT STE. MARIE RIVER.

coming with the white man; he was my friend; his name was Apistsamok. I was glad when I learned that he was coming, and when the white man came to take us away my heart was light; only my mother wept bitterly, and Apistsamok's father and mother too were sad, for they were old and he was their only son. We said good-bye; all the people came to see us go, even Natus-ape; only Hee-pan stayed in his teepee, for he was angry. Then we got into a high carriage and drove many miles over the prairie; we stopped and said good-bye to Mr. Grey, and then went on. That night we camped on the prairie, and the next, but on the third day we came to a town. It was big and there were many white people; some laughed at us, for we had on our blankets and beads, and our hair was long; for Natus-ape made Mr. Yates (for so the white man told us to call him) promise that we should not cut our hair. Mr. Yates was kind to us; he gave us plenty to eat and pictures. By-and-by we went on a train, and after that we came to another town. Here there was much water and many boats; it was strange to us, for we

had never seen so much water. When we went on a boat we were
frightened, and when we got far from land I longed for my teepee. But
soon we got better, and Mr. Yates took us out into a large room where
there were many tables. " Look," said he, pointing to the carved wood-
work round the sides; " the man who made this was one of my boys,
and learned carpentering in my home." I said nothing, but in my heart
I wondered. On the second day we left the boat, for we had come to
the place where Mr. Yates lived. We drove a little way along a road,
and soon we saw in the distance many people coming; they were Indian
boys and girls. They were running and laughing and shouting; they
were glad to see Mr. Yates, but they looked very much at us. They
were all dressed like white people, only we wore blankets. We stopped
in front of a large house. Here there was a white woman and some
white children; they all seemed glad and happy, but they talked much
to Mr. Yates and looked often at us. Then we went indoors and into a
big room, and all the boys and girls had tea. After that Mr. Yates
told me to say good-bye to my sister, for she was going with the girls
to the other home, for they did not live here. Soon after that a bell
rang, we went into a big room, and Mr. Yates read in his own language
from a book; all the boys sang a hymn in the English language. Mr.
Yates then prayed, and after that we all went to bed.

I have not room to tell of all we did or of all we had to learn.
Everyone was kind to us, but many things seemed very hard. No one
knew our language but Mr. Yates, and we could not talk the English, so
it was hard for us to understand what they wanted us to do. Our
clothes seemed strange to us, for Mr. Yates gave us the white men's
dress and took away our blankets. At night they made us take off our
clothes, and in the morning put them on again, and it seemed to us
much trouble for nothing. There were so many bells, and when one
rang we always had to do something—eat, or sleep, or do school, or work
outdoors, or sing, or go to church, or play,—and it was hard to know
what each bell meant. It was hard to have to do just what you were
told, and it was hard to feel that we were in a strange land, among
strangers, and far from our tribe. But in a few months it got better,
we got more used to the ways of the white people. I began to want to
learn the books and to be as wise as the other boys. I wondered that some
of them seemed to care so little about working and spent so much time
in play. Apistsamok was not like me, he cared not for the books,
therefore they taught him a trade. He was a bootmaker, and worked
half the day with many other boys making boots; he liked this, and
often showed his work to me. We were very happy, though we
sometimes felt a wish to see the prairie and the Indian teepees. Every
Sunday the girls came to church and stayed for dinner, and in the
afternoon the brothers and sisters walked and talked together. I asked

Anistapitaki if she was happy, and she said, Yes, she liked the girls and their way of living better than the Blackfoot way, but the lessons were hard.

It was not long before the winter came. Deep snow covered the fences, the river was covered with ice, and the boys wore moccasins on their feet and warm clothes. Apistsamok did not like the cold; when the winter came he used to cough much and get weak. This winter it was just the same, his cough was very bad. Mr. Yates used to look anxiously at him many times. Once he said to me, " Did Apistsamok ever have a cough like this before?" " Yes," I answered. "I wish I had known that before," said Mr. Yates; and after that he would not let Apistsamok go out on very cold days. But in my heart I felt sad, for my friend got very thin, and his cough was worse than it had ever been before. "When the warm weather comes, I will take you home," said Mr. Yates to him one day. Apistsamok smiled, but afterwards he said to me, "I feel much sick, Mianami, my friend; something says to me in my heart, You will never go back to your teepee and your tribe; when the long days come and the sun is warm I shall not be here." I said nothing, for it is not the way of Indians to talk much, but my heart was heavy, for I knew he spoke the truth. Many times did Mr. Yates speak to us of the white man's religion, of the God who made us and all the world, and of the Saviour who died for us. At first it was hard to believe, for it was different to our religion, but by-and-by it seemed to me better than ours. The white man had no sun-dance, and none of the evil practices of the Indians, and soon we believed that theirs was the true religion. One day we had been very busy, putting up green things in the church, for it was near Christmas. Mr. Yates had told me all about what Christmas meant, and I listened eagerly, for it seemed to me a beautiful story. I went to see Apistsamok soon after; he was in the hospital, in bed, for he was very ill now. I told him the story and he liked it. By-and-by Mr. Yates came in; after he had talked to us for some time, he asked us would we like to be baptized. We knew what he meant, for he had often spoken of it, and we said "Yes." " Soon, then," said Mr. Yates, "it shall be done." Christmas-day was very nice. I saw my sister; she came to church, and after church we had a great dinner; but many times I thought of my friend lying in the hospital. In the evening we played some games and sang some hymns, and then the girls went home. A few days after there was a Christmas-tree; it was very pretty; I got many presents, and I carried some over to Apistsamok; they pleased him much, he sat up and looked at them and laughed; then I was glad. It was nearly two weeks after when Mr. Yates baptized us. It was on a Sunday; Apistsamok was very weak, he looked white and strange. His Christian name was Arthur and mine John, after Mr. Grey and Mr. Yates. When it was over the others went away, but I stayed. Presently Apistsamok said, "Mianami, my friend, I am getting very weak; soon I shall die. My mother will be sad, for she has no other son but me; tell her I have much love for her; I send her a pair of boots which I made for her. Tell her not to weep, tell her not to cut off her fingers, for it is not good. Mianami, my spirit will go to the white man's God, for I am His child now. Keep the white man's religion, Mianami, and we shall again see each other. Farewell, my brother." Thus spoke my brother, my friend Apistsamok, and I said farewell and went away very sad. That night I awakened suddenly from my sleep; it was dark, but I heard a strange sound. It was the church bell; oh! so low it went, it filled my heart with fear. Some of the boys woke also; they spoke in low tones, and soon I heard the word "Apistsamok": then I knew that Apistsamok was dead. . . .

The next day Mr. Yates took me to see him. His face was calm and there was a smile upon it. There were many flowers round him. I looked long upon him, and wondered how it was that I had never before seen a dead man with a smile upon his face. Then I thought it is the Christian religion which has made Apistsamok glad, and in my heart there arose a desire to teach my people of the true God, that they too might die smiling and at peace like Apistsamok.

It is years since that happened, but I never forgot that wish. I worked hard that winter; in the spring I went to see my people with Mr. Yates, and I comforted Apistsamok's father and mother and told them of his last words. Then I came back with Mr. Yates, and for eight years I worked, fitting myself to become a Missionary to my people. For four years now have I lived amongst them; many of the old people are dead, but there are many left who are still heathen and there are few to teach them. It is hard work, for the Indian loves his ways and religion even as the white man loves his. But if the white people would but help, it could be done. Oh, white men, you have taken much from the Indian; what better can you give him in return than a knowledge of the true God, and a helping hand to lead him forth from darkness into light?

NOTES OF THE MONTH.

ON February 9, a farewell service was held in the Chapel in the Society's house. The service was a celebration of the Holy Communion, at which an earnest address was given by Canon Mason. Five new Missionaries sailed for India the next day, and ten days later the Rev. R. R. Winter left England to return to his work at Delhi. There were many communicants.

ESSINGTON, in the Diocese of Caledonia, in British Columbia, was the scene of the work of the Rev. A. H. Sheldon, whose sad death, by drowning, took place last year. The Bishop now writes to describe the state of the Mission under his successor :—

"The population is steadily increasing, the hold of the Church stronger, the morals purer, and sound knowledge through the schools extending.

"Port Essington has already become the chief centre of trade in the diocese, and is likely to keep the lead. But still it is a rough place, with so many elements of evil in force that strong men are wanted to grapple with them.

"I rejoice that Mr. Brown has resolved to remain there. On all hands it is acknowledged that he has, almost single-handed, wrought a remarkable reformation in the neighbourhood.

"He has nearly doubled the capacity of the Church and filled it. The school in memory of the late Mr. Sheldon is finished, paid for, and in constant use. The dispensary is also in full swing, and many hundreds of patients prescribed for.

"At my last Confirmation there, besides whites and Indians, there were six Chinese confirmed. On the same day I baptized four Indians in the same church. The Chinese alone bought a new American organ, costing, I think it was £35, and presented it to the church.

"At Aberdeen, across the Skeena, six miles distant, services have been taken by either Mr. Brown or Mr. Cope every Sunday. The same at Balmoral, where the new church is just completed. Likewise at Sunnyside, where the materials for a church are on the ground, ready for construction.

"Port Essington has, you will see, become a prolific mother of churches, while yet in her youth.

"Under God's blessing all depends on the stamp of clergy at work. We must have dash, order, and devotion."

WE are grieved to hear that the Bishop of Barbados is very seriously ill.

"ISLAM as a Missionary Religion" is the title of the latest addition to the series of books on "Non-Christian Religious Systems" issued by the S.P.C.K. It is by the Rev. C. R. Haines, who has written other works relating to both Missions and Islam. Mr. Haines gives a good historical description of the advance of Islam, from the days of

Mohammed, in India, China, Malaysia, Europe, and Africa. He regards its progress as due to the joint and skilful use of both the agencies of force and persuasion. . . . Since Islam claims a political as well as a spiritual supremacy, it is difficult to see how, while remaining the same, it can survive the loss of temporal dominion. . . . Christianity in India is increasing, relatively, very much faster than Islam.

THE Rev. A. M. Hewlett has just returned to Madagascar after his furlough in England. He was in time for the dedication festival of the Church of St. James at Tamatave, which was consecrated eleven years ago.

"It is very encouraging, on coming back, to find that, though our numbers are small, there seems to be a real earnestness and love for the Church amongst those who do come. The attendance at the English evensong on Sundays has averaged 15 for the five Sundays since our return, and the offerings at those services average 9s. 6d. Last Sunday I spoke of the anniversary of St. James' Day, and, though we could not arrange any special gathering for the English part of the congregation this year, I asked them to help in the expenses of the feast we proposed to give to the native members of the church and school. There were several very generous responses both in money and in kind, so that, the feast being paid for, I am able, with the consent of the donors, to begin a little fund towards the re-painting of the church. A thorough puttying and painting of the outside will cost £40, and prudence demands that it should be done at once. The interior is beautiful wood, light and dark, and is, I am happy to say, untouched by the paint-brush. In the same way I have just managed to preserve the inside of the new Mission-house, which is of lovely red wood, from the brush, but the outside I had to paint, at an expense of £24. 16s., to preserve it from sun and rain.

"To return to our festival. On Tuesday the school-boys, with Rajaobelina and Andrianjakoto, the two catechists who are with me at present, made an expedition, in which I was very sorry not to be able to join them, to fetch palms and other green things to decorate the church; and on Wednesday, the Vigil, we all turned our attention to making it beautiful. There was also a good deal to do in buying and killing an ox for our feast. About five we had our first vespers, or evensong, with a short sermon on the Epistle for the day, and the new hymn we had taught the children for this occasion, a Malagasy version of

'Hark! the sound of holy voices,'

to the beautiful tune 'Deerhurst.'

"The next morning began with the Holy Eucharist at seven. Sixteen communicated, including our own party and the teachers. On the conclusion of the service we made a procession, repeating Psalms xxx. and cxxvii., to this new Mission-house, where we held a short service, dedicating it to God's glory, and praying that a faithful succession of priests might never be wanting here.

"About half-past nine we sung Mattins, at which the church was fairly filled, and then we made our way to a pleasant spot under the mango-trees, just north of this. After a couple of hours' play, we ate our lunch on banana leaves instead of table-cloths and plates. I suppose about 150 partook—at all events, the ox was finished. Then we gave some little prizes to those twenty-five or thirty children who had been diligent in school during our absence in England. We gave dolls to the girls and shirts to most of the boys. Ratsimatahotra, one of the chief officers of the Betsimisaraka, honoured us with his presence. He is seldom absent from church on Sundays, and is always cordial and helpful. I feel towards him much as an English parson does towards his squire, when he is a hearty Churchman. There were several other officers and gentlemen there, and as we came home tired out, they went to the 'Battery' to their various Government duties. I thought it nice that they should get away to join us. We certainly did not give them as good care as they might have had at home. Amongst the women present was the ever-faithful Mary Celestie, the very first person baptized by Mr. Holding, as appears by our Baptismal Register under date November 13, 1864.

"Our Festival Day closed with evensong at four o'clock, to which all the children came back.

"To-morrow we keep as 'Sunday within the Octave' of our Dedication Feast. I hope to celebrate in Malagasy at seven and in English at eight; preach after Mattins at nine, catechise at three, and preach in English at four. Our collections—not much more than £1, perhaps—are to go as an offering from the daughter church towards the completion of the cathedral. I leave here on Tuesday to be present at the consecration on St. Laurence's Day, and I am afraid, with that and the Synod and the journeys up and down, I shall have to be away four Sundays.

"I have just started off four men carrying the church bell back to Mahasoa. It was hurled down and broken in the hurricane of February 22 last year, and has only now got mended. On it is inscribed,

A.S. MDCCCLXXVI

ROBU EPO.

LAUS DEO.

It was, I believe, given to Bp. (Robert) Kestell-Cornish by that enthusiastic campanologist, the late Mr. Ellacombe, the beloved patriarch of Clyst St. George. A sister bell, somewhat larger, is in the bell turret, seen in the accompanying photograph of the west end of our church here. The western porch, as repaired after the hurricane, shows a want of painting, which I hope may stir up someone to help us in that undertaking. The new Mission-house is to the south-east of the church. I hope to send you pictures of it at some future time."

ON Trinity Sunday, June 16, 1889, an ordination was held by Bishop Caldwell in St. Peter's Church, Kodaikanal, Pulney Hills. Four natives and one European were ordained: three as priests and two as deacons. Up to the time of the ordination there were twenty-five deacons in all in Tinnevelly and Ramnad, of whom twenty-one were in Tinnevelly and four in Ramnad. At the same time there were twenty priests in all in both districts, of whom there were seventeen in Tinnevelly and three in Ramnad. The existence of so large a number of deacons may require explanation. Some of them had been ordained with the intention that they should be allowed to remain deacons, if not permanently, yet at least for a considerable time, to allow persons of higher intellectual attainments and greater ability to be advanced to the priesthood before them. For this reason a selection only was made on this occasion of those who were already in deacon's orders—viz., two from Tinnevelly and one from Ramnad. There were special reasons why each of these persons should now be admitted to priest's orders without further delay. In addition to the deacons newly admitted to the priesthood, there were two additions on this occasion to the order of deacons. These were Mr. A. Heber Thomas, B.A., of Ramnad, an Oxford graduate, who was appointed to read the gospel, and Mr. A. M. Satyanathen Naidu, of Kulasagarapattanam, in the Nazareth district, originally a convert from the Alvar-Tirunagari Anglo-Vernacular School.

FROM the Lytton Indian Mission, in the Diocese of New Westminster, the Rev. E. L. Wright reports many details of interest in his visitation of the various stations included in his district. For instance, going on from Zookht, where the Indians are about to build a little church so that the services can be held in it instead of in the Nicola village court-house, he came, after a journey of twenty-three miles, to Quieskina.

"This is a small 'reservation' situated on the other side of the Nicola River. The small band of Indians, numbering about twenty, is presided over by a medicine man, who, two years ago, refused to allow the children to be baptized, and the adults to give their names for baptism. The people have now refused to listen to him any longer, and at this visit brought five children for holy baptism, and nine adults gave their names for baptism and confirmation, and three for confirmation. I had prayers and instruction and five infant baptisms."

A FRIEND has sent us the following cutting from the *Times of India.* Its interest is less in its being a specimen of hypocrisy and fraud among those eminent for heathen piety, than as an indication of the curious working of man's untutored religious instinct. We may marvel why can the Yogi have thought the supposed miracle suitable to his religious character, or the people have been impressed by such exercise of the " holy man's wonderful powers " :—

" We have already learned from Professor Oman's charming volume on Indian life that the Yogi is not always what he seems. He is sometimes, in fact, an arrant impostor, and in such cases probably has not been regularly apprenticed to his business at all. When an apprenticed Yogi has squatted down with feet doubled up, arms crossed, and head bent, and has, in due accordance with prescribed rites, murmured the mystic syllable 'O'm' twenty millions seven hundred and thirty-six consecutive times—an operation which will occupy him for eight months and a half—the chances are he has no burning desire to go in for trickery. A very odd case, however, is reported from Jodhpore, near Calcutta. A Yogi has been in the neighbourhood for some days and has been the object of much reverence and innumerable offerings. He was smeared with dirt of the regulation quality, and rendered formidable by much yellow ghastliness. He gave out a day or two ago that at a certain hour he would transform a man into a goat, and that the miracle could be witnessed by all and sundry for the small charge of four annas per head. He had what we believe is technically called a 'good gate,' and producing the unhappy victim of his magical powers (who looked, we are told, supremely unconcerned at his fate), he duly crammed him down into a hole in the earth. The hole was a sort of diminutive tunnel, and from its other end, after weird spells and uncanny mutterings and many mysterious passes, the Yogi produced, amid the astonished cries of the crowd, a live goat. The man had been transformed as promised, and the crowd melted slowly away awestruck at the holy man's wonderful powers. At nightfall, when the coast was clear, the man who had been converted into a goat crawled out of the hole, and demanded the price of his secrecy, rupees twenty-five —a sufficiently reasonable sum one would think in the circumstances. The Yogi, rashly covetous, declined to give more than rupees ten, and, on his confederate losing his temper, threatened to make him lose his head also, with the assistance of a knife. Undaunted by threats, however, and serene in the knowledge that his cause was just, the man made his way to the police thana, and had the too covetous Yogi locked up. He is now awaiting his trial, and doubtless feeling rather sorry for his attempt to 'bear' the market."

IN September we inserted a letter from the Rev. W. H. Elton, of North Borneo, which contained an appeal for £30 a year to enable him to station a Catechist at Kudat, where there are about 100 Christian Chinese, in addition to others in the neighbourhood. We are glad to be able to say that the appeal has been responded to, and the required amount is now promised, and that for the first year already sent out.

ON Saturday, August 10, the Cathedral for the Diocese of Madagascar, St. Lawrence, Antananarivo, was consecrated by the Bishop. It was on St. Lawrence's Day that the huge island was first discovered, four centuries ago, by the Portuguese, who gave it the name of St. Lorenjo. From the account of the proceedings in the *Madagascar Times* we take the following:—

"As early as half-past six in the morning a considerable crowd of neatly dressed Malagasy had filled the stone stairway and the precincts of the Cathedral, and the Holy Communion was celebrated at 7 A.M. in the Malagasy language by Bishop Kestell-Cornish. Soon after eight o'clock the service was ended, and great crowds immediately began to assemble to obtain admission for the Consecration Service, which was fixed for 10 A.M., and before the commencement of the service nearly 2,000 people were seated. His Excellency the Prime Minister, with his suite, arrived at a few minutes before ten, and was met at the terrace by Mr. Pickersgill, Her Britannic Majesty's Vice-Consul, with Colonel St. Leger Shervinton and Major Graves, British Officers in the Queen of Madagascar's service, who were in full uniform, and who escorted the Prime Minister to a raised pew near the choir, Her Britannic Majesty's Vice-Consul sitting on his left.

"Some fifty to sixty foreigners were present at the service, and by careful management at the doors perfect order and quietness reigned after the procession had entered the Church, although twice the number of natives would have entered had the building been capable of holding them, or had they been permitted to make the experiment.

"The procession left the old Church a few minutes before ten, consisting of forty-five choristers, seven native ordained deacons, five English clergymen, and the Bishop, his pastoral staff being carried by the Rev. E. O. MacMahon, acting as the Bishop's Chaplain. The procession arrived at the west door as the last verse of 'Onward, Christian Soldiers,' rang through Andohalo, and, after the usual prayers and responses, a loud knock at the door was responded to by a deacon, and, the door having been opened, the procession walked up the nave chanting the Twenty-fourth Psalm.

"Bishop Kestell-Cornish followed the form used at the recent consecration of the Truro Cathedral. That the service was singularly impressive and imposing no one who attended could deny. The choir of chosen voices simply enraptured the immense congregation, as the familiar strains of Anglican music ascended through the arches. The Bishop began by consecrating the font at the extreme west end, and thence by degrees proceeded to different parts of the Cathedral, ending with the pulpit and the altar, after which he received the pastoral staff from his Chaplain, and then formally dedicated the building to be used for no other purpose than a house of prayer, and pronounced it 'holy' in the name of the Father, the Son, and the Holy Ghost.

"This being completed, Mendelssohn's anthem, 'How lovely are the messengers,' set to the Malagasy translation, was beautifully rendered, after which the Rev. A. M. Hewlett, M.A., preached the sermon on the text of Col. l. v. 24. Mr. Hewlett is remarkably facile in the language of Madagascar, and his quiet calm expression, and his attitude in the pulpit, demonstrated that he was speaking with intense earnestness and feeling, and he is certainly a born preacher. His sermon made a great effect upon the natives—we are quoting their own opinions—and everyone listened to the end in breathless silence.

"Following the sermon came a hymn, during the singing of which a collection was made amounting to £22, or $110, and a Blessing then concluded the Morning Service."

FOLLOWING upon this, not inaptly, we have a letter from the Rev. C. P. Cory showing how earnestly the spirit of self-help in the native Church of Madagascar is being fostered, how the Missionaries are with great self-sacrifice paying native teachers and bearing other Mission expenses out of their own pockets, and how many demands for teachers are refused and openings for work neglected for lack of means :—

"During the last five years a sum of not less than $1,000 has with great difficulty been collected from the natives as the nucleus of an endowment fund; the interest on this money has already enabled us to reduce by one-sixth all salaries paid to native teachers throughout Imerina. Also, I should like to state that the expenditure in Imerina has been considerably reduced since 1885, many teachers having been removed, and the whole district consolidated, so that, where there was formerly a teacher receiving from $5 to $6 a month, there is now one that receives but a dollar. Also, that very much work has been refused both in Imerina and on the coast; and that, in accordance with our last Synod rules, no church can or has been put upon the Block Grant in Imerina that does not build its own church and pay for its own school-master since that date."

SUGGESTED SUBJECTS FOR PRAYER.

For the Missionaries recently gone forth to India, and for those returning to their work there.

For the Australasian Church, and especially its vacant sees.

For South Africa, and especially that the Church may be helped and blessed in her work among the Europeans and the natives attracted by the mines.

For Madagascar, and the strengthening and extension of the Church's work in that land.

THE SOCIETY'S INCOME.

Abstract of RECEIPTS *and* PAYMENTS *from January 1 to September 30.*

	GENERAL FUND	SPECIAL FUNDS
Subscriptions, Donations, Collections, &c.	£20,939	£11,116
Legacies	8,301	107
Dividends, Rents, &c.	3,006	2,798
TOTAL RECEIPTS	£32,246	£14,021
PAYMENTS	£65,537	£13,670

The Receipts under the head of Subscriptions, Donations, and Collections for the General Fund from January 1 to September 30, in five consecutive years, compare as follows : 1885, £21,993 : 1886, £19,931 ; 1887, £21,904 1888, £20,483* ; 1889, £20,939.

* In addition, the Treasurers received in 1888 Securities of the value of £25,296 as "A Thankoffering to Almighty God for the extension of the Church in the Colonies and Dependencies of the British Empire and beyond it"; also other Securities of the value of £2,268 as a Trust Gift, *the Income only being available.*

THE MISSION FIELD.

THE FIELD IS THE WORLD. THE SEED IS THE WORD OF GOD.

DECEMBER 2, 1889.

WIDENING HORIZONS.

THE last number of a closing year would seem to be a fitting occasion for taking a brief retrospect, and for discovering where we stand, and what we have done, and what lies before us. While in this, as in all other works of fallible men, there is much room for humiliation and self-reproach, there is, nevertheless, so much of assured progress visible on any intelligent retrospection, that those who have taken part in our work may thank God for His blessing which has rested on our labours. The extension of our empire, perhaps in some cases against our will, is a patent fact. It would seem as though, however much statesmen may deprecate the responsibilities of rapidly extending dominions, those dominions will grow in spite of all, as by a law external and irresistible. The same things are being reproduced, and the same feelings obtrude themselves, in the smaller sphere of our work. In a valuable paper on "The Spiritual Counterpart to Imperial Destiny," which appeared in our pages in January 1888, there occurred the following thoughtful passage: "Divine Providence seems to have been leading us forward, or we might almost say hurrying us onwards, with breathless speed to a greatness and influence beyond our utmost imagination. We find ourselves the centre of an influence which grows day by day and year by year; and we increase, moreover, from time to time our territorial possessions. And so we have almost learned to look upon ourselves as being destined for yet higher eminence, and to believe in what the Bishop of Durham called some time since the 'Imperial Destiny of Great Britain.' Nor can it be merely foolish pride when such men as Bishop Lightfoot refer to the idea at solemn seasons such as a Church Congress; rather must we regard the expansion of England as an admitted fact on which we should meditate humbly and solemnly, that we may try to understand the Will of God concerning it. The outspread of the various branches of the English-speaking race must have a wide influence upon the future of the world."

The Society's original constitution pointed to its expanding with the growth of the British Empire, and wonderfully has it fulfilled the objects of its founders. It may claim the credit of having planted the Church in the great majority of the British Colonies; but being in an unique sense the Missionary organ of the Church of England, it has followed not merely the growing empire but the flag of Great Britain, which floats over all seas. Whether it has been a wise policy thus to attempt to occupy regions so vast that only enormous resources can cope with their necessities is a matter of opinion. As a matter of fact it has been found impossible to turn a deaf ear to those, Bishops and others, who have given themselves to the work of carrying the Gospel to remote and heathen lands, and who have looked to the Society's ill-replenished treasury to provide them with things material. The consequence is that the Missions everywhere are weak and undermanned, and natural progress is arrested by insufficient machinery.

This growth of the Society's work has been so gradual and natural that many of its warmest friends may be pardoned if they have not marked it, just as many patriotic citizens have taken the growth of our empire as a thing of natural development.

From the Society's point of view, such an attitude on the part of Churchmen is disastrous. Thinking that as the Society has done well in the past it will do well in the future, they continue their help on the scale of long-ago, when the field of its work was only a portion, and a small portion, of what it is to-day, and its income not proportionately less but even much larger than now.

We think, then, a brief retrospect of certain features in the Society's work and position twenty years ago, and a comparison of its work and needs to-day, will be interesting to our readers, and possibly beneficial to the Society's exchequer, if it impresses the moral which we shall hope to deduce.

Taking, therefore, a glance at the work twenty years ago, and comparing it with the story of to-day, we find that there was in 1869 no mention in the Annual Report of the Dioceses of Lahore or Rangoon, of Japan or North China, of Pretoria, or of Madagascar. There was no work at all being done in Japan, in North China, or in Fiji. There was Mission work being done on a small scale in Lahore and Rangoon, which formed part of the Diocese of Calcutta, and there was a feeble struggling Mission on the low-lying east coast of Madagascar. The Society's responsibilities to these countries in the present year involve an expenditure of nearly £17,000; in 1869 probably as many hundreds of pounds would have met all demands.

In 1869 the Society's grant to Rupertsland was £275—all that was asked for, and probably all that was needed. The colony was then a vast hunting-ground, from which immigrants were warned off. The great Canadian Pacific Railway had not then laid its iron trail across that country and joined two oceans; it had not entered into the dreams of the most patriotic of Canadians. In twenty years the single diocese has become six; the Society has largely helped in the endowment of two, has contributed greatly to the endowment of St. John's College at Winnipeg, and of the clergy in the original Diocese of Rupertsland, and its annual expenditure in this ecclesiastical province is now nearly £6,000, as against £275 in 1869.

Events altogether beyond the Society's control have, in some cases, interfered with its policy of gradually reducing grants to colonial dioceses. Rules must never be allowed to stand in the way when wisdom points to their supersession. This has befallen in the West Indian Dioceses. In 1869 the Diocese of Antigua received £125, and the Diocese of Nassau, always the least fruitful in all elements of commercial prosperity, £250. Thus the West Indies cost the Society £375 per annum. The Windward Islands, which formed part of the Diocese of Barbados, the island of Trinidad, then grouped in that Diocese, and Jamaica, had ceased to be beneficiaries of the Society's money. But in the next decade the policy of disestablishment and disendowment was carried out in the West Indian Islands. To have withheld prompt and liberal relief would have been to sacrifice all that had been done in the past. The Society helped to endow the Dioceses of Antigua and Nassau by grants of large sums, providing for the latter on the death of Bishop Venables an Episcopal stipend for his successor, and its expenditure on these Churches in 1889 is £2,000, as compared with £375 in 1869. Similarly, in view of the very interesting evangelistic work carried on in the Diocese of Guiana, the expenditure has grown from £390 in 1869 to £820 in 1889.

In 1873 a grant of £100 was made to a solitary clergyman at Pretoria; five years later the Society promoted the endowment of a Bishopric, and guaranteed a stipend to the Bishop until the endowment should be completed. The diocese now receives £900 per annum. In 1869 the expenditure in the then Dioceses of Grahamstown and Natal was £7,000 per annum; in the four dioceses which cover the same area it is now nearly £9,000.

In 1873 a small Mission, consisting of two priests, was sent to Japan, and in 1874 a similar body went to North China. Little or nothing was known of the countries, and everything was a venture of faith. Now there is a Bishop in Japan, with a good clerical staff around him. One of the pioneers to North China is now Bishop of that Mission, and the Society is spending about £3,500 per annum in those countries.

In 1874 the Society was enabled to secure the consecration of a

N 2

Bishop for Madagascar, whom it has maintained up to the present time. The Bishop has now 16 ordained missionaries, and the Society's expenditure is £3,200 per annum, as compared with £700 per annum in 1869.

When the Fiji group were added to the roll of our colonies in 1875, the Society felt bound to take them under its care, and two priests are now ministering to the pioneer settlers in those remote islands.

In 1885 the conquest of Upper Burmah added to the British dominions a heathen country larger than the United Kingdom, with a population of more than four millions of souls. The Society has Missions, which by comparison with some others may be called strong, at Mandalay and at Shwebo, and ought to extend Christian stations towards the frontiers of China. It is not easy to estimate the cost of those Missions, which form part of the Diocese of Rangoon, but it is very considerable.

Then from time to time, within the limits of older fields of work, there spring up gregarious movements which demand prompt and immediate care, and involve large expenditure. Thus, in 1869, the Kol Christians came over as a body, and some thousands, with their Lutheran ministers, were adopted by the Society. At this day there are about 13,000 souls with a clerical staff of 20, of whom 15 are natives. In 1872 new ground was broken in Western India, and a Marathi Mission was founded in the Nagur district, where there are now some 4,000 Christians,' and, alas! only four missionaries. In the following year, the Karens in the Toungoo mountains of Burmah were received in large numbers into our Communion. There are now in the two groups of villages 3,800 baptized persons, more than 1,300 communicants, and seven ordained missionaries. All of these Missions have come upon the Society's treasury.

But greater than all, there was the remarkable movement of 1878 in Tinnevelly, when about 30,000 souls within the limits of the Society's Missions were moved to become inquirers and disciples. The task of shepherding these multitudes taxed all resources to the utmost. An appeal to the Christian Church at home produced some £10,000, and the Society's increased expenditure in the Diocese of Madras bears witness to the strain which this remarkable movement has laid on it.

If it be assumed from these statements that the Society's resources have increased in a ratio corresponding with its extended work, the inference will be wrong. There has been growth, of course. For example, in 1869 it received in subscriptions, collections, and donations £63,636, while its normal income under the same item has, on one occasion, reached £80,000, and may be taken at an average of between £78,000 and £79,000. There have been years rich in legacies, and there have been responses to special appeals, sometimes disappointing, sometimes truly generous. The exceptional and ever-growing demands have been met by reductions in the grants to the older colonial dioceses—reductions made not without consideration, and in pursuance of the fixed policy which throws a colonial diocese year by year more and more on its own resources as those resources naturally grow. It may be taken that little or no hardship has been inflicted by this policy, but rather that a healthy spirit of self-help has been stimulated. To take only one or two examples—in 1869 Newfoundland received £4,100, where now it receives £2,900, and it has in that time increased its clerical staff about 30 per cent.; in 1869 the Australasian dioceses received £2,250, they now receive £450.

But all along proper and legitimate growth has been checked by lack of means, and apparent injustice has been done to many dioceses. Why, for example, it has been asked, should Pretoria receive £900 per annum, and Grahamstown £3,000 per annum; Bloemfontein £1,000, and St. John's £2,530, and Maritzburg £2,125? It is perfectly true that the respective requirements of the several dioceses are by no means represented by the help which they receive; but the fact is that, in consequence of the restricted means at the disposal of the Society, younger dioceses, such as Pretoria and Bloemfontein, could have received help commensurate with their just claims only by reducing the help given to Grahamstown and Maritzburg and St. John's, just when to have done so would have destroyed all that had been attained by years of work.

The moral of all this is, then, that had the Church at home been more liberal, the Church abroad would have been stronger and ready sooner to stand on its own feet.

Now a word for the present and the immediate future.

To some it may seem that experience is thrown away in the councils of the Society, if with the knowledge of the past it enters on fresh fields. But it must do so. There are voices that it is sinful to refuse to hear, and there are ventures of faith now to be made, as fields open and opportunities multiply, on a scale of which the past knew nothing.

For several years the Society has been calling attention to two countries as demanding the care of the Church. These are New Guinea and Corea. In the first it seemed to be the duty of the Australian Churches, now well settled and numbering many wealthy members, to find its immediate sphere of work. Those Churches have received large help in the past. In some portions of Australia, State aid for many years poured year by year enormous sums into their treasury; their Bishoprics are sufficiently endowed; they have the means of education in abundance, and they had received nearly £250,000 from the Society. It is for the spiritual benefit of Churches so situated that they should stretch out into the regions beyond and sow there the seed which long ago was planted in their own land. And there is every reason to hope that our just expectations will be realised; but it seemed necessary that the first step should be taken by the Mother Church, and accordingly the Society sent out last month the Rev. A. A. Maclaren, well known to many of our friends as an earnest and able "deputation," and has voted a lump sum of £1,000 towards the New Guinea Mission.

On All Saints' Day, the Rev. C. J. Corfe, having accepted the call of our President, was consecrated Bishop of Corea, a heathen country with a population of eleven millions. This Mission will be conducted on the community principle: the Bishop and the clergy whom he hopes to secure will live a common life with a common fund; and when it is stated that, with its present resources, the Society has not been able to guarantee more than £650 per annum, it will be seen that this Mission starts with the seal and symbol of apostolic poverty very visibly stamped upon it. A special fund has been opened, and it is hoped that not a few will contribute to it.

Nor is this all. Methods of colonisation are now rapidly changing, and lands are peopled at a rate that was as impossible as it would have been incredible some years ago.

The North Borneo Company, which has secured a large territory in that island, which has been one of the Society's fields for more than forty years, has gladly given its co-operation, and has liberally assisted the Rev. W. H. Elton, whom the Society has sent to Sandakan, the capital.

Our readers have for some months been following the steps of the Bishop of Bloemfontein in the journal of his adventurous travels, of which the last instalment appears in our present number. The whole of the country through which he passed was sparsely populated; some of it may almost be called a desert. According to all the precedents of the past, it would have been long, very long, before even our national spirit of enterprise had colonised those regions, and we may say without boasting that colonisation is an art in which the Englishman excels beyond all comparison. But, as has been said, methods are changing. It is not now the poor who can no longer bear the pressure of life at home who seek in new countries the homesteads and the independence denied to them at home. It is capital, in volume unlimited, and directed by wealthy and shrewd companies or syndicates at home, which now seizes on enormous countries, and throws across their area a network of railways, canals, telegraphs, and "floats" other ventures for the opening of coal-fields, for the working of gold-mines, and generally for developing all the latent capacities of the country.

Immediately on the return of the Bishop of Bloemfontein to his home there was a stir in the South African Church, which in its poverty

saw the duty of extending her frontiers at least up to the Zambesi, the
northern limit of the Bishop's journey. Ways and means make the
Church's action slow. Capital has no such difficulty. Every loan that is
"floated" is subscribed many times over, and money has to be rejected
because it is offered in volume greater than can be employed. Speculation
is active and eager; risk of loss is incurred, and gladly; and so within
the last few weeks a gigantic company has been founded under royal
charter, which will at first occupy a region one third greater than
Germany, which is to be known as British Zambesia. In the words of
the *Times* of October 22 :

"The principal field of operations of the British South African
Company, according to the charter, shall be the region of South Africa
lying immediately to the north of British Bechuanaland, and to the
north and west of the South African Republic (the Transvaal), and to the
west of the Portuguese dominions. No western limit, it is seen, is stated ;
that was perhaps unnecessary, as of course it is settled that the 20th degree
of east longitude marks off the widest German claims. Ample room is
thus left to the company for the expansion of its territory, and the
charter expressly stipulates that it is at perfect liberty to do so by every
legitimate means, east and west and north. The company is authorised
to acquire whatever other concessions it can, including 'All or any rights,
interests, authorities, and powers of any kind or nature whatever,
including powers necessary for the purpose of government and the
preservation of public order in and for the protection of territories,
lands, or property comprised or referred to in the concessions and
agreements made as aforesaid, or affecting other territories, lands, or
property in Africa or the inhabitants thereof.' In short the company is
empowered to govern the territories embraced in its charter in the
name and in behalf of the interests of the British Empire."

Thus in a few years this corporation, resembling as it does in some
features the old East India Company, will have occupied the country up
to the borders of the Congo and Lakes Tanganyika and Nyassa. The
Lake Companies, which are at present colonising that country, are ready
to be absorbed into Zambesia, while on the north-east the British
Imperial East Africa Company is tending from the Victoria Nyanza in
a south-westerly direction, and will at no distant day meet the others.
The influx of Englishmen and English capital into the two South
African Republics will soon make those countries English in influence,
language, and sentiment, and there can be no reasonable doubt that
England will have the dominating power over the whole of the
continent. A skeleton map is given to enable our readers to verify our
words.

We must here lay down our pen. But we doubt if anyone will
challenge the heading of this paper and deny that our horizons are

widening, wherever we look.　To our readers we would say, Lift up your eyes and see; lift up your hearts; lift up holy hands and pray that you and

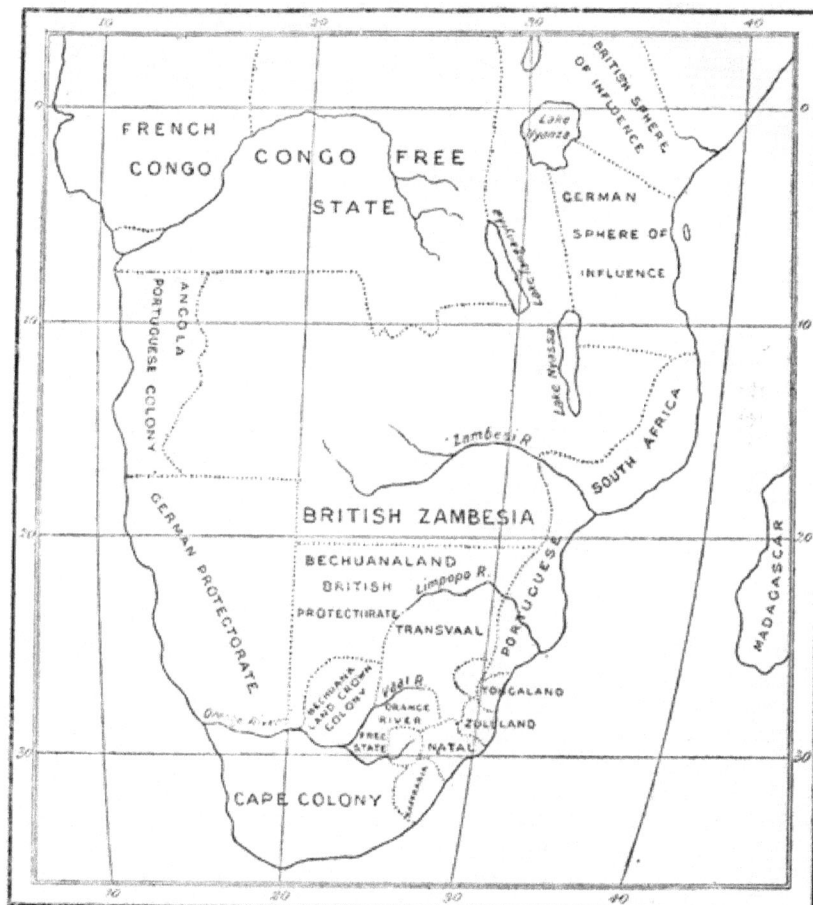

all your brethren in the fellowship of our Communion may have grace to rise up to the great opportunities which God puts in our way to try our faith and to test our love.

ENGLISH SETTLEMENTS IN NORTH CHINA.

BY THE REV. W. BRERETON.

AT the request of the Bishop, writing from England, I visited Tientsin and its vicinity, in February, to consult, with all who might be interested in the matter, about the Bishop's proposal to appoint a clergyman for English work at Tientsin; and I renewed my visit with the same object in April. My visits have resulted in sundry promises of yearly subscriptions towards a clergyman's income when the Bishop finds a man for the post and sufficient money wherewith to pay him.

I went by rail from Tientsin to Tangku, and thence to Tangshan. The former is an important station, deriving its name from a miserable-looking native village, close to the well-known Taku forts, and is on the north bank of the river, the town of Taku being on the south bank, a little further down. The place is likely to become the great maritime coaling station of North China, and also a centre for the distribution inland of foreign merchandise. Even the architectural display of a large coaling station would improve the landscape, for all round, as far as the eye can reach, stretches a treeless barren plain of mud impregnated with soda and other salts. I received a very kind welcome from the resident-engineer and his wife, the daughter of an English rector. What a contrast between her life in an English country rectory, with the parish church hard by, and her life in a mud cottage on the edge of a barren salt plain, looking out upon a wide tidal river, the sight of whose waters suggests sloppy pea-soup, and far away from the sound of church bells and the means of grace! On my first visit on Sunday I administered Holy Communion at Tangku, and in the afternoon we crossed the river to Pilot Town, a suburb of Taku, where I met a considerable congregation of English and American sea-captains, pilots, and their families, about thirty souls. We had service in the pilot office. I was told that my visit was the first they had ever received from a clergyman of the Church of England since the foundation of the settlement, shortly after the war of 1860. The majority of the congregation were members of our Church. The Roman and the English Methodist Missions have

TINTERN.

converts in the adjoining native town. The ministers of the latter Mission frequently hold an English service in the pilot office. Practically my visit was, to the Anglican Mission in this Diocese, the discovery of a little colony of Church people in need of the means of grace, but perhaps through long disuse, not very conscious of their need ; and yet the place lies in the direct track of all the steamer traffic in and out of Tientsin, a fact which may give rise to reflections not very pleasing.

At Tangshan, which is half a day by rail from Tangku, I was very kindly received by the engineer-in-chief of the railway and the mining companies and his wife. Tangshan is the northern terminus of the eighty-five miles of railway constructed and open to traffic. The growth of this place dates from the sinking of the coal mine ten years ago by the Chinese Engineering and Mining Company. Formerly it was a mere hamlet. Now it is a considerable Chinese town, with a European suburb, having neatly laid streets lighted with gas. I was told that they employed daily at the coal mine three thousand men above and below ground. The work is carried on under the supervision of English engineers, mechanics, and overmen, who, with the wives and children of a few, number in all twenty souls. An English Methodist missionary holds an English service every Sunday afternoon. The country around is fertile, and also rich in minerals, especially coal and iron. There are native steel works and also native potteries in the neighbourhood.* The combination of Chinese life and European scientific methods and appliances, situated thus far inland, away from any treaty port, Tientsin being eighty-five miles off, suggests the picture of a piece of modern English colliery and railway industries set down in the middle ages. The district is said by experts to be of great importance, as likely to become one of the busiest mining and manufacturing centres in North China.

My two visits to Tientsin confirm me in the conviction that a clergy-man for *English* work at Tientsin and the outlying places, such as Taku, Tangku, and Tangshan, is unquestionably *the first need of this Diocese.*

Years of observation lead me to the suspicion, if not to the conviction, that the Church of England in North China, as a whole, is losing more than it gains. We are making some progress among the heathen—slow and small indeed, but yet, viewed over a course of years, distinct progress. But, on the other hand, in the largest centre of foreign activity in the Diocese, a centre where English trade and influence preponderates, our Church unmistakably loses ground simply by the continued absence of its ministrations ; and, to me at least, it seems no exaggeration to say that, as a set-off against every Chinaman whom we baptize, must be placed the fact of the sympathies, and in some cases the formal allegi-

---

* since writing the above, I have been informed that the Mining Company has begun experiments in silver mining somewhere in the neighbourhood.

ance, of an English Churchman alienated from the church of his baptism, and often lost to all care for religion. A decidedly religious man in a place like Tientsin would be almost a miracle of staunch Churchmanship if he did not feel strongly drawn to throw in his lot with Rome, or with Protestant Dissent, for to these, under God, belong the merit of keeping alive religion in the place.

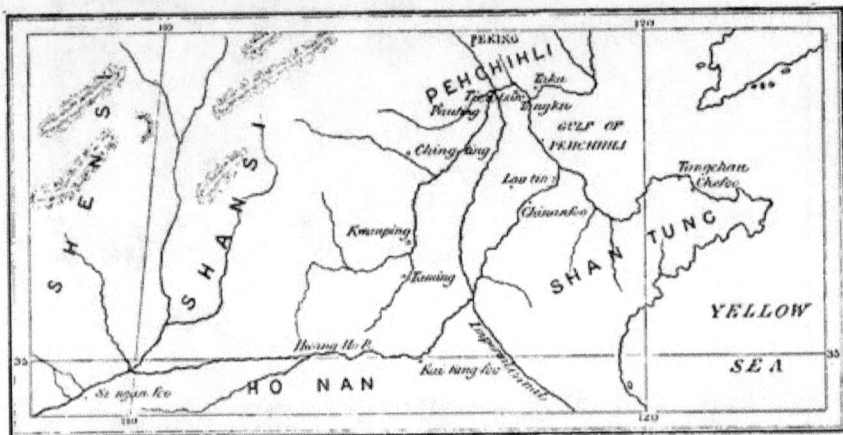

Tientsin is the point of divergence of the natural highways, of the distribution of imports and exports, and of the distribution of European residents and European civilising ideas and methods in this part of the Chinese Empire, and therefore, in my opinion, it is the natural and obvious basis for English work in this Diocese, and most probably for Chinese work as well.

UNDER THE ROCKY MOUNTAINS.

INCHER CREEK, in the Diocese of Saskatchewan, is a mission to which the Rev. H. Havelock Smith was appointed as the first clergyman in May last year. He thus describes the place and his work :—

" The members of the Church are scattered over a vast field, which can only be thoroughly worked ' in the saddle.' The settler is an intelligent man, in many cases having had university education. All are of the ranching type, and need constant looking up. The life of the Western man is not conducive to the keeping alive of spiritual life, and I find great indifference among many towards religious and pious thought and instruction, and many who are not altogether insensible to the gifts of grace.

" This parish is widely extensive, about 1,500 square miles. The population I am not quite certain of, as I know of no trustworthy census ever having been taken, but should put it down as not exceeding 800; the village of Pincher Creek itself does not exceed 150 or 200, and has two resident ministers—a clergyman of the Church of England, and a minister of the Presbyterian body—and a visiting Methodist and Roman Catholic, so that the spiritual life is not dead by virtue of lack of evangelists.

" My parish is, indeed, a lovely portion of Southern Alberta, under the very smile of the Rocky Mountains on the west, the Porcupine Hills on the north, and prairie lands east and south. From the mountain gorges sweep down torrents of rivers, clear, sparkling, and cool, adding beauty and health to the surrounding plains, broken, as they are, by undulating hill and dale. Along the river-bottoms there is a heavy growth of timber, and, until you reach the foot-hills of the mountains, the only timber to be seen. Upon the prairie flats and hillocks browse the cattle and horses of the ranchmen, sometimes seen in large bands, and at other times scattered in smaller herds over the countless knolls and hills of the river banks and bottoms, reminding one of the ' cattle upon the thousand hills.' There is a striking grandeur about the mountains, seen, as they are, at a distance of some twenty miles, towering high, till sometimes the peaks are lost amidst the clouds. How they speak to us of Nature's God! How they chill the idea of man's greatness; and yet he is sovereign of all, under the rule of the Almighty!

"There are in this district some thirty Church families, and some twenty-five individuals not included in families. The communicants' roll has gradually increased, till it now has reached some forty-three, thereby giving us the privilege of sending two lay delegates to our Diocesan Synod. In January last we had the pleasure of a visit from our Diocesan, who expressed himself thoroughly satisfied with the progress

A GLIMPSE OF A VALLEY UNDER THE ROCKIES.

being made. We are looking for a second visit soon, as he has returned from his visiting tour in the Saskatchewan country.

"The parish raises annually $540 towards the clergyman's stipend, which is supplemented by your Society's grant of $480. The Bishop is anxious that the stipend should reach $1,200, as, owing to the expensive nature of even necessary things, it is almost impossible to do with less.

"Travelling is expensive, and our yearly visit to attend the Diocesan

Synod, which must be made overland, is a heavy tax when hiring becomes necessary. I have, as I am the farthest West, about 135 miles to travel to reach Calgary. At our first meeting, which was held in February of this year, and at which all the clergy of the newly formed Diocese of Calgary were present, I was obliged to leave on Sunday afternoon. I had a service at 12 o'clock, left at 2.30 P.M., and preached in Macleod at the 7 o'clock service, a distance of thirty-three miles, doing the distance in three hours and three-quarters in the saddle. During Lent

A PEAK OF THE ROCKY MOUNTAINS.

of this year I did the journey every alternate Wednesday, to give addresses to a congregation of a brother clergyman. This, besides my usual knocking about, gives some idea of what the ordinary work of a missionary in this country is. I have only one out-station, which I visit every third Sunday, and of this I can but speak most encouragingly, for ever since its foundation the services have been well attended, and Holy Communion administered every six weeks."

FROM BLOEMFONTEIN TO THE ZAMBESI: A GREAT MISSIONARY JOURNEY.

BY THE BISHOP OF BLOEMFONTEIN.

BACK TO MATABELELAND, AND HOME.

(Concluded from page 425.)

FTER the Gaza men had left Sipiro's, the Bishop exchanged presents with the chief, and took every opportunity of making known the object of his visit, and told the people that if teachers came to them they must treat them well, and not ask for presents. Their reply was, "Your oxen are very well, and it is nice to see a white man so close." The journey back to the wagons was made uncomfortable by a cold rain which continued till about 11 A.M. next day. The Bishop, however, went on his way, and records that at night "the carriers were perfectly quiet during my reading and prayers, and John interpreted a little address which I gave on Christ's telling the disciples to take the little child for their example."

On September 10, the Bishop spent some time with the chief, Goto, who gave him considerable information concerning the country, and said that the land of the Gazas was "seven days away," *i.e.*, a man with nothing to carry could reach it in seven days. Then the chief had his present, and the wagons moved off towards Umtigeza's town. But the walk in the rain from Sipiro's gave the Bishop and others who were with him fever, which made travelling far from easy. The Bishop suffered probably more than any other, for his chest was affected, and on September 15, he says:

"While I was talking with someone I began to lose consciousness for a second or two, and then became stupid, and lay down in the wagon as it was going on; and I was almost sure that an old enemy was at my lungs. Edward made me meal and mustard plasters in pairs— large ones that went all round me."

He writes on

"*September* 16, *Sunday.*—I believe that a good many Mashona came to the wagons. Edward tried to buy some eggs from them, but they would not sell any. I had my poultices on and off all day. I forget how far Sydney Smith lived from a doctor, but I would far sooner not be 1,000 miles from one. But I know that if Almighty God intends me to come safely home nothing can stop me.

As though to comfort me, a little calf appeared to-day, bringing milk with it, I hope.

"*September* 17, *Monday.*—We made two very good treks to-day, over very easy country, except where the trees were thick. I did not leave the wagon except to go to the tent when we stopped. I think that the evil has been warded off my lungs, but I suppose that I have some fever, and do not care to eat what I have to eat. It is very uncomfortable, but might be much worse. I suppose that it is more felt by a person who is not well, but the temperature seems nearly always to be too hot or too cold. Then one part of my body is very hot, and another very cold; my legs seem to have a permanent chill in them, which asserts itself immediately they are not taken great care of. Jelly is ill with fever. None of the other men except the Matonga are really ill now, but they are not *well*. It is a strange thing that one day's cold rain could affect every one as it did. There must be something very malarious in the earth.

"*September* 18, *Tuesday.*—If I had not known that I must have slept a good deal, I might have said that I passed the night in trying to find a comfortable position in which to do it. I was told that a sable antelope was near the wagons, so I got up, and missed it, and went to bed again. Then my men told me that it was still not far off, so I again got up, and shot it.

" We had prayers; and one trek brought us to the Umviati River, an uninteresting stream here, and, as far as we could see, impassable for a wagon; for where there are not rocks there are quicksands. So I dressed, and rode out to find a place where we might cross, and failed to do so. But I shot another sable antelope, and was glad to give the Mashona who were with us some meat to eat.

"I was very uncomfortable again in the evening. My temper has been gradually becoming very bad, but I hope that I seldom show it, except to Jelly. One can only be angry with people for moral faults; there is no sense in being angry at mistakes, whatever consequences may be involved. Though before the men I laugh at my difficulties, a good many of them seem to get upon my nerves. I think I shall always have the greatest patience and sympathy with people who have irritable nerves owing to too much work. Last night I had an uncomfortable feeling of not being sure of what I was saying."

Gradually, however, the Bishop and his men got better, and overcame the difficulties in their way—they were many and great—until October 2, when he writes :

" As it is necessary for our oxen, if we wish to keep them strong, to travel by night, we do so, one man going in front with a lantern. The far greater ease with which the oxen travel, and the greater pace they go, much more than make up for the difficulties connected with travelling in the dark. It is amusing to see John, who at one time was almost angry at the idea of travelling unless it was quite light, because wild beasts would frighten the oxen, now ready and pleased to drive on in the dark, because it is far better for the oxen. We used also to have elaborate arrangements at night for keeping away the lions, but I think I have laughed the men out of the idea of the need of them.

"*October 4, Thursday.*—We have now left the pure Mashona people, and those in front of us for some distance are a mixture of Mashona and Matabele ; but there are very few people at all about here.

"*October 5, Friday.*—By night travelling, and having made Jelly alter the loading of his wagon, and taking some of his weight on to my wagon, we are doing distances which are very good.

"Jelly is an interesting study, as being recommended by a high-class trader, when compared with my own men ; showing, I think, that a far higher class of servant is produced by the Missionary than the ordinary employer of the country. I think that he will look back on the months that he has been with me as a kind of penal servitude, but we are all on very good terms, and the camp is very happy ; there does not seem to be a jar or a complaint of any kind, except that some of the men's feet are sore."

By this time Matabeleland had been fairly re-entered, and the entry on October 8 in the Diary runs thus :

"After the morning trek, at our resting place a large number of people came to the wagons. They were neither Mashona nor Matabele, but a mixture of both.

"One of Lobengula's sons is here, and sent me a polite message. All along the road we hear of men being called up, and of 'impis' going out.

"Late in the evening we crossed the Dubainzi River—sandy and difficult. The oxen are beginning to show signs of sickness, they have been eating some poisonous grass possibly.

"*October 9, Tuesday.*—The Tschangani River was crossed early, and when the wagon stopped I rode with John to Miati, about five treks distant in a wagon. I sent for my letters, then went to Mr. Elliott, the London Missionary here, and was most kindly received. They had heard that I was coming, and had received a false account of our being shut up by the Gaza people.

"The whole place here is excited and unsettled. The gold adventurers, a few of whom have come asking permission to go into Mashonaland, have made the whole Matabele nation most nervous. Mr. ——, who is the most northerly trader in South Africa, now that Mr. Wisbeach is dead, tells me that a few days ago, when he was coming from the chief's, the men at the Umbezweni kraal ran out at him and another man with him, pulled off their hats, beat their horses, and drove them back. The talk of the Matabele is about a white 'impi,' which they assert is coming.

"*October* 10, *Wednesday.*—I am making an arrangement with Mr. Elliott to leave my wagon and take his on in exchange. I am going to sell some of my things, which will give money to pay the men and buy new oxen. Mr. Elliott gives me four oxen with his waggon. My oxen being tired is the penalty that I and they have to pay for the pace of our journey, though it is a sort of comfort to find that other people's oxen are worse than mine, and yet have done much less work.

" Re-packing and making a wheel occupies us at present.

"*October* 13, *Saturday.*—News came from the chief's kraal of the excited state of the people. Mr. Rees passed through a village where the people ran out, crying 'Beat the white man,' but when he told them that he came from here, they were quiet. He says that no one will work in the fields from fear of the white 'impi' which they say is coming; and one woman asked him whether, when it came, it would kill children 'so high, or so high,' giving different heights, apparently those of her own children.

" Nothing can be greater than the cordiality of the London Missionaries about my journey. When I told Mr. Rees, who has been on the Lake Tanganyika, of the time we had done our Zambesi walk in, he said that I could not have gone on long at that rate, which I suppose was true. He did not expect that I should get over the mountains and valley at all."

With reference to Mission work in Matabeleland, the Bishop says:

" I have no idea of a Mission among the Matabele. It would be a fatal error to try and force our Church in among the London Missionary work in Matabeleland. The Roman Catholics tried, but were sent south. Lobengula asked them where their wives were. They told him that they did not believe in wives. He then asked them where were their mothers, and they are said to have given some answer to the same effect. His reply might have come from the wisest and best of men: it was: 'I do not wish anyone to teach my people who does not believe in mothers and wives.'"

The Bishop stayed at Iniati till the 16th, having started his wagons on their way towards the chief's kraal the day before. Then he rode after them with John, taking also with him a boy for Shoshong from Mr. Elliott. Little was done on this day beyond reaching the waggons and moving them further towards Hope Fountain. On October 17 the Bishop writes:

" At about daybreak I rode with John to the river near the Umbezweni kraal, and took off the saddles under a bank, where we could not be seen. When I began to pass the kraal some of the people there jumped on to their huts, some ran in different directions to cut us off. They shouted a good deal; but all that could be understood was, that they thought that I was one of the people who had come to fight against them. We made a round and reached the track before the leading man, who was encumbered with a gun. Some seem to have followed us a good distance, but we made a shorter cut than they, and so saw them no more.

"I paid my respects to Lobengula as I went by his kraal at Umvutja. He was 'making medicines' in his goat kraal. Then I went on to where the Administrator, Sir Sidney Shippard, and Captain Gould-Adams were encamped. The Administrator's escort seems to have been a good deal annoyed since coming into Matabeleland : once the natives were so violent that a fight seemed imminent. Had they fired no white man would probably have been alive by now. I hear that the Umbezweni regiment have been petitioning the King to be allowed to kill the present Indunas, whom they do not consider patriotic, and also all the white people in the country—*i.e.*, the gold-diggers, who are asking to be allowed to go into Mashonaland.

"I called on the chief, who was very polite. I told him where I had been, and what I had done. I told him, also, that I did not think he need be afraid of white people living in Mashonaland, because they would die there. At which he laughed, and said that 'they would see for themselves.' I then thanked him for his civility, and asked permission to leave the country; when he said that I had not asked him for much —for gold, or such things—and that I could go. I told him that I did not wish to bring my wagons round by this place, as my oxen were tired, and he intimated that they need not come. (This is said to be the first time that he has allowed a wagon to go through without coming to him.) Then I informed him that I wished to keep the horse, my present to him, till I arrived at Kanya, from which place I would send it to him. He agreed, and quite understood that it was a gift and not a payment for anything. After that we talked a good deal about other things, but, as the present is an inopportune time for asking permission to settle a Mission in Mashonaland, I said I would talk about that some other time. When I took leave he was very polite ; but he amused himself a good deal by saying, 'Good bye, young man.'

"*October* 18, *Thursday.*—I had intended to go to Hope Fountain, but the Administrator wished me to go with him and Major Gould-Adams to the chief, which we did late in the afternoon. Mr. Moffatt went also, and Mr. Helm interpreted. Sir Sydney explained that he had come to pay a friendly visit ; that he had no connection with the men who were asking for gold concessions ; and that England did not want the country, but wished to prevent other people taking it. Another meeting was arranged for to-morrow.

" *October* 19, *Friday.*—A child of the chief has died ; so the interview is postponed.   He and his wives go into the country around as a sign of mourning, and he has to be purified by certain ceremonies before he can attend to business again.   Should anyone touch a dead body he is not allowed to see the chief for a ' moon.'

" I rode to Hope Fountain.

" The Government post is lost, owing to the Shoshong men, who were carrying it, meeting a Matabele ' impi ' which was going to attack the imaginary English ' impi.'   The bag was thrown away, and the men ran back.

" I sold some of my provisions to a colonist who is trying to get an entrance into Mashonaland.

" *October* 20, *Saturday.*—I sold some more of my stores, and exchanged photographic apparatus and other things for five oxen with Mr. Helm.   He has been most kind.   Whether I or the London Society Missionaries go into Mashonaland seems the same to him—the work of God will be done.

" *October* 21, *Sunday.*—I sent on the wagons to the Komalo River last night to stay there over to-day.

" I gave an address to a few natives in the school-chapel belonging to the Mission, and in the evening held a little service for the two Missionaries and their people.

" *October* 22, *Monday.*—I sent a message to the chief by Mr. Helm saying that I was leaving to-day, but that I hoped to come and visit the Mashona people again.

" John has gone home."   Elsewhere the Bishop says of this man :— " I think that it is his mother who wants him at home.   I gave him a very good present besides his wages.   He has been invaluable to me, and I am very sorry at losing him.   I have John ' Selous,' a Griqua, in his place.

" Jelly wished to be allowed to put four young oxen in at once, and I foolishly allowed him to do so.   This folly ended in our going about three miles in as many hours, and my being ' put in ' the wagon ; for in avoiding one of the wild creatures I stepped back into a great hole, and sprained my ankle.

" The grass is miserably bad in most parts.   I have lost six oxen, and am trying to reach the Impakwe river, where the grass is good.   I hope the people will appreciate my hurrying back, for it certainly is very unpleasant, and also expensive, as the oxen can only do about half what they could have done had I waited till the rains came."

For the next two or three days travelling was difficult, but not eventful.

On October 25 the Bishop says :—

" The road is now chiefly down-hill, as the Matabele highlands are

ending. The heat is most oppressive. There are no signs of rain. We
stop in the early morning just below the ascent to the pass, called the
Tiger Pass, which separates the high country from the low country.

"There is a village of Makalaka near here, where the women are far
more decently dressed than the Matabele women. The men follow the
disgusting fashions of the Matabele. After crossing the pass we stopped
at Mangwe's Brook.

"*October* 26, *Friday.*—During the early trek two men in a wagon
came to meet me. They said that they had come round from the
Transvaal by the eastern part of Matabeleland, that they had been a
good deal annoyed by the natives, and at last stopped by the Chief's
orders. It was a most dangerous thing to do. They wished to know
about the line to be drawn between Lobengula's and Khama's country,
which I had no right to tell them about (the dispute being as to whether
the Shashi or Maeloutsi River is the boundary). One of them, a tester of
gold-reefs, said that he wanted the question as to whether he might dig
between the Shashi and Maeloutsi settled at once in one way or another;
at which I smiled. It appears that somebody has paid, or agreed to
pay, to somebody else, a large sum of money for the right to dig here,
if the chances of finding gold are such as are described; but no one is
allowed to go into the country that is in dispute between Khama and
Lobengula.

"We stopped at water, for the heat of the day was excessive.
Moving very slowly at about 5 P.M. we travelled for about two and a
quarter hours, then rested an hour, during which the Administrator and
Major Gould-Adams and their waggons came up. They are travelling
faster than I do. Even for their journey to Matabeleland, after going
round by the Crocodile river to settle the dispute between Khama and
the Transvaal, they bought new oxen at Umoubja, then borrowed a
whole team from Khama, and have another one waiting to meet them
from Shoshong. I have no intention of trying to keep up with them.
They have my gold friends of the morning with them, who have been
arrested by Lobengula, and ordered to leave the country under the
'escort' of Major Gould-Adams. Some other gold people are travelling
with them, thinking it best to go together.

"I started away, and travelled to about 1.30, then rested and went
on again at 3.45, and arrived at the Umquesi River at about 8.30 A.M.
This is a very beautiful river when there is water in it. It is never quite
dry; now there are only pools; but the water can be drunk without
fear of being made ill by it. The grass, also, is very good. The oxen
will have a rest here for a day or two."

During this rest the Bishop discusses in his Diary the position of the
Portuguese on the Zambesi, concerning which other men with a larger
experience of them than he had have written, and the state of the Matabele

country and people. With reference to the Matabele, there can be no
doubt that they were then much excited against the white men by the
persistent attempts of the gold-seekers to obtain a position in the land,
and by the false reports of a white "impi" coming to attack them.
There was evidently real danger of an outbreak ending in the massacre
of every white person in the country. That danger was averted probably
by the wise action of Lobengula, who, what with one thing and another,
must have been sorely tried just then. That in less than a year the
position should be so greatly changed—*i.e.*, that at the request of Lobengula himself Matabeleland should be taken under British protection—
neither the Bishop nor anyone else seems to have anticipated.

Only the ordinary incidents of travel are recorded by the Bishop until
November 1, when he reached Tati, the principal goldfield—so far as was
then known—of Matabeleland. He then says :

"I rode for two treks and walked for one. I find that my legs are
somewhat helpless; I think that I must be getting tired. We reached
Tati early. The people seemed to have been annoyed a good deal. I forget
how many 'impis' they say have come to Tati. All the workings have
been stopped, and the outlying stores broken into. A trader's wagon
was looted, and about £60 worth of goods taken. A message was
brought from the Chief to-day, saying he was angry with his men for
stopping the works, but the manager thinks it is useless to go on while
the country is in its present state. One of the two men carrying the
letters seems to have been caught and badly beaten.

"I have exchanged eight thin tired oxen for six fat good ones, which,
I think, is not a bad bargain. I have sold nearly everything that anyone would buy, have left one wagon to be sold, and put twenty oxen
into my own wagon, which gives the best chance of getting through the
country in front. I hear that the wagons ahead of us have divided into
two parties, so as to allow the water holes to fill again before the second
party come on."

Upon leaving Tati nothing of importance occurred, except the part-
ing with Jelly, until Khama's country was reached. There some gold-
diggers were found living in two tents, who were very careful not to cross
the Macloutsi, they being on the side of the river which was undoubtedly
Khama's territory. On Sunday, November 4, there was a very nice service with the men, and the Bishop says :

"I gave an address on the difference between a Christian and a
heathen nation; and indeed standing here between the two forms of
government—Khama's and Lobengula's—the difference is very striking.
We had an afternoon service especially for the white men who stay
here, or somewhere on the river, to look after the gold-diggings."

For days after this the road lay through a kind of desert, a thirsty
land, and both men and cattle suffered accordingly. The visit to

Shoshong, Khama's capital, is certainly the most noteworthy event recorded in the remainder of the Bishop's Diary. This is it:

"*November 15, Thursday.*—We reached the Mahalapsie River, not so easily as I should have wished, and here Mr. Heeney and one of his men met me, and rode over the hills into Shoshong with me. We called on Mrs. Hepburn on our way down the Pass into the town—the largest (having a population of 20,000) and by very much the best-ruled native town in South Africa. No brandy or beer of any kind is allowed to the natives or the white men. The people are not even allowed to make the Kaffir corn beer. One store stands prominently dismantled, from which a trader has been ejected, who would continue after warning to sell brandy to the people. Khama has had a great deal of trouble about this question, but now he rules white men and natives equally strictly.

"*November 16, Friday.*—I slept last night at Mr. Heeney's, and early this morning went to see the Chief, who was most courteous, offering me a guide by the Lopepe Road, if I wished to go by it, telling me that my wife had seen his wife a good many times when she was here, and expressing himself pleased to hear that the men whom he had sent with me had done well. It is impossible to imagine a greater contrast between this cleanly, good-looking, educated gentleman, studiously polite even to every child who salutes him, an example in life to all his fellow-Christian and heathen subjects, so good a soldier that his father had to recall him from a kind of exile into which he had been sent on account of his being a Christian in order to fight for him—the 'noble savage not contaminated with Christianity.'

"I had a long talk with Khama in the afternoon about his people, and the line of action he would take in the event of his country being attacked. They live crowded together in one town on account of the place being a natural fortress, and will probably continue to do so till there is no longer any danger from the Matabele. I asked him whether in any particular whatever he considered that any of his people had deteriorated by becoming Christians. "None whatever," was his reply. I then asked if he thought they would be worse soldiers. He said that a people who became Christians, and therefore gave up raiding, would not, from want of practice, be good for aggressive warfare, but for defending their country he thought them just as good.

"*November 17, Saturday.*—The wagon came in, and I sold some things, and then wrote letters telling the clergy from Mafeking to Kimberley on what days I intended to be with them."

Our space will not permit us to follow the Bishop from Shoshong to Mafeking, interesting though his experience was, and we therefore close the narrative of his journey, destined we hope to lead to a wide extension of the Church's Missionary work, with his arrival at Mafeking:

"*December 4, Tuesday.*—We were about 2½ hours from Mafeking, in the tired state of our oxen, when I rode forward by myself after breakfast into the town. My pony was quite tired out, which is hardly to be wondered at, since he has made the round from Bloemfontein, Kimberley, through all parts of the journey where horses went, and back to here. I was alone, and not sure of the road, so that the tin roofs of the town, as soon as I had made certain that it was not a mirage, were a pleasant sight. The officials were most kind.

"*December* 5, *Wednesday*.—It is strange that I should have arrived exactly on the day on which I told the Mafeking people I intended to be with them ; nor could I without great expense, have arrived one day sooner. Here I leave my wagon for sale, and arrange for such things as I leave to be sent down to me.

"I shall do what is needed here so far as is possible, and then visit Vryburg, Phokoane, Barkly and Kimberley, on my way to Bloemfontein.

"However inefficiently I may have carried out the journey, I trust that through the whole of it I have tried to do my duty."

[NOTE. —He who has had the privilege of preparing the Bishop of Bloemfontein's Diary for the *Mission Field* has had personal experience of the distress connected with travel in the plain of the Zambesi ; he has talked also with men who have travelled in Matabeleland and the regions adjacent ; and from their experience and his own, he cannot refrain from saying that the Bishop's journey is an admirable instance of Christian Missionary enterprise, and not inferior to any other achievement in South African travel.]

THE END.

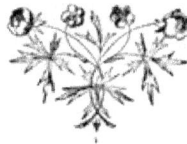

THE CHILDREN'S CORNER.

THE STORY OF SATTHIANATHAN, A NATIVE CLERGYMAN IN SOUTHERN INDIA.

I WAS born at Alvar Tirunagari in the year 1860. My father is a respectable landlord and owner of property in the neighbourhood. In religion he is a Hindu of the Vishnuvite sect. He paints on his body eighteen marks of Vishnu, and wears a massive garland of sacred beads called *Rudra aksha* (Siva's eyes) round his neck. He is much respected by Hindus on account of his piety, and is held in great reputation in the place. My elder brother, Samuel Reugiah Naidu, was the first convert to Christianity in the town, and he continued a steadfast servant of Christ up to the time of his death, which took place in the year 1886.

When I was five years old my education was begun in a native vernacular school, but, as my father saw my taste for learning, he resolved to send me to the S. P. G. Mission School in my native place. The Holy Scriptures were taught there daily. When I was only a boy of thirteen I was sent to a High School at Palamcotta, where I was unfortunately left to the care of a pensioned military officer who ill-treated me, and consequently I left the school and went home. The next year I was sent to the Sawyerpuram Seminary, and there also, having no proper person to look after me, I shortly afterwards went home and discontinued study. My father entertained high hopes of me, so he sent me once more to the High School at Palamcotta, but during the two years of my life there I neglected my studies and associated with wicked boys. As I knew that my father was in a good position in life, I was not anxious about passing any of the examinations which qualified for employment in Government service or elsewhere. My brother, whom I mentioned above, and who was educated in the S. P. G. Mission School at Alvar Tirunagari, was at this time baptized at Nazareth, and my father, in great fear lest learning English should lead me also to reject Hinduism, refused help, and I was obliged to return home once more.

My whole attention was now directed to persecuting my Christian brother, and in combination with my father and relations we sought by every means to bring back my dear brother to Hinduism. All our attempts proved fruitless, and only strengthened him in his faith. He formed a society of religious inquirers which numbered twenty-one, and who resorted daily after sunset to the river-bed, where they held long religious discussions and concluded with extempore prayer. At this time I was unwilling to hear anything about Christianity, and never cared to see what went on at these meetings, though several times I did my best to be a great nuisance to the meeting. When I was about eighteen years old, my brother's bright example affected me, and I sought the help of the Rev. A. Pichamutthu who was then the Head Master of the Mission School at Alvar Tirunagari. He often spoke to me about Christianity, and created in me a desire to examine for myself the different religions ; the first, that of the Hindus ; the second, that of the Mahommedans ; and the third, that of the Christians. I thought by this means that I might choose the best if I were only once acquainted with them all. In this way I went carefully through them all. Nor was I satisfied with this examination only, for I often went to the Rev. A. Margöschis at Nazareth, from whom I received advice and clear explanation of what seemed to me some difficult matters in Christianity. Pamphlets, tracts and religious books were also abundantly supplied me. Now God's time was drawing near. He had compassion on me, and He visited me with a severe illness. When all hope of my recovery was given up, my brother approached my bed and whispered a few words in my ear, urging me to become a Christian without delay. I at once resolved to become a faithful disciple of Christ the Saviour of the world, regardless of what the consequences might be, and from that time forward my sickness began to abate and I got quite well again.

My brother's hands were now strengthened, and we both determined to set to work towards the extirpation of demon worship amongst our people. A demon named Madasamy was worshipped as the tutelar deity. Sacrifices of every kind, except human, were offered to it at the birth of each child, and special sacrifices were made once a year at an immense cost, to which all our relatives contributed. There is an interesting story told regarding the origin of this demon. He was formerly a barber-physician from Malabar, and he had saved up some money earned by his profession. One of my ancestors was said to have secretly murdered him, and to have taken from him all that he had, and thereupon the wrath of God was kindled against his murderers, and it was thought that the soul of the barber was transformed into a devil and created evils amongst them. One midnight my brother and I went with axes and broke down the image of stone dedicated to this evil spirit, and shattered it to pieces. This bold act irritated our people, who drove us both from home and starved us.

Alvar Tirunagari at this juncture was visited by several Missionaries

and Evangelists. There are ten large pagodas dedicated to the various
heathen deities in the town, besides numerous small ones. These pagodas
are disfigured with strange figures and pictures. This town is built
upon the bank of the river Tâmpurapurney which is considered very
sacred by the Hindus. There is a funny story told in the Purânas of a
certain dog of the place which happened to swim over the river on a day
named Yegathâsi, a fast day sacred to the Hindus. The dog being
unable to find anything to eat swam across to the other side of the river,
but again finding nothing it stayed there the whole night. On the
morning of the next day called Thuvathasi, on which Hindus eat early
in the morning, it swam back to the town, and feasted itself with the
remnants of food thrown away. The god Vishnu, delighted at this dog
which had bathed in the sacred river, and had fasted and feasted like
one of his own devotees, descended from heaven, and, having taken it
alive, drove back with it in his chariot to heaven.

The Rev. A. Margöschis, the superintending Missionary, frequented
the Mission School, and sending for the young men he gave them spiritual
advice and encouragement. Bishop Caldwell delivered two or three
addresses to the Hindus in the pandal before the largest pagoda. One
of the Cowley Brotherhood also visited the town, and preached very
earnestly to the Hindus, and stirred the hearts of the young men in a
wonderful way. With some other young men I followed him to Nazareth
to hear a course of sermons in the church there.

On the 23rd of December 1878 the Evangelists from Nazareth
made a second visit to the town, accompanied by Rev. Mr. Margöschis
and Messrs. Hubbard and Bullivant, and they baptized Sankarem Pillai
and Samuel Sarkunam Naidu and thirty others by the side of the bridge
of the river, a great multitude of people from the town being present on
the occasion. There is no proper church at Alvar Tirunagari, though
land has been bought for one, so the river water was used for the
baptism. They then proceeded to the heart of the town, and in a convenient place at the foot of the great temple they preached very boldly.
The audience was estimated to be about two thousand people. Men,
women and children climbed up to the tops of the houses around in
order to listen. Some heard attentively and others threw stones, one of
which went quite close to the head of the preacher, who continued his
address regardless of impending danger. A week after, on the festival
of our Lord's Circumcision, Jothynayagam Pillai and myself, known up
to this time as Subbiah Naidu, were baptized by the Rev. A. Margöschis
in the Nazareth Church. I took at my baptism the name of Arthur
Margöschis Satthianathan, to perpetuate the name of the kind gentleman who influenced my conversion. Jothynayagam Pillai, who sowed
the Gospel seed in the hearts of his pupils, was a Hindu schoolmaster.
But it was God's good pleasure to separate him from us by early death.

He died very peacefully in the Nazareth Hospital, on the 26th of August 1880, and was interred in the cemetery there. N. Muthiah Naidu and Manikam Pillai were also admitted into the Church by holy baptism. The former was baptized in the Mission School of the place by Mr. Margöschis, Bishop Caldwell being then present. He is now a student in the S. P. G. Theological College, Madras. When the latter was baptized at Alvar Tirunagari itself, his house was set on fire by his relatives; he himself was burnt and escaped, but he entered the burning house again to save his old mother. Had not the Rev. A. Margöschis, the Medical Missionary, treated him in his dispensary, he would probably have died, he was so badly burnt.

After this we were accustomed to assemble for our daily services in the girls' school, where we went in procession, singing through the streets during the chief festivals, and having a band of music, torches lighted, and flags flying. We were anxious to *show* that we were Christians and to lead others on to follow us.

Our relations now awoke, and in great wrath began to do many frivolous and cruel things against us. When the bell was rung for prayers, my father used to beat a brass plate, so that he might not hear the bell. Sometimes he feigned madness, and went about the streets almost naked. I was several times beaten, dragged about, and driven from home. Attempts were made to kill me. I was once taken by force to a place near Palamcotta, and shut up in a room for the whole night. At daybreak I managed to open the door and ran away. Another desperate attempt was now resorted to to kill our souls. All our relations assembled in a place and began to tempt us in various terrible ways. But God's Spirit speaking for us and strengthening us at this perilous time, we did not yield to the evil wishes of our enemies. They produced a bond which had been circulated in several villages and signed by all our relations. By this bond they were prohibited even to speak to us, or to have any sort of dealings with us. Thus, entirely forsaken and renounced by our relatives, we had recourse to the benevolence and kindness of the Rev. A. Margöschis, who shared in our afflictions and troubles. Whenever he visited us in our town, my father heaped upon him abuses and threats for making Christians of his only two sons. But for all this, we were steady in the Faith, God helping us.

Defeated in this way, our relatives now applied themselves to the powers of magic. A small leaden plate, bearing the names of the converts and their patron Missionary with several cross lines called Chuckram, and some spells called Manthram, was buried in the ground at the entrance of the girls' school. It was their foolish belief that this plate would endanger our lives. Some way or other the magic plate got to the surface, and was handed over to Mr. Margöschis. Through all we saw that it was God who delivered us out of the hands of our enemies and preserved us from so many dangers, which cannot be related in detail. Had not God moved the mind of the Missionary to show his tender love to us, we should have been swallowed up by the ravening wolves, and the little flock, being scattered abroad, would have become a prey to the wild animals. "Blessed be the name of the God of Israel, for His mercy endureth for ever."

When I was twenty years old Mr. Margöschis sent me to the C. M. S. College at Palamcotta, and in a year's time I was, by the valuable instruction of the Rev. H. Schaffter, enabled to pass the Matriculation Examination of Madras University. Of the 45 candidates sent up from the College, only seven passed, and I headed the list. Next year, 1880, I married a Christian girl, educated in the Sarah Tucker Institution, at Palamcotta. In the year 1881 I was recommended to be admitted to the S. P. G. Theological College, Madras, and to be trained for the ministry. I delayed and hesitated to join the College. My wife was seized with sickness, and I was dangerously ill. Then in my calamity I remembered God's past mercy, and attributed it to His hand. I formed a firm resolution to devote my life to Christ my Master.

In the month of June 1883 I was sent up to the College, and had the privilege of being trained by Doctor Kennet and Rev. F. H. Reichardt. In four years' time I finished my course, and passed the Cambridge and Oxford Preliminary Examination of candidates for Holy Orders in the first class.

On Trinity Sunday, June 10, 1889, I was ordained a deacon by the Right Rev. Bishop Caldwell, in St. Peter's Church at Kodaikanal, and am now in spiritual charge of two congregations numbering a thousand Christians. "Blessed be God, who hath not cast out my prayer, nor turned His mercy from me."

NOTES OF THE MONTH.

ON All Saints' Day the Right Rev. Charles John Corfe, D.D., All Souls College, Oxford, was consecrated in Westminster Abbey, as the first Bishop of Corea, by the Archbishop of Canterbury. His Grace was assisted by the Bishops of London, Carlisle, Oxford, Southwell, and Lincoln, and B shop Mitchinson.

The Bishop of Reading and the Bishop of Derby were consecrated on the same occasion.

WE extract the following passage from the eloquent sermon preached by the Ven. Dr. Gifford on the occasion :—

"To-day another leader in that great enterprise is to be consecrated in our sight and sent forth to Corea, a tributary, but almost independent kingdom, of the vast empire of China. For more than twenty years the Bishop-designate has been serving God most usefully, most happily, as a chaplain in the royal navy. He has still fourteen years to serve, in the order of nature, before he could be compelled to retire. Nothing short of the Archbishop's call, which he humbly believes to be a call from God, would have led him to sever his connection with a work in which he has always had the greatest spiritual profit as well as the most real happiness. In leaving the service prematurely, and leaving it—as I may say from my own knowledge—amid universal regret, he forfeits his right to a full pension, and has only a retiring allowance of £100 a year on which to depend for sustenance in sickness or old age. The bishopric has no endowment whatever. The Society for the Propagation of the Gospel makes a grant of £650 for five years, and this sum must go as far as possible in maintaining four or five priests, who will live together in some sort of community, bound by no vows either limited or lifelong, but by strong and common links of steadfast and holy purpose, and by the constraining love of Christ, and of the souls for which He died. At present the Bishop has no one with him, but stands alone in this brave enterprise. Like the Patriarch when 'called to go out into a place which he should after receive for an inheritance,' he will go out literally not knowing whither he goes, into a land which he has never seen, knowing only that dangers and difficulties await him in a country rarely visited by Europeans, and in which the name of Christian is an object of hatred and contempt. Of the Bishop's intentions with regard to his work he naturally shrinks from speaking at large, lest he should either say too little or too much. But I cannot withhold from you the satisfaction of hearing some few at least of his own exact words :—

"'Experience (he says) teaches me that I shall have to modify considerably any plans I may propose to myself when I am actually face to face with my surroundings. Before going out, however, I intend everywhere to enlist men rather than to beg for money; and to ask God to give me, if it please Him, men who will sacrifice a great deal more than I have for His service. If money comes, I still hope that we may use it rather to build schools and hospitals, and provide stipends for clergy in different ports and towns (as God gives us

openings) rather than upon ourselves. I want, if possible, to insist strongly on the advisa-
bility of all my fellow-helpers volunteering to work without assured stipend. It is a
stupendous work, and I crave your earnest and constant prayers. . . . . I must lean entirely
on God. Nothing but this will save the Mission.'"

BISHOP CORFE'S consecration is a definite step in the beginning
of the new Mission to Corea. This is no small sphere of work
upon which the Society has entered. Another of equal newness and
importance is New Guinea, the first Missionary of the Church of England
for which land, the Rev. A. A. Maclaren, sailed on October 31, the day
before the Bishop of Corea's consecration.

BISHOP SARGENT'S honoured career was closed by death on
October 12. He has spent the whole of his ministerial life as a
Missionary of the C.M.S. in Southern India. Ordained deacon and
priest in the same years as Bishop Caldwell, 1841 and 1842, he was
consecrated with him on March 11, 1877, in Calcutta Cathedral, by the
Bishops of Calcutta, Madras, Bombay, and Colombo to be an assistant-
bishop to the Bishop of Madras, it being arranged that he should exercise
such functions in regard to the C.M.S. Missions in Tinnevelly as were
to be exercised by Bishop Caldwell for those connected with the S.P.G.
Bishop Sargent was the author of works on theology and antiquities, and
enriched the Tamil language by translating into it Paley's " Evidences."

OUR readers will be glad to know that the circulation of the *Mission
Field* continues to grow satisfactorily. At the beginning of the
year we announced a very large increase, and this has been added to
considerably since. It is, however, at the beginning of a year that new
subscribers are most numerously found, and we hope that we may be
able to speak of a still larger circle of readers next year.

WE would especially call attention to the system of parochial
circulation which for the last three years has been in successful operation. Parcels containing not fewer than twenty copies of the
Mission Field are sent each month at half-price and post free if the cost
be prepaid for the year. A large number of parochial associations
now avail themselves of the advantage of this system; and there can be
no doubt that an association in which month by month Missionary information is thus disseminated, and the Missionary spirit encouraged,
must be more prepared than it otherwise would be to take its share in
the great work of forwarding by prayers and alms the Missionary cause.
There may be, too, some hope of spiritual gain to the individual reader

himself, as he learns what his fellow-soldiers under the Master's Banner are doing to enlarge the Kingdom.

IN February we gave some account of Fiji and the work of the Church in that distant colony. Mention was especially made of the work which had been begun among the island labourers who have been brought to Fiji principally from the Solomon Islands. For their benefit a "Polynesian school" was founded, and the Rev. W. Floyd now writes from Levuka that eight adult Solomon Islanders were baptized on

LEVUKA, FIJI.

Whitsunday, "the first-fruits of Melanesia in Fiji." Four of them were shortly afterwards solemnly admitted to the choir. He adds that the Chinese in Levuka are now flocking to the Church.

Both Mr. Floyd, of Levuka, and Mr. Jones, of Suva, write to express their thanks for the increased grants voted by the Society for next year. Mr. Jones writes cheerfully of his work, and speaks of the offerings of the congregation for completing the church and other purposes. He says that Suva has now one of the nicest churches in the South Pacific, and that it is not only an ornament to the town, but is built of the best materials.

AT Boulogne-sur-Mer £2,000 is still required for defraying the cost of the Society's new Church of St. John. A private individual has promised to double any sums given for this object between October 20 and Christmas Day. Contributions are received by the Society's Treasurers.

GENERAL VIEW OF LEVUKA.

WHAT policy is to be pursued with regard to Tristan d'Acunha we do not know. On every ground it is desirable that the eighty inhabitants of this desolate island should be removed to some place—in South Africa or elsewhere—where not only would they be in a position of greater material comfort, but would be relieved from the isolation which lowers their mental standard. The Rev. E. H. Dodgson, who went to be their clergyman and teacher in 1880, came to England a few years ago in the hope of arranging for their deportation. He returned in 1886 hoping that this plan might soon be carried out. As it has not, he has remained with his flock. How he thus cuts himself off from England and communication with any friends, the fate of his last letter illustrates. He sent it on April 16, and it reached the Society, *via* Calcutta, on October 29. He says that the Tristanites are "willing, and more than willing, to settle elsewhere," but that they are "as much in prison here as if they were at Portland or Dartmoor." He thus states the difficulty as to their leaving:—

"Their whole property consists in house, land, and stock; they would have to begin life as *absolute paupers*, even if they *did* get a passage into the world, for such property is not easily carried in the pocket. As long as they *are* here, they can make a living (of a sort) from hand to mouth, but for a lot of large families of children and elderly people to throw themselves upon the world as paupers would, of course, be utter madness."

Mr. Dodgson goes on to speak of there being no alternative between the Tristanites having a clergyman to themselves, and their being left altogether destitute of spiritual ministrations.

"It may seem unreasonable to make any fuss about such a mere handful of people (less than eighty) when so many thousands of the heathen are yet uncared for, but the Tristanites are *not* heathen, but Christian colonists—more or less English—*imprisoned* on a little rock in mid-ocean."

It is to be hoped that the Government may be able to take steps for removing the Tristanites; but, whether they do or not, we think that it is

TRISTAN D'ACUNHA.

not only the few souls on that inhospitable rock who are benefited by the example of devotion shown by him who gives up so much to minister to them in sacred things.

PRESIDING at the annual meeting of the Wirral and Birkenhead Branch of the Society, on October 15, the Bishop of Chester said that he could not conceive any cause which had a clearer and a stronger claim on every Churchman and Churchwoman, and certainly not less upon the Bishop of a home See, than the cause of Missionary work. It was very satisfactory to come there and learn from the general work of the Society, and especially in Birkenhead, that it had made signal progress, so much so that it caused them to take new courage.

"We are aware that stones can be thrown at the windows of the Missionary house.

We have all heard of criticisms which turn up again and again with a sort of galling recrudescence—criticisms levelled against the work of Missionaries.

"I would say that the wisest policy with regard to these things is to reverse the motto of the Volunteers, which is 'Defence not Defiance,' and I would propose that our motto with regard to these criticisms shall be 'Defiance not Defence.' No doubt some of the criticisms are well intended, and some are well informed, but a number of them are mere ignorant cavillings and carpings. We have so much to do that we cannot spare time to deal with petty and irrelevant matters. I think that the whole policy of the Church with reference to the Missions could be summed up in the three words, 'Reform, inform, and perform.' As to reform, it is the duty, and safety, and to the success of every institution, whatever it may be, whether secular or sacred, to be constantly endeavouring to reform itself and to improve its methods.

"Let us look calmly round on all sides, and see in what respects we can learn from other Missions and religious denominations. It is a great stumbling-block in the way of the progress of the Christian Church to have so many divisions among ourselves. I think we should lay stress over and over again upon the waste and weakness wrought by these things. I believe that one reason why we take so little interest in the Missionary work of the Church is because we know so little about it, and I would that every clergyman were his own deputation in his own parish. Churchmen should look upon our Colonial Church and Missionary work as their own frontiers and outposts, and should spend upon them special thought and sympathy. We must do something in the way of contributing, and getting more contributors, and not content ourselves with mere pious platitudes."

BY a strange error, which we much regret, the *Mission Field* for November spoke of the Farewell Service with Missionaries going out to India as taking place on February 9 instead of October 9.

FROM Malote, in the Diocese of Pretoria, the Rev. C. Clulee reports that his principal converts, the brothers of the chief, " have, almost unaided, quarried stones, made bricks, and built a good portion of the walls of a Mission School Chapel, which," he adds, " is very encouraging."

FORWARDING the simple and beautiful story which occupies this month our Children's Corner, the Rev. A. Margöschis, of Nazareth, under whom Mr. Satthianathan Naidu is working, remarks :—

"At Alvar Tirunagari, the conversions have all been amongst what are popularly termed the 'high castes,' and the Brahmins themselves have not been untouched. In these days of keen criticism of Missionary policy it is of first-class importance to note that all the conversions at Alvar Tirunagari have been the direct result of the Mission School in the place, and of the influence exercised thereby in the example and teaching of the schoolmasters employed there. The conversion of the heathen is a matter of such primary importance that earnest men will not be willing to decry any effort made for CHRIST; and although teaching Hindus in a Mission School may not be so popular as what is called *direct* evangelistic work, yet surely it would be a great mistake to use all our efforts in one direction and to neglect other modes of work which have in the past produced satisfactory results. There are diversities of gifts and diversities of operations, but it is the same Spirit who worketh in all."

Satthianathan's story mentions Jothynayagam, and of him Mr. Margöschis writes :—

"This young man was a Hindu teacher who kept a private school for caste pupils,

He frequently came to me, and I was rather astonished one day when he asked me if there would be any objection to his keeping 'Sunday School' for his boys. As he was a heathen at the time, and, as far as I knew, had shown no actual signs of his intention to forsake Hinduism, I was rather puzzled, but I told him that of course I was not in a position to forbid him keeping a Sunday School if he thought proper to do so. He had between twenty-five and thirty boys, chiefly Brahmins in his school, and he taught them Scripture history and the principles of Christianity as far as he knew them. If a Christian teacher had gone near the school, the pupils would all have been withdrawn, but when this Hindu teacher, with the mark of Vishnu on his brow (and this was what chiefly misled me), taught Christian truth and morality, no one thought it necessary to object. Within a year or so afterwards, the teacher confessed Christ openly, and when he was dying he begged to be carried to Nazareth, to escape the non-Christian funeral which his heathen relatives would have provided. He received the blessed Sacrament with great devotion, and fell asleep in full hope of a glorious resurrection. A small stone cross in the Nazareth cemetery now marks all that is mortal of one of Christ's most humble and earnest disciples. Several of his boys are still what we term in the Mission field, 'Enquirers,' or seekers after God. May they find Him and join their teacher in the land of light and truth, where too may we all meet."

IN June we printed a report from the Rev. W. Nicolls, of his Mission work at Moose Jaw, in the Diocese of Qu'Appelle. He has now moved to Whitewood, in the same Diocese. Whitewood is chiefly inhabited by English people. Mr. Nicolls writes :—

"There is a small church of lumber sufficient for present needs. The town of some 300 people is on the main line of the Canadian Pacific Railway, supported now by an agricultural district. There are about twelve Church families."

Besides this place, he has six out-stations in his Mission, in working which he is assisted by a lay reader. These stations are at distances of twenty, thirty, twelve, five, ten, and thirteen miles from Whitewood, in different directions. The efforts of the Church people in such places to erect and furnish churches are always encouraging. For instance, Mr. Nicolls speaks of Wapella, a small town, as at present with a very small church of lumber :—

"The latter is simply a converted shanty, 16 feet by 12. Lately it has been almost wrecked by the wind. The people are going to build a church of stone 36 feet by 24. The townspeople have dug the stone and prepared it for hauling, and the country people (farmers) have been drawing it to the church site with their teams. The total cost is estimated to be about $850. There are nineteen Church families connected with this centre. They are working well."

Forest Farm he describes as a district entirely composed of Church people who have moved up from Manitoba.

"They are very willing to work, and are to build a log church 30 × 20. The logs are to be hauled this winter from the Qu'Appelle valley, five miles north. There are about eighteen Church families. They have no school at present, though hoping soon to build one."

FROM North China the Rev. W. Brereton reports that he has lately been occupied with the preparation for the printers of a portion of the Prayer Book in the Mandarin dialect. It is a revision made by the Bishop of a previous translation.

" We cannot in Chinese have both a clear, readable type and a handy Prayer-Book, so the book has to be bound in more than one volume. The Calendar and Tables of Lessons were very dry work. . . . I reckon that between preparation of manuscript and reading of proof, Mr. Chary and myself read out to each other in a loud voice the whole Calendar and Tables of Proper and Daily Lessons eight times. This piece of information is not very stimulating to people at large, but it is very satisfactory to us to have the whole undertaking piloted safely through a Chinese printing house, and an extra satisfaction to know that it is the first attempt at a complete translation into Chinese of the English Calendar and Tables of Lessons."

CANON WIDDICOMBE, of the St. Saviour's, Thlotse Heights, Mission, in Basutoland, and the Diocese of Bloemfontein, reports during three months the baptism of seven of his most promising catechumens, viz., six Basuto and one Coolie.

"Among them were two children of Jonathan Molapo, the chief of the district of Linbe, and a daughter of the late Paramount Chief of the Basuto, Moshesh."

We must quote the sentences that follow :

" My coadjutor, the Rev. J. Deacon, is energetic and untiring in itinerating among the heathen villages, and in rapidly acquiring the language of the country. He relieves me of the lion's share of the riding, as I am getting too old for much of that sort of work, after almost thirty years' service in South Africa.

"Our new church is now roofed in, and, if all goes well, we hope that it may be ready for dedication by Christmas, or at the latest by Easter.

"There is a magnificent field of work open to the Church in Basutoland, but, alas ! we have neither the men nor the means to enter upon it at all adequately. May the Lord speedily send forth more labourers into this far distant corner of His vineyard."

THE Rev. R. R. Winter, who has just returned to Delhi, would be grateful to anyone who would send him the *Church Quarterly* and the *Spectator*. Other Missionaries would be glad to receive the *Guardian* in the same way. Their names and addresses will be gladly given at the Society's office.

SUGGESTED SUBJECTS FOR PRAYER.

For Africa, that the Church may be able to make use of the opportunities offered there.

For the new work to be undertaken in New Guinea and Corea ; for the Bishop of Corea ; and for the Rev. A. A. Maclaren who is going as the first Missionary of the Church of England to New Guinea.

For the Diocese of Madras, and the building up of the Native Church in it.

For the Church at home, that it may realise more fully its Missionary opportunities and responsibilities.

MONTHLY MEETING.

THE Monthly Meeting of the Society was held at 19 Delahay Street, on Friday, October 18, at 2 P.M., the Rev. B. Compton in the chair. There were also present J. M. Clabon, Esq., C. M. Clode, Esq., C.B., the Master of the Charterhouse, General Gillilan, Colonel Hardy, General Lowry, C.B., Canon Lucas, General Maclagan, Canon Mason, B.D., Rev. J. Frewen Moor, General Sawyer, General Tremenheere, C.B., S. Wreford, Esq., *Members of the Standing Committee* ; and the Rev. J. Adams, J. Boodle, Esq., Rev. J. A. Boodle, Rev. H. J. Day,

Dr. De Tatham, Rev. J. J. Elkington, Rev. Dr. Finch, Rev. H. Halford-Adcock, Rev. S. Coode Hore, H. Laurence, Esq., Rev. J. H. C. McGill, Rev. J. Maconochy, Rev. G. C. Reynell, Rev. H. Rowley, Rev. Canon Scarth, and W. E. Sharpe, Esq., *Members of the Society.*

1. After prayers, the minutes of the last meeting were read.

2. The Treasurer presented the abstract of receipts and payments from January 1 to September 30, printed on page 440 of the *Mission Field.*

3. The Secretary read letters from the Bishops of Calcutta, Madras, Lahore, and Bombay, on the allegations that Government Educational officials in India had acted in opposition to Christianity.

4. Power was given to affix the Corporate Seal to documents relating to Axenstein Church, Land at Kuching, and St. John's College, Newfoundland.

5. Read letter, dated August 15, 1889, from the Lord Bishop of Pretoria, as follows :—

"I have delayed answering your circular of May 28, for a reason which I trust you will account sufficient—the desire to show gratitude in a tangible form, by sending a draft for the Treasurers, for the amount of collections for the Society made in the Diocese. This was delayed for one parish's remittance, and I have now the pleasure of sending a draft for £47 6s. 6d. and the list of contributing parishes, which I am happy to say, for the first time, includes every one of the number.

"I also enclose my own cheque for £2. 2s., in the hope I may be able to revive and continue the annual subscription of former days.

"All this will show that our gratitude for aid is very real, and I would ask you to express it to the Board. We are most grateful for your aid, the steady regularity of which keeps us going. I only wish you could see how we go on, with what difficulties we have to contend, and what demands to meet, and you would treat us more like you do our older neighbours, with much more liberal aid. But for what you have done and do, God bless you."

6. The Right Rev. G. E. P. Blyth, Bishop for Jerusalem and the East, addressed the members. His lordship described the wish of the Eastern Church for connection with the Church of England, and mentioned several interesting instances of the interchange of courtesies between the patriarch and himself. At an Ordination held by Bishop Blyth in Jerusalem, bishops and clergy representing the various Oriental churches attended.

The Bishop proceeded to speak of the Jews in Palestine, and of their rapid increase from eight thousand in 1841, and twenty thousand in 1883, to seventy thousand at the present time. The Jews find Christianity as represented by the Church of England to be most attractive to them. It is impossible for the Eastern churches in Palestine to attempt Missionary work.

His lordship referring to the work of the chaplains in Egypt and Cyprus, and at Beyrout, expressed a hope for the Society's help in this department.

7. All the candidates proposed at the meeting in June were elected into the Corporation ; and the following were proposed for election in December :—

Rev. C. Hardy Little, St. Martin's, Brighton ; Rev. Norman Thicknesse, Limehouse, E. ; Rev. Herbert Stewart, Ramsgill, Pateley Bridge, Yorks ; Rev. W. Bellars, Margate ; Rev. Wentworth Watson, Monmouth ; Rev. W. Fredk. Cosgrave, Hunwick, Willington, Co. Durham ; Rev. Canon G. Buckle, Wells, Som.; Rev. Preb. E. C. S. Gibson, Theol. Coll., Wells, Som.; Rev. W. F. Rose, Worle, Weston-Super-Mare ; Rev. A. Thompson, Wells, Som.; Rev. J. P. Hewett, Norton Fitzwarren, Taunton ; E. D. Bourdillon Esq., Pitminster, Taunton ; Rev. George Porter, Wickford, Battles Bridge, Essex ; Rev. R. H. Bagnall, Barkestone, Bottesford, Nottingham ; Rev. C. Hannibal Crossley, Nowton, Bury-St-Edmunds; Rev. Gilbert C. F. J. Moor, St. Andrew's, Worthing ; Rev. J. M. Hodge, 38 Tavistock Place, Plymouth ; Rev. A. H. Stocker, Ovington, Alresford ; Rev. H. R. Hanson, All Saints', Portsea.

THE SOCIETY'S INCOME.

Abstract of RECEIPTS *and* PAYMENTS *from January 1 to October 31.*

	GENERAL FUND	SPECIAL FUNDS
Subscriptions, Donations, Collections, &c.	£25,009	£12,211
Legacies	8,715	107
Dividends, Rents, &c.	3,904	3,569
TOTAL RECEIPTS	£37,628	£15,887
PAYMENTS	£71,097	£14,279

The Receipts under the head of Subscriptions, Donations, and Collections for the General Fund from January 1 to October 31, in five consecutive years, compare as follows : 1885, £25,361 ; 1886, £23,210 ; 1887, £25,576 ; 1888, £24,776* ; 1889, £25,009.

* In addition, the Treasurers received in 1888 Securities of the value of £25,296 as " A Thankoffering to Almighty God for the extension of the Church in the Colonies and Dependencies of the British Empire and beyond it "; also other Securities of the value of £2,268 as a Trust Gift, *the Income only being available.*

INDEX

ARMS OF THE SEE OF CALCUTTA.

www.ingramcontent.com/pod-product-compliance
Lightning Source LLC
Chambersburg PA
CBHW031811270326
41932CB00008B/388